Managerial styles

Philosophies
Contingencies
Perceptions
Individual problems
Interpersonal communi-
cations

Chapter 10

Motivation

Needs
Satisfiers and dis-
satisfiers
Expectancies and con-
tingencies
Management by objectives
Job enrichment

Chapter 11

Leadership

Power and influence
Traits
Contingency models
Substitutes for leadership

Chapter 12

Groups

Roles
Models
Contingencies
Procedures for group
problem solving

Chapter 13

Conflict

Contingency model
Role conflict
Interpersonal conflict
Intergroup conflict

Chapter 14

**Organizational
change processes**

Need for changes
Resistance to change
Change model
Approaches

Chapter 15

**Challenges to
management**

Changing world
Changing managerial
processes
Changing behavioral
processes

Chapter 16

Management: Contingency Approaches

SECOND EDITION

Don Hellriegel

COLLEGE OF BUSINESS
TEXAS A & M UNIVERSITY

John W. Slocum, Jr.

COLLEGE OF BUSINESS
PENNSYLVANIA STATE UNIVERSITY

ISBN 0-201-02854-9
BCDEFGHIJ-HA-798

To Lois and Gail

Preface to the Second Edition

The basic objective of this revised edition remains the same as that in the first edition—to help prepare students for managerial careers. The managerial concepts, techniques, and skills that make up the book were selected because of their usefulness to managers. To achieve this end, we have had to integrate materials from the diverse approaches to the study of management. The strategy was not to present to the reader different approaches, but to integrate these approaches for the solution of managerial problems.

It is our position that management is a discipline. Management is not just a collection of experiences from successful managers, but rather an organized body of knowledge, with its own concepts, techniques, and needed skills, a good many of which are discussed in this book. Management is also people. Every achievement of management is the achievement of a manager. Every failure is a failure of a manager. People, not "forces" or "facts," manage. The vision, integrity, and dedication of managers determine whether there is management or mismanagement. Whether you will manage successfully is not determined solely by what you will learn in this or other courses, how smart you are, or how well motivated you are to apply new learnings to the job. Successful management also has to do with your personality and management style. How you influence others will significantly influence your managerial success.

Anecdotes are used frequently to drive home the essentials of management. Although a considerable volume of research related to management has taken place since the first edition of this book, it was not our purpose to critically examine it. Rather, we have integrated research findings into the text only when they are meaningful and relevant. As a result, we feel that clear and productive explanations of concepts have been achieved.

Another objective of this book is to be primarily descriptive rather than quantitative. We have simplified and included only those quantitative models that offer operational managerial solutions. The integration of quantitative materials with other materials lets the instructor use as much or as little of these as desired without omitting a major portion of the text.

Written for the introductory course in management, this book presents a distinctive contingency approach, which seeks to understand the interrelationships within and among the various parts of an organization. Each function, department, or work group can be analyzed separately or as a unit related to other departments, functions, and work groups within the organization. When the production department, for example, acts in response to various marketing department orders, we say that the production department's behavior was "contingent" on the demands placed on it by the marketing department. Hence a contingency approach to management occurs where the behavior of one department, individual, work group, or entire organization is dependent on its relationship to others. The basic notion is: "*If* the marketing department can sell 100,000 typewriters, *then* the production department will use plan A. *If* we sell only 50,000 typewriters, *then* plan B should be used."

Does the contingency approach provide a cure-all for solving all management problems? The answer is *no;* this approach does not provide us with the five easy steps to be a better manager. Cookbook approaches, while seemingly practical and easy to understand, are usually shortsighted and don't work. Many practical approaches to management look deceptively simple: If you follow certain principles, then you will be a more effective manager. The promise is that "anyone can be an effective manager if he or she will only try the medicine."

Knowing what to do can be learned; you can be taught about management, about the skills associated with the process of management, and about awareness of your managerial behavior. Fundamental contingency concepts might be more difficult to grasp, but they will help you to a more thorough understanding of real management situations. This book is certainly not intended to be the "only way" that managers manage. Rather, it is designed to show that a contemporary manager can benefit from an integrated approach to the study of management.

The discussion questions at the end of each chapter are directly related to the text material. Additionally, the sections on management incidents are presented so that students can demonstrate their ability to apply the managerial concepts and techniques discussed in the text. These incidents are set in a variety of different types and sizes of organizations and include problems of women, minorities, and all levels of management. The incidents were selected from a large number of exercises that were classroom-tested at Ohio State University, Pennsylvania State University, and Texas A & M University.

Like the first edition, the book is organized into four major parts. A significant addition to the second edition is the inclusion in each chapter of specific contingencies facing a manager. Part I, "Foundations," has been revised in a substantial way, primarily by the fuller explanation of the contingency approach in Chapter 1. Another significant change is the inclusion of cases, such as A&P, K-Mart, and AT & T. We have also tried to more clearly indicate the historical contributions in the management literature.

Part II is titled "The Managerial Processes." Chapters 4–9 focus on such areas as organizational design, decision making, planning, and control. This section is arranged so that the organizational-design issues are discussed before the functions of management. We feel that presenting a macro view first has some merit, because we can use the concepts in these chapters to understand the basic management functions. Chapters 5 and 6 have been revised to bring them more in line with the needs of both students and instructors. The recommendations of adopters and nonadopters have been carefully considered, and many of the suggestions have been used in this part of the book. In addition, there are many more company examples than in the first edition to highlight the concepts discussed and less use of mathematical symbols and notations in Chapter 7. The contingency model of planning added to Chapter 8 provides a useful view of where the various planning techniques and approaches fit into the organization. In Chapter 9 the corrective model of control has been reworked, and the contingencies influencing control are more clearly identified and developed.

Part III, "Behavioral Processes," also has been reworked. Chapter 10 has been totally reorganized to include materials on communication, managerial styles, and perception. This chapter sets the stage for the other chapters in this part. The chapter on motivation now includes a section on task design. The last part of each of these chapters has been expanded and is more narrative, discussing the nature of the concepts and their advantages and disadvantages. The chapter on groups has been substantially revised to better illustrate the contingency approach and the day-to-day management implications of the concepts, models, and techniques presented. Chapter 14, on conflict, has been restructured to more clearly show the causes of the three major levels of conflict, their effects, and the mechanisms for managing each. Moreover, the contingency model of conflict has been revised, and its application to the three levels of conflict has been worked in throughout the chapter. Applications of key contingency concepts through illustrative problems have been added throughout this part.

Part IV, "The Process of Change," has added new dimensions on social responsibility, career planning, and the role of women in management. The integration of various change practices has been worked into Chapter 15, and a new model of the change process has been developed.

Numerous other changes and improvements have been made that need not be mentioned here, but taken in total they will, we hope, make this edition better organized and more relevant for the student and a better teaching aid for the instructor. The book can be used in its entirety, including the managerial incidents, in one term. However, chapters of the book can easily be eliminated, depending on the orientation of the instructor, the objectives of the course, and the role of introductory course in the curriculum. Some knowledge of the social sciences will be of value, but it is not necessary for the student or instructor. College-level courses in mathematics and statistics are not needed.

We are grateful to the many people who helped make this second edition a reality. For excellent support and assistance, we thank the people at Addison-Wesley Publishing Company. For prompt, accurate, and cheerful typing, we thank ten superb secretaries: Marge Bell, Sharalyn Bowersox, Nancy Folmar, Tricia Harrison, Nancy Hillard, Cindi Knippa, Linda Platou, Judy Sorenson, Marie Straka, and Ildiko Takacs. We thank John Slocum (*New York Times*, retired) for the numerous grammatical and stylistic revisions. Without the help of these many people, it is doubtful that the book could have been revised.

Appreciation is also expressed to Dean Gene Kelley and Mike Hottenstein, The Pennsylvania State University, Dean John E. Pearson, Texas A & M University, as well as Dean Ned Bowman, Ohio State University, who were most helpful in providing assistance and other needed resources.

College Station, Texas   D.H.
University Park, Pennsylvania   J.W.S.
November 1977

Reviewer Acknowledgments

We are extremely grateful to the adopters of the first edition who provided numerous valuable suggestions for this revision. We are also keenly aware of the many contributions that our students have made to this edition. We wish to thank those whom we know about and ask those inadvertently overlooked to accept our apologies as well as our thanks.

For the intellectual stimulation and guidance that their reviews have provided us, we are grateful to the following:

David Arnold
UNITED STATES COAST GUARD

Randy Bobbitt
OHIO STATE UNIVERSITY

Rod Chesser
SYRACUSE UNIVERSITY

Pat Connor
OREGON STATE UNIVERSITY

Chester Cotton
CALIFORNIA STATE UNIVERSITY, CHICO

Kirk Downey
OKLAHOMA STATE UNIVERSITY

Patrick Fleenor
SEATTLE UNIVERSITY

David L. Ford, Jr.
UNIVERSITY OF TEXAS, DALLAS

Duane Hoover
TEXAS TECH UNIVERSITY

Steve Kerr
UNIVERSITY OF SOUTHERN CALIFORNIA

Harvey Nussbaum
WAYNE STATE UNIVERSITY

Louis Ponthieu
TEXAS TECH UNIVERSITY

Chet and Janet Schriesheim
KENT STATE UNIVERSITY

John Sheridan
PENNSYLVANIA STATE UNIVERSITY

David Sprague
WESTERN ILLINOIS UNIVERSITY

Harriet Stephenson
SEATTLE UNIVERSITY

John Stinson
OHIO UNIVERSITY

Gordon Taylor
WESTERN ILLINOIS UNIVERSITY

Hobart Tredway
WESTERN ILLINOIS UNIVERSITY

Carlton Whitehead
TEXAS TECH UNIVERSITY

7
Models of Decision Making   196

8
Planning Process   232

9
Control Process   268

Part III
Behavioral
Processes
300

10
Managerial Styles   304

11
Motivation   332

12
Leadership   366

13

Group Process   396

14

Conflict Process   430

Part IV
The Process of Change
468

The Foundations

FOUNDATIONS

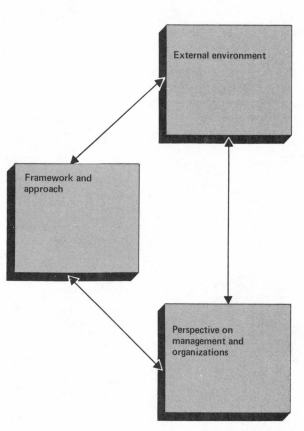

PART I

Part I, designed to set the stage for the entire book, establishes the general managerial issues and problems that will be considered in more depth in Parts II, III, and IV. Part I considers management and organizations as a whole by considering the external environment of organizations, the general patterns for managing the internal operations of organizations, and the different types and combinations of skills needed by managers.

In Chapter 1, the universal nature of organizations and management is emphasized. Our blending of systems, behavioral sciences, and traditional approaches for developing the contingency viewpoint is presented. The types of skills—human, technical, and conceptual—needed by all managers are explained.

Chapter 2 traces the importance of the external environment in managing organizations. Neither a person nor an organization is an "island." Rather, managers and organizations are constantly influenced by and trying to influence the major parts of their external environment. Thus an overview of the impact of the cultural, political, and economic systems on management and organizations is presented. Today's culture, with its diverse values, provides a dynamic setting for organizations and managers.

Chapter 3 discusses the two major perspectives in the practice and study of management—how these perspectives have evolved through the practice of managers and the contribution of scholars. The closed-system perspective has made many contributions to the management of the internal operations of organizations, especially under stable or nonchanging conditions. The open-system perspective emphasizes that an organization has a number of interacting parts and can be considered only in relation to its external environment. Through the use of various contingency approaches presented throughout the book, it will be possible to recognize the contributions both of these perspectives can make to the complex job of managing organizations.

1

The Framework and Approach

FOUNDATIONS

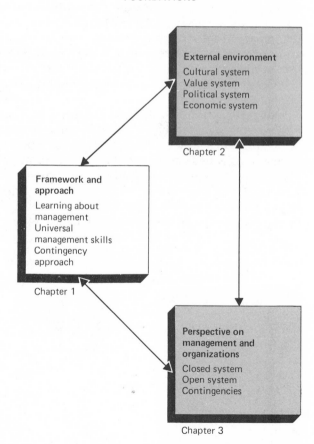

External environment

Cultural system
Value system
Political system
Economic system

Chapter 2

Framework and approach

Learning about management
Universal management skills
Contingency approach

Chapter 1

Perspective on management and organizations

Closed system
Open system
Contingencies

Chapter 3

The objectives of this chapter are to develop your understanding of:

the importance of the formal study of management in modern societies;

the types of skills needed by all managers;

the main underlying viewpoints in this book for learning about management, including the systems, behavioral sciences, and traditional viewpoints;

the use and significance of the contingency approach for applying these three viewpoints; i.e., there is no single best way for managing, but not all ways are equally effective; and

the territory, or subject areas, included in the book.

Managers and aspiring managers are bombarded by a battery of recommendations each time they are exposed to a book, magazine, course, or seminar
concerning management. These sources include such recommendations as:
increase the closeness of supervision, substitute machines for labor, decentralize authority, centralize planning, use sensitivity training, cut prices, improve product quality, eliminate rules, permit conflict as well as a number of
general prescriptions for improving organizational and managerial effectiveness. Although there may be few absolute dangers in such recommendations
and prescriptions, managers may find them relevant and useful only when
evaluated from a particular perspective and in particular situations. One of
the major objectives of this book is to assist you in developing the conceptual
(mental maps), human, and technical skills needed by all managers to accurately diagnose a problem and take proper action.

A second major objective, which follows from the first one, is to suggest
the knowledge and skills needed to know when and how to use different
practices, principles, models, and techniques. This chapter is designed to set
the stage and present the broad outline for the rest of the book.

LEARNING ABOUT MANAGEMENT

On the surface, it may appear that this book is intended only for those individuals who will be in formal management positions, e.g., president, vice-
president, division manager, product manager, sales manager, supervisor, foreman. A common theme in these position titles is that they are likely to include
responsibility for the work of others as well as to possess a certain degree
of formal authority to "command" others. Much of the content of this book
will also be of value to individuals not formally designated as managers, however. Parent Teacher Association leaders, school board members, religious
officers, fraternity or sorority officers—all can benefit from this book. Why?
The answer is that management occurs "whenever there is effort consciously
directed toward the attainment of a goal by individuals."[1] We might broaden
this definition even further by suggesting that management also includes the
creation of new goals. Several years ago, for example, McDonald's created
a new service goal of providing a breakfast menu at many of its hamburger
outlets. This new service goal was probably added in order to contribute to
McDonald's profit goal.

In the broadest sense, employees need to engage in certain management
processes if they exercise some degree of judgment or discretion over how
and when they perform their work or supervise the work of others. Thus
salespersons may "manage" if they plan their daily calls and decide how to
organize their sales presentation after obtaining certain information from the
prospective customer.

Importance

The study of management is important to all citizens because organizations,
which are strongly influenced by their managers, have a profound and in-

creasing impact on our lives. Sometimes, in fact, we are said to be living in an "organizational society" or a "managerial society." At the minimum, some examination of management and organizations is useful in helping us deal constructively with the managers and organizations that prevail in practically every area of our lives—from supermarket manager to hospital administrator.

For those who aspire to or already occupy managerial roles, the formal study of management is an important aid in acquiring or increasing the conceptual, human, and technical skills so necessary for managerial effectiveness. This is not to suggest that on-the-job experience is unimportant. Formal management education and experience are not really substitutes for each other. Rather, they should complement and build on each other over a lifelong process of self-development. Accordingly, this book puts forth no pretentious claim about making you into a successful manager. For even though formal learning through books and the classroom is an essential foundation, there are several limitations in this approach. For example, actual experience provides an intensity of learning which is difficult, and for many forms of learning impossible, to duplicate in the classroom. Learning to manage solely from experience can be slow, costly, and inadequate. Lessons to be learned must wait for the occurrence of events which provide the opportunity for experience. This limitation is especially critical for events that occur infrequently. Lessons are costly when learned only after the consequences of the decisions are known. For example, the need for better quality control might be identified only when sales fall off because customers complain about shoddy goods. Finally, experience can be inadequate because it tends to ignore the wealth of knowledge that has been accumulated to help managers. In sum, the formal study of particular techniques, skills, and models is relevant to real-world problems, and good management is not simply a seat-of-the-pants exercise.

Learning Objectives

Four general learning objectives may be served through the formal study of management and organization. These learning objectives, which are similar to the objectives of the scientific method, involve description, understanding, prediction, and control.

Your motivation for learning about management may vary widely. At the most fundamental level, you might be interested only in *describing* an organization and its management. In other words, what has happened or is happening? At the next level, which builds on the previous one, you become more concerned with "why" questions. To state that employee turnover is 20 percent per year is descriptive, but when you are able to identify why this turnover is taking place, you are reaching the level of *understanding*. By building on the purposes of description and understanding, you can become involved with *prediction*. If you found that much of the turnover was accounted for by female employees who had difficulty in obtaining satisfactory care for their small children, you might *predict* that a child-care center at the plant would go a long way toward eliminating this cause of turnover. *Control,* the most inclusive purpose, refers to the manager's ability to influence and direct various factors to obtain desired results.

These four objectives need to be interwoven in the active process of managing. Unfortunately, the current state of knowledge in the complicated field of management is not sufficiently advanced in all of the topic areas in this book to always reach the learning objectives of prediction and control. For example, in attempting to increase an individual's work motivation, we are able to identify some key factors and conditions that are likely to affect an individual's motivations (e.g., challenging work, money, praise). We are also able to speak in terms of the general likelihood that certain courses of action to increase work motivation might have particular effects. For example, let's assume that a person wants a challenging job that provides personal recognition. An assembly-line job is not likely to increase this individual's motivation. However, we are not able to predict or control with certainty an individual's motivation to work because one's wants and needs may change over time.

Ultimate Objective

Nothing has been said as to whether management will have favorable or unfavorable consequences for the public, employees, suppliers, customers, or managers themselves. No one lives in a moral and ethical vacuum. The dilemmas and responsibilities facing managers are especially heavy because their need to "control" people and other resources creates special problems. For example, decisions to promote, demote, or dismiss certain individuals can have major impacts on their professional and personal lives. It is imperative that these decisions be made as objectively as possible and on the basis of merit.

Although the formal study of management should help an individual become a better manager, this is not the ultimate objective. To manage well is a *means,* not an end in itself. The ultimate objective of management is to satisfy specific needs of society or individuals. To do this, Drucker suggests:

There are three tasks, equally important but essentially different, which management has to perform to enable the institution in its charge to function and to make its contribution:

—the specific purpose and mission of the institution, whether business enterprise, hospital, or university;
—making work productive and the worker achieving;
—managing social impacts and social responsibilities.[2]

Management is the key *activating* part of the organization in ensuring that these three essential tasks are performed. This is not to suggest that management acts alone in performing these tasks. Rather, management probably has the greatest power and influence, relative to any other group within or external to the organization, in determining whether these tasks are performed effectively or ineffectively. Some of these other groups are government, unions, specialists or professionals, customers, and suppliers.

Fig. 1.1. Learning about management.

Summary

Figure 1.1 summarizes and suggests the interrelatedness in the ideas presented so far and provides the broad foundation for the strategy of this book. These ideas may be summarized as follows:

1. Managers are faced with a battery of recommendations for improving effectiveness;
2. Work experience, although necessary, is not sufficient for developing managers of the future;
3. The formal study of management and organizations serves a number of learning objectives, each of which can be related to the problems currently confronting managers;
4. The attainment of these learning objectives should lead to good management practices;
5. Good management should result in effective organizations that fulfill a specific societal need.

The feedback loop in Fig. 1.1 also suggests that the study of effective organizations is one of the major sources of the knowledge and skills needed for learning about management and organizations.

UNIVERSAL MANAGERIAL SKILLS

The challenges facing managers of all institutions—both private and public— are immense. These challenges range from improving the productivity of organizations to dealing with the increased skepticism by large segments of the population toward organizations and their right to survive.[3] Nonetheless, the challenges and problems must be dealt with by individuals—managers—singly or in groups.

A useful framework for thinking about the basic and observable skills needed by all managers for effectively dealing with the numerous challenges and problems confronting them has been proposed by Katz.[4] He says that the three basic skills needed by all managers can be classified as *technical, human,* and *conceptual.* The relative degree and mixture of the skills needed by a particular manager will depend on the level of management and the types of responsibilities assigned. The mix of skills needed by a production foreman is likely to be quite different from that needed by a coordinating group vice-president. The production foreman is likely to need relatively high technical and human skills, whereas the group vice-president is likely to need relatively high conceptual and human skills.

The use of the word skill "implies an ability which can be developed, not necessarily inborn, and which is manifested in performance."[5] The following separation of these skills into three distinct categories is useful for the purposes of discussion. In practice, however, these skills are closely interrelated, and it is often difficult to tell where one begins and another ends.

Technical Skill

Technical skill refers to developing an understanding of and ability to perform specific kinds of activity. These activities involve methods, procedures, and techniques. It is probably easy to visualize the technical skills of design engineers, market researchers, and accountants. Of the three skills, technical skill is the most concrete and is most often emphasized in educational institutions and on-the-job training programs.

In the late 1950s, business schools came under considerable attack for placing too much emphasis on the development of students' technical skills at the expense of developing their human and conceptual skills. This technical-skill orientation may still be found in courses in accounting, statistics, computer programming, mathematics, finance, and business law. Other basic business courses, such as management, marketing, and business policy, are likely to focus less on technical-skill development. However, the development of technical skills is crucial for increasing efficiency of operations. This skill is likely to be of relatively greater importance for lower-level managers, especially those involved with physical operations, such as in a production plant, than for higher-level managers. (The development of technical skills is not strongly emphasized in this book. However, some attention is given to technical skills in Part II, which includes chapters on organizing, decision making, planning, and controlling.)

Human Skill

Human skill refers to the ability to lead, motivate, manage conflict, and build group effort. Whereas technical skill emphasizes working with "things" (techniques or physical objects), human skill focuses on working with people. We give this topic considerable attention, especially in Part III, which includes chapters on individual styles, motivation, leadership, groups, and conflict. Human skill is a vital part of the job of all managers, regardless of level (foreman versus vice-president) or function (production versus marketing). As mentioned earlier, one of the major tasks of management is to make work productive and the worker achieving, because organizations have only one true resource—people.

Although managers are fond of saying that people are their greatest asset, we agree with the view that "the traditional approaches to the managing of people do not focus on people as a resource, but as problems, procedures, and costs."[6] We hope that this book will play some role in the development of the human skills needed by managers for dealing with organizational members as valuable assets.

Conceptual Skill

Conceptual skill refers to developing such abilities as: (1) seeing the organization as a whole and its relationship to the external environment; (2) understanding how the parts and functions of the organization depend on one another and how changes in one part can affect all of the others; (3) knowing how to diagnose and assess different types of management problems; and (4) using models or frameworks for managing true-to-life management problems.

The development of conceptual skill involves thinking in terms of the following: "relative emphasis and priorities among conflicting objectives and criteria; relative tendencies and probabilities (rather than certainties); rough correlations and patterns among elements (rather than clear-cut cause-and-effect relationships."[7] A strong thrust throughout the book is the goal of developing your conceptual skill, which is often more difficult than the learning of concrete technical skill. Thus to avoid confusion, we have made extensive use of concrete incidents and cases to illustrate the concepts and models discussed.

Summary

The relative need for technical, human, and conceptual skills at different managerial levels is suggested in Fig. 1.2. This figure indicates that lower-level managers need substantial technical skills, moderate amounts of human skills, and small amounts of conceptual skills. Middle-management people need substantial human skills, but only moderate amounts of technical and conceptual skills. Finally, higher-management people need substantial conceptual skills, moderate amounts of human skills, and lesser amounts of technical skills. Obviously, these are generalizations, and there are important exceptions. For example, first-level research and development managers are likely to need substantial conceptual skills.

To a greater or lesser degree, every manager needs to possess some com-

Fig. 1.2. Relative skill emphasis for different management levels.

bination of technical, human, and conceptual skills. This book gives relatively greater emphasis to the development of the human and conceptual skills needed by managers. Technical skills, although extremely important, are often emphasized in other types of basic courses in schools of business as well as on-the-job training.

So far, we have discussed why it is important to learn about management and the types of skills needed by managers. With this background, we can now explain the general framework for this book.

GENERAL FRAMEWORK

There are four major, interrelated components of this book. The first component consists of the three basic *viewpoints* toward management and organizations. These viewpoints are particular ways of looking at and dealing with different aspects of management. The three—traditional, systems, and behavioral sciences—viewpoints can be integrated and/or used as appropriate to the management problem. In brief, the *traditional* viewpoint emphasizes stability and orderly management through the application of principles. The *systems* viewpoint emphasizes relationships and the interdependencies among the parts of the organization and the external environment. The *behavioral sciences* viewpoint emphasizes the organization's key resource—people.

The *contingency approach,* the second component of our general framework, enables us to draw on the strengths and contributions that have been made by the traditional, systems, and behavioral science viewpoints. According to the contingency approach, the processes, strategies, and techniques for dealing with management problems will vary according to the circumstances or situations. For example, if the external environment of an organization is changing rapidly, the internal management practices needed will be different from those needed if the external environment is relatively stable.

The contingency approach provides a more sophisticated and integrated understanding of management. Moreover, it shows how the three viewpoints can complement one another and provides a comprehensive means for diagnosing specific management problems. In sum, there is *no single viewpoint* that provides an adequate umbrella for the varied management situations issues and problems considered in this book.

The third major component in our framework is the *territory,* or subject areas of the book. The territory consists of three major parts, each of which helps integrate our understanding of the management and functioning of organizations. These parts are the *external environment* of organizations; *basic managerial processes,* such as organizing and planning; and *behavioral processes,* such as motivation and leadership. Each of these parts is examined, with emphasis on the need for different strategies and practices given various contingencies. For example, a number of concepts and research findings are useful for understanding individual motivation. The motivational profile of blue-collar workers tends to be substantially different from that of scientists; thus the causes and probable solutions for motivational problems are likely to vary for these two groups. Therefore, a manager must use a contingency and diagnostic perspective to handle these types of problems.

The decline in the usefulness of universal principles is a consequence of

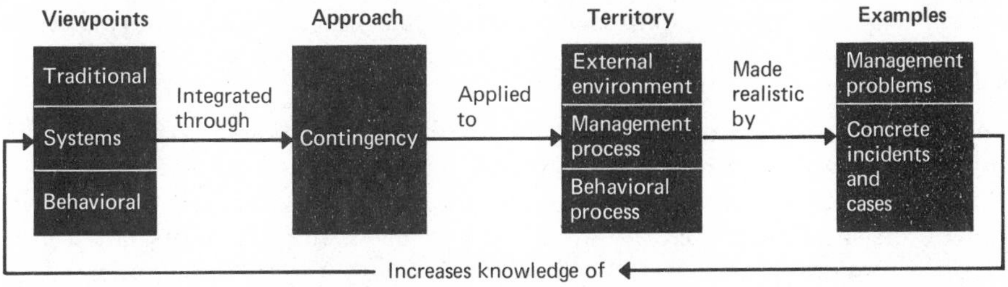

Viewpoints		Approach		Territory		Examples
Traditional Systems Behavioral	Integrated through	Contingency	Applied to	External environment Management process Behavioral process	Made realistic by	Management problems Concrete incidents and cases

— Increases knowledge of ◀—

Fig. 1.3. General framework for the study of management.

the growing body of knowledge in management. This knowledge now limits the usefulness of principles formerly presumed to hold under all conditions. This development seems to parallel the experience in other professional fields, such as medicine, law, and education.

Words such as *concept, theory, process,* and *function* have little meaning unless they can be related to something "real." To overcome this problem, true-to-life examples and case studies of organizations are used as the fourth component to our general framework. Actual managerial problems are presented that may be diagnosed and solved with a knowledge of the three viewpoints as applied through the contingency approach to the territory covered in this book. Moreover, incidents and cases are introduced to show the practical relevance of the viewpoints, contingency approach, and the territory. The general framework for the study of management used in this book is summarized in Fig. 1.3. The feedback loop from the examples to the approaches component implies that the "ways of thinking" and the body of knowledge about management are very much influenced by the activities of real organizations and real managers.

Viewpoints

An examination of the traditional, systems, and behavioral science viewpoints to the study of management and organization will show that they can be complementary and interdependent. Keep in mind that we will be presenting only some of the basic common threads in each of these viewpoints. Thus the differences among those writing from the traditional viewpoint, for example, will not be discussed here.

TRADITIONAL VIEWPOINT

The traditional viewpoint refers to a body of knowledge that management can use to create order and stability within the organization.[8] The emphasis is on formal management processes, such as organizing, decision making, planning, and controlling. The treatment of these management processes tends to focus on finding the one best way and the establishment of universal principles. The formal, heavy emphasis on the organizational point of view is illustrated in the definitions given to the planning and organizing processes:

Planning, that is working out broad outline the things that need to be done and the methods for doing them to accomplish the purpose set for the enterprise;

Organizing, that is the establishment of the formal structure of authority through which work subdivisions are arranged, defined and coordinated for the defined objective.[9]

Implicit in the definitions above and explicit in the traditional viewpoint is a relatively simple assumption about the organization's key resource—people. Traditionalists tend to write about the planning and organizing processes, among others, as though people at work, especially nonmanagers, are interested *only* in money and/or job security. This may be true in some cases; in others, not. This "sometimes-yes-sometimes-no" approach is the essence of the contingency approach. Therefore, rather than concluding that a particular way of organizing recommended in the traditional view is invalid, we will suggest that it may be effective given certain contingencies, such as routine tasks, a stable external environment, and organizational members who accept this form of organization.

SYSTEMS VIEWPOINT

The systems viewpoint is a way of observing, thinking, and solving problems.[10] Compared to the traditional and behavioral science viewpoints, the systems viewpoint is less a body of knowledge about management and more a way of considering management problems and issues.

Every individual, group, or organization can be viewed as a subsystem of a larger system and as interdependent with other subsystems.[11] For example, you may recall a time when you were under considerable pressure and tension and soon thereafter experienced a severe headache or nausea. In simplified terms, your psychological subsystem triggered reactions in your physiological subsystem. Similarly, any business organization is a system composed of various human and nonhuman subsystems. Nonhuman subsystems might include the impersonal aspects of the control, planning, and decision-making subsystems of the organization. Furthermore, that business organization can also be viewed as a subsystem of the parent corporation, which itself is a subsystem of the nation's economic system.

The relevant level or type of system depends on the specific situation facing a manager. The economist trying to forecast the national level of unemployment, for example, would not need an analysis of a single work group. On the other hand, a manager faced with the problem of high absenteeism would find little help in an analysis of expected capital expenditures or consumer attitudes about future spending plans.

The systems viewpoint, then, is concerned with the parts or structure of subsystems, the relationships among these parts, and the interdependencies between the subsystems and their higher-level systems.[12] In a more formal sense, a system consists of objects and relationships between attributes of the objects.[13] The "objects" are not so much the *physical* parts of the system (people, buildings, machines, and money) as the *functions fulfilled* (roles played) by the respective parts. In this book, we shall limit our concern to such areas as the decision-making, controlling, and leadership functions of management.

Attributes may be thought of as the characteristics (properties) of objects. For example, decision making may be differentiated by such attributes as degree of centralization, degree of certainty, and amount of (decision-making) freedom available to organization members.

The *relationships* which need to be analyzed among the environmental, managerial, and behavioral parts depend on specific contingencies. For example, the communication process, by which decisions are created, evaluated, and transmitted, might need to be examined if trouble arose within the decision-making subsystem. Similarly, relationships between the leadership and motivation processes might be analyzed in other situations, because research has demonstrated that different leadership styles have varying effects on the motivation of individuals to work. These and many other types of relationships will be discussed throughout the book.

The systems approach to the study of management is useful because it keeps us from snatching at simple cause-and-effect relationships. It also cautions us against a false sense of certainty about the definition of the problem, as well as the ultimate answer to any given management problem. Although the systems viewpoint constantly directs our attention to complex relationships, it does *not* provide us with concrete answers for dealing with such relationships.[14] In any event, managers may experience many emotions—joy, frustration, achievement, and sometimes ambiguity—in their efforts to understand the relationships among key subsystems, with their patterns, variety, and complexity. But the struggle is worthwhile if the end result is more effective management of the organization.

BEHAVIORAL SCIENCE VIEWPOINT

Behavioral science is a body of knowledge about how people behave, why they act as they do, and what the relationship is between human behavior and the larger environment.[15] The importance of the behavioral science viewpoint to the study of management becomes apparent when one realizes that *only people* act and have goals.[16] Organizations act and have goals only as a result of decisions made by people. The need for a behavioral science viewpoint in developing managerial (especially the human and conceptual) skills has been forcefully expressed as follows:

> Of all the subjects which he might undertake to study formally, none is more appropriate for the businessman-to-be than human behavior. It is not the general or liberal values alone that justify the inclusion of this topic in the business curriculum. The very nature of the firm and of the manager's role in the firm suggests that every person anticipating a responsible position in a modern enterprise needs a substantial amount of knowledge about human behavior. Thus, we stress human behavior as an element in the undergraduate business curriculum, more for its professional implications than for its general educational significance, although the latter is far from unimportant.[17]

However, the application of behavioral science insights, although generally applied from a systems point of view, is nonetheless more limited than is a totally integrated approach. For example, a behavioral science approach would be concerned with the design and functioning of the numerous forms of human-machine systems (such as assembly lines) which are utilized by organizations; this book is not. Rather, our interest focuses on the interpersonal

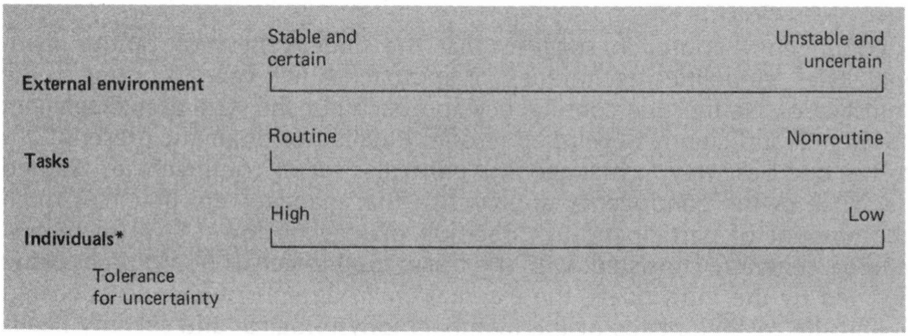

External environment	Stable and certain	Unstable and uncertain
Tasks	Routine	Nonroutine
Individuals*	High	Low
	Tolerance for uncertainty	

*Other dimensions possible, such as unskilled to professional workers, positive to negative attitudes toward management, and primary concern with lower-level needs (physiological and security) to primary concern with higher-level needs (esteem and self-actualization).

Fig. 1.4. Three key contingency variables.

personalities may result in various levels of effectiveness in different types of positions.

In brief, one of management's goals in using the contingency approach would be to create an appropriate match-up among the external environment, task, and individual contingency variables. For example, one type of harmonious match-up would exist if the external environment were stable and certain, the tasks to be performed were relatively routine, and most organizational members had a low tolerance of uncertainty.

IMPLICATIONS FOR DEVELOPMENT OF MANAGERIAL SKILLS

The contingency approach should serve as an aid in developing the technical, human, and conceptual skills needed by all managers. All of these skills are based on your *diagnostic* ability. The contingency approach places heavy emphasis on investigation, observation, and examination in the determination of management problems and possible courses of managerial action. It continuously challenges you to think analytically and to perceive the environment and yourself through many different "pairs of glasses." This is the essence of enhancing your diagnostic ability.

At a more applied level, the contingency approach helps you to develop the technical skills for determining the techniques and methods that are likely to be effective for different circumstances. Human skills are needed for dealing with various "people" problems and issues. For example, in Chapter 14, we present a basic conflict model that suggests the need for different conflict-management strategies and styles, given different contingencies. Finally, the emphasis on diagnosis and complex relationships should contribute directly to the development of your conceptual skills.

In sum, the contingency approach focuses on: (1) "if-then" relationships; (2) the idea that although there is no one best way to manage, ways are not equally effective; (3) action guidelines for determining the most likely form of effective management, given certain contingencies; and (4) the development of diagnostic ability. The contingency approach will be applied to a range of managerial issues, topics, and problems, as explained in the next section.

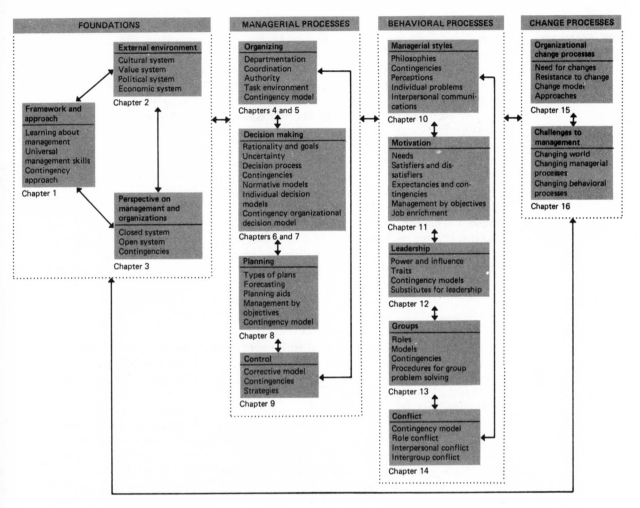

Fig. 1.5. Territory of this book.

The Territory

The territory, or subject areas, to which the traditional, systems, and behavioral science viewpoints will be applied through the contingency approach is shown in Fig. 1.5, which also identifies the chapters within which each of the content areas is discussed. The arrows and feedback loops convey the idea of mutual relationships and interdependencies between the parts and chapters. Although various possible relationships between and within these parts and chapters are explained throughout the text, you will probably find it easier to think of each chapter as being interdependent with the others.

We begin with a discussion of the effects on organizations of the external environment and some of its parts, presenting several of the interdependencies between the external environment (i.e., cultural, economic, and political systems) and organizations. Although the dimensions and scope of the external environment are practically infinite, we focus only on those aspects of the cultural, political, and economic systems which seem to have the most direct impact on organizations and their managers.

Several general models for understanding organizations as a whole are discussed in Chapter 3. Managers' choices (whether conscious or subconscious) about which general model or combination of models to use will influence the form and character of the managerial and behavioral processes of their organizations.

The managerial processes, which include organizing, decision making, planning, and controlling, are discussed in Chapters 4–9. The behavioral processes, which include styles, motivation, leadership, groups, and conflict, are presented in Chapters 10–14. The discussions of organization change processes (Chapter 15) and the future (Chapter 16) present a number of major interactions between the managerial and behavioral processes. The feedback loop from the change section (see Fig 1.5) indicates that changes within organizations can and do have external impacts on the cultural, economic, and political systems. Of course, the reverse is also true.

Summary

Whether or not you are or intend to be a manager, you need to learn about management. Effective organizations and the needs of society cannot be realized without effective management and managers, and all managers need certain technical, human, and conceptual skills.

The general framework for the study of management employed in this book was laid out in Fig. 1.3. The traditional, systems, and behavioral science viewpoints will be integrated through the contingency approach. This approach will in turn be applied to the major territory of management, including the external environment, management processes, and behavioral processes. The practical and realistic nature of this territory will be demonstrated through the use of numerous examples of applied management problems, concrete incidents, and true-to-life cases. Finally, the study of real organizations will increase your knowledge of the usefulness of and limitations to the three viewpoints.

The bridging strategy throughout the book is the contingency approach, which focuses on "if-then" relationships and the development of conceptual skills through improvement of your diagnostic ability. The general theme of the contingency approach is that there is no one best way to manage and that any two ways will not be equally effective.

The territory of management to be presented in this book was overviewed and outlined in Fig. 1.5. This framework will be repeated at the beginning of each part to help you maintain a picture of the "whole" and develop a better feel as to where you have been, where you are at the moment, and where this book is taking you.

The discussion questions at the end of each chapter can trigger your creative potential. For example, you might reflect on the content areas studied and their relevance for understanding your own and others' behavior in organizations. Or you might think about new types of relationships between the content areas which weren't considered, but might be worthy of further analysis. We hope that this type of creativity can be stimulated by discussions with other students and your professor. The possibilities for reflection, introspection, and speculation are endless. Your active involvement in such activities will make the book more meaningful to you here and now, as well as in future managerial roles. In sum, this book should serve as an aid in the development of needed managerial skills.

Discussion Questions

1. What are the learning objectives for studying management and organization? Use a specific example to explain how one builds on the other.

2. A firm has a problem of coordinating between its district branches and central headquarters. How might the communication element be analyzed from the systems viewpoint, and how might the interpersonal element be analyzed from the behavioral science viewpoint?

3. Explain the usefulness and limitations of the contingency approach.

4. Think of some problem you have recently experienced within an organization. Then try to diagnose this problem through the use of the contingency approach. In doing this, you should be concerned with undertaking a diagnosis rather than with arriving at a solution.

5. If possible, identify at least three courses you have taken and explain how they have contributed to the development of your technical, human, and conceptual skills.

Management Incidents

JOHN TAYLOR

John Taylor is a production foreman for the United Steel Association, Inc. Lately, his monthly production quota has not been met, and John has found himself "in trouble" with his boss. John reports that the problem is in the area of raw materials; he never seems to have adequate stocks. Jim Zack, his superior, realizes that this is a problem, but reports that it is John's job to handle scheduling. (Apparently John didn't realize this; as a result, he has been experiencing increased anxiety.)

How could Mr. Zack analyze this problem if he used: (1) the systems viewpoint; (2) the behavioral science viewpoint; (3) the contingency approach?

JANE CARTER

Jane Carter is 23 years old and fresh out of college with a bachelor's degree in business. Despite a tight job market, Jane landed a job as a supervisor in one of the manufacturing plants in her home town. This plant produces refrigerators. Jane is to be a supervisor in one of the departments that has the task of final assembly of refrigerators. She is to supervise twelve individuals; eight of them are in their early twenties, and the other four are in their early fifties.

The 12 workers are paid a low hourly rate plus a group-incentive rate. The latter is based on a combination of the number of refrigerators assembled plus the quality of the group's work. A variety of standards is used by the quality control department to inspect and assess the degree of quality of the assembly department's work. A standard quality control form is completed by the quality control department for each refrigerator. Based on a rather involved formula, the group-incentive pay would be reduced in "proportion" to the severity of the quality problems found in the assembly work.

There are only two restrictions on Jane's freedom in running her department. First, the weekly production goals established by higher management must be met. Second, the general personnel policies and rules must be followed. No union represents the production workers, and they do not appear to want to form one.

Jane has just completed a three-month orientation program to the plant as a whole. Somewhat unstructured, this program consisted primarily of spending several weeks in each of the departments in the plant, except the one over which she will be supervisor. It's Sunday afternoon, and Jane is thinking (and feeling a little anxious) about officially assuming the position of supervisor on Monday morning.

1. What contingency variables should Jane be thinking about?
2. How might differences on each of these contingency variables be important influences on her management style and practices?
3. What types of management skills is Jane going to have to emphasize in the first two months and in the long run?

REFERENCES

1. E. Schell, "Everybody Is a Manager," in *The Manager's Job,* ed. R. Livingston and W. Waite (New York: Columbia University Press, 1960), p. 50.

2. P. Drucker, *Management: Tasks, Responsibilities, Practices* (New York: Harper & Row, 1973), p. 40.

3. "America's Growing Antibusiness Mood," *Business Week,* September 17, 1972.

4. R. Katz, "Skills of an Effective Administrator," *Harvard Business Review* **52** (1974): 90–101.

5. *Ibid.,* p. 9.

6. Drucker, *op. cit.,* p. 308.

7. Katz, *op. cit.,* p. 101.

8. R. Miles, *Theories of Management: Implications for Organizational Behavior and Development* (New York: McGraw-Hill, 1975), p. 38.

9. L. Gulick, "Notes on the Theory of Organization," in *Papers on the Science of Administration,* ed. L. Gulick and L. Urwick (New York: Columbia University Press, 1937), p. 13.

10. J. Buckley, "Goal-Process-System Interaction in Management: Correcting an Imbalance," *Business Horizons* **14** (1971): 81–92.

11. F. Kast and J. Rosenzweig, "General Systems Theory: Applications for Organization and Management," *Academy of Management Journal* **15** (1972): 447–465.

12. D. Katz and R. Kahn, *The Social Psychology of Organizations* (New York: Wiley, 1966), p. 18.

13. A. Hall and R. Fagen, "Definition of System," *General Systems* **1** (1956): 18.

14. A. Melcher, "Theory and Application of Systems Theory: Its Promises, Problems, and Realizations," *Organization and Administrative Sciences* **6** (1975): 3–9.

15. M. Wadia, "Management Education and the Behavioral Sciences," *Advanced Management* **36** (1961): p. 8.

16. J. Ritchie and P. Thompson, *Organization and People: Readings, Cases and Exercises in Organizational Behavior* (St. Paul: West, 1976), p. 1.

17. R. Gordon and J. Howell, *Higher Education for Business* (New York: Columbia University Press, 1959), p. 166.

18. R. Mathis and J. Jackson, *Personnel: Contemporary Perspectives and Applications* (St. Paul: West, 1976).

19. F. Luthan, *Introduction to Management: A Contingency Approach* (New York: McGraw-Hill, 1976), p. 29.

20. J. Newstrom, W. Reif, and R. Monczka, *A Contingency Approach to Management: Readings* (New York: McGraw-Hill, 1975).

21. J. Lorsch and P. Lawrence, *Studies in Organization Design* (Homewood, Ill.: Richard D. Irwin and Dorsey Press, 1970).

22. F. Fiedler, "Style or Circumstance: The Leadership Enigma," *Psychology Today* **3** (1969): 38–43.

2
External Environment

FOUNDATIONS

External environment

Cultural system
Value system
Political system
Economic system

Chapter 2

Framework and approach

Learning about
management
Universal
management skills
Contingency
approach

Chapter 1

Perspective on management and organizations

Closed system
Open system
Contingencies

Chapter 3

The major objectives of this chapter are to:

suggest new ways for thinking about differences in cultures and how these differences can act as an important contingency;

develop your understanding of the importance of the political processes that always take place between an organization and groups external to it, e.g., customers, regulatory agencies, and suppliers;

increase your knowledge and skill in the use of six major political strategies used by the managements of all organizations in dealing with their external environments;

demonstrate the importance of the economic system to management and how market structure acts as a contingency to influence the amount of managerial decision-making discretion.

The systems and behavioral science viewpoints, as applied through the contingency approach, require that management explicitly recognize forces that are external and internal to the organization. The external environment directly or indirectly influences the organization's: (1) *internal practices and processes,* such as the formal structure; (2) opportunities for *continued survival and growth;* and (3) *degree of discretion* (freedom and autonomy) that can be exercised by management.[1] Today, virtually every major management problem is affected by some aspect or group from the external environment of the organization.

The external environment of organizations is comprised of the cultural, political, and economic systems. These systems are treated as part of the external environment primarily for the sake of convenience. It is obvious that organizations are *part* of the environment; they not only are influenced by it, but can also change it. For example, values, a crucial element of the cultural system, are not just outside the organization; they impact on various processes and activities inside the organization as well.[2]

This chapter specifically focuses on the external environment and suggests some of its broad implications for management. One of the essential activities of all organization is the continuous need to adapt to and cope with changes in the external environment.[3] With the external environment of organizations becoming more erratic, unpredictable, and complex, it is essential for managers to have a high level of conceptual and human skills for coping with their changing environments. This chapter places primary emphasis on the development of your conceptual skills for dealing with the external environment.

We will discuss only some major dimensions of the cultural, political, and economic systems that interact with organizations and must, therefore, be understood and dealt with by managers. The groups that can play a role in the cultural, political and economic systems and can thus impact on management are wide-ranging. Of course, management can and does directly impact these groups as well. Some of the groups of direct significance to management are customers, suppliers, competitors, unions, regulatory groups (government), etc.[4]

CULTURAL SYSTEM

Concept of Culture

Since 1960 culture has increasingly been used as an important contingency variable for explaining differences in the behavior of organizations and management. The emerging field of comparative management has relied especially heavily on cross-cultural studies. However, there is no single definition of culture. The term has been variously defined as a society's attitudes, beliefs, and values; as all those features characteristic of a society's stage of advancement; and as all of a society's social, political, educational, legal, and economic characteristics.[5] The first definition is the one we find most useful.

Role of Culture

INTERPLAY WITH MANAGEMENT

There is a direct interplay between the culture and management; many management practices are, at least in part, based on the beliefs, customs, and political system of the culture within which the organization is operating.[6]

The importance of appreciating culture differences is especially significant for
the management of multinational corporations. For example, between 1960
and 1974, private American direct investment abroad rose from about $32 bil-
lion to over $110 billion; foreign private direct investment in the United States
rose from about $7 billion to $20 billion.[7] With the prospect of Volvo, Volkswagen, Toyota, and many other foreign firms opening plants in the United
States, it appears that foreign firms are establishing operations in the United
States at an accelerating rate.

HELPS ANSWER BASIC QUESTIONS

The behavior of organizations and their members has to be understood within
a cultural context, because that context helps people answer the following
types of questions:

1. *What is reality?* Culture influences how we perceive and interpret our
   environment. For instance, it helps us define such things as safe and dangerous conditions and the importance of time, and it determines whether
   we explain events in terms of physical or supernatural causation.
2. *What is valuable?* Culture defines what we consider important and what
   gives meaning to our lives. For example, culture determines the significance of wealth and how it is used.
3. *What means are available?* Culture creates and maintains the know-how
   and technologies that enable us to pursue our goals. For example, as major
   cultural institutions, schools and colleges create and transmit knowledge
   so that a skilled work force will be available to serve the goals of other
   institutions.
4. *What are the proper standards of conduct?* Culture defines the accepted
   rules of behavior that organizations and individuals are expected to follow.[8]

In 1976 it was disclosed that some of the largest multinational business
firms in the United States had paid millions of dollars in bribes to politicians
and government officials. The resulting furor suggests the gap that can sometimes exist between standards and actual conduct. However, the commitment
to a high moral tone in management had earlier been reaffirmed as follows by
Clifton Garvin, Jr., chairman of Exxon: "An overly ambitious employee might
have the mistaken idea that we do not care how results are obtained, as long
as he gets results. He might think it best not to tell higher management all that
he is doing, not to record all transactions accurately. . . . He would be wrong
on all counts. . . . We don't want liars for managers."[9]

In contrast, people in some other countries appear to accept bribery and
influence peddling as a normal standard of conduct. This cultural difference
has been used as the major rationalization by executives of American multinational organizations for offering bribes in foreign countries. Since everyone
else was bribing, they argued, they were forced to do so as well to remain
competitive.

However, even though different countries may have different cultures, a
culture does not necessarily have national boundaries. In other words, there
could be more than one culture in a given country.[10] For example, although

Table 2.1. The cultural continuum

Cultural dimensions	Cultural continuum	
	Traditional	Complex
1. Amount of formal education	Little	Extensive
2. Extent of factory-type jobs	Few	Many
3. Attitude toward new experiences (both with people and in new ways of doing things)	Tendency to reject	Tendency to accept
4. Belief in science and medicine	Passive and fatalistic	Active and optimistic
5. Level and complexity of goals for one's self and children	Low and few	High and many
6. Punctuality (wanting people to be on time and showing an interest in planning)	Unimportant	Important
7. News events	Limited to local news	Concern with national and international news
8. Institutions which satisfy needs	Few, with emphasis on family	Many, with changed role of family
9. Geographic	Tendency toward rural	Tendency toward urban

A. Inkeles, "Making Men Modern: On the Causes and Consequences of Individual Change in Six Developing Countries," *American Journal of Sociology* 73 (1968): 215. Reprinted by permission.

the United States has a dominant cultural pattern, distinct subcultures also exist. One such subculture is the "counterculture" hippie movement, which seems to represent a movement toward a more basic, or traditional, culture. The basic differences between traditional and modern cultures are summarized in Table 2.1. Of course, cultures are not rigid *or* static, traditional *or* modern. Rather, most cultures undergo continuous change and also provide some freedom within which individuals and organizations can maneuver.

Cultural Differences as a Contingency

Although this section serves to illustrate culture as a contingency, keep in mind that we are "painting with a broad brush." Thus there can be major differences in managerial practices and the like within any particular culture.

A number of cultural dimensions are used to identify and characterize cultures. These dimensions can be measured along a continuum ranging from traditional to complex, as noted in Table 2.1. Several studies have suggested that the cultural continuum is a useful tool for beginning to appreciate cultural differences. Here we will consider cultural differences relating to employee needs, management style, organization structure, and a composite view of the overall pattern of operation in Japanese firms.

EMPLOYEE NEEDS

One study examined the possible influence of culture on the way a group of workers in the United States and a group in Mexico evaluated their needs for security, social esteem, autonomy, and self-actualization.[11] Both groups worked in plants belonging to the same multinational glass-products company. The study found significant differences in the way the two groups rated almost every one of their needs; the Mexican workers were toward the traditional end of the cultural continuum, whereas the American workers were at the modern end. In general, the Mexican workers placed more importance on the measured needs and were more satisfied than their American counterparts. The data also showed that among the Mexican workers, security was the most important, but the least satisfied need.

The study also emphasized that work has a different significance and plays a different role in the lives of different cultural groups. Of course, tremendous variations can exist among members of a single culture in such things as need satisfaction.[12] For example, the needs of Mexican managers could be more similar to American managers than to Mexican production workers.

Implications for Managers. What can we learn from cross-cultural studies? First, since worker motivation appears to be somewhat culture-bound, a manager can improve the workers' effectiveness only by being sensitive to their cultural background. This is suggested in the frustration stated by an American manager operating in a country with a traditional culture:

> Somehow or other, we just can't get the local people here to assume any responsibility. They won't make decisions unless you tell them what decisions to make. They hate to take the rap if anything goes wrong. They always want to be in a position to put the blame on someone else if the going gets tough. I think there is some cultural trait in these people which makes them shun responsibility. We will always need Americans here in the key jobs because these local people just don't have what it takes to be a good manager.[13]

Second, when a candidate is being considered for a management position outside the United States, his or her ability to adjust to new situations has to be considered. Only by understanding the surrounding culture can a new manager decide how to adapt his or her motivational approach. In a traditional culture, the manager might want to develop a family feeling in the work situation by taking on a parental role. Or, the manager may find it effective to adopt specific rules and regulations to guide employees' actions throughout the entire working day. In a modern culture, on the other hand, the manager may consider it appropriate to adopt a more democratic style of leadership, perhaps encouraging workers to participate in decisions and exercise personal discretion.[14] In each case, the manager needs to take cues from the culture itself.

MANAGEMENT STYLE

Mexican versus American. Some researchers have investigated the way different external environmental conditions affect management philosophies. One such study contrasted American and Mexican management philosophies and concluded:

> Scientific method demands disciplined, patient thinking. From the viewpoint of Mexican managers, scientific method requires intellectual confinement and thus runs counter to their inherent drive for free expression of thoughts.
>
> Through the Mexican psychological makeup there flows a wide stream of passion; they tend toward impatience, impulsiveness, and a disregard for objectivity. Action is important not because it may lead to beneficial results, but because it is the vehicle which allows expression of feelings. And this is the underlying important element: spontaneous expression.[15]

The American penchant for the scientific method doesn't mean that Americans make better decisions. Rather, Mexicans apparently rely more on their inferential ability and recognize redundancy in information far sooner than do Americans.[16]

Chilean versus American. Another study compared American-owned and controlled businesses with comparable domestically owned and controlled firms in Chile.[17] Performances in a wide variety of industries were compared on six measures of effectiveness, such as net profits and return on investment, over a five-year period. The Chilean-owned firms performed substantially better than their American counterparts. Why? In brief, the American firms operated essentially "by the book"—those general policies and guidelines established by the American headquarters. In contrast, the management philosophy of the Chilean firms tended to be highly individualized and was usually based on the personal values of the presidents and local boards of directors.

However, there is also considerable evidence that American firms have done well abroad because of their ability to transfer managerial practices and methods of organization to their international operations.[18]

ORGANIZATION STRUCTURE

Some data suggest that organizational structures may vary partly as a function of cultural differences. One such study compared the organizational structures of 12 large multinational companies based in France, Germany, Switzerland, the United Kingdom, and the United States.[19] The size, technology, ownership situation, and resource requirements of the 12 companies were quite similar.

Several findings are worth noting. First, the European-based firms typically adopted a global structure, whereby all divisional or major managers had worldwide responsibilities. By contrast, the United States–based firms tended to have separate international divisions to direct foreign operations. Interestingly, there appears to be little evidence that one type of structure works better than the other.

Another finding was that the formal superior-subordinate reporting relationships between the corporate headquarters and the overseas units were less structured in the European-based than in the United States–based firms. In addition, United States firms tended to specify more clearly the limits of discretionary authority available to their managers abroad and to rely more on formal, periodic controls. German multinational companies, however, with their emphasis on long-run financial stability, were found to exercise close control over both short- and long-run decisions affecting their subsidiary operations.[20]

GENERAL PATTERN OF OPERATION

A striking case study of the relationship between culture and a general pattern of organization is the "Nenko" system commonly used in the large-scale Japanese organizations which account for about a third of the Japanese labor force.[21] Since the Nenko system is so closely tied to the broader Japanese culture and economy, however, it probably cannot be simplistically transferred to organizations in other cultural and economic settings.[22] Nonetheless, there is some evidence that parts of this system have been successfully implemented in Japanese plants located on the American West Coast.[23]

Employment Security. The Nenko system emphasizes *life-long employment* with a particular firm. After completing one's formal education, the individual joins an organization and is expected to remain until retirement—normally at about 55 years of age. Of course, the obligation is mutual. The large Japanese employer is not supposed to fire or lay off an employee, except in an extreme emergency.

In practice, there has been some loosening up of this pattern of mutual life-long commitment. Some employers have successfully "raided" highly skilled employees from other firms. Employers have also used a higher percentage of "temporary" employees who can be laid off. Even with these modifications, however, there is considerable job security. This often is suggested as one of the reasons Japanese employees are more acceptant of change, especially technological change, than their American counterparts are.

Emphasis on Seniority. The amount of compensation and opportunities for promotion are heavily based on *seniority,* i.e., the length of an employee's service. This Nenko practice is widely accepted because employees tend to have a strong belief that competence (within a job category) increases automatically with seniority. Apparently, individuals in the managerial category are compensated almost entirely on the basis of seniority. After a manager has reached about 45 years of age, however, primarily weight is given to performance and merit.

Group Loyalty. There tends to be an intense sense of *group loyalty* and *shared obligations* under the Nenko system. Cooperation and working as a team is the norm, and individuals tend to think of themselves in terms of the groups to which they belong. This results in a strong feeling of duty and loyalty to the groups. Performance assessments for determining promotability (for people who meet the seniority test) give heavy weight to such criteria as flexibility, group support, and company loyalty. The close and subordinate identity of the individual to the group is illustrated by a typical manager's self-introduction: "I work for Mitsubishi, and my name is Tanaka."[24]

Intergroup Competition. The reverse of the "we" feeling under Nenko is a "they" feeling. Relations within groups discourage competition and encourage harmony and cooperation. However, there is often intense *intergroup competition* among different firms within an industry as well as among separate work groups within a single organization. Such conflicts are often resolved by an appeal to a "higher authority," e.g., higher management or even the "national good."

Group Decision Making. Under Nenko, extensive use is made of a form of group decision making leading to a group consensus. However, this consensus is aimed at *defining the questions* needing attention rather than at deciding what should be done. This process of group decision making is much more time consuming than other methods, such as simply letting one person decide. However, implementation tends to be quicker, since people are more convinced of the merits of what is being done and why.

SUMMARY

Cross-cultural studies reveal culture-based differences between an organization and its environment. Not only is management influenced by its cultural context, but the entire organization may have to adjust the way it relates to its environment. Therefore, management should consider the need to adapt leadership styles and management systems to the characteristics of the organization's cultural environment.

The cultural continuum is a useful tool for making rough comparisons of cultures, and it may also be useful within a given culture. This is especially true for varied and complex cultures such as that of the United States, in which distinct subcultures may be identified. Similarly, even though two cultures may be characterized as complex, they may be very different, e.g., the United States and Japan.

Value Systems

Values and value systems are one of the most important elements for making comparisons between cultures and between groups and individuals within one culture. We can define a value as a basic *concept* that has considerable *importance* and *meaning* to the individual and is relatively *stable,* or unchanging, over time.[25] Terms such as "competition," "property," "equality," and "cooperation" may all be considered to be basic concepts. Any basic concept can be assessed by determining its importance (high, medium, or low) and meaning (e.g., "successful," "right," or "pleasant") for the individual. Thus a value represents one of the concepts determining what is important and meaningful, or significant, to an individual.

A *value system,* then, may be defined as simply the *composite* of an individual's values that normally fit into some *pattern* and *hierarchy,* or ordering by importance. Moreover, a value system often consists of concepts that are compatible with and supportive of one another. For example, of the four values presented above, "competition" and "property" are likely to be highly compatible with each other and somewhat less so with "equality" and "cooperation."

IMPORTANCE OF VALUES TO MANAGEMENT

It is important for all individuals, especially managers, to appreciate the significance of values and value systems. Although the role of values will be cited throughout the book, for the moment let's just consider the general significance of personal values to management, which have been summarized by England as follows:

1. Personal value systems influence the way a manager looks at other individuals and groups of individuals, thus influencing interpersonal relationships;
2. Personal value systems influence a manager's perception of situations and problems;
3. Personal value systems influence a manager's decisions and solutions to problems;
4. Personal value systems set the limits for the determination of what is and is not ethical managerial behavior;
5. Personal value systems influence the extent to which a manager will accept or resist organizational pressures and goals;
6. Personal value systems influence not only the perception of individual and organizational success, but its achievement as well.[26]

Of course, personal value systems will influence nonmanagers in similar ways as well. We now turn to the types of concepts that can go into a value system. The variations in the significance assigned to these value concepts will show differences in value systems and their impact on people's decisions and behavior.

VALUE FRAMEWORK

The value framework presented in this section is drawn from the work of England and his associates.[27] Because of its complexity, we will highlight only certain aspects of their value framework.

Identification and Assessment of Value Concepts. England and his associates identified 66 concepts (values) for assessing managers' personal value systems. These 66 concepts were then categorized into five classes: goals of business organizations, personal goals of individuals, groups of people, ideas associated with people, and ideas about general topics. The 66 concepts and their categorization into each class are shown in Fig. 2.1.

To assess an individual's values, a questionnaire listing the 66 concepts was developed. Respondents are asked to react to each concept in terms of

Goals of business organizations	Personal goals of individuals	Groups of people
____ Employee welfare	____ Achievement	Semiskilled workers
____ High productivity	____ Autonomy	Highly skilled workers
____ Industry leadership	____ Creativity	Customers
____ Organizational efficiency	____ Dignity	All employees
____ Organizational growth	____ Individuality	Government
____ Organizational stability	____ Influence	Unskilled workers
____ Profit maximization	____ Job satisfaction	Labor unions
____ Social welfare	____ Leisure	Managers
	____ Money	Me
	____ Power	My boss
	____ Prestige	My company
	____ Security	My coworkers
	____ Success	My subordinates
		Owners
		Stockholders
		Technical staff
		White-collar employees

Ideas associated with people	Ideas about general topics
____ Ability	____ Authority
____ Aggressiveness	____ Caution
____ Ambition	____ Change
____ Compassion	____ Competition
____ Conformity	____ Compromise
____ Cooperation	____ Conflict
____ Honor	____ Conservatism
____ Loyalty	____ Emotions
____ Obedience	____ Equality
____ Prejudice	____ Force
____ Skill	____ Liberalism
____ Tolerance	____ Property
____ Trust	____ Rational
	____ Religion
	____ Risk

Fig. 2.1. Value framework of concepts within five classes. (G. England, O. Dhingra, and N. Agarwal, "The Manager and the Man: A Cross-Cultural Study of Personal Values," *Organization and Administrative Sciences* **5** (1974): 9. Used with permission.)

its *importance* and *meaning* to themselves. The importance of a concept is determined by having the individual rate it as high, average, or low; for meaning, the individual rates each concept as being "successful," "right," or "pleasant." Thus individuals might view the same concepts as important, but for somewhat different reasons.

You might find it useful to make a rough diagnosis of your own values. You could then compare yourself with some of the findings to be presented or use the diagnosis as a basis for discussion with your classmates. On a separate sheet of paper, rate each of the 66 concepts' importance (high, average, or low) and meaning ("successful," "right," or "pleasant") to you. To develop a general idea of your expressed value system, first underscore the concepts you indicated as having high importance within each of the five

classes. Then, for those concepts indicated as highly important within each
class, look for a pattern to the meaning you assigned them.

Value Orientations. Normally one of three value orientations emerges from a person's responses on the questionnaire. A *pragmatic* value orientation exists within a class if the individual tended to respond to highly important concepts as "successful." This type of individual is said to be guided more by a concern for whether a certain course of action will work and how successful or unsuccessful it is likely to be. Thus there tends to be an emphasis on "practicality" versus "idealism."

An *ethical-moral* value orientation exists within a class if the individual tended to respond to highly important concepts as "right." This type of individual is said to be guided more by a concern for whether a certain course of action is "right" or "wrong," "moral" or "immoral." The debate in 1976 over the practice of giving bribes to obtain business in other countries was based in part on conflict between pragmatic and ethical-moral value systems. Some American executives, off the record, stated: "Although we don't like to give bribes, it is necessary to get the orders, and this is an established way of doing business in certain countries." In contrast, other executives stated: "It's wrong, that's why we don't and won't do it, so there's no other issue to consider."

The third type of pattern is a *self-satisfaction* value orientation, which exists if the individual tended to respond to highly important concepts as "pleasant." This type of individual is said to be guided more by a concern for whether a certain course of action will maximize his or her own self-interest. Thus there tends to be an emphasis on increasing personal pleasure and decreasing pain (hedonism).

The potential usefulness and implications of this value framework are provided by highlighting value orientations of managers within and across cultures and American managers versus labor leaders.

CULTURAL DIFFERENCES

There are both differences and similarities in value orientations of managers across cultures. With respect to similarity, organizational goals such as efficiency, growth, and stability tend to be considered as important concepts across cultures. Moreover, there can be major differences among managers within a given culture. Among the managers studied in each country, certain managers were found to have a strong pragmatic orientation, some an ethical-moral orientation, and others a self-satisfaction orientation. Managers within a culture can also be characterized as "hard" or "soft." "Hard" managers placed high importance on ambition, obedience, aggressiveness, achievement, success, competition, risk, and force; "soft" managers placed high importance on loyalty, trust, cooperation, compassion, tolerance, employee welfare, social welfare, and religion. Where do you rank on the "hard"-"soft" continuum? Do you tend to fall into one pattern or the other?

With this background and qualification, we can highlight some of the broad similarities of managers within a given country. This also serves to highlight differences in value patterns of managers between cultures. The value patterns for American, Japanese, Korean, Indian, and Australian managers have been sketched by England and his associates as follows:

1. American managers:
   a) Large element of pragmatism
   b) Low importance of social values
   c) Emphasis on traditional organizational goals, such as profit maximization, organizational efficiency, and high productivity
2. Japanese managers:
   a) Very high element of pragmatism
   b) Value magnitude very high (size and growth)
   c) Low value on conflict and its open expression
   d) Motivation for work seems more a product of forces external to the organization than internal to the organization
3. Korean managers:
   a) Large element of pragmatism
   b) Low value on most employee groups as significant reference groups
   c) Low importance of political and social values
   d) Generally low value on organizational goals
4. Indian managers:
   a) High degree of moralistic orientation
   b) High relevance on political values
   c) Value on stable organizations with minimal or steady change
   d) Value on personal goals and status orientation
   e) Value on a blend of organizational compliance and competence
   f) Low value on most employee groups
5. Australian managers:
   a) High degree of moralistic orientation
   b) High emphasis on social and political values
   c) Low value on such concepts as achievement, success, competition, and risk.[28]

As suggested earlier in the chapter, value patterns are important because of their potential impact on interpersonal relationships, perceptions of situations and problems, decisions and solutions to problems, what is and is not regarded as ethical behavior, and the like. This is further illustrated by comparing the general value pattern of American managers with a sample of American labor leaders.

AMERICAN MANAGERS VERSUS LABOR LEADERS

An individual's value pattern is likely to be influenced somewhat by the requirements and expectations of his or her position and organization. Also, individuals are likely to seek out or remain in positions that are somewhat consistent with their value patterns. Accordingly, striking differences have been found in the value patterns of American managers and American union leaders.[29] One major difference is that union leaders seem to emphasize an ethical-moral value orientation; managers, a pragmatic value orientation.

The two groups were asked to indicate the relative importance of organizational goals, including employee welfare, organizational efficiency, high productivity, organizational stability, industry leadership, organizational growth, social welfare, and profit maximization. The union leaders, as a group, considered employee welfare the most important and profit maximization the least important organizational goal. The managers ranked these goals the other way around. Similarly, ambition, ability, and skill were important values for managers, whereas trust, loyalty, and honor were much less important. Just the reverse was found for union leaders.

It is apparent that these contrasting value patterns help explain why the two groups approach various issues from contrasting and even conflicting directions. You might want to take a moment again and see how you compare with the union leaders and managers on the value patterns just outlined.

DIVERSITY IN AMERICA'S VALUES

An in-depth analysis of the historical roots of American values is beyond the scope of this book. But some background on the evolution of the Protestant and Judeo-Christian ethics is needed for understanding the diversity in America's values today.[30]

Calvinism. Calvinism was the dominant strain of reformed Christianity in America, and it fostered the development of the so-called Protestant ethic. This ethic, characteristic of America from about 1620 to 1930, emphasized the acquisition of property (material wealth) and competition. The Calvinists believed in predestination, namely, that only a few people are chosen for God's kingdom. Consequently, each individual faced the anxiety of trying to determine whether he or she was among those chosen for Heaven. Since worldly success was interpreted as a sign of election, a premium was placed on hard work and acquisitiveness. Thus the Protestant ethic, through Calvinism, was compatible with and supportive of the emergence of American capitalism.

Judeo-Christian Ethic. The Judeo-Christian ethic, with its emphasis on cooperation and equality, appears to be in conflict with the Protestant ethic. But since 1930, it has been gaining prominence in the United States. The Protestant ethic seems to be consistent with autonomy in decision making and the exclusive pursuit of profit in business. The Judeo-Christian ethic calls for the use of a different value framework. In 1975 *Business Week* recognized this shift in a special three-part series.[31] One impact of this value shift has resulted in the expansion of the role of the federal government in the United States today and the push for equality.

The emergence of this ethic in the business sector and some of the dilemmas it poses are dramatically apparent in a report published by the Committee for Economic Development (CED). This report, which was strongly influenced by 50 executives who are trustees of CED, represents a significant departure in the *expressed* social responsibilities of business enterprises in America. The attempt to blend the Protestant and the Judeo-Christian ethics can be found in numerous sections of the report. The following citation illustrates this attempt.

Current profitability, once regarded as the dominant if not exclusive objective, is now often seen more as a vital means and powerful motivating force for achieving broader ends, rather than as an end in itself. Thus, modern managers are prepared to trade off short-run profits to achieve qualitative improvements in the institution which can be expected to contribute to the long-run profitable growth of the corporation.[32]

Although such statements leave many questions unanswered and create new conflicts for the manager, they do represent a major shift in American attitudes from earlier periods. Cornelius Vanderbilt (1794–1877), for example, was the very personification of competitive and acquisitive values, and he amassed $100 million from investments in the railroad industry. He felt that the public had no business meddling in his railroads: "Law! What do I care about the law? Hain't I got the power?"[33] Compare this statement with the CED quote!

We do not want to give the impression that most managers have accepted the values expressed in the CED report or that they even consider them to be relevant criteria in decision making. This would not be at all consistent with the value pattern of American managers presented earlier. However, the fact that a group of executives expressed the desirability of incorporating other values into the decision-making process may represent the beginning of a major change in American management.

Implications for Management. As suggested in Fig. 2.2, the Calvinistic tradition and Judeo-Christian ethic underlie the diversity and conflict in the values of contemporary America. To us, this implies the inevitability of conflict, ambiguity, disorder, and muddling through certain decisions. There is no single unifying thread which a manager can use as a "guiding light" in making all decisions. Different solutions to recurring problems may easily be rationalized by apply-

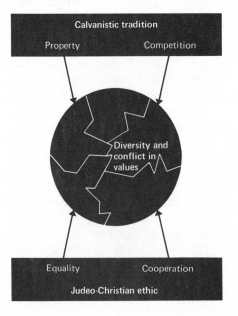

Fig. 2.2. Diversity in contemporary values.

ing different values. On the other hand, a manager could experience consider-able conflict, when faced with several possible solutions to a problem, if each alternative seemed to satisfy a different value. In such a case, it may be neces-sary to trade off one value for another.

Current prescriptions for resolving these uncertainties are themselves con-flicting and range from B. F. Skinner's call for the "intentional design of a culture and the control of human behavior"[34] to a plea for greater personal growth and freedom.[35] Obviously, prescriptions such as these represent value judgments of the first magnitude. It is not our intention to assert the right prescription. Rather, we want to emphasize some of the complexity and diversity with which the modern manager is faced.[36]

Summary

One useful definition of culture is that it comprises a society's value orienta-tion. Therefore, there is a close relationship between culture and management practices. Values and the diverse value patterns in American culture and be-tween cultures are an important factor in the decision-making process. En-gland's value framework can be used to highlight the difference in managerial values that can exist within organizations. In sum, we began with a cross-cultural emphasis, proceeded to a discussion of a value framework for considering values of individuals and groups, and ended with a presentation of the diversity of values which seems to prevail in contemporary America.

POLITICAL SYSTEM

Importance of Political System

The political system can be considered a subsystem of the cultural system. Since values and conflicts in values are often expressed through political pro-cesses, it is logical to discuss the political system after discussing values. Busi-ness, educational, and religious organizations, among others, typically try to influence the political system in order to enhance the likelihood of their own survival and the attainment of the values they cherish. This means that business and other organizations may use direct or indirect political processes to influ-ence the behavior and even the survival of other organizations. Consumer groups, for example, have tried to influence business organizations primarily through government units.

Our comments on the political system will be highly selective, focusing on the external dimensions of the political system as they relate to management. We will focus primarily on the major strategies organizations have used to influence and respond to the political environment.

POLITICAL SYSTEM AND BUSINESS

In its broadest implications, the political system includes the decision-making components of a social system as well as those components involved in ob-taining support for these decisions from the environment. Therefore, an orga-nization's political environment extends beyond governmental institutions, as

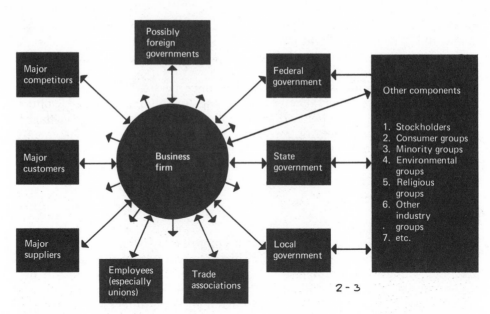

Fig. 2.3. Some components of a business firm's environment.

important as these might be, to the whole complex of groups, institutions, and individuals possessing power to influence decisions and behavior. For the business firm, these sources of influence include trade associations, major customers, government agencies, and other components.[37]

Figure 2.3 identifies the diverse components of the external environment of business firms—especially of large corporations—with which political processes often occur. These components can both influence and be influenced by businesses. The extent to which managers have to deal with each component will vary over time as issues come and go. Customers, suppliers, and employees are commonly regarded as key participants in the economic system, but are included in the political environment because of the interaction that occurs among economic, social, and political forces.

Figure 2.3 also suggests that the influences on business firms are as diverse as the contemporary value system in America. But as Epstein concludes: "Although the political power of business firms and their managers is very real and pervasive, it does not presently constitute a danger to the American pluralistic democracy."[38] This is because legislation, rulings, decisions, and programs that are contrary to the desires of significant corporate interests continue to be made. Nonetheless, there is considerable concern that managers in certain segments of the economy, particularly corporations or certain groups, may exert excessive political power.[39]

Political Strategies

Since a firm's external environment is diverse and continually changing, there is probably no single political strategy that managers can use for responding

to or influencing that environment. A strategy is a general approach, usually
expressed in general terms, for achieving a desired objective. In discussing some of the major strategies that organizations have used for relating to their environments, we will focus on the "what is" rather than on the "what ought to be." However, since these latter (normative) questions are extremely important and complex, you may want to think about them as each strategy is examined. Here are three examples of normative questions:

1. How much influence should an organization exert or be permitted to exert in its environment?
2. What forms of influence are appropriate?
3. Under what conditions is it acceptable for the manager to choose particular strategies and tactics?

For example, there may be widespread societal agreement that business firms and other organizations should have the right to lobby before government units. But there is considerable disagreement over the tactics they should be permitted to use to influence the political process.

Six of the major political strategies organizations and managers use to respond to their environment are: cooptation, bargaining, lobbying, coalition, representation, and socialization. In practice, these strategies are not mutually exclusive; they are usually used in some combination. Thus the examples of each strategy often contain elements of the others.

COOPTATION

An organization practices cooptation when it assimilates into its leadership or policy-making structure those elements it views as threatening to its stability or existence.[40] The process of cooptation influences the organization's autonomy—to some extent paradoxically. On the one hand, the coopted individuals or groups become involved in those units of the organization that can influence and shape its future course of action. From this perspective, the organization's autonomy and discretion may be reduced, at least in the short run. On the other hand, cooptation is one way for an organization to adapt to its environment. Individuals or groups which were previously outside of the organization are now in a position to influence its stability and chances of survival—in effect, broadening the available courses of action. In this last instance, we are assuming that these individuals or groups have power that can be used in several ways. It may be used aggressively to stop or change the organization's actions, or it may be used passively by being withdrawn as a source of organizational support.

There are two major forms of cooptation. The first, and most frequently used form, involves *sharing the responsibility* for power rather than the power itself. This is accomplished by bringing individuals or groups into the organization to serve:

1. as members of advisory groups;
2. as members of groups within the organization whose stated powers are subject to the approval or veto of other groups within the organization (this results in a sharing of power in name rather than in fact); and

3. as minority members of groups with power (this results in no actual change in the power structure).

The second and more powerful form of cooptation occurs when, for example, banks are given positions on the board of directors of corporations after loaning them significant amounts of money. Thus the banks may acquire a voice and sometimes what amounts to a veto in further decisions that could result in securing further debt or other long-term obligations.

The most common form of cooptation is the first type. The appointment of Rev. Leon H. Sullivan, a black, to the board of directors of General Motors Corporation in the early 1970s is an example of this form of cooptation. Although Sullivan is able to express the views, needs, and interests of black citizens, he can hardly alter the power structure of GM's 23-member board. For example, at one board meeting, he was the only member to support the Episcopal Church's request that GM pack up and get out of South Africa because of that country's apartheid policy.[41] Sullivan alone cannot make policies, but his membership on GM's board gives him the opportunity to influence the decisions and actions of other board members through persuasion, argument, presentation of proposals, and raising important questions that might otherwise not even be considered. Boards of directors are frequently used for either type of cooptation.[42]

Other examples of cooptation include: (1) forming a group of consumers to advise management on the organization's products; (2) employing nationals in managerial positions in foreign operations; and (3) actively searching for minority or women recruits in order to satisfy demands made by those groups. (However, many women and minority groups have refused to be coopted, insisting on maintaining their independent negotiating (bargaining) status.)[43]

BARGAINING

Bargaining is used extensively within an organization to resolve differences or reach accommodation among its members. Here, however, we will focus on bargaining that occurs with external groups. Bargaining is the negotiation of an agreement between two or more organizations about the exchange of goods or services. More generally, bargaining means that each organization, individual, or group decides what it must do to satisfy the other party or parties.[44] Bargaining occurs as a result of disagreements, but it can happen *only when* the parties also believe that some form of agreement is both possible and beneficial to them. The participants in a bargaining situation typically possess power, i.e., the capacity to give rewards and punishments, in relation to one another. Thus bargaining also implies some degree of mutual control among the parties as well as a process of exchange.[45]

Types of Bargaining Relationships. The types of bargaining relationships that can exist between a business firm and groups in its external environment can be classified in many ways. The one in Table 2.2 was originally developed to explain management-union bargaining relationships. With slight modification, however, it can also be used in considering the relationships between a business firm and *any* of the groups with which it bargains.

Table 2.2. Types of bargaining relationships*

Relationship	Characteristics
Containment-aggression	Party A aggressively attempts to extend its influence over Party B. But Party B aggressively tries to stop or roll back the influence of Party A.
Conflict	Party A never accepts the appropriateness of bargaining with Party B, and therefore actively attempts to eliminate Party B or at least ignores the necessity to bargain.
Power	The parties attempt to obtain the very maximum benefits or advantages from the other parties.
Deal	The leaders of two or more parties negotiate secretly and arrive at agreements which are unknown to their constituencies.
Collusion	This implies that two or more parties reach agreements to maintain some mutual advantages over other parties.
Accommodation	Extreme expressions of power are avoided. The parties are tolerant of one another's demands and accept the spirit of compromise.
Cooperation	The parties exhibit mutual concern over the others' well-being and are concerned about how their action affects the welfare of the other parties. Extreme expressions of power are avoided.
Ideological	The parties adhere to fundamental differences in beliefs or value structures.
Racketeering	The parties, especially their leaders, engage in practices and actions that are generally defined as being corrupt.

* This process may involve more than two parties.
From *Problems in Labor Relations*, 2d ed. by Benjamin M. Selekman, Sylvia K. Selekman, and Steven H. Fuller, Copyright 1958, McGraw-Hill Book Company. Used with permission of the McGraw-Hill Book Company.

1. *Union-Management.* The most widely recognized bargaining relationship is that between management and labor unions. One researcher found that 75 percent of the cases studied involved a moderate form of joint participation.[46] This was often characterized by such traits as:

a) a disposition of union and management to work together on a continuing basis;

b) union influence limited to jobs, work conditions, wages, and fringe benefits;

c) bargaining and grievance settling with little inclination to strike; and

d) a moderate degree of joint problem solving.[47]

In general, bargaining between management and labor in the United States often approaches accommodation and cooperation (see Table 2.2). But this tendency can shift rather dramatically in specific relationships. Given the diversity in the value patterns of managers and labor leaders, this isn't very surprising. For example, an accommodating or cooperative relationship can change dramatically if management makes a surprise announcement that it is going to relocate the plant during the coming year.

2. *Government-Management.* The large-scale involvement of government in business has led to an increasing use of bargaining between government and business. In 1975, for example, the Federal Trade Commission attempted to determine the profits auto companies were making on crash parts. As might be expected, General Motors rejected this position and refused to turn over corporate accounting data. Instead, GM offered the following compromise. "Contingent upon the commission terminating the investigation forthwith and closing its files," GM would (1) publically disclose the retail and wholesale prices of its 13,000 parts; (2) allow most independent body shops in the United States to buy directly from the 27 GM parts warehouses; and (3) etc. In turn, there was discussion within the Federal Trade Commission of trying to force the auto makers to rent out their dies (used to make the spare parts) to any independent stamper wanting to get into the "crash" parts business.[48] Although this issue had not been resolved as of this writing, it is apparent that bargaining processes will be one of the mechanisms for arriving at a decision.

LOBBYING

Lobbying is a process involving direct contact by a lobbyist with a government unit in order to influence legislation.[49] A lobbyist retained expressly for that purpose by a trade association or other membership group would devote some or all of his or her time to legislative matters, even though such activities formed only a part of the group's work. In addition, federal regulatory agencies, such as the Civil Aeronautics Board, the Federal Communications Commission, and the Interstate Commerce Commission, are the target of continual lobbying efforts by the organizations affected by their decisions. Business organizations whose survival and growth depend to any extent on the decisions of these regulatory agencies typically use high-ranking officials in their organizations as lobbyists. For example, every major airline and the three leading broadcast networks (ABC, CBS, and NBC) are represented by corporate vice-presidents in Washington, D.C.[50]

Role of Associations. Lobbying, though often accompanied by bargaining, is a
distinct strategy that most organizations utilize in their relations with government units at the local, state, and national levels. Only the very largest organizations can afford to lobby in their own interest. The more common form of lobbying is carried out by associations and organizations that represent the interests of a group of individuals and organizations. There are approximately 4000 national organizations with some representation in Washington, D.C. An additional 75,000 state and local associations and organizations occasionally call on Washington decision makers. Two of the largest associations representing business interests are the National Chamber of Commerce, which represents 36,000 business and organizational members, and the National Association of Manufacturers, which represents 16,500 member corporations.[51]

Lobbying by AT&T. American Telephone and Telegraph recently led all of the major telephone companies in an all-out lobbying effort in Washington, D.C. The objective was to reverse recent decisions by the courts and the Federal Communications Commission opening up some parts of their $40 billion industry to competition. The telephone companies lobbied Congress to pass a law that would stop competition in long-distance services, permit the telephone companies to acquire the companies that would be put out of business, and eliminate the Federal Communications Commission's jurisdiction over technical and operating standards that affect terminal and accessory equipment attached to local telephone company facilities. These proposals will probably not be enacted in their totality, but they do provide a bargaining stance from which compromises might be developed. The position taken by the telephone companies and the intense opposition to it by the Federal Trade Commission and many other private companies guarantee a long, drawn-out political struggle. Of course, this struggle is essentially concerned with economics, profits, and (hopefully) the public's interest.

Indirect or direct lobbying may be a viable strategy for managers to use in relating to government units that have the power to affect their organizations' activities. Lobbying becomes quite complex when organizations form coalitions—the fourth political strategy available for influencing a firm's environment.

COALITION

A coalition is the combination of two or more organizations or persons to obtain common goals and to increase the members' ability to cope with the environment. Economic self-interest is one of the chief reasons coalitions are formed, especially when they are formed to influence government actions. The three broad categories of economic issues involved are government policy (control of raw materials and taxes), foreign relations (control of foreign sales and investment in overseas plants), and labor relations (mediation/arbitration procedures and use of injunctions).[52]

Some Uses. Coalitions are put together to: (1) oppose or support legislation or proposed heads of regulatory agencies; (2) promote particular products or services (such as oranges and railroads); (3) construct facilities beyond the resources of any one firm, such as generating plants for electric utilities; and (4) represent or push the interests of particular groups, such as women, elderly people, minorities, particular industries, etc.

A coalition, like cooptation, both broadens and constrains the power of management. It is broadening to the extent that it makes possible the attainment of objectives that would otherwise be unattainable. It is constraining to the extent that it requires a commitment to making certain joint decisions in the future. For example, the recent merger of the National Basketball Association and the American Basketball Association is likely to result in new rules for bidding on and recruiting basketball players from colleges. An extension of a coalition may occur when there is a *merger* between two or more organizations. With a merger, each organization ceases to exist in a legal sense and is likely to lose its autonomy.

OPEC as a Coalition. A coalition is likely to exist only as long as each of its members thinks that its self-interest is better realized as a member than as a nonmember. One such coalition is the Organization of Petroleum Exporting Countries (OPEC), which was formed to influence the price of unrefined oil and natural gas so as to "maximize" the income for the member countries. OPEC's power stems from its ability to reduce or cut off the supply of resources needed by other countries. If members of OPEC come to think they could "do better" by acting alone over the long run, the coalition would likely cease to exist or become less influential in pricing and supply decisions.

REPRESENTATION

Whereas cooptation involves bringing external elements into the organization, representation involves encouraging members of one organization to form or join other organizations. The primary purpose of this process is to serve the interests of the representatives' organization. This is a subtle and indirect strategy. School administrators, for example, are often given paid time off and the use of the school's resources to join voluntary associations in the community for the express purpose of obtaining support for the school system.[53] Some of these voluntary organizations might include the Chamber of Commerce, Elks, Kiwanis, Moose, Rotary, United Appeal.

Another form of representation is to have individuals serve on behalf of some group. This form of representation, such as boards of directors, is usually based on some legal requirement.

Role of Boards. In the private sector, boards of directors are usually legally required to represent the interests of the stockholders. This is supposed to be accomplished by having the boards receive (or initiate) and approve all major policies and decisions. In practice, as recent disclosures about corporate price fixing, bribing, and polluting made it appear, the boards of some major organizations could be characterized as "nobody knowing from nothing." Several suggestions for alleviating this problem are to: (1) clearly separate the board from operating management; (2) have a full-time board chairperson; (3) have the chief operating executive report to the whole board, not just to the board chairperson; (4) pay active board members for their efforts; and (5) have boards take initiative and not just react to proposals or other matters brought to their attention by management.[54]

It remains debatable whether such proposals will result in better representation of stockholders and possibly the "public interest." But one certainty remains: The challenges and attacks on the corporate board system are accelerating. Moreover, the possible personal liability of directors for acts of the corporation is increasing daily.[55]

Electric Utility Case. As mentioned, one form of representation involves encouraging members of the organization to join other organizations. This form of representation was used by an electric utility firm in which one of the authors was employed. The utility was located in a large metropolitan area and was privately owned. But the major city in which it was located also owned and operated an electric utility plant about one-tenth the size of the privately owned utility. Ironically, the part of the city served by the publicly owned utility was also served by the privately owned one; some streets had two columns of poles and power lines. The city justified its operation by claiming that it provided a means of evaluating any requests the privately owned utility made for rate increases. The city also claimed that its experience in the power business could be useful if the privately owned utility became "unreasonable" and the city decided to purchase it. As a result, the private ownership of the utility was continuously threatened.

To combat this threat, the private utility encouraged its employees to be active in the community. Employees were "loaned" out to work on public causes, such as United Appeal (Community Chest) campaigns, while continuing to receive full salary. Second, employees were encouraged to run for elective offices and were allowed to be absent or leave work early for this purpose. Finally, employees were encouraged to gain membership and seek leadership positions in community and civic groups which might be able to influence government decision making.

SOCIALIZATION

Socialization is the attempt to indoctrinate people in beliefs or values that are consistent with the interests of the organization or the institution (such as free enterprise) that it represents. It is assumed that if people in the environment accept and support these basic values, they are less likely to be sympathetic toward positions that threaten the organization or its institutional framework.

Societal Socialization. The "American business creed" is a group of beliefs that some business persons try to get others to accept. In its traditional form, the creed advances the idea that a decentralized, privately owned, free, competitive system in which the price mechanism is the major regulatory or control system is desirable and should be perpetuated. Accordingly, the creed dictates that actions interfering with or threatening this system should be opposed and stopped.[56]

Tactics used for societal socialization vary widely. For example, the National Association of Manufacturers and the United States Chamber of Commerce have provided materials for elementary and secondary schools to use in teaching about the American economic system. Another, less commonly used, tactic involves direct appeal to employees through seminars or published materials. One familiar tactic is for individuals, especially those effective at public speaking, to spread a creed in speeches and on television.

Organizational Socialization. Formally or informally, organizations attempt to "mold" their employees, especially new ones, into having certain desired attitudes, styles, and ways of dealing with others and their jobs. Of course, the socialization attempted by top management can be offset or reinforced by the expectations and pressures exerted by an employee's fellow workers. Since organizational socialization will be discussed further in later chapters, we will give only a brief example here.

The increased number of women moving into managerial roles has resulted in the need for new organizational socialization practices. Table 2.3 provides a

Table 2.3. Samples of organizational socialization

Recommen-dations	Managers	
	Women	Men
Dos	Plan your career and take risks.	Be as supportive or critical of a woman as of a man.
	Stress your ambition. Ask: "What can I do to get ahead?"	Practice talking to her if you are self-conscious.
	Speak at least once in every ten-minute meeting.	Let her open the door if she gets there first.
	Take the chip off your shoulder.	Tell your wife casually about a woman peer.
Don'ts	Say: "I worked on . . ." when you wrote the entire report.	Make a fuss when appointing the first woman.
	Imitate male mannerisms or do needlepoint at meetings.	Tune her out at meetings.
	Hang on to the man who trained you.	Say: "Good morning, gentlemen—and lady."
	Leap to serve coffee when someone suggests that it's time for a break.	Apologize for swearing.

"How to Get Along in the Corporate Office," *Business Week*, March 22, 1976, pp. 107–110.

summary of the dos and don'ts for three areas of organizational socialization: (1) women's status as managers; (2) their competence as managers; and (3) their behavior as managers. The recommendations cited in Table 2.3 suggest new types of social behavior for both men and women managers when dealing with each other. These recommendations are attempting to resocialize and change certain sex-role stereotypes as to the behavior and attitudes once considered appropriate for women managers. Due to pressures from women's groups and some government agencies, many organizations are beginning to examine their social practices and policies in terms of equal employment opportunity. For such changes to be effective and lasting, the formal and informal organizational socialization practices will probably have to change.

Summary

All organizations, be they business or nonbusiness, function within an environment. In the political part of the environment, conflicts over topical issues and fundamental values are worked out. Business firms must deal with a variety of components of that environment. To do so, they may use a variety of political strategies—cooptation, bargaining, lobbying, coalitions, representation, and/or socialization.

ECONOMIC SYSTEM[57]

In our discussion of the political system we did not distinguish it sharply from the economic system because the political system determines the general type of economic system operating within a culture. For example, the political system determines the basis for ownership and control of the productive assets in the economic system.

Capitalism is an economic system based on private (individual) ownership of the assets (firms) used to produce the economy's goods and services. Socialism, on the other hand, is based on public (governmental) ownership of the major means of production. Although the American economy is commonly referred to as a capitalistic system, it is more diverse than a single "ism" would imply.

Many of the concepts, models, and research findings presented in this book are applicable to *any* organization. However, some elements of management's role seem to differ according to the type of market structure in which the firm is operating. We believe that the amount of decision-making discretion available to management is substantially influenced by the structure of the market. In other words, market structure is a contingency variable affecting the amount of management decision-making discretion.

Nature of the Economic System

There are four major types of market structure. The traditional market structure best approximates the requirements of capitalism in its pure form. An emerging and increasingly popular interpretation of the contemporary American market structure recognizes the primary role of oligopolies. A more balanced view of the American economic structure is based on imperfect competition and monopolies.

Managers are considerably influenced by the structure of the market in which their organization or its subsystems are functioning. This structure limits management's freedom to enter new markets, the type of market or industry it can enter (which depends on the amount of resources available), the relative amount of control management has over prices, and the quality or quantity of goods produced. The four market structures that influence the area of management discretion are presented next.

PERFECT COMPETITION

Pure capitalism is based on a perfectly competitive market structure. Perfect competition, however, is rarely, if ever, found in the American economy. The industries that come closest to fulfilling this traditional view include aspects of agriculture, forestry, fisheries, construction, and the services and trades.

Basic Characteristics. Since perfect competition requires many firms offering basically the same goods or services to the market, price is a key variable in consumers' purchase decisions. Most of the firms in a perfectly competitive market tend to be small-scale enterprises which require little capital (money) for their establishment. Therefore, it is easy for new firms to be established. In addition, high profits tend to be short-lived, because new firms rush into the field as soon as the profitability of the new market structure is recognized. The ease of entry, in turn, tends to keep the competition at a very high level, driving prices down. Because of these characteristics, this type of market structure experiences a relatively high degree of instability and intense price competition.

Consequences for Management. Perfect competition permits only limited management discretion. Many key decisions affecting the firm's success tend to be externally controlled by market conditions. For example, the prices of the firm's goods and services are strongly influenced by the external market forces of supply and demand. This is readily observed in the wide swings in the price of many agricultural products within a single year. Accordingly, firms tend to react to, rather than anticipate, market conditions.

In addition, there is little separation between ownership and managerial control of these firms. Thus managers tend to be concerned with maximizing profits. Since managers have little control over their environment, they tend to emphasize short-term goals, i.e., those of one year or less.

Managers have little control over prices or the quality or quantity of goods and services acceptable in the marketplace. However, this creates a strange paradox. The firm can sell all of its output at the prevailing market price. There is little advantage to charging less than the market price; a lower price will not enable the firm to sell any more goods than if it had charged the prevailing market price. Furthermore, if the firm charges more than the market price, it will not sell any of its goods or services.

OLIGOPOLIES

Much of the current commentary on the economy focuses on the power of the organizations in oligopolies. Many manufacturing firms, including those in the steel, automobile, chemical, and rubber goods industries, approximate the features of this second type of market structure.

Basic Characteristics. One of the key characteristics of an oligopoly is that there are relatively few producers or suppliers of the particular product or service. For example, three or four firms might provide 70 percent or more of the output for an entire industry (e.g., tires). Competition is based more on differentiating one's products or services and somewhat less on price competition. High barriers to entry usually exist, mainly because of the enormous amount of start-up capital required. For example, few organizations or individuals have the several hundreds of millions of dollars needed to establish an efficient steel plant. Because of these capital requirements, the typical enterprise in an oligopoly is of an extremely large scale.

It would be misleading to suggest that firms in this market structure may not be faced with severe competition in the long run. Between 1970 and 1975, for example, Volkswagen sales in the United States went from about 550,000 to about 275,000, a devastating 50 percent decline. This and other related factors led Volkswagen management to decide to begin producing the VW Rabbit in the United States. Other foreign competition, especially from Japan, had made inroads into the United States. At the same time, the big three American auto makers had lost 20 percent of the domestic auto market to imports. Thus they came out with their own subcompacts. Finally, due to the increased value of the German mark in comparison to the American dollar, VW's prices were pushed up so much that the cars were no longer appealing to economy-minded buyers.[58]

Consequences for Management. Managers tend to anticipate rather than merely react to their environment. Management discretion is expressed through some control over prices and over the quality and quantity of goods and services produced. In the oligopolistic market environment, there is a tacit, if not explicit, cooperation with competitors and other units concerned with the organization.

The concept of countervailing powers is sometimes applied to this market structure. This means that big labor, management, and the government engage in negotiations or bargaining over critical decisions that affect the welfare of the organization. This process of negotiation may reduce the relative influence of the impersonal market forces, which are so prevalent in perfect competition. Since organizations in oligopolies tend to be large, there is frequently a pronounced separation between the ownership of the organization and its control. Typically, direct control of the organization is in the hands of professional managers who may have a relatively small share in the ownership of the organization.

The goal orientations of oligopolistic organizations is varied and complex. They are concerned with long-term survival through control of their environment and growth within it. At the same time, they actively monitor the environment through such units as marketing research to determine what changes they might need to make in their goods and services to remain competitive and grow. Of course, this is probably consistent with long-term profit maximization.

Another effect that this market structure has on management is the high complexity it brings. The large-scale enterprise with its many technological and environmental interdependencies creates enormous coordination problems for management. In addition, extensive planning networks, which have time horizons of five years or more, are established to ensure the future survival and growth of the organization. Characteristics such as these create an environment in which management must exercise considerable discretion.

IMPERFECT COMPETITION

The American economy has often been analyzed in terms of both perfect competition and oligopolies. Actually, it is more complicated than this. Imperfect competition, a third type of market structure, is a hybrid of perfect competition and oligopolies and thus offers a more balanced view. Firms in the imperfectly competitive market structure include many services (e.g., barber shops), retail and wholesale trade, and some construction organizations.

Basic Characteristics. Imperfect competition is like perfect competition in that firms tend to be extremely profit-conscious and have numerous competitors, there is a relatively free movement of resources in and out of the market structure, and managerial control is primarily in the hands of owners. But imperfect competition is also like an oligopoly in that managers confront segmented markets because of perceived differences in goods and services. Also, there is some protection from direct price competition; consumers often have imperfect information about available alternatives, distance barriers, and time barriers. In other words, a firm may enjoy some protection from price competition because it provides differentiated goods and services in the right place and at the right time.

Consequences for Management. Managers have some discretion over prices and the form and volume of the goods and services produced. Managers tend to anticipate market conditions by initiating decisions with respect to the variables noted. But this market structure permits ready competition from other firms because of the moderate capital requirements needed for entry. Consequently, a market niche, once established, tends to be short-lived.

MONOPOLIES

A monopoly exists when a single organization (seller) provides virtually all of a service or good. One approximation of a monopoly is price-regulated public utilities, e.g., telephone companies, electric utilities, and firms providing natural gas.

Basic Characteristics. Unlike oligopolies, legal monopolies are protected from direct competition by government regulations, and they exist and survive with the permission and under the supervision of a government agency. The government has direct control over the prices charged by the firm for its goods or services. The rationale for direct control is based on the assumption that the government should protect the consumers because there is a lack of choice available to them. This protection takes the form of government rules, regulations, procedures, and inspections over the public utility.

This is not to suggest that a monopoly can charge as high a price as desired without affecting revenue and the demand for its services and goods. For example, Franklin Boilor, the head of the United States Post Office (a monopoly) recently observed: "It is clear from recent experience that there is a lot of price elasticity in our business. As rates go up, our volume declines. If we continue what we are doing, we could destroy the Postal Service."[59]

Consequences for Management. One of management's main concerns in price-regulated public utilities is the survival of the organization as a privately owned firm. Top managers in public utilities are involved to a great extent in the political strategies discussed previously. You might recall, for example, our previous discussion of AT&T's recent lobbying activities in Washington, D.C. On the other hand, these managers tend to have little discretion over organizational goals. For example, managers in an oligopoly may decide to enter into the production of completely new types of goods and services. But the charter of the public utility may limit the types of services it can provide. In some instances, this restriction is overcome by establishing holding companies. Also, the job tenure of managers in price-regulated public utilities is probably somewhat more stable and secure than in the other market structures.

Some managers in price-regulated public utilities have taken considerable initiative to gain a degree of control over those individuals or government agencies that are supposed to be regulating them. By these means, they have been able to enhance the amount of discretion available to them.

Discretion and Market Structure

Figure 2.4 gives a rough indication of the amount of managerial discretion available in different market structures. The vertical axis shows the amount of man-

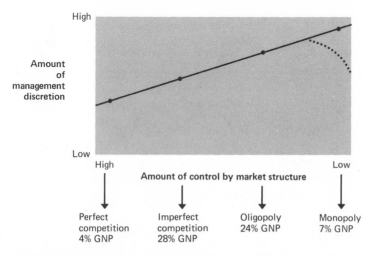

Fig. 2.4. Relationship between management discretion and market structure.

agement discretion; the horizontal axis shows the amount of control the market structure exerts on the organization. As the figure shows, the amount of management discretion available increases as one moves from perfect competition toward a monopoly. At that point, however, the direct control and influence of government agencies may actually reduce managerial discretion (as suggested by the dashed line). But where the public utility has gained some control over its regulator (such as a public utility commission), managerial discretion may be relatively great. Thus of the four possible market structures, price-regulated public utilities are likely to experience the most variation in management discretion.

Finally, Fig. 2.4 shows the relative contribution of the types of market structure to the gross national product (the total dollar value of the goods and services produced within a given year in the United States). Firms in the four market structures account for approximately 63 percent of the GNP; government accounts for the remainder.

Summary

This chaper has discussed some of the ways in which the cultural, political, and economic systems influence and are related to the management of organizations. The effects of these systems will also be presented, as appropriate, in later chapters.

Some of the major implications of our discussion for managerial practice are the following:

1. The cultural system emphasizes the value patterns that exist within a society. These value patterns play a fundamental role in influencing the nature of and how the political and economic systems operate.
2. Leadership styles and managerial practices are somewhat influenced by cultural setting.
3. Values can play an important role in managerial and individual decision making.
4. The value patterns in the United States are diverse and thus provide the basis for some of the conflicts, ambiguity, and disorder in contemporary society.
5. Organizations are increasingly faced with external environments that place conflicting demands on the organization. These conflicting demands occur over topical issues and fundamental values and are often dealt with through political strategies. These strategies include cooptation, bargaining, lobbying, coalition, representation, and socialization.
6. Finally, the degree of discretion available to management is probably influenced by the type of market structure in which the firm or one of its divisions is operating. These market structures are perfect competition, imperfect competition, oligopolies, and monopolies.

Discussion Questions

1. Research has shown that the more successful American managers tend to emphasize certain of the 66 value concepts listed in Fig. 2.1 and to de-

emphasize others. (a) Identify the nine concepts that you think have been found to be positively related to managerial success; (b) identify the twelve concepts that you think have been found to be negatively related to managerial success.

2. At the beginning of the chapter, we suggested that culture helps its members answer four basic questions. Apply the following versions of these questions to your own culture: (a) How is the importance of time defined? (b) What is defined as valuable? (c) What are three universally accepted proper standards of conduct within organizations?
3. Do you think that American culture has too much of an emphasis, especially in the business sector, on property (acquiring material wealth) and competition or on equality and cooperation? Explain.
4. If a community claims that a firm has polluted a nearby river, what actions might management take to reduce that pressure?
5. What are some of the dangers of using cooptation to deal with the external environment? Do you feel that this type of strategy should be used only when other strategies have failed?
6. How would the management of a large Kansas wheat farm differ from that of a large producer of steel? Who would have more options available for action? Explain.

Management Incidents

BOB OR SAM

Assume that as the purchasing manager in a large rubber company, you are evaluating two senior clerks for a newly created position of assistant manager in your department. Both have worked for you for the past five years and are equally competent. However, the two men differ in the following ways:

Bob Strawser is a very creative man who has been continually making suggestions for improvement in office procedures. Although not all of his ideas are practical, in the past you have adopted some of his suggestions. Bob is sincere, hard working, and can be helpful to others. He is, however, not a very popular man in the department, because other employees do not like procedural changes and extra pressures which they think are unnecessary at times.

Sam Smith, equally efficient as Bob Strawser, is not a "man of ideas," but he is very congenial and well liked. He goes out of his way to help others whenever they have problems. He is definitely contributing to the good morale of your department. He enjoys his reputation as a kind man.

1. What personal value concepts seem to be dominant in each person (see Fig. 2.1)?
2. Whom would you recommend?
3. Why?

---

* The first two incidents are adapted by permission from G. W. England, O. Dhingra, and N. Agarwal, "The Manager and the Man: A Cross-Cultural Study of Personal Values," *Organization and Administrative Sciences* 5 (1974): 67–69.

DEALING WITH "OBSOLETE" ENGINEERS

You are the manager of the Research and Development Department. In your section are ten engineers who specialize in a phase of engineering in which there have been great breakthroughs in knowledge. As a result it is only the engineers who have graduated in the past few years who are trained with respect to the new knowledge.

As the manager of this section, you have been asked to make a recommendation about retraining the "obsolete" engineers or letting them go and hiring recent graduates. Retraining would take about six months of full-time study on the part of the "obsolete" engineers, and it is not certain that all of them would successfully complete training. You know that these ten engineers have made significant contributions to the company in the past and have an average tenure of seven years.

1. Which of the following would you recommend?
   a) Retrain all of the engineers and have the company pay all retraining costs.
   b) Retrain all of the engineers and have the costs of retraining shared equally by the company and the individuals.
   c) Retrain only those engineers who are judged to be "trainable" and have the company pay all retraining costs.
   d) Retrain only those engineers who are "trainable" and have the cost of retraining shared equally by the company and the individuals.
   e) Do not retrain. Retain only those engineers who can continue to make significant contributions to the company.
2. What values are implicit in your recommendation?
3. Would any of the political strategies discussed in this chapter be useful in dealing with this problem? Explain.

ANDREW CARLSON

Andrew Carlson is a recent graduate of the business school of an American university. He has just been hired by a large American-based corporation with plants in many countries. Because of Andrew's extensive experience in management before he returned to school, his first assignment is as the plant manager of a new, small plant in Mexico.

Prior to leaving for his new post, Andrew has come to you for advice on what he should look for in the way of differences between the United States and his new post in Mexico. Moreover, he would like some guidelines for being a successful manager.

REFERENCES

1. D. Mileti and D. Gillespie, "An Integrated Formalization of Organization-Environment Interdependencies," *Human Relations* **29** (1976): 85–100.

2. P. Connor and B. Becker, "Values and the Organization: Suggestions for Research," *Academy of Management Journal* **18** (1975): 550–561.

3. P. Hunsaker, W. Mudgett, and B. Wayne, "Assessing and Developing Administrators for Turbulent Environments," *Administration and Society* **1** (1975): 312–327.

4. W. Dill, "Environment as an Influence on Managerial Autonomy," *Administrative Science Quarterly* **2** (1958): 409–443.

5. L. Megginson and E. McCann, "Applicability of Management Principles in Underdeveloped Economics," in *International Handbook of Management,* ed. K. Ettinger (New York: McGraw-Hill, 1965).

6. P. Drucker, *Management: Tasks, Responsibilities and Practices* (New York: Harper & Row, 1973). *Also see:* G. Barrett and B. Bass, "Cross-Cultural Issues in Industrial and Organizational Psychology," in *Handbook of Industrial and Organizational Psychology,* ed. M. Dunnette (Chicago: Rand McNally, 1976), pp. 1639–1686; W. Evan, "Culture and Organizational Systems," *Organizations and Administrative Science* **5** (1974/75): 1–16.

7. A. Krut, "Some Recent Advances in Cross-National Management Research," *Academy of Management Journal* **18** (1975): 538–549.

8. J. Thompson and D. Van Houten, *The Behavioral Sciences: An Interpretation* (Reading, Mass.: Addison-Wesley, 1970), pp. 22–27.

9. "How Companies React to the Ethics Issue," *Business Week,* February 9, 1976, p. 78.

10. K. Roberts, "On Looking at an Elephant: An Evaluation of Cross Cultural Research Related to Organizations," *Psychological Bulletin* **74** (1970): 327–350.

11. J. Slocum, M. Richards, J. Sheridan, and C. Altimus, "The Relationship Between Leadership Style and Job Satisfaction in Traditional and Modern Cultures," *Quarterly Journal of Management Development* **2** (1973): 221–228.

12. M. Haire, E. Ghiselli, and L. Porter, *Managerial Thinking: An International Study* (New York: Wiley, 1966); L. Cummings, D. Harnett, and O. Stevens, "Risk, Fate, Conciliation, and Trust: An International Study of Attitudinal Differences Among Executives," *Academy of Management Journal* **14** (1971): 285–304.

13. F. Harbison and C. Myers, *Management in the Industrial World* (New York: McGraw-Hill, 1959), p. 388.

14. G. Lauter, "Sociological-Cultural and Legal Factors Impeding Decentralization of Authority in Developing Countries," *Academy of Management Journal* **12** (1969): 367–378.

15. E. McCann, "Anglo-American and Mexican Management Philosophies," *MSU Business Topics,* 1970, p. 21. Reprinted by permission of the publisher, Division of Research, Graduate School of Business Administration, Michigan State University.

16. J. Kernan and L. Schkade, "A Cross-Cultural Analysis of Stimulus Sampling," *Administrative Science Quarterly* **17** (1972): 351–358.

17. W. Wright, "Organizational Ambient: Management and Environment in Chile," *Academy of Management Journal* **14** (1971): 65–73.

18. A. Ruedi and P. Lawrence, "Organizations in Two Cultures," in *Organization Design,* ed. J. Lorsch and P. Lawrence (Homewood, Ill.: Richard D. Irwin and Dorsey Press, 1970), pp. 54–83.

19. H. Schollhammer, "Organizational Structures of Multinational Corporations," *Academy of Management Journal* **14** (1971): 345–365.

20. J. Daniels and J. Arpan, "Comparative Home Country Influences on Management Practices Abroad," *Academy of Management Journal* **15** (1972): 305–315.

21. This section draws heavily from: T. Oh, *op. cit.;* H. De Bettignies, "Japanese Organizational Behavior: A Psychocultural Approach," in *Management Research: A Cross-Cultural Perspective,* ed. D. Graves (San Francisco: Jossey-Bass, 1973), pp. 75–93; P. Drucker, *op. cit.;* K. Odaka, *Toward Industrial Democracy: Management and Workers in Modern Japan* (Cambridge, Mass.: Harvard University Press, 1975).

22. T. Oh, "Japanese Management—A Critical Review," *Academy of Management Review* **1** (1976): 13–25.

23. L. Kraar, "The Japanese Are Coming—With Their Own Style of Management," *Fortune* **41** (1975): 116–122.

24. De Bettignies, *op. cit.,* p. 86.

25. G. England, "Organizational Goals and Expected Behavior of American Managers," *Academy of Management Journal* **10** (1967): 107–117.

26. G. England, O. Dhingra, and N. Agarwal, "The Manager and the Man: A Cross Cultural Study of Personal Values," *Organization and Administrative Sciences* **5** (1974): 1–97.

27. *Ibid.*

28. *Ibid.,* pp. 88–89.

29. G. England, N. Agarwal, and R. Trerise, "Union Leaders and Managers: A Comparison of Value Systems," *Industrial Relations* **10** (1971): 211–226.

30. R. Erickson, "The Impact of Cybernetic Information Technology on Management Value Systems," *Management Science* **16** (1969): B40–B60.

31. "Equalitarianism: Threat to a Free Market," *Business Week,* December 1, 1975, pp. 62–65; "Equalitarianism: Mechanisms for Redistributing Income," *Business Week,* December 8, 1975, pp. 86–90; "Equalitarianism: The Corporation as Villain," *Business Week,* December 15, 1975, pp. 86–88.

32. Research and Policy Committee, *Social Responsibilities of Business Corporations* (New York: Committee for Economic Development, June 1971), p. 22. Reprinted by permission.

33. N. Gros and H. Larson, *Casebook in American Business History* (New York: Appleton-Century-Crofts, 1939), pp. 359–373.

34. B. Skinner, "Beyond Freedom and Dignity," *Psychology Today* **5** (1971): 37–80.

35. E. Koprowski, "Cybernetics and the Death of God," *Management of Personnel Quarterly* **7** (1968): 17–27.

36. G. Cavanagh, *American Business Values in Transition* (Englewood Cliffs, N.J.: Prentice-Hall, 1976).

37. M. Zald, "Political Economy: A Framework for Comparative Analysis," in *Power in Organizations,* ed. M. Zald (Nashville: Vanderbilt University Press, 1970), pp. 221–261.

38. E. Epstein, *The Corporation in American Politics* (Englewood Cliffs, N.J.: Prentice-Hall, 1969), p. 303.

39. A. Berle, *The American Economic Republic* (New York: Harcourt, Brace and World, 1963); R. Barber, *The American Corporation: Its Power, Its Money, Its Politics* (New York: Dutton, 1970); G. McConnell, *Private Power and American Democracy* (New York: Knopf, 1966).

40. P. Selznick, *TVA and the Grass Roots* (New York: Harper Torchbook, 1966), pp. 13–16.

41. "A Black Director Pushes Reform at GM," *Business Week,* April 10, 1971, pp. 100–103.

42. J. Pfeffer, "Size and Composition of Corporate Boards of Directors: The Organization and Its Environment," *Administrative Science Quarterly* **17** (1972): 218–228.

43. W. Chalmers and G. Cormich, eds., *Racial Conflict and Negotiations* (Ann Arbor: Institute of Labor and Industrial Relations, 1971), p. 17.

44. J. Thompson and W. McEwen, "Organizational Goals and Environment: Goal-Setting As an Interaction Process," *American Sociological Review* **23** (1958): 23–31.

45. S. Levine and P. White, "Exchange as a Conceptual Framework for the Study of Interorganizational Relationships," *Administrative Science Quarterly* **5** (1961): 583–601.

46. M. Derber, W. Chalmers, and M. Edelman, *Plant Union-Management Relations: From Practice to Theory* (Urbana, Ill.: Institute of Labor and Industrial Relations, 1965).

47. M. Van De Vall, *Labor Organizations* (Cambridge, England: Cambridge University Press, 1970), p. 72.

48. "GM's Plan to Blunt an Auto Parts Probe," *Business Week,* October 16, 1975, p. 26.

49. U.S. Senate, Special Committee to Investigate Political Activities, Lobbying, and Campaign Contributions, *Final Report* (No. 345), 85th Congress, 1st Session (May 31, 1957), p. 8.

50. L. Kohlmeier, Jr., *The Regulators* (New York: Harper & Row, 1969), p. 72.

51. D. Hall, *Cooperative Lobbying—The Power of Pressure* (Tucson: University of Arizona Press, 1969).

52. *Ibid.,* p. 46.

53. J. Price, *Organizational Effectiveness: An Inventory of Propositions* (Homewood, Ill.: Richard D. Irwin, 1968), p. 117.

54. C. Brown, *Putting the Corporate Board to Work* (New York: Macmillan, 1976).

55. "The SEC Looks Harder at How Directors Act," *Business Week,* February 2, 1976, p. 56.

56. F. Sutton, S. Harris, C. Kaysen, and J. Tobin, *The American Business Creed* (Cambridge, Mass.: Harvard University Press, 1956).

57. The basic sources used in the development of this section include: R. Caves, *American Industry: Structure, Conduct, Performance,* 2d ed. (Englewood Cliffs, N.J.: Prentice-Hall, 1967); G. Grossman, *Economic Systems* (Englewood Cliffs, N.J.: Prentice-Hall, 1967); and A. Solo, *Economic Organizations and Social Systems* (New York: Bobbs-Merrill, 1967).

58. "Why VW Must Build Autos in the U.S.," *Business Week,* February 16, 1976, pp. 46–51.

59. "Why the Post Office Can't Break Even," *Business Week,* March 29, 1976, p. 63.

3

Perspectives on Management and Organizations

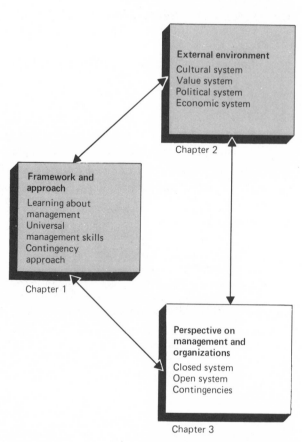

FOUNDATIONS

External environment

Cultural system
Value system
Political system
Economic system

Chapter 2

Framework and approach

Learning about management
Universal management skills
Contingency approach

Chapter 1

Perspective on management and organizations

Closed system
Open system
Contingencies

Chapter 3

The objectives of this chapter are to:

discuss a model of bureaucracy, its application to modern organizational problems, and the modification of its original concepts;

examine the scientific-management model and its underlying managerial assumptions;

discuss the administrative-management model and Fayol's contribution to it;

discuss the nature of the human-relations model and how it grew out of the traditional-management school of thought;

present a summary and overview of the closed-system perspective.

discuss the characteristics of open systems in terms of the organization's behavior;

indicate two major system variables and the impact of these variables on the effectiveness of two large, complex organizations;

present a systems framework for the analysis of employee behavior.

Organizations—manufacturing firms, the United States government, prisons, educational institutions, volunteer organizations—are everywhere in our modern society, but our understanding of them is often limited and fragmented. What we know or think we know about organizations comes from a variety of disciplines—sociology, psychology, economics, anthropology—each with its own perspective. Many current management practices still bear the imprint of practitioners and management theorists who lived and worked during the early part of the twentieth century. Although we are concerned primarily with today's organizations and management practices, there is value in looking at the traditional views and in tracing their development. Current views are not completely distinct from and unrelated to the traditional views; they evolved from earlier views. Moreover, many current management practices are influenced and guided, either consciously or unconsciously, by these traditional concepts.

Organizations are created to achieve specific goals. Much of the early writing on organizations resulted from the search for improved efficiency and productivity. This goal led management practitioners and scholars to view the organization as a closed system. That is, they concerned themselves only with those activities that would lead to improved efficiency, e.g., simplifying the activities performed by production workers. Thus there seemed to be an underestimation of factors that scholars could neither control nor understand—employees and the political, economic, and cultural environment in which the organization operated. Closed-systems models dealt with the conditions thought to maximize rational behavior and performance.

Organizational roles and decisions were geared toward goal achievement and making the organization more and more rational in the pursuit of its goals. Thus the closed system focused on the establishment of a means-end chain to maximize the efficiency of the organization. This goal could be accomplished by emphasizing structure, formalizing relationships, and setting forth useful principles about employees and the organization's environment.[1]

We also look at organizations from an open-system perspective. This perspective is based on the assumption that an organization contains more factors than we can fully comprehend and that it interacts with its environment. Boundaries separate organizations from one another. But the organization doesn't exist in a vacuum. The organization's external environment can affect its internal structure and employees' behavior(s). All organizations have their own boundaries, and these boundaries limit the types of services undertaken by the organization. For McDonald's, Burger King, Kentucky Fried Chicken, and Fish & Chips, for example, the boundary is the fast-food industry. These firms do not sell automobiles, tires, TV's, or mobile homes; nor do they compete with organizations selling these consumer products. Rather, their focus is limited to the food industry and within that, the fast-food segment. Firms within these boundaries have similar organizational structures and recruit, train, and promote similar types of personnel. The technology in all of these firms is similar and all operators cater to a particular type of clientele. All of these organizations form an open system; that is, they exchange information, energy, and materials with the external environment. For example, Burger King receives inputs of money, people, meat, vegetables, beef, and other resources; transforms these inputs through its production process; and exports a variety of hamburgers and soft drinks. According to the open-system view, the organization (Burger King) is dependent for its survival and efficiency on an exchange of goods and services with its environment. The organization has a number of interacting parts and can be considered only in totality and in relation to its external environment.

One point needs clarification. When speaking of organizations as open systems, we mean that they are "relatively" open systems. In fact, most biological organisms and social organizations are "partially open" and "partially closed." Open and closed are a matter of degree. Therefore, the use of closed- and open-system perspectives in this chapter should not be taken as representing two ends of a continuum. Rather, writers have different viewpoints for examining organizations. Closed-system thinking considers the organization as a self-contained, deterministic unit. Only limited aspects of the internal operation of the organization are considered, and the approaches to decision making, motivation, and the internal structural arrangements of roles are highly formalistic, without reference to the external environment.

CLOSED-SYSTEM PERSPECTIVE

Four types of organizational theories form the closed-system perspective. Bureaucracy, scientific management, administrative management, and human relations are the four models we will consider here.

Bureaucracy

Max Weber, a German social historian who lived at the turn of the twentieth century, is the individual most closely associated with the bureaucratic model. Writing in the early 1900s, he was interested in studying not only the structure of complex organizations, but also the broad economic and social issues facing society. Thus his ideas on bureaucracy represent only a part of his total thesis on social theory.

One of the first to deal with the problems of organizational complexity, Weber developed the bureaucratic model in an attempt to analyze the structural relationships in complex organizations.[2] He regarded proper staffing and structure as essential ingredients of organizational efficiency. Efficiency was to be achieved through the use of authority based on a manager's position in the organization. Those in higher-level positions were to have more authority and were presumed to have greater expertise than those lower in the organization. Each member of the administrative staff was to occupy a position that had specific amounts of power, salary, and expertness (determined by technical competence). There was to be a set of rules and regulations specifying relationships between positions. Defining positions according to jurisdiction and place in the hierarchy would permit appointing experts to a position and establishing rules and regulations for categories of activity. Motivating proper performance of officials was to be accomplished by providing salaries and patterns of career advancement. According to Weber, the decisive reason for the advancement of bureaucratic organizations was their purely technical superiority over other forms of organization. The following caricature of bureaucratic reality none-theless provides an overview of bureaucracy.

The Bureaucrat's Prayer

Oh, Thou, who seest all things below
Grant that thy servants may go slow;
That we may study to comply
With regulations til we die.

Teach us, O Lord, to reverence
Committees more than common-sense;
Impress our minds to make no plan
And pass the baby when we can.

And when the Temper seems to give
Us feelings of initiative,
Or when, alone, we go too far
Recall us with a circular.

'Mid fire and tumult, war and storms,
Sustain us, Blessed Lord, with forms,
Thus may thy servants ever be
A flock of perfect sheep for Thee.

—Anon

CHARACTERISTICS

Seven organizational characteristics are usually associated with a bureaucratic organization: a formal system of rules and regulations, impersonality, division of labor, hierarchical structure, life-long career commitments, a legal authority structure, and rationality.[3] These dimensions will be briefly described.

Rules and Regulations. A formal system of rules and regulations controls the decision-making behavior of all employees. Bureaucracies are based on the idea that rules and regulations help provide the order needed to reach the organization's goals. Adherence to these rules and regulations ensures uniformity of procedures and operations regardless of the individual manager's personal desires. Thus personnel can enter and leave the organization, but the rules and regulations ensure the organization's stability over time.

Rules and regulations also provide a means by which top management can coordinate the efforts of various employees. The typical "red tape" that each student must go through to register for course work in many colleges, for example, has stayed the same for years, even though registrars have come and gone. This red tape gives the college a stable registration procedure. Thus we should not assume that all rules and regulations are bad for the organization.

Impersonality. Reliance on rules and regulations leads to impersonality. Al-though this term often has negative connotations, Weber believed that im-personality guaranteed managers' job security. All employees were subject to the same rules and regulations and were thus saved from the personal whims of others. Superiors were bound to rate subordinates on performance and ex-pertise rather than on personal and/or emotional considerations. In other words, impersonality was designed to preserve objectivity and the individuality of the bureaucrat.

Passage of equal opportunity legislation in the early 1960s updated this concern with impersonality. Today employers cannot ask potential employees about their sex or race on the application form. The purpose of this rule is to protect candidates from the personal whims of personnel officers who might screen out applicants on the basis of sex or race.

Division of Labor. The manager must perform official duties which are assigned on the basis of specialization and expertise. Specialization enables the organization to take advantage of the particular skills a member possesses and help that person develop these skills through repetition and practice. When the tasks are broken down into subtasks, the individual can be assigned to perform these subtasks, which are essentially simpler and more repetitive than the total-task requirements. The individual is able to learn the tasks and the necessary skills quickly. These steps lead to increased efficiency by the individual and therefore less reliance by the organization on the skills of a particular person. With extremely simplified jobs, personnel replacement is eased and relatively simple. When a jobs opens up, the person to fill the position can be chosen solely on the basis of his or her qualifications.

There are a number of consequences of specialization. For example, managers may use specialization to hold on to their positions in the hierarchy. For example, according to Fig. 3.1, the manager of industrial relations is a specialist in worker-management grievance and disciplinary procedures. Lower-level managerial personnel (e.g., foremen) must consult with the industrial relations person before taking disciplinary action against an employee. In this case, the industrial relations person's decision-making power is based on expertise in interpreting the management-union labor agreement.

Hierarchical Structure. Most bureaucratic organizations have a pyramid-shaped hierarchical structure, as in Fig. 3.1. Each level in the hierarchy represents a different degree of authority. Typically, power and authority increase with level in the hierarchy, with each lower-level position being under the control and direction of a higher-level position.

The degree of authority at a particular level may be defined in terms of the range of discretion permitted. The higher the level, the wider the range of discretion and status symbols (e.g., bigger office, higher pay, private secretary) allowed.

A well-defined hierarchy lessens the organization's dependence on its members and discourages emotional aspects of behavior. In Fig. 3.1, the relationships between the six hierarchical levels are clearly defined, with superiors responsible for subordinates' actions and as well as for their own decisions to successively higher managerial levels. Through the hierarchical structure, the behavior of all employees can be integrated to achieve the goal(s) of the organization.

Life-Long Career. To the manager in a bureaucracy, employment is a life-long career commitment. Weber believed that managers should be appointed to positions in accordance with their technical qualifications and that they should regard the position as their primary occupation. In essence, the individual's techni-

Fig. 3.1. Organization chart of Standard Steel Corporation.
(Standard Steel Division of Titanium Metals Corporation of America, Burnham, Pa. Used with permission, 1978.)

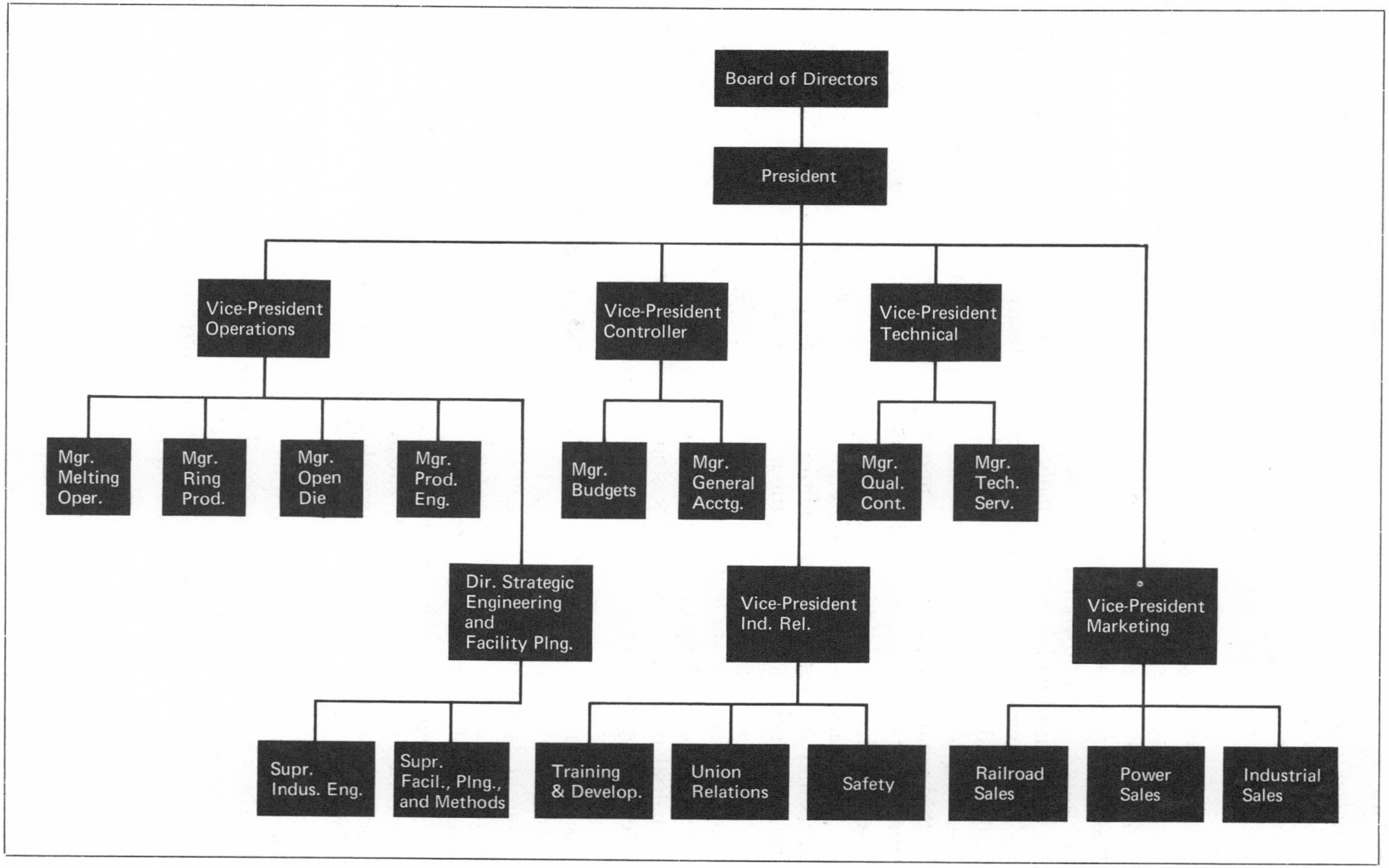

cal qualifications alone were sufficient for continued employment; job security

was guaranteed as long as the individual was qualified. Entrance requirements
(e.g., level of education) ensured technical qualification rather than reliance
on "pull" (patronage).

Job security, tenure, incremental salaries, and pensions were used to ensure
the devoted performance of official duties, without regard to pressures from
individuals external (i.e., political) to the organization. Promotion was granted
on the basis of examinations to determine the individual's technical competence to handle the demands of the higher role. For example, promotion
through civil service ranks is determined by technical qualifications and seniority. Technical qualification can often be determined by examination results,
amount of formal education, and previous work experience. Thus a GS-7 position in the federal government requires less education, experience, and technical
skills than does a GS-8. The assumption is that there is a close correspondence
between organizational level and expertise.

Authority. The framework created by rules and regulations, impersonality,
division of labor, and the hierarchical structure is tied together and changed
through the formal system of *authority*. Weber identified three types of organizational authority structures. The first type, *traditional* authority, carries the
force of tradition or custom. The divine rights of kings and the authority of the
tribal witch doctor are examples of traditional authority; it rarely occurs in
modern organizations.

Charismatic authority, the second type, occurs when subordinates voluntarily comply with their supervisor and suspend their own judgment because of
the extraordinary capacities, strengths, or powers of the leader. Often social
movements are headed by charismatic leaders, e.g., Jesus Christ, Adolf Hitler,
and Martin Luther King.

Rational authority is the only type based in law. A superior is obeyed not
because of his or her personal (charismatic) qualities, but because of the individual's position in the organization's hierarchy. This system of authority is
most appropriate in a bureaucracy, because legal authority is based on a body
of rules accepted by the members of the organization. Procedures to fill these
roles must be consistent with those accepted rules and regulations.

Rationality. Rationality brings order to a system of activities intended to achieve
a goal. The organization should be ordered on the basis of "logic" and "science." The activities of the organization's members should be directed toward
the goal. If activities are goal-directed, resources (financial and human) can be
more effectively utilized. In bureaucratic organizations, rationality is achieved
through goals. The organization has a general goal, which is then broken down
into subgoals for each hierarchical level and/or department. If these departments all reach their goals, the general goal will be reached. It is assumed that
individuals in the organization essentially accept that goal as a given when they
accept their positions in the organization. Members have an obligation to
achieve the goals set by the organization. Organizations enhance their rationality through both the hierarchical structures and position descriptions which
limit organizational members' choice of goals.

According to Weber, bureaucratization developed for several reasons. First, as organizations became larger, administrative tasks increased in both number and complexity. More managers were hired, and each manager was assigned a functional area based on his or her expertise. Second, Weber believed in the technical superiority of bureaucratic organizations, citing their emphasis on impersonality, strong organizational structure, and high degree of specialization. Noting the advancement of bureaucratic principles in such organizations as the army, church, university, and state government, Weber reasoned that bureaucracy was necessary to foster efficiency in complex organizations.

DEGREE OF BUREAUCRACY

The seven characteristics of bureaucracy can be used to place organizations along a continuum from high bureaucratic orientation to low bureaucratic orientation. As indicated in Fig. 3.2, organizations do not fall at either extreme of this continuum. Rather, they vary in the degree to which they exhibit the various characteristics.

One of the problems in transforming these seven dimensions into an over-all rating is that of measurement. For example, one organization may be highly bureaucratic on division of labor and low on structure, whereas in another organization these characteristics are reversed. Are these two organizations equally bureaucratic? Although this scaling technique leaves a number of such questions unanswered, it is nonetheless a useful device.[4]

In general, government agencies, such as the Department of Defense, rank high on these dimensions and can therefore be placed near the bureaucratic end of the continuum. On the other hand, most research and development laboratories, such as the RAND Corporation, rank low on these characteristics and can thus be placed at the other end of the continuum.

But ranking organizations is more complex than this. An organization's departments can vary considerably in their degree of bureaucratization. For example, General Motors, K-Mart, and Mack Trucks are centrally located on the continuum (see Fig. 3.2). Their research and development departments, however, are likely to be less bureaucratic than the organization as a whole. Similarly, the companies' production departments, concerned with producing standardized goods, such as automobiles and refrigerators, would be more bureaucratic. Thus only in the broadest sense can an organization be "placed" on this continuum. Therefore, Fig. 3.2 is best suited for making comparisons in assessing the degree of bureaucratization in an organization. It suggests important variables and the relations to look for among the dimensions.

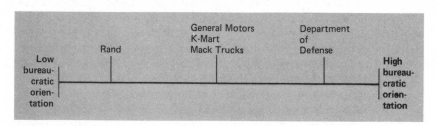

Fig. 3.2. Continuum of bureaucratic characteristics.

Table 3.1. Anticipated and unanticipated effects of bureaucracy

Characteristics	Anticipated benefits	Unanticipated effects
Rules and regulations	Efficiency	Rigid rules
Impersonality		Red tape
Life-long career commitments		Lack of communication
Hierarchical structure		Slow decision making
Detailed job descriptions		Technological incompatibility
		Alienation of employees

POSSIBLE NEGATIVE EFFECTS OF BUREAUCRATIC BEHAVIOR

The same organizational and management practices that make bureaucracy potentially superior to other forms of organization can be used in ways contrary to organizational efficiency.[5] As shown in Table 3.1, although a bureaucracy is intended to be highly efficient, in practice its characteristics may give rise to many unanticipated harmful effects.

Rigid Rules. Rigid adherence to rules and regulations for their own sake permits little individual discretion and creativity. Bureaucracy means routinization and exact task specification, as well as an ever-increasing set of rules, procedures, and programs to control the individual's behavior. This can in turn lead to reduced motivation to perform, higher turnover, and shoddy work. Also, people may develop preferences for dealing with problems in their own special way.

Protection of Authority. A study of the Tennessee Valley Authority revealed that the central problem was the need for delegation of power and decision-making rights to lower-level organizational members.[6] This need had emerged from the increasing complexities of the task. However, the lower-level members chose to neglect the organization's goals in favor of more limited personal goals that would maximize their own self-interest and prestige within the organization. Several of these individuals had become "empire builders," valuing power, status, and pay. These people brought in unneeded subordinates, added more space and physical facilities, and used work projects. This suggests that bureaucracies may encourage employees to perform at a minimally acceptable level in terms of productivity and efficiency and to be apathetic toward the organization's goals.

Poor Decision Making. Large, complex organizations are highly dependent on decisions being made on time. Delays in reaching one decision may cause delays in reaching others. In a highly bureaucratic organization, adherence to the rules, regulations, and procedures may be regarded as more important than high-quality, timely decisions. In such cases, adherence to rules and regulations becomes a value in and of itself. Formalism and ritualism ensue. Decisions are delayed until all red tape has been cleared and the petty insistence on the privileges of power and status has been played out.

Incompatible with Technology. Differences in technology may also make the universal application of the bureaucratic model impossible. For example, in the automobile industry, each work station along the assembly line contributes its own (small) part to the total car. In this context, bureaucracy has worked fairly well for most American automobile manufacturers. However, workers making Mercedes cars are not on a highly automated assembly line, but rather are grouped in teams; a team assembles each car, and places its stamp of approval on each of its cars. Here the technology is more of a craft, which simply doesn't fit the assumptions of the bureaucratic model. In sum, technology may have a greater impact on certain elements of an organization's structure (especially those related to work flow) than it does on the administrative or managerial staff.[7]

Incompatible with Values. Professional values, such as science, service to professional organizations, and innovation, may be incompatible with the bureaucratic values of efficiency, order, and stability. Since professional individuals are increasingly associating with large organizations and assuming more important places in organizations, this criticism is very important. For example, to the bureaucrat, authority is related to hierarchical position; to the professional, authority derives from personal competence or technical expertise that resides outside of the formal organization.[8] Routinization of work and standardization of procedures are of prime importance to the bureaucrat; the professional, by contrast, stresses the uniqueness of the problem and advocates change through research and development.

CONTINGENCY VIEWS OF BUREAUCRACY

The modern view is that although bureaucracy is not "dead," managers must recognize its limitations and negative effects. James Webb, former administrator for the National Aeronautics and Space Administration, used a bureaucratic-type organizational structure, but relied on real-time feedback rather than on position-based authority.[9] Under this plan, four levels of hierarchical authority, frequently working simultaneously with a variety of information networks, were used in launching the Apollo projects. This particular adaptation of the model was made to meet the particular needs of NASA.

Another view is that bureaucracy functions best when large amounts of routine work are to be accomplished. Lower-level employees handle the bulk of the work by simply following rules and regulations. It is only the exceptional case, one to which the rules do not apply, that must be called to the attention of supervisors, who make decisions (to change the rules, make exceptions to the rules, or ignore the case) that are passed down to subordinates. Lower-level employees are not expected to use discretion and can be evaluated on the basis of how well they conform to the rules.

Few, if any, organizations are currently operating under all of the conditions described by Weber and indicated in Fig. 3.2. Modifications in the bureaucratic model have been caused by an environment that emphasizes innovative and dynamic structures (such as matrix and project structures, which will be discussed in Chapter 5), new technologies, and political and social values. In this new environment, the creative organization is becoming the rule rather than the exception.[10]

Scientific Management

At the beginning of the twentieth century, industries were becoming larger and more complex. Haphazard management, previously sufficient, was now inefficient. Managers were no longer involved with the production process; they had to spend more of their time on administrative (planning, scheduling, staffing) problems. Managers also had difficulty in keeping abreast of the technical methods of production and therefore no longer had a basis for judging a fair day's work from the increased number of employees.

The changing technology had created a need for specialists who understood production operations and who were well versed in the solution of common problems that threatened operating efficiency. Frederick Taylor, a mechanical engineer, and his associates focused on the human aspect of the new machine-oriented production system. Their goal was to define precisely all aspects of the worker-machine relationship. This would enable them to specify the most efficient actions a worker should take to complete a given task.[11]

Taylor believed that there was only one best way to perform a given task. Taylor, like Weber, believed that an organization should be governed by definite, predictable methods, logically determined and written into laws. Efficiency could be increased by having workers perform repetitive tasks that did not require problem-solving activities; furthermore, performance should be described in behavioral terms (e.g., number of units produced per shift).

TIME-AND-MOTION STUDY

The nature of the task was determined by time-and-motion study, which was made to restrict a worker's activities in performing a task and to ensure that these activities were the most efficient to completing the task. Efficiency was measured in terms of time and costs.

Another objective of time-and-motion study was to make the job highly routine and efficient. Eliminating wasted effort and detailing a specific sequence of activities would minimize the amount of time, money, and effort needed to produce a product. A standard method and time for task accomplishment could not be stated unless other factors, such as machine speeds and feeds, supply of raw materials, were standardized as well. Thus Taylor and his associates undertook an analysis of work flows, supervisory techniques, worker fatigue, and inventory storage.

VIEW OF WORKER

Taylor's view of the worker stemmed logically from his methods and the tasks studied. The only relevant behavior was the worker's physical ability. The worker's capacity to produce, muscle durability, and fatigue were the major factors Taylor examined. Speed in task performance was assumed to be related to skill, degree of manual dexterity, and the level of effort expended. According to Taylor, workers should be selected on the basis of these physical characteristics and not on psychological ones, such as emotions, personality, or learning potential.

Taylor believed that workers' underlying motivation was money. Scientific management was based on the assumption that workers would be rational and follow management's orders in order to gain extra money. A differential piecework system was recommended as the primary pay system. A worker would receive not only a higher wage for meeting a standard, but also a higher rate for all pieces produced, not merely those exceeding the standard. Clearly, employees would work harder if they could double their wages. It was assumed that management would be most receptive to this because increases in productivity would more than compensate for the higher labor costs. For example, a worker who produced 100 automobile tires was paid $100.00. A worker who produced 110 tires would be paid $120.00. The 100 tires was the standard for which the company paid $1.00/tire. Because the ten extra tires were in excess of the standard, the worker's rate was adjusted for all 110 tires produced.

FUNCTIONAL FOREMANSHIP

Taylor's idea of functional foremanship was based on his principle of specialization. To Taylor, who viewed expertise as the only source of authority, the gap between authority and managerial expertise was a problem. Since one foreman could not be expected to have expertise in all of the tasks supervised, the foreman's particular area of specialization was the same as the area of authority. This, of course, created the need for multiple foremen for each worker. This led to the concept of functional foremanship. Workers would have eight foremen—one each for planning, production scheduling, time-and-motion studies, and discipline, as well as four on the shop floor to deal with such matters as maintenance of machinery, speeds and feeds of materials into the machines, etc.

CONTINGENCY VIEW OF SCIENTIFIC MANAGEMENT

Worker-management cooperation was the essential condition for the implementation of scientific management. Because Taylor believed that his concepts would enhance workers' economic status, he could foresee no conflict between workers and management. In fact, he believed that his methods would reduce the instances of industrial conflict and act as a major force in resolving it. Management was expected to: (1) develop a technique for each factor affecting a worker's task and replace the old seat-of-the-pants methods; (2) scientifically select, train, and develop workers; and (3) guarantee a division of work and responsibility, with management assuming the planning functions associated with the task and workers performing the task.

Although many applications of Taylor's principles are still used by industrial engineers today,[12] such as time-and-motion studies and Gantt charts,[13] his strategies have been strongly criticized. Taylor's analysis made no provision for sociological and psychological variables; he neglected such factors as the informal organization, conflicts of interest between workers and managers, multiple goals of workers, and differences in perception. Taylor also assumed that: (1) the organization's goals were known to all employees; (2) tasks could be broken down into their simplest elements and were repetitive; (3) the output of the production process somehow disappeared (i.e., he did not care about the areas of marketing or sales); and (4) resources—machines, workers, and the like—were always available in uniform qualities.

SUMMARY

Perhaps the critical element for management in Taylor's scheme was the standardization of every task. The crux of the system was time-and-motion study, whereby the most efficient methods for task completion could be isolated, routinized, and used to develop standards and pay rates. The emphasis on standardization suggests that the worker was thought of as a tool or machine to be regulated, handled, and programmed by management as easily as any other tool to achieve the organization's goal. For the organization, this suggests a closed-system perspective in which production is guarded against variability in materials and low inventory and is routinized so as to better predict and control performance.

Administrative Management

Scientific management focused on the shop level and worker-machine relationships. Administrative management was concerned with the structure of the entire organization.[14] This model evolved during the early 1900s and is most closely identified with Henri Fayol, a French industrialist whose most famous work on management was not translated into English until 1949.

Fayol claimed that essential similarities in structure and processes among organizations could be identified. For example, he asserted that any organization's structure can be viewed both vertically and horizontally. Vertical structure is the hierarchy created by delegation of authority and responsibility from the top downward; horizontal structure is the variety of functions carried out, e.g., finance, marketing, production.

This model focused on the formal aspects of the organization's structure and minimized the effects of the human factor. Accordingly, a clear distinction is made between the position and its occupant. Management's main tasks are to: (1) discover a set of functions necessary for the organization to reach its goal, and (2) group tasks so as to maximize productivity and efficiency and minimize cost.

MANAGEMENT FUNCTIONS

Management's basic functions were to plan, organize, command, coordinate, and control. Planning involves forecasting and preparing to meet the future and is the responsibility of top management. Command, the directing and structuring of subordinates' tasks, is based on authority and the level of the manager in the organization's hierarchy. Coordination, like command, is an essential aspect of the control process and is closely related to the formal authority structure of the organization. Coordination, the most important function, is the means by which the organization and its managers achieve goals; coordination gives hierarchical form to the organization. Through control managers could check the actual performance of subordinates against the organization's rules, regulations, and standards.

From these five basic functions, Fayol developed fourteen principles, or guidelines, for managers. These principles were to replace the rules of administration previously based on intuition and are discussed further in Chapter 4.

PROCESS OF MANAGEMENT

Fayol was also interested in the process of management. "Management" is usually defined as "a process of getting things done by people who operate in organized groups." Fayol's analysis of management is based on the five managerial functions and such specific techniques as budgeting, quality control, and industrial engineering.

CONTINGENCY VIEW OF ADMINISTRATIVE MANAGEMENT

Fayol's analysis provides a means by which the five managerial functions and principles for implementing these functions are put into effect. However, his framework lacks clarity, since it suggests nothing about the logical arrangement of these functions and principles. It did, however, establish broad guidelines for management practitioners that were better than seat-of-the-pants or intuitive approaches.

General Characteristics of Three Models

These three models are still used, criticized, and referred to by current management practitioners and writers. Therefore, it is useful to pinpoint the similarities and differences among the three models.

1. All three models emphasize the formal aspects of the organization, e.g., task components, role relationships, authority, and hierarchy. All three focus on the substantive aspects of rational work, organization, and the science of management. In effect, the infancy stage of management was concerned with the formal relations among departments, task, and structural elements of organizations. Seat-of-the-pants management practices were replaced with sound theoretical and scientific concepts.

Although it was surely recognized that people had feelings and interacted socially in the organization, the overriding focus was on performance. For example, Taylor was concerned with eliminating the senseless antagonism between workers and management. His wage-incentive system was intended to provide workers with a just monetary reward for their work. Similarly, the bureaucratic model gave attention to job security, career progression, and protection of the worker from the manager's arbitrary whims. This suggests that Weber was concerned with the individual in the organization. However, none of these models dealt with informal or social relationships and the psychological aspects of work. Rather, they all assumed that sound job analysis and well-written rules and regulations would help ensure efficient performance.

2. All three models were concerned primarily with efficiency—the cost-

benefit ratio. The principles of scientific management, administrative management, and bureaucracy were seen as fostering efficiency as the major standard against which to judge employees' performance.

3. All three models highlighted the role of the manager. The bureaucratic model suggested that a strong relationship exists between expertise and organizational level. A superior was to be obeyed by subordinates on the basis of not only his or her higher position, but also presumed greater expertise. A similar inference can be drawn from the emphasis on structure in the administrative-management model and the stress on the managerial planning in the scientific-management model.

These similarities may be seen in Table 3.2. Division of labor, hierarchical arrangements of positions, and rules and regulations were the chief ingredients in these models. Decisions were made to maximize the economic benefits to the firm, and economic efficiency was the major criterion. The organization's employee was thought of as an instrument of production whose behavior was influenced solely by economic rewards. Even today, time-and-motion studies prescribe the movements most appropriate for performing a task most efficiently. By focusing on such factors as speed and output, these studies ignore the psychological aspects of work performance.

4. An important difference among the three models was the part of the organization emphasized. In scientific management, the unit of study was the shop floor and the individual's relationship to the task. Administrative management focused on the whole organization and developed principles leading to

---

Table 3.2. Overview of the bureaucratic, scientific management, and administrative management models

I. Structure
1. focus on
   a) division of labor
   b) hierarchical and functional processes
   c) structure
   d) span of control
2. assumptions are implicit
3. emphasize principles

III. Leadership
1. single leader
2. chosen on merit
3. chosen by superiors
4. relies on authority in position
5. leader's task to achieve organizational (rather than subordinates') goals
6. unitary goal

II. People
1. machines
2. economic or job-security motives only
3. must adjust to job
4. unaffected by fellow workers (no groups)
5. can be hired and fired as need arises

IV. Decision making
1. consciously rational
2. full knowledge of alternatives and consequences
3. efficiency sole value criterion
4. maximizing decisions

overall organizational rationality. The bureaucratic model was concerned with both the organization and the society in which it functioned.

Human Relations

The last of the four closed-systems models, the human relations model, differs from the three other models in terms of both tactics and details. This model arose as a reaction to and rejection of the emphasis on structure in the other models. Ironically, human relations began as a research project in the spirit of scientific management. The original goal of the famous studies at the Hawthorne plant of Western Electric in the late 1920s was to determine the relationships between worker performance and such factors as heat, light, and fatigue.

As the experimenters in the Hawthorne plant varied these factors to observe their effect on workers' performance, they discovered that the data were contrary to the basic ideas of scientific management. Production rose to extremely high levels under the poorest working conditions. For example, as the lighting level was decreased by set increments until the employees could barely see to do their work, the output increased.

After two years of study, the researchers turned to psychological and sociological factors to explain the unexpected results. They began studying the social organization of the plant rather than the formal organization. The researchers examined the determinants of work-group behavior in interaction with the organization's structure and culture—in short, the interactions of individuals working together. Thus workers were no longer perceived as isolated individuals, but rather as group members whose behavior was greatly controlled by group norms (standards of behavior) and values.[15]

ASSUMPTIONS

The researchers soon realized that workers do not always behave and react to management's mandates or according to economic "logic," but rather to the logic of sentiment. Several basic assumptions of the human relations model are:

1. Workers are basically motivated by *social needs* and obtain a sense of identity through association with others;
2. Workers are more responsive to the social forces of the *peer group* than to the incentives and controls of management.
3. Workers are responsive to management to the extent that a supervisor can meet a subordinate's social and acceptance needs.[16]

BANK WIRING STUDY

One researcher related how the Hawthorne plant's Bank Wiring group controlled the output of the wiremen and soldermen by adopting the following code:

1. You should not turn out *too much work*. If you do, you are a "rate-buster."
2. You should not turn out too *little* work. If you do, you are a "chisler."

3. You should not tell a supervisor anything to the detriment of a fellow worker. If you do, you are a "squealer."[17]

The findings from this study showed the potential strength of the informal organization. Informal social interactions were based on sentiment (feelings) which occurred within the framework of the formal organization's policies, rules, and procedures. In the behavior code above, for example, the group levied sanctions, including ostracism and not helping these individuals in their work, on those who broke its norms. Such norms may reduce competition among workers and increase cohesiveness (group solidarity). Thus the main functions of norms are to allow group members to increase their control over their environment, to lessen their dependence on management, and to increase their social satisfaction and emotional stability.

CONTINGENCY VIEW OF HUMAN RELATIONS

The human relations approach tried to solve organizational problems by focusing on the individual and the work group while ignoring the formal organization. Such organizational factors as the power structure, the nature of the task itself, and the technology employed remained largely external to the analysis. Basic societal factors too were left out of consideration. For example, conflicts in the power structure might result not from poor communications or bad interpersonal relations, but from differences in interests; one group's gain might be another's loss. On a societal level, if market competition necessitated the introduction of new technology but the workers resisted, what should management do? If human relationists had viewed groups in terms of strategy and bargaining, they would have realized the utopian character of the strategy of full worker participation in decision making. On the other hand, if organizations were to practice such internal democracy, the result would probably be a radical transformation of the political and economic institutions of society.

On the individual level, the human relations strategy reduced all problems to matters of emotion. There was a persistent attempt to show that the human being is not entirely "rational." But an emphasis on sentiment minimizes the importance of the very real rational problem-solving processes that do occur.[18]

SUMMARY

The human relations model emphasized the organization as a social system that emerged from the interactions among individuals within the organization. Thus it was stressed that workers do not necessarily behave and adhere to the rules and regulations of management or behave according to economic rationality. The logic of sentiments and group norms was quite different from that of management as prescribed in the bureaucratic, scientific-management, and administrative-management models.[19]

The goal of the human relations model was basically to integrate the informal and formal organizations. Informal norms and values were assumed to provide a buffer between workers and management. The informal organization was seen as allowing groups to increase their control in the work setting while also providing the worker with a major source of satisfaction and emotional stability.

Table 3.3. Comparisons of closed-system models

Area	Rational-economic	Human relations
Objectives	Economically oriented; profit stated in nonhuman terms	Employee-oriented; concern for welfare of human, benefit programs; group help, implementation
Communication systems	Close control; formal channels; concern for and attempt to control informal grapevine	Deemphasis on formal systems, information to all, encourage bypassing; communicate directly; group communications
Control systems	Very close; management-established quotas "countable"; measurable individual incentives and control	Control based on *groups*; peers provide control, social pressures
Decision making	No participation—manager *must* make all the decisions; technically best decisions desirable	Group participates in decision making; interested more in acceptance of decision than in technical aspects
Structure	"Tall" structure and very detailed regulations; highly organized; authority-based	"Flatter" structure; room for groups to form and operate
Leadership styles	Autocratic; manager makes all decisions and announcements; decisions oriented to results that will provide most economic returns	Leader should fulfill the needs and desires of the group; results emerge from group; group oriented to democratic process
Reward	Economic rewards; tangible, individual incentives	Group incentives—economic as well as social; rewards stem mostly from peers; fringe benefits strong

Modified from E. Schein, *Organizational Psychology*, Englewood Cliffs, N.J.: Prentice-Hall, 1965, pp. 47–56; and W. Scott, "Technology and Organization Government: A Speculative Inquiry into the Functionality of Management Creeds," *Academy of Management Journal* **11** (1968): 301–313.

Comparison of the Closed-System Models

The implications of the human relations model for management and the organization are quite different from those of the other closed-system models. Table 3.3 contrasts the central ideas flowing from the human relationists with those of the other three models. The underlying philosophy of the human relations model is that human dignity in the work place should be restored and that the objectives of the organization should be directed toward the employees' welfare rather than just toward profits. The human relationists favored participatory management, whereby a group leader seeks out group advice and emphasizes group rewards (as opposed to economic incentives alone), as the basis of motivation. Managers had to have effective social skills, in addition to technical competence.

The importance of specialization, hierarchy, role relationships, and principles of organization for the achievement of organizational goals was modified by the apparent ability of the informal organization to resist formal goals and determine level and quality of output. The human relationists sought changes in the formal structure and task's design that would give the employees more freedom and initiative to make the job satisfying and challenging. In contrast to the formal hierarchical structure of the organization, with its numerous organizational levels, "flatter" structures were proposed that emphasized teamwork, open communication channels between management and the workers, and encouragement of informal groups. The small group served as the primary determinant of members' satisfactions and control over performance of the task itself.

OPEN-SYSTEM PERSPECTIVE

A very different way of looking at organizations is offered by the open-system perspective. The various organizational functions and processes are not considered as isolated elements, but as parts reacting to and influencing the larger environment. Thus decisions by a manager in one part of the organization can have repercussions throughout the organization, because all of its parts (subsystems) are linked.

Since it first appeared around 1960, the open-system model has become an important part of management thought and practice.[20] Today the open-system model can be applied to such areas as operations research, organization development, human resource systems, management information systems, and sociotechnical systems. The contingency model presented in Chapter 1 is a logical extension of the systems approach to management. Throughout this book, we attempt to present an open-system perspective through a contingency approach. For example, a contingency approach to organizational design is discussed in Chapter 5.

The open-system model can be used to answer broad, systemwide questions such as:

1. What are the basic parts of the system?
2. How are these parts interdependent?

Fig. 3.3. The open-system model.

3. What processes are used to link the parts and carry on adjustment to one another?
4. What are the goals of the system?

In this chapter we will be emphasizing the need to study the organization as a whole rather than as parts isolated from one another or from the environment.

General System Model

The organization can be seen as a number of interdependent parts, each of which contributes to *and* receives something from the whole. In turn, the whole organization is interdependent with its external environment. An open system is a "system [involved] in exchange of matter with its environment, presenting import and export, [the] building up and breaking down of its material components."[21] In other words, open systems exchange information, energy, or materials with their environments.

Figure 3.3 is a simplified version of the organization as an open system. The organization (1) takes in various forms of information, energy, and materials from its environment; (2) acts on these inputs by transforming, or changing, them; and (3) sends out to the environment the transformed information, energy, and materials. More commonly, the inputs to an organization are people, materials, machines, money, and management. Outputs are typically identified as goods and services. For example, in examining a university from an open-system perspective, the inputs are the students, faculty members, physical and financial resources, and administrators. The students' learning activities are the transformation process; the output is in the form of knowledgeable students. When the former students become employees of other organizations, they become inputs again, and the cycle is repeated.

For the student to gain knowledge, all parts of the system (faculty members, physical and financial resources, and administrative staffs) should work together to reach the goal. If the university can no longer attract students, faculty, and other needed resources, it ceases to exist. During 1976, for example, 150 colleges closed their doors because they could no longer acquire inputs—primarily students—from their environment.

Properties of Open Systems

The open-system model provides a significant new strategy for examining such properties as: interrelated subsystems, differentiation, holism, goals, feedback, negative entropy, stability, adaptation, and equifinality. Each of these properties provides a necessary element, or building block, in the open-system model.

Any organization consists of a number of parallel, higher-level, and lower-level subsystems. The outputs of one subsystem can provide some of the inputs of another subsystem, as shown in Fig. 3.4. The interrelationship between subsystems is conveyed by arrows. This property can be portrayed with a simple example, but remember that the number and forms of interrelationship are much more complex in reality.

Let's assume that each of the input→transformation→output subsystems shown in Fig. 3.4 can be presented by positions in the organization, such as salesperson, sales manager, production manager, and vice-president of marketing. We shall trace the flow of communication between these parts as a consequence of a customer order. At the first (lowest) level, the sales manager gives input to a salesperson—to make a sales presentation to XYZ Corporation. Transformation occurs when the sales presentation results in a huge order (output).

Naturally, the salesperson then gives a copy of this order to the sales manager (input at level 2). Because the order needs to be filled quickly, the sales manager decides to write a memo (transformation) to the production manager indicating the importance of the order, especially since it's from a new customer, and urging cooperation. At the same time this memo (output) is being sent to the production manager, the sales manager also prepares (transformation) a memo to the vice-president of marketing, indicating receipt of the order and forewarning the superior of some possible static from the production people because of the short delivery time promised.

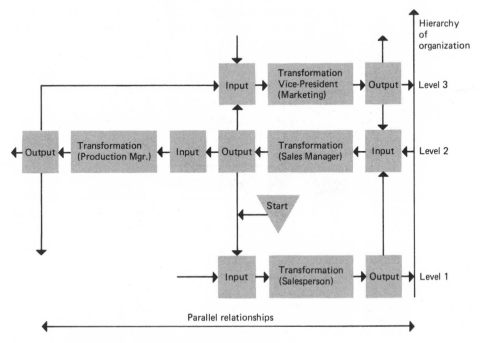

Fig. 3.4. Simplified model of interrelated subsystems.

After receipt (input) of the memo, the vice-president of marketing decides (transformation) to congratulate the sales manager by telephone (output) and to advise checking with production or a superior in the future before accepting orders with such tight time constraints. After hearing this (input), the sales manager starts thinking (transformation) that it might be desirable to set up some kind of system to avoid the problem of accepting delivery dates which might not be met.

In the meantime, the production manager has received (input) the memo from the sales manager and is furious about the tight time schedule; production people are already working ten hours a day plus Saturdays. Deciding to bring this problem to a "head" because it has happened too often in the past, the production manager prepares (transformation) a memo for the vice-president of marketing (after getting clearance from the vice-president of production). The memo (output) is hand-carried to the office of the vice-president of marketing (input).

This example shows how viewing an organization as a group of interrelated subsystems enables one to become aware of the possible interactions *among* and *within* organizational units. Since these interactions account for numerous management problems (such as the one illustrated), the need for analyzing and understanding them is obvious.

DIFFERENTIATION

Open systems tend to become more complex, or differentiated. As applied to organizations, differentiation is "the state of segmentation of the organizational system into subsystems, each of which tends to develop particular attributes in relation to the requirements posed by its relevant external environment."[22] To take an extreme example, General Motors has many specialized subsystems (units) to cope with its varied problems (e.g., air pollution, safety). As of 1977, each of GM's more than 30 major divisions also had major subunits, such as production, engineering, marketing, finance, and personnel. Many of these subunits are a natural consequence of the corporation's size, diversity, and the growing complexity of its worldwide environment. For example, General Motors' annual sales are greater than the tax receipts of all but a dozen or so countries. Its sales are also greater than the combined tax revenues of New York, New Jersey, Pennsylvania, Ohio, Delaware, and the six New England states. GM's size is evident in the fact that it employs 700,000 individuals and operates 127 plants in the United States and 45 other countries.

Differentiation can also be seen in a comparison of advanced industrial societies with developing countries or with earlier periods of industrial societies. For instance, the more than 20,000 distinct occupations and 8000 types of manufacturing industries in the United States indicate an extremely high degree of differentiation and complexity in the industrial sector.

HOLISM

Differentiation suggests the need for recognizing a system as something different from and *more than the sum of its parts*. This is because the interactions among and between the units *and* the characteristics of each of the units help determine the total system. The system becomes a totality when the units are *integrated.* Integration, then, is the process of achieving unity of effort among the various subsystems in order to accomplish the organization's task.

The process of integration can be illustrated by a simple example. Most business organizations have marketing, finance, and production units. Each of these units creates outputs. But the output of the whole organization is not simply the sum of the outputs provided by the marketing, finance, and production units. Rather, the output of the organization is the result of the *integration* of these units. Thus it is integration that makes the organization a whole. But as applied to the study of organizations, holism is, at best, only a partially realized concept. The holistic concept has been used to a greater extent and with greater success in developing an understanding of some of the organizations' parts than for its totality. Therefore, you will find, in this and other books, much more discussion and data on the interactions within particular subsystems.

GOALS

Organizations are established to do something; they perform activities toward some end. It might appear obvious that all organizations seek to increase productivity, but organizations actually vary a great deal in their emphasis on productivity. Quality may take precedence over quantity in one organization, with the reverse true in another organization.

Multiple Goals. The answers to the questions "What is a means to achieve a goal?" and "What is a goal?" depend on whose point of view is being considered—society, the customer, the investor, the worker, the top executive, and the like. For society, the justification of a steel company's existence may be to produce needed goods with minimal pollution to the environment. For customers, the goal of the steel mill might be to produce certain kinds of goods and deliver them on time; for investors, to maximize their return on investment; for workers, to have a stable job and good working conditions; for top executives, to make the best steel for the lowest price. Thus an organization can have *multiple goals* which can be pursued all at once or in some sequence, and some goals may be in conflict.

Typical organization goals fit into four basic categories:[23]

1. *Societal goals*—goods and services demanded by society;
2. *Output goals*—specific types of consumer goods, educational services, and the like;
3. *System goals*—desired organizational states or conditions, e.g., growth, stability, profits—which can be satisfied regardless of the output or product goals;
4. *Product goals*—the characteristics of goods and/or services being produced, e.g., quality, quantity, availability, uniqueness, and innovativeness.

Unfortunately, goals do not always fit neatly into one of these categories. But since we want to illustrate the variety of goals that organizations pursue, some classification scheme is necessary, and we will therefore overlook this limitation.

For the DuPont Corporation, a conservative fiscal policy is a *system goal.* This large corporation repeatedly states that its goals are high profitability and return on capital investment. Although DuPont can generate a substantial amount of capital internally, it could have grown even larger if it had increased capital expenditures by borrowing funds from banks at very low rates. By deciding not to do this, DuPont has needed a higher rate of return on new investments (in products, new plants) than its competitors, which have grown faster than DuPont. Since the mid-1960s, therefore, DuPont has lost its commanding leadership position in the chemical field.

Certain *product* goals have distinguished Daimler-Benz, the makers of Mercedes cars, and Timex from other organizations. With Mercedes, quality itself is a goal. The people who work at this plant are conscious of the quality standards and take a great deal of pride in their workmanship. Short-run gain may be sacrificed to maintain quality. Mercedes-Benz dealers cater to a select clientele and produce only a limited number of cars each year. By contrast, the goal of Timex is quantity—the mass production of watches. This company's leadership believes that most people do not want to pay the cost for extreme accuracy or incur the cost of cleaning and repairing watches. Thus a Timex watch has a relatively short life, but the low price tag means that customers can afford to buy new watches. Since Timex watch designs are simple, the company can use cheap, unskilled labor in a mass-production process. (With the introduction of the digital watch, Timex is also trying to capture a group of customers who want quality products.)

Subgoals. Each subsystem moves toward one or more subsystem goals. In a business organization, the production unit might have the general goal of producing goods of a given quality at the minimum cost; the marketing unit might have a goal of increasing sales by a certain percentage each year; and the finance unit might have a goal of minimizing the cost of borrowed money. Subsystem goals are organizational subgoals; they help the firm reach its higher-order goals, as suggested in Fig. 3.5.

Of course, business firms do not exist solely to meet their own goals. Generally, the organizational goals of profit, growth, and survival are subgoals of the larger economic system. In theory, at least, the goal of the American economic system is to provide for the consumers' welfare through the allocation of resources and the production and distribution of goods and services. Business firms are permitted to pursue their goals, within limits, because they help achieve other goals such as consumer welfare.

A & P: A Case Study.[24] At the end of 1963, the Great Atlantic and Pacific Tea Company (A & P) was the nation's largest retailing organization, in terms of sales. Although Sears, Roebuck and Company displaced A & P as the largest retailer at the end of 1964, A & P continued to rank as the largest grocery chain until 1972, when it was overtaken by Safeway Stores, Inc. For 104 years, or until 1964, A & P had been highly successful in terms of profitability and sales growth. During the years 1964–75, sales remained stable but earnings began to decline; stock that had sold for $71/share in 1964 was down to $11/share in 1975. The decline in earnings was matched by its sharp decline as a leader in the retailing field.

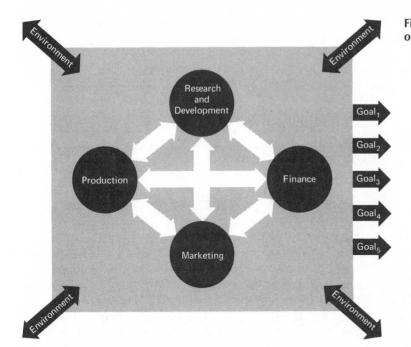

Fig. 3.5. System of goals.

85

OPEN-SYSTEM PERSPECTIVE

The company was founded in 1860 by George Hartford, who had become virtually the sole owner by the time of his death in 1917. Previously he had established a trust to hold his stock for the benefit of his children and their children. Two of his sons, John and George Ludlum, were the principal architects of the A & P organization between 1917 and 1951. When John died childless in 1951, his will established the John Hartford Foundation as the recipient of his stock. When 92-year-old George Hartford died in 1957, his stock too went to the John Hartford Foundation. Many people feel that his style of management over his 77 years with the company was the source of A & P's biggest problem.

During the late 1960s, A & P had systems goals and product goals. The organization's failure to alter or expand these goals in response to changes in the environment was a major factor contributing to its decline. A & P's system goals were stability, conservative fiscal policies and high dividend payments, and growth primarily through increased market shares by utilizing existing stores. Stability was maintained by the company's unchanging policy of promoting only from within the organization; all of A & P's executives had come up through the ranks. A & P's view was that since certain basic techniques of food retailing had proved successful for more than a century, there was no reason to change now. The management of A & P had the expertise necessary to operate city stores, but was unfamiliar with the complexities and uncertainties of the new suburban market. In order to move into the suburban market, A & P would have had to bring in outside managers, which would have meant breaking the tradition of promoting from within. Furthermore, since these individuals would be responsible for handling problems for the organization, they would expect a place in top management and would therefore be able to influence the organization. A & P continued to follow a goal that was no longer appropriate, and the organization gained a reputation for "slow-moving, complacent management" and "managerial ultraconservatism."

The second system goal of A & P was to refrain from borrowing money, a policy initiated by the founder and perpetuated ever since. This policy permitted A & P to pay high dividends to its stockholders. Although A & P did not plan to enter the suburban market, it nonetheless needed capital for distributing its earnings in the form of cash dividends. In 1965, many of A & P's stores were old and in poor physical condition. But rather than break its tradition of no long-term debt, the company allowed its stores to remain in poor condition. A & P customers began shopping at the newer, more modern stores of its competitors.

A & P also sought to increase the market shares of its existing stores. The company had earned a reputation for being a price leader within the food retailing industry, and it believed that its reputation would continue to attract customers. However, the discount grocery stores entering the market during the late 1960s were able to match or better A & P's price and also offered more attractive surroundings.

These various systems goals of A & P were in conflict. The organization sought to achieve growth by utilizing existing stores, which severely limited its growth possibilities. Real growth potential lay in the suburban market, but A & P's other goals of stability and freedom from long-term debt prevented it from entering that market.

A & P's product goal was to provide quality foods at a low price. One of the keys to profitable food retailing is rapid turnover of inventory, which compensates for the low profit margins. During the late 1960s, A & P offered its customers credit cards and trading stamps. The results were disastrous and created large losses. Rather than cover these losses by borrowing and break the A & P tradition, however, the organization passed the losses on to the customers in the form of higher prices. More customers deserted. In an effort to win some of them back, A & P initiated its Where Economy Originates (WEO) plan in early 1972. Stores were turned into warehouses. Products in their packing containers were placed in the aisles. Only one or two check-out lanes were open. Customers had to bag their own groceries. Employees were not normally available to assist the customers. Prices were slashed. People did begin switching to A & P, but prices were so low that the company was losing money. When A & P was forced to begin raising prices, customers again flocked to stores offering better service and more attractive surroundings.

To increase profits, other food chains had begun selling nonfood items, which offered a higher profit margin. A & P, however, refused to do so. As one A & P divisional president stated, "There is a higher profit margin on nonfoods, but it's just not our business." Again, the failure to alter goals and, in turn, the corporate structure in response to environmental changes led to a decline in A & P's profits.

In early 1975, the board of directors ended its 115-year tradition of promoting from within, electing outsider Jonathan Scott as the chairman of the board. Scott's task was to get things turned around. He closed 1200 of A & P's 3500 stores that were too small to operate efficiently and has planned the construction of new stores. The new stores, to be located in shopping centers, will offer wide selections of food and nonfood items. In 1975, Scott also initiated a new trademark for the company: "Price and Pride." Although it is still too early to fully evaluate Scott's programs, sales for the second quarter in 1975 were only eight percent less than sales for the previous year, and, of course, operating costs were down substantially.

FEEDBACK

The use of feedback permits managers to determine whether progress is being made toward goals. The variety of feedback mechanisms is endless—test results, performance evaluations, awareness of other people's feelings, bank statements, etc. Feedback is all around us.

Two types of feedback exist for complex open systems—positive and negative.[25] *Negative* feedback, the more common type, is the comparison between current behavior and predetermined standards or goals. For example, the normal human body temperature is 98.6°F. Deviations from this standard become known through a feedback mechanism, e.g., a fever or chills. Feedback for organizational subsystems is more complex. Organizational goals or standards against which the feedback is compared *can and do change* over time. A college student who continues to receive feedback in the form of C's may begin studying more or seeking out better learning techniques in order to get the desired A's. If the student still gets C's, she or he may make further attempts to correct the deviations, but may also begin to experience frustration and anxiety. Gradually, however, the goal level may shift to that of C grades; thus the C grades obtained and the goal of C grades match.

Negative feedback can also be *learned and created*. Nothing in the organization automatically provides for negative feedback. Instead, managers must allocate resources and provide the techniques to obtain negative feedback. Of course, once management establishes the feedback mechanisms, they may take on the appearance of being automatic. For example, in some supermarkets, inventory updating occurs on a daily basis through the use of special labels that pass through sensors at the check-out counter. These sensors send data to a computer that provides daily inventory and other information on each shelf item. This inventory sheet is then compared with the numbers of each item (goals) management feels should be carried. A decline from this goal or standard represents a deviation, which is corrected by reordering (new input).

The second general form of feedback, *positive* feedback, is often ignored, even though it has considerable significance for humans and organizations. Negative feedback is used to help the system remain stable by returning it to predetermined standards. Positive feedback encourages the system to change.

Assume that the president of a business firm obtains feedback that profits are 20 percent above the goal for the first six months of the year. Does the president respond by stating the need to correct for this type of deviation from the goal? Of course not! Most likely the president will encourage behavior which will lead to the same or greater financial performance during the next six-month period. We can also explain positive feedback in our example of the student who was having grade problems. Before, we assumed that the goal was A grades and that the C's were negative feedback. Now, assume that the goal is C's, but that the experience is A's. Should the student attempt to correct for this deviation by bringing his or her grades down to the C level? Possibly! Or, being an adaptive and changing being, the student might shift the *goal* to that of B or even A grades. The grade information in this situation becomes a form of positive feedback.

In sum, the same information which is fed back into the system can be characterized as either negative or positive. If used as a basis for returning to or maintaining the status quo, the information is considered negative feedback. If used as a basis for changing the goals or internal structure of the system, the information is regarded as positive feedback.

NEGATIVE ENTROPY

Negative and positive feedback provide one means for offsetting or reducing *entropy,* or "a movement to disorder, complete lack of resource transformation, and death."[26] A key assumption is that if left undisturbed, the system will remain closed; change occurs only if energy is deliberately imported from the environment. Disorder and randomness are likely to develop in an organization unless it is opened by input in the form of information, energy, and materials. Inputs counteract the natural tendency toward entropy. In the human system, food and medical supplies are inputs that offset the negative entropy of hunger and disease.

Business firms, governmental units, educational establishments, and other types of organizations, by contrast, do not have such physical limitations and may therefore exist indefinitely under conditions of negative entropy. The business firm acts to ward off or reduce entropy by: (1) maintaining a reserve of cash to increase its ability to survive if suddenly confronted by a general economic depression or loss of major markets; (2) selecting and training its members to meet present and future demands on the system; and (3) seeking and utilizing technology to lower production costs. Although organizations may survive under adverse conditions, most organizations are relatively short-lived. Most of the giants in American industry today are less than 100 years old. The ability of these organizations to stop or prevent entropy over the long run remains an unanswered question.

STABILITY AND ADAPTATION

Open systems are also stable and adaptive. Stable open systems are self-regulating, much as thermostats and automatic steering devices are. When disturbed, a stable system will actively attempt to return to its previous state. Negative feedback systems facilitate this process. Stability attempts to maintain: (1) the parts or structure of the system (and its subsystems); (2) the relationships between the parts; and (3) the interdependencies between the subsystems and their higher-level systems.[27]

Adaptation, on the other hand, is concerned with significant changes in each of these three maintenance factors and the possibility of further growth in the system. Growth occurs through the creation of new and different parts, relationships, and interdependencies. Adaptation also implies that the feedback control loops make possible self-direction or at least adaptation to a changing environment. Although stability and adaptation may often be in conflict, they

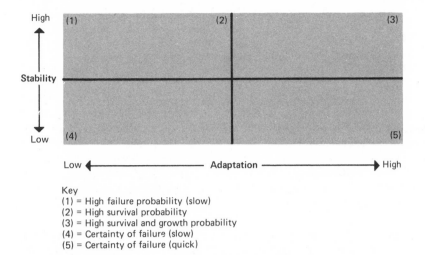

Key
(1) = High failure probability (slow)
(2) = High survival probability
(3) = High survival and growth probability
(4) = Certainty of failure (slow)
(5) = Certainty of failure (quick)

Fig. 3.6. Combinations of stability and adaptability for organizations.

are not at opposite ends of a single continuum. The choice is not stability *or* adaptation. Rather, both are needed.

Figure 3.6 shows a simplified model of stability and adaptation as separate, although interrelated, dimensions of human and organizational systems. Organizations can vary greatly on these two dimensions. Also, the various combinations of these two variables lead to different consequences. The five consequences presented in the key to Fig. 3.6 are illustrative, rather than exhaustive, of the possibilities. Further, an organization can shift on this chart over time.

Figure 3.6 shows that organizations with high stability and low adaptiveness (1 in the model) tend to be rigid and, over the long run, most likely to fail. But if these organizations exist in environments that are not changing too rapidly and have built up negative entropy (e.g., cash reserves, inventory levels, etc.), the process of failure may be slow. Organizations that tend to react to rather than anticipate changes requiring adjustments (2) have a strong survival probability. Organizations with both high stability and adaptation orientations (3) have a high probability of both survival and growth; making the most of negative and positive feedback, these organizations can react quickly and anticipate changes both internally and externally. Possibility 3 is probably the ideal toward which many business firms strive.

Organizations with low stability and low adaptation (4) are virtually certain to fail quickly. Of course, the rapidity of failure for an ongoing organization will depend on the amount of negative entropy it possesses when it moves into possibilities 4 or 5. Organizations in cell 4 tend to be rigid and apathetic. Their slow, inadequate feedback mechanisms result in expenditures of resources long after adjustments are needed.

Finally, organizations in cell 5 would also face certainty of failure. Rather than exhibiting rigid and apathetic behavior, their attempts to adapt result in chaos and confusion. Active change efforts might falter because of inadequate or nonexistent feedback on the consequences of these changes, as well as confusion about the direction and purposes of the changes.

S. S. Kresge: A Case Study.[28] S. S. Kresge and Company illustrates possibilities 1, 2, and 3 in Fig. 3.6. Kresge has shown the most dramatic growth of any American retailer within the past decade, growing from eighth to third largest nonfood retailer in the United States, behind Sears and J. C. Penney's. This rise is even more outstanding when one considers that most other large merchandisers suffered from recession problems in 1974–76.

Entering the dime store business in 1897, Sebastian S. Kresge used his $8000 in savings to buy a half-interest, with J. G. McCrory, in a store in Memphis, Tennessee. A year later these men opened a second store, in Detroit, Michigan. In 1899 Kresge founded the company in his own name. By 1912 the company had 85 stores with an annual sales volume of $10.3 million. That represented a lot of sales, because the stores stocked no items that sold for more than $.10.

By 1916 the company had 150 stores and faced its first major decision. Inflation brought on by World War I was limiting what could be sold for a dime, so a decision was made to raise the limit to $.25. By adapting to its changing environment (cell 2), the company reported sales of $51 million by 1920. Shortly thereafter, a chain of dollar stores was started.

After World War II, the company made plans for expansion because of changes in the retailing field. It expanded into new merchandise markets and opened more stores. By the late 1940s the chain had 696 stores, 61 of them in Canada, and a sales volume of $251 million. In the early 1950s, however, the president reported a decline in sales and profits. In an attempt to understand this problem, the president commissioned a team of experts to identify Kresge's strengths and weaknesses, study its competitors and the entire retailing market, and recommend a course of action to maintain Kresge's growth and profitability. After two years of study, the experts indicated that new discount stores were hurting Kresge's profits the most. Since the report also indicated that there were no national discount stores, the president decided to move Kresge into the discount business, while keeping the variety stores as long as they were profitable. This decision reflects characteristics of cell 3—high adaptation to the environment and high stability in terms of goals.

The first K-Mart opened in a Detroit suburb in 1962, and 17 others opened the same year. By 1966 when founder Sebastian Kresge died at age 99, company sales had reached $1 billion, and the total number of company stores had reached a record 915, including 162 K-Marts. At the end of 1976 the company had 1663 stores in the United States, Puerto Rico, Canada, and Australia. Of these stores, 1206 were K-Marts, 366 were Kresge variety stores, and 91 were Jupiter stores (small, limited-stock discount operations). Sales for fiscal 1976 were $8.4 billion, and the president has predicted that sales will reach $12 billion by 1980. Store openings continue at the rate of two a week.

Throughout its history, Kresge had successfully adapted to its customers' wants and needs. According to the senior vice-president for sales and general merchandising, the average K-Mart customer is between 22 and 44, parent of two children, lives in a mortgaged home, and has an annual income of between $12,000 and $20,000. K-Mart marketing surveys continually are taken to understand changes in consumer buying patterns. For example, in the 1974–76 recession, K-Mart found that people with higher incomes were shopping in their stores, an increase in do-it-yourself products, and a phenomenal growth of cloth diapers, as the sale of disposable diapers had dropped off.

K-Mart's own merchandise represents about 18–20 percent of sales. The ratio has not changed much, and the company does not plan to change it. In 1976–77 K-Mart started to market its own major appliances. These products will have to compete, in terms of price and service, with the national brands that K-Mart also carries.

W. T. Grant: A Case Study.[29] The W. T. Grant Company had long been known throughout the retailing industry for its steady increases in sales and profits over its 69-year history. In its heyday, it was one of the nation's largest retail chains. On October 2, 1975, the Grant Company reported a negative net worth and was forced to file for bankruptcy under Chapter 11 of the Federal Bankruptcy Act. On February 12, 1976, Grant agreed to liquidate all its operations within 30 days; it had total assets of $512.1 million and liabilities of $1.1 billion, even after closing 715 of its 1074 stores and laying off 50,000 employees. The impact of the W. T. Grant's fall, second in dollar terms only to Penn Central's collapse, jarred the business community and left more than 8000 suppliers with more than $70 million in uncollectable bills for merchandise, newspapers holding the bag for $2 million in advertising, and 27 banks stuck with $640 million in loans.

In 1906 William T. Grant invested his life savings of $1000 to open his first store in Lynn, Massachusetts. Customers flocked to the store. The store was an instant success because it was the only store to offer a convenient location, a large variety of software goods, and above all reasonable prices. For a number of years, there was no strong competition for Grant's. After his initial success in Lynn, Grant began to plan an expansion program to satisfy the needs of consumers in other locations. For more than 50 years, the goals of Grant stores remained the same—to offer customers a large variety of reasonably priced goods in a convenient location. From 1906 to 1966, W. T. Grant personally directed the company to be sure that his policies and goals were not changed.

Throughout the 1960s and part of the 1970s, the W. T. Grant Company began new programs to expand store size and the number of merchandise lines carried. When a new president took over in 1966, the founder's basic philosophy was changed; a variety of high-ticket durables (TV's, radios, freezers, washers and dryers, etc.) was offered, as well as a wider number of merchandise lines. Sales and profits jumped to a record high in the mid-1960s.

The reasons for Grant's change were obvious. During the mid-1960s the company stood back and watched several of its competitors (K-Mart, Sears, Montgomery Ward, among others) successfully expand into high-ticket items. When Grant's decided to adopt a similar policy, its expansion had to be rapid enough to allow it to catch up with its competitors.

The purchase of a television or major appliance is a sizable expenditure for most families. Extending credit to customers may ease their burden and at the same time raise the sales figures for the individual stores. The major drawbacks of credit are the uncertainty created for the company in terms of unpaid bills and fraudulent uses of credit. To guard against these possibilities, Grant's accepted Master Charge and Bank Americard in its larger Grant City stores and also set up its own credit card company. These policies were effective, and Grant's was able to expand its credit sales to 25 percent of total sales very quickly.

During this period, Grant's also expanded into new locations. The company closed some of the older, less profitable stores in the downtown areas and opened larger Grant City stores in small shopping centers. Between 1963 and 1973, Grant's opened 612 stores and expanded 91 others. Grant's management chose not to locate in large mall-type shopping centers, citing the problems of too much competition and traffic. This decision had mixed results; it did increase convenience for some customers, but it also caused Grant City stores to miss out on the large volume of consumer activity associated with large malls. Since only a few local merchants were usually located in the same shopping center as a Grant City store, the management was hoping that the "one-stop shopping" aspect would draw enough customers to their locations. When this strategy began to fail, Grant's began selling items below cost in an attempt to generate traffic. However, most customers came into the stores to buy these loss leaders, but failed to purchase other merchandise. Selling merchandise below actual costs created cash-flow problems for Grant's entire operation.

During 1971 and 1972, sales continued to climb, but due to the large capital expenditures for the credit programs, profits leveled off in late 1972 and started to decline. The 1972 sales decrease was the first in the company's history. The effect of the sales decrease was compounded by an increasing cost of goods-sold figure and a rising rate of interest on short-term notes payable. With sales and profits declining, a new president, an individual who had come up through the ranks as a finance officer, was appointed.

Conditions grew worse until October 1975, when the company collapsed. The company had to borrow millions at high interest rates to finance its credit business. In addition, attention to store operations fell off. Sales went down further. When profits were down in the early part of 1974, collections of credit accounts also slipped. In early 1974, there were allegations that some of Grant's executives had accepted kickbacks from real estate landlords, and a complete shake-up of top management occurred in June 1974. The chairman of the board and the president left the company, and a new man, who had a solid background in merchandising, was brought in to head the company operations. He immediately fired 11,000 employees and closed 125 unprofitable stores. For the fiscal year ending January 31, 1975, Grant reported a loss of $177.3 million. The new president and his staff sought to deemphasize credit and return to the traditional business of soft goods and accessories that the founder, William T. Grant, had believed in.

Despite growing difficulty in paying its bills, the company managed to get the banks to extend their loans again and again. Rumors persisted that the Federal Reserve Board had quietly pressured the banks to keep the big retailer alive. As losses mounted, the board of directors brought in another new president in April 1975. Between April and October 1975, he and his staff met almost daily with the banks. But the company continued to lose money and ended the

first half of 1975 with a reported loss of $113.3 million. On October 2, 1975,
the W. T. Grant Company went into bankruptcy.

According to Fig. 3.6, Grant's approximated possibilities 1, 2, 4, and 5. At first, the company had sought a special "niche" in the retailing market, that of high emphasis on stability and moderate emphasis on adaptation, which was very successful. In the 1960s, the decision not to locate in large shopping malls and adapt to newer customers' wants and desires (e.g., credit plans, large appliances, national merchandise) moved the company from cell 2 to cell 1. The retailing environment had undergone a tremendous change, but Grant's did not move into these markets until it was too late. In an effort to adapt quickly to the changes in the retailing industry, Grant's established a credit policy and began selling large appliances. Grant's was reacting to pressures from the customers, but that is when the company began to decline. The overextended credit policies, the advertisement, and large sale "loss" leaders cut into Grant's financial stability. In an attempt to solve its financial problems, the company's operating problems rose. One last effort was made in early 1975 to return the company to a stable position by reverting to William T. Grant's basic philosophy of selling primarily softwares for cash. Unfortunately, this attempt came too late.

EQUIFINALITY

Equifinality, our last general characteristic of all open systems, simply means that output (e.g., profit, sales) may be reached from different initial conditions and in different ways. This concept has several implications for managers. First, there may be several satisfactory solutions to some problems. Second, two or more organizations faced with the same problem may require substantially different tactics and strategies to solve it. This is based on the assumption that effective solutions are dependent on the unique character of the organization and its environment. Finally, the concept lends credibility to the viability of the contingency approach to management.

Semiconductor Industry: Case Studies. Robert Noyce, chairman of Intel Corporation, and Charles Sporck, chairman of National Semiconductor Corporation, run their respective companies differently, but both companies are among the leaders in the field.[30] Noyce started Intel to seek undiscovered niches in a field where a new technology could create a new market. He identified a new technology and then created a product. Noyce relies on a highly efficient manufacturing operation to back up the marketing effort. Noyce believes that responsibilities and financial rewards should be pushed to the lowest managerial levels; most managerial employees have profited from Intel's strong performance (Intel's stock went from $15.00 in early 1974 to $93.50 in March 1976).

Sporck's major goal at National Semiconductor was to make every line a superefficient, high-volume product line. When he came to the company in 1967, the company had sales of $8 million; by March 1976, sales had risen to $235 million. In March 1974, National's stock was selling at $9; two years later, at $52.00. Sporck stays in close contact with the day-to-day operations. When there is trouble on a product line, he steps in and takes personal control of the product until the trouble is straightened out. The emphasis on high-volume manufacturing has frequently forced many potentially profitable research and development projects to the back burner.

Summary

The systems approach is undoubtedly mind-broadening. It calls attention to social, economic, and technical forces; to goals, structures, people, and environment; and to the various subsystems of the organization, their functions, and their orientations. It indicates that these factors are interrelated and that the relationships are dynamic. What it fails to do, however, is to spell out the precise relationships among these elements. It is not enough to say that all parts of the organization are related. What is needed is a statement of what goals initiate what structural changes in organizations. To a limited extent, the contingency theory of management answers this question.

CONTINGENCY VIEW OF THE MANAGERIAL SYSTEM

The managerial system spans the entire organization by directing the technology, organizing the people and other resources, and relating the organization to its environment. The traditional, or closed-system, management models focused on the fundamental administrative processes—planning, organizing, and controlling—which are essential if an organization is to meet its primary goals and objectives. These basic managerial functions are required for any type of organization (e.g., religious, governmental, educational, or voluntary) where human and physical resources are combined to achieve certain objectives. Furthermore, these functions are necessary regardless of the specialized area of management—finance, accounting, production, or marketing.

Managerial-Systems Model

The managerial system can also be understood by looking within organizations at managerial levels.[31] The managerial-systems model in Fig. 3.7 shows that there are basic differences in the orientation of the managerial system at these different levels.

1. *Technical level.* The technical system produces the firm's goods and/or services. It is here that the organization "does its thing"—producing bicycles, toothpaste, typewriters; providing health care or fire protection; educating individuals, etc. The problems in this subsystem are technical in nature, imposed by the task itself. Staff personnel—quality-control engineers, industrial engineers, and operations researchers—assist managers at this level. These staff assistants solve the technical problems involved in the actual manufacturing of the firm's product(s).

2. *Organizational level.* The organizational subsystem controls and services the technical system. Organizational-level managers coordinate the firm's internal activities so that the technical system can perform its tasks efficiently and in accordance with the goals and objectives of the firm. Thus the managers

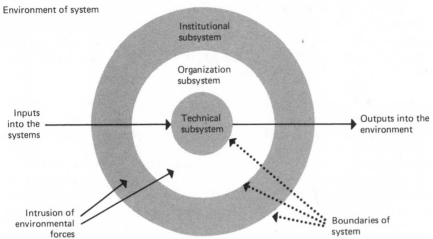

Fig. 3.7. General managerial-system model. (T. A. Petit, "A Behavioral Theory of Management," *Academy of Management Journal* **10** (1967): 349. Reprinted by permission of the Academy of Management and the author.)

in the organizational subsystem influence such matters as which tasks are to be performed, the scale of operations, employment and purchasing policies, marketing, finance, and accounting-related activities. The personnel manager who recruits college graduates is a member of the organizational subsystem. His or her job is to attract to the firm candidates who can assist it in reaching its basic system goals.

3. *Institutional level.* Managers in the institutional subsystem deal directly with the firm's external environments—unions, public, customers, governments—whose support is required for the organization's survival.

In many organizations, these managerial-system roles are performed by different individuals. For example, in the university, the board of regents and the president fulfill institutional-level needs, whereas the deans and department heads are more involved in the organizational subsystem. It is their job to coordinate the activities (e.g., degree programs, athletic programs, continuing-education programs) within the university to achieve the goals set forth by the managers at the institutional level. The faculty members are primarily at technical level. In a hospital, the board of trustees perform primarily at the institutional subsystem level; the administrative staff coordinates aspects at the organizational level; and the doctors, nurses, and other specialists perform at the technical level.

DIFFERENCES BETWEEN MANAGEMENT LEVELS

Most organizations have all three managerial levels, which suggests that they face different situations and therefore perhaps may conflict over important decisions. For example, the people performing the production operations are a part of the technical level, and they should be well versed in the problems involved in manufacturing. The organizational subsystem may be composed of managers representing functional areas such as marketing, finance, and industrial relations. The institutional subsystem is represented by the board of directors, president, and other top executives who interact with the environment. There are often differences in the orientation of the people operating in these different subsystems. Let's compare these briefly.

Technical Manager. The technical manager, concerned with efficiency of output, typically utilizes the methods of scientific management and management science. Technical managers tend to have an engineering point of view and consider the technical subsystem as a logical system of action that can be organized and operated with mathematical precision in the short run. Operations-research techniques, such as linear programming, dynamic programming, queueing theory, and Markov chain analysis, are frequently employed to compute the best combination of resources to produce a given output within a given time.

Institutional Manager. Institutional managers, by contrast, face a wide variety of inputs from their environment, and they are also concerned with how the system's output will be received by clients, consumers, governmental agencies, and the like. The closed-system logic, which emphasizes simple economic maximization strategies, is less appropriate here because the firm may have little control over its inputs. Therefore, managers in this subsystem should have an open-system view and concentrate on adaptive and/or stability goals. The primary task of institutional managers is to take the action necessary to ensure the firm's survival and growth.

Organizational Manager. Organizational managers operate between the technical and institutional levels, and their objective is to coordinate the actions of these two levels. Organizational managers transform the inputs from the institutional managers into a set of decision rules necessary for the technical managers carrying out the production functions of the organization. Organizational managers often need to use the decision strategy of compromise; by comparison, the institutional managers may seek long-run flexibility to enhance the firm's survival in a changing and uncertain market and economic environment. There might also be a substantial loss of production during equipment modification and installation. The vice-president of manufacturing, a member of the organizational level, must therefore reconcile the differences between these two individuals representing different orientations within the same organization.

Implications for Management

The view of the organization as an open system suggests a role for management substantially different from that which it played in traditional models. Traditional management emphasizes economic-technical rationality. This closed-system view was appropriate for the technical level, but not for the organizational and institutional management levels. The human relationists did bring into focus the human side of the enterprise, but neglected the technical, struc-

Table 3.4. The managerial system: technical, organizational, and institutional levels

| Level of subsystem | Some Implications for Managers | | | | |
	Task	Viewpoint	Technique	Time horizon	Decision-making strategy
Technical	Technical, operations, production	Engineering	Scientific management; operations research	Short run	Computational
Organizational	Coordination	Political	Mediation	Short run and long run	Compromise
Institutional	Deal with uncertainty, relate organization to environment	Conceptual and philosophical	Opportunistic surveillance, negotiate with environment	Long run	Judgmental

tural, and environmental aspects. The systems view suggests that managers in various departments face situations which may be different, with varying degrees of ambiguity and potential for conflict. Management is not in full control of all production factors, as suggested by traditional management models. It is strongly restrained by many environmental and internal forces.

Table 3.4 summarizes the implications for managers at each managerial level. The technical subsystem emphasizes closed-system logic, rational decision making, scientific-management techniques, short time horizons, and relies on rules and regulations to maximize the decisions made. The decision strategy is computational, in that all factors affecting productivity can be calculated and those factors that lead to the highest productivity are selected. However, at the organizational and institutional subsystems, different managerial behaviors are needed. For example, at the organizational level the personnel department must coordinate the staffing needs of the entire organization. When two or more departments want to expand their staffs but there is funding for only one position, a compromise decision-making strategy is likely to be used. Finally, at the institutional level, the manager's job is to deal with the firm's external environment (e.g., customers, banks, students) and translate the demands of these groups into services or products that the firm can produce.

Summary

The closed-system approach incorporates the bureaucratic, human relations, scientific-management, and administrative-management models. The bureaucratic model of management and organization focuses on control and authority and includes such dimensions as a well-defined hierarchy, division of labor based on functional specialization, and impersonality. Scientific management sought to improve the efficiency of the individual's work contribution through planning. Henri Fayol's administrative-management theory specified functions and principles for more effective management through planning, controlling, and directing the activities of the workers. Authority was delegated downward, and rules, regulations, principles, and functions were established to guide managerial thinking.

The human relations model, founded by Mayo and his colleagues, initially focused on the physiological conditions in the work place in an attempt to understand worker behavior. Because their results were disappointing, the researchers turned to psychological and sociological factors for understanding workers' behavior. They found workers to be motivated by emotional as well as economic forces. The human relations model has been criticized for employing a closed-system strategy in the study of organizations and thus failing to consider structural variables, conflict, environmental factors, and the like.

In discussing the open-system view of organizations, we noted that an open system is not subject to the process of entropy. Rather, it can maintain a dynamic equilibrium by inputting material, transforming it, and then outputting it to the environment.

The organization can be viewed as having a number of other key characteristics. In general, there is a hierarchy of systems. As the total system becomes more complex, it is differentiated into subsystems to manage the requirements impinging on it from the external environment. Through the use of feedback, the organization maintains a steady state and adjusts to rapidly changing environments.

Level of organization is a major contingency for differentiating managerial systems. Three levels are usually found in the managerial system in complex organizations: institutional, organizational, and technical. The institutional level relates the activities of the organization to its environment. The organizational level integrates the demands from the institutional level with those from the technical level. The technical level is involved with the actual production of the organization's goods or services.

This framework will serve as a basis for our discussion of modern organization design and decision making. In Chapter 5, we shall examine uncertainty in the environment and evaluate its effects on organization structure, goals, and technology. The managerial processes of decision making, planning, and control will then be reviewed.

Discussion Questions

1. Why was the theory of bureaucracy established when there was a tremendous increase in the number and size of organizations?

2. Select an organization and evaluate the degree to which it adheres to bureaucratic concepts.

3. Analyze your own university or college to see whether any of the principles from the administrative-management theorists are being applied.

4. Give your own analysis of scientific management. Evaluate the major contributions and limitations of this traditional model.

5. What is the contingency approach to the study of management?

6. What assumptions concerning "human nature" are represented by closed-system management models?

7. What are the major distinctions between the human relations, administrative management, scientific management, and bureaucratic models?

8. Define "systems."

9. What are the differences between open- and closed-system perspectives to the study of organizations?

10. What management implications can you derive from the A&P, Grant's, and Kresge cases?

11. How does a systems approach affect management practices?

12. Discuss the major differences among the institutional, organizational, and technical subsystems within an organization.

Management Incidents

THE BUREAUCRAT

Major Adams, a personnel officer, had the reputation of being a cautious person. After receiving a training proposal, her first step was to research her extensive library of rules and regulations governing the objectives, goals, number of work-hours, etc. Major Adams rejected the vast majority of proposals, citing the appropriate rule and regulations that she had interpreted as prohibiting the desired training program.

Major Smith, a personnel officer in another unit at the same base, was usually receptive to a proposal and if she thought that the request would serve the objectives of the United States Air Force, she approved it, even if it were contrary to Air Force regulations. When this was pointed out to her, she said, "Sure, I break regulations all the time and everybody knows it. But nobody has ever criticized me for it and besides, our unit has the highest efficiency rating on the base."

General Watson, who supervised both Major Adams and Major Smith, was considering which one to recommend for promotion.

1. Which personnel officer do you think General Watson should recommend for promotion? Why?
2. What do you think about the idea that if the outcome is good, the means to reach it are not important?

LAZARUS DEPARTMENT STORE

The Lazarus Department Store's large shoe department employed about 20 sales clerks. Most of them were loyal and faithful and had worked in the department and store for over ten years. They formed a close-knit social group.

The department store expanded its square footage and hired five new sales clerks in the shoe department within five months. These newcomers soon learned that the old-timers took the desirable time for coffee breaks, leaving the most undesirable times to the five newly hired employees. The old-time clerks also received priority from the old-time cashier; the newcomers waited in line at the cash register until the old-timers had their sales recorded. A number of customers complained to the store management about waiting too long to pay their bills.

In addition, the old-timers frequently instructed the newcomers to straighten shoes in the stock room and to clean displays on the sales floor, although this work was supposed to be done by everybody. The result was that old-timers had more time to make sales and newcomers had less time. Since commissions were paid on sales, the newcomers complained to the department manager about this practice.

1. Explain why these things happened.
2. You are the department manager. What would you do about each of the practices?

HARRISON HOSPITAL*

As an orderly in a local hospital, Robert Millman's duty was to clean and prepare the maternity ward and delivery rooms. Bob's supervisor was the head nurse in the maternity ward on night duty. She in turn reported to the head nurse for that wing of the hospital.

After working several months in this area, Bob detected great hostility between the ward head nurse and the staff physicians. The head nurse was a strict disciplinarian and closely followed all hospital rules and regulations. The staff physicians broke the rules and regulations when it suited them, which was most of the time. The night shift was especially lonely, since few people were around to check on what the physicians were doing. Often the nurses and physicians would play bridge, chess, or just sit and shoot the bull.

---

* Adapted from J. Murray and T. Von der Embe, *Organizational Behavior*, Columbus, Ohio: Merrill, 1973, p. 151.

Gradually it became evident that the head nurse disliked Bob's running errands and playing cards with the doctors. She even complained to her supervisor that the staff physicians were using her subordinates to run errands and that she could not allow this to continue. Of course, Bob liked doing things for the physicians because it gave him higher status in the eyes of other orderlies. Since he wanted eventually to enter college, he believed that helping the physicians was one way of getting a highly favorable recommendation from them.

One evening this entire matter came to a climax when a doctor sent a nurse out of the delivery room for sodium benzoate. The anesthetist had exhausted his supply, and only the head nurse could authorize getting more. The head nurse was nowhere to be found, so the doctor authorized the delivery room nurse to tell Bob to get the sodium benzoate without the head nurse's approval.

Under great anxiety and frustration, Bob secured the sodium benzoate. Shortly afterwards, the head nurse learned of Bob's actions and reprimanded him for not getting her approval. She later complained directly to the head nurse of that wing about the staff physician's actions. Bob told the physicians of the head nurse's actions and asked them to personally talk to the head nurse. They agreed to do so.

1. What happened and why?
2. Use the bureaucratic model to analyze the case.
3. What would you do, as the head nurse, to prevent this from happening again?

REFERENCES

1. For an extended discussion of open- versus close-system perspectives, *see* R. Hall, *Organizations: Structure and Process* (Englewood Cliffs, N.J.: Prentice-Hall, 1972), pp. 14–39; and J. D. Thompson, *Organizations in Action* (New York: McGraw-Hill, 1967), pp. 3–13.

2. *See* L. Hrebiniak, *Complex Organizations* (St. Paul, Minn.: West, 1978); and M. Weber, *The Theory of Social and Economic Organization,* trans. A. Henderson and T. Parsons (New York: Free Press, 1947).

3. This list was compiled from works of P. Blau and R. Schoenherr, *The Structure of Organizations* (New York: Basic Books, 1973); J. Child, "Predicting and Understanding Organization Structure," *Administrative Science Quarterly* **18** (1973): 165–185; and N. Toren, "Bureaucracy and Professionalism: A Reconsideration of Weber's Thesis," *Academy of Management Review* **1,** 3 (1976): 36–46. *Also see* S. Becker and D. Neuhauser, *The Efficient Organization* (New York: Elsevier, 1975).

4. S. Udy, "Bureaucratic Elements in Organizations: Some Research Findings," *American Sociological Review* **23** (1958): 415–418; B. Reimann, "On the Dimensions of Bureaucratic Structure: An Empirical Reappraisal," *Administrative Science Quarterly* **18** (1973): 462–476; R. Mansfield, "Bureaucracy and Centralization: An Examination of Organizational Structure," *Administrative Science Quarterly* **18** (1973): 477–488; and D. Weiss, "Multivariate Procedures," in *Handbook of Industrial and Organizational Psychology,* ed. M. Dunnette (Chicago: Rand McNally, 1976), pp. 327–362.

5. For further discussion, *see* H. Cohen, "Bureaucratic Flexibility: Some Comments on Robert Merton's 'Bureaucratic Structure and Personality,'" *British Journal of Sociology* **21** (1970): 390–399; G. Zaltman, R. Duncan, and J. Holbek, *Innovations and Organizations* (New York: Wiley Interscience, 1973); and R. Presthus, *The Organizational Society* (New York: Vintage Books, 1965).

6. P. Selznick, *TVA and the Grass Roots* (Berkeley: University of California Press, 1949).

7. J. Ford and J. Slocum, "Size, Technology, Environment and the Structure of Organizations," *Academy of Management Review* **2** (October 1977).

8. J. Schriesheim, M. VonGlinow, and S. Kerr, "Professionals in Bureaucracy: A Structural Alternative," in *Prescriptive Models of Organizations,* ed. P. Nystrom and W. Starbuck, North Holland–Timms Studies in the Management Sciences, Vol. 5 (Amsterdam: North Holland, 1978); and R. Satow, "Value Rational Authority and Professional Organizations: Weber's Missing Type," *Administrative Science Quarterly* **20** (1975): 526–531.

9. J. Webb, *Space-Age Management* (New York: McGraw-Hill, 1969).

10. W. Starbuck, "Organizations and Their Environments," in *Handbook of Industrial and Organizational Psychology,* ed. M. Dunnette (Chicago: Rand McNally, 1976), pp. 1069–1123.

11. C. Wrege and A. Perroni, "Taylor's Pig-Tale: A Historical Analysis of Frederick W. Taylor's Pig Iron Experiment," *Academy of Management Journal* **17** (1974): 6–27; and L. Fry, "The Maligned F. W. Taylor: A Reply to His Many Critics," *Academy of Management Review* **1,** 3 (1976): 124–129.

12. J. March and H. Simon, *Organizations* (New York: Wiley, 1958).

13. The Gantt chart plots planned and completed work on one axis and time elapsed on the other. This enables a worker to receive a daily wage regardless of the task and a bonus for completion of the assigned task. For a further explanation, *see* E. Buffa, *Operations Management,* 2d ed. (New York: Wiley, 1968), p. 185.

14. N. Mouzelis, *Organization and Bureaucracy: An Analysis of Modern Theories* (Chicago: Aldine, 1968); and H. Simon, *Administrative Behavior,* 3rd ed. (New York: The Free Press, 1976), pp. 20–44.

15. J. R. Hackman, "Group Influences on Individuals," in *Handbook of Industrial and Organizational Psychology,* ed. M. Dunnette (Chicago: Rand McNally, 1976), pp. 1455–1525.

16. E. Mayo, *The Social Problems of an Industrial Civilization* (Boston: Harvard University, Graduate School of Business, 1945).

17. G. Homans, *The Human Group* (New York: Harcourt, Brace and World, 1950), pp. 48–81.

18. For an alternative explanation of the Hawthorne studies, using an operant-conditioning perspective, *see* H. Parsons, "What Happened at Hawthorne?" *Science* **183** (1974): 922–932.

19. F. Kast and J. Rosenzweig, *Organization and Management: A Systems Approach* (New York: McGraw-Hill, 1974), pp. 81–82.

20. K. Berrien, "A General Systems Approach to Organizations," in *Handbook of Industrial and Organizational Psychology,* ed. M. Dunnette (Chicago: Rand McNally, 1976), pp. 41–62; E. Miller and A. Rice, *Systems of Organization* (London: Tavistock Publications, 1967); and J. G. Miller, "Living Systems: Structure and Process," *Behavioral Science* **10** (1965): 337–339.

21. L. Bertalanffy, *General Systems Theory: Foundations, Development and Applications* (New York: Braziller, 1968), p. 141.

22. P. Lawrence and J. Lorsch, "Differentiation and Integration in Complex Organizations," *Administrative Science Quarterly* **12** (1967): 2.

23. C. Perrow, *Organizational Analysis: A Sociological View* (Belmont, Calif.: Wadsworth, 1970); and H. Simon, *Administrative Behavior,* 3rd ed. (New York: Free Press, 1976), pp. 257–278.

24. B. Loehr, "A&P: A Case Study of Displaced Organizational Goals." Unpublished manuscript, College of Administrative Science, The Ohio State University, March 1976.

25. O. Mowrer, "Ego Psychology, Cybernetics, and Learning Theory," in *Learning Theory and Clinical Research,* ed. K. Adams (New York: Wiley, 1954), pp. 81–90.

26. F. Kast and J. Rosenzweig, "General Systems Theory: Application for Organization and Management," *Academy of Management Journal* **15** (1972): 450.

27. D. Hellriegel and J. Slocum, "Integrating Systems Concepts and Organizational Strategies," *Business Horizons* **15** (1972): 71–78.

28. Abridged from *Columbus Dispatch,* September 7, 1975; *New York Times,* September 19, 1976, and *Wall Street Journal,* December 3, 1976.

29. S. Himes, "W. T. Grant's: A Case Study of Failure." Unpublished manuscript, College of Administrative Science, The Ohio State University, March 1976.

30. "New Leaders in Semiconductors," *Business Week,* March 1, 1976, pp. 40–46.

31. This perspective is abridged from the works of T. Parsons, *Structure and Progress in Modern Societies* (New York: Free Press, 1960), pp. 69–96; T. Petit, "A Behavioral Theory of Management," *Academy of Management Journal* **10** (1967): 346; and J. D. Thompson, *Organizations in Action* (New York: McGraw-Hill, 1967).

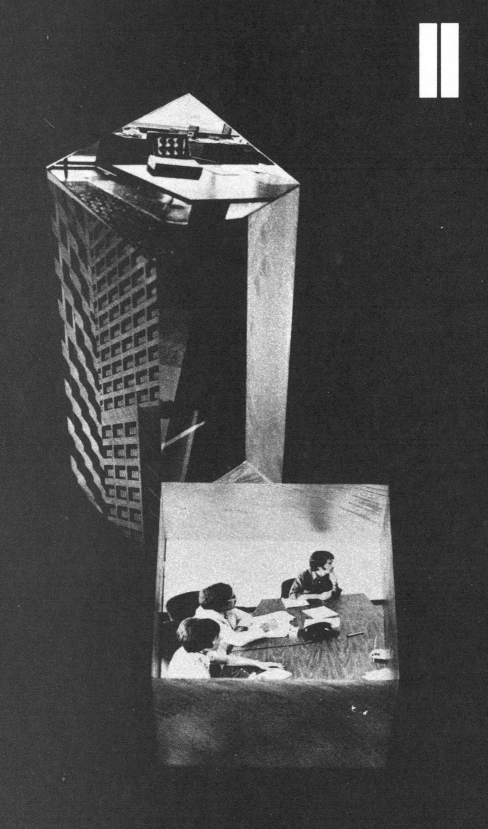

Managerial Processes

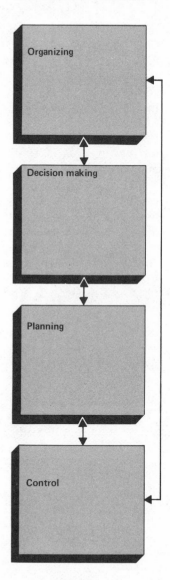

Managerial processes are concerned primarily with the design, planning, and control of the organization, as well as with the decision making these functions require. The central theme for Chapters 4 and 5 is organizational design. Chapter 4 sets forth a number of basic organizational concepts and principles. Basic ways of departmentalizing and achieving coordination are discussed, as well as such concepts as authority, delegation, unity of command, span of control, accountability, and decentralization. The contingencies that influence the application of these various concepts and principles are also developed. Chapter 5 discusses the open-system view of organizational design through a contingency approach. The impact of different external environments on organization design is emphasized by presenting the various forms of decision making, structure, and coordinative devices used by organizations.

The central theme for Chapters 6 and 7 is decision making. Chapter 6 concentrates on developing a framework, or skeleton, of the decision-making process. This leads to an understanding of rationality, goals, uncertainty, differences in decision makers, and several key contingencies that need to be diagnosed as part of the decision-making process. Chapter 7, designed to put "meat and flesh" on the skeleton developed in Chapter 6, is concerned with formal models that may aid the decision maker, descriptive models that explain how individuals often make decisions, and a discussion of a contingency model of organizational decision making that suggests how differences in the situations facing managers require different decision strategies.

The planning process is presented in Chapter 8. This chapter describes the role that planning plays in tying the organization to its environment, examines the sources of information needed to conduct various types of planning, and discusses the major "steps" in the planning process. The contingency framework of planning presented indicates how strategic planning will vary under different conditions. Finally, several planning aids and techniques are explained: the delphi technique, nominal-group technique, modeling, management by objectives, and the Program Evaluation and Review Technique (PERT).

Managerial control processes, the focal point of Chapter 9, involve coordinating workers and equipment toward the goal(s) of the organization. Typically, managers engage in control activities designed to "keep the organization in line." We discuss a framework of formal control systems in organizations and the impact of three major contingencies, including the kinds of power used in the organization, the type of technology, and the level in the formal hierarchy. The second part of the chapter focuses on six strategies of control: human input control, reward-punishment system, formal structure, policies and rules, budgets, and mechanical controls.

4

Organizational Design: Some Basic Considerations

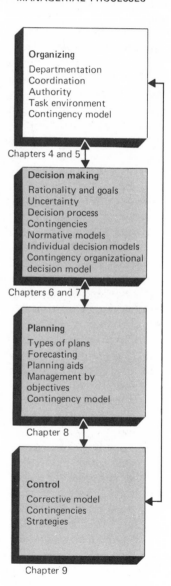

MANAGERIAL PROCESSES

Organizing

Departmentation
Coordination
Authority
Task environment
Contingency model

Chapters 4 and 5

Decision making

Rationality and goals
Uncertainty
Decision process
Contingencies
Normative models
Individual decision models
Contingency organizational
decision model

Chapters 6 and 7

Planning

Types of plans
Forecasting
Planning aids
Management by
objectives
Contingency model

Chapter 8

Control

Corrective model
Contingencies
Strategies

Chapter 9

The objectives of this chapter are to:

develop your awareness of the basic ways for departmentalizing organizations, along with their advantages and disadvantages;

create an understanding of the basic ways of achieving coordination in organizations;

develop your skills in applying the concepts of authority, delegation, and decentralization as parts of the organizing process;

develop your understanding of traditional and contemporary views toward line and staff concepts and relationships in organizations.

One of the purposes of management is to enable people to work effectively toward accomplishing organizational goals. To do this, a structure of roles must be designed and maintained by management. To make the role fully operational, the individual should have a clear concept of the major activities or duties involved, a clear understanding of the relationships of that role with others where coordination is needed, and the needed information to carry out the duties.

In Chapters 4 and 5, we are concerned with the theory underlying an organization's structure. Chapter 4 deals with the nature and purposes of some basic organization activities. As expected from their emphasis on efficiency, Weber, Taylor, and Fayol felt that the fundamental rules for structuring all organizations must be established. We know now that different kinds of organizations require different structures, and this will be examined in Chapter 5. Nonetheless, those fundamental rules are still extremely useful because they do apply to many organizations, especially those that produce products in a standardized manner with relatively unskilled labor, such as automobiles, washing machines, and glass bottles. However, these principles are not ironclad rules, but rather the foundation for understanding how organizing processes affect the behaviors of individuals within the firm.

BASES OF DEPARTMENTATION

Departmentation is the grouping of activities in organization structures.[1] There are four basic forms of departmentation that have proved useful: function, place, product, and customer. Regardless of the type of organizing processes used, each process makes it possible for the organization to group its members with respect to certain basic activities.

Departmentation by Function

Functional grouping of activities is a widely used and accepted managerial practice. It covers what organizations actually do, namely, production, marketing, and financing. Figure 4.1, the organization chart of Diamond Crystal Salt Company, is organized in this manner. (Note that it also has a personnel function.)

Sometimes the basic functions do not really appear on an organization chart, however. For example, hospitals have no marketing departments, and churches have no production departments. Rather, these functions are given other names. Thus, for example, airlines (TWA, KLM, Allegheny) use the terms operations (production), traffic, and finance; large department stores (Lazarus, May Company, J. C. Penney, and Sears) use the terms finance, general merchandising, publicity, and general superintendent. In the latter case, the traditional functions of production, selling, and finance have been combined with other activities.

ADVANTAGES

The most important advantage of functional departmentation is that it follows the principle of specialization, thereby facilitating efficiency in training and

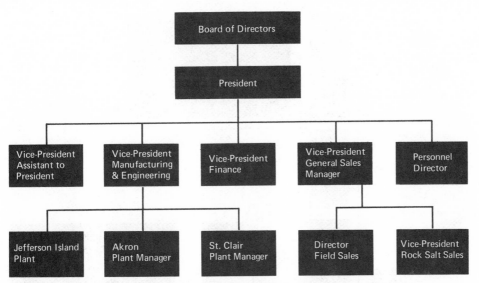

Fig. 4.1. Diamond Crystal Salt Company is organized along functional lines.
(K. White, *Understanding the Company Organization Chart,* New York:
American Management Association, 1963, pp. 158–159.)

utilization of personnel. Functional departmentation is used by such successful organizations as IBM, ALCOA, Eastman Kodak, Sony, and Merrill Lynch. It is also the best way of making sure that the power and prestige of the basic activities being performed by the organization are under control of top management.

DISADVANTAGES

In spite of these advantages, there are some disadvantages of functional departmentation. The size of the geographical area serviced by the firm may call for geographical grouping of activities; the production of numerous product lines designed for certain types of buyers may call for grouping along product or customer lines. In addition, functional departmentation tends to deemphasize the firm's objectives as a totality. Finance people are finance experts, and production people are production experts; the experts often have difficulty seeing the firm as a whole, thus complicating coordination between these activities. In other words, people in the various departments may develop attitudes and other behavioral patterns that involve loyalty to the department, thereby creating "walls" between departments, and considerable effort may be required by top management to promote integration.[2]

Departmentation by Place

Departmentation based on geographic area is a rather common method for organizing physically dispersed firms. The principle is that all activities in a given territory should be grouped and assigned to one manager, on the assumption that efficiency will improve. Place departmentation is used by the

Fig. 4.2. United Airlines' organization chart. (News Bureau Department, United Airlines, Chicago, Ill., 1977. Used with permission.

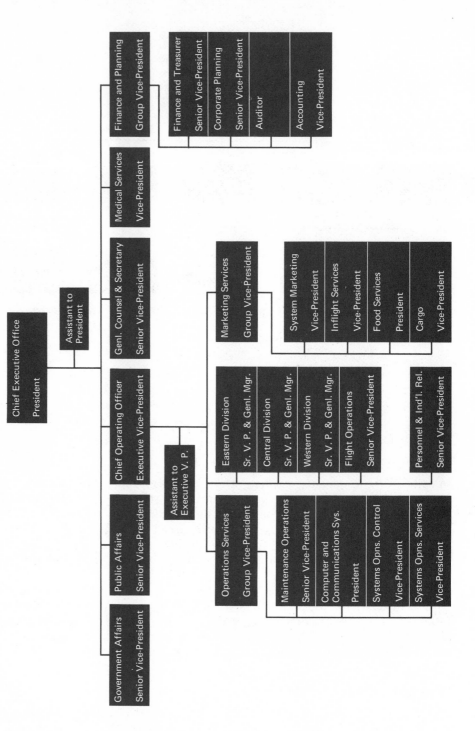

major airline companies. In United Airlines' organization chart (Fig. 4.2), the territories of the three major areas are further subdivided into nine districts (not shown). Other examples of place departmentation are large police departments that divide the city into precincts and department stores that assign floorwalkers, janitors, and window washers to various parts of the store. Similarly, many governmental agencies, such as the Internal Revenue Service, the Federal Reserve Board, the federal courts, and the Postal Service, adopt place departmentation as the basis of organization in their efforts to provide nationwide services. Many multinational firms use this basis of departmentation because of the differences in cultural and legal factors operating in each country. The lack of uniformity in market structures, differences in production methods, and divergent patterns of national traditions and norms make geographical considerations important for the firm's success.[3]

ADVANTAGES

The advantages of place departmentation are primarily those of economy and efficiency. For the production function of the organization, place departmentation would involve establishing plants refining or assembling the same product and distributing the product to an area. By catering to local factors, the production activity could realize gains from providing jobs for local labor, lower freight rates, and perhaps lower labor costs. The marketing function could also benefit from having sales personnel spend more time in sales and less time in travel. They can get to know the customer's needs and, in doing so, serve the customer better. Being closer to the customer may also permit the salesperson to pinpoint what marketing strategy is most likely to succeed.

DISADVANTAGES

Place departmentation requires more personnel with managerial abilities, clearly increases the problems of the central corporate staff to retain control over the operations, and leads to a duplication of many services that could be performed centrally in a functional organization. District managers usually want to have some control over their own purchasing, personnel, accounting, and other services so that they can truly be responsible for the profitability of the operations. As indicated in the disadvantages of functional departmentation, each manager can easily build his or her "empire" at the expense of the entire firm's effectiveness. The reluctance of the district manager to rely on corporate headquarters for services could reflect a management attitude of "I'll show them that it can be done without their help." The duplication of activities also leads to higher costs. For example, for the Internal Revenue Service to have several districts in the United States processing tax forms requires more personnel and expensive computer equipment than if there were just one central clearing house. To ensure uniformity of tax services, extensive rules and regulations are used by the IRS to coordinate the various districts' activities.

Departmentation by Product

The grouping of activities on the basis of product has been an emerging trend in large multiproduct companies, such as GM, Ford, Procter & Gamble, Gen-

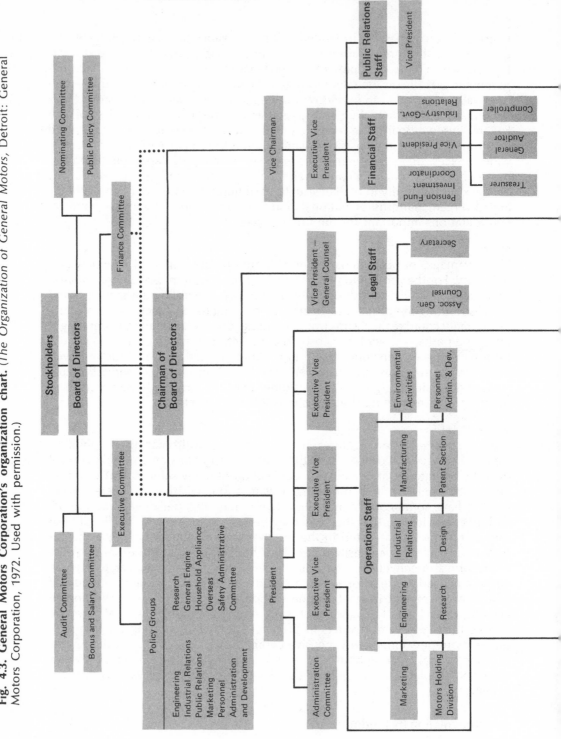

Fig. 4.3. General Motors Corporation's organization chart. (*The Organization of General Motors*, Detroit: General Motors Corporation, 1972. Used with permission.)

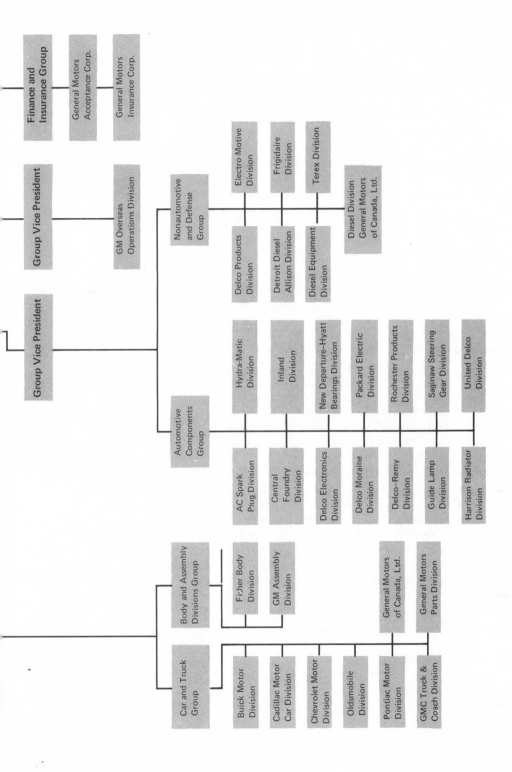

eral Foods, Corning Glass Works, and Mack Trucks. Typically, these organizations once had a functional basis of departmentation, but their growth and subsequent managerial problems made functional departmentation uneconomical and led to a reorganization on the basis of product.

This strategy permits top management to delegate extensive authority to a product-line manager over the manufacturing, sales, service, and engineering functions that relate to a given product or product line. General Motors' organization chart (Fig. 4.3) reflects this as one of the corporation's bases for departmentation. Each division—Chevrolet, Buick, Pontiac, and so on—has considerable operating autonomy, with its own manufacturing plants, sales force, distribution centers, and research and development staffs. Product managers are given a considerable degree of profit responsibility by top management for their specific product lines.

ADVANTAGES

Departmentation by product line eases the problems of coordination and makes use of the individuals' expertise and knowledge in specific areas. For example, the sales effort of a particular individual may be maximized when that person is discussing nuclear power plants, solar energy units, or laser beams, each of which is best sold by an expert thoroughly familiar with the product. Product departmentation is especially useful if the firm's volume is high enough to warrant employing such experts.

Product departmentation may also require highly specialized capital equipment. For example, Westinghouse must use highly specialized equipment in the production of nuclear turbines for the generation of electrical power. If such equipment is used to full capacity, economic gains may be realized in the manufacturing, assembling, and handling of the product. Westinghouse, for example, has also found that the coordination between the sales and engineering efforts in the production of these power-generation plants can be easily maintained by grouping activities by product line. Corporate headquarters of Westinghouse has also found that profit responsibility can be pinpointed to each vice-president. When the vice-president is required to supervise sales, engineering, service, and cost functions, headquarters can set predetermined profit goals for the management and can evaluate more intelligently the contributions of each product line to total profit. If the product line is unprofitable, as was the home entertainment product division of Westinghouse, the product line may be dropped completely, with little disturbance to other parts of the organization.

DISADVANTAGES

The disadvantages of product departmentation are very similar to those encountered in place departmentation. That is, both require that the firm have a large number of personnel with the needed managerial talent available to staff the product lines, and there are dangers of increased costs through the duplication of activities. Top management also has to be aware of the increasing control costs. At General Motors, for example, enough decision making is placed in the hands of the executive committee (see Fig. 4.3) so that this group

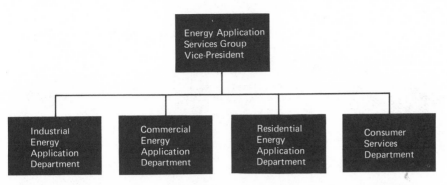

Fig. 4.4. Organization chart for Cleveland Electric Illuminating Company's Energy Application Services Group. (Public Information Department, Cleveland Electric Illuminating Company, Cleveland, Ohio, 1977. Used with permission.)

can integrate decisions made by the various product-line managers to keep the entire company's goals in order.

Departmentation by Customer

The grouping of activities to reflect the interests of different customers is commonly found in business firms. Customers are the key to the way many utilities are organized, because the various customers make varied demands on the utilities services. Figure 4.4 shows the marketing group for Cleveland Electric Illuminating Company; the marketing group is divided according to the four different customer groups served by this utility company. Customers are the key to the way activities are grouped, and the heads of all groups report to one manager.[4]

ADVANTAGES

This type of departmentation is often used when the various needs of the customers must be met by the organization. For example, Standard Steel Corporation sells to both wholesalers and industrial buyers. Wholesalers want steel of a dependable quality, quantity, and suited for the ultimate use of their customers. Industrial buyers want a product that will save money, is of high quality, plus a service that includes installation and repair of the product, and sometimes the training of employees as well. Each of these markets is served by different groups of marketing specialists at Standard Steel.

DISADVANTAGES

The major disadvantage of customer departmentation is the difficulty coordinating this type of grouping and functional, place, and/or product groupings. Managers, to maintain (or get) sales, may want to give some customers privileges (rates, entertainment, discounts) that cannot be given to all of the firm's customers. Another disadvantage is the possibility that capital equipment

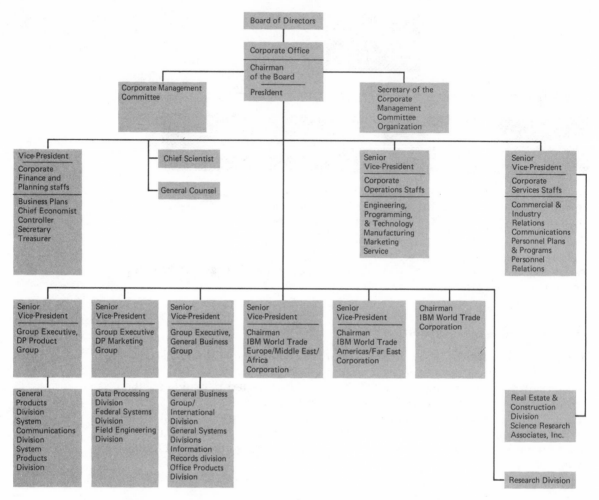

Fig. 4.5. Corporate organization for IBM. (Public Relations Department, International Business Machines, Armonk, N.Y., 1977. Used with permission.)

might be left unused until other orders are filled. In recessions an entire customer market, such as small machine shops and tool and die operations, may disappear.

Factors Influencing Departmentation

The bases of departmentation discussed are by no means exhaustive. Departmentation is not an end in itself, but simply a method of grouping activities to facilitate the achievement of the firm's goals. As we indicated, each method has its advantages and disadvantages. The selection of a particular departmentation strategy depends on the type of situation facing the firm. Because of the relative advantages of each type of departmentation, most complex organizations use several of these strategies in grouping activities. For example, at the senior vice-president level at IBM, the work is grouped according to product, as indicated in Fig. 4.5. The managers reporting directly to the vice-president are members of a particular operational or product grouping.

Another point to be considered is the use of different groupings within a functional area. For instance, Arrow Plastics and Rubber Company has place departmentation for both the production and sale of all of its products except toy dolls, which is a product department. Thus in this firm, a department manager is employing two bases (place and product) for grouping activities at the same organizational level. Arrow asserts that the objective of departmentation is not to build rigid structures, but to group activities that will best contribute to achieving the company's goals.

The mixing of departmentation in practice is, then, merely a reflection of the operation of the principle of division of work and the enormous complexity of the organizing problem. Dividing the work is the initial step, but there remains the problem of relating subordinates to supervisors and departments to one another. This involves coordination. The concepts basic to achieving coordination are the unity of command, span of control, and delegation of authority.

CONCEPTS OF COORDINATION

It has often been said that good people can make any organization effective. It has also been found that ambiguity in an organization is a good thing in that it forces teamwork, since people know that they must work together and cooperate to get anything done. Teamwork is especially relevant in team sports; although coaches may spend hours practicing against "foreign" teams, the actual game situation is one of ambiguity for both offensive and defensive players. However, during practice sessions, coaches develop players who want to cooperate and work together most effectively. To do this, players need to know the part they are to play in any cooperative effort and how each player relates to the others. Coordination is required to design and maintain these systems of roles.

Unity of Command

According to traditional-management theorists, such as Taylor, Fayol, and Weber, one manager should be in charge of an area of responsibility. Moreover, a chain of command should be established so that all organization members know to whom they report and who reports to them. No confusion should exist among the individuals responsible for organizational activities over who gives orders and who implements them. The unity-of-command principle forms the basis for the hierarchy found in most organizations.

The *scalar principle* refers to the chain of direct authority relationships from manager to subordinate throughout the organization.[5] The basic idea

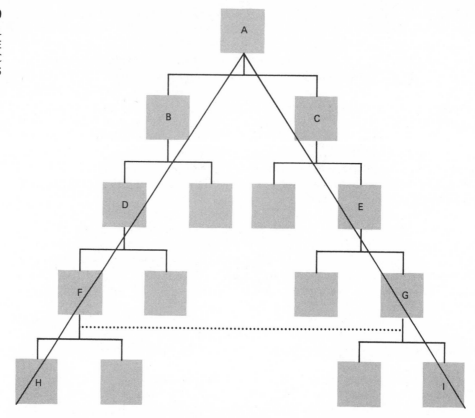

Fig. 4.6. The scalar principle. (Adapted from H. Fayol, *General and Industrial Management,* trans. C. Storrs, London: Pitman, 1963, p. 34.)

of this principle is that every employee should know his or her area for responsibility in the organization and that no one individual should report to more than one superior. If this principle is followed, subordinates know who delegates authority to them and to whom matters beyond their authority must be referred.

The basic scalar principle is indicated in Fig. 4.6. Suppose that F needs to contact G. Adherence to the unity-of-command principle requires F to follow the chain of command to A and then go to G. Of course, it would be much quicker for F to go directly to G, as indicated in the dotted line. Nonetheless, Fayol believed that the communication between F and G should be approved or authorized by their respective superiors (D and E) and that D and E should be informed of the outcome of F and G's discussions. Neither F nor G would be accountable to anyone except D or E.

The unity of command grew out of the organization's needs for cooperation to achieve certain organizational goals. One way to ensure that this cooperative activity takes place with the least cost is for management to adopt an organizational structure in which every employee knows who his or her superior is. Obstacles to performance caused by uncertainty and confusion of assignments can be clarified by one's immediate supervisor.

Span of Control

Span of control deals with the number of subordinates who report directly to a superior.[6] The problem of span of control is as old as organizations. The problem arises from the belief that a manager's mind is not complex enough to supervise too many people. This belief has been fostered by military organizations' finding that narrow spans of control were most effective in combat situations. Traditional-management practitioners also specified that the number of subordinates reporting to any one manager should range between four and twelve.

In actual experience, one finds a variety of practices. In a survey of 100 large companies, the American Management Association found that the number of executives reporting to the president varied from 1 to 24; only 26 presidents had 6 or fewer subordinates, and the median number was 9.[7] Comparable results have been found by other researchers.[8] One consistent result is that in large organizations (those with at least $1 billion sales), the span of control at the top tends to be no more than 12, with the span decreasing as company size decreases.

However, such findings are of limited usefulness. First, they typically measure the span of control only at or near the top level of the organization. Span of control here is hardly typical of that throughout the organization. Second, since many of the participating companies report varying spans of control, it is hard to generalize the findings. Perhaps more important is that simply reporting what companies do in practice is not the same thing as specifying what they "ought" to be doing. Just because the president of General Motors in 1975 had two vice-presidents reporting to him and one of these vice-presidents had thirteen managers reporting to him does not make that pattern "correct." A further limitation is that some managers tend to regard the span of control as an end in itself and to measure the effectiveness of their organization in terms of clarity and completeness of a fixed number of employees reporting to any one supervisor. The creation of a fixed span is *not* completely desirable, as we shall see shortly.

GRAICUNAS' FORMULA

Several management scholars have attempted to quantify the span-of-control principle to make its application more precise. In a paper published in 1933, a French management consultant, V. A. Graicunas, analyzed superior-subordinate relationships and developed a mathematical formula based on the geometric increase in complexities of managing as the number of subordinates reporting to a single supervisor increases.[9] Although the formula may not be applicable in every situation, it does serve as a guideline for managers because it focuses on three important issues in span of control: (1) the number of subordinates directly reporting to a given supervisor; (2) the relationship between the superior and each possible combination of subordinates, and (3) the cross-relationships that develop when one subordinate must deal with another.

From an analysis of these three issues, Graicunas developed the following formula to give the number of all possible types of superior-subordinate relationships requiring managerial attention. Where n represents the number of subordinates reporting to a manager and C represents the total possible contacts, the number of all kinds of relationships will be represented by

$$C = n(2^n/2 + n - 1).$$

The results of this formula are shown in Table 4.1. The data clearly show that a geometric increase in the number of possible relationships occurs if the number of subordinates increases arithmetically. For example, by adding a fifth subordinate, executives increase the possible relationships for which they are responsible by 127 percent (from 44 to 100). The data also indicate that the complexity of the manager's job resulting from the addition of one subordinate is potentially the greatest beyond spans of five.

The usefulness of this formula is somewhat limited, however. First, managers may do more than just manage; for example, a sales manager may also do some selling. Second, the formula ignores workers' interdependence. For example, the work of two subordinates may be so closely related as to require continual coordination (e.g., operating room nurses, air traffic controllers). Also,

Table 4.1. Possible relationships with a variable number of subordinates

Number of subordinates	Number of relationships
1	1
2	6
3	18
4	44
5	100
6	222
7	490
8	1,080
9	2,375
10	5,210
11	11,374
12	24,708
18	2,359,602

H. Koontz and C. O'Donnell, *Management: A Systems and Contingency Analysis of Managerial Functions*, 6th ed., New York: McGraw-Hill Book Company, 1976, p. 287. Used with permission of McGraw-Hill Book Company.

the relationship may be only intermittent (e.g., relay members of a track team). Do different conditions require different spans of control? Third, what about the managerial ability of the superior? It is more likely that supervisors with exceptional managerial talent will be more successful in regulating their time and frequency of contacts with their subordinates and therefore use wider spans of control than executives with lesser talents. Fourth, if a subordinate has been a member of the organization for a long time and has developed appropriate patterns of behavior, a superior might spend less time with him or her than with a newcomer experiencing organizational life for the first time.

CONTINGENCY FACTORS AFFECTING SPAN OF CONTROL

There is no "right" number of subordinates a manager can effectively supervise. Rather, there are several general factors that affect a superior's span of control. The National Conference Board lists the following general factors to be taken into consideration in determining the optimum span for a given situation:

1. the competence of the superior and subordinate;
2. the degree of interaction between departments being supervised;
3. the extent to which the supervisor must carry on nonmanagerial work;
4. the similarity or dissimilarity of activities being supervised;
5. the incidence of new problems in the supervisor's department;
6. the extent of standardized, objective rules and procedures within the organization;
7. the degree of physical dispersion of activities.[10]

LOCKHEED EXAMPLE

One company that has attempted to use some of these variables for an answer to the span-of-control problems is Lockheed Aircraft Corporation. After a large-scale study, Lockheed found that six factors were important in determining span of control.[11] Although the study was aimed at the middle-management group in which the spans were only three to five, i.e., narrow, and although the underlying variables used at Lockheed were not precisely the same as those suggested by the National Conference Board, there were many similarities.

The variables Lockheed used for its analysis are shown in Table 4.2. These six variables (labeled "span factors" in the table) were then given a weighting score (indicated in parentheses), which was based on the analysis of the 150 middle managers and department directors studied at Lockheed. After the scores for a given manager's position had been determined, that person could compare the total span-factor weighting to determine his or her suggested span of control. For example, let's assume that a first-line foreman supervised subordinates performing identical tasks in close physical proximity; the task itself was simple and repetitive, required little subordinate training and minimum contact with others, and had little planning. In this case, the foreman would receive a score of 11. On the opposite end of the continuum would be a manager who was supervising employees who were performing fundamentally distinct functions, who were geographically dispersed, who were performing highly complex and varied tasks that required close and constant supervision in coordination with others, and whose tasks required extensive planning.

Table 4.2. Degrees of supervisory burden within span factors (numbers show relative weighting)

Span factor

Similarity of functions	Identical	Essentially alike	Similar	Inherently different	Fundamentally distinct
	(1)	(2)	(3)	(4)	(5)
Geographic contiguity	All together	All in one building	Separate building, one plant location	Separate locations, one geographic area	Dispersed geographic areas
	(1)	(2)	(3)	(4)	(5)
Complexity of functions	Simple repetitive	Routine	Some complexity	Complex, varied	Highly complex, varied
	(2)	(4)	(6)	(8)	(10)
Direction and control	Minimum supervision and training	Limited supervision	Moderate periodic supervision	Frequent continuing supervision	Constant close supervision
	(3)	(6)	(9)	(12)	(15)
Coordination	Minimum relation with others	Relationships limited to defined courses	Moderate relationships easily controlled	Considerable close relationship	Extensive mutual non-recurring relationships
	(2)	(4)	(6)	(8)	(10)
Planning	Minimum scope and complexity	Limited scope and complexity	Moderate scope and complexity	Considerable effort required, guided only by broad policies	Extensive effort required; areas and policies not charted
	(2)	(4)	(6)	(8)	(10)

H. Koontz and C. O'Donnell, *Management: A Systems and Contingency Analysis of Managerial Functions*, 6th ed., New York: McGraw-Hill Book Company, 1976, p. 295. Used with permission of McGraw-Hill Book Company.

This manager would receive a score of 55. The higher the score, the smaller the suggested span of control.

Despite these rather crude methods, Lockheed was able to eliminate one level of supervision and to widen the span of middle management, with a consequent reduction in supervisory costs. Although the index was successfully used by Lockheed, the company's management is quick to point out that use of these factors and their corresponding weights should not be used blindly. A manager still must rely on judgment. The model is intended to be used only as a general guide which, when supplemented with judgment based on experience, may assist the manager in making more effective span-of-control decisions.

BEHAVIORAL ISSUES

There has been a considerable amount of span-of-control research by behavioral scientists interested in the operation of small groups. Group size is the major behavioral variable affecting span-of-control relationships.[12] Several relevant conclusions emerge from this body of research:

1. Group cohesiveness (attraction of one individual to a group) is best with approximately five members. A smaller group does not provide sufficient interaction for cohesiveness, and a larger group tends to break down into subgroups or cliques.
2. Small groups tend to generate higher member satisfaction than do larger ones, largely because of the opportunity for participation by those members who want it.
3. As groups become larger, the demands on the leader become more exacting and complex and require him or her to become more directing. This leadership style is needed because of the difficulties of coordinating the efforts of the larger group.

In summary, some confusion has arisen from specific statements about the ideal maximum number of subordinates who should report to any one supervisor. There is, of course, no one such number. Rather, the maximum number of subordinates a manager can effectively manage is a function of several contingency factors, as well as several behavioral consequences. Although there is probably a magical limit, that number will vary in accordance with the contingency factors and the importance attributed to them by the manager and the organization.

AUTHORITY STRUCTURE

The underlying thread that makes the division of work and its coordination possible is the authority structure of the firm. The authority structure is the means by which activities can be placed in a manager's job and the coordination of the organization's activities carried out. Thus authority is the manager's tool for exercising considerable discretion in creating an environment conducive to individual performance. Authority is the cement of the organization's structure.

Authority provides for the direction and control of the flow of decisions from the top of the organization downward through the unity of command. "Authority" is the term for the rights needed to carry out one's organizational obligations. Executive authority includes, therefore, the rights of decision and command with respect to the organizational activities of one's subordinates. For example, if A tells B to perform a task, B may not perform it. But if B does, there are two possible reasons. First, A may have convinced B by providing certain information that has led B to perform the task. Second, B may have accepted A's decision without really giving the decision any thought, feeling that it was A's right to do so. This second instance is an example of Weber's legitimate authority. Traditional-management theorists (see Chapter 3) maintained that authority always comes from top management and is legitimized by the person in that role.

Chester Barnard, president of New Jersey Bell Telephone Company from 1927 to 1948, maintained that authority flows in the opposite direction, from the bottom up.[18] This view is known as the acceptance theory of authority. Barnard realized that not every decision made by one's immediate supervisor could be consciously analyzed, judged, and either accepted or rejected. Rather, most decisions or orders fall within a subordinate's "zone of indifference." If a decision falls within the zone, the subordinate will comply without question; if it falls outside the zone, the person will question whether to accept or reject it. The width of the indifference zone depends on the degree to which rewards exceed the burdens and sacrifices. A manager's asking a secretary to take some dictation probably falls within the secretary's zone, because it is a part of the job description. The manager's asking the secretary to dinner, however, probably falls outside that zone, and the secretary may refuse to comply. If we merge the traditional definition of authority with that of Barnard, we can define authority as a superior's right to command and the subordinate's acceptance of a superior's right to command.

Responsibility

Responsibility may be thought of as an owed obligation, one acquired when an individual accepts an assignment of certain objectives, activities, and duties. The manager has duties to carry out and is responsible for the actions of his or her subordinates. Since authority is the discretionary right to carry out assignments and responsibility is the obligation to accomplish them, it follows that authority should correspond to responsibility. Responsibility for actions can be neither greater nor less than authority. For example, there are real limits to the decision a foreman can or should make and to the authority and responsibility he or she should have. A production foreman has no authority to change a salesperson's compensation; a regional sales manager has no authority in somebody else's region. A production foreman usually lacks the competence and the knowledge to work out adequate pay plans for salespeople.

Accountability

Organizational authority is the degree of discretion conferred on people to make it possible for them to use their judgment. If a subordinate accepts the manager's decision and it falls within his or her zone of indifference, the manager can hold the subordinate accountable. Accountability is the subordinate's acceptance of a given task to perform because she or he is a member in the organization. Accountability also requires each member of the organization to report on his or her discharge of responsibilities and to be judged fairly on the basis of his or her record of accomplishment. In the secretary-manager example, the secretary is accountable to the manager for dictation. Thus accountability, unlike authority and responsibility, always flows from the bottom up. It is an explicit contract to perform certain task-related activities in return for some reward, usually money.

Oftentimes authority and responsibility are misused. For example, a college book salesperson who is given authority to work a given geographical territory cannot be held responsible for making faculty members choose certain books. However, the sales manager has the authority to use certain resources to obtain sales where possible. In this case, the proper balance between authority and responsibility is reached when the sales manager manages his or her territory in the best way possible.

Delegation of Authority

Most failures in effective delegation occur not because of the manager's lack of understanding of the principles of delegation, but because of unwillingness to apply them in practice. Three basic personal attitudes affect the delegation of authority. First, a manager must be willing to give another person a chance. Decision making always involves some discretion for the decision maker, and this means that a subordinate's decision might differ from the one the supervisor would have made. Second, the manager must be willing to give subordinates the right to make decisions. One reason for the Ford Motor Company's sales decline in the late 1920s was that Henry Ford, Sr., did not permit subordinates to make decisions. He had to confirm every purchase and make sure that he understood every production operation. Unfortunately, this took vital time away from activities that the chief of a large corporation should have been undertaking. Third, a manager must trust his or her subordinates. Delegation assumes that the manager trusts the subordinate to act responsibly. Many managers do not delegate, believing that the subordinates are not trained enough, cannot handle people, have not developed sufficient expertise to make judgment decisions, or do not have sufficient facts in the situation. Sometimes these considerations are true, but all too often they reflect the manager's distrust of subordinates and unwillingness to delegate decision-making authority.

Centralization-Decentralization

Whether authority should be concentrated or dispersed throughout the organization is a question not so much of what kind, but how much. Authority is a fundamental aspect of delegation. There is neither absolute centralization nor absolute decentralization. No one manager makes all decisions; total delegation would eliminate the need for managers. In other words, there is a continuum of centralization and decentralization. In addition, an organization may be relatively centralized in some functions and relatively decentralized in others.

Authority is delegated when a superior gives decision-making discretion to a subordinate. Clearly, supervisors should not delegate more authority than they have, nor should they delegate all of their authority, in effect passing on their job to their subordinates. The process of delegation involves the determination of results expected, the assignment of tasks and delegation of authority to accomplish them, and the responsibility for the task's accomplishments. In practice, these processes are impossible to split.

DECENTRALIZATION

Decentralization refers to both a high degree of delegated authority and a basic management philosophy. It requires a careful selection of what decisions to delegate and those to hold near the top, selection and training of personnel to make decisions, and the formulation of adequate control mechanisms.

General Motors is partially decentralized; its divisions are Chevrolet, Oldsmobile, Cadillac, Pontiac, Buick, Allison, and Frigidaire. Corporate strategy, formulated by top-management committees, provides unifying guidelines for decisions that are made by division-level executives. Each operating division has the authority to purchase, manufacture, and distribute its products. Similarly, each division is evaluated by two objectives: (1) base pricing, which measures the productive efficiency and rate of return on capital invested in each of the divisions; and (2) share-of-market standing, which indicates how well the division is competing in the marketplace as a seller. Thus the organization of General Motors benefits from centralization of planning, financing, and staff services, while at the same time it derives its additional advantage from on-the-spot, decentralized decision making.[14]

Many other major corporations, such as General Electric Company, E. I. duPont de Nemours & Company, and Sears, Roebuck & Company, have implemented the idea of decentralization very successfully. Others, such as General Dynamics, have suffered major financial setbacks while attempting to implement this strategy. There are no universal benefits to be derived from decentralization, although several factors appear to be important.

Because managers operating in a decentralized structure have to make decisions, they are being *prepared for promotion* into positions that will require greater authority and responsibility. Decentralization encourages the professional development of managers. That is, during this apprenticeship period managers must adapt and prove themselves to the company. They are being compared with others, and this may lead to a *healthy achievement-oriented* atmosphere within the firm. General Electric's statement of company goals notes that decentralization fosters the development of all of an individual's *human resources.*[15] The development of generalists rather than specialists is encouraged, thereby facilitating succession into positions as general managers.

However, not all companies have gained from a decentralized design. For example, prior to 1957 General Dynamics had decentralized authority, although the company president made almost all of the decisions through continual direct communication with the operating divisions. When the president died in 1957, the new president was unable to effectively coordinate the diverse interests of the 11 divisions and direct them toward a common corporate goal. Formal communications were poorly developed, since the previous president had used a system of frequent visits to each division. From 1960 to 1962, the Convair Division of General Dynamics lost over $435 million on the Convair 880/990 commercial jet, yet the new president communicated with the head of this division *fewer than ten times*.[16] Lack of information about the operations of each division ultimately culminated in the loss of any semblance of control. When Convair's costs began to get out of hand, critical production delays developed, and key sales were lost, General Dynamics' management was unable to cope with the crisis. Even the board of directors was not informed when the vice-president of the corporation personally negotiated a sale of aircraft to American Airlines which, if finalized, would have produced a substantial loss for the firm.

CONTINGENCIES AFFECTING DECENTRALIZATION

It should be clear from General Dynamics' experience that not all companies have benefited from the decentralization of decision making. Although the temperament of the individual manager often affects the extent to which authority is delegated, other factors also enter in.

Costliness of the Decision. This is perhaps the overriding factor determining the extent of decentralization in an organization. As a general rule, the more costly the decision to be decided, the more probable it is that the decision will be made by top management. The cost of a decision may be in dollars or in such intangibles as the company's reputation in the field, competitive position, or employee morale.

In many firms, top management may feel that it cannot delegate authority over the expenditure of capital funds. In General Motors Corporation, the financial aspects of that company's operations are centralized under an executive vice-president (see Fig. 4.3), who reports to the chairman of the board of directors rather than to the president.

Uniformity of Policy. Managers who value consistency invariably favor centralization of authority. The management may wish to assure customers that they will all be treated alike with respect to quality, price, credit, delivery, and service. Uniform policies have definite advantages in the areas of cost accounting, statistics, and financial records because they enable management to compare relative efficiencies of various departments. The administration of a union-management labor agreement is facilitated through uniform policy with respect to wages, promotions, vacations, fringe benefits, grievances, and other matters.

History of the Firm. Whether authority will be decentralized depends on the firm's past history. Marshall Field and Company and International Harvester Company have shown a marked tendency to keep authority centralized. Similarly, when Henry Ford, Sr., the founder of the Ford Motor Company, ran the organization, it was highly centralized. Ford took pride in having no organizational titles in top management except those of president and general manager; he insisted, to the extent possible, on making all decisions in the company himself. Other companies, such as Sears, Roebuck & Company, have a history that fosters decentralization.

Availability of Managers. Underlying decentralization of authority is the assumption that competent and well-trained managers are available to make decisions. Too often there is a shortage of good managers. To have decentralization, many corporations ensure the adequate supply of trained managers by pushing decision making down through the organization and permitting managers to make mistakes that involve little cost. In this manner, the organization is actually developing managerial potential, because it feels that the best training is actual experience.

Control Mechanisms. Even the most avid proponents of decentralization, such as General Motors, duPont, and Sears, believe that controls are needed to determine whether performance is conforming to plans. To decentralize is not to lose control, as happened in General Dynamics. One cannot expect good managerial performance at any level of organization without some way of knowing whether it will be used properly.

Environmental Influences. The contingency factors affecting the extent of decentralization dealt with so far have been internal to the organization. Such external factors as governmental controls, national unions, federal and state regulatory agencies, and tax policies are also important factors affecting the degree of decentralization within a firm. Governmental policy in the employment of minorities, for example, makes it difficult to totally decentralize authority in the hiring decision(s). If the federal government limits the number of hours worked and the minimum wages to be paid, the local manager cannot freely establish wages and hours outside of these guidelines.

The impact of national unions on long-term contracts also has a centralizing influence on many organizations. So long as departmental managers can individually negotiate the terms of the labor contract, authority to negotiate may be delegated by top management to these managers. But where national unions bargain with the entire company, e.g., General Motors, Goodrich, the National Football League, and many other international firms, a company can no longer chance decentralization of certain decision-making prerogatives to local management.

LINE AND STAFF RELATIONSHIPS

Traditional theorists suggested that an organization with both line and staff functions would offer the best potential for growth. In the typical manufacturing organization, for example, the *line* person is concerned with the achievement of the organization's objective through delegation of authortiy, work assignments, and supervision of others. The *staff* person, on the other hand, indirectly influences the work of others through the use of suggestions, recommendations, and advice.

This distinction between line and staff is usually easy to establish in a manufacturing organization. Line units denote a *command* relationship; staff

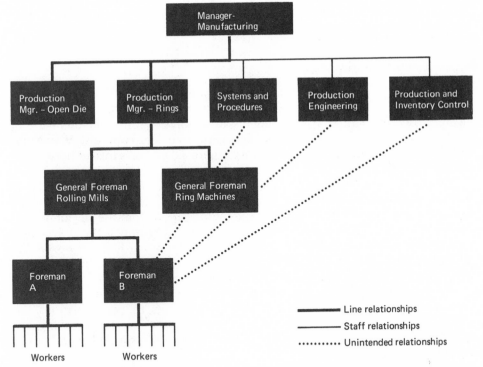

Fig. 4.7. Line and staff relationships.

units, an *advisory* relationship. In a nonbusiness organization, such as a hospital or university, this distinction between line and staff is less clear. In a hospital, the physicians (technical staff) treat the patients, and the administrators concern themselves with hospital maintenance. Similarly, in a university, the faculty (professional staff) works toward the fulfillment of the basic objectives of the institution through teaching and research, and the administrators (deans, vice-presidents, etc.) are involved in the supportive and auxiliary functions.

According to traditional theory and practice, staff departments are supposed to *assist line departments* in work that requires *technical expertise* and detailed attention. Staff people become experts in a given field, and line managers rely on them for specialized advice. Figure 4.7, which shows a production department of Standard Steel Company, illustrates this condition.

In Standard Steel's manufacturing division, the staff performs three types of specialized assistance: systems and procedures, production engineering, and production and inventory control. Staff specialists also prepare and process data which line managers need for making decisions. For example, the production and inventory-control department customarily collects data on the cost of making a late delivery to an important customer, the number of jobs completed in each shop per day, and the level of inventory that should be stockpiled per product for anticipated demands. These experts on data analysis work closely with the systems and procedures personnel. When these experts have studied their problem(s), they submit their recommendations to the manager of manufacturing, who accepts the appropriate recommendations for implementation by line managers.

Types of Staff Authority

When staff functions are separate from the line organization, as in Fig. 4.7, a decision must be made as to what authority the staff personnel should be given. Observation of staff departments in action suggests that there are at least four types of authority relationships: staff advice, compulsory staff advice, concurring, and command authority. Figure 4.8 portrays this authority continuum for staff units.

Many staff activities are *purely advisory* in nature. The manager is *free to seek* (or not seek) the advice of staff specialists. The manager who is looking for a new operations researcher may seek information from the personnel department as to the average starting salary for such personnel, the universities most likely to have qualified young candidates, and the like. However, the *acceptance or rejection* of comments and information given by the personnel department is the *prerogative* of the department manager.

In the case of *compulsory* staff advice, the manager must at least listen to the appropriate staff agency, but need not follow its recommendations. Although such a procedure does not limit the manager's decision-making discretion, it ensures that the manager has *made use of the specialized talents* of the appropriate staff agency.

Concurring staff authority requires that the *line and staff managers agree* on the particular course of action to be followed. This procedure expands the staff manager's authority and restricts the line manager's decision-making discretion to areas in which there is mutual agreement on a particular course of action. Thus, the manager of the operations department and the head of the personnel office must agree that certain criteria are valid, certain universities should be visited, and the like. Decisions involving the recruitment of operation researchers are made jointly. When agreement cannot be reached, the issue is moved to the level of the organization where one individual has authority over both the line and the staff units.

The strongest form of staff authority occurs when the line grants *limited command authority* to a staff unit, permitting it to give orders and expecting that other organizational units will comply. If the personnel department has the authority to screen prospective candidates and reject those who do not meet quality standards, the personnel department is exercising *command au-*

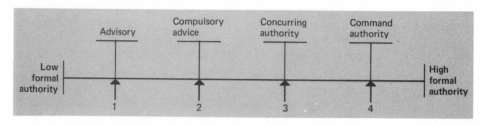

Fig. 4.8. Continuum of authority for staff units.

thority in the area of hiring. In many organizations, personnel and industrial-relations departments exercise command authority over the use of psychological testing, hiring policies and procedures, employee counseling, and related employee activities and benefits.

Line and Staff Conflicts

Authority problems between line and staff units have created much friction and conflict in organizations. There are many reasons for these conflicts, but we shall examine only some of the major ones.

One factor aggravating line-staff conflict is that of *personal characteristics.* A group of line and staff managers was asked to rank the desirability of personality traits on the basis of their importance to the success of the respondents' management positions.[17] Traits included characteristics such as forcefulness, imagination, independence, cooperation, adaptability, and caution. The results indicated that *staff* managers felt that they had to be more *cooperative, adaptable,* and *cautious* (to succeed in their jobs) than did line managers.

A comparison between line and staff personnel in three industrial plants led another researcher to conclude that staff people were generally younger, better educated, more concerned with dress and appearance, had different recreational interests, and came from different backgrounds than did the line people.[18] *Line* people are generally oriented toward *advancement with the company; staff* people, toward *advancement in their profession.* The former see their future in terms of loyalty to the organization; the latter, to their profession. This difference in commitment and loyalty to the organization can lead to a conflict in interests. Thus, for example, scientists may be interested in making a contribution to their field with the development of a new product, whereas their manager is interested in getting the product into consumers' hands and recovering the costs for research and development.

A second source of conflict is the fact that staff units are usually located higher in the organization and are often called on by top management to make reports and analyses of operating divisions. Thus they acquire *informal command authority,* much to the dismay of line personnel. These staff efforts are often perceived by line managers as attempts to control and check on the line units. For example, consider the unintended relationship, using Fig. 4.7. The dashed line represents informal functional authority acquired by each staff person from the line officer. In our case, let's assume that the production engineer notices that Foreman B's section has been incurring unusually high costs. In this discussion with Foreman B, the staff person notices that the foreman shows a general lack of respect for the engineer's capabilities and work. After the general foreman of rolling mills and the manager of manufacturing receive the staff person's report, they ask the specialist to explain why Foreman B's engineering costs are out of line. Relating the uneventful meeting with Foreman B, the production engineer complains of an inability to influence the foreman.

The two managers realize that these costs must be kept under control, and they arrange a meeting with the foreman to explain why costs must be kept down and that the production engineer has spent a great deal of time and effort on developing procedures to cut costs. After the meeting, the production engineer has a very pleasant conversation with Foreman B, who now seems very receptive to the staff person's ideas. Realizing that both the manufacturing and rolling-mill managers relied on the production engineer as an authority on engineering costs, the foreman no longer viewed the specialist as a "staff" person, but as an individual with *authority in this area*. Eventually, the acceptance of staff recommendations and suggestions by lower management, as representative views of top management, tends to create an authority link that is quite different from the prescribed formal arrangements. This is often more representative of the real working relationships of the group. The consequences, as indicated by the dashed lines in Fig. 4.7, are unintended but real.

Of course, not all conflict between line and staff managers is inherently bad or adversely affects the performance of a line unit. In many cases, these differences have some merit and can lead to better decisions. In the situation involving the foreman and the production engineer, the former's lack of attention to costs prevented the unit from operating at peak efficiency, and the production engineer's overriding concern with only the cost aspect was probably too narrow a focus on the problem. In this situation, the compromise solution ultimately worked out incorporated the thinking of both the production engineer and the foreman. What is important to the organization is that the disruptive effects of conflict be minimized and that constructive resolution of conflicting viewpoints be effected. Intraorganizational conflict and methods to reduce disruptive conflict will be discussed further in Chapter 14.

Location of Staff Units

The location of staff specialists in an organizational structure is usually determined by the differences between the general and specialist staffs. If the services of a staff department are used extensively throughout an organization, the unit may need to be located relatively high up in the organization, as shown for General Motors in Fig. 4.3. A functional general staff is usually found at the top of most large corporations. In the case of General Motors, offices that handle corporate legal, public relations, marketing, finance, and manufacturing problems constitute the general staff. These staff offices are usually headed by vice-presidents who are in policy-making positions rather than in charge of operating units. For example, in General Motors, the vice-president in charge of industrial relations is given responsibilities for personnel and industrial-relations policies for all divisions. This staff unit handles selection of the psychological tests to be used in screening prospective employment candidates and the development of brochures for use by division personnel managers outlining the company's benefits and promotion policies.

If a staff group is assigned to provide needed services to a specific line function, the unit should be located near that function. At Standard Steel, for example, the production and inventory-control staff people report to the firm's manufacturing manager, because a major portion of their work is provided to manufacturing, as indicated in Fig. 4.7. Staff specialists perform supportive functions (some of which would have to be performed by a line manager if staff specialists were not present) in a specific area and usually report to the line officer of that division.

Summary

A basic problem facing all managers is how to organize their tasks and personnel to achieve the organization's goal(s) most effectively. The basic process of grouping activities is departmentation. There are four strategies for grouping activities—function, place, product, and customer—and each has specific advantages and disadvantages. Each of the bases of departmentation raises the problem of how the manager can coordinate the activities of the various groups. The basic concepts of coordination are the scalar principle and span of control.

The scalar principle refers to the chain of direct authority relationships from superior to subordinate throughout the organization. In nearly every organization there is a problem of determining how many individuals should report to one manager. The span-of-control principle addresses this problem. A number of contingency factors affect how wide a manager's span of control should be to maintain an effective department.

The authority structure of an organization is the means by which the organization maintains its viability. *Authority* refers to the manager's right to command and the subordinate's acceptance of this right. *Accountability* flows from the bottom of the organization upward and refers to the subordinate's acceptance of a given task to perform. *Responsibility* is an owed obligation and should go hand in hand with authority. Whether authority should be concentrated or dispersed throughout the organization refers to the degree of centralization or decentralization. However, although decentralization is closely related to delegation of authority, it also reflects a basic underlying philosophy of the organization and its management.

Most large organizations employ staff groups to provide specialized assistance to line management. The power granted to staff groups by line management may vary from primarily advisory to actually making decisions in specified areas. In many large organizations, both general and special staff departments have been created to make recommendations and decisions with respect to the solution of organizational problems. Authority and personal discrepancies between line and staff officers have been at the root of some conflicts within organizations.

Discussion Questions

1. Why is departmentation of activities needed?

2. What is customer departmentation?

3. What is functional departmentation?

4. What is place departmentation?

5. What is product departmentation?

6. What is the principle of unity of command?

7. What is the principle of span of control? List some of the important contingencies affecting the span of control.

8. Why do some managers hesitate to delegate?

9. How do accountability, authority, and responsibility differ?

10. How may an organization decentralize its authority structure?

11. Why has there been conflict between line and staff for so long and in so many companies? What are the roots of this conflict?

12. Identify several positions in an educational, military, or business organization and classify them as either line or staff. What were some of the problems that you encountered in performing this task?

Management Incidents

PEACHTREE HOSPITAL

The administrator and the personnel director of a large hospital were discussing problems of the hospital's organizational structure. It has been their practice to meet at least bimonthly to review the operations of the hospital and the staffing situation. The hospital had been open for less than one year, and the staff had spent the better part of its time recruiting and training employees. The administrator believed that sufficient time had elapsed to "shake down" the hospital staff and that organizational problems encountered would be "exceptions" to policies on the books. However, the administrator was presently concerned with the high turnover (over 45 percent for nurses and LPs), absenteeism, uncleanliness of the wards, and loss of medical supplies.

The personnel director argued that these were still "start-up" problems and would be solved within another month or so. The administrator, who believed that the organization's charts, job descriptions, and policy manuals clearly covered all areas, couldn't understand the problem. Furthermore, all of the hospital's personnel had been trained by the hospital, and many had had several years of experience with other hospitals before coming on board with this new hospital.

The personnel director agreed with many of the points raised by the administrator, but added that formal organization charts and job descriptions did not ensure that employees would behave correctly. However, the personnel director did agree to conduct a survey within the hospital to determine the extent to which employees understood the organization.

The questionnaire was completed by nearly all 1200 of the hospital's workers, administrators, doctors, nurses, maintenance workers, and others. The questionnaire included more than 150 items dealing with a variety of issues concerning the organization's structure. The results were tabulated, and a summary was prepared for the administrator. Some of the important findings were:

1. Twenty-five percent of the orderlies and maintenance workers felt that there was uncertainty concerning the goals of their job;

2. Thirty percent of the orderlies and maintenance workers felt that they

often had difficulty in obtaining job-related information from their supervisors;

3. Thirty percent of all workers could not name their immediate supervisor;
4. Thirty-five percent of the administrative staff felt that they were not given authority commensurate with their responsibility;
5. Tweny percent of the nurses did not know their decision-making rights;
6. Forty percent of all workers did not know whether they were performing line or staff functions in the hospital.

The hospital administrator was shocked to read these statements.

1. What would be your response to the administrator if you were the personnel director?
2. What are some authority and responsibility problems in the Peachtree Hospital?
3. What seems to be the major problem area?
4. How would the administrator know that the structure of the hospital was the most efficient?

THE TACK COMPANY*

In December 1976, the Tack Company franchised eight large chains, totaling over 750 stores, in order to reach a previously neglected market. This was in addition to more than 14,000 existing independent dealers already selling electrical appliances. Although the general sales manager, Ms. Smith, knew that this would create more work for the 200 salesmen, she also knew that it would help the division's profit picture. It was decided that Mr. Kelley (Ms. Smith's old boss) would head the department. Although Mr. Kelley was nearing retirement and rarely agreed with Ms. Smith's policies, it was felt that through her management and organizational ability, she would be able to quickly turn the department into a profitable venture.

Within six months, many of the independent dealers began to complain and threatened to cancel their franchises with Tack. Because the chain stores were buying in quantity, they were severely undercutting the independent dealers' prices. Because of this situation, Ms. Smith sent letters to all Tack zone managers and personnel, which in effect stated that the independent dealers are important to the company.

Although there was no indication of a previous problem, in December 1977 the chain stores began to complain that Tack's salesmen were ignoring them. Mr. Kelley authorized an investigation, and within three weeks he had the results. The results showed that all stores received contact when taking on Tack products, but only 20 percent of the stores had had at least one subsequent contact up to the time of the study. Mr. Kelley knew that unless this situation improved, the chain stores would switch to other suppliers. Therefore, he sought answers as to why the contact was so poor for the chain stores.

1. How was the company organized? To whom were the salesmen responsible?

---

* Adapted from J. Murray and T. Von der Embe, *Organizational Behavior,* Columbus, Ohio: Merrill, 1973, p. 183.

2. What was the relationship between Ms. Smith and Mr. Kelley?
3. What would you do to correct the problem?

THE DYNAMIC CORPORATION

The Dynamic Corporation is a national manufacturing firm that produces and sells toys and games. Prior to 1972, the company specialized in adult toys, but in 1973 the toy market for children became so lucrative that the Dynamic Corporation decided to compete in that line too. Adult games have no single, correct strategy and therefore require a great deal of thought on the part of the player. In true adult games, such as checkers, bridge, chess, there is no one right way to win; everything depends on what one's opponent does and on one's own skill.

After an intensive study of the children's toy market, Dynamic Corporation decided to market children's toy dolls. The doll industry's volume is estimated at $450 million annually, and the large producers, such as Mattel, spend well over $1 million in research and development.

In 1977, because of growing sales, the management of Dynamic Corporation was considering a reorganization. At the time, the firm was organized along functional lines (see Fig. 4.1). However, Trudy Smith, the president of the company, thought that it might be wiser to change to product departmentation. Some of the marketing people thought so too. The production department, however, felt there was more to be gained from a functional departmentation. The finance and accounting department people seemed indifferent.

The president's reorganization plan was to set up three product divisions: baby toys, young girl's toys, and adult games. The baby toys and adult divisions accounted for over 60 percent of the firm's sales, but the young girl's division was growing rapidly. According to the marketing research department, sales for the girl's division would soon catch up.

1. Draw the proposed reorganization chart.
2. What are the advantages of product departmentation over functional departmentation?
3. What recommendations would you make to the president? Explain your reasons as much as possible.

REFERENCES

1. A. Melcher, *Structure and Process of Organizations: A Systems Approach* (Englewood Cliffs, N.J.: Prentice-Hall, 1976), pp. 191–213.

2. J. Price, "The Impact of Departmentalization on Interoccupational Cooperation," *Human Organization* **27** (1968): 362–367; and A. Kover, "Reorganization in an Advertising Agency: A Case Study of Decrease Integration," *Human Organization* **22** (1963–1964): 252–259.

3. J. Simonetti and G. Boseman, "The Impact of Market Competition on Organization Structure and Effectiveness: A Cross-Cultural Study," *Academy of Management Journal* **18** (1975): 631–638; and L. Franko, "The Move Toward a Multidivisional Structure in European Organizations," *Administrative Science Quarterly* **19** (1974): 493–506.

4. M. Hanan, "Reorganize your Company Around its Markets," *Harvard Business Review* **52,** 6 (1974): 63–74.

5. H. Fayol, *General and Industrial Management,* trans. C. Storrs (London: Pitman, 1963), p. 34.

6. P. Evans, "Multiple Hierarchies and Organizational Control," *Administrative Science Quarterly* **20** (1975): 250–259; W. Ouchi and J. Dowling, "Defining the Span of Control," *Administrative Science Quarterly* **19** (1974): 357–365; and J. Child, "Parkinson's Progress: Accounting for Numbers of Specialists in Organizations," *Administrative Science Quarterly* **18** (1973): 328–348.

7. *Business Week,* August 18, 1951, pp. 102–103.

8. G. Fisch, "Stretching the Span of Management," *Harvard Business Review* **41,** 5 (1962): 80–81.

9. A. Graicunus, "Relationship in Organization," in *Papers on the Science of Administration,* ed. L. Gulick and L. Urwick (New York: Institute of Public Administration, 1937), pp. 183–187.

10. J. Stieglitz, "Optimizing the Span of Control," *Management Record* **24** (1962): 25–29.

11. H. Koontz, "Making Theory Operational: The Span of Management," *Journal of Management Studies* **3** (1966): 229–243.

12. R. House and J. Miner, "Merging Management and Behavioral Theory: The Interaction between Span of Control and Group Size," *Administrative Science Quarterly* **14** (1969): 451–466.

13. C. Barnard, *The Functions of the Executive* (Cambridge, Mass.: President & Fellows of Harvard College, 1938).

14. P. Drucker, *The Concept of the Corporation* (New York: John Day, 1946).

15. R. Cordiner, *The New Frontiers for Professional Managers* (New York: McGraw-Hill, 1956), pp. 55–57.

16. R. Smith, "General Dynamics: A Crisis of Control," *Corporations in Crisis* (New York: Anchor Books/Doubleday, 1966), pp. 67–112; and "General Dynamics: Winning in the Aerospace Game," *Business Week,* May 3, 1976, 86ff.

17. L. Porter and M. Henry, "Job Attitudes in Management: V. Perceptions of the Importance of Certain Personality Traits as a Function of Job Level," *Journal of Applied Psychology* **48** (1964): 305–309.

18. For an excellent review, *see* A. Filley, R. House, and S. Kerr, "Professionals in Organizations and Line-Staff Relationships," in *Managerial Process and Organizational Behavior,* 2d ed. (Glenview, Ill.: Scott, Foresman, 1976), pp. 380–409; and P. Browne, and R. Golembiewski, "The Line-Staff Concept Revisited: An Empirical Study of Organizational Images," *Academy of Management Journal* **17** (1974): 406–417.

5

Contingency Approaches to Organizational Design

MANAGERIAL PROCESSES

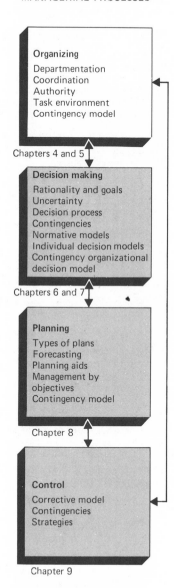

Organizing

Departmentation
Coordination
Authority
Task environment
Contingency model

Chapters 4 and 5

Decision making

Rationality and goals
Uncertainty
Decision process
Contingencies
Normative models
Individual decision models
Contingency organizational
decision model

Chapters 6 and 7

Planning

Types of plans
Forecasting
Planning aids
Management by
objectives
Contingency model

Chapter 8

Control

Corrective model
Contingencies
Strategies

Chapter 9

The objectives of this chapter are to:

describe the relevant environments of organizations;

present a contingency model of organizational design;

present strategies that organizations have used to adapt to their environment;

analyze different forms of decision making, structure, and coordinative devices used by organizations in various environments;

describe the role of chief operating officer in different environments facing different pressures.

We all know that organizations differ. These differences occur in what the organizations do, how they make decisions, how they are structured, and how effective they are in doing their tasks. Managers need to understand what these differences are, what conditions give rise to them, and how they can be explained. In this chapter we will discuss the relationship between the organization's structure and the environment in which it operates.

As indicated in Chapter 3, one of the primary differences between the closed- and open-system approaches to the study of organizations is their underlying assumptions about the external environment. The closed-system approach emphasizes things that are controllable by the organization through use of rules, regulations, job design, recruitment practices, and structure. The environment of the organization, being more unpredictable, is relatively ignored, assumed to be a given or neglected in favor of focusing on making the internal operations of the organization as efficient as possible. The open-system approach assumes that the organization and its environment are in an active relationship with each other. Just as individuals learn to adapt to their environment, so too must organizations. The structure of the organization and its departments must be keyed to the environment in which it is operating. Each department of the organization provides some function that is needed in order for the entire organization to survive. Organizations survive because they have adapted to the environment in which they are functioning.

In Chapter 4, we discussed some of the basic principles in management. These principles are still applied today in most effective organizations. However, with the contingency approach, the manager needs to become familiar with the internal and external conditions facing the organization before deciding on the appropriateness of one of the basic management principles (unity of command, scalar principles, etc.). Effective organizational design results not from the use of management principles, but from matching appropriate principles with the particular set of conditions facing the organization. Under certain conditions, classical bureaucratic rules and regulations may be very appropriate; under other conditions, they may not.

DEFINING THE ENVIRONMENT

In the broadest sense, the environment is everything external to the organization's boundaries. However, it may be more useful to think of the environment as (1) the general environment, which affects all organizations in a given society, and (2) the specific task environment, which affects the individual organization more directly.[1]

Many of the societal, or general, environmental forces that influence organizations were discussed in Chapter 2. Some of these forces are cultural, technological, educational, political, sociological, and economic. Frequently, managers take these conditions as given, with little recognition of how they affect the internal operations of organizations. These conditions set the general characteristics under which all organizations operate. For example, although the large state universities operate in different specific environments (individual states), they have many similar characteristics. Professors and students find that Ohio State University, Penn State, Colorado, and Texas A&M have many more

similarities than differences. Throughout the United States, city governments
of a particular size have similar structures and problems, as do the states'
public school systems.

143

DEFINING THE
ENVIRONMENT

The Task Environment

An organization operating in the general environment may not be directly
influenced by all of these conditions, nor can it respond to all of them. The
task environment comprises the specific forces relevant to the decision-making
processes of the organization.[2] The task environment is made up of groups
beyond the organization's own boundaries that provide immediate inputs,
exert pressures on decisions, or make use of the organization's outputs. The
sudden shift of American consumers away from gas-guzzling cars in 1975 to
more economical cars caused a major slump in car sales and caused automobile manufacturers to lay off thousands of workers. The automobile industry's
task environment had changed. The general economic recession during 1975
was the general environment for all firms, including automobile manufacturers.
The general environment is the same for all organizations in a given society.
The task environment may be different for each organization.

The distinction between the general and task environments is not always
clear-cut. Forces in the general environment are continually breaking through
to the task environment of the organization. For example, until the mid- or
late 1960s, universities had been able to maintain barriers to the general environment. During the Vietnam War, and especially after the Kent State shoot-
ings in May 1970, conditions in the general environment, such as international
conflicts, political activities, minority-rights movements, and women's lib,
became relevant forces in the universities' task environment.

Conditions in the general environment may also bring other institutions
into the relevant environment of the organization. When equal opportunity
legislation was passed in 1964, for instance, many firms had to change their
hiring procedures as well as the criteria used for promotion. Federal legislation
to control the quality of air caused shifts in types of fuel and the design of
American- and foreign-made automobiles.

RELEVANT CONDITIONS

The relationship between the general and task environments is illustrated in
Fig. 5.1. The figure also shows the managerial subsystems for the firm, including
the institutional, organizational, and technical levels. The organization's task
environment can be thought of as a subset of the general environment. Only
the relevant conditions in the task environment affect the organization's performance. The five factors composing the relevant task environment are general
enough to encompass all types of organizations—voluntary, service, business,
educational, religious, custodial, and military. The two factors we will discuss
—market and technological factors—are most useful in analyzing problems in
the management of organizations.[3]

Market Factors. Organizations produce some sort of product, service, or value
for a particular set of individuals. These individuals use the products—tele-

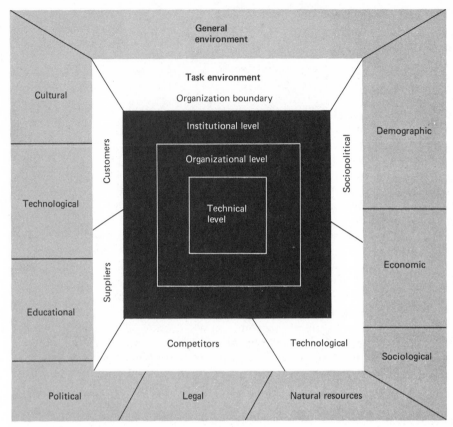

Fig. 5.1. Relationship of general and task environments to the organization.

visions, cars, hamburgers, books, pens—for many different things. People also use many services—welfare, consumer protection, the Better Business Bureau. Organizations like the Better Business Bureau and Planned Parenthood provide information to individuals. Hospitals provide a wide variety of services for individuals.

Markets may vary along several dimensions—time, size, shape, and cost. Some markets exist for only a very short time, but recur periodically. For example, the demand for fireworks around the Fourth of July is very high, then drops off sharply until the following July. Other markets vary by cost, shapes, and size. Sales of pocket calculators rose from $4 million in 1971 to an esti-mated $28 million in 1976. When the pocket calculator was introduced on the market in 1971, the average price was $247.00. Today, it seems that almost every month, a new, less expensive, smaller, and more complex instrument is put on the market. The market for transistorized calculators has expanded rapidly, whereas the market for slide rules, formerly used in making calcula-tions, has declined.

Fast-shifting consumer preferences have also shortened the life cycle for many products. Approximately 55 percent of the products sold today did not exist ten years ago, and of the products sold then, about 40 percent have been taken off the shelf. In the pharmaceutical and recording industries, a product is often obsolete within six months.

Technology. The technological segment of the task environment has two parts. The first is the availability of the mechanical means for production of goods and services and possibly the replacement of human effort. This aspect emphasizes such things as automated production lines, computer systems, monitoring equipment, and other hardware. How these hardwares are brought into the firm and set up are important tasks of the managers at the technical or production level. The technical advances within the organization cannot be carried any further than the technology available in the environment or created by the organization through its own research and development efforts.

But the economic or social costs of some technological advances may be too high for the organization. Large department stores, such as J. C. Penney, Sears, Roebuck & Company, May Company, and K-Mart, have their own data-processing centers for charge accounts, whereas a local store might still bill customers by a hand-posting method.

The second aspect of technology refers to the accumulated knowledge about the means to accomplish tasks. In this sense, technology is the skill and brains of individuals. It is the application of science to real-world problems. Accountants may use the computer in performing their task, but they also utilize the given knowledge of accounting procedures in accomplishing the task.

CHARACTERISTICS OF THE TASK ENVIRONMENT
We have defined the relevant task environment of an organization as having both market and technological factors. Although other aspects of the task environment could undoubtedly affect the design of an organization as well, most of the research has concentrated on these two dimensions of an organization's task environment.[4]

The central theme of the contingency approach with respect to organizational design is that the degree of change and complexity in the task environment affects an organization's hierarchy, departmentation strategy, coordination mechanisms, and control systems. A firm that produces a stable product in a market with little technological innovation and relatively few competitors confronts a different organization-design problem than does a firm that provides a rapidly changing product or service in a growing, competitive market. The first environment is stable; the second, changing or uncertain. The degree of change in a firm's task environment may be thought of as a continuum ranging from stability to instability. These two states of the environment have substantial implications for the internal structure of the organization, the type of individual who is likely to be effective in the organization, and the type of management practices used in the organization. In general, firms operating in changing environments require internal organizational structures different from those of firms operating in stable environments.[5]

The Stable Environment. A stable environment is characterized by:

1. products and services that have not changed much in recent years;
2. lack of technological innovations;
3. a stable set of competitors and customers, with few new competitors;
4. stable political, economic, and social conditions;
5. consistent government policies toward regulation and taxation.

Changes in a stable environment are relatively small. When they do occur, they have a minimal impact on the internal operations of the organization. Top management can keep track of what is going on and make virtually all necessary policy decisions alone. Companies in the brewing, insurance, candle-making, coal-mining, glass container, and food-staples (e.g., flour and gelatin) industries operate in relatively stable environments. Although there may be slight changes in the product, e.g., the introduction of low-calorie beer in the brewing industry, these changes can be easily incorporated into the existing organizational structure.

Changes in a stable-environment product are likely to be in size (e.g., amount of beer produced, number of life-insurance policies or loaves of bread sold). Such changes probably will have little impact on the structure of the organization. The product itself is unlikely to change significantly, and there will be little need to change the production process. Managers in the technical core of the organization are not faced with changes in production processes. Firms in highly stable environments are likely to develop extensive distribution systems and invest heavily in capital equipment. These firms adapt to changes in demand by changing the size of the work force, not by changing the product or the method of production. For example, in the brewing industry, the method of production requires a high capital investment and an extensive distribution system (e.g., beer distributors, trucks, warehouses). If there is a shift in demand, alterations in the production system would emerge rather slowly, because the final product is still beer. Anhauser-Busch, Schlitz, or Carling, for example, would reduce the number of employees if beer sales dropped off rather than seek new products (e.g., making wine or "hard" liquor). Change in the production and distribution systems would be too costly.

A stable environment provides a high level of predictability. Firms operating in this environment are able to use common business indicators for their planning and sales efforts. The United States Department of Commerce prepares annual output projections for various industries, based on changes that have occurred in the industry over the last ten years. Firms operating in stable environments can use these indices for forecasting market changes and sales trends.

The Changing Environment. A changing environment is characterized by:

1. products and services that have been changing moderately or continually;
2. major technological innovations, which may make the old technology obsolete;
3. an ever-changing set of actions by competitors and customers;
4. unpredictable and changing governmental actions, reflecting political in-

teractions between the public and various groups for consumer protection, pollution control, and civil rights;

5. rapid changes in the values of a large number of individuals.

Firms in this type of environment are likely to feel an ongoing need to adapt their internal structures to the environment. In an unstable environment, customers, prices, demands, etc., are changing. Products based on consumer preferences must be changed to meet new preferences and fads. Organizations in the electronics, pharmaceutical, and watch industries operate in changing, unstable environments.

When the technology is also changing, new ideas and concepts must be generated quickly, and these new ideas can affect the way in which the product is manufactured or the product itself. In the electronics industry, breakthroughs in integrated circuits and miniaturization have affected the nature of the product itself. The introduction of electronic digital watches has had a tremendous impact on the market. For centuries, Swiss-made watches dominated the industry. The Swiss firms were independent and stressed the craftsmanship that went into each watch. When the technology of the industry changed from hand-wound to electronic and digital watches, the Swiss were unable to meet the competition of the new innovations. As a result, the entire Swiss industry has suffered declining sales and revenue.

In the United States, the high cost of labor, intense competition, and lack of governmental protection created a different set of environmental conditions for the watch industry. Only two firms—Timex and Bulova—were able to survive changes in their task environment; they innovated successfully to meet the demands of the new technology. According to Ardith Rivel, a vice-president at the Benrus Corporation, electronic digital watches that had been selling for $125 to $135 a few years ago sold for less than $30 in 1976.[6] Watches with light-emitting diodes and liquid-crystal displays have changed the nature of the entire industry. As the technology changed, more watch makers gradually began producing electronic digital watches, and prices dropped rapidly.

Environment-Organization Link

Organizations face different task environments. The underlying assumption of the contingency approach is that organizations will adapt to these environments by designing their structures to fit the demands of the environment.[7] Some organizations will not adapt their structure(s) and will instead try to change the nature of the environment. As indicated in Chapter 2, some strategies used by organizations to respond to changes in the environment are co-optation, bargaining, lobbying, coalition formation, representation, and socialization. Where a stable technology exists, as in the safety-razor, fountain-pen, or leather industries, firms may spend large amounts of time and advertising to avoid a technological breakthrough that will radically alter the industry. For example, when the electric razor was introduced to the public in 1938, both the American Safety Razor Corporation and Gillette Safety Razor Company were one-product companies, and both engaged in large-scale marketing campaigns to prevent the electric razor from dominating the shaving market. Only during 1956–58 did sales of electric razors exceed those of razor blades. Since 1958, razor blades have regained and maintained their sales lead.

Some firms have managed to retain their organizational structures in spite of changes in the environment. However, most organizations adapt their structures to the demands of the environment. Many organizations interact with environments having both stable and changing characteristics. Marketing and technological factors may take on characteristics ranging from high stability to high instability. Firms confronting a stable market and technological environment will probably perform routine operations, be fairly formalized, have centralized decision making, and/or rely heavily on rules and regulations in running the organization. This environment does not require a complicated organization structure and/or decision-making rules. But to deal successfully with a changing environment puts a premium on a decentralized organization structure and on managers keeping informed about external developments. Also needed are a flexible communication system that bypasses the formal hierarchy when necessary to bring specialists together and a structure that can give emphasis to new products and services when opportunities are detected. Perhaps most needed in a changing environment are people who can accept ambiguity (uncertainty) as they change tasks and positions on various teams where they must cooperate with people of differing backgrounds and from different functional areas.

CONTINGENCY APPROACHES TO ORGANIZATIONAL DESIGN

Organizational structures will differ according to the conditions of their task environments. That is, the organization's subsystems (institutional, organizational, and technical) will differ, depending on whether the market and/or technology are stable or changing. Table 5.1 provides an overall framework for developing the contingency approach to the design of organizations. The two key factors are stability and homogeneity. Stability refers to the amount of change in the dimensions in the organization's task environment over time.

Table 5.1. Contingency designs of organizations

Homogeneity	Stability	
	Stable	Changing
Homogeneous	I	II
Heterogeneous	III	IV

Adapted from J. Thompson, *Organizations in Action*, New York: McGraw-Hill, 1967, p. 72.

That is, are the number of customers, suppliers, manufacturing methods, and price structures stable or changing? Homogeneity, on the other hand, refers to the degree to which the task environment is segmented—numerous buyers, customers, and sellers, or few buyers, customers, and sellers. A heterogeneous task environment has many buyers and different types of customers and sellers; a homogeneous task environment, few buyers and limited types of customers and suppliers. The resulting four quadrants present different kinds of problems to the organization and therefore require different organizational structures.

Homogeneous and Stable Task Environments (I)

The bureaucratic form of organization structure is probably most appropriate when the market and technology are stable and homogeneous. Changes in technology are few, the markets served are fairly well defined, and there is stability in both suppliers and customers. As indicated in Chapter 3, bureaucracy is characterized by a high degree of centralized control at the top administrative level and a fairly rigid hierarchy. Lines of authority and responsibility are clear, jobs are well defined through the use of detailed position descriptions, and each manager has clearly specified goals. Promotion through the organization is based on expertise and seniority. Individuals who do get promoted will probably have the same viewpoint as those who promoted them. Thus members of the management team have a high degree of similarity in point of view, attitude, and background. Most likely there will be a small proportion of managers to workers.

Information needed by managers at the institutional level (e.g., presidents) from the task environment is gathered from technical reports published by the government and other sources, such as trade magazines, trade meetings, and general business news sources. This information is then sent to lower-level managers, who are not actively involved in the decision-making process. It is the job of the chief operating officer to maintain the status quo by making all the decisions.

Bureaucratic organizations have been criticized for failing to adapt and cope with the environment. However, if the environment is stable and homogeneous, the hierarchical form of organization is precisely the kind of structure needed to cope effectively with the task environment. To have a different organizational form under these conditions would likely lower the success of the organization. In a study of 20 industrial firms in the United Kingdom, Burns and Stalker found that firms operating in stable and homogeneous task environments (e.g., rayon mills) were more successful when they adopted a "mechanistic" system of management.[8] The dimensions of the mechanistic management system are as follows:

1. organizational problems and tasks are broken down according to specialized functions;
2. coordination occurs through the formal hierarchy;
3. the job duties and responsibilities assigned to each position are defined precisely;
4. the structure of control, authority, and communication is hierarchical;

5. interaction between members of the firm follows the chain of command;
6. greater importance and prestige are attached to internal rules and regulations than to general knowledge, expertise, and skill;
7. the behavior of all workers and managers tends to be governed by rules and regulations.

The tasks performed in the bureaucratic organization's technical level are routine and repetitive. That is, a standard way of performing the job is established and routinized through the use of time-and-motion study or other principles of scientific management. Tasks are repetitive; all members are usually assigned only a few tasks which are performed over and over, day after day. The limited skill required by the task can lead to the workers' increasing demand for employment stability. It is easy to replace workers, since probably a large pool of unskilled labor is available to perform the task. Production workers have very limited control over what they do and how they produce the work.

These types of firms are highly capital intensive rather than labor intensive. Managers need to know how to design and maintain the production system so that it can achieve maximum productivity with the equipment. Bureaucratic organizations in the private sector often require a high volume to break even, and even minor fluctuations in productivity can adversely affect the economies of the system. When the Teamsters union struck Anheuser-Busch in 1976, first-quarter profits for the world's largest brewing company dropped 44 percent. The strike reduced beer sales for the month of March 1976 by an estimated 2.5 million barrels and cost the company $13 million in potential profits. Although other organizations struck by a union might also report losses, the depreciation and costliness of capital equipment made this problem more critical for Anheuser-Busch.[9]

Because the market is relatively unchanging, channels of distribution are probably fairly well defined and standardized. A successful distribution system might require ten years or more to set up. New distribution channels will be opened only if the current methods become highly inefficient. It is likely that the organization will have a great deal of influence over the distribution system. The effective marketing strategy is to educate customers to adapt their wants to the available products. Thus, for example, each brewing company spends millions of dollars each year trying to convince consumers that its beer is "lighter," "less filling," and "tastes better."

McDONALD'S: A CASE STUDY
A quick analysis of a franchise organization can highlight organizations facing a stable, homogeneous task environment. The typical franchise organization, such as McDonald's, Kentucky Fried Chicken, The Pancake House, or Dunkin' Donuts, operates in a homogeneous market environment. Competitors have similar promotional strategies and production technology. Technology tends to remain relatively constant, and the potential market (fast food) is defined as homogeneous for all firms. The managers of the franchise have market-oriented goals, short-term horizons for service and future markets, and are more likely to be preoccupied with getting the job done (highly produc-

tion-oriented) than with maintaining good interpersonal relations (low "people" orientation).

The integrative mechanisms employed by McDonald's, for example, include not only a detailed organizational structure, but also continual service (in terms of bookkeeping systems, company troubleshooters, advertising) to ensure that the franchise managers conform to McDonald's rules and regulations. McDonald's operations manual is a 385-page detailed book covering the most minute facet of operating an outlet, e.g., what stock and equipment, such as cigarettes, gum, candy, and pinball machines, are not permitted on store premises. One of 30 field-service managers visits the franchise manager monthly. Franchise owners must send weekly financial reports to the company and must attend a three-week intensive training program at the so-called Hamburger U. in Elk Grove, Illinois. There, new managers are trained in techniques for regulating production so that the service standard ("No customer has to wait for more than 50 seconds") is always met; they are taught how to organize the grill, shake, and counter workers into an effective team. The new managers also learn the strict standards for personal grooming, are introduced to a few variations in types of food to suit regional tastes, and are indoctrinated in dealing with college students as customers and employees.

The company also provides the franchise manager with a different maintenance reminder for each day of the year (e.g., "Lubricate and adjust potato-peeler belt" or "Contact snow-removal company"). Because each member of the McDonald's organization has a specified role, it is not difficult to get integrated programs of action. Extensive collaboration among headquarters departments leads to unity in the franchises. For example, the design department at the parent organization works closely with the site and location department to ensure that each franchise meets the standards set by the organization and also blends in with the general atmosphere and appearance of the community. Once these departments have reached an agreement, the franchise operator must erect the structure according to the plans set for that location. As Fred Turner, McDonald's president since 1968, says: "In an age when so many Americans are on the move, one of our main assets is our consistency and uniformity. It's very important that a man who's used to eating at a McDonald's in Hempstead, L.I., knows he can get the same food and service when he walks into one in Albuquerque or Omaha."[10]

SUMMARY

Firms operating in a homogeneous and stable environment:

1. have a relatively fixed or stable market share;
2. try to maximize production efficiency;
3. attempt to maintain competence in the product or service line currently offered;
4. have "mechanistic," or bureaucratic, form of internal structure;
5. have a mass-production technology, which permits few exceptions, requires a heavy capital investment, and provides employees with routine jobs;
6. believe that the role of the chief executive officer is to create distribution

channels to reach customers, maintain the status quo, and/or make small-increment product changes as needed.

The mechanistic organization has been found to be effective because it can adapt and cope with the demands of its task environment. Given a stable and homogeneous task environment, the bureaucratic organization is likely to be effective.[11] The stability of the environment means that organizations need to maintain set relationships with the environment if they are to remain effective.

Homogeneous and Changing Task Environments (II)

Firms operating in this task environment are faced with the problem of changes in customers' attitudes, habits, and tastes, but not their number. That is, the firm is still dealing with a relatively homogeneous group of buyers, etc., but the services and products these individuals want keep changing. Since the significant changes are likely to take place in the marketing sector of the task environment, the top managers of the organization need to stay in close contact with the customers' changing desires. In general, product changes in the task environment will reflect style or design changes more than they do radical product changes. For example, Schlitz's introduction of "light" beer reflects a change in the style of brewing beer rather than in the product line.

The major task of the chief operating officer in this task environment is to monitor the environment for changes and then make decisions as to how the organization should adapt to them. Appropriate changes in the product should improve the organization's distinctive competence in the industry and hopefully stimulate demand. Decisions by corporate presidents and their staffs (members of the institutional level) have a long-term impact on the firm. Once built, the productive facilities are relatively inflexible and can be changed only at major expense; the total investment is likely to be large, and development of a market is long-range. The major task of organizational members at the institutional level is to maintain and create new product markets that can be produced by the firm.

A hierarchical form of organization is likely to be effective and should probably resemble the "mechanistic" form. However, individuals performing the marketing and other functions dealing with the task environment are likely to have more decision-making power, because they must monitor the changes in the environment and relay them to the appropriate members of the organization. If the market isn't present, one must be created to gain economies of scale. In 1890, for example, Standard Oil Company gave free kerosene lamps to the Chinese peasants to create a market for their kerosene. In this case, Standard Oil created a new product and then sold it to a homogeneous group of customers.

The type of environment confronting organizations in quadrant II leads to programmed production tasks performed within a stable technology. A process type of production technology is usually found in this quadrant. That is, the end products of an oil refinery are determined by the process it uses. Slight changes in the process can change the octane rating of gasoline from 89 to 95 or leaded gas to unleaded gas. The refinery makes these process changes in order to meet the changing wants and demands of customers, other businesses, and governmental regulations. All process-production companies, including chemicals, milk processors, paint manufacturers, and plate-glass plants, concentrate on a few products, but segment the market enough to capture the changes in the customers' tastes. Pittsburgh Paints, for example, offers its customers 200 different shades of colors. Each of these paints is appealing to a homogeneous set of consumer tastes.

Process production requires very high capital investment and a high volume to break even. The typical process plant in the chemical or plate-glass industry can operate profitably only at or near peak capacity. It has a great diversity of product mix, requires high skill on the part of schedulers, maintenance, and other managers, but low skill on the workers' part.

SUMMARY

Firms operating in a homogeneous and changing task environment:

1. have a relatively fixed market share, and adjustments are made or created to gain production efficiency;
2. try to improve the economies of scale;
3. have as their major marketing strategy the improvement of their distinctive competence by making minor modifications in the product itself;
4. have a mechanistic form of organization, but less so than firms in quadrant I;
5. use a process technology, which allows for few exceptions, programmed job descriptions for operations workers, and heavy capital investment;
6. believe that the chief executive officer should search for information in the task environment concerning the changing styles, habits, or attitudes of the firm's customers.

Heterogeneous and Stable Task Environments (III)

Firms operating in this task environment have relatively constant customers and suppliers, but there are a great number of them. Conglomerates, such as Dart Industries, SCM, AMF, Walter Kidde, Indiana Head, and Gulf Western, typically operate in this type of task environment. The job of top management is to stay in close contact with a continually changing consumer or client group by monitoring changes in the market. Changes are generally made in the product's style or design to reach new customers.

A hierarchical, or mechanistic, type of authority structure is likely to prevail throughout the organization. Control systems to monitor the changes in and adapt to the environment will be developed in such a way as to be keyed by decisions made in the marketing department. In conglomerates, the structure is highly differentiated. Each firm within the conglomerate is assigned specific responsibilities, product lines, and targets for profitability. For example, each division of Textron, Inc. (Homelite Saws, Bell Helicopter, Talon Zipper Company) is a profit center responsible for its own sales, marketing research, and manufacturing processes. A top executive of Textron, Inc., stated that his firm wants to give the management of acquired companies independence to run the company. Because of the independence of divisions within Textron, coordination is needed only in the financial area. This coordination is achieved through Textron's annual budgeting process.[12]

General Motors too operates in a heterogeneous and stable task environment. GM is decentralized along product lines—e.g., Pontiac, Frigidaire, Delco, Oldsmobile, Chevrolet—and is able to respond effectively to changes in each product's environment. Each of GM's product divisions is a profit center responsible for its own sales and manufacturing processes. The divisions' activities are coordinated through financial and administrative committees. The financial committee provides guidelines for capital expenditures, methods of accounting to be used by each product manager, rate of return on investment, and other financial matters; the administration committee is concerned with long-range planning activities, production and sales policies, purchase commitments, and the like. Day-to-day operating decisions are handled at the product-manager level; long-term decisions, which require coordination among the various product lines, are handled by top management committees.

Since the type of task environment confronting firms operating in this quadrant is relatively stable, the usual production process is mass production, whereby parts are assembled in standardized ways. The enormous number of Japanese Buddhist temples built between A.D. 700 and 1600 may look quite different, yet each temple was put together out of essentially standardized parts, e.g., beams standardized as to width and length, standardized roofing and roof tiles, standardized intervals between the various levels of a pagoda, and so on. The individually distinctive features, e.g., doors or iron grilles or the ornamentation of the tiles on the roof's edge, were added at the very end. Japanese temples, built of wood, burned down again and again. But they always could be rebuilt exactly from the drawings showing only the exterior appearance.

General Motors often points out that there are so many options on its cars—colors, body styles, seat fabrics, accessories, and so on—that the customer can actually choose from millions of different final-product combinations. More important is the fact that all GM passenger cars use the same frames, the same bodies, and very substantially the same engine, braking systems, lighting systems, and the like. Yet the cars look different, have different characteristics, and represent a great variety of combinations of basic standardized parts because each customer wants something different. Henry Ford, who in 1928 said, "The customer can have a car in any color as long as it's black," treated the market as homogeneous. Customers did not like this uniformity and began to buy automobiles from manufacturers who gave them various color combinations. Similarly, American Motors is at a very real disadvantage in the automobile market because it has to turn out a fair diversity of end products—at least in looks and styling—without General Motors' volume.[13]

Insurance companies also fall into this quadrant. The services they offer vary because their clientele's needs for insurance (fire, health, losses at sea, life, burglary, and so on) vary. However, insurance companies process their clients in standardized ways that resemble mass production. The input and output for insurance companies are standardized. The input is a standard form, and the output is the payment of a check. Only the amount of the check varies, and this amount, of course, is determined in advance by the policy itself.

Mass-production technologies are usually labor-intensive. They require a high volume to break even. Top management needs managers who are highly skilled in the maintenance and design of the operating system, but it needs individuals with little judgment in its operations. For example, the typical insurance company has numerous highly qualified actuaries, computer experts, etc., who design life insurance programs. Insurance companies also employ thousands of low-skilled clerks to handle the paperwork of processing clients' claims, payments, and adjustments.

SUMMARY

Firms operating in the heterogeneous and stable quadrant:

1. have a relatively fixed share of the market;
2. try to improve its economies by planned change;
3. aim to improve the distinctive competence of each product it produces in order to segment the market into easily identifiable customers;
4. use a mechanistic form of organization, with profit centers created for each product;
5. use mass-production technology;
6. believe that the chief executive officer should gather data from the task environment and integrate all products.

Heterogeneous and Changing Task Environments (IV)

Many managers today believe that they face this type of environment, which is characterized by continually changing products or services, major technological innovations, and rapid changes in the values and behaviors of customers, suppliers, and other parties in the organization's task environment. Successfully dealing with such an environment puts a premium on creativity and sensitivity to the task environment and depends on a type of organization structure different from that found in the other environments. Perhaps most of all, the heterogeneous, changing environment requires people who can accept ambiguity, as they change tasks and positions on various teams where they must cooperate with people of differing backgrounds and perspectives.

In a large organization, the various departments have different task environments. Some of Westinghouse's departments operate in fairly stable task environments (e.g., broadcasting, consumer products); others, in more changing ones (e.g., power systems, industry and defense products). To be effective, Westinghouse must facilitate the departmentation of structure and employee attitudes toward tasks and goals for various task environments. Departments operating in stable task environments will probably have "mechanistic" structures. It is important to realize that the task environments of the departments within an organization may differ from one another. The structure of each department reflects its unique task environment. When we discuss different management systems, therefore, keep in mind that one organization can have multiple management systems, each attempting to adapt to its own task environment.

Table 5.2. Organizational differences between the mechanistic and organic management systems

Factor	Mechanistic	Organic
General structure	Emphasis on rules More formality Limited autonomy in decisions Narrow job definition	Less rigid structure Fewer rules and policies Greater discretion in decisions More job scope
Objectives	Short-range/cost	Long-range/development
Bases of authority	Position power Commitment to organization Centralization	Skill and expert power Commitment to self and discipline Decentralization
Bases of compensation	Level and relative importance of the position Increases based on "merit" and tenure	Quality of training and experience Increases based on experience in area of competence (maturity curves)
Evaluation criteria	Objective measures Focus on results as outcomes Short time span between performance and results	Subjective criteria Focus on activities rather than results Long time span between performance and results
Organization climate	Rules-oriented formalism	Innovation-oriented
Status	Lower	Higher

Adapted by permission from H. Tosi and S. Carroll, *Management: Contingencies, Structure and Process*, Chicago: St. Clair Press, 1976, p. 461.

Table 5.2 shows some of the differences between the internal structures of organizations in the homogeneous/stable (mechanistic) and heterogeneous/changing (organic) quadrants. Although we recognize that any particular organization may not have all of these characteristics, they seem to be very prominent.

In their study of 20 industrial firms in the United Kingdom, Burns and Stalker also found that when firms were facing novel, unfamiliar areas in both the market and technological situations, a fundamentally different kind of management system became appropriate. This management system was not the "mechanistic" one that was successfully used by firms facing stability in the market and technological environment. Firms operating in the electronics industry had relatively flexible organizational structures. A number of plans were devised specifically to meet the situation at hand, and there was a deliberate attempt to avoid clearly defined functions and lines of authority. Communications, aided by committee meetings, tended to flow easily outside of the formal organization structure. Individual jobs were defined as ambiguously as possible so that they could develop to fit the changing needs of the task. The dimensions of this type of management system, labeled "organic," are shown in Table 5.2. Although it is beyond the scope of this chapter to discuss all of the differences between "mechanistic" and "organic" management systems, we shall discuss differences in personnel and organizational structure.

PERSONNEL DIFFERENCES

Several researchers have concluded that different kinds of management systems will attract and retain individuals with different value orientations.[14] Table 5.3 summarizes some of the differences between individuals in mechanistic and organic management systems.

Tolerance for ambiguity refers to the individual's ability to function effectively in uncertain situations. A person with high tolerance can make decisions under conditions of unclear job definitions, unclear lines of authority and responsibility, and high degrees of uncertainty about the criteria of performance evaluation. A person with a low tolerance for ambiguity has a need for the structure and definition of activities usually found in mechanistic management

Table 5.3. Some individual differences between members in mechanistic and organic management systems

Mechanistic	Factor	Organic
Low	Tolerance for ambiguity	High
Low	Integrative complexity	High
Toward position power	Attitudes toward authority	Toward autonomy
Low	Individualism	High
Low	Outside reference groups	High
Low	Professional values	High

Adapted from S. Tosi and S. Carroll, *Management: Contingencies, Structure and Process*, Chicago: St. Clair Press, 1976, p. 467.

systems. The stability of the task environment fosters adherence to rules and regulations in order to achieve maximum efficiency. Managers in the organizational and technical subsystems are evaluated on how well they follow orders from top management.

Integrative complexity is an individual's capacity to deal with a variety of information, understand it, and integrate it in order to solve problems. Managers in charge of research laboratories have a greater need for this skill than do managers in charge of production-line operations. The production-line manager is concerned more about scrap, production efficiency, downtime, and other technical problems than about marketing, accounting, finance, and other organizational problems. On the other hand, the manager of an R&D laboratory should be concerned with all of these business problems as they affect the laboratory; as the task environment is changing, the problems in these basic business areas are likely to change in scope and magnitude for the manager.

Several researchers have found that individuals working in organic management systems have higher educational levels than those in mechanistic systems.[15] In general, those with higher educational levels are less tolerant of directive leader behavior. Managers in changing task environments tend to have a greater preference of autonomy than do managers in more stable task environments. On the other hand, managers in mechanistic organizations prefer the strong authority relationships provided by the organization's hierarchy and its rules and regulations.

Managers and professionals with an inside-the-organization orientation are sometimes referred to as "locals," whereas those who identify with outside reference groups are called "cosmopolitans." Cosmopolitans adhere to what they perceive to be the values of their profession and are less committed and loyal to the organization's values and norms than are locals.[16] Professionals and scientists tend to be cosmopolitans because of their expertise and problem-solving abilities and are typically employed in organizations in changing task environments. Professionals are concerned less with money and promotions, value the scientific approach, and are more concerned with the intrinsic nature of the job (e.g., feelings of achievement, challenge) than are locals. These different perspectives and value orientations can create hostility and dissatisfactions in organizations employing a large number of professionals and line managers.

ORGANIZATION STRUCTURE

Perhaps one of the most effective ways to approach the problem of coordinating units with different tasks, values, and people is to create the appropriate organization structure. This requires that management keep informed about the changes in each environment. The structure of the organization should facilitate the collection of information from customers, suppliers, competitors, governmental agencies, and a multiplicity of action groups (e.g., civil rights, consumer protection, environmentalists) so that management can make better decisions.

Establishing effective means for dealing with problems of uncertainty and the management of diverse specialists can be accomplished through the *matrix* form of organization. In the matrix, or project, organization, individuals from various departments are assigned to one or more project teams to work together for the duration of the project. Hughes Aircraft Company, for example, is organized into five product lines—space and communications, industrial electronics, Hughes international, a research center, and research laboratories. When Hughes Aircraft is awarded a contract, the work is performed by the divisions that have the needed specialists. Thus if the contract is awarded to the Systems Division, the manager of that division determines the extent to which other divisions may be used in completing the contract. The impact of a newly awarded contract requires that a large number of people in various divisions work closely together to complete the contract. The continuous influx of new contracts, with subsequent allocation of products or tasks to all divisions, places continual burdens on a product or functional organization. Hughes's handling of its contracts necessitates changes not only in the numbers and orientations of people, but also in the mix of managerial, professional, and technical personnel required to complete any given project. The pressures from new technological advances and short lead times have made it necessary to establish some type of organizational structure to coordinate all of the various activities associated with a particular project.

Matrix management really represents a compromise between functional and product departmentation. In the functional organization, each department has its own specialists (e.g., accounting, marketing, personnel, production); in the product organization, all of the different specialists needed to produce a given product are in the same unit. Functional organization obviously makes it more difficult to achieve coordination of the different specialists, whereas product organization usually does not allow specialists sufficient access to other specialists and can lead to too many specialists of a certain type working at less than their capacity on a particular product.[17]

A useful way to think about the differences among functional, product, and matrix organizational forms is presented in Fig. 5.2. This figure indicates that organizational designs may range from the purely functional to the purely product organization. In the functional organization, heads of the various functions make all decisions that affect their departments. Their authority is based on their positions in the organization's hierarchy and its policies, rules, regulations, and job descriptions. The coordinating mechanisms used by the functional manager include functional task forces, teams, managers, and departments. For example, if the personnel department has a problem, the manager of that department can create a task force to examine critically the problem and then report back to the entire department with its recommendations. On the other hand, a product organization, such as General Motors, places the decision-making responsibilities on each product manager (e.g., Pontiac, Chevrolet, Oldsmobile, etc.). These managers make decisions in a semiautonomous manner with respect to the other product managers. In the product organization, the coordinating mechanisms also include task forces, teams, managers, and departments, but they are concerned primarily with one product. The matrix form of organization uses advantages of both the product and functional forms of departmentation.

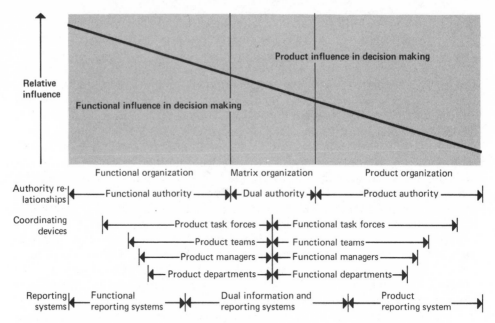

Fig. 5.2. Continuum of organizational designs. (Adapted from J. Galbraith, "Matrix Organization Designs: How to Combine Functional and Project Forms," *Business Horizons* **14** (1971): 37. Copyright 1971 by the Foundation for the School of Business at Indiana University. Reprinted by permission.)

An example of a matrix organization is shown in Fig. 5.3. Program units consist of program coordinators who represent product groups. For example, the Hughes Aircraft Company has seven product groups. The program unit focuses on the coordination of the functional units and tries to maintain a balance between the needs of the product groups and the needs of the functional departments. The staff service unit(s) (see Fig. 5.3) are concerned primarily with planning, budgeting, scheduling, and other support activities for the entire company. The executive committee consists of the top executive and at least one top manager from the program unit, staff service unit(s), the project director, and each functional department. One duty of this committee is to serve as a top-level integrating mechanism. The functional departments provide the expertise and knowledge in their specialized area, such as marketing, research, and production. The project director is concerned about meeting schedules within budgetary limitations and in producing the output within previously planned specifications.

The project director staffs a project with members from the functional areas. The assignment patterns may vary as follows: (1) full time for the duration of the project; (2) full time for one phase of the project; (3) part-time assignment; and (4) contract services from the functional department. In this last assignment pattern, the functional specialist never becomes part of the project team; rather, the project manager arranges for certain services from the functional department. In engineering, for example, the project may not be able to utilize certain specialized personnel or equipment all of the time; a solid-state physicist may be needed only occasionally, and the project may need only part-time use of an expensive environmental test laboratory or prototype shop.

The technology used in each stage of the project is likely to change. The basic work is performed in homogeneous stages. In the building of a traditional single-family house—one of the oldest examples of project management—there are four stages: (1) digging the foundation and pouring concrete for the foundation walls and basement floor; (2) erecting the frame and roof; (3) installing plumbing and wiring equipment in the walls; (4) finishing the interior. Each stage of the building process requires different types of workers and different technologies. It is the job of the contractor to get the order and then integrate the skills of the various craftsmen to erect the home. Each of the

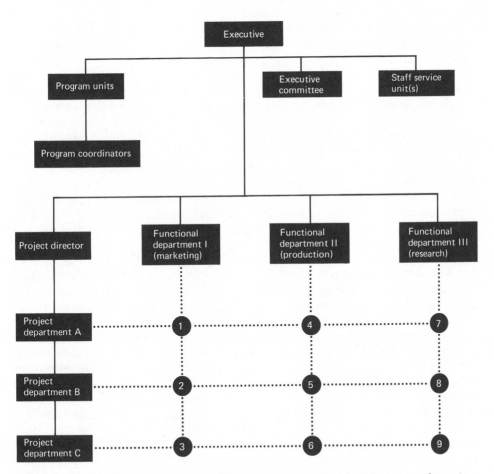

Fig. 5.3. Simplified matrix structure. (Adapted and modified by permission from A. Delbecq and A. Filley, *Program and Project Management in a Matrix Organization: A Case Study,* Madison: Wisconsin Graduate School of Business, University of Wisconsin, Madison, 1974, p. 16.)

craftsmen is also a specialist who has been trained in the technical functions, e.g., electrician, plumber, carpenter, plasterer, carpet worker, etc. Similarly, in the space industry, NASA's great success was due to the integration of activities of its far-flung offices, centers, contractors, and subcontractors. Computer systems helped, but the single most important integrative element was the energy and commitment of various project managers, who traveled between the various differentiated contractors to discuss problems and promote concern for the entire mission.

The project manager's authority and influence flow in different directions from those described by some classical-management theorists. A project manager's authority flows horizontally, across the superior-subordinate relationships existing within the functional activities of an organization. Throughout the life span of a given project, personnel at various levels and with varying skills must contribute their efforts to allow for the sequential development of the project. For each new project awarded the firm, new lateral information-decision-making networks must be worked out which may differ significantly from those used in the functional organization. In essence, the project manager has no clear-cut communications channels, but is faced with a web of communications that frequently crosses vertical lines of authority and involves outside subcontractors as well. Authority is *de facto* and stems from the project manager's charge from top management to get the project done within time and cost constraints. In practice, the project manager must rely heavily on alliances built with peers through negotiations, knowledge, and resolution of conflict. The building of these relationships supplements the lack of formal authority over all of the resources needed to complete the project. Success will partly depend on the project manager's ability to influence other organizational members through the use of informational and communication inputs rather than just his or her formal authority in the organization. Authority cannot be dictated in advance because of the changing nature of project work and the dynamics of project organizations, where many competing projects vie for the firm's scarce resources (e.g., personnel, capital, machinery).

The matrix form of organization, although effective, is not a cure-all. Conflicts arise between managers of different projects and between project managers and functional managers. In addition, the individual members of the project team (indicated in the circles in Fig. 5.3) often receive incompatible requests from their two managers (functional and project) and therefore experience considerable role conflict and job stress. The emphasis on flexibility rather than on permanency of job assignments strongly affects the employees who work for organizations using project management. Insecurity about future employment after the project's completion, career retardation, and personal development are concerns expressed by employees. Therefore, they may feel less loyal to the organization and are more likely to report that they are frustrated on the job than are employees in a more conventional, functional type of organization. As the project begins to "phase out," members attempt to latch onto new projects for fear of being laid off. In some instances, the organization cannot absorb these employees in other projects either because of the cycle stage of the project or because of the lack of contract awards. Thus fear of possible unemployment causes special problems in project organizations.[18]

The matrix, or project, structure is in operation at the TRW Systems Group of TRW, Inc., for the development of earth satellites, landing modules, etc. An internal TRW document describes this structure as follows.

TRW Systems is in the business of application of advanced technology. The company's organization has been expressly planned for effective performance of the projects that comprise our business and for flexibility for future shifts in this business.

The hardware work that we do is awarded by our customers in bid packages that usually involve a number of technical fields and integration of hardware from these into a single end item. We have several hundred of these projects in operation at a time. They range in people assigned from three or four to several hundred. Most of the projects are small—only a few fall in the "large hardware projects" category we are mainly concerned with here.

From the standpoint of personnel and physical resources, it is most efficient to organize by specialized groups or technologies. To stay competitive, these groups must be large enough to obtain and fully utilize expensive special equipment and highly specialized personnel. If each project had its own staff and equipment, duplication would result, resource utilization would be low, and the cost high; it might also be difficult to retain the highest caliber of technical specialists. Our customers get lowest cost and top performance by organization and specialty.

For these reasons, the company has been organized into units of individual technical and staff specialties. Each customer's needs call for a different combination of these capabilities.

A way of matching these customers' needs to the TRW organization elements that can meet them is necessary. The project system performs this function.

In the project system, a project office is set up for each customer program. The project office reports to a company manager of appropriate rank in the organization with cognizance in the technical area of the project. The over-all project organization is similar for each project. The project manager has over-all management responsibility for all project activities and directs the activities through the project office and substructure described in the following. The project office is the central location for all project-wide activities such as project schedule, cost and performance control; system planning, system engineering, and system integration; and contract and major subcontract management. Assistant project managers are appointed for these activities as warranted by project scope.

The total project effort is divided into subprojects according to the technical specialty involved, thus matching the TRW Systems' basic organization structure. Each subproject has a subproject manager who takes project direction from an assistant project manager. The subproject manager is responsible for performance in his specialty area to the supervisor of the organizational element that will perform the subproject work. The subproject manager is the bridge between the project office and this organizational element. The members of the next subordinate level of management in that organization take project direction from him. The work is further subdivided and performed within their organizations.[19]

The document also describes how people interact in a matrix structure.

In an organization like TRW, when getting a job done cuts across departmental boundaries, contact with a large number of other people is a way of life ... because of the necessity for interaction of a technical and personal nature, the team approach is viewed as the most manageable system. Since the teams comprise a heterogeneous group of technical specialties and individuals, conflict is understandable enough. . . .

As one executive expressed it, ". . . groups and individuals in TRW derive the necessary discipline from the job itself and the preciseness of the technological and support specialties required to get that job done effectively. We focus on the problem and organize ourselves to solve that particular problem."

Because people are encouraged to do things "a different way," and because the company has designed a system in which a man's responsibility emerges from the job to be done, he must obtain the cooperation of others over whom he has little traditional, direct authority. . . . "Making the matrix organization really work can be difficult and frustrating; we attempt to reduce the difficulties by encouraging openness and cooperation," comments a training specialist. "If openness exists, a man can devote his time and energies to the real job of making an effective organization, instead of politicking and empire building which dissipate energy and drain off effort that ought to be used constructively on the job."[20]

Although project management has been confined mostly to the aerospace and construction industries, it may find increasing application in many other areas where there is increasing demand for advanced technology and sequential development of related subsystems. Project management in other sectors, such as transportation systems, urban renewal, and pollution control, may provide important innovations in the structure of industries operating in these sectors.

Summary

Structure should be derived not from abstract principles, but from the organization's markets, technology, and task environment. Standardization and stability are desirable in mechanistic management systems operating in stable task environments. On the other hand, when the task environment is unpredictable, innovative organizations, such as the matrix form, are needed to provide more flexibility in the organization's response to the environment. Although the relationships are not inevitable or certain, the usual association of structure, technology, task environment, and management systems is as illustrated in Table 5.3.

Table 5.3. Summary of organizational design relationships

Homogeneity	Stability	
	Stable	Changing
Homogeneous	1. Market share: relatively fixed and predictable	1. Market share: need for identification and minor adjustment; relatively fixed and stable
	2. Firm's objective: maximization of current product line	2. Firm's objectives: improve economies of operation to maximize product line
	3. Market strategy: Maintain competence in product line	3. Market strategy: improve distinctive competence by creating demand for product(s)

Table 5.3. Summary of organization design relationships (cont.)

Homogeneity	Stability	
	Stable	**Changing**
	4. Organization form: mechanistic	4. Organization form: fairly mechanistic
	5. Dominant Technology: mass production or assembly line; programmed tasks, heavy capital investment; few product exceptions; low skill requirement for workers	5. Dominant technology: continuous process; few exceptions in inputs, but varied final products; low skill requirement for workers, high skill requirement for managers and designers of system
	6. Role of chief executive officer: little active search in the task environment; maintain status quo; create effective distribution channels to get product(s) to customers with minimal cost(s)	6. Role of chief executive officer: commitment to a conservative search process in the task environment; create demand for product(s) through advertising media
Heterogeneous	1. Market share: changing	1. Market share: varied and unpredictable
	2. Firm's objectives: maintain ability to adjust to varied needs of customers	2. Firm's objectives: develop effective problem-solving methods to cope with uncertain task environment
	3. Market strategy: contingency planning; search for advanced information	3. Market strategy: adapt to change in the market and technology
	4. Organization form: mixture between organic and mechanistic; profit centers	4. Organization form: organic
	5. Dominant technology: mass production, few exceptions, and capital intensive	5. Dominant technology: craft or job shop; many exceptions; no dominant technology
	6. Role of chief executive officer: adaptive planner and searching for information in the task environment	6. Role of chief executive officer: secure orders for the firm; active search for information in the task environment

Consistency in management is not necessarily a virtue. All parts of a large organization need not be similarly structured. Manufacturing consumer products or electric lamps, for example, is much different from designing nuclear power systems and defense systems, although all of these activities are taking place at Westinghouse. Each department of the organization is responding to its own task environment. Since manufacturing an automobile is different from designing a missile defense system, these two units in GM should not be similarly structured, nor should they attract and retain the same type of personnel. The emerging organizational principles offered by the contingency approach are designed to promote the responsiveness of the organization to the demands of its task environment.

Discussion Questions

1. What is a stable environment? What structure tends to characterize organizations in such an environment?

2. What is a changing environment? What structure tends to characterize organizations in such an environment?

3. What is a "mechanistic" organization?

4. What is an "organic" organization?

5. Provide some examples of firms operating in the different quadrants in Table 5.3.

6. What is the relationship between an organization's technology and its structure?

7. How is project management accomplished?

8. Discuss the role of the chief executive officer in stable/homogeneous and changing/heterogeneous environments.

Management Incidents

CONTINENTAL BAKING COMPANY

The Continental Baking Company makes bread, cakes, rolls, and frozen pastries for sale in retail grocery stores and supermarkets. More than 750 employees in the Columbus, Ohio, plant work on three shifts. More than 600 of the employees are unskilled and perform various machine, baking, and packaging operations necessary to produce the 50 varieties of bakery products. Because of sanitation considerations established by the Ohio Board of Health and the time sequence involved in the kneading, rising, and baking operations, tasks are specifically defined and restricted by rules and regulations. The firm has six other plants scattered throughout the United States and markets its products in all 50 states.

Ohio State University is also located in Columbus. The Special Education Division, operating under the College of Education, has its own classroom and laboratory for children between the ages of 5 and 15. The program, dependent primarily on federal and state funds, is experimental. The 40-person staff consists of psychologists, teachers, and educators who are specialists in working with children who have special learning problems, such as dyslexia, or who are mentally handicapped. The variety of programs ranges from regular classes of up to 15 students to one-to-one teaching.

1. How would you expect the structure of the two organizations to differ? Why?
2. How would you describe the task environments of the two organizations? Would this affect the type of individual likely to be attracted to and retained in the organization?

HONEYWELL CORPORATION

In 1970 Honeywell purchased General Electric's computer business. The purchase involved seven GE plants, more than 27,000 employees, and 7000 computers that GE had in the field. One of the GE management concepts that Honeywell was thinking about adopting was called the "mission concept." Through this concept, various systems specialists, no matter where they were geographically situated, were given a worldwide task to plan, design, develop, manufacture, and market computer systems. GE believed that it could capitalize on existing expertise, whether it was in College Station, Texas, or New York City. GE found that a small-computer specialist living in New York City might be needed to correct a small-computer problem in Seattle.

1. How was GE organized?
2. If you were the president of Honeywell, would you adopt this "mission concept"? Why?

NITTANY LION COMPANY

The Nittany Lion Company, a specialized job shop making quality woodworking tools, has a single organization with approximately 50 employees. These employees describe themselves as "jacks of all trades, masters of none." Foremen, especially skilled, have good relationships with top management. The company is six years old and was formed by two graduates of the local university.

Recently a strong demand for the company's products has increased the size of the work force from 50 to 200. The number of products have been reduced, and production has become specialized. The few high-selling products are demanding more and more production time. There is a seven-month backlog of customer orders. A primary function of top management has become appeasing irate customers. As a result, internal coordination between the various departments has suffered. The need for a larger work force has forced the company to hire machine operators rather than general machinists. Supervisors have complained about the large amount of "instructional services" now needed in their jobs.

1. What has happened in the firm's task environment?
2. What is the relationship between technology and organization structure?

REFERENCES

1. W. Starbuck, "Organizations and Their Environments," in *Handbook of Industrial and Organizational Psychology*, ed. M. Dunnette (Chicago: Rand McNally, 1976), pp. 1069–1123.

2. H. Downey and J. Slocum, "Uncertainty: Measures, Research and Sources of Variation," *Academy of Management Journal* **18** (1975): 562–578.

3. J. D. Thompson, *Organizations in Action* (New York: McGraw-Hill, 1967).

4. For further elaborations on how technology affects organization structure, *see* C. Perrow, "A Framework for the Comparative Analysis of Organizations," *American Sociological Review* **32** (1967): 194–208; J. Woodward, *Industrial Organization* (London: Oxford University Press, 1965); and P. Blau, C. Falbe, W. McKinley, and P. Tracy, "Technology and Organization in Manufacturing," *Administrative Science Quarterly* **21** (1976): 20–40.

5. *See* P. Lawrence and J. Lorsch, *Organization and Environment: Managing Differentiation and Integration* (Boston: Graduate School of Business Administration, Harvard University, 1967); "Differentiation and Integration in Complex Organizations," *Administrative Science Quarterly* **12** (1967): 1–49; P. Khandwalla, "Viable and Effective Organizational Designs of Firms," *Academy of Management Journal* **16** (1973): 481–495; and R. Duncan, "Characteristics of Organizational Environments and Perceived Environmental Uncertainty," *Administrative Science Quarterly* **17** (1972): 313–327.

6. *Wall Street Journal*, April 16, 1975.

7. P. Hirsch, "Organizational Effectiveness and the Institutional Environment," *Administrative Science Quarterly* **20** (1975): 327–344; D. Darran, R. Miles, and C. Snow, "Organizational Adaptation to the Environment: A Review." Paper presented at the Seventh Annual Meeting of the American Institute for Decision Sciences, November 7, 1975, Cincinnati, Ohio; R. Duncan, "Modification in Decision Structure in Adapting to the Environment: Some Implications for Organizational Learning," *Decision Sciences* **5** (1974): 122–142.

8. T. Burns and G. Stalker, *The Management of Innovation* (London: Tavistock, 1961), pp. 120–122.

9. *Columbus Dispatch*, May 3, 1976.

10. J. Lukas, "As American as McDonald's Hamburger on the Fourth of July," *New York Times Magazine* **41,** 424 (1971): 5, 22–29.

11. C. Anderson and F. Paine, "Managerial Perceptions and Strategic Behavior," *Academy of Management Journal* **18** (1975): 811–823.

12. R. Pitts, "Strategies and Structures for Diversification," *Academy of Management Journal* **20** (1977): 197–208.

13. P. Drucker, *Management: Tasks, Responsibilities and Practices* (New York: Harper & Row, 1974).

14. J. Lorsch and J. Morse, *Organizations and Their Members: A Contingency Approach* (New York: Harper & Row, 1974); K. Downey, D. Hellriegel, and J. Slocum, "Individual Performance and Elicited Uncertainty." Paper presented at the 19th Annual Midwest Academy of Management, St. Louis, Missouri, April 24, 1976.

15. Lorsch and Morse, *op. cit.*; R. Hall, "The Concept of Bureaucracy: An Empirical Assessment," *American Journal of Sociology* **69** (1973): 32–40.

16. J. Schriesheim, M. VonGlinow, and S. Kerr, "Professionals in Bureaucracy: A Structural Alternative," in *Prescriptive Models of Organizations*, ed. P. Nystrom and W. Starbuck, North Holland–Timms Studies in the Management Sciences, Vol. 5 (Amsterdam: North Holland, 1978).

17. J. Galbraith, *Designing Complex Organizations* (Reading, Mass.: Addison-Wesley, 1973).

18. C. Reeser, "Some Human Problems of the Project Form of Organization," *Academy of Management Journal* **12** (1969): 459–467.

19. H. Rush, *Behavioral Science: Concepts and Management Application* (New York: National Industrial Conference Board, 1969), pp. 158–159. Reprinted by permission.

20. *Ibid.*

6

Essentials of Decision Making

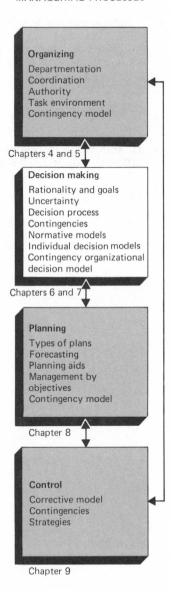

MANAGERIAL PROCESSES

Organizing
Departmentation
Coordination
Authority
Task environment
Contingency model

Chapters 4 and 5

Decision making
Rationality and goals
Uncertainty
Decision process
Contingencies
Normative models
Individual decision models
Contingency organizational
decision model

Chapters 6 and 7

Planning
Types of plans
Forecasting
Planning aids
Management by
objectives
Contingency model

Chapter 8

Control
Corrective model
Contingencies
Strategies

Chapter 9

The objectives of this chapter are to:

enhance your conceptual and technical skills for diagnosing several key contingencies that need to be considered as part of your decision-making process;

develop your understanding of rationality, the nature of goals, the degree of uncertainty, the nature of the decision maker, and other environmental influences in the decision-making process;

develop your conceptual and technical skills for evaluating differences and similarities in models of decision making in terms of their purpose, degree of openness, and how they compare to the general process of decision making.

What should the objective of the sales department be for the next six months? Should we decrease the price of product X? If so, by how much? Would a different organizational structure improve our effectiveness? What conditions can we create to increase the motivation of the plant workers? What changes are taking place in the external environment that might create new opportunities for us and/or the need for internal changes?

The common theme in all of these questions is that someone must engage in decision-making processes and make decisions. Management is the art of "getting things done." Many of the chapters of this book are concerned with providing suggestions to improve your technical, human, and conceptual skills for knowing when and how to "get things done." For example, Chapters 4 and 5 suggested how you might structure organizations differently, depending on various contingencies. This knowledge was intended to aid you in your decisions about the design of formal organizational structures. Thus decision making is a crucial individual and organizational activity that cuts across and includes all of the topic areas in the book, such as organizational design, planning, control, leadership, and motivation. It has even been suggested that decision making is *the* single most important organizational activity for managers.[1]

For our purposes, a model of decision making refers to a framework for explaining how certain types of decisions are made or should be made. This chapter lays the groundwork, and Chapter 7 presents some models of decision making. This chapter does not deal with the commonplace decision problems (such as motivating employees or choosing a leadership style) faced by management on a daily basis. These problems are discussed fully in Chapters 11 and 12. Rather, the concepts and models of decision making presented in this and the following chapter help managers "decide how to decide."

SOME CONTINGENCIES INFLUENCING DECISION MAKING

The contingencies included in this section are limited to those that typically play a role (even though an unconscious one at times) in all types of decision problems. These types of contingencies also have an important role in your understanding of the decision-making models presented in Chapter 7. The contingencies we will consider are degree of rationality, the nature of goals, the degree of uncertainty, the nature of the decision maker, and the amount of time available for making the decision.

Before contingencies can have any influence, several preconditions must exist for meaningful decision making to take place by an individual or organization. Meaningful decision making is likely to take place only if the answer to the following questions is yes.[2]

1. *Is there a gap or difference between the present (existing state) and some desired goal (state)?* This gap may initially be more in the form of some vague sense of dissatisfaction with the present.

2. *Is the decision maker (individual or organization) aware of the gap?* For example, in 1976 a dissident group of the Teamsters claimed that the union's leadership was undemocratic and was exploiting its power for personal gain. At the national convention in 1976, the president of the Teamsters stated that

there would be no changes because there was no need to, and he publicly told the dissidents to "go to hell." In other words, the formal leadership perceived no gap between the present and desired states with respect to the decision issues raised by the dissidents.

3. *Is the decision maker motivated to reduce or eliminate the gap?*

4. *Does the decision maker have the resources or ability to reduce or resolve the gap?* For example, although you might like to open up a McDonald's outlet, unless you could raise about $250,000, there would be little meaning in engaging in further decision making as to how this might be accomplished.

If the questions above cannot be answered in the affirmative, it is unlikely that meaningful decision making can take place.

Rationality

How often have you told (or felt like telling) another person that his or her course of action was irrational? Although accusing others of irrationality is a common emotional response, we need to consider it in a more systematic manner. Much of the thinking and writing on decision making is concerned with the rationality of the decision itself, the decision process used, and the decision maker.

RATIONALITY OF THE DECISION ITSELF

A decision is considered rational if it maximizes goal achievement within the limitations of the environment in which it is made.[3] This definition, however, assumes that the goal is known; it leaves no room for evaluating the "rationality" of the goal that is to be attained through the chosen course of action. In other words, "rationality" must include consideration of *goals* as well as *means.* An example is the turmoil over the discovery of bribes being made by some American corporations to foreign politicians and individuals. To the American executives, the bribes may have represented a decision that was perceived as necessary to attain the goal of securing certain orders. From this view, the bribes may have looked like a rational decision. If other values and goals applied (e.g., fair play and honesty), the bribes may well appear to be an irrational decision.

RATIONALITY OF PROCESS

The concept of rationality often emphasizes the process to be used in arriving at decisions. The basic steps in a rational decision-making process include:

1. collecting and analyzing all information relevant to the decision issue (goal or problem);
2. determining preferences according to some measuring device (such as money or amount of satisfaction);
3. selecting the alternative that maximizes the decision maker's utility (such as money or amount of satisfaction).

The individual who follows these steps would presumably approach the requirements of a rational decision-making process.

The degree of rationality of the decision process is illustrated by a study of how a sample of graduating seniors from the business school of a university went about the decision to interview certain firms.[4] The students seemed to fall equally into three groups. The "maximizers" felt that the organizations differed significantly in salary, career opportunities, advancement potential, and working conditions. The only way they could actually collect and analyze the information on firms was to take as many interviews and get as many job offers as possible. Based on what they were looking for, they would then "rationally" choose the best offer. "Minimizers," by contrast, simply tried to minimize the number of interviews by getting one offer and taking it. They tended to believe that all firms were about the same and did not feel that a choice of employment opportunities was important. Finally, the "validators," in between the other two groups, tried to get their favorite offer (very subjectively determined) and then get just one more interview to see if their favorite was really a good one. In terms of rationality of the decision process, it would appear that the "maximizers" were the most rational and the "minimizers" the least rational; the maximizers more closely followed the steps in the rational decision-making process.

IRRATIONALITY

As suggested above, rationality—of both the decision and the process—can be thought of as forming a continuum. This continuum, which ranges from rationality to irrationality, suggests that there can be "more or less" of rationality and irrationality. For example, in the example of job-seeking behavior by college seniors, the validators appear to be more "rational" than the minimizers, but not as "rational" as the maximizers.

Irrationality in a person or organization is usually associated with defying the laws of reason and logic or going against something considered rational by other groups or individuals. It is often easier to make judgments as to irrationality over "means" than over "goals." For example, a residential-building contractor interested in minimizing the cost of building houses would probably consider it irrational to have the carpenters use only hand hammers for driving nails when speedier and low-cost power hammers are readily available.

Many times rationality or irrationality depends on the values and goals of the particular individual. For example, students who occupy the administration building on a university campus, in an effort to force the institution to increase the support to its minority-student program, may regard their actions as highly rational. Given their goal and the alternative means available, they may be rational from their own viewpoint. To the president, board of directors, and other groups within and outside the university, however, the students' actions may be viewed as disruptive and irrational. An indication of the community's view of the irrationality of the act might take the form of arrest and prosecution of the offenders. Does this mean that every act that can lead to arrest or punishment is, by definition, irrational from someone else's point of view? Possibly! But this approach also suggests the inadequacy of viewing all decisions on a rationality-irrationality continuum without regard to other contingency factors, such as differences in values and goals.

BOUNDED RATIONALITY

175

SOME
CONTINGENCIES
INFLUENCING
DECISION MAKING

Bounded rationality is an especially useful concept because it emphasizes the limitations to the rationality of decision makers and partially explains the conflicts and differences in decisions arrived at by individuals, even when they appear to have the same information. The bounded-rationality concept provides a general description of the day-to-day decision processes of most individuals. In brief, it refers to the tendency of decision makers to satisfice, engage in a limited search of alternatives, and make decisions with inadequate information and control of the factors that are likely to influence the outcomes of their decisions.[5]

Satisficing. Satisficing means that an individual does not set an optimum goal in a decision problem, but instead establishes a very limited range of goals that would be satisfactory. For example, one goal of a business firm might be to maximize profits. However, profits are often expressed as desired goals, such as a 15 percent rate of return on investment or a 10 percent increase in profits over the previous year, which may not represent maximizing behavior. Similarly, satisficing seemed to be taking place for the college students who had the goal of obtaining only one or two job offers, even though they had many interviews for jobs.

Limited Search. Bounded rationality assumes that the individual or organization undertakes a very limited search of the possible alternatives which might be used to obtain the desired goal. The individual is assumed to consider alternatives only until finding one that appears to provide an adequate means for obtaining the desired goal. Of course, the attempt to obtain information about all possible alternatives could "freeze" the decision maker. College graduates who attempt to evaluate every possible position in the world for which they might be qualified in order to choose the best one might die of old age before obtaining all the necessary information to make a decision. Of course, maximizing behavior recognizes there are costs of time, energy, and money in the identification and assessment of alternatives. The key difference in the concept of bounded rationality is that decision makers stop considering alternatives as soon as they hit on one that seems acceptable for reaching their goal. Thus some of the college students took only as many interviews as necessary to get one or two job offers.

Inadequate Control and Information. Bounded rationality holds that some factors outside the control of the decision maker will influence the actual results of their decisions. The state of the future, which is determined by numerous factors, influences whether the goals are reached. Management might make a decision (after an extensive decision process) to purchase a number of automatic stamping machines to make disc brakes for automobiles. With the reduced cost of labor going into each piece produced, the machines would pay for themselves within two years. But management did not anticipate the resistance to the machines by the union members and the decline of automobile sales. As a result, the automatic machines were not effectively used, and the "payback" period was eight rather than two years.

In sum, bounded rationality suggests that decision makers frequently have incomplete information on their decision problem. This adds further credibility to the idea that rationality is typically tied to a limited frame of reference, whether it be that of an individual, group, or organization.

Although this discussion has not totally resolved the role of rationality in decision making, it has served to highlight the different viewpoints and complexities to rationality. As mentioned earlier, one of the preconditions for decision making is the existence of a gap between the present (existing state) and desired goals (state). Once goals have been established, they are often used as a standard or criterion for evaluating the effectiveness of decisions intended to reach the goals. However, the concept of goals, in relation to decision making, can be a rather complex matter.

Goals

One of the most important decision problems facing all individuals is the identification of goals. Managers in the organizational (marketing, production, personnel, finance, and accounting) and institutional (presidents, vice-presidents, boards of directors) subsystems are especially responsible for the formulation of goals. The amount of discretion available to a manager in the formulation of goals will vary widely, depending on his or her level in the organization, the degree to which the determination of types and levels of goals has been formally decentralized, and the degree of personal influence the manager has with his or her superiors and others.

NATURE AND IMPORTANCE

From an organizational point of view, goals are results to be attained. These goals may also be termed objectives, ends, missions, purposes, standards, deadlines, targets, and quotas. Regardless of the label, goals specify a state of affairs that some members think desirable for their organization. The goals set forth may not necessarily prove to be effective for the organization's long-run survival and growth. Henry Ford's goal of producing only black Model-T Fords was ultimately detrimental to the company's success. A&P's goal of promoting only from within, not having an active management-development program, and not adequately expanding in suburban markets enabled Safeway to take over the leadership in the food retailing industry.

It is possible for an organization, using relatively rational decision processes for its means, to establish what some individuals might regard as irrational goals. Of course, value judgments and the frame of reference of the parties can also play a role in such a debate. The consumer often serves as the final judge of the rationality of a business firm's action goals. W. T. Grant's goals of selling only softwares at low prices was an appropriate subgoal for increased profits before 1950. Unfortunately, Grant's realized too late that its customers wanted other merchandise and services.

The importance of this example lies in a more general idea, namely, that the types and levels of goals represent a continuous decision problem facing all organizations, whether they are business, religious, governmental, military, educational, or health institutions. Although the more general goals of the organization may not change, there is a continuing need for adjusting subgoals to changes in the task environment. The general goals of survival, growth, and profitability for a business firm remain relatively stable. But its subgoals with respect to the types of goods and services provided may show significant shifts over time. Kresge's (K-Mart) change of goods and services in the mid-1960s to capture a new type of customer, the discount shopper, is an example of a change in subgoals (see Chapter 3).

HIERARCHY-OF-GOALS FRAMEWORK

The general and formal goals presented in organizational charters, public pronouncements by executives, and annual reports may not be much help in understanding the behavior and decisions made by managers of organizations. These statements are purposely general and ignore the many informal goals members pursue.

The organization can be portrayed as a *hierarchy of goals.* Each goal may serve as a means or an end, depending on one's viewpoint. The hierarchy-of-goals framework, which is sometimes referred to as the means-end chain, provides a way to systematically link the goals of lower-level units with those of higher-level units in the organization. The goals established for each unit should direct the members' behavior and decision-making efforts in each unit.

Presumably, the goal for each lower-level unit creates a form of tunnel vision for members by directing their energies toward a limited area of activity and results. This is necessary to obtain the efficiencies in specialization of labor. The goals of a particular department are regarded as means when they represent a decision strategy a higher-level unit has chosen for attaining its own goals. From the standpoint of the members within the department or other lower-level organizational units, the same statements would be regarded as goals rather than means. All large organizations consist of numerous means-ends chains.

Application of Hierarchy-of-Goals Framework. The hierarchy-of-goals framework can be illustrated through an analysis of a large electric utility employing about 5000 individuals. (For purposes of illustration, the means-end chain is presented for only a limited number of organizational units. Figure 6.1 shows several goals of the electric utility in a means-goals (ends) staircase. That is, a goal at one level becomes a "means" for the level above, which has a new, higher goal of its own.

Taken from the company's manual, the goals in Fig. 6.1 have been abridged and are numerically illustrative rather than actual. The manual actually presents several goals at each level. As you read *down* the means-goal staircase, the goals become narrower in scope and more specific. To portray the hierarchy of goals for the entire organization, dozens of means-goal staircases would be needed. In the marketing division alone, means-goal staircases would have to be presented for (1) the Community-Development Section of the Area-Development Department, (2) Commercial Sales Department, (3) Eastern Sales Department, (4) Industrial Sales Department, and (5) the Marketing Services Department.

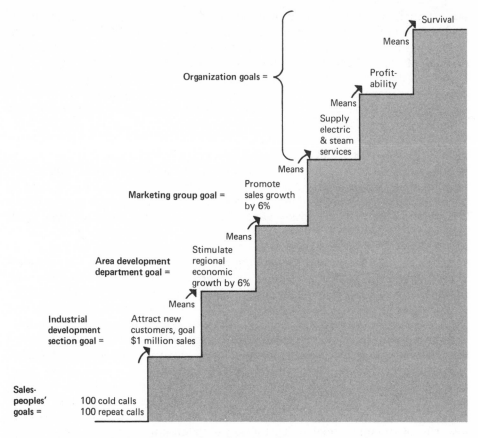

Fig. 6.1. Hierarchy of goals for part of an electric utility.

Problems with Hierarchy of Goals. The hierarchy-of-goals framework suggests that organizational decision making is an orderly, conflict-free process as long as everyone keeps to his or her goals. In this condition, goals are *not* likely to be an important contingency variable in the decision-making process. However, goals become an important contingency variable when two or more decision makers are engaged in the same decision problem but possess different goals.[6]

Management might have a goal of keeping pay increases to 7 percent, whereas the union's goal is to get 10 percent increases. The decision-making processes likely to occur under the contingency of "agreement of goals" or "disagreement over goals" are discussed in the next chapter (and Chapter 14, on conflict). Thus there are several problems and limitations to the hierarchy-of-goals framework worthy of mention.

1. *Nonacceptance of Assigned Goals.* The hierarchy-of-goals framework implies that the individuals will accept and support the goals assigned to their role or unit whenever they engage in a decision-making process. However, individuals participate in many roles, e.g., employee, parent, spouse, church

member. In each of these roles, the individual has particular goals. If conflict occurs between the goals of some of these roles, the individual cannot simultaneously satisfy all of them. One of the more dramatic illustrations of this seemed to occur when Elliot Richardson, head of the Justice Department in 1973, chose to resign rather than fire Archibald Cox (head of the special unit set up to investigate Watergate) as ordered by President Nixon.

2. *Conflicts between Units.* The means-goal staircase does not illustrate the inevitable conflicts between organizational units. The marketing unit's goal of increased sales may conflict with the production unit's goal to produce at a minimal cost per unit of output. The marketing people might decide that the way to increase sales is through a greater variety of products or lines of the same product. However, the production people, given the goals of efficiency of output, may prefer to standardize outputs and schedule long production runs to achieve the lowest unit cost.

3. *Suboptimization.* When goals are interdependent, maximization of one goal can reduce attainment of one or more of the others.[7] A student may decide to study as many hours as needed to earn all A's, a goal requiring a total commitment to long hours of study. Although this student seeks to optimize this goal, he or she may become more miserable each term, because this behavior has produced an undesirable result in terms of other personal goals. The decision to study long hours may prevent the student from attaining goals of satisfactory interpersonal relationships, recreational activities, or involvement in campus political activities. Under the assumptions made, one can conclude that the individual has suboptimized in terms of the goals of his or her *total* self.

The possibility of suboptimization is widespread in organizations with a high degree of division of labor and many different organizational units. Each organizational unit of a public utility, for example, has goals that serve as means for attaining higher-level goals. If the manager's performance is evaluated only in terms of the attainment of the goals of the work unit, his or her decisions may be influenced accordingly. For example, this may lead the area-development manager to attempt to maximize departmental interests, even though this might have adverse consequences on other departments. The area manager may want the salespeople in industrial sales to spend more time obtaining information about companies which are thinking about expanding or relocating. However, excessive attention to such activities might interfere with the salespeople's primary goal of increasing energy use by present customers.

Suboptimization can usually be avoided through strong leadership from each higher level, various management-development programs, and appropriate reward systems. These devices encourage managers to maintain a broader perspective than indicated by the narrowly defined goals of their work units. Suboptimization is not inevitable; rather, it occurs only when optimization in one part reduces *goal attainment of the whole system.*

Uncertainty

Goals and the consequences of decisions for attaining goals are usually concerned with the future. The likelihood of a particular future environment oc-

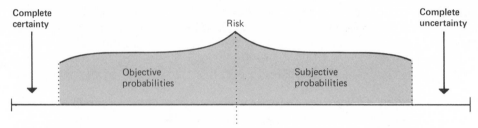

Fig. 6.2. Continuum of states of nature.

curring can vary considerably. Thus one of the contingencies influencing decisions and the decision-making process is the degree of uncertainty about the future. Decisions are made under three sets of future conditions or states of nature—certainty, risk, and uncertainty. It may be useful to think of these states of nature as lying on a continuum varying from certainty to uncertainty, as shown in Fig. 6.2. Note that the risk condition is further divided into objective probability and subjective probability.

The manager's level in the organization may be related to the likelihood of encountering decision situations with these different states of nature. Managers in the technical subsystems (e.g., foremen, machine operators, assemblers, and others concerned with actually making the product) are more likely to experience decision situations under conditions of objective and subjective probabilities. Managers in the institutional subsystem (e.g., presidents and vice-presidents) more often encounter decision situations involving states of nature under subjective probabilities and uncertainty.

CERTAINTY

This condition exists when the decision maker has complete knowledge of the results, or "payoffs," of the alternatives for solving the problem. The decision is relatively easy once a manager has identified the alternatives and the results associated with each. The manager simply chooses the one with the best results, or "payoff." If all other things are equal, for example, we would expect a purchasing manager to purchase a standard grade of paper from the supplier who offers the lowest price.

In actual practice, of course, the decision process is not quite so simple. There are usually many possible alternatives, and it would be extremely time-consuming and expensive to calculate all of them. But the manager who decides not to investigate all of the possible alternatives can never be certain that the best alternative was chosen. Decision making under certainty for the manager is probably infrequent. There are probably some decision issues, especially within the technical subsystem, that approach certainty. For example, the decision to work employees overtime who are engaged in routine tasks is likely to be done with the expectation that at least a certain number of additional units will be produced. The cost associated with this overtime can be determined with near certainty. In general, decision making under "certainty" and objective probability occurs with the more routine and repetitive decision problems facing management.

Decision making under conditions of *risk* assumes that enough information exists to predict the likelihood of different states of nature (future conditions). The amount of this information and the interpretation of it by managers can vary widely, as implied in the terms "objective probability" and "subjective probability" in Fig. 6.2.[8]

Objective Probabilities. Here the manager can assign, with relative "certainty," the probability or likelihood that each of the possible states of nature will occur. Although uncertain as to which state of nature will in fact occur, the manager may, by examining past records, be able to determine the probability, or likelihood, that a given one will occur. For example, life insurance companies are not able to determine which of their policy holders are likely to die when. However, they can often establish "objective probabilities" of how many of their policy holders, in various age and other categories, will die in a particular year. Of course, their objective probabilities are often based on the expectation that past experience will be repeated in the future.

Subjective Probabilities. A common decision situation for managers involves states of nature with subjective probabilities. In this condition, the manager assigns probabilities to the alternative states of nature on the basis of his or her belief that each will occur. Thus the probabilities assigned are often unique to the manager (another manager may assign different probabilities to the same possible states of nature). The basis for the assignment of subjective probabilities might depend on the manager's intuition, previous experience with similar decision situations, other "experts'" opinions, personality traits (such as risk taking versus risk avoidance), and other factors.

For example, what effect would a ten percent price increase have on the average amount of popcorn sold per theater customer? The decision maker might believe that there is a 30 percent chance that there would be no impact on popcorn sales, a 60 percent chance that sales would drop off by 5 percent, and a 10 percent chance that sales would drop by 10 percent. As you might expect, subjective probabilities and uncertainty are more often the state of nature for dealing with nonroutine, nonrepetitive, and complex decision problems.

UNCERTAINTY
In this condition, the manager (though possibly able to identify the various states of nature that might occur) has no information or insight to use as a basis for assigning probabilities to each state of nature. In the most extreme case of uncertainty, there may not even be a basis for speculating about the different states of nature, let alone their probability of occurrence. Dealing with uncertainty is especially central to the job of managers in the institutional subsystem.[9]

The decision by the French and British governments to collaborate on constructing a supersonic passenger plane was a major decision under conditions of uncertainty. When the plan for constructing the Concorde was announced in 1962, the estimated development cost was $150 million. By 1976 that cost had spiraled to over $2 billion. It has been decided that the first batch of 16 Concordes will be the last. At $60 million per plane, the Concorde costs about twice as much as a Boeing 747 and burns about three times as much fuel per passenger mile as the 747. It is 5 to 17 times as polluting, depending on the specific pollutant. Moreover, the noise levels and possible harm to the ozone layer remain as severe problems.[10] In short, many of the present-day concerns about the Concorde were not thought of as relevant problems in 1962 or were not expected to be problems.

Nature of the Decision Maker

Personal differences may be an important contingency, especially in states of nature involving subjective probabilities and uncertainty, which rely so much on personal perceptions and interpretations of the environment and alternatives. In Chapter 2, we discussed how differences in personal value systems can influence managers' perceptions of problems and the identification and assessment of alternatives. The role of individual differences in decision making and other issues is explored in depth in Chapter 10, which focuses on individual styles. Here we will mention one type of individual difference that appears to be important to managerial decision making—the tendency to accept or reject risk and uncertainty.

Managers willing to take risks (high–risk takers) are more likely to accept the uncertainties associated with job changes than are low–risk takers.[11] Apparently, high–risk takers open themselves up to greater gains and losses than do low–risk takers. The task environment of an organization can be uncertain and risky. A top-management group unwilling to take risks could create a problem of slow response to changes in the task environment and being continuously scooped by competitors. This situation had characterized A&P until its new president took office in 1975.

Some research also suggests that older people are "more afraid of failure and demand a surer thing, when dealing with financial risks."[12] This may be one of the reasons that some companies in rapidly changing task environments, such as IBM, now have policies requiring their top executives to "retire" at age 60 or younger.

Important decisions almost always involve a fair degree of risk to oneself and/or the organization. Individual differences with respect to risk taking might be summarized as follows. A high– or moderate–risk taker views the acceptance of risks (including uncertainty) and the opportunity to obtain rewards as being positively related to each other, up to some point. In contrast, the low-risk taker (high–risk avoider) tends to make decisions where the risk (including uncertainty) is the least. This means that the probability of the outcome is relatively great. This can also result in the risk avoider accepting the certainty of a known "loss" over the risk in decisions that could lead to great gains or larger losses.[13] For example, a risk-avoiding employee may decide not to take a new job even though his or her present job is somewhat dissatisfying and is not likely to get better. Instead, the person may decide that the present job is predictable and offers seniority protection.

Amount of Time

Managers frequently find that they have to make more decisions than they have the time to process systematically.[14] Sometimes the perceived need to make decisions quickly becomes a source of conflict between certain staff specialists and managers. The staff specialists accuse the managers of letting time pressures push them into a "crisis" style of decision making. In turn, the managers charge the staff specialists with wanting to "study decisions to death" and use elaborate techniques that take too long.[15]

Under time pressures, an individual's decision-making process may change in two fundamental ways.[16] First, the person is likely to give *greater weight to negative information.* In other words, the possible "losses" or risks from the decision are focused on more than the possible rewards are. For example, what would your decision be if you received a phone call offering you a job and telling you that you could also continue your education on a part-time basis? Most people, if given only a few hours in which to decide, would say no. If you had a month to arrive at such a decision, the outcome might still be the same, but it might well be a "closer" decision.

Second, the decision maker tends to *consider fewer aspects* or dimensions to the decision problem. The decision maker tends to redefine a complex problem as a simple one. During the 1974–75 recession, for example, many organizations had to cut back quickly on their work forces. Some managements simplified this complex problem by requiring every department to cut back by a fixed percentage. This decision ignored the possibility that some units could contribute more to overcoming the financial difficulties created by the recession or that some units were relatively more overstaffed than others. Of course, the ten percent cut-back approach may have been chosen because higher management didn't want to deal with the internal politics and power plays that would likely take place under a policy of differential treatment.

Summary

Several key contingency variables are likely to influence the nature of the decision-making process and the decisions actually reached. These contingency variables are degree of rationality, goals, degree of uncertainty, nature of the decision maker, and the amount of time available for making the decision. Of course, these contingencies are not all necessarily relevant in every decision problem. The nature of the decision and time availability may have little impact on routine decision problems for which well-defined procedures have been established.

CLASSIFICATIONS OF DECISION MODELS

The many dimensions of decision models can be classified as in this chapter, although our classifications do not exhaust the possibilities.[17] Specific decision models may be differentiated according to the classifications of purpose, degree of openness, and process. This framework provides a useful guideline for comparing differences and similarities in the decision models and should assist the manager in deciding on the decision model(s) which are most helpful in coping with various types of decision problems.

Purpose

The purpose of decision models can be classified as either normative (i.e., "what should be") or descriptive (i.e., "what is"). Managers are likely to use both. In fact, conflict may develop between a manager who is discussing the decision problem from a "normative" perspective and the other is using a "descriptive" model. Agreement on the frame of reference to be taken toward the decision problem can reduce this as a source of unnecessary conflict or confusion. Of course, this is not to imply that the parties will necessarily agree on the type of normative or descriptive model which best fits the situation.

A *normative* decision model prescribes "what should be" and how decisions should be made. The United States Constitution is a normative model; it establishes a broad framework of standards against which potential and actual decisions are to be judged. A company's plans and stated goals provide a normative framework that helps establish standards of correctness for organizational decision makers.

A *descriptive* decision model, on the other hand, explains "what is." The federal population census taken every ten years is a descriptive model of the socioeconomic characteristics of the population in the United States. A firm's income statement is also a descriptive model; it summarizes the financial affairs of the firm over a specified period of time.

Although the normative/descriptive distinction is one of the more useful ways of classifying decision models, the two types should not be regarded as polar opposites. They are simply different and tend to meet different managerial needs. Several examples of both normative and descriptive decision models will be presented in Chapter 7.

Degree of Openness

Decision models can vary in their degree of openness. Open decision models tend to be more effective when the state of nature is uncertain or involves the use of subjective probabilities. Closed decision models are often effective under conditions of certainty and objective probabilities. The use of open or closed decision models should depend on the nature of the decision problem.[18]

CLOSED DECISION MODEL
A closed decision model describes a situation in which there is a known set of alternatives and the manager selects a decision by a rational process. This model assumes that:

1. goals are predetermined and therefore are not a central part of the decision problem;
2. the decision problem is relatively simple, routine, and recurring;
3. all of the alternatives and outcomes can be determined or defined;

4. the process of analysis involves identifying and ranking all of the alternative strategies;
5. the decision maker attempts to maximize or satisfy a goal level.[19]

More frequently, decision situations at lower levels of the organization lend themselves to solution through the use of relatively closed models.

OPEN DECISION MODEL

Open decision models view the decision process and outcomes as much more uncertain. This type of decision model often assumes that:

1. goals are *not* necessarily predetermined, but may represent an important part of the decision problem;
2. the decision problem is relatively complex, nonroutine, and infrequent;
3. several parties may be involved in the decision problem, each seeking goals which are somewhat conflicting;
4. there is a lack of information about the decision problem and the likely consequences of each of the alternatives.

The decision-making processes (strategies) used in open decision models are presented in the next chapter. Open decision models are often relatively more important for managers in the organizational and institutional subsystems of the organization.

Process

The process of decision making refers to general methods or steps that are implicit or explicit in decision models. The three processes presented here are concerned primarily with "rational" decision making and represent normative processes. The third process, which incorporates the important aspects of the first two, considers the decision-making process as dynamic and ongoing.

INDUCTIVE DECISION PROCESS

The inductive process involves creating a model from which an existing outcome can be predicted. A deductive approach, by contrast, involves developing of a model to show an outcome which was not apparent from an analysis of the real world.[20] The elements and the sequential flow of the inductive decision process are summarized in Table 6.1.

Application. The intuitive use of the inductive process can be highlighted with a simplified example. Noting a decline in morale and an increase in absenteeism and turnover (observation), a manager wrestles with various alternatives and arrives at the prediction that a profit-sharing system will change these conditions (hypothesis). Because of uncertainty that this alternative will actually work, the manager decides to introduce the profit-sharing plan into only one of the firm's divisions. This division is geographically separated from the others, but engages in activities similar to those of the other divisions and has the same morale problem. The introduction of the profit-sharing system is a manipula-

Table 6.1. The inductive decision process

Elements	Explanation
Observation	Empirical observation of facts, reported events.
Hypothesis	Statement of prediction (if x is done, then y should result).
Experiment	Test through manipulation of variables.
Results	Confirm or reject hypothesis.
Theory	Statement of functional relationship among variables.

Reprinted with permission from Arthur I. Bachrach, *Psychological Research: An Introduction*, 2d ed., New York: Random House, Inc., © 1965, p. 55.

tion of the rewards provided to the employees (experiment). What happens? After some time has passed, the manager makes further observations to confirm or reject the hypothesis (results). To the manager's dismay, there has been *no improvement* in morale or rate of absenteeism and turnover. If there had been improvement, the manager could have drawn some conclusions about the relationship between profit-sharing plans (the independent variable) and morale, turnover, and absenteeism (the dependent variables). Although this approach does not meet all of the requirements of theory development, the manager would probably make decisions in terms of his or her personal experience of the situation.

DEDUCTIVE DECISION PROCESS

Why did the manager choose to test the profit-sharing plan in the first place? It could be partly due to the use of the deductive process in this decision problem. The starting point of the deductive decision process is the development of premises or assumptions. These premises indicate what should be observed under a specific set of conditions. If the expected results are not observed, the premise (theory) is considered false. In our example, the manager's deductions (premises) might include various assumptions about the nature of people and their motivations at work. Thus the manager might have assumed that: (1) employees are motivated only by money; (2) the greater their opportunity to earn money, the more they are likely to work hard and steadily; (3) greater profits can be obtained through higher commitments to work and reduced turnover and absenteeism; and (4) a profit-sharing plan should be an effective strategy for resolving these problems.

A second aspect of the deductive process is that some theories have premises that are primarily beliefs or values. These deductions cannot be tested through observations, because: (1) the state of the art precludes adequate measurements; (2) the theory is based on pure logic rather than on the "real world"; (3) the theory serves normative purposes. Nonetheless, deductive theories may be particularly useful to managers in the planning aspects of their roles. Robert Kennedy implied the usefulness of deductive theories in his statement: "Some men see things as they are and say 'Why?'; I dream of things which never were and ask 'Why not?' "

Managers and scientists typically find it useful to work back and forth between induction and deduction in decision problems. These processes should be viewed as mutually beneficial rather than competing, because both contribute to problem solutions. In addition, each process often incorporates elements of the other.

As will be seen in the next section, the processes of decision making universally *prescribed* for managers are deeply imbedded in the scientific approach. However, it is much more useful to think of part of the manager's role as that of an *applied scientist.*

DYNAMIC DECISION-MAKING PROCESS

Managerial decision making is a dynamic, ongoing process. It is not a fixed technique or a decision made at a specific point. This general, dynamic process is presented in Fig. 6.3.

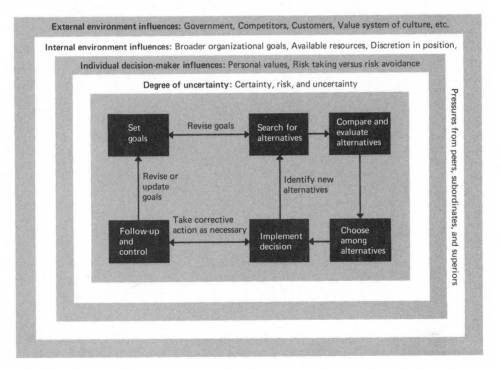

Fig. 6.3. The dynamic process of managerial decision making. (The "inner core" of this figure is adapted from *The Managerial Decision Making Process* by E. Frank Harrison. Copyright © 1975 by Houghton Mifflin Company. Reprinted by permission of the publisher.)

Four "layers" influence and surround the general decision-making process a manager might undertake. Of course, additional "layers," such as availability of time for making a decision or the presence of agreement or disagreement over the goals, could have been included as well.

The first (outer) layer consists of *external environmental influences,* e.g., government, competitors, customers, and societal values. For example, affirmative action requirements being enforced by government agencies have pressured many managements to set goals with respect to the employment of women and minority groups. The alternatives for reaching such a goal have also been influenced by expectations that firms will advertise available positions in minority-oriented newspapers, interview at women's colleges, and the like. The second layer, *internal environmental influences,* includes such factors as the broader organizational goals, the resources available for dealing with the decision problem, the amount of decision-making discretion in the position (a plant manager can't normally make unilateral changes in a collective bargaining agreement), and the pressures that might be exerted in decision problems by superiors, peers, or subordinates. The third layer of influences on the decision-making process is simply the *nature of the individual decision maker.* Thus the goals established, the alternatives identified, and the alternative chosen could be influenced by one's personal values and/or tendency toward risk taking or risk avoidance. Finally, the fourth "layer" surrounding this general decision-making process is the *degree of uncertainty* existing in the decision problem.

Of course, the relative impact of the four layers of influence will vary with the type of decision problem. The following discussion of the "core" of the process is based on Harrison.[21]

Setting Goals. The first element in this dynamic process is to set the goals to be achieved. The goals spell out the results desired—what is to be achieved by when. For example, a goal may be to reduce turnover to an annual rate of five percent within six months (the date should also be specified). Of course, the establishment of goals is itself often a major decision problem requiring a consideration of alternative goals, comparison and evaluation of alternative goals, choice of goal, etc.

Search for Alternatives. Second, alternatives that might help achieve the desired goal must be sought. This search might take the form of seeking information within and external to the organization, engaging in creative thinking, and analyzing the possible causes of the problem and courses of action (i.e., identifying alternatives). If there do not appear to be any meaningful alternatives for reaching the goal, it may be necessary to change the goal.

Compare and Evaluate Alternatives. Once the alternatives have been identified, they need to be compared and evaluated. This element in dynamic decision making attempts to zero in on the expected results (outcomes), including the relative costs of each of the alternatives. (Several of the specific techniques for undertaking the comparison and evaluation "step" are presented in Chapter 7.) Depending on the results expected, the alternatives may fall into one of four categories, as follows.

1. A *good alternative* is likely to lead to desirable results for the decision maker. The cost of implementing the alternative is expected to be less than the gains.
2. A *bland alternative* is unlikely to produce positive or negative results for the decision maker. The federal government's promotion of WIN (Whip Inflation Now) buttons and the accompanying rhetoric in 1975 was probably an example of a bland alternative for dealing with inflation.
3. A *mixed alternative* is likely to have both positive and negative results for the decision maker. For example, a manager may insist that subordinates deal in a particular way with a problem, because it is the technically best solution. The possible resentment created in the subordinates may result in their half-hearted efforts to implement the solution, thus reducing the potential "payoff" from the technically superior decision.
4. A *poor alterative* is likely to lead to negative results for the decision maker.[22] The decision by Grant's to drastically reduce credit requirements to its customers was apparently a poor alternative for stimulating sales. In 1974 alone, the company had to write off $92 million in bad debts. This decision was one of several key errors leading to the firm's bankruptcy.

Choose Among Alternatives. Decision making is popularly associated with the "act of choice." But "choice" is really only one small step in the decision-making process. Many employers complain that recent college graduates, when given a project, tend to present and discuss only one alternative. Without an explicit comparison and evaluation of alternatives, the only alternative made available to a superior is that of accepting or rejecting the choice being presented! The validity, "rationality," and limitations of a preferred choice become easier to understand and appreciate if all of the steps of the dynamic decision-making process are included in the report to a superior.

On the surface, choosing among alternatives might appear to be straightforward. Unfortunately, however, there are often difficulties in choosing among alternatives when the decision problem is complex, nonroutine, and involves high degrees of risk or uncertainty. Several of these difficulties can be summarized as follows.[23]

1. Two or more alternatives might appear *equally attractive*. This could justify further comparison and evaluation of the remaining desirable alternatives. Or, the decision maker could choose by flipping a coin.
2. If *no single alternative* is likely to meet the desired goal, it may be desirable to implement two or three of the alternatives identified. The goal of reducing turnover, for example, might be dealt with through a combination of alternatives, including changes in selection practices, compensation systems, working conditions, and managerial leadership practices.
3. The decision maker may be *confused* and *overwhelmed* in the choice element because there are too many attractive alternatives. This might require lumping like alternatives together into groups and taking a second, more intense look to compare and evaluate them.
4. There may be *no alternative* (singly or in combination) that will accomplish the desired goal. This may require a further search for alternatives or a revision in the desired goal to make it less demanding.

Implement Decision. In one sense, the "action" step of decision making begins with the implementation of the chosen alternative(s). A good decision is not necessarily a successful one. As suggested earlier, a technically outstanding decision may be offset by inadequate acceptance, especially by those individuals who must implement it. If the decision cannot be implemented, an effort should be made to identify new alternatives. We will have more to say on this in later chapters.

Follow-up and Control. Implementing the decision will not automatically lead to the desired goal. Rather, the decision maker must use various strategies and techniques to prevent and/or take corrective action if the implementation element starts to go off course.

Since many of the layers surrounding the decision process are changing, the follow-up and control phase may also indicate that there is a need to revise and update the goals. Thus the "feedback" provided in this step could pinpoint a need to reactivate the entire decision-making process.

Summary. The dynamic process of managerial decision making outlined in Fig. 6.3 is probably most useful for nonroutine, complex, one-time decision problems. These decision problems usually involve a high degree of risk and uncertainty. On the other hand, routine, recurring, and less complex decision problems may not require all of the steps set forth in Fig. 6.3. If, for example, a particular type of decision problem tends to recur often, there would be no need to repeatedly implement a search for alternatives. Most likely, a policy or procedure would be established to handle such a decision.

Summary

Several contingencies can make a difference in a manager's decision-making process. These contingencies are the degree of rationality, goals, the degree of uncertainty in the decision problem, the nature of the decision maker, and the amount of time available to make a decision.

Decision models can be classified in a variety of ways. These classification schemes are especially helpful in understanding where and when the various decision models can be used. Our classification framework of decision models includes purpose (normative versus descriptive), degree of openness (closed versus open), and process (inductive, deductive, and dynamic decision making). The dynamic decision process provides a framework for highlighting a number of influences on the decision-making process and determining which elements should be adhered to for rational decision making.

The concepts of decision making presented in this chapter should serve as a useful foundation in assisting managers "to decide how to decide." Having established the "skeleton" of decision making, our concern in the next chapter is to "flesh it out" by presenting decision models. These models are designed to serve as aids for dealing with different types of decision problems.

Discussion Questions

1. What is the difference between rationality of the decision itself and rationality of the process of decision making? If possible, identify a personal example of a situation in which the decision seemed rational, but the process of decision making did not.

2. Why can an organization sometimes expect individuals, who are limited by the concept of bounded rationality, to make reasonably "rational" decisions?

3. Develop a hierarchy-of-goals framework for yourself. Begin with the taking of this course as the lowest subgoal (means).

4. Define "suboptimization." Give an example from either your work or college experience. Is there any way by which your example could be corrected?

5. What is meant by decision making under the states of nature of uncertainty, risk, or certainty? Give a personal example of different decision problems you encountered that seemed to have been made under these three conditions.

6. How can the "nature of the decision maker" influence the decision-making process? Give one example of how "your nature" seemed to influence your decision making in an organization.

7. Use the inner core of the dynamic decision-making process presented in Fig. 6.3 to identify one desired goal and work your way through the first four "steps" in this process. You should identify at least four alternatives in the "search for alternatives step."

Management Incidents

PRESIDENTIAL DECISION MAKING*

"The biggest poker pot I ever raked in, I won with a pair of nines." The company's president paused for effect before his waiting executive group. "The point I'm trying to make is this: A sense of relative values and timing—waiting it out and hanging in there when the big chips are flying and the signals are confusing—is the key in our business, just as it is in poker. Lately we've had to call some stiff bets—extreme interest rate fluctuations, an unprecedented sales drop, and a big inventory buildup. Our stock hasn't come back like it should have, either.

"Well, what do we do?" he asked. "Do we fold and wait for the next hand? Cut the dividend? Close down the new research center? Spin off your

---

* Taken from B. Bridgewater, D. Clifford, and T. Hardy, "The Competition Game Has Changed," *Business Horizons* **18** (1975): 5–20. Reprinted by permission.

business, Al?" (This with a glare at the manager of the troubled WHIZ division, a high-technology growth business entered in the late 1960s that had consistently beaten its sales targets—and consistently lost money.)

"That might look like plain common sense under the circumstances," the president continued. "But I think we'd be damn shortsighted to take those kinds of steps. I'm convinced that we still hold winning cards. Know what's going to happen when the economy finally absorbs this last oil price increase completely, the Fed wakes up, and consumers start feeling the tax cut? Well, I'll tell you. By the end of the year, inflation's going to taper off to 5% or less, interest rates will settle back to normal, and our customers will start spending again. Now when that happens, do we want to be caught short of capacity?

"Of course we don't. If we're agreed on that, let's refigure the equity issue we planned for the fourth quarter, take another cut at the capital budget, tighten up where we can, and hold on to our cards for the next round." And so, rejecting the alternative of major strategic or structural change, the president and his executive group turned to a searching discussion of cost-reduction possibilities.

The president's metaphor is that business competition is a poker game. High stakes, a shrewd sense of his competitor's strengths, weaknesses, and likely next moves, and thoughtful management of his own resources—the common themes were there.

1. What assumptions did the president make about the states-of-nature contingency? Do you agree or disagree? Why?
2. Does the concept of bounded rationality seem to fit the president? Explain.
3. Identify the hierarchy-of-goals framework implicitly being used by the president.
4. How would you assess the president's decision making in comparison to the dynamic process of managerial decision making in Fig. 6.3?

ALCOHOLISM DECISION PROBLEM

Alcoholism is a part of business. It affects nearly ten million individuals, not including their families, friends, and employers.

The economic cost associated with misuse of alcohol in the United States is estimated at $25 billion dollars a year. Moreover, most alcoholics are involved in the work force. Accordingly, alcoholism is a part of business, and a very costly one at that.

There is strong evidence that the majority of problem drinkers in the United States are located in rather stable economic circumstances and favorable family environments. There have been attempts to use the family circle as the springboard for early identification and intervention. However, this approach has proved futile in many situations. In recent years, it has often been suggested that the "springboard" should be the workplace, with particular focus on identifying the developing problem drinker. The rationale for company involvement in this area is partially based on such findings as a strong positive correlation between problem drinking and absenteeism, medical claims, greater conflicts between fellow workers and supervisors, decreased productivity, and the like.

A number of larger organizations have been successful with programs designed to reduce the problem of alcoholism. However, even these "successes" have in no way solved the problem. Assume that you have been assigned the decision problem of developing a program to reduce the rate of problem drinkers in your company from 10 percent (present state) to five percent (desired goal) within two years.

1. How might you diagnose or assess the nature of this decision problem with respect to the following contingencies: degree of rationality, goals being pursued, degree of uncertainty in the decision problem, and nature of the decision maker?
2. How could you apply the dynamic process of managerial decision making (see Fig. 6.3) to this decision problem? What are some of the limitations in Fig. 6.3 for dealing with this type of decision problem?

REFERENCES

1. H. Simon, *Administrative Behavior: A Study of Decision-Making Processes in Administrative Organization,* 3rd ed. (New York: Free Press, 1976).

2. K. MacCrimman and R. Taylor, "Decision Making and Problem Solving," in *Handbook of Industrial and Organizational Psychology,* ed. M. Dunnette (Chicago: Rand McNally, 1976), pp. 1397–1453.

3. R. Dahl and C. Lindblom, *Politics, Economics, and Welfare* (New York: Harper & Row, 1953), p. 38.

4. W. Glueck, "Decision Making: Organization Choice," *Personnel Psychology* **27** (1974): 104–110.

5. H. Simon, *op. cit.,* pp. 38–41, 240–244.

6. C. Perrow, "The Analysis of Goals in Complex Organizations," *American Sociological Review* **25** (1961): 854–866.

7. D. Miller and M. Starr, *Executive Decision and Operations Research,* 2d ed. (Englewood Cliffs, N.J.: Prentice-Hall, 1969), p. 48.

8. For a more detailed discussion of these concepts, *see* S. Kassouf, *Normative Decision-Making* (Englewood Cliffs, N.J.: Prentice-Hall, 1970), pp. 26–29, 46–52.

9. R. Mack, *Planning on Uncertainty* (New York: Wiley-Interscience, 1971), p. 1.

10. R. Taylor, "The Concorde: Going Nowhere Fast," *MBA* **10** (1976): 55–56.

11. L. Williams, "Some Correlates of Risk Taking," *Personnel Psychology* **18** (1965): 297–309.

12. R. Ebert and T. Mitchell, *Organizational Decision Processes: Concepts and Analysis* (New York: Crusk, Russak, 1975), p. 78; *see also* V. Vroom and B. Pehl, "Relationship Between Age and Risk Taking Among Managers," *Journal of Applied Psychology* **55** (1971): 399–405.

13. E. Harrison, *The Managerial Decision-Making Process* (Boston: Houghton Mifflin, 1975), pp. 151–158; *see also* J. Dickson, "The Adoption of Innovative Proposals

As Risky Choice: A Model and Some Results," *Academy of Management Journal* **19** (1976): 291–303.

14. H. Mintzberg, *The Nature of Managerial Work* (New York: Harper & Row, 1973).

15. C. Grayson, "Management Science and Business Practice," *Harvard Business Review* **51** (1973): 41–48.

16. P. Wright, "The Harassed Decision Maker: Time Pressures, Distractions, and the Use of Evidence," *Journal of Applied Psychology* **54** (1974): 555–561.

17. Miller and Starr, *op. cit.*, pp. 145–162.

18. P. Nutt, "Models for Decision Making in Organizations and Some Contextual Variables which Stipulate Optimal Use," *Academy of Management Review* **1** (1976): 84–98.

19. M. Alexis and C. Wilson, *Organizational Decision-Making* (Englewood Cliffs, N.J.: Prentice-Hall, 1967), pp. 148–161.

20. R. Dubin, *Theory Building* (New York: Free Press, 1969), p. 9.

21. E. Harrison, *The Managerial Decision-Making Process* (Boston: Houghton Mifflin, 1975), pp. 22–40.

22. V. March and H. Simon, *Organizations* (New York: Wiley, 1958), p. 114.

23. M. Homes, *Executive Decision Making* (Homewood, Ill.: Richard D. Irwin, 1962), pp. 90–92.

7

7

Models of Decision Making

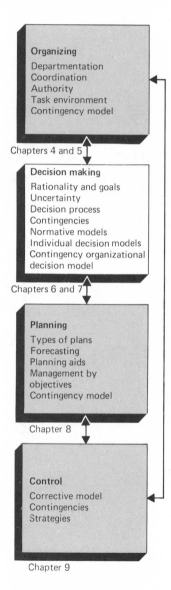

Organizing
Departmentation
Coordination
Authority
Task environment
Contingency model

Chapters 4 and 5

Decision making
Rationality and goals
Uncertainty
Decision process
Contingencies
Normative models
Individual decision models
Contingency organizational
decision model

Chapters 6 and 7

Planning
Types of plans
Forecasting
Planning aids
Management by
objectives
Contingency model

Chapter 8

Control
Corrective model
Contingencies
Strategies

Chapter 9

The objectives of this chapter are to:

develop your conceptual and technical skills in knowing when and how you can utilize the normative decision models;

develop your conceptual and human skills in the use of individual decision models for understanding and predicting how and why individuals are likely to respond to certain types of decision problems;

develop your conceptual, technical, and human skills in the use of the composite organizational decision model;

increase your conceptual skill by developing an appreciation of the differences in managerial decision situations, which can range from routine, certain, and well-defined decision problems to nonroutine, uncertain, and unstructured ones. There may also be uncertainty and/or strong disagreement between individuals over the goals to be attained.

Chapter 6 emphasized the types of contingencies that need to be diagnosed in "deciding how to decide" and that help explain why people "decide as they do" in various decision-making situations. The chapter also described several general perspectives toward decision making—*normative* (i.e., telling a decision maker how to analyze a decision problem) and *descriptive* (i.e., describing how decision makers actually make their decisions). Chapter 6 provided a basic framework of decision making. We can now use that framework to discuss specific decision models that provide concrete illustrations of the themes in Chapter 6.

Three major classes of decision models are presented in this chapter. *Normative* decision models are typically recommended for the solution of decision problems involving economic factors, such as prices to be charged and number of units to be produced. These models, which may be thought of as tools to improve the effectiveness of managerial decisions, are normative because they prescribe logical approaches for solving certain decision problems.

Individual decision models, by contrast, explain and describe some aspects of how people actually make decisions. Thus these models are descriptive rather than normative. As such, they help in understanding how and why people reach some of the decisions they do. Because individuals have different values and goals, one person's decisions may appear to be illogical and inconsistent to others.

Finally, the composite *contingency* organizational decision model focuses more on decision processes of the organization and its departments. It includes some ideas from both the normative and individual decision models and suggests a strategy of decision making that may be most effective given *different contingencies* in the *problem situation.*

NORMATIVE DECISION MODELS

Normative models prescribe how decisions should be made.[1] The models show step-by-step procedures for helping managers solve certain problems that influence goal attainment. A rough approximation of a general normative decision model was presented in Fig. 6.3. The "inner core" of this model prescribed the following elements and sequence to the decision-making process: set goals, search for alternatives, compare and evaluate alternatives, choose among alternatives, implement decision, follow up and control. In one way or another, the specific normative decision models presented here contain most of the basic elements of the "inner core" of this skeleton framework.

Normative decision models: (1) seek rationality and goal maximization by helping decision makers arrive at the one best decision (or combination of decisions); (2) assume that the goal(s) are known and agreed on, (3) assume that some degree of information about the decision problem can be provided, and (4) assume that the state of nature in the decision problem can range from certainty to subjective probabilities (high risk, which approaches uncertainty).[2] Normative decision models are most easily used when the decision problem is routine, certain, and well defined. They are likely to have limited use when (1) goals cannot be defined or agreement cannot be reached over the goals; (2) it is difficult to identify alternatives and obtain concrete information on alternatives; and (3) agreement cannot be reached on the effects of the various alternatives.[3]

Managers may derive a number of potential *benefits* from the use of normative decision models. These potential benefits can be summarized as follows:

1. A manager's informal thinking is more likely to focus on the crucial elements of a decision problem.
2. Hidden assumptions and their logical implications are more likely to be brought out into the open and made clear. This is because normative decision models require the specific identification of assumptions and the assessment of different alternatives.
3. The reasoning underlying a recommendation may be more effectively communicated. If all assumptions, alternatives, probabilities, and the like are laid out in the open, the reasons for the final recommendation should be easier to follow.
4. A manager's judgment can be improved and the area in which judgment has to be exercised might be reduced.[4] This is because there is usually a great emphasis on defining the true nature of the problem, collecting relevant information, and quantifying where possible.

As mentioned above, however, normative decision models may have limited or no use in certain types of decision problems. There are also several other *obstacles* and limitations to the use of normative decision models:

1. Only a small percentage of all managers are aware of the possibilities of such models and know how to use them successfully. Over time, the educational process should eliminate this obstacle.
2. These models can become so complex and the analysis so time-consuming that they could result in an unacceptable delay of critical decisions.
3. They may simply be less practical and economical than traditional decision-making approaches.

Based on a survey of 20 major companies utilizing normative models, Brown concluded that the development of these models appears to be far ahead of managerial application.[5] This may be partly due to inadequate technical skills on the part of many managers in the use of such models. It may also be due to the fear by some managers that the use of these models could reduce their personal power or ability to control as well as show up weaknesses in their own decision making.

Normative decision models have been developed for dealing with various decision problems. We will present only the broad outline of three common normative decision models—the break-even model, the payoff-matrix model, and the decision-tree model.

Break-Even Model

The break-even model may prove useful for decisions concerned with projecting profits, controlling expenses, and determining prices. It shows managers the basic relationships between units produced (output), dollars of sales revenue, and the resultant levels of costs and profits for an entire firm or one of its product lines. The model can be developed from historical data or from estimates. A break-even model based on historical data might be used to make year-by-year comparisons of a product line. It can also be used to determine what shifts seem to be taking place between units produced and costs per unit. A break-even model based on data estimates may be helpful as a starting point in the analysis of investment decisions.

MAJOR VARIABLES AND RELATIONSHIPS

The major variables in the break-even model include the following:

1. *Fixed costs*—those that remain constant regardless of the number of units produced. Within a limited span of time (such as one year) and output levels, the following types of costs might remain fixed: insurance premiums, real estate taxes, administrative and supervisory costs, and mortgage payments on the physical plant.
2. *Variable costs*—costs that tend to vary with changes in the number of units produced, although they do not necessarily vary proportionally for each additional unit of output. Variable costs might include direct labor, raw material, packaging, and transportation.
3. *Total costs*—the sum of the fixed and variable costs associated with different levels of production.
4. *Total revenue*—the total dollars received from sales for different numbers of units sold.
5. *Profits*—the excess of total dollar sales over total dollar costs associated with certain levels of production.
6. *Loss*—the excess of total dollar costs over the total dollar sales associated with certain levels of production.
7. *Break-even point*—the point at which total costs equal total sales. It may be expressed in terms of total dollar revenues or total units produced.

Figure 7.1 presents one type of break-even model in chart form. It shows one set of possible relationships between the seven variables explained above. The vertical axis in Fig. 7.1 represents the dollar range of sales and/or costs. The horizontal axis represents ranges in units produced (outputs). The relationships between these variables are plotted to show losses, profits, break-even point, and variable costs for various production levels.

APPLICATION

The break-even model is often a useful starting point for some types of investment decisions. In an actual case, two individuals were trying to determine whether they should open a copying service near the campus of a college. The investors were thinking of producing only Xerox copies and had collected bits and pieces of information about actual and estimated costs. The cost structure of the Xerox copies had also been determined. Thus the investors were ready to estimate: (1) the operating losses to be expected with different levels of sales; (2) the break-even point; and (3) the operating profits to be expected with different levels of sales. The required capital investment was only $3000, so the investors decided to focus on recurring costs (e.g., rent, manager's salary,

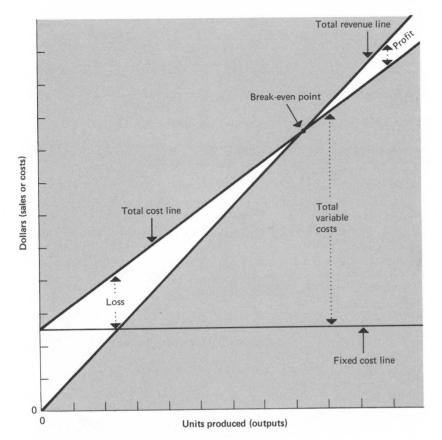

Fig. 7.1. The break-even model.

advertising, paper, lease of machine, etc.) and to exclude the capital investment from the break-even model. The data in Table 7.1 were used to develop the *monthly* break-even model.

Figure 7.2 shows a break-even model for the copy service firm. The model is based on calculations from the data in Table 7.1. There are several important things to note in the model. First, the firm will need to sell about 60,000 copies per month in order to break even. Second, the firm has high fixed costs but relatively low variable costs. The fixed costs are $2150 per month, and the variable costs range up to $1120 at 95,000 Xerox copies. After the break-even point, profits rise sharply for each additional Xerox copy sold. Since the total costs per Xerox copy sold are relatively stable, the key determinant of success is to *stimulate adequate market demand*. Placing ads in the local and student newspapers, giving introductory discounts on prices, and guaranteeing satisfaction are examples used by the firm to stimulate demand. Charging different prices or leasing the Xerox machine on different payment plans would lead to other break-even points. The estimated break-even model of the copy firm closely approximated its actual experience.

Table 7.1. Development of monthly break-even model

Fixed costs		Monthly basis
Rent (includes heat and electricity)	=	$ 250
Manager's salary and fringe benefits	=	450
Fixed part-time help: (30 hrs per mo × $2.00 per hr)	=	60
Advertising	=	150
Lease of Xerox machine (2400 model)*	=	1200
Miscellaneous supplies	=	40
Total fixed costs	=	$2150

Constant variable costs		Per Xerox copy produced
Paper (4 mills)	=	$0.004
Toner (ink) and developing fluid	=	0.002
Total	=	$0.006

Other variable costs		Per Xerox copy produced
Part-time help (needed after 40,000 copies have been produced per month)	=	$0.01

Revenue		
Estimated revenue per Xerox copy (actual prices range from 5¢ to 2¢ per copy, depending on the number of copies of a single sheet)	=	$0.045

* Lease arrangement provides for producing up to 95,000 copies at the fixed rate of $1200 per month. Beyond 95,000 copies, the lease rate is $0.006 per copy. The leasing corporation performs all services on the machine.

LIMITATIONS

Although the break-even model is a useful decision aid, there are several limitations in its application. The basic assumption that expected profits depend on various levels of units sold may be misleading. Profits are also influenced by impersonal market forces, such as changes in the price or quality of competing products. Changes in production processes (such as increased automation) or improved marketing effectiveness (such as a new television commercial that really "sells") may also influence profits. Or, a decline in general business activity might shift the relationships between the variables.

These limitations can be partially overcome by developing several break-even models, each constructed on the basis of different sets of assumptions

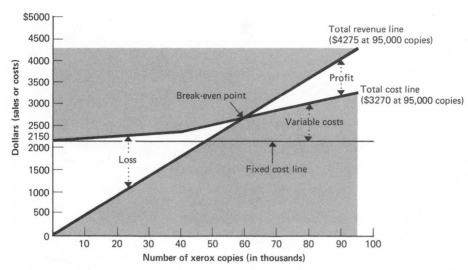

Fig. 7.2. Monthly break-even model for a copy service firm.

and estimates. A manager may still need to consider additional factors or more complex relationships than those brought out in the break-even model. Some of these will be discussed in the following sections on the payoff matrix and decision tree.

Payoff-Matrix Model

A second normative model for analyzing decision problems is the payoff matrix, a useful managerial tool for helping evaluate the alternatives in a particular decision situation.[6] The payoff matrix assumes that the decision maker is able to both identify desired goals and specify the alternatives (strategies) for dealing with the decision problems. The payoff-matrix model can be applied to many decision problems. It can help answer such questions as whether to make a long-distance call on a person-to-person or station-to-station basis, increase or decrease the price of a product, or make a particular investment.

BASIC VARIABLES AND RELATIONSHIPS

A matrix is a two-dimensional array of figures or symbols arranged in rows and columns. A symbolic payoff matrix, which assumes that the states of nature fall under the categories of subjective or objective probabilities, is shown in Table 7.2. The basic variables in the payoff-matrix model are defined as follows.

1. *Strategies (S)*—the alternative decisions that might be made or followed. They are shown symbolically in Table 7.2 as $S_1, S_2, S_3 \ldots, S_n$. In the previous example, the different prices to charge for Xerox copies might represent the alternative strategies.

Table 7.2. Symbolic payoff matrix

Strategies (alternatives)	Possible states of nature				
	N_1	N_2	N_3	$\ldots$	N_m
	Probability that each state of nature will occur				
	P_1	P_2	P_3	$\ldots$	P_m
S_1	O_{11}	O_{12}	O_{13}	$\ldots$	O_{1m}
S_2	O_{21}	O_{22}	O_{23}	$\ldots$	O_{2m}
S_3	O_{31}	O_{32}	O_{33}	$\ldots$	O_{3m}
.	.	.	.		.
.	.	.	.		.
.	.	.	.		.
S_n	O_{n1}	O_{n2}	O_{n3}	$\ldots$	O_{nm}

2. *States of nature (N)*—the future set of conditions that could prevail in the environment and are relevant to the decision problem. They are shown symbolically in Table 7.2 as $N_1, N_2, N_3 \ldots, N_m$. As related to the previous example, they could refer to different levels of expected market demand for Xerox copies.

3. *Probability (P)*—the likelihood that each state of nature will occur. The sum of the probabilities must always equal 1.0. It is always assumed one of the alternative states of nature will occur. A matrix with four states of nature could have probabilities of 0.1, 0.2, 0.2, and 0.5 (equals 1.0). The symbolic payoff matrix in Table 7.2 assumes that the decision is to be made under conditions of risk, which can involve either objective or subjective probabilities. States of nature could also involve certainty or uncertainty. If certainty were the condition, the payoff matrix would show only one state of nature. If uncertainty were the case, the payoff matrix would not show any probabilities with the possible states of nature. The probabilities are shown symbolically in the model as $P_1, P_2, P_3 \ldots, P_m$.

4. *Outcome (O)*—the "payoff" that can be expected for each possible combination of strategy and state of nature. A payoff can be either a profit or loss. For example, O_{11} in Table 7.2 shows the outcome, or payoff, if the first state of nature (N_1) did occur and the first strategy (S_1) was chosen. Thus each such outcome is labeled a *conditional value*.

STATES OF NATURE

Certainty Condition. In making a choice from the available strategies under conditions of certainty, only a part of the typical payoff matrix is needed, because the future is known. Table 7.3 shows a payoff matrix under certainty. A manager would simply need to identify the strategy that provides the most

Table 7.3. Payoff matrix under certainty

Strategies	State of nature (N_1)		Example
S_1	O_{11}	=	\$1000 profit
S_2	O_{21}	=	\$ 900 profit
S_3	O_{31}	=	\$2000 profit

favorable outcome ("payoff"). In Table 7.3, three strategies are possible, each yielding a different total profit. Since strategy S_3 yields the highest profit, it should be selected.

Risk Condition. The payoff matrix is most useful under conditions of risk (either objective or subjective probabilities). To work toward a decision when the matrix consists of two or more states of nature, one must calculate the expected values for each strategy. *Expected values* provide a "weighted" average outcome for each strategy. The expected value for each strategy is the sum of all outcomes (conditional values) after they have been multiplied by their probability of occurrence. For example, the symbolic expected values for the payoff matrix in Table 7.2 can be presented as follows (where EV = expected value):

$$EV_1 = P_1O_{11} + P_2O_{12} + P_3O_{13} \ldots P_mO_{1m}$$
$$EV_2 = P_1O_{21} + P_2O_{22} + P_3O_{23} \ldots P_mO_{2m}$$
$$EV_3 = P_1O_{31} + P_2O_{32} + P_3O_{33} \ldots P_mO_{3m}$$

$$\cdot \qquad \cdot \qquad \cdot \qquad \cdot \qquad \cdot$$
$$\cdot \qquad \cdot \qquad \cdot \qquad \cdot \qquad \cdot$$
$$\cdot \qquad \cdot \qquad \cdot \qquad \cdot \qquad \cdot$$

$$EV_n = P_1O_{n1} + P_2O_{n2} + P_3O_{n3} \ldots P_mO_{nm}.$$

APPLICATION

Let us assume that the president of a university is trying to decide how many seats to add to the football stadium. The information available and assumptions established are as follows:

1. All of the seats at most of the games during the past two years have been occupied.
2. If more seats had been available, additional tickets could have been sold.
3. The president and administrative staff believe that the football team should be good, if not excellent, during the next two or three years, because of the many first-team sophomores and juniors.
4. A modular seating system has been decided on because of its low cost

and excellent quality. The modular system being considered comes in package units of 4000 seats.

5. Moderate increases (4 percent per year) are anticipated in the student population of 30,000 and the local town population of 100,000. The town is located 30 miles from a major metropolitan area.

Based on the factors above, the president has decided to consider four strategies and has developed estimates of subjective probabilities for four levels of demand for additional seats (states of nature). It has been determined that the total costs associated with each module of new seats (4000 seats) will be $10 per seat per year during the period chosen to pay for the construction costs. The maximum potential revenue per season will total $25 per seat.

Calculating Conditional Values. The outcome, or conditional value, for the first year can be determined for each strategy and state-of-nature combination by using the following equation:

$$CV = (R \times Q_D) - (C \times Q_C),$$

where CV = conditional value, R = revenue per seat, Q_D = quantity of seats demanded, C = total costs per seat, and Q_C = quantity of seats constructed. Thus if 4000 seats are demanded (Q_D) and 4000 seats are constructed (Q_C), the equation can be applied as follows:

$$CV = (\$25 \times 4000) - (\$10 \times 4000)$$
$$CV = \$100,000 - \$40,000$$
$$CV = \$60,000 \text{ (profit)}.$$

On the other hand, if 16,000 seats were constructed (Q_C) and only 4000 seats were demanded (Q_D), there would be a loss of $60,000. For this situation, the equation can be applied as follows:

$$CV = (\$25 \times 4000) - (\$10 \times 16,000)$$
$$CV = \$100,000 - \$160,000$$
$$CV = -\$60,000 \text{ (loss)}.$$

The conditional values show what would happen *if* each demand and seat expansion combination did occur. The conditional values for each possible combination are presented in Table 7.4. Note that there is *no* consideration of the probabilities associated with the states of nature (different possible demands). The calculations are also based on the fact that the effective demand for each strategy cannot exceed the number of seats constructed.

Calculating Expected Values. Table 7.5 shows four levels of demand for seats and the corresponding subjective probabilities assigned by the president. The president believes that there is a 50 percent probability that 4000 seats will be demanded, but only a 5 percent probability that 16,000 seats will be demanded.

From the information contained in Tables 7.4 and 7.5, we can develop the expected value matrix by multiplying each conditional value by the probability of occurrence assigned to each state of nature. For example, the expected

Table 7.4. Conditional values for stadium-expansion decision (in $ thousands)

Seats constructed	States of nature (demand for seats)			
	4,000	8,000	12,000	16,000
4,000	$ 60	$ 60	$ 60	$ 60
8,000	20	120	120	120
12,000	−20	80	180	180
16,000	−60	40	140	240

Table 7.5. Possible demand for stadium seats

Seats demanded	Probability of demand
4,000	0.50
8,000	0.30
12,000	0.15
16,000	0.05
	1.00

Table 7.6. Expected values for stadium-expansion decision (in $ thousands)

Strategies	States of nature (seats demanded)				Total expected value (in thousands)
	4,000	8,000	12,000	16,000	
Seats constructed	Probability of demand				
	0.50	0.30	0.15	0.05	
4,000	$ 30	$18	$ 8	$ 3	$59
8,000	10	36	18	6	70
12,000	−10	24	27	9	50
16,000	−30	12	21	20	23

value for constructing 4000 stadium seats and having a demand of 4000 seats would be determined as follows:

$$EV = CV_{4000} \times P_{4000}$$
$$EV = \$40,000 \times 0.50$$
$$EV = \$20,000$$

The expected value for each of the other combinations is shown in Table 7.6. The expected value for constructing 8000 seats is $70,000. Given the information and assumptions in this problem, the optimum solution would be to construct 8000 seats.

EFFECTS OF DECISION MAKERS

Under conditions of subjective probabilities, the nature of decision makers can strongly influence the results from the payoff-matrix model. Three factors in the actual behavior of individuals under conditions of subjective probabilities (risk) and uncertainty are especially important. First, decision makers' perceptions and attitudes toward the conditions of risk and uncertainty can vary.[7] As mentioned in Chapter 6, decision makers who are high–risk takers may assign higher probabilities to certain states of nature than low–risk takers. Second, perceptions of risk can vary over time for a particular decision maker. A decision maker's preference for risk may lessen with age. Third, managers are generally "biased" toward conservatism (low–risk taking).[8] Managers seem to give too much weight to the most negative consequences (highest potential loss) of each strategy. Although this approach may be effective in avoiding great losses, it typically precludes the possibility of great gains as well, because high–risk decisions frequently have high potential payoff.

Decision-Tree Model

The decision-tree model may be more useful than the payoff-matrix model under certain conditions, especially if a sequence of decisions must be considered to analyze the initial decision problem. The decision-tree model is useful when a decision problem can be broken down into a sequence of logically ordered smaller problems. The solutions to the smaller problems can then be combined to provide a solution to the larger decision problem.

For relatively simple problems, the decision-tree model may be unnecessary. Its use is frequently appropriate for complex decision problems that have significant financial implications. These may include decision problems in marketing, investment in research, pricing, plant expansion, and new ventures or acquisitions. In short, the decision tree is an effective tool for assessing choices, risks, objectives, and monetary gains.[9] It highlights the interactions among future decision strategies, possible states of nature, and present decision strategies.

BASIC VARIABLES AND RELATIONSHIPS

Although the number of calculations and branches on a decision tree can become complex, the really critical elements in its construction are the assumptions and probabilities from which the payoffs are developed. The basic variables and steps in the development of a decision tree are summarized as follows.

1. The *skeleton, or framework,* of the decision tree first needs to be developed. The skeleton is made up of *nodes* (represented by small circles and rectangles) and *lines* that indicate connections between the nodes. The nodes may represent: (a) a decision choice that may be taken, (b) an outcome (event) from an action that is taken, and possibly (c) the probabilities of the various states of nature. Then, each of the outcomes is linked to a subsequent action. Through this process, every "reasonable" alternative course of action is considered and followed to its conclusion.

2. The *various probabilities* and/or other data are entered in the appropriate places. For example, the probabilities are often entered adjacent to event (outcome) nodes.

3. The *"optimal" course of action* is determined by an analysis of the decision tree.[10]

APPLICATION

The president and staff of Emperor Products Corporation, a medium-sized electronics-component manufacturer, were trying to decide whether to increase the current production output of one of Emperor's products by installing an additional semiautomatic machine or by putting its employees on overtime.[11]

One-Year Decision Tree. After much discussion, they agreed that there was a 0.60 subjective probability that sales would increase 20 percent and a 0.40 subjective probability that sales would drop by as much as 5 percent. After developing figures on the dollar consequences for only the next year, they reached the following conclusions:

1. *Strategies*—overtime versus one new unit of equipment;
2. *States of nature*—sales rise (0.60 probability) versus sales drop (0.40 probability);
3. *Net cash flow*—the net cash-flow implications of the alternative strategies are shown below:

Strategies	Cash flow	
	New equipment	Overtime
1. 20% sales rise	+$460,000	+$440,000
2. 5% sales drop	+$340,000	+$380,000

A simple decision tree was constructed to take into account the probabilities of the two events (Fig. 7.3). The decision tree suggests that the expected payout would be $416,000 for the overtime alternative and $412,000 for the new-equipment alternative. At this point, the "best" decision appears to be the overtime alternative.

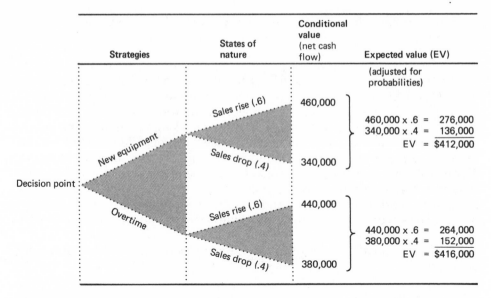

Fig. 7.3. One-year decision tree: new-equipment decision.

Two-Year Decision Tree. The executives decided to further evaluate their apparently "best" alternative (strategy) by extending the decision-tree model another year. After extensive discussion, they concluded that the longer-term prospects for the product in question were excellent. Accordingly, they worked out the following probabilities:

1. If sales did drop 5 percent the first year, there was a 0.80 subjective probability that they would increase 20 percent in the second year and a 0.20 probability that sales would increase by only 10 percent.
2. If sales rose by 20 percent in the first year, they expected a 0.50 probability that second-year sales would increase 20 percent and a 0.50 probability that sales would increase by 10 percent.

Based on these probabilities, they worked out a two-year decision tree (Fig. 7.4). By working backward in the decision tree from right to left, we can compute the expected cash flow for the entire two-year period. The expected values (cash flows) may be calculated for each state of nature and related to each strategy. The decision tree can also be reduced and simplified by using only the highest value at each strategy node. The executives followed this process and discovered that over the two-year period, it would be advantageous to purchase a new unit of equipment now. You can determine the relative wisdom of this choice by using Fig. 7.4 and following the procedures outlined above.

Summary

So far we have highlighted three specific normative decision models. These models prescribe step-by-step procedures for analyzing certain types of decision problems. These models should be viewed as aids rather than as sub-

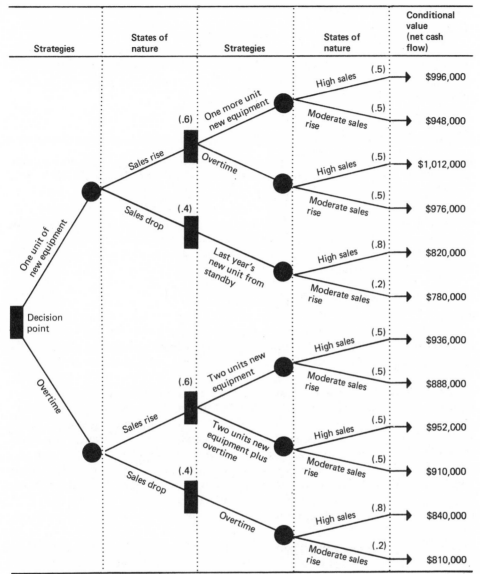

Fig. 7.4. Two-year decision tree: new-equipment decision. (E. A. McCreary, "How to Grow a Decision Tree," *Think Magazine*, April 1967. Reprinted by permission from *Think Magazine*, published by IBM, copyright 1967 by International Business Machines Corporation.)

stitutes for managerial judgments. Normative models often depend on the formulation of managerial judgments, such as the goal(s) to be attained, the specification of the problems, the assumptions made, and the probabilities used.

Normative decision models emphasize how decision makers ought to approach problems. We now turn to *descriptive* models, which focus on the processes and forces which help explain the "what is" of decision making. Three such descriptive models are the adaptation decision model, the inequity decision model, and the heuristic decision model.

Adaptation Decision Model

The adaptation decision model provides a way of explaining how individuals modify their goals as a consequence of their experiences.[12] The processes in this model frequently occur without the individual's being consciously aware of them. In Chapter 3, this model was illustrated in the discussion of how a student's grade goals might change over time, depending on the grades actually achieved. We suggested that when the actual grades exceeded the student's grade goals, the grade goals would rise. When actual grades were less than the goals, grade goals would tend to decline.

BASIC VARIABLES AND RELATIONSHIPS

Figure 7.5 summarizes the variables and processes in the adaptation decision model. This model identifies three distinct time periods through which the decision maker passes. The continual feedback loops suggest that adjustments can occur in both goals and alternatives.

Period 1. The decision maker is assumed to possess some type of goal hierarchy, which may consist of action goals. The stimulus for action is the gap, or difference, in the individual's experience and goals—the difference between "what is" and what the individual wants "to be." Because of this difference, the decision maker generates and analyzes alternatives that might reduce this gap. As suggested by the concept of bounded rationality, the generation of alternative courses of action to reduce this difference is likely to be quite limited, continuing only until the decision maker finds a satisfactory alternative. Thus the alternative chosen may not actually represent the maximum, or optimal, alternative.

Period 2. Next, the decision maker begins to compare the alternative courses of action, using a subjective process to determine the relative advantages and disadvantages of each alternative. One of the alternatives is tried, and the outcome of the alternative is determined.

The value (importance) of the outcome is also determined subjectively. Two individuals may experience the same objective outcome, such as a 10 percent increase in salary, but its value may vary for each individual. One individual may be very materialistic and value money highly, whereas the other may be quite happy with fewer material goods.

Period 3. This is a critical time period, because the individual may engage in adaptive decision making by considering additional goals and alternatives.

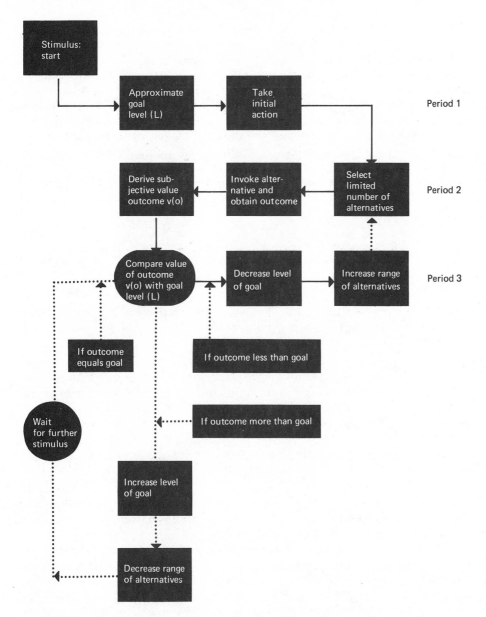

Fig. 7.5. Adaptation decision model. (Adapted by permission from M. Alexis and C. Z. Wilson, *Organizational Decision-Making,* Englewood Cliffs, N.J.: Prentice-Hall, 1967, p. 160.)

During this period the individual compares the value of the outcome with the established goal level.

Over the long run, a person's decision making takes one of three courses. If the outcome is about equal to the goal level, the decision maker would be satisfied and would simply wait for further stimulus. If the outcome is greater than the goal level set, the decision maker might begin to increase the goal level and decrease the number of alternatives considered. In other words, if the alternative gets what is desired and more, the individual has little motivation or incentive for generating other alternatives. Finally, if the outcome is less than the goal level, the individual is likely to experience disappointment. Initially, the decision maker might even try the same alternative again and raise the goal level. If this is not effective, the decision maker, over the long run, is likely to reduce his or her goal level, thereby increasing the likelihood of considering more alternatives. In sum, the adaptation decision model focuses on the sequence of decisions that may result from the perception of a problem (problematic stimulus) and the process by which individuals adjust their goals.

APPLICATION

One of the authors was once involved in the establishment of firms which provided Xerox copies at relatively low prices. The adaptation decision model can be applied in this situation.

Period 1. The initial stimulus was a felt gap between present income and desired income. The author considered a number of investment alternatives and their widely varying risks and payoff possibilities.

Period 2. Your author, along with a partner, decided to establish a firm to provide low-cost Xerox copies near the campus of a large university. Several key factors led to this decision: (1) the potential for a large payoff relative to the small investment needed; (2) the ability to control losses and to know that the largest losses possible should the firm fail would not be exorbitant; and (3) the initial market advantage of providing Xerox copies at half the price asked by the university, with no other private competition in the community.

Period 3. The month-by-month sales and profit increases were greater than the preestablished goal levels of the partners. As the months passed, therefore, they redefined acceptable levels of sales and profits.

After about a year, a new alternative emerged. The partners decided to branch out by establishing another copy firm in a different city. Although several locations were considered, the partners did not really evaluate alternative types of investment possibilities. They opened their new outlet next to a large university in another city. This appeared to be a low-risk decision, since there were so many similarities with their first investment situation.

Unfortunately, the outcome was much less than the partners' desired goal level. Within one month, two other private competitors established similar firms. The next several months were traumatic for the two partners. Drastic price cutting to drive out the competition was pointless; the partners knew that market demand was insufficient to support three private copy firms. After several months, the partners closed the outlet, since they were far from reaching the needed break-even point. The partners decreased their goal level to that of operating their one outlet at a profit. Since this experience, they have not even thought of opening another outlet.

Inequity Decision Model[13]

The inequity decision model provides managers with a framework for understanding and predicting behavior of employees in such areas as motivation, individual performance, and compensation systems. It provides a *partial* explanation for individuals' decisions and actions as a consequence of perceiving conditions of equity (justice) or inequity (injustice).[14] Problems of inequity can arise in any situation involving a direct relationship and comparison between two or more individuals, e.g., subordinate and superior, worker and coworker, husband and wife, teacher and student, girlfriend and boyfriend. When two individuals exchange something, one or both of them may perceive the exchange as inequitable. The inequity decision model holds that an individual who perceives an inequity in comparison with other individuals will be motivated to reduce that inequity. The greater the perceived inequity, the greater the motivation to undertake decision making and actions to reduce it.

BASIC VARIABLES AND RELATIONSHIPS
There are six basic variables in the inequity decision model.

1. *Inputs*—the contributions each individual perceives as bringing to the exchange relationship. The following types of variables may be relevant inputs in the employment situation, for example: education, intelligence, experience, seniority, age, sex, level of responsibility, hazards, physical and mental effort required, personal appearance, and health.

2. *Outcomes*—the benefits or rewards an individual receives in an exchange relationship. In the employment setting, common outcomes are salary, stock options, seniority benefits, fringe benefits (retirement and sick pay), opportunity for advancement, interesting work, safe and comfortable working conditions, and status symbols, e.g., a larger office, better desk, and impressive title.

3. *Recognition*—the acknowledgment of the inputs and outcomes considered as part of the exchange relationship. Difficulties can arise in exchange relationships because the individuals, often subconsciously, are not in agreement on the factors to be included as inputs and outcomes. New workers may feel that current performance should be the only factor given a heavy weighting in pay increase decisions, whereas older workers may feel that seniority should be the primary input factor.

4. *Relevance*—the significance assigned to inputs and outcomes by the parties in the exchange relationship. For example, two individuals might recognize an input factor but give different weights to its significance. Thus younger workers might believe that current performance should be given a 70 percent weight in pay-increase decisions and seniority only 30 percent; older workers may reverse the importance given to these two inputs.

5. *Person*—any individual (or group) for whom equity or inequity exists.

6. *Other*—any individual (or group) used as a reference point for making comparisons with a person's inputs and outcomes. Some "other" groups are firefighters versus policemen, plumbers versus electricians, rubber workers versus auto workers, males versus females, and blacks versus whites.

MODEL

The inequity decision model is shown below. Inequity exists whenever a person perceives that the ratio of his or her outcomes or inputs is unequal to the ratio of outcomes to inputs of some other person or group. This can occur when two individuals are in a direct-exchange relationship or when both are in an exchange relationship with a third party.

$$\frac{\text{Outcomes}_P}{\text{Inputs}_P} \quad < : \quad \frac{\text{Outcomes}_O}{\text{Inputs}_O},$$

where P = person, O = other, : = proportional, < = less than, — = divided by.

The inequity decision model emphasizes the decision process involved in evaluating and reacting to an individual's (Person) perception of his or her inputs and outcomes relative to those of somebody else (Other). Inequity is always a relative matter and exists if the outcomes divided by the inputs for Person are not proportional to the outcomes divided by the inputs for Other, as perceived by Person.

APPLICATIONS

Let's consider two hypothetical examples under conditions of inequity and equity, respectively. We will also assume that Person can assign numerical values to all of the variables making up the outcome and inputs. Person perceives that her weekly salary of $200 (outcome) is extremely low relative to her education, experience, and responsibilities (inputs). Similarly, she perceives that the $300 weekly salary paid to a new organizational member who has no experience and fewer responsibilities is too high. Thus an inequity exists:

$$\frac{200_P}{400_P} \quad < : \quad \frac{300_O}{150_O}$$

$$1/2 \quad < : \quad 2.$$

Now suppose that Person perceives her outcomes as reasonable, in proportion to her inputs, and perceives the outcomes of Other as being similarly reasonable, relative to Other's inputs, even though Other's outcomes are twice as great as Person's outcomes. This condition of equity might occur if a superior has more experience and job responsibilities (inputs) than a subordinate does. This condition can be described as follows:

$$\frac{200_P}{200_P} \quad : \quad \frac{400_O}{400_O}$$

$$1 \quad : \quad 1$$

Person's values, attitudes, and group memberships are important factors that influence his or her perception of the existence and intensity of the inequity. The perception of inequity usually motivates the individual to reduce it. The strength of motivation depends on the amount of inequity perceived.

DECISIONS AND ACTIONS FOR REDUCING INEQUITY

From a decision-making perspective, a key question is how to reduce inequity. Bear in mind, however, that the strength of the available empirical evidence for all means of reducing inequity varies considerably.[15] Some of the means available for reducing inequity are the following.

1. *Increase inputs.* John may increase his inputs when they are inadequate compared to Barbara's inputs. This could occur if John and Barbara were receiving the same pay, but Barbara was producing much more than John. John might decrease the perceived inequity by increasing his effort to achieve greater equality or quantity of output.

2. *Increase outcomes.* John may try to increase his outcomes if they are low in relation to Barbara's outcomes and to his own inputs. If John's pay is low compared to Barbara's and her inputs, the inequity could be reduced through a wage increase.

The attempt to increase outcomes was apparently one of the factors contributing to the long strike in 1976 by the rubber workers in the tire industry. The rubber workers contended that the equity relationships between them and the auto workers had been lost over the previous three years. The rubber workers felt that they needed a substantial pay increase to reestablish an equitable relationship between them and the auto workers.

3. *Leave the situation.* When John perceives inequity of any type, his decision may be to simply "leave the field" or situation. Thus he might quit his job (turnover), obtain a transfer, or be absent frequently. In a study of 900 hourly workers employed in ten shops of a branch of Boeing, for example, there were greater perceptions of inequity in the four high-turnover shops than in the six low-turnover shops.[16]

4. *Distort the situation.* John may increase or decrease his inputs and outcomes through psychological distortion or rationalization. Distortion is most likely to occur with respect to the degree of personal significance attached to each of the inputs and outcomes, but as a means of reducing inequity, it is likely to "work" only up to some threshold level. Distortion might occur if John feels inequitably treated when Barbara received the promotion to manager that he felt was rightfully his. Over time John may convince himself that the responsibilities (inputs) required in the job really aren't worth the rewards (outcomes): "Who wants all the hassle" or "Life's too short to have to put up with all of that" or "I would have had to give up too much of my time with my family. It's not worth it."

SOME MANAGEMENT IMPLICATIONS

First, the inequity decision model provides a relatively simple way of explaining and predicting an employee's feelings and reactions toward various organizational rewards. Managers must be concerned with the level *and* the perceived equity in the distribution of rewards, such as pay, fringe benefits, promotions, and status symbols. Second, the model cautions managers to be aware of the relevant "Other" that an individual or group uses as a basis for comparisons. Third, the inequity decision model suggests that managers should consider how different combinations of rewards can have an additive effect on the total perceived outcomes, as well as which rewards can be substituted for others. Finally, as managers make organizational changes, they should try to achieve some type of balance between inputs and outcomes that are considered valid by the employees.[17] For example, some companies offer employees a large package of benefits from which to choose. Younger employees might select generous hospital benefits and vacation time in the summer, whereas older employees might choose to put more money in pension plans and various stock-option alternatives.

Heuristic Decision Model

The adaptation and inequity decision models explain some personal decision processes and the consequences of certain experiences on decisions and behavior. In contrast, the heuristic decision model helps to explain how individuals can and do deal with unstructured decision problems (such as how to meet long-term energy needs).

The heuristic decision model refers to sophisticated "trial-and-error" approaches that rely heavily on the knowledge and judgment of the individual decision maker. More formally, "heuristic is a cue, technique, or rule that reduces search for a solution and/or offers a novel insight into the problem area. Heuristics illuminate or expose promising paths to solutions; for example, 'when in doubt, punt' is a heuristic."[18] Although a heuristic is intended to aid in the solution of a problem, there is no guarantee that it will do so.[19]

RELATION TO PROBLEM STRUCTURE

Heuristics can be used in one or more of the following stages of solving relatively unstructured problems: (1) searching for ways to help find or define the problem; (2) searching for ways to help structure the problem to make it solvable; (3) finding ways to generate the most likely alternative solutions; and (4) finding ways for gathering and interpreting information based on one's experiences.[20]

Highly structured decision problems can be defined quantitatively and solved by computational techniques. Unstructured problems, on the other hand, are difficult to solve because: (1) the key variables in the problem are symbolic or verbal rather than numerical (such as deciding who would make the best vice-president of production); (2) the goals to be obtained are often vague and stated nonquantitatively (such as deciding what the firm's social responsibilities are); and (3) for many practical problems, adequate computational techniques are simply not available.[21]

The degree of problem structure for managers and workers often varies according to their level in the organization.[22] For example, when alternatives are "objective" and ready-made, as might occur for machine operators and shift foremen, a high problem structure exists. As organizational level rises to department foremen, division superintendents, and plant managers, alternatives become more subjective and personal, i.e., constructed by the manager.

In certain types of organizational units, such as research and development or marketing research, however, classification by problem structure may be inadequate, because the professional employees located low in the formal hierarchy may be dealing with problems that have little structure. For example, market researchers attempting to anticipate consumers' preferences five years from now are dealing with a low-structured decision problem.

SOME HEURISTIC APPROACHES

Heuristics often provide partial solutions and guesses to problems rather than optimal or even satisfactory solutions. These approaches can be used in one or more stages of the decision-making process (such as definition of goals or identification of alternatives).[23] Heuristic approaches frequently employed by managers in organizations include hierarchy of goals (means-end analysis), planning, and the use of analogies.[24]

Hierarchy of Goals. The hierarchy-of-goals approach, presented in Chapter 6 (see Fig. 6.1), involves: (1) making a judgment as to the general goal to be achieved; (2) searching for a set of general means for accomplishing the goal; (3) using each of these means for achieving these subgoals; (4) etc.[25]

Planning. Planning involves creating a future course of action to accomplish goals for tomorrow. A variety of heuristic techniques (such as Management by Objectives) can be used in planning. Planning, a key part of the managerial process, is explored in Chapter 8.

Analogies. Analogies are one set of the many heuristic approaches used for creatively dealing with low-structured problems.[26] Personal, symbolic, or direct analogies, used in creative decision making, make the "familiar strange" and the "strange familiar."[27]

In the *personal-analogy* approach, the person attempts to find personal significance in the problem. For example, in considering a new pay policy, management may try to assess some impacts by pretending to be the employees who will be affected by it. The *direct-analogy* approach, by contrast, involves the comparison of parallel situations. For example, an organization is analogous to a person in that both have goals, inputs, outputs, equilibrium states, etc. Alexander Graham Bell used direct analogy by studying the human ear when he invented the telephone. The *symbolic-analogy* approach involves abstract reasoning and relationships. A number of scientific insights have been stimulated through symbolic analogies. Thus radio waves have been made analogous to the waves on the ocean, and solar winds have been made analogous to the movement of hydrogen atoms through space.[28]

In sum, the heuristic decision model refers to the various approaches and techniques used by individuals to deal with decision problems that are nonroutine and unstructured. Thus there is considerable concern with the application of individual judgment, intuition, and past experience to the decision problems.

Summary

The adaptation, inequity, and heuristic decision models are only three of the many ways for describing and explaining individual decision making. Each of these models focuses on a particular aspect of individual decision making and should be interpreted and evaluated in terms of its limited goals. Each of these models should be relevant to managers for understanding their own and other people's decision processes.

CONTINGENCY ORGANIZATIONAL DECISION MODEL

The organizational decision model provides a third major way of understanding the broad, complex subject of decision making. Our interest in organizational decision making is threefold: (1) to examine several of the major decision contingencies which can confront organizations and their subunits; (2) to present the major decision-making strategies that may be appropriate under different contingencies; and (3) to identify the types of organizational structures that may be effective for coping with these decision contingencies.

The organizational decision model presented here is closely related to the contingency model of organizational design developed in Chapter 5. Both models are concerned with the degree of uncertainty in a decision problem. A highly structured decision problem involves certainty, or low risk; a low-structured one involves high risk and uncertainty. The organizational decision model presented here considers *any* general type of decision problem, whereas the model presented in Chapter 5 focused only on organizational *design* decisions. Moreover, the model here is somewhat more complex, because it considers the possibilities that the organizational decision makers will have different goals and/or beliefs about cause-and-effect relationships. The organizational decision model helps managers to determine the decision strategy that is likely to be effective under different contingencies.[29]

Contingency Variables

The contingency organizational decision model is based on the interaction of two basic contingency variables—beliefs about causation and goal preferences.

BELIEFS ABOUT CAUSATION

This variable refers to the amount of agreement or disagreement between two or more individuals (managers or other) as to the cause-and-effect relationships of past, present, or future actions. This variable can be thought of as a con-

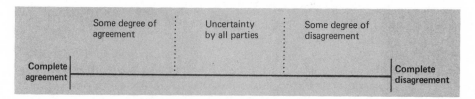

Fig. 7.6. Continuum of beliefs about causation.

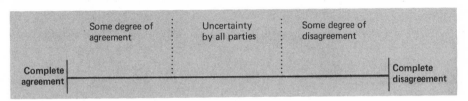

Fig. 7.7. Continuum of goal preferences.

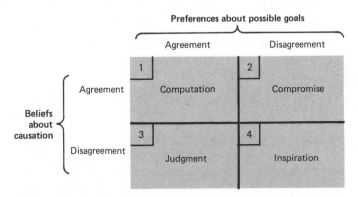

Fig. 7.8. Contingency organizational decision model.
(Adapted by permission from J. Thompson, "Decision
Making, the Firm, and the Market," in W. Cooper *et al.*,
eds., *New Perspectives in Organizational Research*, New
York: Wiley, 1964.)

tinuum, ranging from complete agreement to complete disagreement between
the parties as to the perceived cause-effect relationships in a decision problem.
Although atypical in organizational settings, it is possible that none of the parties involved in a decision problem will hold any beliefs about causation. These
ideas are suggested in Fig. 7.6.

Disagreement over beliefs about causation may be illustrated by a marketing problem. Sales managers may contend that more of the marketing budget
should go into hiring additional salespersons so as to increase sales. In contrast,
the advertising and promotional managers may claim that sales could be improved by using more of the marketing budget in media advertising and other
promotional approaches.

PREFERENCES ABOUT POSSIBLE GOALS
The second basic contingency variable is the preferences (priorities) by the par-
ties toward possible goals. This variable too forms a continuum, as shown in
Fig. 7.7, ranging from complete agreement to complete disagreement.

Decision Model

By cross-classifying the variable of causation and goal preference, we can assemble the contingency organizational decision model. The four cells in Fig. 7.8

show four major types of decision situations for managers: *Cell 1*—agreement about both causation and goal preferences; *Cell 2*—agreement about causation but disagreement about goal preferences; *Cell 3*—disagreement about causation but agreement about goal preferences; *Cell 4*—disagreement about both causation and goal preferences. The types of decision-making strategies which may be effective for each of the four combinations have also been inserted in the appropriate cells.

Managers of a single organization may be faced with different decision situations; therefore, it may emphasize different decision strategies (i.e., computation, compromise, judgment, or inspiration) in different departments. Furthermore, a single department might experience all four decision situations as it deals with different problems. Managers need to be sensitive to these differences because: (1) they may try to force a decision strategy into a situation for which it is not suited, leading to reduced organizational effectiveness; and (2) there may be sound reasons for departments in the organization to differ in their decision strategies.

COMPUTATIONAL STRATEGY

Here, decision making is a relatively mechanical and technical process. This strategy involves problems for which there are well-established procedures that can be systematically followed to arrive at a decision. Such programmed decisions are appropriate for repetitive, routine problems.[30] Some of the types of problems for which a computational strategy can be used are: opening a charge account in a department store, processing savings deposits or payroll checks, and assembling an automobile. Of course, the initial creation of programs and procedures to handle problems such as these may involve the use of the judgment strategy.

A department facing primarily computational decision problems can be designed as a bureaucracy and can use a mechanistic system of management. For example, the check-processing department of a bank (technical subsystem) is likely to make the most use of the computational strategy, whereas the bank's loan officers (organizational subsystem) who deal with businesses will need to use additional strategies.

JUDGMENT STRATEGY

Managers use the judgment strategy when the relative effectiveness of the available alternatives cannot be proved. Here, the decision makers have the same goal preferences, but disagree or are uncertain about cause-and-effect relationships. The individuals may have available many of the same "facts" related to the decision problem, but perceive and interpret them differently.

Some of the types of business problems that rely on the judgment decision strategy stem from the following questions. What combination of employee benefits will have the maximum impact on stimulating employee productivity? Which advertising program will have the greatest impact on company sales? What combination of workers and machines will result in the lowest cost per unit, yet maintain high quality? What is the best combination of stocks to hold for obtaining maximum growth in the value of the firm's investments?

Organizations often use a number of the same organizational structures for situations requiring the judgment and compromise decision strategies.[31] These structural arrangements can include boards of directors, executive committees, project organizations, interdepartmental committees, special task forces, teams, superior-subordinate meetings, and the like. For example, the negotiation of a labor-management contract usually involves the use of management teams and union teams. To arrive at a contract, both parties will probably need to use the judgment and compromise strategies.

The judgment strategy sometimes involves majority voting. Presumably, all participants have an equal voice (one vote–one person) in the final decision choice. This is not to imply, however, that the individuals have equal influence or control in the total decision problem.

COMPROMISE STRATEGY

If one goal preference can be satisfied only at the expense of another goal preference, the decision-by-compromise strategy may be required. In this situation, the parties may perceive and interpret the "facts" in a similar manner, but disagree over the desirability of the goals and values that will be served by the available alternatives.

Some of the types of business problems that may require the compromise decision strategy include: (1) the price to be charged a major customer for the services or goods provided by a firm; (2) the amount of pollutants that should be permitted in automobile emissions as judged by the Environmental Protection Agency and the automobile manufacturers, respectively; and (3) the amount of service wanted by an industrial sales manager from the marketing research department versus the ability and willingness of the marketing research manager to provide the service demanded.

As mentioned previously, many of the same structural arrangements (i.e., boards of directors and task forces) are utilized for judgmental and compromise decision strategies. In some instances, however, the structural arrangements could differ somewhat. For instance, the judgment strategy is assumed to require the widest possible participation. In the case of a trade union, this could involve voting by all its members. On the other hand, the compromise strategy generally requires a decision unit small enough to permit active involvement and interactions among representatives from the concerned factions. The collective-bargaining process between the United Rubber workers and the tire firms normally involve only a handful of representatives from the union and each company. Of course, the judgment strategy is applied when the union members vote to either accept or reject the "package" their representatives have arrived at through the compromise (bargaining) strategy. Other examples of representative structures include trial juries, the United States Congress, and the United Nations Security Council.

INSPIRATION STRATEGY

This strategy, the least typical of the four, may be necessary and effective in a decision situation characterized by confusion because the individuals cannot agree on cause-and-effect relationships or goal preferences. The decision-by-inspiration strategy is often implemented through two tactics. First, the parties may try to imitate their more successful counterparts. For example, several years ago Burger King began to copy McDonald's general promotional strategy, especially through television. Second, the parties may bring in well-known executives or prestigious consultants who tell them what their goal preferences should be and how to attain them. Naturally, this still does not guarantee success. A&P seemed to use this tactic in bringing in an outsider as the new president and giving him a "free hand." By 1976, he had initiated many changes that appeared to be having positive results.

IMPLICATIONS FOR INTERNAL POLITICAL PROCESSES

The use of the judgmental, compromise, and inspirational strategies is both part of and a consequence of political processes within organizations.[32] In Chapter 2, we presented some of the political strategies for dealing with groups *external* to the organization. At the middle and higher levels of management, many of these same strategies may be used in dealing with other individuals and groups *internal* to the organization.

Bargaining (compromise) may be extensively utilized to resolve differences to reach accommodation among organizational members. Members within an organization may form a *coalition* to represent their common interests on a particular decision problem.[33] For example, all of the workers may get together and sign a petition to protest a new overtime policy. Individuals or groups within the organization may *lobby* managers who have the power to make judgmental decisions. Sales managers may lobby higher management to allocate more of the marketing budget to the hiring of more salespersons. Within the organization, *cooptation* may be used by higher management in establishing "junior-executive boards" of younger managers. These boards may serve as advisory groups to higher management, but they don't exercise any real power.

Summary

The contingency organizational decision model attempts to both capture the complexity and diversity of organizational decision making and be consistent with some of the internal political processes. The model is both descriptive and normative. It is descriptive in recognizing the various types of decision-making situations that may face managers. It is normative in suggesting the strategies that should be utilized in different decision situations. Changes in the decision situation of the manager typically requires like changes in the decision strategy used.

COMPARISONS OF DECISION MODELS

The similarities and differences in the seven decision models presented in this chapter can be compared by using some of the dimensions presented in Chapter 6—degree of uncertainty, nature of the decision maker, amount of time available, purpose, degree of openness, and process. Table 7.7 highlights the similarities and differences in the seven decision models on the basis of these dimensions. These assessments represent our interpretation of the "best fit" on

Table 7.7. Comparative analysis of decision models

Dimensions for comparison of decision models	Normative decision models			Individual decision models				Organizational decision making	
	Break-even	Payoff matrix	Decision tree	Adaptation	Inequity	Heuristic		Contingency organizational decision model	
Degree of uncertainty	Certainty Risk	Certainty Risk Uncertainty	Certainty Risk Uncertainty	Not considered	Not considered	Risk Uncertainty		Certainty Risk Uncertainty	
Nature of decision maker	Not considered	Not considered	Not considered	Considered	Considered	Considered		Considered	
Amount of time	Not considered	Not considered	Not considered	Not considered	Not considered	Not considered		Not considered	
Purpose	Normative	Normative	Normative	Descriptive	Descriptive	Descriptive and normative		Descriptive and normative	
Degree of openness	Semiclosed	Semiopen	Semiopen	Mostly open	Mostly open	Open		Open	
Process	More deductive	More deductive	More deductive	More inductive	More inductive	Inductive and deductive		Inductive and deductive	

each dimension. Thus there is latitude for debate and discussion on some of the assessments assigned to certain of the models.

Let's briefly review each of these dimensions in relation to the decision models. The *degree of uncertainty* focuses on whether the decision model considers decision problems under conditions of certainty, risk, and/or uncertainty. The payoff matrix explicitly recognizes that decisions are made under a variety of conditions. Earlier, in our example of the football stadium expansion problem, the university president and administrative staff had to assign subjective probabilities (risk condition) to the likelihood of different numbers of seats being sold. On the other hand, the adaptation decision model does not explicitly consider the degree of uncertainty that might be involved in making choices.

The second dimension, the *nature of the decision maker,* considers whether the decision models address the possible impact that differences in individuals could have on their dealing with decision problems. For example, the subjective probabilities used in the decision-tree model will be strongly influenced by a decision maker's preference for risk taking. But the decision-tree model provides no direct recognition of such individual differences or what to do about them. On the other hand, the adaptation decision model directly recognizes that the unique personality and goals of the decision maker can strongly influence the alternatives considered and decision choices.

The dimension of *amount of time* focuses on whether the decision models recognize the influence of having to make decisions under tight versus loose time constraints. We do not feel that any of the decision models directly considers this factor; none of the models gives direct recognition or guidance as to the impact of tight versus loose time schedules on decision making. This dimension is indirectly recognized in the use of some type of heuristic. For example, when pressed for a quick decision on a potentially high-loss problem, many individuals seem to follow the heuristic of choosing the least risky alternative. The cliché that seems to come closest to this situation is "A bird in the hand is worth two in the bush."

Purpose refers to whether the decision model is normative (prescribing how decisions should be made) or descriptive (explaining how individuals and organizations actually do make decisions). For example, the break-even model is clearly normative, because it identifies the types of variables and relationships one should consider for certain problem situations, such as whether to make an investment. On the other hand, the organizational decision-making model is both descriptive and normative. It is descriptive in laying out the basic decision-making situations likely to confront a manager, but normative in telling the manager the decision strategy (e.g., computation or judgment) that is likely to be most effective in different decision situations.

The fifth comparative factor, *degree of openness dimension,* refers to how much the models are open or closed. A closed decision model assumes that goals are known, alternatives can be identified, and the alternatives can be objectively weighed and compared. Of course, open decision models tend to have just the opposite characteristics. In our view, none of the seven decision models is completely closed. The break-even model is perhaps the most closed; the organizational decision model, the most open, because goals are not always known or agreed on, the alternatives are not easily identified, and the alternatives cannot easily be weighed and compared.

Process is concerned with whether the decision model relies on the inductive or deductive process. You will recall that the inductive process starts with observations, moves to hypotheses, and ends up with a theory, or statement of functional relationships among variables. The deductive decision process, on the other hand, starts with the development of assumptions. As suggested by our labeling of these models in terms of decision process, none of them is purely inductive or purely deductive. The normative decision models (i.e., break-even, payoff matrix, and decision tree) tend to be more deductive. On the other hand, the adaptation and inequity decision models tend to be more inductive. Finally, the heuristic and organizational decision models tend to use a rich combination of both inductive and deductive processes.

Summary

Three normative models are the break-even, payoff matrix, and decision-tree models. They all prescribe techniques for dealing with certain types of decision problems. By contrast, the adaptation inequity, and heuristic models are descriptive. They allow one to analyze what actually occurs in individuals' decision-making processes. The contingency organizational decision model emphasizes two contingency variables that can influence the strategy of decision making—beliefs about causation and goal preferences. This model also recognizes the contributions provided by both the normative models and individual decision models.

Discussion Questions

1. When can a decision-tree model be more effectively used than the payoff-matrix model?

2. When can a payoff matrix be more effectively used than a break-even model?

3. Why aren't normative models used more frequently by managers?

4. Why should you, as a future manager, be interested in models of decision making?

5. If possible, what personal example can you provide that seems to represent the process of the adaptation decision model? (Your example could be from a school or work setting.)

6. If possible, what personal example can you provide that seems to represent the process of the inequity model? (Your example could be from a school or work setting.)

7. How could the individual decision models help someone be a more effective manager?

8. How might differences in individuals' perceptions influence their use of the contingency organizational decision model?

9. The contingency organizational decision model assumes that two or more individuals will often be involved in the same decision problem. What assumption does this model tend to make with respect to the relative power of these individuals? How could differences in individual power influence the use of the contingency organizational decision model?

Management Incidents

JIM SMYTHE

Jim Smythe, director of personnel for the Djohn Company, was assigned the task of reconstructing a compensation program for five upper-middle-level managers of the company. The Djohn Company manufactures electronic circuit breakers for Pratt-Whitney jet engines. Jim knew that the available budget for these five men was $240,000. Jim also gathered the following data on each of the five managers:

Manager 1—purchasing; has a staff of 20; recently experienced personal financial difficulties; has ten years seniority with the company; age 55.

Manager 2—manufacturing; has a department of 1000; holds MBA degree and is a "man on the move"; has several offers from other companies; one year's seniority; age 35.

Manager 3—finance; has staff of 50; has CPA degree; 25 years seniority; outstanding company record; age 65.

Manager 4—marketing; has a department of 200, mostly salesmen (industrial); 15 years seniority; excellent service record; has a BS in marketing; age 42.

Manager 5—research and development; has a staff of 20 professional employees; R & D is vital to this company, since it has an expanding technological environment; has a Ph.D. in engineering; has six months seniority; age 50.

1. What decision models outlined in this chapter appear to be relevant to this situation:
   a) from the personnel director's point of view?
   b) from the manager's point of view? (Assume that the managers are aware of the salary reconstruction assignment.)

STELLA UNIVERSITY

As president of this university, you have recently heard about increasing concern over grading practices and policies. In general, the faculty seems to feel that grading standards need to be tightened up. The students, on the other hand, feel that the grading standards need to be loosened up. They believe this will give them a better chance of getting good jobs or gaining admission to graduate school.

1. By using the contingency organization decision model, what decision strategies might be effective in dealing with the problem?

2. What use, if any, could be made of the computation, compromise, and judgment strategies for dealing with one or more parts of this decision problem?

REFERENCES

1. S. Kassauf, *Normative Decision Making* (Englewood Cliffs, N.J.: Prentice-Hall, 1970), p. 3.

2. P. Nutt, "Models for Decision Making in Organizations and Some Contextual Variables which Stipulate Optimal Use," *Academy of Management Review* **1** (1976): 84–98.

3. A. Van De Van and A. Delbecq, "A Task Contingent Model of Work-Unit Structure," *Administrative Science Quarterly* **19** (1974): 183–197.

4. P. Moore, "Technique versus Judgment in Decision Making," *Organizational Dynamics* **2** (1973): 69–80.

5. R. Brown, "Do Managers Find Decision Theory Useful?" *Harvard Business Review* **48** (1970): 78–89.

6. R. Schlaifer, *Analysis of Decision Under Uncertainty* (New York: McGraw-Hill, 1969).

7. J. Hammond, "Better Decisions with Preference Theory," *Harvard Business Review* **45** (1967): 123–141.

8. R. Swalm, "Utility Theory: Insights into Risk-Taking," *Harvard Business Review* **44** (1966): 123–138.

9. J. Magee, "Decision Trees for Decision-Making," *Harvard Business Review* **42** (1964): 126–138.

10. D. Miller and M. Starr, *Executive Decisions and Operations Research*, 2d ed. (Englewood Cliffs, N.J.: Prentice-Hall, 1969), pp. 452–464.

11. The substance of this example is drawn from E. A. McCreary, "How to Grow a Decision Tree," *Think Magazine*, April 1967, pp. 7–12.

12. M. Alexis and C. Wilson, *Organizational Decision-Making* (Englewood Cliffs, N.J.: Prentice-Hall, 1967), pp. 158–162.

13. J. Adams, "Toward an Understanding of Inequity," *Journal of Abnormal and Social Psychology* **67** (1963): 422–436; R. Goodman and A. Friedman, "An Examination of Adams' Theory of Inequity," *Administrative Science Quarterly* **16** (1971): 271–288.

14. M. Deutsch, "Equity, Equality, and Need: What Determines which Value Will Be Used as the Basis of Distributive Justice," *Journal of Social Issues* **31** (1975): 137–149.

15. J. Campbell and R. Pritchard, "Motivation Theory in Industrial and Organizational Psychology" in *Handbook of Industrial and Organizational Psychology*, ed. M. Dunnette (Chicago: Rand McNally, 1976), pp. 105–110; D. Middlemist and R. Peterson, "Test of Equity Theory by Controlling for Comparison of Co-worker's Effect," *Organizational Behavior and Human Performance* **15** (1976): 335–354.

16. C. Telley, W. French, and W. Scott, "The Relationship of Inequity to Turnover Among Hourly Workers," *Administrative Science Quarterly* **16** (1971): 164–172.

17. O. Belcher and T. Atchison, "Equity Theory and Compensation Policy," *Personnel Administration* **33** (1970): 22–33; P. Goodman, "Effect of Perceived Inequity on Salary Allocation Decisions," *Journal of Applied Psychology* **60** (1975): 372–375.

18. F. Shull, A. Delbecq, and L. Cummings, *Organizational Decision Making* (New York: McGraw-Hill, 1970), p. 89.

19. D. Taylor, "Decision Making and Problem Solving," in *Handbook of Organizations,* ed. J. March (Chicago: Rand McNally, 1965), pp. 73–74.

20. P. Gordon, "Heuristic Problem-Solving," *Business Horizons* **5** (1962): 43–53.

21. H. Simon, *Decision Rules for Production and Inventory Controls with Probability Forecasts of Sales* (Pittsburgh: Carnegie Institute of Technology, 1958), p. 3.

22. N. Martin, "Differential Decision in the Management of an Industrial Plant," *Journal of Business* **28** (1956): 249–269.

23. F. Kast and J. Rosenzweig, *Organizations and Management: A Systems Approach,* 2d ed. (New York: McGraw-Hill, 1974), p. 432.

24. A. Newell, J. Shaw, and H. Simon, *The Process of Creative Thinking,* RAND Corporation, 1959, p. 1320.

25. J. March and H. Simon, *Organizations* (New York: Wiley, 1958), p. 190.

26. I. Summers and D. White, "Creativity Technique: Toward Improvement of the Decision Process," *Academy of Management Review* **1** (1976): 99–107.

27. W. Gordon and G. Prince, *The Operational Mechanisms of Synectics* (Cambridge, Mass.: Synectics, 1960).

28. C. Gregory, *The Management of Intelligence* (New York: McGraw-Hill, 1967), pp. 198–199.

29. This model is modified and adapted from J. Thompson and A. Tuden, "Strategies, Structures and Processes of Organizational Decision," in *Comparative Studies in Administration,* ed. J. Thompson *et al.* (Pittsburgh: University of Pittsburgh Press, 1959); J. Thompson, "Decision-Making, the Firm and the Market," in *New Perspectives in Organizational Research,* ed. W. Cooper *et al.* (New York: Wiley, 1964).

30. H. Simon, *The Shape of Automation for Men and Management* (New York: Harper & Row, 1965), pp. 58–59.

31. R. Duncan, "Modifications in Decision Structure in Adapting to the Environment: Some Implications for Organizational Learning," *Decision Sciences* **5** (1974): 122–142.

32. A. Pittigrew, *The Politics of Organizational Decision-Making* (London: Tavistock, 1973).

33. R. Cyert and J. March, *A Behavioral Theory of the Firm* (Englewood Cliffs, N.J.: Prentice-Hall, 1963).

8

8
Planning Process

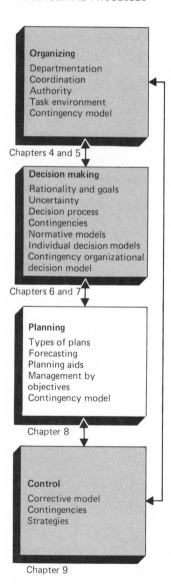

Organizing
Departmentation
Coordination
Authority
Task environment
Contingency model

Chapters 4 and 5

Decision making
Rationality and goals
Uncertainty
Decision process
Contingencies
Normative models
Individual decision models
Contingency organizational
decision model

Chapters 6 and 7

Planning
Types of plans
Forecasting
Planning aids
Management by
objectives
Contingency model

Chapter 8

Control
Corrective model
Contingencies
Strategies

Chapter 9

The objectives of this chapter are to:

comment on why some planning efforts fail, the use of planning, and the relative accuracy of planning;

develop a clear understanding of the nature of planning as it relates to decision making, the general types of activities and goals involved in the planning process, the major types of plans, and the range of comprehensiveness in planning;

develop your conceptual skill for understanding how the planning process will vary under different contingencies;

increase your skill in obtaining and using information in the planning process;

develop your skill for knowing when and how to use various planning aids and techniques, such as the delphi technique, nominal-group technique, modeling, Management By Objectives, and the Program Evaluation and Review Technique (PERT).

Businesses and organizations can survive only if they are able to manage change. The organization that manages change well will progress and grow. As the rate of change in the organization's task environment increases, new and better ways must be found to understand, anticipate, deal with, and monitor changes in the environment. Planning is the key management function for dealing with change in a positive, purposeful way.[1]

Planning is the formalized decision-making process of establishing goals and strategies at various levels in the organization. Successful planning usually involves the top managers of an organization. Their major concerns in planning are to: (1) *anticipate* and *avoid* problems in the future; (2) identify *opportunities* in the future; and (3) develop *courses of action* that will help the organization reach its desired goals. Top-management planning begins as a process for helping managers to deal with unstructured decision problems that are characterized by novelty, complexity, and uncertainty.[2]

As a means of dealing with uncertainty and change, some managers apply planning through two extreme profiles. "Paralysis by analysis" is "planning" by deferring or simply not making important decisions. "Extinction by instinct," by contrast, occurs when managers are so concerned with immediate problems and take such pride in making quick, clear-cut decisions that they fail to adequately plan for the future of the organization.[3] Ideally, managers will continuously weigh the relative costs and benefits associated with the different degrees of planning as they strive to deal with and create change.

THE SCOPE OF PLANNING

Contrary to popular impressions, formalized planning is not limited to the giants of business. A study of 93 moderate-sized companies found that all but four of them used a formal approach to planning.[4] The planning periods for these firms ranged from one to ten years, with most using a five-year time frame. Although virtually all of the plans involved specifying formal goals, there was considerable variation in the other dimensions of the plans, such as the means to be used and the resources required.

Despite the benefits to be gained from planning, such efforts often fail.[5] First, planning is risky and uncertain. As one high-level planning manager at General Electric noted: "No amount of sophistication is going to allay the fact that all your knowledge is about the past and all of your decisions are about the future."[6] Some of this uncertainty can be reduced and the capability for responding to unlikely future possibilities developed through *contingency* planning. Contingency planning simply means considering alternative future possibilities and developing a plan for each of them. For example, to avoid a disaster, events of low probability (i.e., flow of foreign oil to the United States will be cut off) but great impact should be planned for.

Second, unanticipated changes may be taking place so rapidly that only the most general and limited planning is possible. In this situation, planning might focus on creating an organization that can respond rapidly. Third, strategic plans may be made without adequate consideration of how they will be implemented or who will be responsible for implementing them. Fourth, there is an all too common tendency to simply project into the future what has happened in the past. One consultant attests to this widespread failure: "Maybe 95 percent of all companies really don't pay too much attention to the future. They react to history that is anywhere from one day to a few centuries old."[7] Although this may be an exaggeration, it does suggest that relying on historical experience to deal with the future has severe limitations, especially when the changes under way don't simply represent more or less of the same. Finally, too often a sharp separation is made between planning and implementation. Related to this is the idea that managers who must implement a plan should usually have some *participation* in its development.

Although strategic plans are concerned with a risky and uncertain future, plans made for short time periods, e.g., one or two years, are reasonably accurate. Somewhat surprisingly, long-term plans of five years or more have proved to be reasonably accurate despite the longer time horizons.[8] As mentioned earlier, this accuracy is increased when contingency planning is undertaken and there is continuous updating and replanning. When this pattern is followed, the planning process becomes a way of life, especially for top and upper-middle managers.

These statements provide further support for our general theme that organizations can effectively plan for the future and thereby provide some control over their destinies. Some individuals even claim that formal organizational plans are beginning to have national side effects in determining the rate of capital goods spending, inflation, and corporate borrowings. As a consequence, the national economy may be increasingly affected by corporate plans rather than by impersonal market forces or governmental actions.[9]

ELEMENTS OF PLANNING

Relationship to Decision Making

All planning is decision making, but not all decision making is planning. Planning, as an area of decision making, incorporates several special characteristics: anticipatory decision making, a system of decisions, and the creation of desired future states.[10] *Anticipatory decision making* is deciding what to do and how to do it *before* action is required. Although this process can be highly informal, our focus is on formal planning which precedes action. The *system of decisions* refers to the interconnections between one decision or set of decisions and other decisions. For example, the decision (plan) to obtain a college degree creates the need for dozens of other, interrelated decisions, e.g., which college to attend, when to start, and where to live. This system of decisions has the properties of an open system and therefore usually has no simple beginning or ending point in organizations. The *creation of desired future states* is, simply, the establishment of a goal. For example, in the 1950s Kresge's set a goal to move into the discount business, since this was a rapidly growing market and there were no national discount stores. As a result of creating this desired future state, K-Mart stores literally blanket the United States today.

Planning activities are a conscious decision process made up of the following steps:

1. establishing goals;
2. identifying opportunities and anticipated problems;
3. accumulating information;
4. relating of bits of information and beliefs;
5. establishing assumptions;
6. forecasting future conditions;
7. developing and choosing among alternative courses of actions;
8. ranking or selecting total plans which will achieve the best balance of ultimate and secondary objectives;
9. establishing policies;
10. establishing standards and means for measurement of adherence to the plan of action.[11]

Most of these activities are discussed in the remainder of the chapter.

Goals

An effective organization must be capable of maintaining its stability as well as adapting to change. The planning process can help to meet both of these goals.

MAINTAINING STABILITY

By assisting in integrating (coordinating) the physical and human resources of an organization, planning may contribute to the maintenance of stability. The predetermined courses of action established through planning are means for partially predicting and controlling the organization's future actions. Plans enable one unit to anticipate the actions of other units with which it is interdependent.[12] For example, Ford Motor Company develops monthly and quarterly plans with the tire companies to deliver a certain number and type of tires to its various production plants.

There is growing evidence that planning units or departments are also being created to achieve internal integration between the major divisions and departments of an organization. The need for integration becomes especially acute when the departments are highly differentiated in terms of products, geographical areas, and clientele served.[13] These planning units may also be used to facilitate adaptation.

FACILITATING ADAPTATION

Organizations' attempts to adapt and innovate are usually expressed in their long-range strategic plans, which often specify goals, strategies, and action programs aimed at identifying new markets, products, and services. The use of long-range planning to facilitate adaptation is extremely important.[14] Most adaptive organizations expend considerable effort on planning activities by developing alternative strategies and tactics in anticipation of different changes in the environment and gathering and analyzing information about environmental changes and reactions to the organization's present outputs. Ford Motor Company's introduction of the Pinto in September 1970 is a classic example of adaptive behavior.[15]

The Pinto was the first American-made car created specifically to compete "head-on" with small-car imports, especially the Volkswagen. In 1968 the market planners and economists at Ford had perceived and anticipated several environmental forces:

1. imports would increase from 7 percent in 1967 to 14 percent in 1975 (1.5 million units);
2. Ford's domestic volume would decrease by 240,000 units if imports increased by 750,000 units annually;
3. General Motors would soon enter the subcompact market;
4. Volkswagen's share of the small-car market would increase in the years ahead.

These and other factors led Ford planners to specify three prime objectives for the Pinto:

1. its size was to be the same as the Volkswagen sedan;
2. its cost of ownership was to equal that of the Volkswagen: competitive purchase price, equivalent fuel consumption, built-in durability and reliability, comparable serviceability, lower maintenance costs, and competitive parts prices;
3. its comfort, convenience, and appearance were to be better than Volkswagen's: wider tread and lower height for better stability; better maneuverability, ventilation, and heating; easier front- and rear-seat entry and exit; more interior room, and wider option availability and distinctive styling.

These objectives provided criteria for evaluating the numerous subplans and decisions that needed to be made to introduce the Pinto. By relating the objectives for the Pinto to Volkswagen, the Ford planners were also given a firm base of comparison, which reduced ambiguity and uncertainty about the correctness of their course of action. The success of the Pinto suggests that Ford adapted to the environmental change at that time fairly well. When the energy crisis hit, Ford was able to successfully make a further adaptation in the Pinto by introducing the four-cylinder MPG model.

Types of Plans

STRATEGIC PLANNING

Nature. Although there is no universally accepted description, strategic planning can be broadly defined as "the process of deciding on the objectives of the organization, on changes in these objectives, on the resources used to attain these objectives, and on the policies that are to govern the acquisition, use, and disposition of these resources."[16] Strategic planning is usually associated with a long time horizon, e.g., five or more years, but *not always*. For example, a company's plan to acquire a major subsidiary may have a time span of less than one year from the initial conception of the plan to its implementation, yet this plan meets the requirements of strategic planning.

It may be more reasonable to suggest that the *effects* of strategic plans are likely to be felt for extended time periods. Strategic plans may be concerned with the overall organization and/or subunits such as production, marketing, financing, and human-resource administration. In sum, a good strategic plan will concern itself with an analysis of such things as organizational goals; environmental forces, strengths, and weaknesses; and the present as well as the desired position of the organization.[17]

Role of Top Management. Strategic planning usually receives primary emphasis at the top (institutional) level of the organization. Top-level managers have the primary task of coping with the uncertainty created by uncontrollable and unpredictable forces in the organization's task environment. Two of the major techniques for coping effectively are: (1) scanning the environment for threats (such as invasion of imports into the domestic automobile market) and opportunities available to the organization; and (2) developing cooperative and competitive strategies for dealing with environmental forces.

Both of these strategies require a long-term time horizon and use of the judgmental and compromise decision strategies. For example, during the development of the Boeing 747, the emergence of many unanticipated problems required changes in the original plan. One major problem area was the weight and thrust of the new Pratt and Whitney engine. This created the need for extensive problem solving and negotiations among top managers of Boeing, Pan American, and United Aircraft (the producer of the Pratt-Whitney engine). The agreement arrived at forced Boeing to revise its plans in the carrying capacity of the plane, sales price, and the like.[18]

Significance. Top management's concern for strategy has often been found to be an important ingredient in successful companies' strategic planning. One study of firms in the food-processing industry demonstrated this point with a rather interesting approach.[19] An analysis of the themes and content of the annual reports for 82 firms in food processing revealed striking differences between the top 25 percent of the companies and the least successful 25 percent. The annual reports of the less successful companies:

1. had more complaints about the weather;
2. had vigorous complaints about price controls;
3. talked less about the coming changes in their environment, about product/market portfolio, and about their future direction;
4. were less inclined to mention changes in their organizations;
5. were less clear in their plans to cope with the energy crisis; and
6. were less clear in their plans to respond to the worldwide demand for protein.

The common characteristic in the themes for the more successful food-processing companies, by contrast, was their focus on anticipating and avoiding problems, identifying opportunities, and developing courses of action. In sum, strategic planning should be a dynamic, ongoing process rather than an annual event. It should provide the glue that directs and binds together the diverse activities of a complex organization.[20]

Questions. The strategic-planning process is concerned with the basic questions that define and redefine the organization's nature and purpose. As you read down the following list of questions, note that they move from the current strategy and associated problems and missed opportunities to new strategies that might be considered to a specific strategy that *should* be followed.

1. Record current strategy:
   a) What is the current strategy?
   b) What kind of business does management want to operate (considering such management values as desired return on investment, growth rate, share of market, stability, flexibility, character of the business, and climate)?
   c) What kind of business does management feel it ought to operate (considering management's concepts of social responsibility and obligations to stockholders, employees, community, competitors, customers, suppliers, government, and the like)?
2. Identify problems with the current strategy:
   a) Are trends discernible in the environment that may become threats and/or missed opportunities if the current strategy is continued?
   b) Is the company having difficulty implementing the current strategy?
   c) Is the attempt to carry out the current strategy disclosing significant weaknesses and/or unutilized strengths in the company?
   d) Are there other concerns with respect to the validity of the current strategy?
   e) Is the current strategy no longer valid?
3. Discover the core of the strategy problem:
   a) Does the current strategy require greater competence and/or resources than the company possesses?
   b) Does it fail to exploit adequately the company's disctinctive competence?
   c) Does it lack sufficient competitive advantage?
   d) Will it fail to exploit opportunities and/or meet threats in the environment, now or in the future?
   e) Are the various elements of the strategy internally inconsistent?
   f) Are there other considerations with respect to the core of the strategy problem?
   g) What, then, is the real core of the strategy problem?
4. Formulate alternative new strategies:
   a) What possible alternatives exist for solving the strategy problem?
   b) To what extent do the company's competence and resources limit the number of alternatives that should be considered?
   c) To what extent do management's preferences limit the alternatives?
   d) To what extent does management's sense of social responsibility limit the alternatives?
   e) What strategic alternatives are acceptable?
5. Evaluate alternative new strategies:
   a) Which alternative *best* solves the strategy problem?
   b) Which alternative offers the *best* match with the company's competence and resources?
   c) Which alternative offers the *greatest* competitive advantage?
   d) Which alternative *best* satisfies management's preferences?
   e) Which alternative *best* meets management's sense of social responsibility?
   f) Which alternative *minimizes* the creation of new problems?

6. Choose a new strategy:
   a) What is the *relative significance* of each of the preceding considerations?
   b) What should the new strategy be?[21]

The results of *failing* to consider or adequately address these types of fundamental questions and consider "radical" alternatives are well documented. Many times a strategic failure occurs for all of the firms in a particular industry. For example, firms in the film and camera industry didn't develop a film-camera system that would provide finished prints instantly. Polaroid, which had not been involved with either film or cameras, invented and marketed such a system. Similarly, IBM, a computer company, was the first to develop the electric typewriter. Firms already making typewriters were instead working to improve the manual typewriter. Another example is the development of the automatic washing machine by Bendix, a firm in the aeronautics and automobile parts business.[22]

Sears Roebuck: A Case Study.[23] The strategic decisions (incorporated into strategic plans) are said to account for the dominant position Sears has enjoyed in the retailing industry within the United States. These decisions, made at different points in the firm's history, have involved internal, external, or both types of forces. The ten strategic decisions can be summarized as follows:

1. As the farm population was now using automobiles and coming to town, Sears decided in the mid-1920s to add retail stores to its catalogue business;
2. Forming a unique management structure that remains its core today, Sears decided to centralize merchandising (all buying, promotional, and advertising operations) in Chicago and to control store operations from territorial headquarters;
3. Having decided to control the cost, quality, and quantity of its merchandise by drawing up its own specifications, Sears today is responsible for the design details of 95 percent of the goods it sells;
4. Its post–World War II decision to aggressively expand by relocating old stores and adding new stores in new locations gave Sears many prize locations as the population moved west and into the suburbs;
5. By deciding in the mid-1950s to expand its sale of soft goods in retail stores, Sears changed from a hardware store featuring tools and fishing tackle to a full-line department store;
6. The more recent decision to play up style and fashion along with economy modernized Sears' image and made the firm one of the largest mink and diamond merchants in the country;
7. Setting up a service organization, despite its low or zero profitability, has supported the sales of Sears' durable goods;
8. Diversifying into insurance and other financial services through its Allstate operation created a subunit that one day may become as big as Sears itself;
9. A series of decisions to invest in supplier corporations not only increased Sears' prime strength in distribution, but has also led to some sizable capital gains;

10. Finally, a series of decisions to invest heavily in superior personnel, accomplished in part through large-scale training programs (200 to 500 college graduates a year), promote from within, offer generous profit-sharing plans, and permit employees to purchase Sears' own stock for the profit-sharing fund, has given Sears superior management in considerable depth.

TACTICAL PLANNING

Managers and specialists in the organizational and technical subsystems are primarily involved in tactical planning, which is based on computational and compromise decision strategies.

Nature. Tactical planning is typically concerned with (1) current activities and those in the near future (one year or less); (2) control and integration of current operations; and (3) current allocation of resources, especially through the budgeting process.[24] The main purpose of tactical planning is to facilitate system maintenance; strategic planning, by contrast, enhances system adaptation. Another difference is that tactical planning relies heavily on structured decision making, whereas strategic planning emphasizes innovative and unstructured decision making.

Significance. Despite their differences, strategic and tactical planning must be integrated into a well-designed planning system. Each type of planning provides the basis for the other. For example, Bell and Howell has incorporated tactical and strategic plans into one overall company plan. A 60-month (5-year) "moving" plan consists of both strategic and tactical plans for all parts of the organization; the "moving" plans are reanalyzed and updated quarterly.[25]

Comprehensiveness of Planning

One way to measure the comprehensiveness of planning is to assess the number of people or units within or outside of the organization that will be affected by the plan. The greater the number of people and units impacted, the greater the comprehensiveness of the planning process. Comprehensiveness can also be defined as the intensiveness and extensiveness of the planning process. *Extensive* planning considers all of the major parts, including goals, means, resources, and control.[26] The *intensity* of the planning process is determined by the depth and thoroughness of analysis undertaken for each of these parts.

GOALS

Goals are the future ends, or objectives, to be served. Managers and other organizational members must answer such basic questions as: Why does the organization exist?; What is it?; and What should it become? In the early 1960s, for example, Ford Motor executives decided that the company's business was not primarily the production of cars and trucks, but rather making items, regardless of their form, to move people and goods. Thus the long-term goal of the company is to become a diversified transportation company.[27]

Impact. Broadening a firm's overall goal can have considerable impact on the direction of the organization and the types of alternatives it evaluates. The process of goal formulation in planning may often be fluid; the goals arrived at will be a complex function of the interplay among the external environment, the motives of individuals who have power over the organization's resources, the coalitions formed through bargaining processes, and the internal social system.[28] Because of the interplay of these forces, the real goals of an organization are not always consistent with the official goals, such as those stated in its planning document or in its executives' public relations speeches.

Contingencies. It is commonly prescribed that the strategic planning process should result in very *specific goals* for key areas of the firm. The nature of such goals might be illustrated as follows:[29]

1. to increase return on investment to 14 percent after taxes within four years;
2. to increase commercial sales to 70 percent of total sales and reduce military sales to 30 percent over the next five years;
3. to reduce long-term debt to $20 million within three years;
4. to design and implement a matrix organizational structure in the research and development division within two years;
5. to design and implement a Management By Objectives system through the first level of supervision over the next three years.

It is often desirable to specify goals in this manner under certain contingencies. If the environment is not too turbulent, shifting, and uncertain, it is probably desirable to identify goals with detailed specificity. Concrete goals have certain advantages. They are powerful motivators (if accepted), they can reduce the expenditure of time and energy spent in exploring alternative futures because they already know what needs to be accomplished, and they provide a measure of stability and sense of direction.

Under certain other contingencies, however, it may be more desirable to use general *directional goals,* which are primarily qualitative. Of course, a complex organization could use a combination of specific and directional strategic goals. Directional goals and planning might occur when the environment or subenvironment is very turbulent, shifting, and uncertain or one is engaged in the early planning phases of a project with considerable uncertainty.[30] The advantage of directional goals is that they preserve flexibility and help managers continue to consider possibilities for wholly new goals and opportunities. If top managers have little personal tolerance for dealing with rapid change and uncertainty, they are likely to find the use of directional goals stressful and anxiety provoking, however.

MEANS

A critical element in planning is determining how to achieve the desired goals. However, the degree of detail spelled out in the means can vary considerably —from broad statements of policy to general programs to specific procedures and rules (see Fig. 8.1). Fundamental policies concerned with the organization's purpose and ways of doing business are at the top of the pyramid. From these

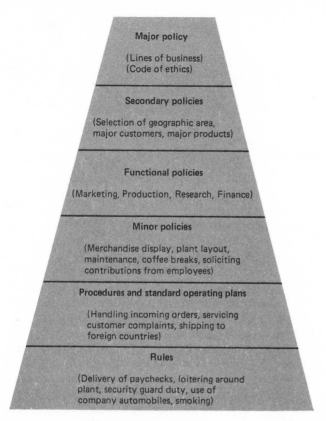

Fig. 8.1. Pyramid of means. (Reprinted with permission of
Macmillan Publishing Co., Inc., from *Top Management
Planning* by George A. Steiner. Copyright 1969.)

major policies are developed means of lesser importance and scope, which
shade into rules and procedures.[31]

Continental Oil Company: A Case Study.[32] The long-range plan of the Continental Oil Company, a major producer and marketer of petroleum products,
forms a pyramid of means, as follows:

1. *General policies*—a summary of the goals and major policies;
2. *Programs and procedures*—specific programs to implement the proposed
   policies and goals for each of the organization's functional areas. Goals are
   expressed in quantified terms, such as dollar sales and percent share of
   the market within defined time periods. In addition, the labor, money, and
   facilities needed to implement these programs are spelled out. To highlight the degree of change called for by the plan, the major deviations from
   previous plans are indicated, as well as the rationale for such changes.
3. *Financial results*—the anticipated effects of the programs and procedures
   are prepared for one-, two-, three-, four-, and five-year periods. The effects

considered include such financial dimensions as net income, capital expenditures, return on investment, and cash flow.

Following the presentation of the general policies, programs and procedures, and financial results for the company as a whole, subplans for each operating department are outlined and detailed in a similar manner.

Resource Requirements

This part of the planning process refers to the amounts and types of resources required for the several plans, as well as their allocation to the various units in the organization. Five major categories of resources are necessary to make a plan operational: money; facilities and equipment; materials, supplies, and services; and personnel. The dollar costs associated with these resources are most visibly expressed in the budgets that organizations prepare in support of the plan.

An effective budgeting process will help ensure that future funds for the required resources are available. Generally, budgets are either operational or strategic. *Operational* budgets tend to be tied to tactical plans and have short time horizons, i.e., one year or less. The bulk of an organization's annual and monthly budget is operational, because it designates the funding needed for maintaining current operations within the present goal framework. Operational budgets are used primarily for control purposes, thereby helping maintain an organization's stability. In contrast, *strategic budgets* include all expenditures *except* those needed to provide existing products or services with existing methods.[33] Strategic budgets are concerned with changes in resources and the purposes to which they are put, thereby facilitating adaptation.

Control

Since Chapter 9 is devoted to the control process, here we will present only a few highlights. Control can be either anticipatory (preventive) or corrective in character. Control is *anticipatory* to the extent that it predirects behaviors or feelings before they occur. In this sense, a plan represents an "advanced" control mechanism. The parties to a plan can anticipate, with some degree of predictability, the actions of other parties by virtue of the requirements of the plan. In this situation, there is likely to be a heavy emphasis on rewards as a way to increase the probability of advance cooperation.

Corrective control, the type most frequently thought of as control, involves taking corrective action when differences are found between the desired and actual conditions. The relationship between control and planning exists because the variations from the plan provide the signal that corrective action is needed.

ITT: A CASE STUDY

ITT's comprehensive planning system places heavy reliance on the control component. The ITT president and top-level product-line managers set the basic quantitative goals for the organization's 400 operating units, which function in some 60 countries. Within these goal constraints, the group- and division-level managers develop plans, subject to review, to meet these goals. ITT's preventive controls are expressed through the assigned quantitative goals. Corrective controls are revealed in ITT's information system, which requires reporting of deviations from goals, reasons for such deviations, and the proposed corrective actions.[34]

The disclosures in 1975 and 1976 of ITT's illegal political contributions and involvement in the affairs of foreign countries, particularly Chile, suggest that the top management of ITT sought to obtain control over segments of the task environment as well. ITT, apparently, regarded these activities as a means to ensure the company's own stability. Of course, these activities ran counter to the broader social values in the United States and other countries.

CONTINGENCY VIEW OF STRATEGIC PLANNING

We can now pull together and reinforce a number of points and ideas presented so far in this and previous chapters that have a direct bearing on strategic planning under different contingencies. To do this, the contingency approach to organization design, presented in Chapter 5, will be used. Figure 8.2 provides this overall framework and suggests the nature of the strategic-planning process under varying situations.

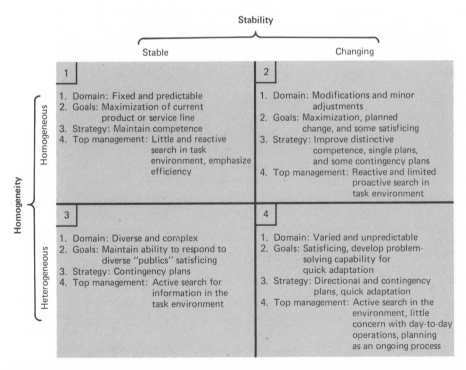

Fig. 8.2. Contingency framework of strategic planning.

As we said in Chapter 5, the *degree of stability* refers to whether the organization's task environment changes over time or is relatively stable. That is, are the customers, suppliers, ways of manufacturing the product, and price structure stable or changing? The *degree of homogeneity* refers to how similar or dissimilar the parts of the organization's task environment are. The task environment of a firm with many types of suppliers, customers, and technologies is "heterogeneous." A task environment with few types of suppliers, customers, and technologies is "homogeneous." The resulting four quadrants suggest the differences in strategic planning that are likely to be found.

Significance

Since the framework and characteristics of each of the cells in Fig. 8.2 were considered in depth in terms of organizational design in Chapter 5, only some of the significant highlights for strategic planning will be mentioned here. First, top managers should probably consider their strategic-planning process from a contingency perspective.[35] Thus there is no one best way for engaging in strategic planning. Rather, it should depend on the current task environment of the organization and the one the organization is moving toward.

Second, the complexity, uncertainty, and turbulence in the strategic-planning process can vary widely among firms.[36] Firms in cell 1 (e.g., local dry cleaner and can manufacturer) in Fig. 8.2 are likely to experience the lowest amount of complexity, uncertainty, and turbulence; those in cell 4 (e.g., a manufacturer of atomic energy plants and a university), the most. This can be readily seen by analyzing Fig. 8.2 in terms of the expected domain, goals (objectives), strategy, and role of top management for firms within each of the four cells.

Third, top management needs to recognize that the task environment of major divisions or departments of complex and diversified organizations, such as Westinghouse and General Electric, can vary substantially. Therefore, the strategic-planning process may have to vary between departments and divisions for maximum effectiveness. For example, a universally imposed strategic-planning process which is effective for established product divisions might create havoc for a new-ventures division and the research and development division.

Fourth, the contingency framework for strategic planning suggests that management can easily get trapped by its own planning processes. An organization in a particular task environment may fail to perceive that its task environment is changing, because the planning processes being used creates blinders as to how and what the top managers are likely to perceive in the task environment.

In our judgment, one of the reasons the rapidly changing task environment of some organizations has been dealt with so poorly is due *not* to the lack of a planning process, but to the lack of an *appropriate* planning process. Too many managements continue to utilize planning processes appropriate to a stable and homogeneous task environment. They should, however, be moving toward some use of planning processes appropriate in a heterogeneous and changing task environment. For example, state universities are often required by their state legislatures or central governing boards to use planning processes that are appropriate to a stable and homogeneous task environment. However, the greatest planning needs in universities usually are in changing and heterogeneous task environments.

INFORMATION INPUTS TO PLANNING

Forecasting is often regarded as providing one of the main sources of information for the planning process, especially strategic planning. The view of information inputs to planning is broadened here by recognizing other ways available to search for information, the kinds of information sought, and the sources from which it is obtained. Information is critical to the planning process, as well as to all of the other managerial and behavioral processes. The information inputs of interest here might be called "strategic information" because of their use in developing strategic plans.

Means of Scanning

Scanning refers to the exposure to and perception of information. The means of scanning can vary from an undirected, fortuitous, and subconscious observation to a purposeful, predetermined, and highly structured inspection.[37] Within this broad range, there appears to be a continuum of four identifiable means of scanning, as shown in Fig. 8.3.

UNDIRECTED VIEWING
Undirected viewing involves the manager's exposure to and perception of information that has no specific purpose. The information inputs are great in number and varied in substance and source. Although much of this information is readily dropped from attention, it can be valuable as a means of reducing one's natural tendency toward tunnel vision, i.e., perceiving and processing only information which seems to be of immediate relevance. For the most part, undirected viewing does not have major effects on planning activities.

CONDITIONED VIEWING
Conditioned viewing involves a degree of purposefulness by the manager in the reception of the information inputs. The manager is receptive to these information inputs and is willing to assess their significance. There is a natural

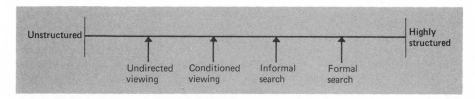

Fig. 8.3. Continuum of means of scanning.

tendency to *react,* or respond, under conditioned viewing. For example, a vacationing motel manager who notices that new firms are being established to provide camper and trailer sites for travelers may begin wondering whether to add this service.

INFORMAL SEARCH

Informal search is a modest step from a reactive pattern toward a *proactive* orientation. There is a limited and relatively unstructured effort to seek out information for a specific purpose, e.g., keeping an eye out for certain types of information, letting others know of information needs, actually soliciting information.

In 1951 Charles K. Wilson took his family on a vacation from Memphis, Tennessee, to Washington, D.C. They stayed in motels which he thought were expensive, small, and uncomfortable. He sensed that the growing number of motorists would have a need for decent accommodations. When he returned to Memphis, Wilson decided to construct a motel which had all of the services he had missed on his trip. He became the founder and chairman of Holiday Inns.[38] Since Wilson had previously exhibited an entrepreneurial orientation and was continuously looking for business opportunities, it appears that this incident more closely fits the informal-search approach.

FORMAL SEARCH

This is a highly proactive scanning process deliberately undertaken to obtain information for specific purposes. This scanning process may call for formal plans, procedures, and methodologies for obtaining information inputs. Organizational units most likely to conduct a formal-search procedure are research and development departments and marketing research departments.

The use of formal forecasting techniques also fit this category. An example of the costs for not engaging in formal search, along with some humor, has been reported this way:

> Some years ago the Pioneer Tool & Die Co., of Akron, Ohio, built a baitless, odorless, automatic trap that catches mice by the dozens. This device, about the size of an attaché case, lures curious rodents, one at a time, through a hole and trap door and along a corridor that eventually leads to their deaths. The company built 5600 of these traps and lost $63,000 when only 400 were sold at $29.95 each. The company finally scrapped 5000 traps and at this writing is still trying to sell 200 at $15 each. Mr. Zinkann, the president of the company, says, "our big mistake was that nobody ever found out whether anyone wanted to buy a mousetrap as elaborate as ours for the original high retail price."[39]

The failure of the Edsel automobile serves as a continuous reminder that even with an elaborate formal-search process, the success of a plan is by no means guaranteed. The manager may simply have a better idea of the sources and amounts of uncertainty inherent in planning decisions.

Kinds of Information

There are several kinds and sources of information inputs relevant to strategic planning. The research findings we present are based on a study of managers

Table 8.1. Relative importance of classes of external information for 190 managers

Information classification	Percent of first-choice responses	Information categories
Market	58%	Market potential Structural change Competitors and industry Pricing Sales negotiation Customers
Technical	18%	New products, etc. Product problems Costs Licensing and patents
Broad issues	8%	General conditions Government actions, etc.
Acquisition leads	7%	Leads for mergers, etc.
Other	9%	Suppliers, etc. Resources available Miscellaneous
Total percent	100%	

Adapted from F. J. Aguilar, *Scanning the Business Environment* (New York: Macmillan, 1967), p. 43.

from 41 companies, most of them manufacturers of chemical products for use by other industrial firms.[40] Although these findings are significant and may well be representative of a broader population, they may not be representative of practices in all industries. We do, however, feel that the framework within which the empirical findings fit can be applied generally.

Table 8.1 provides a classification of four kinds of strategic external information. It shows the relative importance of each classification, as perceived by the responding managers, and the information categories included within each classification.

With 58 percent of the first-choice responses in terms of relative importance, market information is obviously the dominant classification. Because the chemical industry is usually regarded as being very technologically oriented, the findings become even more important. It might have been expected that the technical-information category would receive more first-choice responses in this industry. On the other hand, since competitors often represent the most immediate potential threat to the success and survival of a firm, his finding isn't too surprising.[41]

Sources of Information

Related to the classes of information managers regard as important are the sources used to obtain such information. This discussion centers on an identification of the sources for obtaining the different kinds of information. Figure 8.4, which provides one way of classifying information sources, distinguishes between sources inside (within) the firm and those outside (external to) the firm. Within each of these categories, a further distinction is made between personal and impersonal sources.

The manager's responses show that personal sources far exceed impersonal sources in importance (71 percent versus 29 percent). This suggests the importance of personal-communication networks in the manager's world of work. To a surprising extent, the managers rely on face-to-face exchanges for much of the information they find valuable. It may also suggest that the individual moving into a manager's role, or preparing for one, will want to sharpen his or her interpersonal-communication skills.

The information sources discussed so far, though having applicability to the planning process, are also intimately related to the other managerial processes such as organization, control, and decision making. Information inputs which have been of special importance to planning are usually identified as the domain of forecasting.

Outside sources	Personal	Customers, suppliers, business and professional associates, bankers, etc.
	Impersonal	Trade publications, newspapers, trade shows, technical conferences, etc.
Inside sources	Personal	Subordinates, peers, or superiors
	Impersonal	Scheduled meetings, regular reports and notices, etc.

Fig. 8.4. Classification of information sources.

Forecasting

Forecasting, a major component to any planning process, differs from planning in the following ways. Forecasting is usually concerned with predicting, projecting, or estimating future events or conditions in the organization's environment that are mostly outside of the direct control of its management. Planning, on the other hand, is more encompassing, because it is concerned with identifying goals, strategies, alternatives, etc., that are within the control of management.

It is increasingly recognized that forecasting should go beyond traditional economic and technological forecasts. There are increasingly attempts by some firms to forecast change in the cultural (values) and political systems as well. The available forecasting technologies are quite varied and can become extremely complex, but here we will only illustrate several of the tools and approaches for aiding the forecasting process.

The foundation of all forecasting is some form of extrapolation, which involves the attempt to project some tendency from the past into the future.[42] The simplest, and many times most misleading, form of extrapolation is the linear, or straight, projection of a past trend. In the 1950s, for example, several producers of baby foods assumed that birth rates would be a simple projection of the past. They ignored the weak, but significant, information signals that were available in the environment, i.e., increasing acceptance of the pill and the changing values and attitudes on the part of women as to their role in society.[43]

There are, of course, more varied and sophisticated extrapolation forecasting techniques. Among two of the many approaches available as aids in forecasting are the Delphi technique and simulation models.

DELPHI TECHNIQUE

The Delphi technique involves the systematic refinement of experts' opinions to arrive at a general consensus about the future.[44] Since this method relies on experts' opinions about the future, it is obviously not fail-safe. However, increased accuracy (relative to a single expert's opinion) derived through a collection of experts' opinions has been obtained with the Delphi process.[45]

The Delphi technique has gained considerable recognition as a forecasting device. In 1966, TRW, a major advanced technology firm, began to use it for planning studies in such diverse fields as space, transportation, and housing. In 1968, LTV, a large conglomerate, began to use it as a tool of technological forecasting. An application in a more basic industry was made by the Goodyear Tire and Rubber Company in its planning of future tire research.[46] In recent years, the Delphi technique has also been applied to help identify problems, set goals and priorities, and identify problem solutions. Thus it has certainly grown beyond being only a forecasting technique. Since Delphi does not require face-to-face contact, it is a useful technique for involving experts and others who cannot come together physically.

Basic Process. The basic process in the use of the Delphi technique can be summarized as follows.

1. A questionnaire is sent or given to the experts. It requests numerical estimates of specific technological or market possibilities, e.g., expected dates, volumes, and developments, as well as assigned probabilities.

2. A summary of this first round is prepared. It may show the average, median, and quartile ranges of responses.

3. This summary report is fed back to the participant (but always anonymous) experts, requesting them to revise their earlier estimates if they feel it appropriate.

4. A new summary is prepared and fed back, but this time those experts whose responses significantly deviate from the median are asked to justify their forecasts.

5. Summaries are again revised and fed back along with the justifications. Now justifications of counterpositions are sought.

6. Finally, the counterpositions are fed back with the request for additional reappraisals.

Each of the following ten questions is concerned with future possible developments in the typical American business firm within the next several decades.

In addition to giving your answer to each question, you are also being asked to rank the questions from 1 to 10. Here "1" means that in evaluating your own ability to answer the questions, you feel that you have the best chance of making an accurate projection for this question relative to the others; "10" means that you regard that chance as relatively least. Please rank all questions such that every number from 1 to 10 is used exactly once.

Rank (1-10)		Question	Answer* (year)
_____	A.	In your opinion, in what year will women serve as presidents of at least five of *Fortune Magazine*'s 500 largest corporations?	_____
_____	B.	In what year will most boards of directors of publicly held corporations contain members who represent primarily the consumer rather than the stockholders?	_____
_____	C.	In your opinion, in what year will managers regularly be paid for working a 20 hour work week?	_____
_____	D.	By what year will business have effectively reduced its pollution of the environment to a nondangerous level?	_____
_____	E.	In what year will top management in half of the largest 100 manufacturing firms rely on computerized systems as their primary tool for planning?	_____
_____	F.	By what year will the use of mind stimulating drugs be employed by 10% of the chief executives as an aid in determining corporate policy alternatives?	_____
_____	G.	In what year will energy prices make operations unfeasible for most American industrial corporations?	_____
_____	H.	By what year will the M.B.A. degree be a minimum requirement for entry into the management training programs of most corporations?	_____
_____	I.	In what year will prime interest rates make it totally prohibitive for corporations to expand their plant capacities?	_____
_____	J.	In what year will most financial statements reflect a significant level of accounting for social costs and assets (e.g., pollution, welfare and human resources)?	_____

Never is also an acceptable answer.

Fig. 8.5. Delphi questionnaire. (Prepared by Dr. Harvey Nussbaum, School of Business Administration, Wayne State University. Reprinted by permission.)

In short, the heart of Delphi is a series of questionnaires. The first question-naire may include broadly worded questions, but with additional rounds, the questionnaires become more specific, because they are built on responses to the preceding questionnaires. Figure 8.5 provides an example of a Delphi ques-tionnaire that has been developed for student and class use. You might want to take a few minutes now and answer these questions. Note that the question-naire attempts to assess judgments about selected possible future development in the typical American business firm within the next 20 years.

SIMULATION MODELS

Simulation models are often used to forecast the effects of possible changes in the environment and/or decisions by management on the performance of the organization as a whole or one of its departments. The objective of a simula-tion model is to obtain the essential qualities of reality without actually ex-periencing the particular reality. Simulation models are intended to let man-agement take a contingency approach to the future by forecasting the effects of numerous "if-then" questions. A simulation model might help forecast the effects of different rates of inflation on sales and profits, for example. *If* inflation is 8 percent and management continues its past decisions and policies, *then* the effects on profits might be forecast as a 6 percent decline. If inflation is 12 percent and management continues its past decisions and policies, then the effects on profits might be forecast as a 20 percent decline.

A simulation model could help a manager deal with such questions about the future as the following.[47] First, what effects will a changed economic en-vironment have on the organization if the key decisions and policies of man-agement are not changed? Second, what effect will the change of a particular decision or policy have on the firm when it is made to anticipate or respond to certain environmental changes? Third, are there combinations of manage-ment decisions and policies that can enable the firm to compensate or capi-talize on changes in the economic environment?

The types of environmental factors in a simulation model could include inflation rate, short-term interest rate, tax rate, and operating costs. Some of the management decisions and policies included in simulation could be prices charged, pricing response time (the frequency with which prices are updated), growth rate in units sold, dividend policy, operating cash, depreciation, capac-ity expansion plans, and the like. The performance measures included in a simulation model could be an income statement, financial ratios (such as debt/equity ratio, return on equity, and earnings per share), and balance-sheet statements.

Without worrying about the mechanics of simulation models, we note that the important point is that management may be able to better forecast the effect of numerous "if-then" questions on profits, sales, earnings per share, etc.

Applications. Simulation models can be used for virtually any problem or functional area (i.e., finance, marketing, personnel, and production) where there is a concern with forecasting. Let's consider two of these applications.

The IBM World Trade Corporation, which is responsible for IBM's interna-tional business, makes major use of computerized simulation models. The elements of its simulation models, expressed in mathematical equations, include: (1) present operational activities; (2) forecasts about internal and external changes such as costs, prices, investments, labor productivity, etc.; and (3) extrapolation of past performance. The effects of various planning alternatives and assumptions are obtained through predicted data on sales forecasts, revenue comparisons, income and expense accounts, etc.[48]

Management and unions are utilizing computer simulation for the development of their collective-bargaining plans and for anticipating the long-run effects of each other's proposals. The vice-president of corporate planning at American Airlines stated:

> When our pilot contract was under negotiation recently, the union requested a new limitation on the number of flight hours each pilot would fly per month. We were able to feed this limitation into our computers and relate it to production levels we had planned over the next five years. We were able to determine exactly what our crew costs over the five-year period would be with new flight hours and to compare them with present costs.[49]

Limitations. Because the future is rarely the same as the past, managers can mislead themselves if they base simulation models entirely on historical relationships and data. As one authority put it: "To do so would be like steering the ship by watching its wake."[50] Accordingly, a high degree of judgment and skill is needed to construct simulation models for forecasting purposes.

Even the most sophisticated forecasting and planning systems will not prevent sudden changes and surprises. The "petroleum crisis," for example, created a discontinuity for many societies and major corporations which had modern forecasting and planning systems. Some of these firms simply weren't looking into this possibility. Others had forecasts of Arab action, but apparently felt that the probability was too low to warrant action or chose to suppress the bad forecasts from consciousness. William Woodside, President of American Can, notes that there is a strong tendency to ignore, suppress, or reject forecasts warning of crisis: "The roughest thing to get rid of is the Persian messenger syndrome, where the bearer of bad tidings is beheaded by the king. You should lean over backwards to reward the guy who is first with the bad news. Most companies have all kinds of abilities to handle problems if they only learn about them soon enough."[51]

PLANNING MODELS AND AIDS

This last part of the chapter is intended to develop your conceptual and technical skills in the use of three specific planning models and aids: Management By Objectives (MBO), nominal-group technique, and Program Evaluation and Review Technique (PERT). Our classifying these techniques as planning models and aids is judgmental, however, because they are intimately related to other processes, especially those of control, motivation, and change. Although these planning models and aids may overlap in certain respects, the use of one does not prevent the application of the others in an organization.

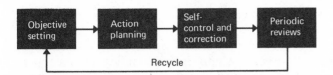

Fig. 8.6. Basic process of Management By Objectives.

Management By Objectives

Management By Objectives (MBO) is both a *philosophy* of management and a *process*. It is a philosophy which emphasizes a "proactive" rather than a "reactive" way of managing. Thus MBO tries to help an organization influence its future rather than only respond to other forces or manage by crisis. Management By Objectives also places a high value on increased *employee participation* in work-related matters at all levels of the organization. (The behavioral and motivational aspect of MBO will be discussed in detail in Chapter 11.)

BASIC PROCESS[52]
MBO consists of a series of interdependent and interrelated elements, as summarized in Fig. 8.6. (In the discussion that follows, keep in mind that we use the terms "objectives" and "goals" interchangeably.)

Objective Setting. The distinguishing feature of MBO is the establishment of objectives (also called *goals, targets,* or *purposes*) for all organizational departments and as many individuals as possible. The objective-setting stage should provide clear answers to two basic questions: Why are we here? and If this is why we are here, what should be accomplished? Consistent with the hierarchy-of-goals-framework discussed in Chapter 6 (see Fig. 6.1), the objective-setting process is likely to include development of objectives at the following levels:

1. long-range goals that determine what the organization is and what it is trying to become;
2. more specific organizational objectives that are often quantitative and include time periods, e.g., an objective to increase return on investment to 14 percent within three years;
3. objectives for the various divisions and departments, e.g., the production department's reduction of the volume of electrical energy utilized per unit of output by 10 percent within one year;
4. individual job objectives, e.g., for a machine operator to reduce, within 12 months, waste and spoilage to 5 percent of all materials used.

As suggested in these "steps," the objectives often specify levels of achievement in *quantitative* and *time-bounded* terms. In other words, the quality and quantity of achievement expected within a defined period of time is specified for each division, department, and individual. The objectives to be achieved become the standards against which effectiveness is evaluated. Thus *quantitative* objectives for a sales manager might be to: (1) increase sales by 5 percent;

(2) maintain private-label sales at 7 percent of total sales; and (3) keep expenses for advertising promotion at last year's level. The sales manager could also be accountable for such *qualitative* objectives as: (1) developing a sales quota system for all salespeople; (2) preparing and recommending an incentive-compensation system for area managers; and (3) adjusting advertising emphasis from wholesalers to consumers. This contrasts with traditional systems that claim to measure effectiveness by rating individual performance on factors such as health, judgment, ability to deal with others, cost consciousness, job knowledge, initiative, and so forth.

Participation in the establishment of objectives by as many affected people as practical is generally recommended. When objectives are unilaterally established and implemented, MBO is likely to be viewed by participants more as a means of measurement and control than as a planning and motivational system.[53] If MBO is used as a club to pressure higher performance, it might be expected to fail or to have limited success.

There are several underlying themes in the objective-setting process. First, it should force managers and others to realize that there is *no* single objective for the organization, its component departments, or individual members. Second, MBO makes explicit the reality that objective setting involves risk and uncertainty in the inevitable balancing and trade-offs between objectives. Finally, the objective-setting process requires management to be more *explicit* about relative *priorities* and to analyze the relationships between objectives, subobjectives, and the actual behavior of members in the organization.[54]

Action Planning. After the objectives and their interrelationships have been established, action planning should be done with respect to the means, or "how," of accomplishing them. Action planning focuses on the methods and activities for accomplishing the desired objectives. If MBO is approached in a logical design, the action plans will depend on the specified objectives.

The comprehensiveness of action plans can vary widely. In more stable and less complex environments, management needs less action planning, because the means used are likely to be routine and standardized. In contrast, the activities that might be part of the action plan for a vice-president of marketing whose objective is to increase sales volume by 10 percent within 12 months might look like this:

1. release the new product that has been developed to supplement the product line;
2. evaluate the feasibility of a reduction in price to stimulate demand for the existing product line (products X and Y);
3. upgrade the effectiveness of sales personnel in selected geographical areas;
4. increase the rate of delivery for products X and Y.[55]

Self-Control and Correction. A comparison of objectives and action plans may suggest two major courses of action: *corrective actions,* in the form of revised means, or a thorough *reanalysis* of the objectives themselves. The objectives established should probably be reviewed several times a year as a part of the overall planning process.

Self-control and correction also means that employees at each level in the organization will be given the responsibility and opportunity for controlling their own behavior in performing the necessary activities to achieve the objectives. Self-control and correction is a relative concept that suggests that the immediate superior should spend less time and effort in continuously watching subordinates and telling them what to do and how to do it.

Periodic Reviews. This element means there should be systematic and scheduled reviews to measure and discuss progress, identify and resolve problems, and revise, drop, or add objectives. Although these reviews look to the past, there is considerable emphasis on determining the significance and lessons from the immediate past for dealing with the future.

The appraisal of an individual's performance during these periodic reviews strives to put a greater emphasis on mutual problem solving between the superior and subordinate. In some other approaches, by contrast, the superior acts more judgmentally, simply telling subordinates their weaknesses, strengths, and pay raise (if any) for the coming period. The mutual problem-solving approach requires subordinates to *participate* in reviewing their own performance. The superior encourages this by asking them to identify obstacles, problems, and courses of corrective action. Since objectives have been previously developed and (hopefully) agreed on, the review process also focuses more on actual achievements of the individual. This is in contrast to evaluating personality traits or subjective characteristics such as "conscientious," "enthusiastic," "creative," and the like. As suggested in Fig. 8.6, the periodic reviews should be a source for obtaining inputs to future objective setting. Thus the MBO process recycles over time.

PUREX CORPORATION: A CASE STUDY

A longitudinal study in 15 manufacturing plants of the Purex Corporation suggests some of the achievements and problems which might be experienced with a newly established MBO program.[56] The two-year time frame of the study involved an analysis of company records, including productivity data, and employee attitudes toward the MBO program. Seventy-four responses were obtained from the three managerial levels in the plants. Nonmanagerial employees were not included in the study and were apparently not a direct part of the MBO program.

Effectiveness. There was a significant increase in the levels of objectives set forth during the study period. The levels-of-production objectives increased from 97 percent to 104 percent, a 7 percent increase during the 2½-year study period. As might be expected, the actual attainment of the objectives set forth also improved. Moreover, productivity, which indicates the relative efficiency for attaining the objectives, increased about 9 percent from the theoretical standard. Toward the end of the study period, productivity increases began to taper off, however, perhaps because of the reduction of excessive "fat" in the organization. The managers felt that the MBO program provided two major advantages: (1) improved planning and control, and (2) increased motivation for better individual performance.

Problems. The Purex case also indicates that an MBO program is not a cure-all for solving all management problems. These limitations may be due to poor implementation, as well as to problems inherent in the MBO system itself. The major problem areas were: (1) the feeling expressed by lower-level managers (especially foremen) of not fully participating in the setting of objectives affecting them; (2) the general view by all levels of management that the system created burdensome and excessive paperwork; (3) the excessive emphasis on quantitative measures; and (4) the perception by some managers that MBO was being used as a device to squeeze extra work from them without corresponding rewards. Twelve of the 74 respondents reported that the MBO system was being used as a "whip" and/or felt it "treats people like statistics." Only 12 of the 33 foremen responding reported participation in setting objectives according to the spirit and intent of the program. Seven respondents said that there was adjustment of figures and inaccurate reporting. Thirteen managers thought that production objectives, which are more easily measured and quantifiable, were being emphasized at the expense of others, especially quality objectives. Some of the other motivational and behavioral aspects of these results are covered in Chapter 11.

MIXED RESULTS

As with any managerial process, the relative effectiveness of Management By Objectives is likely to be strongly affected by the behavioral forces operating in the organization.[57] Thus the research results on the effects of MBO are mixed. Also, some of these research results are difficult to interpret because the philosophy and processes of MBO were never fully implemented. In any event, two contrasting views of Management By Objectives can be presented:

1. The MBO programs which are likely to be most successful include (a) conscious emphasis on goal setting; (b) frequent interaction and feedback between subordinates and superiors regarding progress toward objectives, stumbling blocks, or the need for revised objectives; and (c) opportunities for participation, even though the final decisions may be made higher up in the organization.

2. When MBO is used as a top-down club, it is likely to be ineffective.[58] More important, if the values of organizational members are strongly antagonistic to the philosophy and processes of MBO, it is probably doomed to failure. Challenges such as these indicate the need for considerably more research on the effectiveness of the full-scale normative MBO model.

Nominal-Group Technique

A more limited planning aid, as compared to Management By Objectives, is the nominal-group technique. It is a special-purpose technique especially useful for dealing with planning tasks that require idea generation, creativity, and the exercise of judgment by a group of people. This technique is designed to deal with planning situations in which group members with different backgrounds and skills need to pool their judgments to create or identify a desirable course of action.

BASIC PROCESS

The nominal-group technique has the following characteristics:[59]

1. a group of about seven to ten individuals;
2. members, working alone in separate rooms or around a table in full view of one another, silently write down their ideas about the nature of the problem or alternative solutions to the problem, if it has already been identified;
3. at the end of some time period (e.g., 10 to 15 minutes), members share their ideas in a structured format, i.e., each member presents, in round-robin fashion, only one idea in each round;
4. a recorder writes a short, paraphrased version of each idea, as it is presented, on a flip chart or board until all ideas, possibly 18 to 25, have been expressed. There is no recorded identification of ideas with members;
5. each idea is then openly discussed by asking for clarification or stating support or nonsupport of it;
6. each member privately and in writing rank-orders the ideas in order of preference; the group decision or recommendation would be in the mathematically pooled outcomes of the member rankings of each idea.

POTENTIAL ADVANTAGES

The nominal-group technique can be particularly effective in the early exploratory phases of planning, because it encourages creativity and diversity of viewpoints. The process helps reduce a variety of inhibiting forces in most groups, including management planning meetings. The potential advantages of the nominal group technique can be summarized as:

(1) with no criticism allowed, participants are more willing to share ideas that are not yet well developed; (2) since there is no discussion, the nominal groups do not fall in a rut by focusing on one particular train of thought; and (3) because contributions are not evaluated, the nominal group can concentrate all of its time and energy on the specifically assigned task. Beyond this, (4) nominal grouping prevents dominance of strong personalities (formal or informal group leaders) since they have no persuasion opportunity. Also, (5) the expression of minority opinions and ideas is encouraged since criticism is not allowed. Finally, (6) incompatible, conflicting ideas are more likely to be expressed because feelings of inferiority or defensiveness among group members are minimized.[60]

APPLICATIONS

Although the nominal-group technique is a relatively new form of social technology, its use is increasing in private and public organizations alike, e.g., the federal Department of Agriculture, General Motors, state employment agencies, and universities. The nominal-group technique has been applied in a wide variety of planning situations, ranging from exploratory research to consumer participation in the planning process of organizations.[61] In our judgment, the nominal-group technique will be increasingly applied to planning tasks in the future.

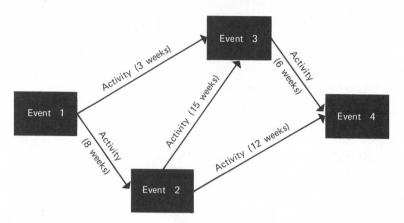

Fig. 8.7. Basic PERT network.

Program Evaluation and Review Technique (PERT)

This special-purpose planning aid represents one of the possible techniques of *action planning*. PERT is often used as a planning aid in production activities or for research and development projects.

BASIC PROCESS AND ADVANTAGES
PERT consists of five major elements: a network, resource allocation, time and cost considerations, network paths, and the critical path.[62] Let's consider these elements and their interrelations.

Network. A basic network, which represents the foundation of the PERT approach, is shown in Fig. 8.7. The network, a diagram of the sequential steps that must be performed to accomplish a project or task, consists of events, activities, and relationships. *Events* are points of decision or accomplishment of some task; *activities* occur between events and are the physical or mental efforts required to complete an event.

Activities are usually broken out in the network when different individuals or departments are to be held responsible for them. The relationships between the basic tasks are indicated by the desired sequence of events and activities in the network. For example, event 3 cannot occur until activities 1 and 2 have been accomplished. If these activities are the responsibility of different managers, they must coordinate their work.

Resource Allocation. To undertake the activities needed, resource requirements, such as labor, material, equipment, and facilities, need to be estimated. The availability of these resources will be a key influence on the length of time between events and the costs associated with each activity.

Time and Cost. PERT's principal value is its ability to aid management in reducing time and cost expenditures. The cost considerations may be expressed in the form of subbudgets, or estimated costs for each specified activity against which actual costs can be compared.

Given the resource constraints, time estimates for each activity can then be made. Figure 8.7 shows that the activity between events 1 and 2 should require eight weeks, for example.

Critical Path. A path is the sequence of events and activities that should be followed over the course of a project. A complex network may consist of dozens or even hundreds of activities and paths. Of course, work may take place along each of the different paths separately and concurrently. The length of the entire project is determined by the *path with the longest elapsed time.* To shorten a project, activity in the longest path should be the focal point for managerial attention. Since the longest path determines the shortest possible completion time, it is called the *critical path.* The critical path in Fig. 8.7 requires a total elapsed time of 29 weeks and can be calculated by adding the number of weeks scheduled to complete the activities between events 1 and 2, 2 and 3, and 3 and 4.

APPLICATIONS

The first major application of PERT occurred in 1958, when it was used in the United States Navy's Fleet Ballistic Missile Program, more popularly known as the Polaris Missile Program. PERT was credited as a major contributor to the two-years-early completion date of this program.[63]

Some governmental agencies require companies with whom they have contracts to use PERT. This technique has far-ranging action planning applications, such as in filming a movie, building a plant, diversifying into a new business, or introducing a product.

After a project is under way, PERT becomes less of a planning aid and more of a control mechanism. This is because it can monitor, through the periodic reporting system, the variances by comparing actual versus the planned elapsed times and costs for each activity.

Summary

Planning, one form of decision making, often incorporates the concepts and models explained in Chapters 6 and 7. The exception principle was utilized in this chapter; we emphasized only the concepts and models which, in our judgment, bear heavily on the process of planning.

As a way of developing your conceptual and technical skills in the complex area of planning, the chapter was organized into four major parts. The first part provided an introduction to the reasons planning fails, its uses, and relative accuracy. Planning is useful in maintaining stability and facilitating adaptation. The second part of the chapter provided a framework for considering the general features of planning. It included a discussion of the activities, nature, purpose, types, and comprehensiveness. The third part of the chapter set forth a contingency view of strategic planning to indicate how it might differ for organizations with different degrees of change and diversity in their environments. The most difficult planning problems occur in heterogeneous task environments under changing conditions. In contrast, planning is easiest in homogeneous task environments under stable conditions. Since information and the lack of it is so crucial to the planning process, we then focused on information inputs. One aspect is the nature of forecasting, for which two techniques are commonly used—the Delphi technique and simulation models. The last part of the chapter presented three applied planning models and aids—Management By Objectives, nominal-group technique, and Program Evaluation and Review Technique. The planning models and aids can all be used in the same organization and at the same time. The behavioral aspects of planning will be considered more directly in Chapter 11, which focuses on motivation, and Chapter 15, which deals with processes of organizational change.

Discussion Questions

1. What is the difference between strategic planning and forecasting?

2. Explain the similarities and differences between the Delphi technique and simulation models.

3. If an organization's strategic plans are always 100 percent accurate, does this mean that its managers are good planners? Explain.

4. How would you compare and contrast strategic planning and tactical planning?

5. If you were developing a five-year plan for yourself, what issues, goals, and areas would be included as part of your strategic and tactical planning, respectively?

6. Use the Management By Objectives model to develop an analysis of the experiences you had in your last job. You should assess this experience in terms of how consistent or inconsistent it was with the basic MBO process in terms of objective setting, action planning, self-control and correction, and periodic reviews.

7. What is the difference between contingency plans and taking a contingency view of strategic planning?

8. Can the contingency view of strategic planning be applied to planning for yourself? Explain?

9. Use the Program Evaluation and Review Technique (PERT) to develop an action plan for the successful completion of this course.

Management Incidents

THE COACH'S NEW JOB

You have recently been appointed Head Football Coach at All-American University. Previously you were assistant coach at three different universities during the past ten years. All of the schools you were affiliated with had mediocre win-lose records. The university you are joining has had an even worse win-lose record. In all of the previous jobs and as a student athlete, you observed one common theme—poor or no planning. With your bachelors degree in business, you are acutely aware of the prominent role of strategic planning in most successful firms. In your previous jobs, you were continuously frustrated and put down by the head coaches whenever you brought up the need for some strategic planning.

The university administration has given you a four-year contract, a moderate increase in the budget for the coming year, and a relatively free hand. Because the central administration feels that a good football team can attract students and create favorable public relations, your only mandate is to develop a "winner." You intend to invest substantial energies in strategic planning. You are convinced that this will avoid the crisis atmosphere and management by reaction and hindsight so evident in the other football operations with which you had been affiliated. You should feel free to make whatever assumptions are necessary to deal with the following questions.

1. What concepts, tools, and approaches would be of primary importance in this strategic-planning process?
2. Give a concrete example of each of the concepts, tools, and techniques identified in the first question.
3. Where would you place your situation in terms of the contingency framework of strategic planning shown in Fig. 8.2? What implications would this have for your approach to strategic planning?

JEWEL COMPANIES*

The Jewel Companies, Incorporated is headquartered in Melrose Park, Illinois. It has approximately $2 billion a year in sales. The company operates several hundred supermarkets. Many of these supermarkets are connected with drugstores opened by the company. Jewel Companies has also branched into self-service department stores, convenience food stores, restaurants, and the manufacturing of food products.

The planning process of Jewel was described by Howard O. Wagner, its executive vice president, as follows:

The organization has changed substantially in recent years. During the 1950s, the company operated with a five-year expansion plan. This planning was restricted to the corporate level. Since then the company has become widely decentralized. The operating companies have their own management staffs and largely operate independently.

All of the operating companies have short-term annual budgets, which are very detailed and extended to the store level. The operating companies submit their plans to corporate management for review. Long-range planning is done mainly at the operating-company level. Each company submits detailed state-

---

* Reprinted by permission of the publisher from *Long Term Profit Planning* by E. Weinwarm and G. Weinwarm. © 1971 by American Management Association, Inc., pp. 126–127.

ments of funds required, including inventories and other current requirements, and profit projections. Many of the stores are leased from corporate-controlled real estate companies.

A three- to four-day conference of top executives of the corporation and the subsidiaries is held annually, away from headquarters. At that time the long-range plan is reviewed and another year is added. The long-range plan now covers three years. Management feels that a longer period would be unrealistic in view of the number and rapidity of unforeseeable changes in this industry.

A capital planning committee makes the final allocation of available funds, and the operating companies then plan the use of their respective shares. A minimum return of 10 percent on investment is required and is considerably higher for riskier projects. The analysis is based on the discounted cash-flow technique.

There is no separate planning organization or staff. Top management of the corporation and the operating companies, with their staffs, do the planning. Management believes that this method is economical and works satisfactorily. The company has been highly successful in regularly exceeding the growth rate of the industry.

Special attention is given to recruitment and training of personnel and the development of the supervisory and executive personnel needed to support the planned expansion programs. There have been no problems in staffing new facilities from the available inventory of trained personnel.

1. What concepts and approaches seem to be illustrated in this description of the planning process at Jewel Companies?
2. How might you characterize the Jewel Companies' "situation" (or situations) in terms of the contingency framework of strategic planning shown in Fig. 8.2?
3. Based on the limited description presented above, do you feel that there should be any changes in or additions to the planning process at the Jewel Companies? Explain.

REFERENCES

1. M. Kami, "Business Planning As Business Opportunity," in *Preparing Tomorrow's Business Leaders Today*, ed. P. Drucker (Englewood Cliffs, N.J.: Prentice-Hall, 1969), p. 103.

2. H. Mintzberg, D. Raisinghani, and A. Theoret, "The Structure of 'Unstructured' Decision Processes," *Administrative Science Quarterly* **21** (1976): 246–275.

3. G. Steiner, "Does Planning Pay Off?" *California Management Review* **5** (1962): 37–39.

4. J. Bacon, *Planning and Forecasting in the Smaller Company* (New York: Conference Board, 1971).

5. M. Sashkin, "Failures in Planning," in *Introduction to Management: Readings and Discussion*, ed. M. Sashkin and H. Nussbaum (Lexington, Mass.: Xerox Individualized Publishing, 1975), p. 75.

6. "Interview: Does GE Really Plan Better?" *MBA* **9** (1975): 43.

7. A. Roalman, "Why Corporations Hate the Future," *MBA* **9** (1975): 36.

8. R. Vancil, "The Accuracy of Long-Range Planning," *Harvard Business Review* **48** (1970): 98–101.

9. D. Ammer, "The Side Effects of Planning," *Harvard Business Review* **48** (1970): 32–44.

10. R. Ackoff, *A Concept of Corporate Planning* (New York: Wiley/Interscience, 1970), pp. 2–4.

11. R. Murdick, "Nature of Planning and Plans," *Advanced Management Journal* **32** (1967): 37.

12. J. Emery, *Organizational Planning and Control Systems* (New York: Macmillan, 1971), p. 113.

13. M. Arhriya, "Planning as Integration," in *Studies in Organization Design,* ed. J. Lorsch and P. Lawrence (Homewood, Ill.: Richard D. Irwin and The Dorsey Press, 1970), pp. 168–186.

14. D. Thunes and R. House, "Where Long-Range Planning Pays Off," *Business Horizons* **13** (1970): 81–87; J. Friedman, "A Conceptual Model for the Analysis of Planning Behavior," *Administrative Science Quarterly* **12** (1967): 225–252; D. Kruckeberg, "Variations in Behavior of Planning Agencies," *Administrative Science Quarterly* **16** (1971): 192–203.

15. Adapted from "Ford Motor Company Case," in *Marketing Management,* D. David (New York: Ronald Press, 1972), pp. 547–568.

16. R. Anthony, *Planning and Control Systems: A Framework for Analysis* (Boston: Harvard University, Graduate School of Business Administration, 1965), p. 24.

17. L. Gerstner, Jr., "Can Strategic Planning Pay Off?" *Business Horizons* **15** (1972): 5–16.

18. L. Sayles, "Technological Innovation and the Planning Process," *Organizational Dynamics* **2** (1973): 68–80.

19. E. Bowman, "Strategy and the Weather," *Sloan Management Review* **17** (1976): 49–62.

20. R. Vincil, "Strategy Formulation in Complex Organizations," *Sloan Management Review* **17** (1976): 1–18.

21. Frank F. Gilmore, "Formulating Strategy in Smaller Companies," *Harvard Business Review* (May–June 1971): 80. Copyright © 1971 by the President and Fellows of Harvard College. All rights reserved.

22. Sayles, *op. cit.*

23. J. McDonald, "Sears Makes It Look Easy," *Fortune* **69** (1964): 120–123.

24. W. Hall, "Corporate Strategic Planning—Some Perspectives for the Future," *Michigan Business Review* **24** (1972): 16–21.

25. C. Percy and W. Roberts, "Planning the Basic Strategy of a Medium-Sized Business," in *Long-Range Planning for Management,* rev. ed., ed. D. Ewing (New York: Harper & Row, 1964), pp. 106–114.

26. *See* Ackoff, *op. cit.,* p. 6.

27. F. Secrest, "The Process of Long-Range Planning at Ford Motor Company," in *Managerial Long-Range Planning,* ed. G. Steiner (New York: McGraw-Hill, 1963), p. 237.

28. W. Hill, "A Behavioral Model of the Formation and Displacement of Corporate Goals," *Southern Journal of Business* **4** (1969): 1–17.

29. A. Raia, *Managing by Objectives* (Glenview, Ill.: Scott, Foresman, 1974).

30. M. McCaskey, "A Contingency Approach to Planning: Planning with Goals and Planning without Goals," *Academy of Management Journal* **17** (1974): 281–291.

31. G. Steiner, *Top Management Planning* (New York: Macmillan, 1969), pp. 266–269.

32. J. Cecil, "Continental Oil Company: Long-Range Planning," in *Managerial Long-Range Planning,* ed. G. Steiner (New York: McGraw-Hill, 1963), pp. 186–196.

33. Anthony, *op. cit.,* p. 54.

34. W. Cain, "International Planning: Mission Impossible?" *Columbia Journal of World Business* **5** (1970): 53–60.

35. C. Hofer, "Toward a Contingency Theory of Business Strategy," *Academy of Management Journal* **18** (1975): 784–810.

36. C. Anderson and F. Paine, "Managerial Perceptions and Strategic Behavior," *Academy of Management Journal* **18** (1975): 811–823.

37. F. Aguilar, *Scanning the Business Environment* (New York: Macmillan, 1967), pp. 19–21.

38. "Rapid Rise of the Host with the Most," *Time Magazine,* June 12, 1972, pp. 77–82.

39. B. Burton, "Who Needs It?: Firms Strive to Avoid Introducing Products that Nobody will Buy," *Wall Street Journal,* March 6, 1967.

40. Aguilar, *op. cit.*

41. D. Cleland and W. King, "Competitive Business Intelligence Systems," *Business Horizons* **18** (1975): 19–28.

42. D. Bell, *The Coming of Post Industrial Society: A Venture in Social Forecasting* (New York: Basic Books, 1973), pp. 196–210.

43. I. Ansoff, "Managing Strategic Surprise by Response to Weak Signals," *California Management Review* **18** (1975): 21–33.

44. A. Delbecq, A. Van de Ven, and A. Gustafson, *Group Techniques for Program Planning: A Guide to Nominal, Group and Delphi Processes* (Glenview, Ill.: Scott, Foresman, 1975).

45. D. Roman, "Technological Forecasting in the Decision Process," *Academy of Management Journal* **13** (1970): 127–138.

46. A. Fusfeld and R. Foster, "The Delphi Technique: Survey and Comment," *Business Horizons* **14** (1971): 63–74.

47. S. Wheelwright, "Management by Model During Inflation," *Business Horizons* **18** (1975): 33–42.

48. H. Schollhammer, "Long-Range Planning in Multinational Firms," *Columbia Journal of World Business* **6** (1971): 79–86.

49. G. Steiner, ed., *Managerial Long-Range Planning* (New York: McGraw-Hill, 1963), p. 60.

50. V. Hammond, III, "Do's and Don'ts of Computer Models for Planning," *Harvard Business Review* **52** (1974): 112.

51. Roman, *op. cit.,* p. 37.

52. Adapted from Raia, *op. cit.*

53. H. Levinson, "Management By Whose Objectives?" *Harvard Business Review* **48** (1970): 125–135; O. McConley, "MBO—Twenty Years Later, Where Do We Stand?" *Business Horizons* **16** (1973): 25–36.

54. P. Drucker, "What Should You Expect? A User's Guide to MBO," *Public Administration Review* **36** (1976): 12–19.

55. Raia, *op. cit.*, p. 71.

56. Adapted from A. Raia, "A Second Look at Management Goals and Controls," *California Management Review* **8** (1966): 49–58.

57. H. Tosi *et al.*, "How Real Are Changes Induced by Management by Objectives?" *Administrative Science Quarterly* **21** (1976): 276–306; J. Ivancevich, "Changes in Performance in a Management by Objectives Program," *Administrative Science Quarterly* **19** (1974): 563–574.

58. S. Kerr, "Some Modifications in MBO as an OD Strategy," *Academy of Management Proceedings* (1972): 42.

59. Delbecq, Van de Ven, and Gustafson, *op. cit.*, pp. 7–10, 17–18.

60. T. Green and P. Pietri, "Using Nominal Group to Improve Upward Communications," *MSU Business Topics* **22** (1974): 40.

61. Delbecq, *op. cit.*

62. This discussion is based substantially on *New Uses and Management Implications of PERT* (New York: Booz Allen and Hamilton, Inc. 1964). *Also see* R. Schonberger, "Custom-Tailored, PERT/CPM Systems," *Business Horizons* **15** (1972): 64–66.

63. D. Boulanger, "Program Evaluation and Review Technique," *Advanced Management* **26** (1961): 8–12.

9
Control
Process

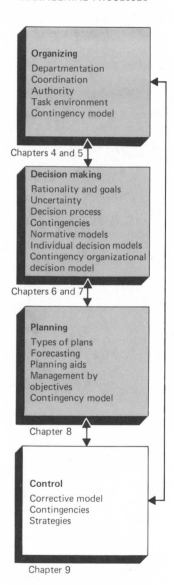

Organizing

Departmentation
Coordination
Authority
Task environment
Contingency model

Chapters 4 and 5

Decision making

Rationality and goals
Uncertainty
Decision process
Contingencies
Normative models
Individual decision models
Contingency organizational
decision model

Chapters 6 and 7

Planning

Types of plans
Forecasting
Planning aids
Management by
objectives
Contingency model

Chapter 8

Control

Corrective model
Contingencies
Strategies

Chapter 9

The objectives of this chapter are to:

develop your skills for using formal control practices that will minimize negative reactions to control;

create a firm understanding of the nature of formal control, its many uses within organizations, and the costs and benefits of control strategies or practices;

develop your conceptual and technical skills for making use of the corrective model of control;

sharpen your conceptual skills in seeing the impact and implications of three major contingency variables on the formal control system—kinds of power used within the organization, the type of technology, and the level in the formal hierarchy; ·

improve your technical and conceptual skills for utilizing six different formal control strategies—socialization, reward-punishment system, policies and rules, formal hierarchy, budgets, and machine controls.

The issues of societal and organizational controls seemed to underlie much of the conflict and unrest that erupted on the campuses and in the streets during the late 1960s and early 1970s. Although the public debate over questions of control have now declined, we should not conclude that the basic issues that fostered much unrest have been resolved. Rather, the approaches for dealing with the issues of control have shifted from attacking organizations and institutions from the outside by riots, boycotts, and the like to working within those institutions to bring about the desired changes.

One of the main purposes of the political system of a society is to resolve issues of control: *who* has the authority to do *what* to *whom*. The means used to resolve issues of control can vary widely, depending on the political, cultural, and economic systems of the society. At one extreme, coercive practices, such as jailing or putting to death those who are challenging the existing controls, have been used in some societies. At the other extreme, participative practices, such as open debate, sharing or eliminating control, and increased rewards, have been used to deal with challenges to the existing structure of controls. Current issues involving questions of control and the practices used by institutions or individuals in our political system can be found in the daily newspaper (i.e., state versus federal control, civil rights for minorities, equal rights for women, government control of business, the executive versus congressional control over foreign affairs, and so on).

Similar challenges to control practices have been taking place within organizations. The fundamental issues of organizational control include such questions as: Who is to control? What forms of control are appropriate or acceptable? How much control is needed? When do increases in control become ineffective for both the employee and the organization? What forces seem to influence the amount and types of controls used within organizations?

This chapter focuses primarily on formal managerial and organizational control. By focusing on internal formal controls, we eliminate many other issues of control with respect to organizations, for control, in its broadest sense, is part of an organization's environmental, managerial, and behavioral systems.

The chapter is organized as follows. First, we discuss the nature of control and present the corrective model of control. Next, we outline three major contingency variables that are likely to influence the relative emphasis on various formal control strategies. Finally, we present six of the formal control strategies often found within organizations.

NATURE OF CONTROL

In its broadest sense, "control" refers to the process by which a person, group, or organization consciously determines or influences what another person, group, or organization will do.[1] Within organizations and society in general, reaction to the word "control" is very negative, often being interpreted to imply restraining, coercing, delimiting, directing, enforcing, watching, manipulating, and inhibiting. This is partially due to the strong belief in such cultural values as individualism and democracy, which appear to be inconsistent with the notion of control. Individualism is based on self-control and some external controls, such as certain governmental laws.

Some laws serve to limit the imposition of control by one group or institution over another. The Bill of Rights acts as a mechanism to limit (control) the actions of the state on its citizenry. This type of mechanism might be thought of as *preventive control*. Preventive control refers to mechanisms designed to minimize the need for taking corrective action. In organizations, rules and regulations and training-and-development programs function primarily as preventive controls. Rules and regulations limit the actions employees can take to reach the organization's goals. It is usually assumed that if the employees comply, the goals of the organization are more likely to be achieved.

The more common view of managerial and organizational control emphasizes a process of *corrective control,* or mechanisms designed to return the individual or department to some predetermined condition. For example, management might believe that theft by some employees has increased. To change this situation, management might now require all employees to enter and depart the building from a common entry and exit area, as well as post a security guard.

Managerial control can be both preventive and corrective in nature, and distinctions between the two types may be found within a single managerial practice. Thus reward-punishment practices may prevent deviations by promising rewards for compliance, as well as attempt to correct for deviations by providing punishments or withholding rewards. A salesperson may be promised a bonus if sales go above a certain level and threatened with dismissal if sales fall below a certain level.

Uses of Controls

Formal control systems, strategies, and practices are put to many uses within organizations:

1. Controls may be used to *standardize performance*. This might be accomplished by supervisory inspections, written procedures, or production schedules.
2. Controls may be used to protect an organization's assets from theft, waste, or misuse. Record-keeping requirements, auditing procedures, and division of responsibilities are some of the tactics of control here.
3. Controls may be used to *standardize* the *quality* of products or services offered by an organization. This might be attained through employee training, inspections, statistical quality control, and incentive systems.
4. Controls may be established to *limit* the amount of *authority* that can be exercised by various organizational positions and levels. The limits on discretion may be expressed in job descriptions, policy directives, rules, and auditing systems.
5. Controls for measuring and *directing employee performance* are common. Merit-rating systems, direct supervisory observation, and reports on output or scrap loss per employee, are illustrative.
6. Managerial *planning* (discussed in Chapter 8) is a major means of preventive control. The process of setting goals helps to define the appropriate scope and direction of the members' behaviors to achieve the desired results.[2]

There are, of course, many other uses of formal controls in organizations. Formal controls are spread throughout every aspect of organizations; control is needed to ensure the stability and adaptability of all organizations. Even so, there remain many unresolved issues, e.g., the amount of control the organization needs to exercise, the appropriate basis of an organization's control system (whether reward- or punishment-centered), and the types of control strategies considered acceptable by the organization's members. Issues of organizational and societal control are intimately related to questions of values. In the People's Republic of China, for example, the intensive socialization of the people, along with the unique Chinese cultural heritage, have led to widespread agreement among the citizenry as to the right of the government to control many aspects of individuals' behavior.

Economics of Control

Formal controls should be recognized as *means* to help the organization achieve its desired results. The costs of formal control systems relative to their benefits must be assessed in the same manner as other organizational processes. Analysis of the economics of control systems, strategies, and practices involves three basic questions:

1. What are the costs versus benefits of various amounts of formal controls?
2. What are the cost-benefit relationships of alternative strategies for controlling the same activity?
3. At what point or for what activities should controls be used?

The economic *benefit* of a formal control system is the difference between its costs and the improvement in performance it creates. For example, when the quality of output is unsatisfactory, is it more economical to: (1) lower the span of control so that superiors can more closely supervise their subordinates; (2) create a system of worker rewards that would increase with increases in quality; (3) substitute machines for humans; or (4) change the points or location of controls to detect errors earlier?

COST-BENEFIT MODEL

A cost-benefit model on the economics of a formal control system is shown in Fig. 9.1. This model suggests that the manager and the organization are faced with a problem of *trade-offs* in deciding on the emphasis to be placed on formal controls. The *horizontal axis,* which indicates the intensity of the formal controls, varies from low to high. The *vertical axis* indicates the dollar costs or benefits of a control practice. For purposes of illustration, the *costs-of-control* curve is shown as a direct function of the amount of formal control. For example, there could be a proportionate relationship between increases in the number of rules and regulations and the costs of using and enforcing them.

We also assume that it is possible to plot the changes in benefits that would exist for each degree of formal control. With a small amount of control, the control structure is so weak that the costs exceed its benefits. As the amounts of formal control increase, a cumulative effect for management might be realized.

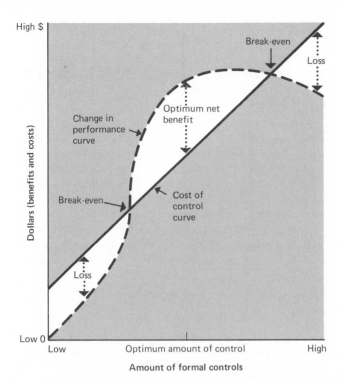

Fig. 9.1. Cost-benefit model of control.

273

NATURE OF CONTROL

Up to a point, the additional increments of formal control practices increase the efficiency of controls management has already established. However, continued increases in formal controls could result in flattening the efficiency curve and lowering performance level. For example, management might acquire net benefits from a reduction in span of control from 20 to 15 employees. Further reductions in the span of control from 15 to 8 employees could result in costs far exceeding the benefits to management, e.g., substantial increases in the cost of managerial control and creation of worker hostility and dissatisfaction because of a feeling of oversupervision and too much pressure. This could lead to accelerated absenteeism, turnover, and worker indifference. The end result could be that the increased formal controls have a negative impact on performance.

Although management may not be able to arrive at the exact point of the *optimum amount* of control, as shown in Fig. 9.1, a range within reasonably narrow limits can probably be determined.[3] Note that the two break-even points shown in Fig. 9.1 indicate the increasing and decreasing effectiveness experienced with additional amounts of formal control.

IMPLICATIONS FOR ROUTINE TASKS
For relatively routine types of tasks and decisions, there is considerable evidence that improvements in information technology, especially through the use of computers, has lowered the relative costs of automated controls (compared to that for human controls). In some cases, like oil refineries and automobile

assembly lines, the only human control is the starting or stopping of the machines.[4] The increasing sophistication in the technology of machine control, along with substantial reductions in their costs, can increase managerial productivity. This is because new technologies, e.g., computer information control, may reduce the number of managers needed to improve their control and coordination of complex organizations.

CORRECTIVE MODEL OF CONTROL

The corrective model of control refers to the process of detecting and correcting deviations from preestablished goals or standards.[5] It places heavy reliance on feedback and reaction to what has already happened.[6] As shown in Fig. 9.2, the development and maintenance of a corrective model of control consists of six interconnected "steps": (1) define the subsystem (e.g., an individual or department); (2) identify characteristics to be measured; (3) set standards; (4) collect information; (5) make comparisons; and (6) diagnose and implement corrections.

Define the Subsystem

A formal control process might be created and maintained for a single employee, a department, or a whole organization. The controls could focus on specific inputs, production processes, or outputs. Controls on *inputs* often limit the degree of variance from standards in the resources utilized within the production process of the organization. This serves to reduce the uncertainty about the quality and quantity of inputs into the production process. For example, at the Joseph P. Schlitz breweries, elaborate controls (including human inspections and laboratory testing) are used to make sure that the water and grains used in the production of beer meet predetermined standards. The *production process* (production subsystem) consists of a web of controls: length of time for cooking the brew, temperature in the vats, sampling of the brew, laboratory testing of it in each stage of the production process, inspection of the beer prior to final packing, etc. Controls on the final *output* of goods and services could range from levels of inventories to monitoring consumer attitudes toward acceptance of the company's goods and services.

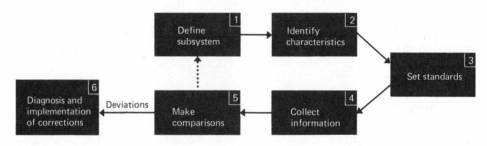

Fig. 9.2. Corrective model of control.

Identify Characteristics

The types of information that can and should be obtained about the subsystem must be identified. The establishment of a formal corrective-control process requires an early assessment of such questions as: What information characteristics are feasible from a technical standpoint? What are the economic costs versus expected benefits associated with obtaining information on each characteristic? Does variation in the characteristic make any difference in the essential performance goals or objectives of the subsystem?

These questions suggest that managers should usually be selective in the characteristics measured. The "Principle of selectivity," also known as Pareto's law, is often a useful guideline in the establishment of controls: "In any series of elements to be controlled, a small fraction, in terms of number of elements, always accounts for a large fraction in terms of effects."[7] The control aspect of a Management By Objectives (MBO) system is based on this principle. The direct control of outputs or objectives enables the control of the few, but vital, elements that can account for major variations in performance. In brewing beer, for example, three of the critical characteristics are water, temperature, and length of brewing time.

Set Standards

Management should establish standards for each of the characteristics being measured. *Standards* are the criteria for evaluating the activities being undertaken by the subsystem.

There are often interrelationships between standards, thus requiring considerable coordination between organizational departments. For example, a consulting firm with goals of providing only the highest-quality services will need to develop an elaborate network of standards for screening its personnel. These selection standards might include a minimum of a master's degree, three years of applicable experience, and the like.

Management is increasingly developing control systems based on performance standards, or statements of the results that exist when performance is satisfactory. For example, American Airlines has established the following types of standards (there are also others) for judging the quality of performance for each of its airport ticket offices.[8] The specific quantitative levels for each of these types of standards approximate the following:

1. *Waiting time*—at least 85 percent of the customers arriving at an airport ticket counter shall be waited on within five minutes;
2. *Baggage mishandlings*—baggage mishandlings by airport ticket salespersonnel, skycaps, and ticket-lift agents shall not exceed 1 per 20 checked and rechecked bags;
3. *Customer impact*—at least 90 percent of airport customer contacts shall be rated acceptable;
4. *Posted flight-arrival times*—at least 95 percent of the flight-arrival times posted in the "will arrive" columns on the arrival board shall be accurate to the degree that the actual arrivals will be within 15 minutes of the time posted.

Collect Information

The collection of information refers to the means used to obtain measurements on each of the designated characteristics. Information could be collected through human (observations by a supervisor) or mechanical (a counting device) means. Information may also be collected by the individual or group whose performance is to be controlled. In some cases, this can result in a loss of meaningful control, especially if money can be diverted to satisfy an individual's or group's personal needs or if those needs aren't being adequately met. In 1975, for example, the new president of Union Planters National Bank of Memphis, Tennessee, found considerable corruption among eight executives and even some clerks. Three of the former employees were sent to jail and several others were indicted. The president claims that executives were getting payoffs in exchange for making shaky multimillion dollar loans. Other employees were found to be simply embezzling money. Why did this happen? According to the new president, the lack of formal controls combined with low pay scales encouraged dishonesty. To solve these problems, he gave a hefty across-the-board pay increase to the bank employees and installed a new control system to prevent shaky loans and detect corruption quickly.[9]

Often employees are motivated to distort or conceal data that can be used as a basis for punishing, demoting, or criticizing themselves. For example, if American Airlines relied on its airport ticket counter employees for the basic data used to calculate performance standards, we might expect some motivation to conceal or distort the data. This might become especially troublesome if the data were then used as a basis for punishing the employees.

Managers often create special departments to act as information collectors by auditing certain activities of other departments. Thus a personnel department might collect data to see that the standards regarding pay raises are being met. Similarly, a controller's department might collect and analyze information to see that expenditures of funds are completed according to certain standards.

Make Comparisons

The process of *making comparisons* refers to determining whether differences exist between the activities and results that are actually taking place and what *should be* occurring. This process involves comparing the information collected with the established standards, which might be contained in written rules, computer programs, or on tap in the manager's memory. A purely comparative activity might occur when a graduate assistant of a professor: (1) obtains the output of student scores on a multiple-choice test from the college's scoring center, (2) compares these scores with the professor's standards, (3) determines the extent to which the students' scores (performances) differ from the standards, but (4) then gives these analyses to the professor for the evaluation of grades because the results are not consistent with the established standards.

If no difference between what is actually taking place and what should be taking place shows up, the department normally continues to function without any intervention.

Diagnosis and Implementation of Corrections

This "step" refers to trying to assess the types, amounts, and causes of the *deviations,* as well as determining and implementing a course of action that would eliminate those deviations. To return to the American Airlines example, let's assume that baggage mishandlings have gone above the acceptable standard. A diagnosis would need to be made of why the mishandlings have increased. Depending on the apparent causes of the deviations, management might consider such corrective mechanisms as further employee training, dismissal or demotion of certain employees, creation of incentive schemes, changed procedures, etc. The actions to implement the corrections in the process may be accomplished by either human or mechanical changes.

Summary

The ability to measure or control a characteristic of a subsystem does not mean that it should be controlled. The corrective model of control just described emphasizes the "Principle of selectivity." This model suggests a framework by which managers can concentrate on the control of deviations or exceptions. This reduces the likelihood of overmanaging and facilitates a more efficient utilization of scarce and expensive managerial resources. The specific nature of corrective and preventive controls within a department is likely to be influenced by three contingency variables—type of power, type of technology, and level in the formal hierarchy.

SOME CONTINGENCIES INFLUENCING THE CONTROL PROCESS

Power

Different control systems, strategies, and practices are closely linked to different kinds and combinations of power used within the organization. Each type of power describes a different relationship between the person subjected to power and the person exercising that power. A general definition of power is "the ability to limit choice," and the types of power by which choice can be limited differ significantly.[10] An organization may use different combinations of five types of power—reward, coercive, legitimate, referent, and expert (discussed more fully in Chapter 12).

REWARD POWER
Reward power refers to a person's or group's perception that another person or group has the ability to provide varying amounts and types of rewards. A common example of this is the superior's granting different pay increases for different levels of performance by subordinates. Managements have often resisted the formation of unions in their organizations because collective bargaining tends to reduce their discretion to reward employees based on different levels of performance. Within business organizations, this is probably the most important type of power use to achieve "control" over people. It is usually considered desirable to base rewards on performance measures. This is

because there should be greater motivation to perform well, especially when the job is not personally satisfying or rewarding.[11]

COERCIVE POWER

Coercive power refers to a person's or group's perception that another person or group has the ability to administer punishments. In the political system, obvious forms of coercive power include physical punishments, e.g., inflicting pain, deformity, or death, and the forceful control over basic human needs. Coercive power in business organizations is commonly expressed through such means as dismissals (or threats of dismissal), demotions, and social pressure.

Social pressure, a subtle form of coercive power, is similar to being hit by a psychological club. One tactic might be for a superior to cut off communications with an individual until he or she shapes up or to continuously monitor the individual's performance or actions. This is what occurred when a senior salesman, who had been with a certain firm for 25 years, decided not to give his "fair share" to the firm's United Fund drive. The company had a schedule indicating each employee's "fair share" so as to reach the firm's goal. This goal was used to justify the company's claim of being socially responsible. The flow of communiction to the salesman from higher levels of management was direct and intense. The appeals for cooperation were strictly of a moral nature; he wasn't threatened with dismissal or demotion. However, the pressures built up. First, there were appeals on two occasions by his immediate supervisor. No change! Then, there were two sessions with the department manager. No change, but weakening! Finally, a 30-minute session with the vice-president of marketing did it. The salesman made out a new pledge in the "recommended" amount.

The employees in this particular department came to interpret the public expression of the firm's recommendation as a required "must." The salesman seemed to react to the battery of communication as a form of psychological punishment. In this as well as most other situations, it is highly probable that other types of power were also operating.

One of the basic problems with control systems based on coercive power is that they tend to create alienation, withdrawal, or aggressive hostilities in those subjected to them. Thus a paradox is created. Coercive power is often justified by management as necessary to gain compliance in order for the organization to attain its goals. But the excessive use of coercive power, as perceived by the employees, may serve to reduce their motivation to comply. It may actually motivate them to withdraw from their work by becoming passive and indifferent participants, creating an even more difficult control problem. To reduce their frustrations, they may also militantly strike back. The massive unionization in the late 1930s was partially a reaction to the coercive power used by some business organizations. In the public sector, some segments of the population view court-ordered busing as an exercise of coercive power by the courts and other government agencies.

LEGITIMATE POWER

Legitimate power, based on the values held by an individual, exists when one person or group believes it is rightful or desirable for another person or group to influence their actions. Thus faculty members are usually viewed as having a legitimate right to assign students grades based on academic performance.

An employee who believes in the institutions of private property and the basic framework of a free-enterprise system may feel that the superior's control of his or her behavior to obtain profits is quite appropriate. In contrast, an employee who believes in public ownership and control of the means of production may interpret managerial controls over his or her work as a form of exploitation. In this case, the superior would be perceived as having little legitimate power, and this would make the superior's control of such an individual much more difficult.

REFERENT POWER

Referent power is based on the desire of one individual or group to identify with or be like another person or group. It is often expressed by copying the actions, style, and beliefs of that individual or group. A manager who defines getting ahead as obtaining successively higher positions in an organization may be especially prone to control through referent power. This individual, placed under an effective manager, may rapidly develop many of the same skills and perceptions as his or her superior. This occurs because of the strong psychological identification with the superior and the need for recognition from that person. In such cases, referent power may be functional for both the individual and the organization.

EXPERT POWER

Expert power refers to a person's or group's perception that another person or group has greater knowledge or expertise and is thus worthy of following. A person might gain expert power through special experience, training, reputation, or demonstrated ability. Professional programs in colleges and universities (e.g., business, engineering, and law) generally create within their students the power of expertise. Many positions in business organizations rely on various types of expertise, e.g., engineers, accountants, statisticians, market researchers, skilled tradesmen, and professional managers.

COMBINATIONS OF POWER

Between organizations or departments, there may be different combinations of the five types of power. The degree to which different combinations of power are effective can vary between organizations as well as between departments of a single organization.[12]

Figure 9.3 shows a hypothetical power graph of the relative emphasis on each type of power in organic and mechanistic managerial systems. An *organic* management system is usually desirable under unstable, complex, and changing task environments. This type of management system is usually decentralized, relies on employee participation in the decision-making process, and is continuously monitoring and adapting to changes in the task environment. A *mechanistic* system, by contrast, tends to be effective when the tasks are routine and the environment is stable. A mechanistic management system is usually centralized, relies very little on employee participation, and emphasizes the development and use of rules and regulations.

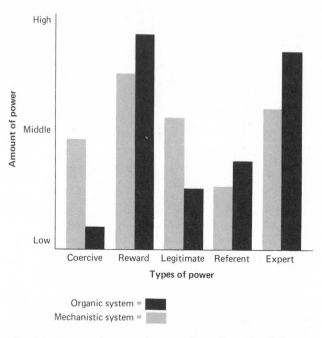

Fig. 9.3. Types of power in organic and mechanistic systems.

Figure 9.3 suggests that there is likely to be more emphasis on coercive power in a mechanistic system than in an organic one; formal, hierarchical authority is a logical basis for integrating and controlling tasks in a mechanistic system. On the other hand, the organic system relies more on mutual confidence between the members to obtain integration and control of activities. This is especially true because the organic system is usually dealing with changing task environments and unstructured decision situations. Expert power, as possessed by engineers and other professionals, is likely to be given more emphasis in the organic system, which emphasizes the importance of personal abilities, self-control, and the contributions of professional expertise to solving the firm's problems. In contrast, the mechanistic system seems to place higher value on the loyalty and obedience of employees to the organization and on legitimate power.

In sum, the control process and structure in a mechanistic system is likely to emphasize: (1) top-down controls; (2) short-term, objective measures; (3) impersonal mechanisms, such as rules, regulations, and machine controls; (4) narrow spans of control; and (5) detailed job descriptions. In contrast, the organic system places less emphasis on these types of control mechanisms and is likely to rely more on: (1) participants' self-control; (2) control through interpersonal contacts—suggestions, persuasion, advice, and information; (3) mutual exchange and long-term control; and (4) control through shared goals and participation in decision making.[13]

Technology

The types of controls found in the technical subsystem of an organization are influenced by the type of technology used—unit, mass production, or continuous process.[14] *Unit-production* technology is the custom manufacturing of individual items, e.g., an aircraft carrier, nuclear power plant, skyscraper, and custom homes. The control system here is likely to emphasize the employee's self-control, managerial surveillance, and control through detailed plans. There is likely to be only a slight use of mechanical controls.

Mass-production technology refers to the manufacture of large volumes of identical or similar goods, e.g., automobiles, baby food, and toothpaste. With this technology, the control system shifts toward impersonal mechanisms and reliance on rules and regulations and mechanical controls, e.g., assembly-line-paced work.

Continuous-process technology is characterized by an ongoing flow of activities for transforming inputs into outputs, with virtually all physical activities being performed by machines. The workers do not so much handle the material itself as monitor the work flow via dials and diagnose work in the production process. Gasoline, milk, soft drinks, and many chemicals are manufactured by continuous-process technology. This type of technology relies heavily on mechanical and other impersonal controls. Thus machines are likely to control other machines, and these controls are based primarily on the corrective model of control presented earlier.

The manufacturing plant of the Sara Lee Company at Deerfield, Illinois, has a continuous-process technology and provides one example of mechanical control. The company's computer system is used to mix, bake, package, freeze, and store 12 different kinds of cakes and can even start goods on their way to the store. "Their computers direct operations at about 15,000 points in the plant, issue 180,000 instructions every three seconds, monitor some 300 variables in the cake-baking process, and scan 200 incoming messages per second."[15]

The interrelationships between type of technology and type of control system are shown in Table 9.1. The means for controlling the production of goods in an organization can vary from personal (self) controls by the worker to impersonal (mechanical) controls. Personal control may be possible because of extensive training and development of the individual. Craftsmen (such as tool and die makers, computer programmers, and electricians) and professionals may be classified at this end of the continuum of control. These types of controls are likely to be strongly emphasized in unit-production technology. At the other extreme of the continuum, there is a strong emphasis on the use of machines, such as computers, to control the production processes. These types of controls are likely to be strongly emphasized in continuous-process technology. Of course, there are a variety of control strategies in between these extremes, e.g., surveillance by managers and reliance on rules and regulations.

In sum, unit technology emphasizes personal control, whereas continuous-process technology is characterized primarily by impersonal control. Mass-production technology represents a blending of personal and impersonal con-

Table 9.1. Interrelationships between technology and control

Continuum of control	Type of technology		
	Unit	Mass production	Continuous process
Self	High	Low	Low
Managerial surveillance	Medium	Medium	Low
Rules and regulations	Low	High	High
Mechanical process	Low	Medium	High

Modified and adapted from E. Burack, "A Commentary and Critique of Four Organizational Behavioral Models," in *Organizational Behavior Models*, ed. A. Negandi and J. P. Schwitter (Kent, Ohio: Bureau of Economic and Business Research, Kent State University, 1970), pp. 11–14.

trol. The major implication of this finding is that managers need to develop controls within the technical subsystem that are consistent with the type of technology being used.[16]

Level in the Formal Hierarchy

Structural characteristics of organizations can also affect the control system. The concern here is with different combinations of the amount and distribution of control at different levels in the organization's hierarchy. The *distribution-of-control* variable refers to the relative control by each level in the hierarchy over the activities of the organization. For example, how much control is exercised by top management relative to first-level supervision? The *amount-of-control* variable refers to the quantity of control by each group or level within the organization. For example, how much of the total control of the organization is exercised by top management, middle management, first-level supervision, and the production workers?

Managers have traditionally been concerned with *distribution* of control in organizations, i.e., who is to have the right to exercise particular types of controls. But the *total amount* of control in an organization may have a bearing on its effectiveness as well. The total amount of control refers to the amount of control held by all groups throughout the organization. If a union has a low amount of control over members' behavior, its effectiveness in bargaining with management is likely to be reduced. Organizational effectiveness might also be influenced by the degree of agreement among the participants with respect to: (1) their perceptions of the actual distribution and the amount of control; and (2) their values as to what the distribution and amount of control "ought" to be. Considerable differences in these perceptions and values could be a source of internal organizational conflicts and dissatisfaction.

Figure 9.4 shows a control graph of the hypothetical profiles for two organizations.[17] The vertical axis shows the amount of control held by each hierarchical level; the horizontal axis shows the range of hierarchical levels typically found in organizations. The profiles for the two organizations represent structures of control that are relatively autocratic. Top management in both organizations has a relatively high degree of control over organizational goals, objectives, standards, and lower-level employees. But there are also major differences between the two organizational profiles. The amount of control held by each level is greater in organization A. This is determined by summing the "amount-of-control" values for all hierarchical levels.

There is some evidence that organizational effectiveness is directly related to the *total* amount of control in that organization. This does not necessarily mean that all levels of the organization need to have a great deal of control. This was suggested in a study of about 250 managers and 1300 employees in the ten plants of one firm.[18] The study concluded that effectiveness at the employee level was associated with a management system in which the control was distributed hierarchically, as in a mechanistic (bureaucratic) system. There was also high agreement among the managers as to the amount and distribution

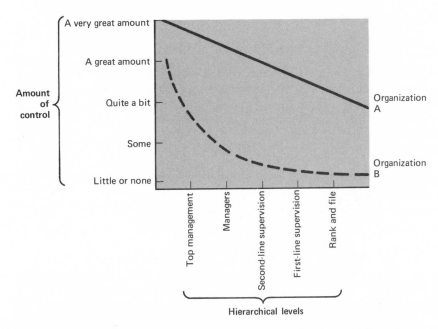

Fig. 9.4. Control profiles for two hypothetical organizations. (Adapted from A. Tannenbaum, *Control in Organizations*, New York: McGraw-Hill, 1968, p. 13.)

of control within the organization. With a mass-production or continuous-process technology, this finding is to be expected. In other settings, such as a research and development unit, it may be desirable for lower-level departments or persons to have relatively higher amounts of control, because their expertise is needed to solve unstructured and nonroutine problems.

Other control structures could be demonstrated by different curves. The curve for *democratic* control structure would rise with lower levels of the hierarchy. In this case, superiors function primarily with and at the consent of the "governed," a situation rarely, if ever, found in American industry. In an *anarchic* control structure, the curve remains low for all hierarchical levels. Since no group exercises primary control and the total amount of control is very low, the organization is likely to be rather weak and ineffective and may become bankrupt. In a *polyarchic* control structure, the curve would be high and relatively flat for all levels. Here, all groups have considerable control, and the organization might function more as a coalition of "equals." Some universities may approximate this profile; the board of trustees, administrators, faculty, and students each have the potential capability of exercising considerable control.

Consistent with the contingency approach, there is no single ideal control system. Rather, the "ideal" system will depend on such factors as the technology used to produce the goods and services, values of the participants, organizational structure, power system, and degree of uncertainty and change experienced by the organization.

STRATEGIES OF CONTROL

In this section we will discuss six strategies of control—human-input control, reward-punishment system, formal structure, policies and rules, budgets, and mechanical controls. These strategies are not necessarily mutually exclusive. Indeed, the control of many activities often requires the use of two (or more) of these strategies at the same time. A combination and interweaving of control strategies probably creates a synergistic effect. In other words, greater control is achieved through a combination of strategies than if each strategy operated independently.

For the most part, our discussion emphasizes the strategies for controlling an organization's employees and managers. There are two reasons for this. First, for most organizations, labor is the greatest cost factor. Second, controlling labor may provide an effective, although sometimes indirect, means of achieving control over the other resources used to create the organization's outputs.

The form and design of each of these formal control strategies depend on many human variables, some of which we shall discuss here. Part III, "Behavioral Processes," also presents ideas and findings which are relevant to a more comprehensive understanding of formal control systems.

Human Input

To increase the probability of effectiveness in any type of organization, managers must control the instability, variability, and spontaneity of individual acts.

Selection techniques provide for the screening of personnel for each position in the organization. Training programs provide for changes in the skills and attitudes of employees. These are two of the means for controlling unwanted kinds of variability. If the organization is to prosper, selection and training controls need to be utilized (prisons and custodial institutions are notable exceptions).

Considerable managerial discretion usually exists over the policies and content of employee selection and training. Much popular interest has been directed at selection and training to determine: (1) the extent to which many of the policies employed accomplish their purpose (a technical question); (2) the legalities of some of these policies, especially with respect to personnel selection on the basis of race, sex, creed, or national origin (social and political questions); and (3) the desirability of using certain selection and training approaches, such as personality tests or sensitivity-training groups (ethical and social questions).

SELECTION

Selection controls are used in hiring people and promoting or transferring employees within the organization. The conditions in the external labor market are likely to have considerable influence on the types and level of selection controls. In a scarce labor market, few candidates are available, and the organization may find it necessary to "lower" its standards or number of controls. To offset the reduced quality of the work force, management might increase its training emphasis or redesign the jobs.

The use of controls in the selection process depends partly on the amount of decision-making discretion and power that the person is supposed to exercise. Two interrelated aspects of the discretion and power in the position to be filled are important. First, how much can the individual's decisions harm or aid the welfare of the organization? Second, how much formal power will the individual have over the use and allocation of the organization's resources? For example, controls are minimal in the selection of file clerks compared to those used in the selection of marketing executives who develop sales strategies, control budgets, and supervise others.

TRAINING AND CONDITIONING

Training is the organization's conscious attempt to change the skills, knowledge, attitudes, values, or motivations of individuals to help achieve its goals.[19] In most types of training, the interests of the individual and the organization are probably compatible. Many professional programs (such as business, engineering, and law) conducted by colleges and universities serve the interests of both the students and the organizations that are likely to employ them. These professional programs provide more than a specific set of skills and technical knowledge. The student is exposed to various social controls, both formal and informal, that can serve to influence individual attitudes, motivations, and values. Similarly, company orientation and developmental programs are usually concerned with forming or modifying attitudes to make them consistent with the needs of the organization. Management development, in contrast to technical and skill training, is often intended to develop in an employee a

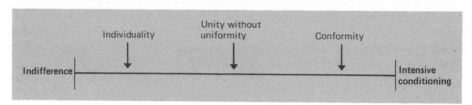

Fig. 9.5. Conditioning range by the formal organization.

sense of commitment to the philosophy and goals of a business organization.[20] Blue-collar employees in routine positions are likely to have little exposure to such programs. Only occupants of discretionary positions, such as those held by managers and specialists, are usually exposed to intensive developmental programs.

The amount of effort an organization puts into *conditioning* individual values, attitudes, and goals ranges from relative indifference to intensive indoctrination, as suggested by Fig. 9.5. Chaos and instability might result if managers had highly incompatible goals, values, and attitudes. At the other extreme is the absolute conformity of the "organization man" stereotype. Intensive conditioning may lead to a static organization, one that is unable to adapt and change. For example, it has been widely reported that in both the Johnson and Nixon administrations, there was little tolerance of members within the top policy group who challenged the existing Vietnam policy and the assumptions on which it was based.

The ideal strategy might be to employ deliberate conditioning to create *unity without conformity*.[21] Many Management By Objectives (MBO) programs and decentralization strategies may provide the means of achieving unity without conformity. This occurs by first encouraging the open discussion of goals, both written and unwritten, that are being pursued. Then an effort is made to reach agreement on the objectives that should be pursued. Finally, the individuals are given some discretion for working toward the objectives in a manner of their own choosing.

Reward-Punishment Systems

Formal systems of rewards and punishments are another control strategy used to direct individuals to fulfilling the requirements of the organization. As suggested earlier, there are wide variations in the form and effectiveness of such systems. Here we present a broad framework showing the range of reward-and-punishment combinations from an extremely mechanistic organization to an extremely organic system.

An *extremely* mechanistic organization attempts to control employee behavior through punishment and the individual's fear of being deprived of the few rewards that are provided by the organization. Such organizations are prisons, prisoner-of-war camps, custodial mental hospitals, and some business firms. The members of these organizations usually have a strong desire to escape from such organizations. The managers of these organizations often

have little discretion in selecting their members and spend little money on
formal training programs.

In the more typical business mechanistic system, however, there are attempts to control employees by emphasizing the exchange of *extrinsic rewards*
in return for the performance of certain designated tasks. Extrinsic rewards are
in the form of wages, pension plans, some types of status symbols (size of
office, access to information, etc.), and job security. At times, the typical
mechanistic system may rely on certain forms of punishments, such as demotions or dismissal. Many business organizations, farmers' cooperatives, some
peacetime military organizations, and labor unions make use of this pattern
of rewards and punishments.

In a highly organic management system, by contrast, there is an attempt
to control employee behavior through the use of intrinsic rewards (i.e., satisfying work), self-control (i.e., personal sense of responsibility for one's work),
interpersonal control (i.e., control through advice and suggestions by those
with the expertise), and a reasonable degree of extrinsic rewards. Organizations approaching this pattern of control include research and development
organizations (especially for managers and skilled personnel), colleges and
universities (especially for faculty and administrators), and voluntary and professional associations.

As suggested in the previous description of moderately mechanistic through
organic management systems, punishment is not likely to be a dominant
control mechanism in most organizations. This is because it is simply not a
very effective method of controlling behavior.[22] However, individuals and organizations do occasionally use punishment (or are perceived as using it) for the
following types of reasons.[23]

1. It may suppress undesired behavior when all other means for modifying
   it have failed;
2. It may be seen as an effective deterrent even when it has little actual
   deterrent effect on the specific individuals who have been punished
   (punishment may reinforce conformity to the prevailing standards by the
   larger group of members);
3. The taking away of rewards may become psychologically indistinguishable
   from punishments (e.g., failure to receive a regular increase in salary may
   be considered a penalty);
4. The desire of individuals to "get even" for harm done to them may cause
   them to seek to punish others; thus revenge or retribution may itself become a source of reward.

A strike may represent a means for management and labor to exchange
punishments and withdraw the rewards that are usually forthcoming in their
relationship. The power of each party to punish the other by refusing to cooperate is occasionally a mutually disastrous experience. This seemed to be one
reason for the failure of the Newark, New Jersey, *Evening News* in September
1972. In 1970, when Media General, Inc., acquired the newspaper for $24
million, the new management felt that the paper was overstaffed and tried to
fire 50 editorial writers. The Newspaper Guild at the *Evening News* called a
strike in May 1971. During the next 11 months, thousands of readers and ad-

vertisers were lost. Before the strike, daily circulation had been 267,000; after the strike, press runs never exceeded 138,000, and some *Evening News* staffers claimed that only about 70,000 copies a day were being sold. With losses approximating $8 million a year, Media General decided to close down the paper.[24]

In sum, the patterns of reward-punishment systems can vary widely between organizations and between departments of a particular organization for controlling peoples' behavior. The general thrust in contemporary America seems to be toward a combination of extrinsic and intrinsic rewards.

Formal Structure

Formal organizational structures are attempts by top management to convey the *pattern of control* it desires for the organization. Organizations typically have formal, written job descriptions based on the tasks and responsibilities of each position. In mechanistic management systems, the position descriptions may be very specific. In organic management systems, the position descriptions are likely to be broader and may consist only of the *types of major goals* expected of the individual in the position. In either case, job descriptions provide limits or constraints on the formal authority or discretion of the individual.

Formal structures also attempt to establish a means of control by prescribing *flows of communication* and decision making. The collection, evaluation, and transmission of information can vitally influence organizational and individual performance. If the formal communication and decision systems provide the individual with too much information or too many decision problems, he or she may feel swamped or overloaded. On the other hand, inadequate amounts of information (or the wrong information) can result in poor decisions and performance.

Formal communication and decision systems are frequently thought of as following the organizational hierarchy. Formal structures can specify lateral and diagonal communication and coordination flows as well. This is apparent in the project form of organization and in some support or auditing units. For example, the personnel department may be delegated the task of exercising varying degrees of control over certain activities, such as affirmative action. If the personnel department has high control over affirmative action, it has functional authority over this particular activity.

Individuals may differ widely in their perceptions of the amount, form, and appropriateness of the formal control to be exercised by an organizational department. These perceptual differences can be the source of interdepartment misunderstandings and conflicts, resulting in decreased effectiveness for the organization as a whole.[25]

Another structural variable that can be altered to affect the control system is the *span of control* (the number of people reporting to a superior). Everything else being equal, it may be possible to increase the control over the activities of each lower level by *narrowing* the span of control. Changing a manager's span of control also provides a partial means of controlling how he or she controls. A *wider* span of control might prevent managers from engaging in undesirable practices, e.g., supervising too closely, creating too much subordinate dependence, and becoming too involved with subordinates on a social and emotional basis.[26]

Policies and Rules

Policies and rules, another major means for exercising control over many organizational activities and functions, define the discretion available in a position or unit as well as indicate mandatory actions. A *policy* is a guide for carrying out action, and it is generally qualitative, conditional, and relational; that is, it is general rather than specific and expresses a condition or relation. The verbs used in stating policies are *to maintain, to follow, to provide, to assist, to use,* etc. Thus a policy might be worded: "Promotions will be based on merit."

A *rule* is a specific course of action or conduct that must be followed. It is established to create uniformity of action and may or may not be prohibitive.[27] An example of a rule is: "Courses may be dropped by the student up through the third week of classes without a grade being assigned."

Flexibility is probably the most basic difference between policies and rules. Policies tend to be made by managers at higher organizational levels, whereas rule making often occurs at all organizational levels.[28] Policy making at General Motors, for example, is the responsibility of the Executive and Finance committees, which are composed entirely of the company's directors. Subcommittees of the Executive and Finance committees include representation from major divisions and departments of the entire organization and frequently develop rules to implement the firm's general policies.

Rules may have both desirable and undesirable consequences for the formal organization. The following summarizes the major consequences of rules:

1. Rules reflect authority, and thus they structure relationships and ensure action consistent with the organization's purposes. For example, rules may define the relative authority of the personnel department and other managers in the organization with respect to the hiring of employees.

2. Although rules may be called on when individual competence or commitment is low, they may reinforce apathy by defining the *minimum acceptable standard* for subordinates. For example, there may be a rule specifying that employees who do not average 300 units of output per week will be subject to a disciplinary layoff. This type of rule may well create negative attitudes toward management and simply motivate the employees to produce 300 units and no more.

3. By focusing undue attention on standards of behavior and operating procedures, rules may inadvertently result in a "means-end reversal" for the organization. This could cause impersonal relations with clients, inflexibility, and resistance to innovation. Following a rule becomes a goal or end rather than a means to an end. For example, a rule may state that the organization will stop serving its clientele at 5:00 P.M. When one of the authors was standing in line at a library on a Saturday afternoon, the clock struck 5:00 P.M. Even

though several people protested, the clerk cited the rule and refused to check out any more books.

4. Rules may receive additional authority from the desire of subordinates to structure working conditions and relationships in a predictable fashion. This creates a domino effect (rules beget rules) as management attempts to deal with hostile worker groups.[29] For example, there may be rules specifying the number of vacation days employees receive based on number of years worked. But conflict might arise between management and workers over how this vacation time should be taken—all at once or spread out. If specific requests cannot be worked out cooperatively and with some give and take on both sides, an elaborate network of formal rules may be developed to specify how vacation time can be taken.

Budgets

Budgets set up targets desired by the organization in the future. These target characteristics are usually expressed in terms of dollars. Nonfinancial characteristics, such as production budgets expressed in units (hours of labor per unit or output, machine downtime per thousand hours of running time, etc.), may also be used.[30]

The control aspect of budgets may be either preventive or corrective. In the *corrective* model, considerable effort may be expended in identifying deviations from the budget. The reported deviations serve as a basis for subsequent managerial action aimed at identifying the causes for the deviation or evaluating whether the budget itself should be changed.[31]

The power of a budget, especially as a preventive control mechanism, depends on viewing it as a bargain or informal contract that has been agreed to by all parties.[32] One study investigated this and other issues by mailing a comprehensive questionnaire to lower-level supervisors to obtain their views about how the company budget was used.[33] They were asked: "Do you feel that frequently budgets or standards are a club held over the head of the supervisor to force better performance?" Twenty percent of the 204 respondents replied yes and 68 percent answered no.

Responses to this questionnaire support the view that budgets are frequently perceived as acceptable by those who must live by them. Of course, 20 percent of these respondents did regard the budget quite negatively. Other research has revealed that budgets may also be viewed with fear and hostility.[34] These reactions are most probable when the organization uses punishments and the threat of punishments to enforce its budgeting system.

Machine and "Automatic" Control

Machines, as a means of control, have developed through several major stages. First, they extended the capability of workers, enlarging individuals' physical control over certain activities. Second, the control function, especially in the production subsystem, became shared. Workers and machines responded to information from each other, creating a mutual control system. Third, a new threshold was reached with automation when machines controlled other machines. Now machines begin to perform the managerial control function and participate with managers in the control process. For example, computers in oil refineries are used to monitor and make automatic adjustments in the production process based on the feedback of data collected from numerous points in the refinery process.

The impact of automatic machine control on management has been reported in a number of studies. One researcher found a reduction of 34 percent in the number of middle-management jobs in a large factory following the introduction of an advanced automated system.[35] *Automation* refers to processes that are primarily self-regulating, or able to operate independently in a wide range of conditions. Automation usually involves joining machines with other machines, especially some type of computer. At one extreme of automation, a person has control merely over the start and stop switches. To date, these applications of automation exist where the environment can be made highly predictable, such as in the production of gasoline, toothpaste, and soft drinks.

The increase in automation and person-machine control in organizations is partially reflected in the exploding information-technology industry.[36] Several instances of advanced machine control in the automobile industry might be noted. Chevrolet installed in its Saginaw, Michigan, brake plant an automated system that controls four stacker cranes, records inventory displacement, directs five miles of conveyors, and diagnoses tool problems for the maintenance staff. Chrysler's computer-controlled system in its Syracuse, New York, plant expands or contracts a boring tool to adjust for the temperature and wear condition of the tool. The system feeds the exact diameters of finished pistons to the machines bearing the cylinder blocks so they can adjust their bit. This makes possible good assembly matches with the available pistons.[37]

In production activities, there has been a steady shift toward machine controls. The shift was initially from human to machine control of nonhuman resources, such as the use of automatic sensors versus visual inspection in the production of steel. With the advent of advanced mass-production technology, machines supplemented other strategies, such as direct managerial surveillance and rules and regulations for controlling production workers. Machines and the interdependencies between them serve as a form of control over the worker's exercise of discretion. In continuous-process operations, a new threshold has been realized, because machines control machines without the direct application of human energy, skill, intelligence, or control.[38]

Summary

The formal control process serves to prevent and correct unwanted deviations from goals and standards. The control process within organizations can be used by management in a variety of ways to achieve goals. Contrary to some popular ideas, however, more controls do not necessarily lead to a more effective organization. First, controls cost money, and controls may not pay for themselves through increased effectiveness. Second, controls, unless carefully de-signed, can lead to unanticipated negative reactions by those who must abide by them.

The corrective model of control probably represents the most common view of the formal control process. The basic "steps" in this process can be used to correct deviations from defined standards through feedback. Three contingencies likely to directly influence the control processes, strategies, and mechanisms used on a particular individual or department are types of power used within the organization, type of technology employed, and the level in the formal hierarchy of the organization.

The last part of the chapter provided a description and analysis of six strategies of control: (1) the control of personnel through selection and train-ing; (2) the use of reward-punishment systems; (3) the formal structure, which helps establish control through position descriptions, specification of com-munication flows, the creation of special units to audit various activities of other units, and the span of control; (4) the development of policies and rules, which are used to guide behavior and decision making; (5) the use of budgets; and (6) the application of machine and automatic controls. These strategies are interrelated, and organizations usually employ some *combination* of them to achieve the control desired.

Discussion Questions

1. Control has been defined as a superior dominating the work life of his or her subordinates. Discuss this statement in the light of your knowledge of the control process.

2. How might the control process used "on" the dean of your school or college differ from that used "on" a sales clerk at the local McDonald's?

3. How might the control process in a marketing research department differ from that in a production department that had the task of bagging potato chips?

4. Based on your own work experience, develop an example of the applica-tion of the corrective model of control. Try to identify each of the "steps" in the corrective model of control as shown in Fig. 9.2.

5. In what ways are control processes likely to differ in mechanistic and or-ganic management systems?

6. Evaluate this statement: "The more the control processes become like those in the organic management system, the more they are likely to be effective."

7. How does organizational level act as a contingency factor influencing the use of control processes and strategies?

8. Why are formal controls important to management?

9. Evaluate this statement: "The fewer the controls in an organization, the greater the likelihood that it will be effective."

Management Incidents

CONTROL AND FREEDOM OF A PURCHASING MANAGER*

Jim Richards was the purchasing manager in a highly centralized company, the Rigid Corporation. Feeling a sense of hopelessness in this situation, he quit and has just taken a similar job with the Hart Manufacturing Company, which two years previously had been reorganized. A planning and control department was created, and Richards was told that a policy of decentralization of authority has been adopted. Richards' predecessor has just been transferred and is not available to instruct him about his new job. Joe Urban, who has served on a continuing basis as a consultant and advisor to the company, was asked to orient Richards. The orientation went much as follows:

Urban: From what you tell me, you will probably find that the methods of management at the Hart Manufacturing Company are almost exactly the opposite of those you have been used to at the Rigid Corporation. You will find that no one here will check how you are doing your job.

Ralph, whom you met this morning, is the head of the planning and control department. He will tell you what materials are needed for production and when. Every six months he will give you a general purchasing program and you will place the orders. You get the specifications from the engineering department. You select the suppliers yourself. You decide yourself about what prices you want to pay.

You will find that for most materials used, we have standard prices. The variance between the price you pay and the standards are carefully followed up by Ralph's department and reported both to you and to your vice-president, who keeps in touch with the market and will step in if he feels that the prices you are paying are too high. Incidentally, if you find a way of getting lower prices, he will step in too—to congratulate you.

But, in any case, he will step in *after* you, under your own responsibility, have placed the purchase order, not before—unless you turn to him for advice, which you may do at any time. In some exceptional cases, he may take the initiative, but you will find this a very rare occurrence.

For planning purposes, the weeks of the year are designated by consecutive numbers. Every week you will receive a release schedule which will tell you what materials, on order but not yet delivered, are needed for production during each of the following eight weeks. As you know, we are short of materials. This release schedule is therefore a very important matter. Check it carefully

* Adapted from Raymond Villers, "Control and Freedom in a Decentralized Company," *Harvard Business Review* (March–April 1954): 89–96. Copyright © 1954 by the President and Fellows of Harvard College. All rights reserved.

when you receive it. If you do not call Ralph within a few days after you have received it, you are considered as having accepted it.

It then becomes your responsibility to supply the materials on time. Any delay will disrupt production. The cost of the disruption will be evaluated by the planning and control department and will be charged against your department.

Richards: You know how suppliers are. They may say yes and yet they don't deliver. They may just say perhaps. What do you want me to tell Ralph, when I receive his release schedule, in a situation where I am 50-50 sure?

Urban: Your position is fully appreciated. But you must realize that in the whole organization, you are *the one* who is in the best position to evaluate the situation. Now, someone has to take responsibility. As you know, a plant cannot have a "perhaps" production schedule or "perhaps" tools on hand or a "perhaps" machine setup. It has to be yes or no. Sometimes we will be disappointed. Everyone agrees that it can happen that you will say yes, and yet the material will not be there on time. But that doesn't lessen your responsibility.

The real issue is how often it will occur and what the damage will be. At the end of the year, two accounts will tell the whole story. The price-variance account will show how active you have been in getting good prices. The time-lost account will show how reliable your deliveries to the production department have been.

In addition, of course, we expect that your materials will be up to specifications—and that you will not systematically protect yourself by refusing to accept Ralph's release schedules.

Richards: What do I do if I think that I cannot get the material in time?

Urban: You call Ralph and tell him so. Nine times out of ten, even more often than that, you will settle the matter between yourselves by changing the production schedule. Your release schedules are issued weekly for an eight-week period. As a rule, this gives you at least four weeks' advance notice, inasmuch as we avoid changing the coming four weeks unless it is absolutely necessary. Now, if you and Ralph cannot see eye to eye, the matter will have to be referred to the executive committee, but you will find that Ralph is pretty good at solving problems.

By the way, let me make this clear to you. Ralph is no more your boss than you are his. If the foreman of the tool room needs to purchase anything, you know that he is not permitted to go and buy it outside. He must send *you* a requisition. Now, this does not make you his boss. You are the head of a service department, available to service him. Ralph is the head of another service department. The release schedule he sends you is a service he renders to you and to the whole organization. It is important for you to understand the spirit in which his department functions.

You will find that the control you are submitted to is very detailed, but it is objective. You receive an assignment. You may accept it or reject it. But if you accept, you must perform. There is no excuse for a failure—no argument either. If you fail, the damage is evaluated. We all make mistakes. The important point is to avoid making too many mistakes and also to understand fully that this extensive control is the necessary balance to the great freedom of action you are being given.

No one will ask you what time you arrive in your office, why you did not show up last Thursday, or whether you have neglected to write to this or that supplier. You are your own boss as far as your function is concerned.

1. What do you think of the control processes and mechanisms used "on" the purchasing manager? Explain.
2. What advantages and problems would you anticipate with these control processes and mechanisms?
3. How would you diagnose the control processes and mechanisms used with respect to the three contingency factors discussed in this chapter, including type of power, type of technology, and level in the organizational hierarchy?

SUPERVISORY CONTROLS

You are the manager of an accounting department for a major industrial firm and have hired a recent college graduate with no supervisory experience to be supervisor of one of your most troublesome sections. In the past, this section has been inefficient, costly, and in general poorly organized. You have given your new supervisor a free hand to reorganize the ten-person section.

Some months later this section was described by a manager as "the most efficient, well-run, disciplined section in the whole firm." However, several employees in this section have recently asked for transfers, and two senior-level employees have retired prematurely. In informal conversations, they have revealed that they cannot perform their duties as they wish.

1. What control concepts and mechanisms might account for these changes?
2. What "human factors" might need to be considered from "here on out" to make sure performance of the section remains at a high level?

REFERENCES

1. A. Tannenbaum, "Control in Organizations: Individual Adjustment and Organizational Performance," *Administrative Science Quarterly* **8** (1962): 236–257. *Also see* G. Giglioni and A. Bedeian, "A Conspectus of Management Control Theory: 1900–1972," *Academy of Management Journal* **17** (1974): 292–305.

2. W. Jerome, III, *Executive Control: The Catalyst* (New York: Wiley, 1961), pp. 31–34.

3. J. Emery, *Organizational Planning and Control Systems: Theory and Technology* (New York: Macmillan, 1969), pp. 28–33.

4. T. Whisler, *Information Technology and Organizational Change* (Belmont, Calif.: Wadsworth, 1970), p. 67.

5. E. Lawler, III, and J. Rhode, *Information and Control in Organizations* (Pacific Palisades, Calif.: Goodyear, 1976).

6. D. Henning, *Nonfinancial Controls in Smaller Enterprises* (Seattle: University of Washington, Bureau of Business Research, 1964), pp. 6–27.

7. R. Boyce, *Integrated Management Controls* (London: Longman's, Green, 1967), p. 21.

8. M. Miller, *Objectives and Standards: An Approach to Planning and Control* (New York: American Management Association, 1956), pp. 77–78.

9. "How a Memphis Bank Stopped Its Crime Wave," *Business Week,* October 27, 1975, pp. 63, 68.

10. J. French, Jr., and B. Raven, "The Bases of Social Power," in *Group Dynamics: Research and Theory,* ed. D. Cartwright and A. Zander (New York: Harper & Row, 1960), pp. 607–623.

11. E. Lawler, III, "Control Systems in Organizations," in *Handbook of Industrial and Organizational Psychology,* ed. M. Dunnette (Chicago: Rand McNally, 1976), pp. 1247–1291.

12. C. Cammann and D. Nadler, "Fit Control Systems to Your Managerial Style," *Harvard Business Review* **54** (1976): 65–72.

13. F. Kast and J. Rosenzweig, *Contingency Views of Organization and Management* (Palo Alto, Calif.: Science Research Associates, 1973), pp. 305–320.

14. J. Woodward, ed., *Industrial Organization: Behavior and Control* (New York: Oxford University Press, 1970); E. Burack, *Technology and Industrial Management* (Boston: Allyn and Bacon, 1972).

15. G. Bell, ed., *Organizations and Human Behavior* (Englewood Cliffs, N.J.: Prentice-Hall, 1967), p. 9.

16. W. Ouchi and M. Maguire, "Organizational Control: Two Functions," *Administrative Science Quarterly* **20** (1975): 559–569.

17. A. Tannenbaum, *Control in Organizations* (New York: McGraw-Hill, 1968), p. 13.

18. J. McMahon and J. Ivancevich, "A Study of Control in a Manufacturing Organization: Managers and Nonmanagers," *Administrative Science Quarterly* **21** (1976): 66–83.

19. C. Haberstroh, "Goals, Programs and the Training Function," in *Management Controls: New Directions in Basic Research,* ed. P. Binini, R. Jaedicke, and H. Wagner (New York: McGraw-Hill, 1964), pp. 268–276.

20. W. Scott, "Executive Development as an Instrument of Higher Control," *Academy of Management Journal* **6** (1963): 191–203.

21. F. Kast and J. Rosenzweig, *Organization and Management: A Systems Approach,* rev. ed. (New York: McGraw-Hill, 1974), pp. 481–484.

22. F. Luthans and R. Kreitner, *Organizational Behavior Modification* (Glenview, Ill.: Scott, Foresman, 1975), and N. Nicholson, "Management Sanctions and Absence Control," *Human Relations* **29** (1976): 139–151.

23. P. Blau, *Exchange and Power in Social Life* (New York: Wiley, 1964), pp. 225–226.

24. "Death in Newark," *Time Magazine,* September 11, 1972, p. 38.

25. D. Henning and R. Mosely, "Authority Role of a Functional Manager: The Controller," *Administrative Science Quarterly* **15** (1970): 482–489.

26. P. Blau and W. Scott, *Formal Organizations: A Comparative Approach* (San Francisco: Chandler, 1962), p. 168.

27. M. Higginson, *Management Policies I: Their Development as Corporate Guides,* AMA Research Study 76 (New York: American Management Association, 1966), pp. 19, 21, 59.

28. L. Sayles, "The Many Dimensions of Control," *Organizational Dynamics* **1** (1972): 21–31.

29. J. Anderson, "Bureaucratic Rules: Bearers of Organization Authority," *Educational Administration Quarterly* **11** (1966): 7–31.

30. A. Stedry, "Budgetary Control: A Behavioral Approach," in *Organizational Decision Making,* ed. M. Alexis and C. Wilsons (Englewood Cliffs, N.J.: Prentice-Hall, 1967), pp. 403–416.

31. A. Stedry, *Budget Control and Cost Behavior* (Englewood Cliffs, N.J.: Prentice-Hall, 1965), pp. 46–50.

32. H. Chamberlain, *Private and Public Planning* (New York: McGraw-Hill, 1965), pp. 46–50.

33. B. Sord and G. Welsch, *Managerial Planning and Control* (Austin: University of Texas, Bureau of Business Research, 1964), pp. 93–99.

34. C. Argyris, *The Impact of Budgets on People* (New York: Controllership Foundation, 1952).

35. T. Whisler and C. Myers, *The Impact of Computers on Management* (Cambridge, Mass.: M.I.T. Press, 1967), p. 31.

36. G. Bylinsky, "Here Comes the Second Computer Revolution," *Fortune* **42** (1975): 134–138.

37. "A Lot More Computers in Detroit's Future," *Business Week,* June 5, 1971, pp. 84–90; "The Smart Machine Revolution," *Business Week,* July 5, 1976, pp. 38–44.

38. D. Sanders, *Computers and Management in a Changing Society,* 2d ed. (New York: McGraw-Hill, 1974).

Behavioral Processes

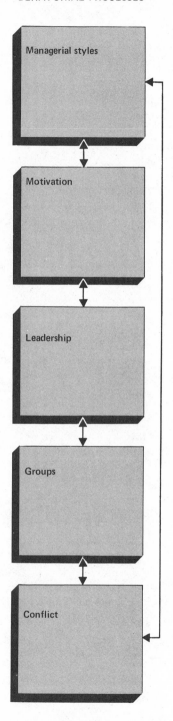

Managerial styles

Motivation

Leadership

Groups

Conflict

Managers get things done through working with others. Motivating, leading, communicating, resolving conflict, and conducting meetings are the interpersonal aspects of management by which subordinates are led to understand and contribute effectively and efficiently to the attainment of the organization's goals. This function is difficult because managers are dealing with a complex of forces about which not enough is known. Individuals differ widely in skills and knowledge, attitudes, learning ability, needs, personality, and values. If people acted as the solar system or a machine does, there would be few human problems for managers to cope with. Unfortunately for managers, however, people are not predictable and do not always do what management wants.

In Chapter 10, different managerial styles, values, and communication processes are discussed. We point out that in addition to being members of various groups that influence behavior within an organization, employees are also unique individuals whose concerns about working with others, attitudes, and values cause them to behave differently. Because executives are managers and thus occupy a superior authority position, they need to understand perceptual processes and how their communications styles impact on employee behavior.

In Chapter 11, we consider the various behavioral theories as they relate to an identification and satisfaction of individual needs. Because managing involves the creation and maintenance of an environment for the performance of individuals working together, it is obvious that a manager cannot do this job without knowing what motivates people. The necessity of building motivating factors into jobs, the staffing of these jobs, and the entire process of communicating with employees is built on a knowledge of motivation. Clearly, for the manager to guide people's activities in desired directions requires knowing, to to the extent possible, what leads people to do things—what motivates them.

Leadership is an important aspect of management. Indeed, as will be made clear in Chapter 12, the ability to lead is one of the keys to being an effective manager. A leader can use various sources of power to influence subordinates. The manager-leader is in a position to facilitate progress and inspire the group to accomplish its tasks. Even the orchestra leader, whose function is to produce coordinated sound as correct tempo through the integrated effort of instruments, relies on sources of power that each business manager possesses. Because of its importance to all kinds of group action, there is a considerable volume of theory and research about leadership. In Chapter 12 we identify several major types of leadership theory and research and outline some of the basic contingencies affecting the kind of leadership style an individual chooses.

Although the behavior of individuals in groups is influenced by the manager's leadership style, the organization's motivational system, and the quality of the organization's communication system, groups often affect the quality and quantity of the organization's products. Chapter 13 focuses on why people join groups, the kinds of problems groups can cause for individuals and for organizations, and the major contingencies affecting the formation of groups in organizations. The knowledge of how effective groups solve problems and remove barriers to group effectiveness are discussed. Most managers can become a lot more effective by trying to understand the resources in a group and knowing when to use and not use a group for problem solving.

The last chapter of Part III deals with conflict. In Chapter 14, we stress that if a management team is to function effectively, a high level of cooperation among group members and between groups within an organization should prevail. The management of conflict occurs when activities desired by the group are based on differences in needs, scarcity of resources, competition or rivalry among group members, or some combination of these differences. The potential value of conflict is also discussed. Often, conflict can be helpful in producing a creative, high-quality decision if managed properly. Conflicts are inevitable, and managers have different styles in resolving them. Diagnosing conflict-handling style will enhance your managerial ability and assist you in becoming a more valuable member of top management's team.

10

10

Managerial Styles

Managerial styles
Philosophies
Contingencies
Perceptions
Individual problems
Interpersonal communi-
cations

Chapter 10

Motivation
Needs
Satisfiers and dis-
satisfiers
Expectancies and con-
tingencies
Management by objectives
Job enrichment

Chapter 11

Leadership
Power and influence
Traits
Contingency models
Substitutes for leadership

Chapter 12

Groups
Roles
Models
Contingencies
Procedures for group
problem solving

Chapter 13

Conflict
Contingency model
Role conflict
Interpersonal conflict
Intergroup conflict

Chapter 14

The objectives of this chapter are to:

develop your understanding about how different managerial philosophies can influence the behavior of employees;

enhance your understanding of the perceptual process;

discuss how individuals cope with problems when joining groups;

explore the dimensions of managerial communication styles;

show how different communication styles affect managers' behavior.

Individuals bring to the organization their own ways of behaving. Although the nature of the task and the organization may attract people with somewhat similar characteristics, employees will still differ in their particular assumptions about people, perceptions, and the factors that affect their interpersonal communication style(s). The way in which people behave in an organization is a function of not only their needs and wants, but also the ongoing philosophy of management. John L. McCaffrey, a former chief executive officer of International Harvester, has stated: "The biggest trouble with industry is that it is full of human behavior."[1] In other words, not all people behave similarly. It is because employees behave differently that managers must have knowledge of perception and communication processes. How a member perceives others and his or her job in the organization will affect that person's expectations about how to behave, how the manager rewards employees, and how "open" or "closed" the individual is to others.

In a number of chapters, we have said that the contingency approach views the organization as an open system, transforming its inputs—raw materials—into goods which it sells to the public as outputs. McDonald's imports raw materials (beef, bread, lettuce, fish, and so on), converts them into hamburgers, milk shakes, etc., and realizes a profit from selling these products. It also recruits employees, trains them, assigns them to jobs, and sooner or later the employees leave the firm by resignation, death, retirement, or discharge.

As an organization grows, efficiency requires that many activities become divided. The organization therefore differentiates into numerous departments. Thus personnel, purchasing, planning, and finance departments evolve while the production department attends to the production process, and advertising and sales departments distribute the product to the customer. Although such specialization may be efficient, it is what individuals bring to the organization that largely determines its effectiveness.

Organizations are designed to tap the energy and commitment of individuals who are to perform jobs, produce work, and achieve the goals of the organization. Many organizational approaches and practices are designed, therefore, on an explicit or implicit model of human nature. The concepts of centralization, decentralization, and span of control, for example, have developed around the problem of controlling and motivating employees. The design of work is heavily influenced by the model of human nature, the chief executive officer, and subordinates. Taylor's scientific-management model assumed that one could hire a person to do a task and that the person would strive to complete the task as quickly and efficiently as possible. It was management's responsibility to plan, organize, and control the inputs to the production process.

Employees learn to understand what the organization's model of motivation is through socialization, the process by which the organization conditions the behavior of its employees. Schein defines organizational socialization as the process of "learning the ropes," of being indoctrinated and trained as to what is important in the organization.[2] Certain behaviors become associated with positive rewards (promotions, increases in salary, status symbols), and other behaviors become identified with negative rewards (demotions, no salary increases, and so on). From birth to death, a person is subjected to the pressure of group norms, values, and rewards that over a period of time develop and shape that person's behavior and attitudes. How an organization socializes its employees depends on management's assumptions about its employees.

Assumptions about people can be self-fulfilling in that certain organizational structures, rules, and practices are created by managers in light of their assumptions about people. Some managers believe that employees are incompetent, possessing little skill, ability, knowledge, and desire to work. A manager with these beliefs will design an organization quite different from that designed by a manager who believes that employees are competent, hardworking, and desire to achieve the organization's goals.

The perceptual process is central to an understanding of human behavior. The way a person "sees" a situation has much greater importance and practical significance for the manager than does the situation itself. People must agree enough about what they "see" to be able to coordinate their efforts, but they must also see the real world accurately enough for the organization to maintain its profitability. Often people find it useful to defend themselves perceptually by distorting or overlooking information which threatens their view of the world.

MANAGERS' PHILOSOPHIES ABOUT EMPLOYEES

The achievement of organizational goals depends on many variables—the environment in which the firm is operating, the structure of the organization, the adequacy of planning and control, the types of decision-making strategies used by management, and the effective use of management approaches and practices. The management philosophy behind each of these factors helps determine job design, leadership styles, motivational plans, and decisions that occur in organizations.

A management philosophy is a logical system of thought applied to a problem, decision, or activity. It is essential in solving management problems, since it provides the basic ideals and beliefs about political, economic, and social forces with which an organization is confronted. All managers operate within a particular philosophical framework that influences their thinking and decision making. A management philosophy helps reduce differences in perception between what is said and what actually occurs in practice. Thus by developing an overall organizational philosophy, managers can evaluate how their relations with subordinates measure up to what is officially stated in the organization's manual. Similarly, when the concepts of philosophy are communicated properly, both managers and nonmanagerial employees will be in a better position to understand the behavior expected of them.

One of the most interesting discussions of two contrasting management philosophies is presented in the work of Douglas McGregor.[3] According to him, superior-subordinate relationships depend on a set of assumptions about the nature of a worker. These he classified as Theory X and Theory Y.

Theory X

The traditional bureaucratic structure, with its pyramid, superior-subordinate relationships, and control systems, suggests that the organization is based on a Theory X philosophy:

1. The average person inherently dislikes work and will avoid it if possible.
2. Because people dislike their work, they must be coerced, controlled, and directed to achieve the organization's goals.
3. The average person wishes to avoid responsibility, has relatively little ambition, and desires security above everything else.

McGregor did not believe that these were inborn human characteristics. However, by observing the way many organizations were managed, he was led to believe that numerous managers assume that employees must be directed and controlled through such devices as external rewards, incentives, threats, and coercion. Theory X does not encourage the development of human growth needs while people are at work.

Theory X assumes that people are motivated basically by money and fringe benefits. It has limited application in motivating people where the important needs are growth and achievement. In sum, Theory X managers are: (1) highly bureaucratic in terms of strict interpretation and application of policies, rules, and regulations; (2) advocates of a highly specialized division of labor, and (3) advocates of economic incentives as the only meaningful way to motivate employees.

Theory Y

McGregor proposed another set of assumptions that he felt presented a much more complete and accurate representation of employee behavior. These assumptions he classified as Theory Y:

1. The average person does not inherently dislike work.
2. Employees use self-direction and self-control in achieving the organization's goals. Punishment and economic incentives are not the only means to obtain motivation.
3. The average person learns and wants to accept responsibility. The avoidance of responsibility, lack of ambition, and emphasis on security are not inherent human characteristics.
4. Many people have the capacity to exercise a relatively high degree of imagination, ingenuity, and creativity in the solution of organizational problems.

The philosophy behind Theory Y implies that it is a management responsibility to establish practices and procedures that promote human growth and development and responsible, cooperative employees. Consequently, if the workers are lazy and produce shoddy products, it is management's responsibility to reorganize the work and control systems to achieve better performance. Theory Y assumes that workers are motivated to achieve organizational goals and are self-directed. Employee commitment to the goals of the organization are affected by management's practices. McGregor suggests that the managerial philosophy of the firm reveals a great deal about the organization's structure, motivational systems, and leadership styles.

In the 13 years before 1962, Avis had never had a profit. Robert Townsend took over the company, and in three years Avis's sales had grown from $30 million to $175 million, and its successive annual profits rose from $1 million to $3 million to $5 million. Townsend attributes his success to his firm belief in Theory Y. When he became head of Avis, he was assured that no one at headquarters was any good and that he should recruit a whole new team. When Avis was sold three years later to ITT, Harold Geneen, President of ITT, commented that he had never seen such depth of management talent. During these three years, Townsend brought in only two new people.[4]

Individual Development

Theory X and Theory Y propose different types of career development for individuals. Theory X assumes that employees are like infants and should be treated accordingly. Infants have very simple needs—to be fed and protected. When infants are hungry, they cry. Hearing the cries, the parents feed the children. Feeding the children may also be a display of love and affection. Children are completely dependent on and submissive to their parents, because they have few abilities of their own. That is, children lack the ability to feed themselves, get dressed, and so on. The parents also represent authority figures, who have power to give or withhold rewards. Parents can provide a wide range of rewards to their children as a means of controlling behavior. Very early in life, children begin to learn how to respond to authority figures. The responses to authority figures learned at home become further developed and reinforced in schools, churches, the Girl Scouts, Boy Scouts, Little League baseball, and many other organizations. Theory X assumes that most adults, including managers, do not advance much beyond this infant stage of development.

Theory Y, on the other hand, assumes that as individuals mature and develop, these basic patterns change. Adults strive for relative independence, autonomy, and control over their immediate world. Individuals develop a self-concept which they bring to the job. This self-concept includes abilities, skills, and attitudes that have been learned while the person was growing up. Whereas the child might have developed superficial abilities in many areas, the adult learns to develop a few abilities in depth. Professional schools (education, engineering, business) within universities, while stressing the importance of a well-rounded education, teach their students skills that will enable them to be effective in their professions. In the business school, the accounting department teaches accounting skills and practices that will enable students to become proficient accountants. Adults are capable of making numerous decisions, thinking in longer time horizons than children, and developing the ability to make numerous contributions to the organization.

The logic behind Theory X and Theory Y as they relate to organizations can be seen in Fig. 10.1. The dimensions have been adapted from the dimensions of bureaucracy presented in Fig. 3.2. The closed-system models of Taylor, Weber, and Fayol assumed that the closer an organization approached the "high" end of the dimensions, the closer it approached the ideal organization. The more

Dimensions	Theory Y	Theory X

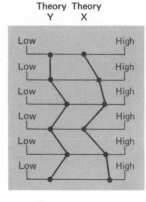

	Theory Y		Theory X
Rules and regulations	Low		High
Impersonality	Low		High
Hierarchical structure	Low		High
Loyalty to organization	Low		High
Top-down authority	Low		High
Division of work	Low		High

Fig. 10.1. Dimensions of organizations in relation to Theory X and Theory Y. (Adapted from C. Argyris, "Personality versus Organization," *Organizational Dynamics* **3**, 2 (1974): 3–17.)

an organization approaches this ideal, the more individuals will be forced to behave like infants.

The notion that the organization should guarantee life-long career paths for individuals is similar to the parental care and feeding of the infant. Rules and regulations established by the organization to control its employees are similar to the rewards and punishments meted out by parents to control the behavior of their children. To Chris Argyris, another noted management theorist, the demands of the formal organization are congruent with the demands parents place on their children (e.g., "Be home at 10 o'clock"; "Wash your face"; "Be nice"), but inconsistent with the needs of adults.[5] Adults want to express their needs on the job, but the formal organization wants these needs suppressed. The logic of the formal organization explicitly states that management should be in control over the key organizational activities. Thus management should be high on the dimensions outlined in Fig. 10.1.

The more an organization approximates the characteristics of the formal organization toward the "high" end of the dimensions, the more individuals will be required to satisfy needs that are like those of children. To the extent that the needs of individuals and the requirements of the formal organization are incompatible, the individuals will experience frustration, psychological failure, short time perspective, and conflict.

According to Argyris, the lower the employee's level in the organization's hierarchy, the lower the amount of control and the fewer the abilities the employee may use, and the greater the incongruency. Subordinates have less control over the nature of their work and have less chance to use their abilities than managers do. Within mass-production industries, restrictions in decision making and skill level are found to go together with increased feelings of psychological stress and social isolation. Low self-determination and job involvement have been reported by workers in mass-production industries, because their jobs are determined by the mechanical pacing of the assembly line, which uses only part of their skills.

Argyris contends that when employees' adult needs are ignored or suppressed by the organization, employees are likely to:

1. fight the organization and try to gain more control by joining a union, sabotaging the work, being absent, and so on;

2. leave the organization;

3. become apathetic toward their work and the organization;
4. downgrade the importance of their work and substitute higher pay as a reward for having to perform meaningless work.

Situational Interpretation

It is difficult to determine the extent of management's failure to provide opportunities for personal growth in industry. At any level within an organization, people who are adjusted to their jobs and to those around them, work steadily and effectively, create few administrative problems, and are well satisfied with the organization are valued by managers.

Argyris assumes that all people want freedom and self-actualization (i.e., opportunity to utilize one's talents to the fullest extent) and that it is somehow morally wrong for individuals to be lazy, unproductive, and uncreative. This may overemphasize some individuals' desire for freedom and underestimate their desire for security. It is also possible that not all people want to self-actualize on the job; be helped, counseled, and nurtured; and derive satisfaction from their job. One author has suggested that

> work, for probably a majority of workers, and even extending into the ranks of management, may represent an institutional setting that is not the central life interest of the participants. . . . Thus, the industrial worker does not feel imposed upon by the tyranny of organizations, companies, or unions.[6]

There are also environmental factors—cultural, economic, legal, political—which might prevent managers from acting in a Theory Y manner. As the environment becomes more turbulent, the organization is faced with unusual demands. For example, in 1973 the federal government, acting on recommendations from the President's Pay Board, mandated that average wages in an organization rise no more than 6.2 percent. Thus even if employees and managers felt that a 10 percent wage increase would reflect the value of their work during the past year, the federal government imposed a limit on this form of recognition. In addition, superior-subordinate collaboration on goal setting may be hampered by the participation of external groups (e.g., shareholders, consumers, taxpayers), as discussed in Chapter 2.

PERCEPTUAL PROCESS

Impressions serve as a basis for a person's getting along with other people. Perceptions also affect numerous organizational decisions, such as those related to hiring, firing, or promoting others.

A manager is often confronted with the task of forming an impression of another person—a new employee, a visiting member from the home office, a staff member she or he had not previously met. The manager's philosophy, needs, and expectations will play a part in the impressions formed. However, one's perceptions about another person may be quite different from that individual's self-perceptions. Person A's behavior is a function of self-perception, but Person B's behavior toward Person A is a function of B's perception of A.

Assume that you are having lunch with two managers from another company to discuss matters of common interest. You know these two only by name and by sight. You meet in the bar and start off with some casual conversation before going to lunch and serious talk. As you do not know these managers well, you will need to pick up a lot of information about them very quickly. In order to have a successful meeting, it will be necessary for you to determine their positions, status, and authority in the organization. If one says, "Marie runs our computer department, and I'm in charge of accounts receivable," exactly what does this mean? "Runs" and "in charge of" are very ambiguous terms. Under whose authority does Marie run the department? How many and what types of decisions can she make? Does their organizational level equal yours? What type of persons are they? Warm? Cold? Efficient? Intelligent? Many such questions run through your mind both consciously and subconsciously. At the same time, you must talk intelligently, figure out their interests, decide whether it would be considered offensive or even childish to tell your favorite off-color joke, and determine whether you are getting across favorably. While all these questions are being answered, you are making statements, nodding when you are supposed to nod, laughing when you are supposed to laugh, and expressing a dozen other emotions at the correct split second. One mistake could show you up as being clumsy or even an idiot.

Now all this activity requires the brain—that human data-processing center —to carry out a fantastic number of operations simultaneously without allowing one message to get crossed or misinterpreted. How? The key word is *selectivity*.

There are two types of selectivity—stimulus and personal.[7] *Stimulus* selectivity refers to those things that are perceived even though one does not want to recognize them. For example, bright lights, loud sounds, a telephone ringing, and extraordinary size are all things which a person cannot normally help but notice. *Personal* selectivity, on the other hand, depends on one's own preferences and expectations of what is to be seen. Personal selectivity involves a manager's assumptions about employees and the frequency with which one has reacted in that way before to a similar situation. A story about three baseball umpires discussing how they call balls and strikes illustrates personal selectivity. The first says, "Some's balls and some's strikes, and I calls 'em as they is." The second says, "Some's balls and some's strikes, and I calls 'em as I sees 'em." The third says, "Some's balls and some's strikes, but they ain't nothing till I calls 'em." The same is true for many of the things and experiences that managers confront daily. Once information is made one's own, it becomes organized into one's personal system for use in making decisions.

Use of selectivity enables a person to put another person into a category even when little information about that other is available. For example, if you know that a man is older than average and little else about him, you may put him into a category involving ideas of greater responsibility, more patience, less energy, and so on. If you see a general office clerk sitting back in his chair with his eyes closed, you may think that the clerk is goofing off, while the senior manager leaning back at his desk with his eyes closed is quite obviously trying to work out a complex situation and is meditating. Seeing the closed eyes of the clerk, you would immediately put that bit of information together with other bits of information you might have about clerks, their work habits, job attitudes, and so on, and conclude that the clerk is goofing off. This may be possible without having to gather any more data or questioning the clerk or making sure that your analysis of the situation was objective. On the other hand, when you see the meditating manager, you immediately conclude that he is working out a problem and wants to have no distractions.

When there is little information and no opportunity for interaction, one then may make maximum use of nonverbal information, such as facial features, general dress, body build, gestures, and so forth. Everyone uses all of these in judging other people. Going back to the example about the luncheon meeting, you probably noticed the two managers' shoes, hair styles, clothing, etc. You also noticed their postures to get an indication to whether they were tense or relaxed. As with all physical cues, a person may make a perceptual judgment without being aware of the information used in reaching a conclusion.

In summary, the basic perceptual process whereby a person takes what is "out there" and makes it a part of one's world "in here" is influenced by selectivity. This selectivity may be based on the person's unique experiences, preferences, and expectations. Unfortunately, selectivity may cause one to ignore or distort data to meet one's assumptions about people. In a general sense, there are four factors that influence one's personal frame of reference: stereotyping, halo effect, projection, and perceptual defense.[8]

Stereotyping

Stereotyping is the grouping together of individuals who seem alike in several ways. "Those guys look like hippies" and "That fraternity is made up of athletes" are stereotypes. Stereotypes may also involve ethnic-group membership, social-class membership, and so on.

Stereotyping has three general characteristics. First, the *categorization* of people requires a classification based on some distinguishable characteristics. These characteristics may be physical (color of hair, skin color, facial features) or based on membership in a group or society. Stereotyping could even be based on distinctive behavior patterns, such as driving expensive sports cars, smoking cigars, commuting, or carrying umbrellas. In other words, stereotyping involves membership in a category which brings forth the perception that such a person has all of the characteristics associated with that category. Second, the *common consensus* is that people who are identified as belonging to a particular category share certain personal attributes. For example, all poorly groomed long-haired young people are lumped together into a category called "hippies," and it is believed that they use drugs, have loose sexual morals, are not interested in holding permanent jobs, and hold antiestablishment values. Sports car drivers can also be put into a class: they dress flashily, are extroverted and aggressive, spend as much time pampering their cars as their girls, and thoroughly enjoy life. Third, stereotyping involves a *discrepancy* between the attributed traits and the actual traits of the person. Thus there are many long-haired young people who dress casually but are also highly responsible, disdain drug usage, are moralistic, and are gainfully employed; similarly, there are many introverted sports car drivers who do not know anything about engines and transmissions.

Halo Effect

The tendency in forming an impression or judgment of a particular person to be influenced by a general impression of that person is known as the halo effect. If you judge a person favorably, you tend to overrate the person on characteristics for which there is no evidence available; if you judge the person unfavorably, you tend to underrate the person on specific characteristics. A manager may single out one characteristic and use this as the basis for judging a subordinate's overall performance. An excellent attendance record could influence a manager's judgment about a worker's productivity, quality of work, industriousness, and so on. Similarly, a manager who perceives a person's performance unfavorably may judge the person as not getting along with fellow workers, as being uncommitted to the company, and having little desire for self-improvement, even when there is no evidence for these judgments.

Projection

This is a method of relieving feelings of guilt and failure by attributing (projecting) fears and socially unacceptable wishes, thoughts, and motives to someone else. A manager who is frightened by rumors of organizational change might not only judge others to be more frightened than they actually are, but also assess various decisions as more frightening than warranted. A general foreman lacking insight into his own failure to make timely decisions might be oversensitive to this trait in his supervisors. If he becomes aware of this fault, for which he feels shame or guilt, it could reduce his feelings of discomfort to focus his attention on similar faults of others. It may comfort him to think that many others possess the same failure, for that means he is not so much an oddball. The salesperson who pads her expense account can be relieved by perceiving many subtle cues that "everyone else" does it too. Projection, therefore, tends to act as a buffer between the "real" world and the world people create for themselves, keeping them from perceiving things that would upset them.

Perceptual Defense

Perceptual defense might be called *putting on blinders* to keep from seeing events that might be disturbing. A person who discovers that a "hippie" lacks most "hippie characteristics" might distort the situation so as to eliminate the inconsistency. Thus inaccurate perceptions prevent people from having to change their stereotypes. Marketing researchers have found that after purchasing a product, individuals will notice and pay attention to advertisements for that product to a far greater degree than they did prior to purchase; the more expensive the purchase, the more extreme this tendency. The reason for this is that the purchase, particularly an expensive one, evokes doubts and second thoughts, creating in the purchaser a need for reassurance which the advertisements provide.

Perceptual defense also occurs within organizations. One study found that an administrator's perception of the company will often be limited to those aspects of the situation which relate specifically to his or her own department, despite the fact that others may attempt to dissuade the manager from such selectivity. Thus the production manager views production-related problems as most pressing; the personnel manager views workers' morale, absenteeism, and grievances as the organization's largest problem.

These perceptual distortions are further complicated by the fact that most interaction occurs at two levels. *Overt* behavior occurs at the outer, obvious level. While this display of behavior is going on, however, a subtle struggle for attention and status, for control and influence, and for liking and warmth is going on in the background—the level of *covert* behavior. A hardheaded executive may overtly resist a splendid idea suggested by a brash young manager because of the hidden fear of one day being replaced by the younger person. This overt behavior on the part of the executive may in turn influence the younger manager to say and do certain things, perhaps even to leave the organization or turn to other pursuits.

One author has described several ways that managers use covert behavior to maneuver their way through the organization.[9] "Hold your coat" is one such tactic; an individual provides moral support for another by doing everything short of going into battle. This is a particularly wise decision if one believes that the individual will go down in defeat and the ultimate victory will enhance one's own position in the organization.

For example, two managers receive raises. Ms. Dinkel receives $2000 and Mr. Helms receives $1000. Dinkel commiserates with Helms and adds that if she were in a similar position, she'd see the boss over this humiliation and threaten to resign. Helms uses this tactic and is forced to resign. Dinkel then receives an additional raise for taking over Helms's duties. The hold-your-coat tactic is relatively safe for Dinkel, because she avoids the boss and does not need to take a position or say or do things to incur the wrath of her boss.

The people a person interacts with during the course of a work day are extremely important in helping or blocking the achievement of one's goals. Thus it is very useful for a person to be able to predict others' behavior. To make such predictions requires generalizations about their future behavior on the basis of scattered bits of their past overt behavior. These generalizations are based on knowledge of other persons in similar categories and on the impressions they make. Without such predictions, one's interaction with other persons would be most disturbing.

The greater one's success in assigning persons to categories with predictable behavior patterns or the better one can fit them under descriptive labels (e.g., student, professor), the better able one is to both predict and organize the many bits of information about them. Information about people can be gathered from "overt" or "covert" means. The importance of covert factors can hardly be overestimated, since they profoundly influence the productivity of a group or, for that matter, of an entire organization. One of the major purposes of the next section is to provide you with a framework for understanding your own behavior in organizations. Interpersonal problems cannot be effectively handled by ignoring them, nor do they disappear if they are ignored. They are usually transformed so that they are not expressed overtly as open hostility, but find their expression through poor task performance, loss of motivation, the indiscriminate opposition of action (subtle ways to do this include using parliamentary procedure, such as tabling motions, offering amendments, setting up committees, etc.), and reliance on perceptual distortions.

INDIVIDUALS' PROBLEMS WHEN ENTERING NEW GROUPS

To deal with interpersonal behavior in organizations, you need to understand some of the basic emotional issues with which the individual is confronted. When you met the other managers at the bar before the luncheon meeting, there was a period of *self-oriented behavior*. This behavior reflects the emotional concerns of each group member. You may feel comfortable discussing football; others may feel comfortable discussing the latest women's fashions. As this self-oriented behavior declines, you begin to pay more attention to one another and to the task to be accomplished. Table 10.1 shows the kinds of personal styles that will help individuals find themselves and also help the group to maintain itself and develop mechanisms for accomplishing its tasks.

The problems an individual faces when entering a new group or interpersonal situation influence his or her style of behavior. Four basic problems that can create tension and anxiety in a new group member are indicated in Table 10.1. An individual's style toward others will emerge from trying to resolve each of these problems as well as attempting to cope with his or her own tensions and anxieties. As the group develops, conditions must be created that permit these same emotional energies to be channeled in the direction of group effort. Let's examine these four problems and their consequences for managers.[10]

Table 10.1. Problems when entering groups

Problems	Resulting feelings	Coping responses (self-oriented)
I. Identity Who am I here?	Frustration	Tough responses fighting, controlling
II. Control and influence Who has the power here?	Tension	Tender responses supporting, helping
III. Needs and goals	Anxiety	Withdrawal and passivity
IV. Acceptance and intimacy		

E. Schein, *Process Consultation* (Reading, Mass.: Addison-Wesley, 1969), p. 35. Used with permission.

Identity

Who am I here? How am I to present myself to others? What type of role should I play in the group? These are the first and foremost problems in choosing a style which will be acceptable to the person and to others in the group. Should I play a dominant, aggressive leadership role (a style which I have used previously with some success), or should I play the tension-reliever role, which has worked for me in other situations? These issues arise because people have a range of possible roles and behavior styles to draw on from past experience. In formal committees, these problems are often partially resolved by the role which the organization assigns. The production engineer is told to join a new-product task force to represent the engineering point of view. But even in this situation, there is still a great deal of latitude for the individual to adopt a style that will satisfy his or her emotional uncertainty and lead to effective task performance. As indicated in Table 10.1, the emotional issue is there, whether or not the individual recognizes it, and it creates tension within the individual, leading to a self-preoccupation. The result is that initially, the individual listens very little to others and demonstrates little concern for their needs.

Control, Power, and Influence

Who has the power in this situation? How much power, control, and influence do *I* have in this situation? Although it can be safely assumed that each member possesses some degree of power, the amount can vary greatly from person to person. One group member may desire to actually influence the task accomplishment of the group, whereas another may wish to control the processes by which the group arrives at its goals.

The dilemma for all group members is that early in the group's history, they do not know one another's needs and styles. People may overtly do a lot of fencing, testing one another out, or experimenting with varied forms of interpersonal styles to relieve their tension (see Table 10.1). However, these behavioral styles may represent underlying drives for power or achievement. The member needs to work through such underlying drives before he or she can carry out any meaningful task activity. The manager must be careful not to mistake an individual's overt behavior for the member's true feelings. Thus the employee who immediately volunteers to help the president of the firm with the United Fund drive in the local community may be doing so in order to be perceived as a valuable employee by the president. The employee who takes over this assignment and meets or surpasses the company quota will be viewed by the president as important to the firm. Employees who want to climb the organization's ladder must help their bosses succeed. Since most transfers or promotions in an organization must have the approval of the immediate superior, an individual's overt behavior may actually be a form of political maneuvering so as to be noticed and eventually get promoted.

One of the pitfalls confronting the head of a newly appointed committee is the risk that he or she may inadvertently prevent this kind of getting acquainted and testing out from happening. If this activity does not occur shortly after a group is formed, superficial decisions may result. Members will not be ready to work on the task or must do their fencing while trying to solve the problem. The end result is to slow down progress and undermine the potential quality of the problem-solving activity.

Individual Needs and Group Goals

Which of my needs and goals can this group fulfill? Can any of my needs be met here? To which of the group's goals can I attach myself? Questions like these raise the anxiety level within the individual (see Table 10.1). Every individual wants the group's goal to include some of his or her personal goals and needs. Preoccupation with this problem may prevent the individual from taking overt action in the group until he or she sees whether or not these personal goals and needs will be satisfied. The problem is that if everyone took this wait-and-see attitude, it would be difficult to get any task activity started. In this situation, the chairperson may rely on any available authority (e.g., the formally stated goals of the committee, the agenda, and the minutes from the last meeting) to move the group out of the starting gate. By setting the goals of the committee, the chairperson is partially solving the problem, but even so cannot be sure that the members of the group will be motivated to achieve the stated goals.

In order to ensure motivated and goal-directed behavior on the part of the group's members, a sounder procedure would be for the chairperson to realize that until members' needs are exposed and shared, it is not possible to proceed. Therefore, sufficient time should be allocated for members to explore what they really want to get out of the group.

Acceptance and Intimacy

Am I accepted by others? Do I accept them? Do they like me? How close to others do I want to approach? When people come together, group norms (standards of behavior) must be developed to help people resolve these questions. For every group meeting, norms must be developed by the group to resolve the issues of acceptance and intimacy. There is no optimal level of intimacy and acceptance for all groups at all times. It depends on the members, on the group's task, on the length of time that the group will spend together, and a host of other factors. But the issues of intimacy and acceptance are always there as a source of tension until working norms have been established to resolve these issues.

Initially the acceptance and intimacy issue will appear in terms of address (Mr., Ms., Dr., Ladies and Gentlemen) and patterns of politeness (senior members speaking before junior members). As the group develops, the issue will center on the formality or informality of the group's procedures. If a group relies heavily on Robert's Rules of Order, the group is probably using more formal procedures to control members' talking than if the group abandons the formal book of rules.

Nonverbal communication also serves as a vital source of feedback about how effectively members communicate their feelings of acceptance and intimacy to one another. Nonverbal communications refer to aspects of behavior more subtle than punching someone in the arm or shouting. Frequently, observed nonverbal messages include directing gazes away from another person to communicate a lack of interest and acceptance, holding the mouth open to communicate enthusiasm (or passion), and placing one's hand on the shoulder to indicate support for the other person's comments or sympathy.

Contingencies Influencing Entry into Groups

Most people can modify their style of behavior when attempting to cope with the emotional problems of identity; control, power, and influence; individual needs and group goals; and acceptance and intimacy. People move toward what is wanted and away from what is feared or disliked. The predominant style of response will depend on two classes of contingencies: (1) the formal structure of the organization and its reward system, and (2) the individual's own personality system.

ORGANIZATION STRUCTURE

A mechanistic organization is more likely to produce withdrawal and/or denial responses than an organically structured organization. A mechanistic management system is characterized by:

1. specialized differentiation of tasks;
2. hierarchical structure of control, authority, and communication;
3. a tendency for interaction between superiors and subordinates to be governed by rules and regulations;
4. the precise definition of rights and obligations and methods into the responsibilities of each job.[11]

The Harrison Bank, a traditional commercial bank, is organized by functional departments, e.g., commercial, loans, data processing, investments. Ten layers separate tellers from the president, and organizational members are given elaborate titles to convey their rank in the hierarchy. The president feels very strongly that the organization structure be formalized and that everyone's specific responsibility, authority, and accountability be made clear. Predictably, these characteristics of a mechanistic design contribute to a limited display of acceptance and intimacy among members of the bank.

An organic management system, by contrast, provides for more frequent changes in roles and position and less emphasis on hierarchical structure. An organic structure requires a greater dynamic interplay between the various members of the organization. The characteristics of an organic system include:

1. the adjustment and continual redefinition of individual tasks through interaction with other employees;
2. a network of structure, authority, and communication which fosters both horizontal and vertical communications;
3. a content of communication that consists of information and advice rather than instructions and decisions.[12]

The Brower Company is a real estate investment firm. The organization's structure is based on the project being investigated at that time. The firm organized a project to market some New Mexican land to buyers throughout the United States. Another project was established to investigate the feasibility of erecting a large-scale shopping center in a semirural area of Pennsylvania. These project arrangements contribute to an organic management system in which employees' emotions are expressed.

Admittedly, the nature of the task environment—commercial banking versus real estate investment—affects the structure of the organization. However, the importance of structure as a contingency affecting employees' behavior cannot be dismissed. A free interplay of emotional responses might lead to initial low job performance, but will in the long run produce a higher level of communication and a stronger, more effective group problem-solving effort. However, if the formal structure of the organization does not permit such emotional growth, the group may never become capable of any real group effort.

Similarly, an organization's reward structure can reinforce certain interpersonal styles and not others. The organization's reward structure (e.g., salary adjustments, status symbols, promotions) may be designed to reinforce styles that generate wanted behavior by employees. The reverse may be true as well. Individuals might be satisfied in a company in which active, creative, and productive behavior is reinforced. The reinforcements available to the manager might include promotion recommendations, salary adjustments, work assignments, and transfers. Therefore, the manager may design a company that reinforces some behaviors and not others.[13]

INDIVIDUAL PERSONALITY

Personality is another contingency factor that may have a marked effect on the style of interpersonal behavior an individual displays in a group. One study examined the influences of Machiavellianism, a personality trait, on job strain and performance of managers.[14] Managers who scored high on the Machiavellian scale were characterized as manipulative, goal-oriented, impersonal, and more persuasive than managers who scored low on this dimension. This study also found that "High Machs" had greater job tension and strain when placed in roles demanding submissiveness than did "Low Machs" and also needed to be in positions of control to a greater extent than did "Low Machs." "High Machs" preferred interpersonal relations to be impersonal, distant, and requiring little interpersonal contact.

To deal with the emotionality that exists and to channel it into effective problem-solving activity, it is essential that the group members and the manager recognize the state of emotionality at a given time. Some of the most common ways of doing this are by:

1. observing what is said (content) and reading "between the lines";
2. noticing facial expressions, actions, and postures of the members, e.g., sagging faces and slumped bodies may suggest extreme relaxation or boredom;
3. realizing that your own feelings, tensions, resentments, delights, or interests can be useful indicators of the group atmosphere, e.g., a member feels thirsty, asks whether others want a drink, and discovers that many do;
4. relating all of the foregoing to the ongoing significant events in the group.

All of these examples stress the importance of understanding the communication process in organizations. Communication is often thought of as the simple transfer of information from one member to another. But as was pointed out earlier, the communication process is wrapped up with feelings of tension, frustration, anxiety, and the like. "Communication style" refers to a whole range of things—whether one is assertive, questioning, funny; whether one's voice is harsh, loud, soft; whether one's words are accompanied by gestures to add emphasis, and so on. Managers are less likely to be concerned about an individual's style as an indicator of personality than about the possible effects of a communication style on others.

INTERPERSONAL COMMUNICATION STYLE

As most people know from analyzing their own communication styles, people not only send the content of a message to others, but also receive and interpret what others say and how they react to that message. Occasionally, the subtle cues of interpersonal communication contradict the content of the message conveyed. For example, a manager may invite subordinates to "come in to speak with me about my problems," but through tone of voice, facial expression, and gestures convey the "real" message: "Don't bother me." Often a person says things in order to "save face," but other cues (facial expressions, gestures) manage to communicate other feelings to the individual.

Johari Window

The concept of communication style is not an easy one to define. Yet if communications are to serve as a central mechanism determining the quality of productivity in most organizations, they are worthy of analysis. The Johari Window is one technique for identifying interpersonal communication styles, their important features and consequences, and it also suggests a basis for interpreting the significance of those styles.[15]

We are using the Johari Window as an information-processing model. Interpersonal communication style and individual effectiveness are measured in terms of information-processing techniques. Managerial performance is thought to be the outcome of various communication styles. The model is a four-celled figure and reflects the combination of two sources of information—self and others. The model, as shown in Fig. 10.2, represents the various kinds of data available for use in communicating to others. Each of the four cells represents a particular mix of relevant information and has special significance for the quality of the communication process.

AREA OF FREE ACTIVITY

The behavior, thoughts, and feelings in this area are known to the person and known to others. It shows the extent of the region of free exchange between individuals with mutually shared perceptions (i.e., people see me the way I see myself). The underlying assumption of the Johari Window is that productivity and interpersonal effectiveness are directly related to the amount of mutually held information. Therefore, the larger this region becomes, the more rewarding, effective, and productive the relationship.

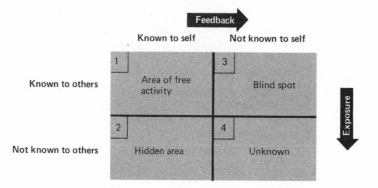

Fig. 10.2. The Johari Window: a model of interpersonal communication processes. (Adapted from J. Luft, "The Johari Window," *Human Relations Training News* **5** (1961): 6–7; *Of Human Interaction,* Palo Alto, Calif.: National Press Books, 1961.)

HIDDEN AREA

The behavior and thoughts known only to oneself form the second area. In a new group, this is a large area, because the members do not know much about one another and each member feels the need to be cautious about how much "self" to reveal to others. The hidden area includes data one perceives as potentially prejudicial (harmful) to a relationship or which one hides out of fear, desire for power, or whatever. This is a protective front or façade that protects the individual's ego. The question is not one of whether a front is necessary, but rather how much is realistically required.

BLIND SPOT

Area 3 represents the behavior and thoughts not known to oneself but apparent to others, e.g., a mannerism in speech or a gesture of which the person is unaware, but which is quite obvious to others. This is seen, for example, in the case of an executive who professes to find performance appraisals quite relaxing, but whose hand trembles, voice cracks, or hand reaches unobtrusively for the third martini or tranquilizer of the afternoon.

All of us operate at times in the blind area; through the process of education and growing up, people learn how to handle these types of behavior. Students who learn that successful managers are aggressive and forceful and that they pay little attention to the human-relations aspect of supervision may begin to reject feelings of warmth as not being part of themselves. They may suppress or refuse to recognize the feelings as their own, when they do occur. However, they might be quite real and highly visible to others.

UNKNOWN AREA

Area 4 refers to behavior and thoughts that are known to neither oneself nor others. Examples of the area of unknown potential are truly unconscious and deeply repressed feelings and impulses, hidden skills, and so on. From time to time, people can become aware of some aspects of themselves which neither they nor the others had known before. Then there is a movement from Area 4 into one of the other areas. For our purposes, this area is of less importance than the other three.

Interpersonal Communication Processes: Exposure and Feedback

The dynamic nature of the model in Fig. 10.2 suggests that movement along the vertical and horizontal regions can enable individuals to change their relationships. Individuals can significantly influence the size of their area of free activity in relating to others by the behavioral processes they employ in establishing their communication style. Within the framework of this model, the enlargement of this area occurs with a reduction of one's hidden area. Thus someone who behaves in a nondefensive, trusting, and risk-taking manner with others may be thought of as contributing increased mutual trust and sharing of data. The process employed toward this end is called the "exposure." It requires the open and candid disclosure of one's feelings, factual knowledge, and the like, in an attempt to share these with others. The exposure process is directly controlled by the individual and may be used to build a trusting relationship.

The need for mutual exposures becomes apparent when one considers the behavioral process required for enlarging the area of free activity laterally, that is, into the person's blind spot. Other individuals can feed back information to the individual about his or her behavior that the individual may not have. A blind spot will be reduced only with cooperation of others and the individual's own prior willingness to deal openly and candidly with others.

Communication Styles and Managerial Impacts

Figure 10.3 extends this discussion by presenting several commonly used communication styles.[16] Each style uses various degrees of feedback and exposure. As might be expected, each communication style has associated with it some fairly predictable consequences for management.

TYPE A

This interpersonal style reflects a minimal use of both feedback and exposure processes. The "Unknown" region dominates this style, indicating withdrawal and aversion to risk taking. The person who uses this style might appear to others as mechanical, uncommunicative, and highly structured. This type of interpersonal style might be found in a highly mechanistic or bureaucratic organization, where personal disclosure and feedback are not rewarded by the organization. Subordinates might describe their manager who uses this style as aloof, cold, and indifferent to their personal needs. The Type A behaviors of managers may also reveal something about the organization. It would probably be tradition-bound, and the overriding need for security might be present. In many respects, Type A managers assume McGregor's Theory X.

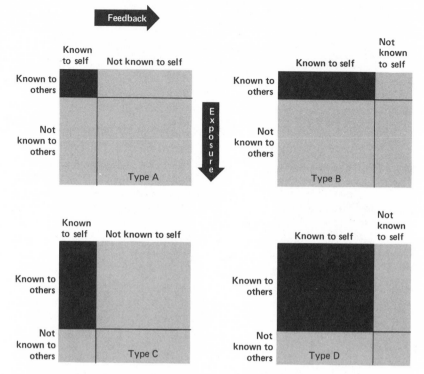

Fig. 10.3. Interpersonal styles. (Adapted from J. Hall, "Communication Revisited," *California Management Review* **15** (1973): 56–67).

TYPE B

Under this approach, there is also an aversion to exposure, but feedback is the only process used and it is overused. An aversion to the use of exposure may be interpreted as a sign of mistrust of self and others. It is therefore not surprising that the "Hidden area" is the dominant feature of this relationship. This style appears to be a probing, supportive interpersonal ploy, and once the hidden area becomes apparent, others will likely leave the relationship. Some managers build a façade to maintain personal control and an outward appearance of confidence. As the Johari Window suggests, those who employ such tactics tend to be isolated from their peers because of the lack of trust and the promotion of a false confidence.

TYPE C

This interpersonal style may reflect ego-striving and/or distrust of others' competence. People who use this style usually feel quite confident of their own opinions and are likely to value compliance from others. They are often unaware of their impact of others' contributions. This is reflected in the dominant "Blind spot" that results from this style. Therefore, subordinates might feel hostility, insecurity, and resentment toward their manager. They will also withhold information or give the manager only selected feedback. Although bureaucratic organizations, with their hierarchical structure and centralized communication networks, are likely to reward the use of this style, so can fear of failure, authoritarianism, need for control, and overconfidence in one's own position. Such traits vary from person to person and limit the communication process.

TYPE D

This represents the ideal state. The conditions for growth and confidence may be created through the use of constructive feedback and exposure. The area of free activity dominates the interpersonal processes. Trust is built slowly, and managers who experiment with Type D processes should be prepared to be flexible and patient with others. Many of the personal problems individuals confront when joining a group (see Table 10.1) surface, and the manager must resist cutting the dialogue short.

Levels of Interpersonal Communication

Most communications occur between two persons within the area of free activity of each person (line A in Fig. 10.4). A second level of communication is the signals or cues picked up from a person's blind self (line B). A third level of communication occurs when one person deliberately reveals a fact that is usually concealed (line C), e.g., "leveling" with a person or "confiding" one's feelings and/or reactions. One person may also communicate his or her feelings to another without either one's being consciously aware of the origin of the feeling (line D).

Various factors may interfere with this communication process, however. If individual A has a very positive self-image, wants to assert his or her opinions to others, and the like, this person's communication style is assertive, clear, and strong. The feedback A has received from others confirms these self-impressions, and thus this person assumes an increasingly strong position in a group.

Individual B, on the other hand, is not secure and expects to have difficulty being self-assertive in a group. This person's communication style is hesitant,

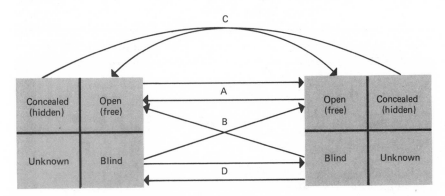

Fig. 10.4. Types of messages in a two-person communication situation.
(E. Schein, *Process Consultation*, Reading, Mass.: Addison-Wesley, 1969, p. 24. Used with permission.)

slow, and low-key. Listeners may assume that B does not have much to say and therefore may "tune out." Under these conditions, B loses more self-confidence, becomes a noncontributor, and increases his or her hidden or avoided area.

In both instances, the final outcome of the respective communication styles is a result of the person's initial expectations which produce a certain style of communication. Given all of the factors which interfere with the communication process between individuals (e.g., stereotyping, halo effect, and emotional issues), it is easy to understand why people fail to communicate effectively. It is the manager's job to help the group make a diagnosis, and it is only through the joint efforts of all of the members in a group that communication difficulties can be overcome.

INITIAL COMMUNICATION PATTERN

What would the Johari Window look like early in the group's development? The area of free activity is relatively small when compared to the others. People tend to engage in behavior in a relatively superficial manner until their underlying emotional problems have been solved. These problems include establishment of an identity, deciding who has the power, deciding which needs and/or goals can be satisfied by the group, and deciding whether or not the individual has been accepted into the group by others.

LATER COMMUNICATION PATTERN

Personal feedback during the life cycle of the group can change the boundaries of the four areas. One powerful effect on a group of an individual, for example, is the exchange of hidden behavior for knowledge of blind spots. During the early stages of a group, members reveal aspects of themselves consciously or subconsciously. After the group has developed norms and a structure to a point where members begin to actively and deliberately feed back feelings and observations about others, the configuration of the areas changes.

How much the individual is willing to share with other group members depends on several things, such as clarity and agreement about goals, methods of problem solving, and personal satisfactions. The work itself must be related to something which is vital to the member and actively involves him or her. The members must be able to achieve some "reward" in return for some "cost" of group involvement. Committee work involves time (a cost) and must be rewarded (a factor in promotion and/or salary increments, for example) if the individual is to continually engage in such behavior. Involvement with emotions is virtually impossible. In a productive effort, however, the emotionality is constructively related to the goals of the group through a process of shared feelings and thoughts.

Channeling Emotionality in Effective Behavior

Emotional reactions are neither good nor bad per se. The function of leadership and organization is to bring these emotions into a constructive relationship to the work task. If the leadership is effective, the work of the group is uppermost, and the emotions express functions which are important. Thus group members inclined toward fight are the initiators, the critics, the evaluators; those inclined toward glossing over may reduce tension with humor or help the group rise to significant problem-solving levels when such behaviors will help the progress of the group. The dependent person may play an important function in helping the group to recognize limits outside the group, and the dependence need is expressed by contributing to group support. Note, however, that, although people tend to use one style (Type A, B, C, or D) which is dominant in their own dynamic system, it is also true that any one person will show, under certain circumstances, a variety of emotions by playing different roles, depending on the organization's reward contingencies and the individual's personality.

Summary

In this chapter, we have examined the various factors that influence the individual's perceptual and communication processes. A person's philosophy of human nature has an impact on what the person will perceive. Two such models are Theory X and Theory Y, and each has a variety of managerial implications. Human beings experience a variety of difficulties in attempting to "objectively" process incoming stimuli, and biases and distortions in perceptions are typical. These biases and distortions are for the most part systematic, making it possible to explain and predict human perceptions.

We next examined some of the causes and types of self-oriented behavior an individual may use when entering a new group. The four basic emotional issues are: (1) identity; (2) power, control, and influence; (3) individual needs and group goals; and (4) acceptance and intimacy. Two major contingencies here are organizational structure and personality, and these contingencies have differing impacts on the causes of self-oriented behavior.

The Johari Window is one technique for understanding the interpersonal-communication process. Many managers report that communication breakdowns are the single most important barrier to organizational effectiveness. The critical factors underlying communication processes are the interpersonal communication styles of the people. The Johari Window can be used as an information-processing model that reflects the interaction of two interpersonal sources of information—self and others. The quality of interpersonal-communication styles has great influence on the organizational practices and procedures used by managers.

Discussion Questions

1. What are the differences between Theory X and Theory Y?

2. Develop a position supporting Argyris's contention that organizations treat employees like infants.

3. What is the connection between Theory X and Argyris's position?

4. What is perception?

5. What factors impede the perceptual process in organizations? Give examples of each.

6. What cues are available to help the manager diagnose the emotional state of his or her work group?

7. Discuss the contingencies that influence the style of behavior exhibited by a member of a work group.

8. What is the purpose of the Johari Window?

9. How can the Johari Window help managers understand the communication process in organizations?

10. Give examples of Type A, B, C, and D styles of interpersonal behavior.

Management Incidents

THE FIVE S's COMPANY

Tom Patterson, project leader for the Five S's Company, has 20 computer programmers reporting to him. These programmers are working on the development of major information systems, and each has been assigned to one of five project teams. Each team is responsible for one of the information systems. Tom Patterson decided that he could handle the administrative functions of his job more efficiently if he delegated more authority to the project teams. Before announcing his decision to all 20 programmers, he decided to discuss it privately with each of the project groups. He wanted to make sure that they understood the reasons why he was thinking of changing the structure of the project team by placing a project leader in each team.

After discussing the proposed change in a morning meeting sandwiched in between other meetings, Patterson later on that day announced his decision for the five project leaders. The following day, Patterson started his two-week vacation.

One morning when Patterson was still on vacation, Randy Sweeney asked Carol Straka to prepare the computer-operator procedure for a system test that had to be run that night. Later that day, Randy asked Carol if the test program was ready; Carol replied that it was not.

Randy asked, "Why not, didn't you have enough time?"

"No," Carol replied, "I had enough time, but where I worked before, that was the task of the project leader."

Randy was visibly upset. "Fortunately, or unfortunately, it is a programming responsibility here, and I asked you to perform that operation. I'm the project leader on this project; now why didn't you do as I asked?"

"You're the project leader?" Carol answered. "To my knowledge, we didn't vote or express any opinions on the matter. Patterson just cut out, and the meeting was too short for me to ask any questions."

1. What has led up to this situation?
2. How could Patterson have avoided this situation?

CENTRE VIEW HOSPITAL

Centre View Hospital will open its doors in a small farming community and has asked you to take the job as its director. Since you have had administrative responsibilities in a larger metropolitan hospital and you and your spouse liked the advantages of living in a rural community, you decided to accept the position. No patients will be admitted during the next month, to permit a final shakedown of the building and the hiring of professional staff and numerous nonprofessional staff. The personnel director already has hired some of your nonprofessional staff from a neighboring hospital and suggests that you and your administrative staff get together to decide about office locations, equipment, and procedures for hiring other staff employees.

1. What are some of the emotional issues that could impair the effectiveness of your first meeting?
2. If you asked a behavioral scientist to assist you in diagnosing the first meeting and the consultant suggested that your area of free activity be enlarged, what does that mean? How would you go about doing this?

COLONY PARTS, INC.

Howard Henry and his family recently moved from Michigan to Altoona, Pennsylvania after living for many years in Michigan. Being a skilled machinist made it relatively easy for him to find employment at the Colony Parts, Inc., a manufacturer of replacement parts for industrial machinery.

From the beginning of his work with the company, Henry was rated as a conscientious and skilled worker. Some of the operations he performed were so intricate that no one else in the company was able to duplicate them with any degree of precision. Although his limited formal education caused some communication problems with the plant's general superintendent, this was seen as a short-term problem that could be overcome in time by Henry's attending evening classes at the local high school.

Unfortunately, Henry's social relations in the plant were far from those expected by his foreman. Refusing to eat lunch or drink coffee with other workers, he seemed highly suspicious of them, even when they approached him in a friendly manner. A similar attitude was exhibited toward his supervisor. Although Henry would take on any assignment given to him, he was extremely reluctant to make any suggestions for improvement of work methods or product design. This was especially frustrating, since his foreman was convinced that Henry had many good ideas for improving work efficiency and product quality. His foreman has asked Henry if he wanted to train some new employees, but Henry's response was: "A worker's responsibility is to do the job and not train employees. That's management's job."

One day the personnel director asked him how he was doing in night school, hoping that this would draw Henry out and get him to reveal what was bothering him. When the personnel director reached for a notebook to take some occasional notes, Henry walked away and refused to work for the rest of the day.

1. What kind of place do you suppose Henry worked in before coming to Colony Parts?
2. What kind of interpersonal style is Henry using? Why?

REFERENCES

1. C. W. Mills, *The Power Elite* (New York: Oxford University Press, 1956), p. 136.

2. E. Schein, "Organizational Socialization and the Profession of Management," *Industrial Management Review* **9** (1968): 1–16.

3. D. McGregor, *The Human Side of the Enterprise* (New York: McGraw-Hill, 1960), pp. 33–34.

4. R. Townsend, *Up the Organization* (New York: Knopf, 1970), p. 34.

5. C. Argyris, "Personality and Organization Theory," *Administrative Science Quarterly* **18** (1973): 141–168.

6. R. Dubin, "Industrial Research and the Discipline of Sociology," *Proceedings of the 11th Annual Meeting, Industrial Relations Research Association,* Madison, Wisconsin, 1959, p. 161. *Also see* J. Maurer, "Work as a 'Central Life' Interest of Industrial Supervisors," *Academy of Management Journal* **11** (1968): 329–339; R. Dubin, J. Champoux, and L. Porter, "Central Life Interests and Organizational Commitment of Blue-Collar and Clerical Workers," *Administrative Science Quarterly* **20** (1975): 411–421.

7. D. Lawless, *Effective Management: Social Psychological Approach* (Englewood Cliffs, N.J.: Prentice-Hall, 1972), p. 33.

8. P. Zimbardo and F. Ruch, *Psychology and Life,* 9th ed. (Glenview, Ill.: Scott, Foresman, 1975).

9. V. Reinhold, *The Corporate Prince* (New York: Litten Educational Publishing, 1971).

10. This section is based on E. Schein's *Process Consultation* (Reading, Mass.: Addison-Wesley, 1969), pp. 31–46.

11. T. Burns and G. Stalker, *The Management of Innovation* (London: Tavistock, 1961), p. 120.

12. *Ibid.,* p. 121.

13. H. Sims, "The Leader as a Manager of Reinforcement Contingencies: An Empirical Example and a Model." Paper presented at SIU Fourth Biennial Leadership Symposium, October 26–28, 1976, Carbondale, Ill.; and B. Hinton and J. Barrow, "The Superior's Reinforcing Behavior as a Function of Reinforcements Received," *Organizational Behavior and Human Performance* **14** (1975): 123–143.

14. G. Gemmill and W. Heisler, "Machiavellianism as a Factor in Managerial Job Strain, Job Satisfaction and Upward Mobility," *Academy of Management Journal* **15** (1972): 51–64.

15. J. Luft, *Of Human Interaction* (Palo Alto, Calif.: National Press Books, 1969); and J. Hall, "Communication Revisited," *California Management Review* **15** (1973): 56–67.

16. Hall, *ibid*.

11
Motivation

Managerial styles

Philosophies
Contingencies
Perceptions
Individual problems
Interpersonal communi-
cations

Chapter 10

Motivation

Needs
Satisfiers and dis-
satisfiers
Expectancies and con-
tingencies
Management by objectives
Job enrichment

Chapter 11

Leadership

Power and influence
Traits
Contingency models
Substitutes for leadership

Chapter 12

Groups

Roles
Models
Contingencies
Procedures for group
problem solving

Chapter 13

Conflict

Contingency model
Role conflict
Interpersonal conflict
Intergroup conflict

Chapter 14

The objectives of this chapter are to:

develop your awareness of the nature of motivation and how it can change over time;

demonstrate how motivation affects employee performance;

create an understanding of how to use three basic motivational theories: need theory, two-factor theory, and expectancy theory;

develop guidelines for effectively motivating employees through Management By Objectives and job enrichment;

identify the contingencies that are likely to play an important role in influencing work motivation and the various approaches designed to increase work motivation.

The topic of motivation at work has received considerable attention in recent years among both practicing managers and organizational researchers. If supervisors are asked to name their biggest work problems, motivation of employees to perform better invariably falls at or near the top of the list. There seems little doubt that motivating employees is one of the most important jobs facing the manager. There seems to be several reasons for this importance.

To begin with, organizations have recently begun to direct more attention toward the human side of the organization. In addition to the need for financial and physical resources, every organization requires people in order to function. There are three behavioral requirements: (1) people must be attracted not only to join the organization, but also to remain in it; (2) people must perform the tasks for which they are hired and must do so in a dependable manner; and (3) people must go beyond this dependable performance and sometimes engage in creative or innovative behavior at work. When the United States Congress ended the draft and instituted a volunteer-based military service, the army faced the tremendous problem of attracting and retaining soldiers. Various incentives, such as financial bonuses for reenlistment, college scholarships, relaxation of training camp standards, and career placements have been used to induce young men and women to join this organization. In other words, the army changed its motivational strategy by focusing more attention on the behavioral, as opposed to the hardware requirements of the organization.

Second, given the ever-tightening limitations placed on organizations by unions and governmental agencies, increased foreign and domestic competition, citizens' lobbies, and trade associations, management is always looking for new ways to maintain and/or increase productivity. Thus organizational effectiveness in many firms can be significantly influenced by management's ability to motivate its employees to direct more effort toward the goals of the organization.

Third, the technology required for production has undergone radical changes during the last two decades. As technology increases in complexity, machines become necessary yet insufficient means of achieving effective and efficient operations. Modern technology can no longer be associated with "automation" and mass-assembly lines. Consider the example of NASA, whose highly complex technology was needed for placing a man on the moon, and developing Skylab. Not only was the technology complex, but also NASA had to bring together thousands of employees who could work at peak capacity to apply the technology required for success. In this instance, NASA had to ensure that it had employees who were capable and willing to use the advanced technology to achieve its goals.

Finally, although organizations have for some time viewed their financial and physical resources from a long-term perspective, only recently have they begun to seriously apply this same perspective to their human resources. Many organizations have established "assessment centers" and encourage their employees to participate in management and organization development programs. Organizations are doing these activities as one means of developing their employees as future resources to be drawn on as the organization develops and grows.[1]

Words can mean different things to people, and even psychologists cannot totally agree what is involved in motivation. The words *needs, drives, desires, wishes, goals,* and *force* are typically used to describe motivation. Motivation has been defined as "an inner state that energizes, activates, or moves and that directs or channels behavior toward goals."[2] This definition has three important characteristics. First, it is concerned primarily with what energizes, or moves, human behavior; second, it focuses on what directs, or channels, such behavior; and finally, it asks how behavior is maintained, or sustained.

Each of these characteristics represents an important factor in our understanding of human behavior at work. First, this definition points to an internal force that drives the individual to behave in certain ways. Second, there is the notion of goal orientation; the individual's behavior is directed toward something. Third, this way of viewing motivation contains a contingency orientation; that is, it considers those forces in the individual and the surrounding environment that give him or her feedback on whether to intensify the drive and direction of energies or to dissuade the person from the course of action and to redirect his or her efforts.

MOTIVATION PROCESS

Perhaps the simplest way to understand motivation is to think of it as a sequence, or process. The basic building blocks of this process are shown in Fig. 11.1. Motivation begins with a need, a felt deficiency. Individuals have many types of needs. Some are innate (e.g., needs for food, water, sex, and sleep), and some are learned (e.g., needs for achievement, affiliation, and power). The learned needs, of course, are much more important to the motivation of employees than are the inborn needs.

Once a need develops, it sets up a drive. A drive is simply the behavioral outcome of a need; it is deficiency with direction. The drive is aimed at a goal which will alleviate the deficiency. A goal in the motivation cycle can be defined as anything that fulfills a need. For example, individuals who have a strong desire to be with others (a high need for affiliation) may attempt (drive) to increase their interactions with those around them (behavior) in hope of gaining their friendship (goal). Therefore, motivation should be thought of as involving needs, drives, behaviors, and goals. All four are important to the manager in understanding the motivation of employees.

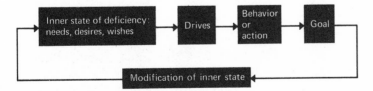

Fig. 11.1. Basic motivation process. (Adapted from R. Steers and L. Porter, *Motivation and Work Behavior,* New York: McGraw-Hill, 1975, p. 7.)

One of the problems in studying motivation is that it cannot be felt, seen, or heard directly through observable behavior. Rather, it is an intervening variable. An intervening variable is used to account for internal (and unobservable) psychological processes that in turn directly affect behavior. Thus motivation, like learning and anxiety, is an "in-the-head" variable. The manager who wants to study the effects of different kinds of incentives (economic, psychological, etc.) must be aware that motivation is an intervening variable and that an employee's motivation can be measured or inferred only from the employee's behavior. But herein lies the problem. In order to study motivation, a manager must measure it. Yet because motivation is not directly observable, the manager must always measure presumed *effects* of motivation, such as performance, turnover, grievances, and the like, and not motivation itself. For example, if we observe that a lathe operator is producing more axles than his coworkers, we can infer that he is more motivated (assuming similar abilities and skills).

BASIC THEORIES OF MOTIVATION

There are numerous theories of motivation. We will look at three theories which managers have used widely by managers—need theory, the two-factor theory, and expectancy theory.

Need Theory

Behavioral scientists often state that all behavior is motivated and that this behavior serves the individual's needs, as was indicated in Fig. 11.1. Without motivation, the individual would not behave, but would be an inert lump, doing virtually nothing. Moved into action by a need, the individual engages in goal-directed behavior motivated by that need and continues to engage in that behavior until the need has been satisfied. The actions serve the need; the behavior is the means by which the need is satisfied. This behavior is often stopped when the goal is reached. For example, a hungry person needs food, is driven by a lack of food, and is motivated by a desire for food in order to satisfy the need. This continuous search for appropriate behavior begins with a felt need and ends with goal-directed behavior that satisfies the need. A. H. Maslow's theory of human motivation is concerned with needs and how the individual's behavior is directed toward the satisfaction of such needs. Therefore, let us examine an individual's needs in more detail, following the need hierarchy of Maslow.[3]

THE NEED HIERARCHY

Maslow's need theory states that people at work are motivated by a desire to satisfy a hierarchy of needs. The significant determinants of motivation, known as needs, appear in a specific ranking, or hierarchy. Those needs which come first must be satisfied to some extent before higher-level needs emerge and become determinants of motivation.

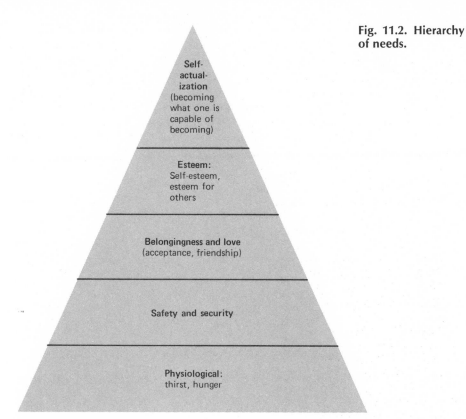

Fig. 11.2. Hierarchy of needs.

337

BASIC THEORIES
OF MOTIVATION

Maslow's framework stresses two fundamental premises:

1. Human beings are wanting animals whose needs depend on what they already have. Only needs not yet satisfied can influence behavior; a satisfied need is not a motivator.
2. Humans' needs are arranged in a hierarchy of importance. Once one need is relatively satisfied, another emerges and demands satisfaction.

Maslow has proposed five classifications of needs in a hierarchy of importance: (1) physiological, (2) safety, (3) belongingness, (4) esteem, and (5) self-actualization. This hierarchy of needs is shown in Fig. 11.2.[4]

Physiological Needs. This category of needs consists of the most basic needs of the human body, such as food and water, which are necessary for survival. *Physiological needs dominate when all needs are unsatisfied.* (Other needs do not serve as a basis for motivation, and it is fruitless to consider any of those higher in order.) Several modern-day management scholars have commented that since this type of situation probably does not arise often in the United States these days, the important needs, at least from a managerial standpoint, would appear to be those higher in the need hierarchy.

Safety or Security Needs. With the physiological needs satisfied, the next higher level assumes importance. These are the safety or security needs, which emphasize protection against danger and economic disaster. From a managerial standpoint, safety needs are the motivation behind attempts to ensure job security and economic security. Today, economic issues are an integral part of the collective-bargaining process. Many unions (e.g., railroad, typographical, steelworkers, and longshoremen) are making demands on management for guaranteed job security and fringe benefits. Similarly, the United States government has passed the "Occupational Safety and Health Act of 1970" to reduce the number of safety and health hazards in the industrial work sphere.

Belongingness and Love Needs. When people's physiological and safety/security needs are satisfied, their needs for belonging and love become important motivators. This level on the hierarchy represents a clear-cut step away from the purely physical needs; nonsatisfaction of these third-level needs may affect the mental health of the employees. This level emphasizes needs for association, acceptance by other people, and for giving and receiving love. The tightly knit work group may, under proper organizational conditions, be far more effective in achieving organizational goals than an equal number of separate individuals.

Esteem Needs. These needs refer to the needs for both self-acceptance and recognition by others that one is a valuable and worthwhile person. The individual needs to feel genuinely respected by his or her peers in and out of the work environment. Satisfaction of these needs leads to a feeling of self-confidence and prestige.

Self-Actualization. The "desire to become more and more what one is, to become everything that one is capable of becoming," is the capstone on the hierarchy. Here are the needs for realizing one's own potential and for continued self-development. Self-actualizing persons must be (1) free from illness, (2) sufficiently gratified in their basic needs, (3) positively using their capabilities, and (4) motivated by some values which they strive for and to which they are loyal.

Although to Maslow these five types of needs form a hierarchy, he believed that decreasing percentages of satisfaction are encountered as lower-level needs are replaced in relative importance by higher-level needs. He speculated that for the average individual, physiological needs are 85 percent satisfied; security and safety needs are 70 percent satisfied; belongingness needs are 50 percent satisfied; esteem needs only 40 percent satisfied; and self-actualization needs are only 10 percent satisfied. Needless to say, the self-actualization needs do not become activated without most of the lower-order needs being somewhat satisfied.

EVALUATION OF MASLOW'S NEED HIERARCHY

Maslow's need hierarchy has attracted a great deal of attention from both academicians and practitioners. Maslow's motivation model is also widely referred to by practitioners, for it is easy to understand, has a great deal of demonstrable common-sense validity, and clearly points out some of the factors that motivate employees in organizations.

Researchers have tested Maslow's need hierarchy in a wide variety of organizations and have arrived at a number of interesting findings:

1. Lower- and middle-level managers are more dissatisfied than top-level managers in attempting to satisfy their esteem and self-actualization needs.
2. At lower levels of management, small-company managers are more satisfied than large-company managers; however, at higher levels of management, the reverse is true.
3. Line managers are more satisfied than staff managers.
4. In the United States and Great Britain, there tends to be a hierarchical satisfaction of needs, as Maslow predicted for managers.
5. Black managers in organizations report more deficiency in need satisfaction than do their nonblack counterparts.
6. Regardless of managerial level or race, there is a tendency for those needs which managers feel are most important (esteem and self-actualization) to be *least satisfied*.[5]

In addition to defining levels of need satisfaction and/or deficiency, Maslow's model has been found to be related to managerial and production employees' performance on the job. Since the need theory contends that human behavior is goal-directed toward fulfilling unsatisfied needs, an individual's need satisfaction should be related to his or her job performance. And, as Maslow's theory would predict, higher-level needs are more closely linked to job performance than lower-level needs are.

Overlapping of Needs. Based on the concept that a single behavior may have a number of needs associated with it, a given need does not have to be fully satisfied before a higher-level need becomes urgent. For example, industrial engineers have found that hunger is a felt need during the midmorning. For most workers, the scheduling of a midmorning coffee break will satisfy this need and thus will no longer serve as a motivator.

It is also important to recognize that this midmorning coffee break may also satisfy the individual's belongingness and love needs. Thus from a practical standpoint, the individual neither chooses nor desires a maximum satisfaction of one level of needs at a time. Instead, the individual is usually content with a satisfactory level of fulfillment. Indeed, Maslow stated, a normal person's needs are partially satisfied and, at the same time, partially unsatisfied.

In terms of the hierarchy of needs, one way to express the interrelationships between needs is shown in Fig. 11.3. This figure shows various levels of satisfaction for the basic needs as well as the number and relative importance of needs existing at any one level. As the basic physiological and safety needs are satisfied, other needs arise, and the peak of satisfaction for each previous need must occur before the peak of the next higher-order need can be reached.

Rigidity of the Need Hierarchy. If able to satisfy two different needs, which one will a person satisfy first? It is not always the lower-level need that will drive the individual's behavior. No doubt you are aware of individuals who have

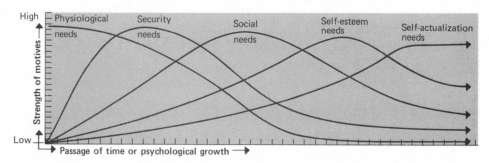

Fig. 11.3. Importance of needs relative to a person's degree of satisfaction. (D. Law-less, *Effective Management: Social Psychological Approach,* Englewood Cliffs, N.J.: Prentice-Hall, 1972, p. 87. Reprinted by permission of Prentice-Hall, Inc., Englewood Cliffs, N.J.)

been willing to sacrifice esteem from others, love, safety, and physiological fulfillment in order to accomplish a personal goal. Listening to the athletes at the 1976 Olympic games, it would appear that esteem and self-actualization needs played an important role in their desire to win.

Although Maslow specified a universal ordering of needs and felt that almost everyone encounters them in that order, he realized that creative persons, entrepreneurs, and professional persons may experience the self-actualization need before lower-order needs are even partially satisfied. Likewise, individuals might skip a certain need level because their environment does not provide opportunities to satisfy that particular need. The artist who lives in poverty but is able to satisfy his or her higher-level needs or the doctor attending medical school and living in student housing would be examples of this situation. Therefore, the need hierarchy has been criticized as being too rigid and not leaving enough room for individual differences. In some cases, we would agree that the hierarchy is too rigid to account for individual differences.

NEED NONSATISFACTION

What happens when needs are not satisfied? Unsatisfied needs cause internal tension, which the individual strives to avoid. Under these conditions, the individual experiences frustration. The football player who works out daily during the summer to make the varsity only to be cut from the squad on the last day is an example of an individual who would probably be quite frustrated. His goal of making the team, the attainment of which would have brought the satisfaction of several needs (e.g., belongingness, esteem, and possibly later financial security), has been blocked.

The ways in which individuals cope with this frustration will vary from person to person. Some people will react in a positive manner (exhibit constructive behavior); others, in a negative manner (defensive behavior). Some patterns, however, are quite common. Figure 11.4 gives a simplified model of reactions to the nonsatisfaction of needs.

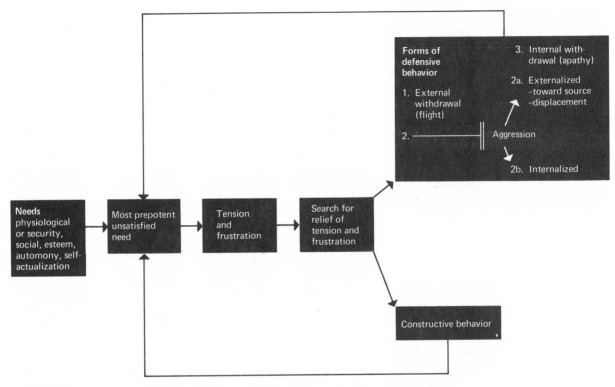

Fig. 11.4. Reactions to nonsatisfaction of needs. (Adapted by permission from B. Kolasa, *Introduction to Behavioral Science in Business,* New York: Wiley, 1969, p. 256.)

Mechanisms for Dealing with Frustration. Nonattainment of a need is frustrating. One mechanism available to people is to leave or withdraw. *Withdrawal* may be physical, e.g., absenteeism and turnover (quitting), or it may be internalized and take the form of apathy. In our football example, the player may transfer to another university (external withdrawal) or remain at the same university and lose interest in football.

Under most conditions, the common reaction to frustration is *aggression,* which is most readily observable as a move outward (e.g., externalized). If there is a direct attack on the source in a way that can alleviate the frustration, this may be reasonable and mentally healthy. On the other hand, it may generate hostility and violence. (This will be discussed in Chapter 14, which is concerned with conflict.) Unfortunately, aggression is sometimes directed toward innocent third parties, a process known as *displacement.* The professor who enters the classroom after an editorial board has rejected his manuscript for publication and who finds fault with everything the class is doing is showing displaced aggression. Your boss who has just received a rough time from *her* supervisor and "snaps back" at you when you ask her a simple question might be another example.

If aggression is internalized, fixation develops. A person who fixates persists in giving the same response that led to the frustration of the need even though the response is improper. The accountant who still gathers data according to procedures learned in college during the 1940s is in trouble when new electronic data-processing techniques are introduced.

Constructive Behavior. On the other hand, you are undoubtedly familiar with many examples of constructive *adaptive* behavior. The incentive worker who is frustrated by the routine of the job may strive for recognition off the job by seeking election to leadership posts in civic organizations or may channel his or her energies into non-work-related activities, such as hobbies and home repairs, to find personal fulfillment. The football player mentioned previously may settle for making the freshman squad or decide to develop his abilities in track. These are only two of the many examples of constructive adaptive behavior which individuals employ to reduce their frustrations and satisfy their needs.

SUMMARY AND COMMENT

A felt need triggers tension which stimulates search behavior on the part of the individual for ways to relieve the tension. If the individual is successful in achieving the goal, the *next felt need* will emerge. If, however, goal attainment is frustrated the person will engage in either constructive or defensive types of behavior. Under either circumstances, the individual returns to the next felt need which emerges.

Business and other organizations have been relatively successful in satisfying their employees' physiological and safety (job security) needs. Fringe benefits, such as supplemental unemployment insurance, workmen's compensation, health and medical insurance, and retirement programs, are examples of how American industry and government agencies provide for employees' lower-level needs. Business has also tried to satisfy the individual's belongingness and affiliation needs by structuring tasks which permit interaction and association with others in many ways. Research has shown that the satisfaction of these needs for employees significantly affects their job performance, but that satisfaction of lower-order needs for managerial employees is not directly related to their performance.

A number of management scholars have commented that employees' higher-level needs cannot be satisfied because their needs are incompatible with those of the organization. Considerable evidence suggests that when employees' needs are frustrated, workers may engage in defensive behavior, e.g., turnover, grievances, slowdowns, absenteeism, and shoddy work. As pointed out earlier, many jobs in the future will require skilled employees to exercise more personal discretion than they are presently exercising, in the repair and maintenance of machinery. Similarly, automation is restricting unskilled workers' contribution to the job by assigning them routine or panel-monitoring tasks which require little use of their abilities and opportunity to satisfy their higher-order needs.

When appraising an organization's effectiveness in providing opportunities for need fulfillment on the job, one must guard against overgeneralization.

It is necessary to look at the position the individual is occupying in the organization, the technological constraints, and the demands of the task in relationship to his or her needs. A manager's success may be a function of his or her ability to satisfy higher-level needs, while simultaneously attempting to satisfy workers' lower-level needs.

Two-Factor Theory

A second frequently mentioned model of motivation is that proposed by Frederick Herzberg and his associates.[6] Herzberg is best known for his "two-factor" theory of motivation, which is concerned with the role that the job and working conditions play in the involvement of employees in meaningful work. This theory grew out of research on the job attitudes and opinions of 200 accountants and engineers.

DEVELOPMENT OF THEORY

The research design of the study was extremely simple, built around the questions: "Can you describe, in detail, when you felt exceptionally good about your job?" and "Can you describe, in detail, when you felt exceptionally bad about your job?" In analyzing the responses, the researchers found that employees named different job experiences or factors related to good and bad feelings about the job. If responsibility led to good feelings about the job, the lack of responsibility was seldom given as a cause of bad feelings. This finding is the most significant aspect of Herzberg's theory of motivation. Rarely were the same kinds of factors named in connection with good and bad feelings about work experiences. In fact, there appeared to be two separate and distinct kinds of experiences. Because the lack of job security, for example, caused dissatisfaction, it didn't follow that high job security caused satisfaction. Since this theory presents two separate kinds of factors—one set that satisfies and another that dissatisfies—it has been labeled the "two-factor" theory.

SATISFIERS AND DISSATISFIERS

Herzberg's research led him to the following conclusions:

1. Some conditions of the job operate primarily to *dissatisfy* employees when they are not present or when they are poorly or improperly managed, but their presence (or their quality) does not build strong motivation. These factors have been labeled "dissatisfiers," or "hygiene," factors, since they are necessary to maintain a reasonable level of "no dissatisfaction." The dissatisfiers were factors associated with the context of the work rather than the work itself. Although he concluded that there are nine hygiene factors (dissatisfiers), Herzberg found that the most important of these were company policies, technical supervision, interpersonal relations, and working conditions.

2. Some job conditions, if present, operate to build a *strong level of motivation* and spur the individual to superior performance. However, if these conditions are *not* present, they do not prove highly dissatisfying. The satisfier factors were named "motivators," or "satisfiers." Herzberg identified seven satisfiers: achievement, recognition, work itself, responsibility, advancement,

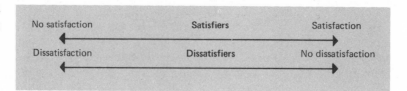

Fig. 11.5. Two-factor continuum.

and the possibility of growth (actual learning of new skills with a greater possibility of advancement).

There is a major difference between the satisfiers and dissatisfiers. The satisfiers (motivators) are job-centered and relate to the *nature of the work itself* and the rewards that flow from performance of that work. Conversely, the dissatisfiers (hygiene factors) are associated with the *context of the work* rather than with the work itself. As indicated in Fig. 11.5, the absence of satisfiers causes a condition of "no satisfaction," but does not contribute significantly to *dissatisfaction*. Similarly, the absence of dissatisfiers causes a condition of "no dissatisfaction," but does not significantly contribute to satisfaction.

Herzberg's model may also be viewed as indicated in Table 11.1, which shows that an explosive situation for management exists when employees perceive no satisfiers and *only dissatisfiers* in the work environment. The consequences of this situation may include high turnover, high grievances, and low performance. If there are satisfiers and no dissatisfiers, management has achieved an ideal situation. That is, all factors which contribute to increased job performance are present, and all those negative factors which contribute to worker dissatisfaction are absent.

In establishing the two-factor theory, Herzberg stressed that motivators give the employee a sense of personal accomplishment through the challenge of the work itself. Real motivation is seen as resulting from the worker's involvement in accomplishment alone, not from the working conditions that are outside of the work itself.

Table 11.1. Combination of satisfiers and dissatisfiers

Organizational climate	Satisfiers	Dissatisfiers
Explosive	No satisfaction	Dissatisfaction
Apathy	No satisfaction	No dissatisfaction
Inequity	Satisfaction	Dissatisfaction
Ideal	Satisfaction	No dissatisfaction

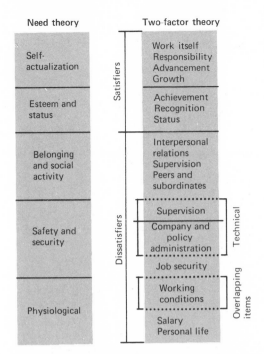

Need theory | Two-factor theory

Self-actualization

Esteem and status

Belonging and social activity

Safety and security

Physiological

Satisfiers — Work itself / Responsibility / Advancement / Growth; Achievement / Recognition / Status

Dissatisfiers — Interpersonal relations / Supervision / Peers and subordinates; Supervision; Company and policy administration; Job security; Working conditions; Salary / Personal life

Technical; Overlapping items

Fig. 11.6. Comparison of need and two-factor theories of motivation. (K. Davis, *Human Behavior at Work,* 4th ed., New York: McGraw-Hill, 1972, p. 59. Used with permission of McGraw-Hill Book Company.)

COMPARISON OF MASLOW AND HERZBERG

Figure 11.6 is a diagrammatic comparison of Herzberg's and Maslow's motivational models. Herzberg insists that the hygiene factors are important and that they, like Maslow's lower-level needs, must be adequately provided if a person is to become a superior performer. If the dissatisfiers are present or increased, the worker becomes concerned about these factors instead of striving for superior performance. Herzberg is suggesting that professional and managerial employees may have achieved a satisfactory socioeconomic level in our affluent society and that the higher-order needs of Maslow (esteem and self-actualization) are the primary motivators. A manager who is disgruntled about a hot office is likely to produce less, but just because management air-conditions the building doesn't necessarily mean that the manager will become more highly motivated to work.

APPLICATION OF THE TWO-FACTOR THEORY

Implementing the suggestions from Herzberg's model may take the form of job enrichment (to be discussed later on in this chapter), removal of certain job controls, and increasing workers' accountability and responsibility. One of the practical applications of the model has been at the Alcar Aluminum Corporation's plant in New York.[7] There are no time clocks at the plant, and production jobs have been designed to give production workers unusual freedom and decision-making responsibility. Workers are told that they can do their jobs any way they think best, as long as the productivity does not suffer greatly.

The underlying philosophy is the "honor system." This system is designed to bring about greater job satisfaction and performance on the part of employees by appealing to their motivators on the job, such as responsibility, decision making, challenge, and the work itself. The results have been encouraging: employee satisfaction is high; tardiness, labor turnover, and absenteeism have been reduced; and productivity has risen.

Several critical contingencies probably influenced the success of this "honor system." First, the plant was nonunionized, which gave management flexibility with assignments to various individuals. Second, management could easily cross-train the employees to help reduce job errors that might be caused by job monotony. Finally, the plant's management was willing to accept attitudes about workers that encouraged greater job freedom through fewer managerial controls (such as time clocks, scheduled breaks, etc.).

EVALUATION OF THE TWO-FACTOR THEORY

Although there is research support of some of Herzberg's claims, the two-factor theory has been criticized on many counts, including methodology and inconsistency with past evidence concerning employee satisfaction and motivation. From a managerial standpoint of these criticisms, we are interested in knowing whether highly satisfied employees are always the most productive ones. Most of the research indicates that there is a fair relationship between an employee's good job attitude and his or her performance. The lack of a strong relationship between job attitudes and performance is illustrated by employees who are highly satisfied with their jobs because they are able to socialize with coworkers, but who have a low motivation for performance. In other words, productivity is a secondary goal to other goals that employees are seeking at work. Increasing the motivators will not always lead to higher performance.

The satisfaction a person receives from performing a job well is called "intrinsic rewards." Intrinsic rewards are similar to satisfiers. That is, a person may feel good after performing the task, may perceive that the work is enjoyable, and may gain a feeling of accomplishment. Feelings of self-esteem may be enhanced when the person believes that he or she is doing something worthwhile. Rewards that are controlled by others in the organization, such as pay, promotion, recognition, fringe benefits, and other dissatisfiers, are known as "extrinsic rewards." The proper performance of the task may also lead to these rewards, which are incentives that are available if the proper motivational strategies are used by the management.

The current viewpoint is that when the individual finds work intrinsically and/or extrinsically rewarding, job satisfaction may increase.[8] Conversely, if the work is monotonous, routine, and provides little rewards, the individual's job dissatisfaction may increase. Therefore, it is believed that satisfaction follows from performance when the performance results in outcomes (e.g., recognition, promotion, self-esteem) valued by the person.

There are serious methodological problems with Herzberg's theory.[9] Although it is not our intent to provide an in-depth methodological critique of the theory, we can summarize the results of several studies carried out to test the theory (see Table 11.2). Employees were asked to think about days when they felt unusually good or bad about their job. As the data in Table 11.2 indicate, being given an interesting task activity is associated with satisfaction, as one would suspect. Being assigned an unpleasant task is related to dis-

---

Table 11.2. Frequency of motivator and hygiene responses

Types of responses	Number as	
	Satisfier	Dissatisfier
1. Task activity	40	39
2. Amount of work	9	27
3. Smoothness of work	11	32
4. Achievement/failure of task	114	64
5. Promotion	20	13
6. Responsibility	33	8
7. Recognition	81	93
8. Money	35	20
9. Interpersonal atmosphere	17	40
10. Working conditions	7	26
All motivators (responses 1–7)	308	276
All hygienes (responses 8–10)	59	86

Adapted from E. Locke, "Nature and Causes of Job Satisfaction," in *Handbook of Industrial and Organizational Psychology*, M. Dunnette, ed. (Chicago: Rand McNally, 1976), p. 1315.

satisfaction. Completion of an assignment is related to good feelings about the job, whereas failure to complete the task is associated with unpleasant feelings. The summary of research indicates that the task is mentioned most often as a source of unusually high or low levels of satisfaction.

When asked to think about a time when he or she felt unusually good or bad about the job, an employee's answer is influenced by the person's memory, what has actually occurred, and his or her tendency toward selective perception. This leads the individual to attribute satisfier responses to self and dissatisfier responses to others. The research indicates that "good days" are associated with: (1) being given an interesting work assignment, (2) recognition from others for good work, (3) an advancement or an increase in responsibility, and (4) achievement from success in completing the task. All of these responses are things for which the *individual* can take full credit, and all produce satisfaction. On the other hand, "bad days" tend to be associated with: (1) being assigned unpleasant work, (2) inability to complete assigned tasks, (3) criticisms from employer or coworkers, and (4) failure to receive rewards that were expected. In general, employees tend to blame bad days on others.

As we stated early in this chapter, motivation is an internal state that drives a person to behave in a certain way. A person may do something in the belief that the effort put forth will satisfy certain goals. In an attempt to understand what goals will be satisfied and what behaviors will be attempted by the individual, Victor Vroom developed an expectancy theory model of motivation.[10] This theory differs substantially from Maslow's notion of a uniform structure of needs and Herzberg's dual class of motivators. Expectancy theory asserts that an individual's motivation to produce at any given time depends on his or her particular goals and perception of the relative usefulness of performance as a path to the attainment of these goals.

EXPECTANCY AND VALENCE

Expectancy theory is based on the assumption that motivation is a process governing choices between behaviors. An *expectancy* is an individual's estimate of the likelihood that some event will occur. In rolling dice, the individual's probability of rolling a five, for example, is one-sixth. The individual perceives the consequences of each alternative action (in this case, numbers other than five) as a set of possible outcomes stemming from a particular roll of the dice. Thus the act of rolling the dice may have five other alternatives, e.g., numbers 1, 2, 3, 4, or 6.

Not all outcomes are desired by the individual, of course. Different outcomes have different valences. *Valences* are anticipated satisfactions (or dissatisfactions) that result from outcome. They are the individual's estimate of the future pleasantness or unpleasantness of an outcome. In the dice example, the individual's desire for a five outcome is greater than for any other number, if he or she desires to win.

Vroom's expectancy theory of motivation emphasizes the individual's expectancies and valences. The motivation to behave can be stated as follows:

Force (motivation) = Σ (Expectancy $\times$ Valence),

where all expectancies and valences a person associated with a particular outcome are considered.

RELATIONSHIP TO PERFORMANCE

Certain expectancies have been found to be related to performance. The first is the "effort-performance" expectancy ($E \rightarrow P$).[11] This refers to the person's expectations about the relationship between the amount of effort expended to the attainment of certain performance goals. For example, each of you is faced with the problem of allocating your time among various activities, e.g., studying, playing sports, dating, eating, and participating in a host of other campus activities. The basic question of the $E \rightarrow P$ relationship is: Which one of these activities is most closely associated with your academic performance? Some students can study very little and still achieve high grades; for others, the process of learning is more time-consuming. The student who can spend little time studying for exams and hardly ever attend class will assign a different set of probabilities to events needed to achieve high grades than the student who

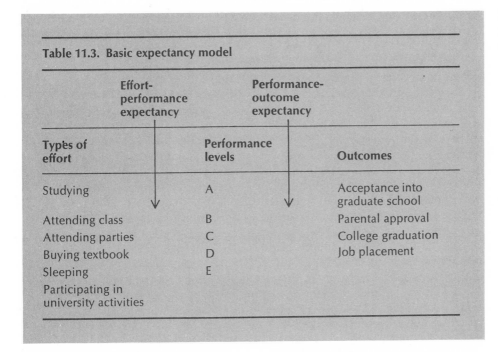

Table 11.3. Basic expectancy model

Types of effort	Effort-performance expectancy	Performance levels	Performance-outcome expectancy	Outcomes
Studying		A		Acceptance into graduate school
Attending class		B		Parental approval
Attending parties		C		College graduation
Buying textbook		D		Job placement
Sleeping		E		
Participating in university activities				

must really keep to the grindstone. A chemistry student with very little self-confidence in his or her managerial skills, for example, may not try to obtain an A in a management course. This student may spend more energy studying for chemistry, a subject area where he or she has higher self-confidence. Similarly, managers with low self-esteem will not try to achieve performance goals they feel they have little likelihood of reaching, even if they desire the rewards associated with reaching those goals.

Another type of expectancy is the "performance-outcome" expectancy (P → O). This refers to an individual's expectations about the relationship between achieving a particular performance level and attaining certain outcomes. For example, a student may feel that a solid B average gives a moderate probability of acceptance into graduate school, parental approval, a high probability of graduation, and a moderate probability of finding a job.

This complex series of behaviors and their anticipated outcomes are taken as a whole to determine the individual's motivation to achieve a certain level of performance. Table 11.3 shows one representation of the expectancy model. The effort-performance activities are studying, attending parties, attending class, buying the textbook assigned for the course, participating in university activities, taking lecture notes in class, and sleeping. For each one of these events, the student can calculate a probability that engaging in the particular activity will lead to a particular grade in the course. Most instructors would like to believe that buying the book, attending class regularly, and studying will enable students to achieve high grades. Sometimes students assign higher probabilities of achieving good grades to other activities, such as sleeping, attending parties, and participating in university activities, than to studying, attending class, etc. The important thing to remember is that the student will choose between those activities which he or she believes will lead to a desired academic grade.

The performance-outcome relationship too is a probability. This refers to the student's attaining certain desired outcomes by achieving a certain level of performance in the classroom. As indicated in the table, each performance level is associated with certain outcomes. A student who earns all D's and F's would have little chance of graduating, being admitted to graduate school, and earning parental approval. In this example, the performance level (academic grades) in and of itself means very little. Grades are important only as means to achieve certain desired outcomes and avoid others. Most students do not want to flunk out of college, would prefer to have parental respect than disapproval, etc. These are outcomes that most students find dissatisfying. To avoid these negative outcomes, students desire grades of A, B, or C and will normally expend effort to achieve these.

Vroom's expectancy theory has shed another insight into the motivational process.[12] Individuals go through a rather complicated and subjective procedure in which they evaluate their perceptions of their abilities to reach performance levels, their preference for the outcomes of each performance level, and the probability that their efforts will be rewarded. Finally, they measure the results against their own needs and wants. Expectancy theory does not provide a concrete theory with which to work from, as given by Maslow and Herzberg. But it does describe a process by which the individual chooses to behave.

MANAGEMENT APPROACHES DESIGNED TO INCREASE WORK MOTIVATION

Many managers can easily differentiate between their good and poor employees and realize the consequences of poor performance on the organization's profits, productivity, and competitive advantage. Solutions have been offered in the form of improved techniques for selecting better employees, training programs to teach needed skills, and motivational plans designed to increase the quality and quantity of performance on the job. The first two solutions are usually performed by industrial psychologists, personnel managers, and other experts. Unfortunately, the manager may still be left with ineffective employees, often described as having motivational problems, after the personnel staff and industrial psychologists have departed.

In attempting to solve or reduce motivational problems at work, two well-publicized performance improvement remedies have been offered. These two approaches are Management By Objectives (MBO) and job enrichment. Both have strengths and weaknesses, and each is applicable to different aspects of the motivational problem. Of course, these approaches are not the only ones management can use to improve the work motivation of employees. Other approaches will be discussed in Chapter 15.

Management By Objectives

Management By Objectives (MBO) is one of the most pervasive management approaches of our time. Literally thousands of organizations around the world are practicing various forms of the system. Implementations may differ sub-stantially, ranging from formal programs to loose agreements on procedures. Regardless of the form, MBO normally includes: (1) defining organizational goals, (2) specifying individual objectives that are consistent with and sup-portive of organizational goal attainment, and (3) reviewing progress toward objectives. However, as the term implies, the fundamental aspect is the com-mitment by individual managers to achieve measurable objectives.[13]

OBJECTIVE-SETTING PROCESS
Setting objectives can assist the individual manager, employee, and the organi-zation in several significant ways. First, objectives help organizational members understand their responsibilities and define priorities for their jobs. Stated ob-jectives answer the question: "What is expected of me?" Second, objectives can stimulate constructive feedback from others, particularly the superior. Third, measurable objectives provide organizational members with an internal feed-back loop that continually signals their progress toward some goal(s). Fourth, objectives can increase the manager's commitment toward goal accomplish-ment. Finally, objectives can be vehicles for enlarging the organizational mem-bers' participation in shaping their own career development and opportunities.

Under an MBO program, a superior and subordinate attempt to reach a consensus on (1) what goals the subordinate will attempt to achieve in a spe-cified period of time, (2) the plan, or means, by which the subordinate will attempt to accomplish the goals, and (3) the means by which progress toward goals will be measured and the specific dates for such measurements. Unless objectives are jointly determined by the superior and subordinate, MBO's po-tential contributions will be greatly limited.

This joint-determination process begins with intensive preparation, focuses on face-to-face objective setting interview, and ends in specific written objec-tives. The joint objective-setting process may also provide an opportunity for two other benefits. First, it can open a channel for effective two-way communi-cations between a superior and subordinate. Second, it can provide a useful mechanism for enhancing managerial and employee potential. Since the key of the objective-setting interview is to gain both participants' active involvement, distortions can occur if the supervisor dominates the interview or conversely abdicates responsibility. The success of the MBO system depends on how well both the objectives and plans are defined, communicated, and accepted.

It is important to note that objectives may be general for the organization or specific for the individual. As indicated in Chapter 8, one of the purposes of MBO is to make it possible to derive specific from general objectives and to ensure that objectives at all levels are meaningfully linked. Sets of objectives for an organizational department determine its activities. A set of objectives for an individual determines his or her job description and can be thought of as a different way to provide that job description.

Performance objectives are developed from the major areas of an indi-vidual's responsibility and activity. The statement of performance objectives should be:

1. clear, concise, and unambiguous;
2. accurate in terms of the true end state or condition sought;

Table 11.4. Objectives of a minimarket food store

Objectives	Measurement used	Review dates	Evaluation (percent of objective achieved)
1. Number of customers attracted to store will be increased by 7 percent monthly	Actual count of sales tickets		
2. Cash outlay per customer will increase 3 percent quarterly	Sales tickets		
3. Promotion of new items will be emphasized by newspaper coupons so that 15 percent of these items sold are paired with coupons	Newspaper coupons		
4. No customer will be kept waiting for more than three minutes at the check-out station	Random sampling of stores during operations		
5. Operating costs will be kept at same cost as in the past year	Accounting records		
6. Part-time employee turnover will be reduced by 20 percent in one year	Personnel records		
7. The ratio of food costs to waste will be reduced by 10 percent each month	Sales and food		

---

3. consistent with policies, procedures, and plans as they apply to the unit for which the objective is set;
4. within the competence of the unit;
5. interesting, motivating, and/or challenging whenever possible.[14]

Some examples of objectives are detailed in Table 11.4. Note that all of these objectives have at least two important components. First, they clearly suggest areas (e.g., sales, waste, personnel size) in which the accomplishment should occur. Second, five of the seven objectives clearly specify a deadline when the objective is to be accomplished, and all objectives specify a level of achievement. The desired level of achievement is the performance level.

AN ACTION PLAN

353
MANAGEMENT
APPROACHES TO
INCREASE WORK
MOTIVATION

The action plan is the means by which the objective is achieved. The action plan should clearly state what is to be done, and all activities needed to achieve the objectives should be stated. The action plan in essence provides an initial basis for a total action program for the individual or department. In General Mills, for each managerial position a statement of accountabilities is included as part of the job description.[15] The statement sets forth, in general terms, the results that a specific position should produce. In preparing General Mills' "Action Plan," a manager consults his or her list of responsibilities and then writes under each statement specific results to be achieved during the year ahead to fulfill that responsibility. After all such responsibilities are fulfilled, the manager and subordinate discuss the action plan, perhaps modifying specific objectives until both can agree that it is a meaningful and obtainable yet challenging plan of action for the year ahead. General Mills advises its managers that the terms they select should be quantifiable, such as percents, ratios, number of, average number of, etc. It is one thing to have an objective "to lower production costs," but quite another to have an objective "to lower the costs of producing the net weight 10 oz box of cereal 7 percent by April 30 by having operations 7, 8, and 9 done by one machine operator." Further, the more precise the statement, the more readily its contribution to successful operations can be anticipated. "To lower costs 7 percent" makes it possible to determine what changes in price or increases in profits can be planned for.

EVALUATION OF MBO PROGRAMS

By far the most frequently mentioned benefit from MBO programs is better management performance. Executives like MBO because they believe it produces results and results that show up on the bottom line of the balance sheet. If an objective is to reduce certain production costs, it can be determined whether those costs have been reduced. In marketing plans to introduce a new product in April, the new product either does or does not appear in April or very shortly thereafter. The evaluation of many MBO programs, however, indicates that they are not without limitations.

At the Purex Corporation, the results of research after an MBO program was started indicated that employees were more concerned about and aware of the firm's goals and future activities.[16] The employees believed that the goal-setting process improved communications and understanding among those involved in the program. A follow-up study, however, showed that many of the participants perceived the program as being a weak incentive for improving performance levels. Evidently they had changed their opinions about the program after it had been in operation over a four-year period. Their reasons for changing their opinions about the program can be placed into five broad categories:

1. Managers reported that the program was used as a whip.
2. The program greatly increased the amount of paperwork.
3. The program failed to reach the lower managerial levels.
4. There was an overemphasis on production.
5. The program failed to provide adequate incentives to improve performance.

Other studies have found similar results. That is, excessive formal requirements imposed by the program—the amount of paperwork to process and complete, forms to update, and information to provide the coordinator of the program—offset the benefits. Managers also tend to overemphasize the quantitative aspect of the criteria. At St. Regis Paper Company, managers are warned not to "get hung up on numbers." Although sound criteria are essential if changes in motivation are to occur, numbers must be used with extreme care. Some managers report that they are so concerned about reaching the objectives that they ignore other work. Managers can reach cost-reducing goals by deferring needed plant maintenance for which an objective may not have been met. Salespersons achieve sales-volume goals by pushing easily sold but low-profit items. MBO can easily be treated as a numbers game rather than a way to manage more effectively.

A company tried to use MBO as a form of management speed-up. Managers were told that they would have to raise their sights and set more demanding objectives because managers in other units had done so. Everyone throughout the entire company was told the same thing. The idea was to make all employees stretch. The strategy did not work, because the employees were realistic enough to know that the only objectives that would be approved were completely unattainable ones. And knowing that they could not reach them, they did not try. In this instance, the utility company adopted MBO as a gimmick for increasing production, and the entire program had to be abandoned just about the time several senior managers began to understand that this was really not MBO.

Another critical factor in the implementation of MBO programs is the supportive managerial climate which pervades the entire organization. Top management cannot assume a passive role. The most effective manner in which to implement MBO is to allow top management to explain, coordinate, and guide the program. Too many firms have begun to manage with objectives only to discover that they have become aware of unsound organizational alignments and poor administrative practices. When top management is involved, changes can penetrate through the entire organization more easily, and lower-level management can see that top management is really committed to the program.[17]

SUMMARY

Management By Objectives is not being offered here as a cure-all for motivational problems, but it is an approach that warrants careful consideration by managers. MBO is an objective-centered approach. The principal emphasis is on mutual goal setting, planning, and problem solving rather than on the production of an informed judgment about an individual's performance by his or her immediate supervisor. The amount and direction of individual growth and job performance are seen to be controlled largely by the quality of the objectives and plans originally agreed on.

Job Enrichment

"Quality of working life" is a subject currently receiving a great deal of attention by management, workers, union leaders, governmental officials, and the news media. In 1974 Governor John Gilligan of Ohio, acting through his Business and Employment Council, established a state-financed Ohio Quality of Work Institute to foster labor-management experiments in democratic work arrangements. In 1972 Senator Edward Kennedy of Massachusetts chaired hearings on worker discontent and introduced in Congress the Workers Alienation Research and Development Act. Supposedly, employees who are dissatisfied with the quality of life at work, as typified by the dull, routine, short-cycle, mechanically paced job of the assembly-line worker, are reacting by restricting output, producing shoddy products, refusing overtime, and contributing to high absenteeism and labor turnover.

A mechanically paced job illustrative of repetitive, dull, routine work is in the paint department of the Ford Motor Company. Work is done in an enclosed booth, to keep the dust from escaping. The booth is white, brightly lit by neon lights, 3 car lengths long, and 15 feet wide. The cars enter and exit through a narrow opening at either end. The job of the individuals who work in this shop is to sand the car smooth before it receives its final coat of paint. The booth is hazy with the dust from the shift before. The primer coat is lead-based, and several employees wear surgical masks. A worker holds a ten-pound air sander in the right hand and sandpaper in the left. It is that person's responsibility to examine the right-hand half of the trunk, roof, and hood. The person opens the passenger door and quickly sands the inside of the door with the sandpaper. Then the entire area is done with the air sander. Any large metal burrs or blobs of paint have to be removed with a scraper that the person carries in his or her apron. Paint runs, grease spots, or specks of dirt have to be ground down to bare metal and smoothed out. Also, the small grille in front of the windshield has to be sanded over three times.

Since the line speed is usually between 55 and 58 cars per hour, the person has to perform all of these operations within 67 seconds. These employees have to plan ahead to get a drink of water: five seconds to the fountain, five seconds for the drink, five seconds back into the booth. The monotony of the line seems to bind the employees together. Small gaps of a few car lengths happen almost every day. Employees are continually peering down the line to see if the gaps are coming. This big hope is that the gap won't appear during one's break. Sabotage is common. Employees force the trunks closed in such a way that the cars cannot be painted properly. In the trim department, where dashboards, mirrors, inside panels, windows, and extras are installed, sabotage is very common, because it is almost impossible to trace the saboteur. As work is done farther down the line, it becomes progressively more difficult to repair, and once the problem becomes apparent, the line must be stopped.[18]

Job enrichment is being touted by many as the solution to such problems. AT&T, Motorola, General Tire and Rubber, General Foods Pet Food Plant, Corning Glass Works, and Maytag have all adopted job-enrichment programs successfully. Job enrichment is concerned with designing jobs to include a greater variety of work content, require a higher level of knowledge and skills, give the worker more autonomy and control over the job, and provide the opportunity for personal growth and development. In theory, job enrichment makes performing the job more rewarding or intrinsically satisfying, which in turn motivates the worker to be more productive. Job enrichment is based on the assumption that enriched jobs will be more intrinsically satisfying to workers who, as a result, will be motivated to perform in a manner that meets or exceeds job requirements.

Contrary to this belief, however, there is growing evidence that not all persons seek to satisfy their needs at work or through work. For these persons, it logically follows that job enrichment would not be perceived as particularly worthwhile. Job enrichment works only for those individuals who have a need to satisfy high-order needs (Maslow's self-actualization and self-esteem) on the job. Thus a major contingency for managers using job enrichment as a motivational device is to determine which workers have this drive to satisfy their high-order needs.[19] Let us examine those job characteristics which may establish conditions for internal motivation for workers who have strong growth needs.

CHARACTERISTICS OF MOTIVATING JOBS

There are three important task characteristics that may be useful in enriching an individual's job.[20] These are: (1) allowing the individual to feel personally responsible for a meaningful portion of the work; (2) providing the individual with outcomes that are intrinsically meaningful or are perceived as worthwhile for the individual; and (3) providing the individual feedback on what is accomplished.

Personal Responsibility. The individual must believe that the work she or he does is "owned" and feel personally responsible for whatever successes and failures occur as a result of the work. This does not mean, of course, that feelings of personal responsibility for work outcomes cannot occur in team projects. All that is required is for team members to feel that their own efforts are important in accomplishing the task at hand. In 1972 Daimler-Benz, which employs 100,000 production workers in Germany, changed many jobs to promote the humanization of work.[21] For example, a truck-assembly unit, which ordinarily would be built around a moving line with 12-minute cycles, was redesigned so that members of a three-person multiskilled group could plan and execute all of the work, including preparation, assembly, adjustment, and welding. The total cycle time, depending on the model, has been stretched from 39 to 41 minutes. Similarly, an assembly unit for shock absorbers, with 12 work stations on a line and five-minute work cycles, was replaced by individual work stations and 25-minute cycles, with workers setting their own pace. In each of the jobs, the team or individual is now fully responsible for a total portion of the manufacturing process. These workers have more job *autonomy* now than before.

Intrinsically Meaningful Outcomes. If employees do not feel that their efforts make much difference to anybody, themselves included, it is unlikely that they will feel especially good if they work effectively. There are at least two ways that work can come to be experienced as meaningful for employees.

First, an employee's job should be a sufficiently "whole" piece of work that she or he can conceive of having produced or accomplished something that makes a difference to people. In other words, the job is high on *identity*. Such jobs provide the worker with a distinct sense of beginning and ending a task and involve the production worker in meaningful operations. At the Bosch

Company in Germany, which employs 50,000 hourly workers, an autoradio assembly line of 60 persons, broken into groups of ten, was redesigned so that now each person does the entire assembly job of the radio.[22] The result has been greater flexibility, elimination of a rigid time pace, and a sixfold enlargement of jobs.

Second, work can come to take on personal meaning by requiring the individual to use a variety of valued skills and abilities. At Bosch, a 15-worker loudspeaker-production unit was broken up into five three-person groups, with each group building the entire speaker and each person learning all of the jobs. This permits shorter production runs for management and far greater flexibility with its personnel. Jobs high on the dimension of *variety* would be expected to provide opportunities for workers to experience this kind of meaningfulness on the job, since high-variety jobs typically tap a number of different skills which may be important to the employee.

Numerous other organizations, such as New York Chemical Bank; Travelers Insurance Company; Merrill, Lynch, Fenner and Smith; American Airlines; and American Telephone and Telegraph, have successfully implemented job enrichment. At the Pet Food Plant of General Mills in Topeka, Kansas, blue-collar workers get a chance to do every major job in the plant, from unloading with a fork-lift truck to making quality-control tests. The workers decide how to spend their time during the working day and are not closely supervised. The results indicate substantial savings in labor and higher job satisfaction; absenteeism averages 1 percent and turnover is about 5 percent, considerably lower than in comparable General Foods plants, and the plant is 30 percent more productive than other, similar plants.[23]

Feedback. Even if the two general conditions discussed above are met, an employee will not experience satisfaction of higher-order needs effectively unless provided with some kind of performance feedback. Such feedback may come from the task itself, another person, a supervisor, or a group of esteemed co-workers.

JOB ENRICHMENT MODEL

A basic model of job enrichment is presented in Fig. 11.7, which shows that the characteristics of individuals combine with the characteristics of the work environment to produce beliefs and attitudes. Job, technology, and organization structure are the crucial aspects of the environment. Organizational effectiveness in turn is a function of the combined behavior of the individuals as modified by the kind of organizational structure and control systems used to coordinate their behaviors. This figure also shows that the external environment is an important influence on both attitudes and organizational effectiveness.

The "characteristics of individuals" element refers to the strength of their self-esteem and/or self-actualization needs and also their concern for pay, autonomy, and interesting work. The "characteristics of job" entry refers to the type of work flow, adequacy of standards, type of technology, and degree to which the job permits the individual to do meaningful work, make meaningful decisions, and receive feedback about job performance. "Employee attitudes" refers to the satisfaction or dissatisfaction that the employee receives from per-

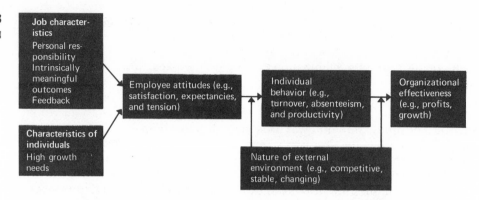

Fig. 11.7. A model of job enrichment. (E. Lawler, "Adaptive Experiments: An Approach to Organizational Behavior Research," in *Readings in Organizational Behavior,* ed. K. Downey, D. Hellriegel, and J. Slocum, St. Paul: West, 1977, p. 7. Used with permission.)

forming the task. The meaningfulness of these internal attitude states is evidenced by the individual's job performance (e.g., turnover, absenteeism, performance, lateness, etc.). Organizational performance is normally measured quite well with respect to financial indicators. There is a considerable amount of evidence showing that the nature of the external environment influences how effective different organization structures are and how individuals will react to new orgnizational designs. For example, the labor market has a strong influence on how employees react to feelings of job dissatisfaction. When jobs are plentiful, employees are much more likely to quit than when jobs are scarce. In Chapters 2 and 5, we indicated that market and technological factors, such as stability, competitiveness, and governmental regulation, influence how effective various organization structures are.

Comparisons of MBO and Job Enrichment

Table 11.5 compares some of the characteristics of MBO and job enrichment in terms of their problem diagnosis, motivational assumptions, reward systems, and motivational implications.[24] The MBO approach assumes that high performance can be achieved when employees know their specified goals, participate in the goal-setting process, and obtain knowledge of their results. All of these processes are assumed to increase employee motivation. The causes of poor performance are ill-defined goals of jobs rather than the content of the job, as in job enrichment. MBO would be appropriate where results of performance are not well understood and performance standards are ambiguous.

The essence of job enrichment is that employees do not like to perform dull, routine, and monotonous jobs. Changes in the content of the jobs will make the work more meaningful and challenging and will increase job satisfaction and performance. Job enrichment assumes that when intrinsic satisfaction (challenge, responsibility) is offered, extrinsic rewards (pay, working conditions) become secondary in importance. Job enrichment also assumes that people require self-actualization on the job and look to their jobs, as opposed to off-job activities, as their primary sources of satisfaction and self-actualization.[25]

What Table 11.5 offers is a contingency approach to the motivation problem. The contingency concept implies that various techniques can be used to solve the motivational problem. *If* the problem is diagnosed as one of job content, *then* job enrichment might be useful. *If* the problem is diagnosed as poorly defined goals, ambiguous performance standards, and employees not knowing what is required of them, *then* MBO might be useful.

Table 11.5. Job enrichment and Management By Objectives: compatible solutions to the motivation problem

Comparison areas	Job enrichment	Management By Objectives
Problem diagnosis	Jobs are extremely monotonous, segmented, and routine. Apathy, absenteeism, and turnover are excessive.	Jobs are ill-defined, and performance criteria are ambiguous and subjective. Employees feel that they do not know where they stand and what is required of them.
Motivational assumptions	Intrinsic rewards from job content (e.g., challenge and autonomy) are the keys to long-run motivation, because people want to satisfy higher-level needs on the job.	People will work to attain objectives to which they are committed, which can be attained by allowing employees to participate in goal setting.
Job-type applicability	Lower-level jobs, which are typically routine and repetitive.	Difficult to apply to higher-level jobs, which often have the most ambiguous objectives or standards.
Time frame for distribution of rewards	Workers receive intrinsic satisfaction upon completion of a challenging job.	Workers receive formal feedback in the appraisal interview, but may receive informal feedback from supervisors at any time.

(cont.)

Table 11.5. Job enrichment and Management By Objectives: compatible solutions to the motivation problem (cont.)

Comparison areas	Job enrichment	Management By Objectives
Motivational implications:		
Positive	Jobs are more interesting and challenging; thus people are motivated to improve quality and to lower absenteeism and turnover.	Reduction of job-related ambiguity, better superior-subordinate communication, and greater effort directed to organizational goals.
Negative	Employees may feel that they have more to say about their jobs than they really do or than management intended. Some employees may not want challenging jobs, but simply a chance to earn money in order to satisfy their needs off the job.	By emphasizing results rather than behavior, MBO can ignore such factors as discretion and judgment and can overquantify job objectives. Employees may feel that their participation in goal setting is not authentic. They may be defensive and anxious about their evaluations and try to cover up their mistakes to make their performance look good.

Adapted from R. Beatty, and C. Schneier, "A Case for Positive Reinforcement," *Business Horizons* **18** (1975): 59. Copyright, 1975, by Foundation for the School of Business at Indiana University. Reprinted by permission.

Summary

There appear to be several reasons why the topic of motivation is receiving greater attention both by those who study organizations and those who manage them. The old simplistic, prescriptive guideline that people work only for money is simply no longer a sufficient basis for understanding human motivation at work. Rather, most behavior is motivated by a person's desire to satisfy unfilled needs. Maslow's need hierarchy is one useful framework for examining employees' needs; Herzberg's two-factor theory is useful in distinguishing between satisfaction with job-content factors and working conditions. Although neither of these theories focuses on individual differences in motivation, Vroom's model seems to hold promise for predicting behavior in organizations where the individual has discretion in the performance of his or her work.

One further point should be made about the three models. They all rely on subjective measures, such as an individual's perceptions and instrumentalities, but the manager must infer the causes of motivation from such subjective measures. Objective measures, such as grievances, turnover, absenteeism, and the like, are the indicators of motivation which can be used to infer a motivated state in employees.

We have also examined two management approaches—Management By Objectives and job enrichment. The supporters of these approaches believe that they can lead to increased motivation, higher job satisfaction, and performance if implemented properly. We do not contend that these approaches are free from limitations; rather, we feel that a contingency notion indicates the proper usage of either approach.

Discussion Questions

1. In what ways do job designs influence employees' work-related attitudes and behavior?

2. Compare and contrast job enrichment and MBO as motivational approaches.

3. Using Maslow's model of motivation, how do you think an American manager's motivation of employees might differ from that of a manager operating in a third-world nation?

4. What reasons might Maslow give for a person's working Saturdays and overtime?

5. How would you distinguish between a need, reward and valence?

6. What kinds of negative behavior might be expected to result from frustration?

7. What are the similarities and dissimilarities between Maslow's and Herzberg's motivational models?

8. Of what practical value is the expectancy model of motivation to managers?

9. What are some ways you could enrich jobs?

10. Distinguish between Herzberg's hygiene and motivator factors. Give examples of each.

11. What are the steps in the motivation process?

Management Incidents

THE H & S COMPANY

The H & S Company specializes in making golf clubs. Recently it abandoned the assembly line in order to allow teams of four or five persons to assemble, inspect, and package a set of golf clubs from start to finish. Teams work in separate rooms and take charge of organization, production, product quality of each club, and group discipline. When the members of a team do not measure up to the team's standards, group pressure is used to make them conform. In extreme cases, the team captain might ask management to have the individual removed from the team. Workers receive a salary which increases with substantial increases in the number of quality clubs produced. Most of the workers are just out of the local high school and: (1) share information among themselves concerning production methods as well as social events; (2) develop high identification with their work groups and frequently socialize off the job together; (3) think of the company as an excellent place to work; and (4) think of new ideas that management could use to cut down production costs. The change from the assembly-line production-line strategy resulted in a 40 percent reduction in the number of management hours devoted to quality control, reduced absenteeism and turnover by 20 percent, and increased production of golf clubs by 15 percent per week.

1. What specific behavioral aspects are apparent in the new team-assembly process?
2. Using Fig. 11.7, how would you account for the reduction in absenteeism and turnover and the increase in productivity of these workers?
3. Using Herzberg's model, explain what happened.

THE SALESMAN PROBLEM

J. P. McNaul was a salesman for the Straka Company, a wholesale drug firm located in Hawk Run, Pennsylvania. One day he was called into his district manager's office and told that he was being terminated at the end of the week. His boss said, "The sales in your territory are only half of what we expected of you, your order size is too small, and the number of new customer contracts isn't enough." J. P. was bitter about the situation, since not once had his boss told him what was expected of him. In fact, J. P. thought that he was doing an excellent job. J. P. then secured employment with the Tricia Company, a newly formed competitor, and was very successful.

1. How would you explain J. P.'s failure at the Straka Company?
2. What could the company have done to prevent this situation?

THE SIMS COMPANY

The Sims Company, a manufacturer of automobile parts and accessories for large department stores who sell these parts under their private labels, is having difficulty in meeting production deadlines and attracting good management talent. Assume that you have been asked to help management set up an MBO program. According to the president of the Sims Company, the overall corporate objective is to obtain a 20 percent sales profit margin. The president said that one way to realize this objective was for the manufacturing division to reduce manufacturing costs by 4 percent within the year.

1. Briefly explain the steps that will have to be followed in implementing an MBO program in this company.
2. What would be some advantages of using MBO in this situation?

REFERENCES

1. R. Steers and L. Porter, *Motivation and Work Behavior* (New York: McGraw-Hill, 1975), pp. 2–6.

2. B. Berelson and G. Steiner, *Human Behavior: An Inventory of Scientific Findings* (New York: Harcourt, Brace and World, 1964), p. 239.

3. A. Maslow, *Motivation and Personality*, 2d ed. (New York: Harper & Row, 1970).

4. Maslow has described two other needs that are less well known than the five shown in Fig. 11.1: cognitive and aesthetic needs. These needs are not opposed to the striving needs, but are complementary to them. The cognitive needs are the need to know or to understand. There seems to be some basis for the existence of cognitive needs, but Maslow did not include this need in his hierarchy. The aesthetic needs are satisfied by moving from ugliness to beauty, but research has failed to support the existence of this need. *See* L. Festinger, *A Theory of Cognitive Dissonance* (Stanford, Calif.: Stanford University Press, 1957).

5. For an excellent review of Maslow's work and the research that it has generated, *see* M. Wahba and L. Bridwell, "Maslow Reconsidered: A Review of Research on the Need Hierarchy Theory," *Organizational Behavior and Human Performance* **15** (1976): 212–240.

6. F. Herzberg, B. Mausner, and B. Snyderman, *The Motivation to Work* (New York: Wiley, 1959).

7. J. McGregor, "The Honor System," *Wall Street Journal,* May 22, 1970.

8. J. Sheridan and J. Slocum, "The Direction of the Causal Relationship between Job Satisfaction and Work Performance," *Organizational Behavior and Human Performance* **14** (1975): 159–172; and E. Locke, "The Nature and Causes of Job Satisfaction," in *Handbook of Industrial and Organizational Psychology*, ed. M. Dunnette (Chicago: Rand McNally, 1976), pp. 1297–1349.

9. A. Filley, R. House, and S. Kerr, *Managerial Processes and Organizational Behavior,* 2d ed. (Glenview, Ill.: Scott, Foresman, 1976), pp. 197–200.

10. V. Vroom, *Work and Motivation* (New York: Wiley, 1964).

11. E. Lawler, *Motivation in Work Organizations* (Belmont, Calif.: Brooks/Cole, 1974).

12. For those interested in a more complete description of the model and the research that it has generated, *see* T. Mitchell, "Expectancy Models of Job Satisfaction, Occupational Preference, and Effort: A Theoretical and Methodological and Empirical Appraisal," *Psychological Bulletin* **81** (1974): 1053–1077; and B. Pritchard, P. DeLeo, and C. Von Berger, "A Field Experiment Test of Expectancy Valence Incentive Motivation Techniques," *Organizational Behavior and Human Performance* **15** (1976): 355–406.

13. S. Carroll and H. Tosi, *Management by Objectives* (New York: Macmillan, 1973); A. Slusher and H. Sims, "Commitment through MBO Interviews," *Business Horizons* **18** (1975): 5–12; and D. McConkey, *MBO for Nonprofit Organizations* (New York: American Management Association, 1975).

14. H. Tosi and S. Carroll, *Management: Contingencies, Structures and Process* (Chicago: St. Clair Press, 1976), p. 320.

15. L. Hrebiniak, "Power and Control." Paper delivered at Alabama A&M University, Huntsville, Alabama, May 28, 1976.

16. A. Raia, "A Second Look at Management Goals and Controls," *California Management Review* **8** (1966): 49–58.

17. J. Ivancevich, "Changes in Performance in a Management By Objectives Program," *Administrative Science Quarterly* **19** (1974): 563–574.

18. Abstracted from R. King, "67 Seconds Per Car," *Washington Post*, September 5, 1976. For other, similar jobs, see J. Hackman and L. Suttle, *Improving Life at Work: Behavioral Science Approaches to Organizational Change* (Santa Monica, Calif.: Goodyear, 1977).

19. L. Porter, E. Lawler, and R. Hackman, *Behavior in Organizations* (New York: McGraw-Hill, 1975), pp. 274–311 provides an excellent review of the theoretical bases for job enrichment; *also see* R. Steers, "Factors Affecting Job Attitudes in a Goal-Setting Environment," *Academy of Management Journal* **19** (1976): 6–16; and H. Sims and A. Szilagyi, "Job Characteristic Relationships: Individual and Structural Moderators," *Organizational Behavior and Human Performance* **17** (1976): 211–230.

20. R. Hackman and G. Oldham, "Development of the Job Diagnostic Survey," *Journal of Applied Psychology* **60** (1975): 159–170; D. Schwab and L. Cummings, "A theoretical Analysis of the Impact of Task Scope on Employee Performance," *Academy of Management Review* **1** (1976): 23–35; and H. Sims, A. Szilagyi and R. Keller, "The Measurement of Job Characteristics," *Academy of Management Journal* **19** (1976): 195–212.

21. Ohio Human Relations Commission, *World of Work Report* **1** (May 1976).

22. *Ibid.*

23. A. Salpukas, "Jobs Rotated to Fight Boredom," *New York Times*, February 5, 1973; and E. Locke, D. Sirota, and A. Wolfson, "An Experimental Case Study of the Successes and Failures of Job Enrichment in a Government Agency," *Journal of Applied Psychology* **61** (1976): 701–711.

24. R. Beatty and C. Schneier, "A Case for Positive Reinforcement," *Business Horizons* **18** (1975): 57–66.

25. R. Simonds and J. Orife, "Worker Behavior versus Enrichment Theory," *Administrative Science Quarterly* **20** (1975): 606–612.

12

12

Leadership

Managerial styles

Philosophies
Contingencies
Perceptions
Individual problems
Interpersonal communi-
cations

Chapter 10

Motivation

Needs
Satisfiers and dis-
satisfiers
Expectancies and con-
tingencies
Management by objectives
Job enrichment

Chapter 11

Leadership

Power and influence
Traits
Contingency models
Substitutes for leadership

Chapter 12

Groups

Roles
Models
Contingencies
Procedures for group
problem solving

Chapter 13

Conflict

Contingency model
Role conflict
Interpersonal conflict
Intergroup conflict

Chapter 14

The objectives of this chapter are to:

make you aware of the differences between a manager and the exercise of leadership;

demonstrate how people obtain their influence in organizations;

illustrate various approaches to the study of leadership and their relationship to organizational effectiveness;

indicate those situations in which the exercise of leadership may have relatively little impact on the behavior of employees and the organization's effectiveness.

From the large numbers of leadership-training programs and the persisting interest of teachers and practitioners in leadership, it is clear that leadership is both an important and complex phenomenon. Since ancient times, writers of various beliefs and philosophies have sought to advise leaders of better methods to increase the effectiveness of their organizations. Particularly influential in the past were such writers as Confucius, Plato, Aristotle, contributors to the Bible, and Machiavelli, who collectively told leaders to be wise, bold, good, willing to compromise, unscrupulous, and well-advised.

Their advice found an eager audience. Many managers think that communication, motivation, and leadership are cure-alls which will solve the problems of their organizations. This state of buyer readiness and the willingness of writers to supply cook-book answers have combined to generate a number of fads in leadership. Strategies—such as "Be democratic" or "Use Theory X"—which have succeeded under one set of circumstances have been applied uncritically to other situations for which they were not well suited. The results have been costly. There are plenty of incentives for managers and administrators to search for better ways to lead and exercise their leadership talents. Top corporate administrators receive high salaries for their ability to increase their organizations' effectiveness.

Managers are the persons in charge of the formal organization or one of its departments. They are vested with formal authority over the department, and this leads to two basic managerial purposes. First, managers must ensure that the organization produces its specific goods and services efficiently. They must design and maintain the stability of the organization's basic operations and must adapt to its changing environment. To accomplish this, managers must create a unified whole rather than direct each department separately. One analogy is a symphony orchestra's conductor, through whose efforts, vision, and leadership instrumental parts become the living whole of a musical performance. But the conductor is only an interpreter of the composer's score. The manager is both composer and conductor. Second, managers must ensure that the organization serves the ends of those persons who control it. They must interpret their particular desires (e.g., annual ten percent growth) and combine these to produce statements of organizational preferences that can guide its decision making.

These two basic purposes are accomplished through the process of leadership. However, most managers spend time on things that are not considered leadership. The sales manager making statistical analyses or placating an important customer or the foreman repairing a tool or filling out a production report—all are necessary activities and have to be done. Similarly, company presidents working through the details of a bank loan or negotiating a big contract or presiding at a dinner in honor of long-service employees do these things because they are the leaders who are expected to handle these activities because of their status and their inspirational, legal, and ceremonial role in the organization.

To accomplish these objectives, the chapter has been organized into three major sections. First, we discuss the nature of the leadership process and sources of power leaders usually have at their command to influence subordinates. Next, we present three major approaches used to understand the leadership process. Finally, we discuss the conditions under which leadership may be substituted for by organizational and/or characteristics usually found in organizations.

NATURE OF LEADERSHIP

Whenever two or more persons get together, who is the leader? Is the leader the person with whom others identify and whom they wish to imitate? Or the person who is most popular in the group? Or the person who exercises influences over the group's decision and behavior? In order to answer these questions, we must be careful to define "the leader" and the leadership process.

What Is Leadership?

Leadership has been defined as the ability to attract other persons to oneself. Leaders are persons others want to follow. Leaders are the ones who command the trust and loyalty of followers—the great persons who capture the imagination and admiration of those with whom they deal. For example, young golfers who admire Jack Nicklaus, Tom Watson, Carol Mann, or Sandra Palmer might try to copy their swings and dress patterns or might use clubs named after these golfing professionals. Teachers in public schools usually point out great people (such as George Washington or Abraham Lincoln) when teaching children about our country's history and often refer to these figures as "born leaders."

Most of the world's work, however, is done by "ordinary" people who work in hospitals, insurance agencies, universities, steel mills, and federal agencies. Among other things, people in these organizations plan, organize, communicate, and accept the responsibility to reach their organization's goals. For example, Ms. Smith works for a large university and has been elected chairperson of the local United Way drive. An important part of this job is to prepare the budget, talk with people, write letters, make phone calls, and perform many other duties that do not directly involve the supervision of others. She is a leader in the sense that she *is able to communicate ideas to others in such a way as to influence their behavior to reach some goals*. She is being asked to get others to act in a way that will lead to an accomplishment of United Way goals.

What, then, do we mean by the term *leadership?* Leadership is something that leaders do, not something they have. *Leadership involves influencing a group's activities toward the accomplishment of certain goals*. It is a process involving the behavior of both a leader and followers.[1]

Even though leadership is something a person does, it should not be confused with activity level. Aggressiveness and the constant direction of others do not necessarily indicate leadership. At times appropriate leadership involves staying in the background so that others may talk or hesitating before making judgments.

Leadership, as an influence process, emphasizes the relationship between two or more persons who depend on each other for the attainment of mutual goals within a specific situation. The dynamics of this situation include the leader, the follower, and the specific situation. The essential feature is that leadership is situational. By such a definition, we distinguish between two elements: (1) a person whose efforts are directed at influencing the behavior, attitudes, and values of another person or persons toward some specified goal in a given situation; and (2) a person who has influence because of his or her position in the organization's hierarchy. This influence process between the leader and the follower(s) is built over time and involves an exchange between the leader and follower.[2]

One of the important features of leadership is that it cannot be studied in a vacuum, but must be studied in group settings. For leadership cannot occur unless one person influences the activities of others—the followers.

In most instances, one cannot really threaten or force people to behave in specific ways. Leadership is the result of an exchange between followers and a leader and must carry satisfaction for both parties. In accepting a leader's ways of doing things, followers voluntarily give up some of their freedom to make decisions. In effect, followers permit another person, the leader, to make certain decisions that affect them in specific situations. In return for permitting themselves to be influenced by another person, followers want to receive certain economic and psychic rewards from the leader. For example, the coach of a sports team demonstrates coaching abilities by leading his or her team to a championship. The players follow the coach's advice on the field and suspend their individual judgments because of the coach's ability to bring psychic and economic rewards to them. Examples of psychic rewards might include a sense of achievement from winning, media focus on the team, or the fulfillment of players' personal goals. Economic rewards might include a bonus for winning a championship, opportunities to make commercial endorsements, etc.

MOTIVATION TO LEAD

Why do people want to become leaders? First, it is important to realize that very few people are forced to assume leadership positions against their wills. Those who are not motivated to become leaders generally choose not to run. Many people are simply not interested in becoming leaders and resist placement in such positions where leadership is required. It is not rare for an employee to decline a chance to be promoted to a supervisor's job or to the executive ranks. Such people are simply not motivated to become leaders in these particular situations.

Even though some persons avoid leadership roles, many others do seek leadership positions. Obviously, then, these people view leadership positions as having a great deal to offer. Consequently, if organizations hope to attract the types of people best able to perform leadership functions, they should be able to identify what it is that attracts people to leadership jobs.

There is little doubt that leadership positions can provide important rewards. Among these are economic rewards. It is highly unlikely that Clairol would have used Dorothy Hamill to advertise its hair products if she had not already won fame as an Olympic skating champion. Similarly, it is most unlikely that Hertz would have offered O. J. Simpson approximately $250,000 to endorse its rental-car service had he not been a successful professional running back. In many organizations, top executives are paid ten to twenty times as much as the lowest-paid employees. *Somebody* thinks that these people are worth such huge salaries.

Leadership, however, is often sought when economic rewards are absent. For example, the team captain, union steward, leader of a church group, and president of a local PTA are not paid for their positions, but people who willingly occupy these positions usually exercise leadership. Why? Leaders also attempt to satisfy psychic needs, and those who aspire to such positions may obtain recognition, esteem, or acceptance.

Followers must make it possible for leaders to satisfy some of these needs. Knowing that one can affect the destiny of others and oneself or being recognized as the best in the field can be important psychic rewards for the leader. This is the price followers pay for the leadership of others. The leader receives rewards from the group, just as group members receive rewards from the leader. Therefore, to remain in a leadership position, the leader must help group members gain satisfactions otherwise beyond their reach. In return, the group satisfies the leader's needs for power and prominence while helping reach organizational goals.

Sources of Power

The preceding paragraphs imply that the leader has certain power or resources to provide (or withhold from) the group in order to help it reach its goal(s). To gain further insight into this influence process, we shall review bases of power available to a leader. (These sources of power were also discussed in Chapter 9.)

Many attempts have been made to identify the sources of power through which one individual may influence another. One of the most useful frameworks for understanding these bases of influence has been developed by French and Raven.[3] These authors have distinguished five different sources of influence: (1) legitimacy, (2) control over rewards, (3) coercion, (4) referent or personal liking, and (5) expertise.

1. *Legitimate power* is based on one's hierarchical position. The corporation president has greater legitimate power than has the vice-president of manufacturing to speak on issues of corporate policy; by the same token, the vice-president of manufacturing has more legitimate power than the first-line supervisor to decide on issues of capital expenditures, work flow, inventory levels, and the like.

2. *Reward power* stems from the leader's control of rewards valued by subordinates. Subordinates who act as their supervisors tell them to do so in part because they believe that their behavior will be rewarded. As indicated in Chapter 11, the motivational process stresses that individuals normally pursue behavior to satisfy a need and reach a goal (reward). Consequently, reward power depends on the leader's ability to provide either intrinsic or extrinsic rewards for subordinates in exchange for their compliance. The supervisor may be able to reward workers through favorable task assignments, vacation schedules, lunch breaks, and pay increases. At Peat, Marwick and Mitchell, a

CPA firm, supervisors distinguish between the good and poor CPA's by giving the poor CPA's "bag" jobs (those jobs in which the clients are usually very difficult to work with). By continuing to give an accountant bag jobs, the company is "saying" that the accountant should start looking for another job and that the person's work is unacceptable to the firm.

3. *Coercive power* is based on fear. If subordinates alter their behavior because they believe that a failure to comply with orders from a superior will lead to punishment, they are responding to coercion. Punishments might be in the form of official reprimands for not following orders, poor work assignments, and a strict enforcement of all work rules.

The behavior resulting from the use of coercion is highly uncertain. Coercion may stop undesired behavior, but it does not necessarily produce desired behavior. The worker who is reprimanded for shoddy work, for example, may simply stop performing the task at all. Additionally, some workers may seek to avoid being reprimanded by falsifying performance reports rather than actually changing the quality of their performance.

4. *Reference power* is based on the followers' identification with the leader. This identification may be based on personal admiration and usually includes a desire by the followers to "be like" the leader. In other words, reference power is usually associated with people who possess admirable personal characteristics, charisma, or good reputations.

5. *Expert power* stems from the perceived and demonstrated competencies of leaders to implement, analyze, evaluate, and control the tasks assigned to their groups. Street gangs usually assess and assign expert power to those who can fight the best; academicians, to those colleagues who write journal articles and books. Expert power is narrow in scope, since a person's expertise is generally limited to specific task areas. For example, a star tennis player with high expert power on the courts may not possess such power in a chemistry class.

Further insight into this framework can be gained by segmenting those sources of power that are based primarily on organizational factors and those based primarily on personal factors. The areas of reward, coercion, expert, and legitimate power are largely specified by the organization. The first-line supervisor is at a lower level in the organization than the vice-president of manufacturing and consequently has lesser amounts of legitimate, coercive, and reward power. A supervisor may have the authority to reprimand a worker, but only the manufacturing vice-president can reprimand the supervisor. Thus position in the hierarchy affects the individual's sources of power.

On the other hand, the areas in which the supervisor can exercise referent power are to a substantial degree left to his or her personal discretion. Some managers possess personal characteristics that make them attractive to subordinates. The formal organization defines legitimate power available to all supervisors and gives them access to rewards and punishments, but the individual manager controls the referent bases of power.

There are other bases of obtaining power, such as exerting effort and interest, location and position, and coalitions.[4] (See Fig. 12.1.) It is not unusual for lower-level managers, clerks, and secretaries in large, complex organizations to assume and yield considerable influence not associated with their

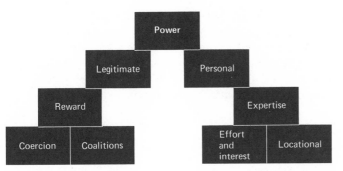

Fig. 12.1. Sources of power.

373
APPROACHES TO
THE STUDY OF
LEADERSHIP

formally defined positions in the hierarchy. Secretarial staffs in universities often have power to make decisions about the purchase and allocation of supplies, the scheduling of classes, and at times the settlement of student complaints. Such power may, in some instances, lead to sanctions against a professor by polite reluctance to furnish supplies and giving others preference in the allocation of typing and secretarial duties. In some large hospitals, ward attendants have been able to influence doctors because the physician has duties that require absence from the ward, and the ward attendants are counted on to furnish vital patient information. This dependence enables ward attendants to use limited sanctions, such as withholding information and disobeying orders, and, of course, gives them influence over the physicians.

Similarly, it is not at all uncommon for lower-level employees to form coalitions to acquire power. A secretary may know the person who manages the athletic ticket office or the one who assigns parking stickers. Such friendships give the secretary the ability to handle informally certain faculty needs that would take a faculty member considerably more time. This ability to handle these services increases the secretary's ability to influence higher-ranking members in the organization.

APPROACHES TO THE STUDY OF LEADERSHIP

In Alfred Sloan's book *My Years with General Motors*, the former chief operating officer of General Motors asks whether or not managerial leadership is a property of the individual or a term describing relationships among members of a group.[5] For years, many people have tried to answer this complex question by turning to all sorts of soothsayers. The analysis of handwriting (graphology), the study of skull shapes (phrenology), and the investigation of the position of the stars and other celestial bodies (astrology) have been employed. To appreciate the complexity and depth of the leadership problem, we shall review several approaches to the study of leadership.[6]

Traitist Approach

For centuries, philosophers and scientists have argued the "great man" theory. Was the destiny of the world shaped by individuals such as Queen Elizabeth I, Winston Churchill, and Alexander the Great? Is there something in these individuals' personalities that enabled them to have a significant impact on the history of the world? Or do such people become leaders because they just happen to have been in the right place at the right time? Depending on your own personal biases, you might answer these questions differently. Under the proper circumstances, there could be an individual whose personality and leadership style fit the situation and who also happened to be in the right place at the right time.

The controversy surrounding this theory has called attention to the "trait" approach to leadership. Much of the early study on leadership was directed at identifying the characteristics of leaders. The basis for this approach is that certain physical, social, personality, and personal traits are considered to be inherent within some individuals and can, therefore, be used in distinguishing leaders from nonleaders. These traits are as follows:

1. *Physical traits*—height, weight, physical attractiveness, vitality, physical stamina, body shape;
2. *Social traits*—empathy, tact, patience, employee-oriented, status, emotional maturity;
3. *Personality traits*—dominance, aggressiveness, extroversion, self-esteem, integrity, confidence;
4. *Personal traits*—verbal skills, judgment, intellectual capacity, achievement-oriented, capacity to work hard, responsible.

Despite the considerable support for the notion that effective leaders have different interest patterns, abilities, and perhaps also some different personality traits than do less effective managers, most researchers have come to regard the "great man" theory as not very effective in predicting leadership. Researchers have failed to identify leadership traits that can consistently be used as standards for designating individuals as either leaders or nonleaders.[7] This does not imply that individual differences have nothing to do with leadership, only that their significance must be evaluated in relation to the contingencies in the situation.

The major criticisms of the trait approach focus on the physical and personality traits. Physical traits have not been found to have a consistent relationship with managerial effectiveness. In the military or police force, for example, members must meet certain minimal height and weight standards in order to perform their tasks effectively. Although these physical attributes may assist individuals in the performance of their jobs, the number of inches of height or the number of pounds of weight do not relate highly to performance.

The empirical work stemming from the concept of leadership as a personality trait has come under considerable question. Some personality traits have been found to relate to managerial success, but the results have not been consistent. For example, some of the personality traits found to relate to a salesperson's success (in terms of sales volume) include gregariousness, risk taking, impulsiveness, exhibitionism, and egocentrism. On the other hand, the personality traits of motivation, intellectual interest, and audacity have been found to relate to a manager who is a "satisficer" and not a "maximizer." *Satisficers* are concerned with the attainment of a satisfactory profit in conjunction with a satisfactory sales volume, whereas maximizers want to increase earnings per share, gross margins, and retained earnings in the firm. *Maximizers appear to seek roles that are likely to receive group attention and in which they can exhibit their strong needs for personal power, impulsiveness, and self-assertion.*[8]

Yet despite its limitations, the trait approach should not be discarded too hastily, for it has made some contributions toward clarifying the nature of leadership. Most universities, for example, are run by educators who hold doctoral degrees and have educational experience; hospitals require the chief of the medical staff to have a medical degree; and Supreme Court justices have legal backgrounds. These can be considered "personal traits." Many managers will agree that individuals with certain personal traits are still more likely to become leaders than others. Such personal traits may include an ability to verbalize feelings and concepts, above average intelligence (but not at genius level), empathy with group members, a degree of insight into group situations, a high level of technical skill in the task(s) the group will be undertaking in its goal-seeking activities, and flexibility in formulating new concepts and ideas. Although none of these personal traits is absolutely necessary, they all predispose the possessor toward leadership.

The one necessary personal trait for those who assume leadership roles is the *motivation to be a leader*. In general, the stronger a person's motivation to be a leader, the more likely it is that the person will achieve a leadership position. Of course, there are many reasons why an individual might desire to become a leader, e.g., an urge to dominate others, devotion to the group and to the group's goals, a high-level aspiration for either self or group, a need for prestige and esteem, and economic rewards.

All of the personal traits mentioned may play a part in influencing the group's choice of a leader. However, contingency factors are often more important than personal traits. People may become leaders because they are in the right place at the right time. They may have specific knowledge or ability that directly fits into the requirements of a leadership role at the time it is available; they may have the greatest seniority among group members; they may be the correct age; or they may have access to important information and the ability to control the flow of this information to other group members.

To summarize, the idea that leadership can be determined by an individual's personality characteristics has proved to be oversimplified. The dream of a method by which the relative amounts of leadership possessed by different people could be measured and the person with the largest amount of this desired trait selected as the leader was unattainable.

Behavioral Approach

If there appear to be no stable personality characteristics that distinguish leaders from nonleaders or effective leaders from less effective leaders, it is still possible that there are some methods or styles of leadership that are more effective than others. Instead of looking at personality of the effective leader, perhaps we should be searching for behavioral indicators of effective leadership. Effective and ineffective leaders may be distinguished not by a battery of psychological tests, but by their characteristic behavior patterns in their work roles.

Interest in the behavior of leaders in their leadership roles emerged during the 1930s and is now evident in two major research programs begun in the late 1940s and carried out at the Ohio State University and the University of Michigan. During the 1930s, two researchers conducted a study with small children to determine the effect of three types of leadership style on their performance.[9] These researchers labeled the leadership styles as autocratic, democratic, and laissez faire.

The *autocratic* leader led by command, and the commands were generally obeyed to avoid punishments. This leader was task-centered and tended to give criticism when productivity slowed down. The *democratic* leader acted in direct contrast to the autocrat, permitting the group to discuss and make decisions, members to work with whomever they chose, and being supportive of the children's work. The *laissez-faire* leader allowed the group total freedom and exerted a minimal amount of personal effort.

The findings indicated that although the quantity of work produced was greater in the autocratic groups, the quality of the work in the democratic groups was superior. Also, when the autocratic leader left the production area, his workers almost completely stopped working (a sign of job dissatisfaction), whereas the performance of those under the democratic leader decreased only slightly in his absence. In general, the laissez-faire style (complete permissiveness and indifference) was not effective in stimulating performance. This style did not produce either higher quality or more productivity than the other two approaches. In fact, there was less work done under laissez-faire leadership, and the work was of poorer quality than in either the democratic or autocratic group.

From this early study, opponents of the behavioral approach have identified three styles of leadership: supportive, participative, and instrumental.[10]

SUPPORTIVE STYLE

Supportive leaders give consideration to the needs of their subordinates and are concerned with their well-being, status, and comfort. These leaders seek to create a friendly and pleasant working climate for employees. Supportive leaders assume that subordinates want to work their best, and they should make it easier for subordinates to achieve their goals. Supportive leaders seek to gain acceptance by treating subordinates with respect and dignity rather than through use of their formal position in the organization's structure or through the use of coercive power. Some typical behaviors of supportive leaders that have been identified by researchers at Ohio State include:

Express appreciation when subordinates do a good job.
Do not demand more than subordinates can do.
Help subordinates with their personal problems.
Are friendly and can easily be approached.
See that subordinates are rewarded for jobs well done.[11]

Proponents argue that supportive leadership behavior is effective because it is more readily accepted by subordinates than are impersonal, autocratic, or task-centered styles. They contend that supportive leader behavior generates goodwill among the subordinates and leads to feelings of high job satisfaction. These attitudes will lead to close cooperation between the leaders and their subordinates, an increase in the motivation of subordinates to work toward the goals of the leader, and a productive work group.

The research evidence basically lends credence to the notion that in groups whose leaders are rate as high in supportiveness, subordinate satisfaction is high and turnover and grievance rates are low. In addition to the attitudes and satisfaction of subordinates, supportive leader behavior has frequently been found to have a positive effect on departmental and individual productivity.[12]

Not all the research evidence has indicated that supportive leader behavior leads to higher job satisfaction and task performance.[13] In such studies, the major contingency was the task. If employees were working on an intrinsically interesting task and/or under conditions of considerable freedom from their supervisor, this style of leader behavior was not strongly related to satisfaction or performance. It thus appears that the task is a *contingency* influencing the relationship between supportive leader behavior and the job satisfaction and performance of subordinates.

PARTICIPATIVE STYLE

Participative leadership is characterized by the sharing of information, power, and influence between supervisors and subordinates. The manager who uses this style of leader behavior treats subordinates as equals and allows them to influence his or her decisions. This style of leader behavior ensures that all subordinates for whom a decision is relevant will have an opportunity to influence the final decision. To accomplish this, participative leaders:

Share information with subordinates.
Seek out opinions, facts and feelings from concerned parties.
Minimize blame-oriented statements.
Encourage the generation of alternatives.
Delay evaluation of alternatives until all have been presented.[14]

As can be seen from these behaviors, participative leaders are actively involved in ensuring that all subordinates participate in the decision-making process. Participative leaders do not give up their roles by becoming members of the group, but they encourage suggestions from subordinates and independent thinking and action. They may, in fact, exercise close supervision by providing information and coaching.

It has been suggested that participation should improve decision making because the subordinate can bring to bear his or her expertise and knowledge on the problem. That is, participative leadership is an effective means of obtaining relevant subordinate expertise and thereby improving the quality of the decision. Other researchers have stated that participation: (1) leads to greater clarity of the means to accomplish goals; (2) enables subordinates to select goals they value, thus increasing the congruence between the individual and the organization; (3) increases the participants' control over what happens on the job (if employees' motivation is higher, having greater autonomy and the ability to carry out their task assignments should lead to increased effort and performance); and (4) increases individuals' ego-involvement in the decision.[15]

Considerable research has been undertaken to determine the effects of participative leader behavior on subordinate satisfaction, performance, acceptance of decisions made by supervisors, and the quality of group decisions. In general, two *contingency* variables seem to affect the results—the *task* and the *personality characteristics* of the individual employee.

If the task itself does not permit the individual to actively participate in the decision-making process or become ego-involved with it, participative leader behavior is seen as having little effect on performance. Simple machine-paced tasks (such as those of an axle assembler on an automobile assembly line or an individual checking to see if there are 157 bolts on the left side of a Vega's door) do not lend themselves to participative leader behavior. On these tasks, there is little to participate in, because the task is controlled by a mechanically paced line. In fact, employees on such tasks might see leader efforts as participation to be a farce or sham.[16]

The participation process is also likely to be more satisfying and rewarding for some subordinates, regardless of the task. This would be expected for subordinates who have a high need for independence and who respect non-authoritarian behavior. Many research studies have shown that participation has its most positive effects on productivity and satisfaction when subordinates are predisposed toward participative leadership.[17]

There is also evidence suggesting that the amount of knowledge possessed by the subordinates and their level of intelligence are important determinants of the effectiveness of participative leader behavior. Subordinates with high intelligence contribute more to the participative decision-making process than do those low in intelligence. Further, when subordinates have knowledge of facts relevant to the decisions and supervisors do not have such knowledge, the participative leader behavior is likely to be more effective than when the opposite conditions prevail.

In summary, for participative leadership to be effective, subordinates must have favorable attitudes toward participation, and the task must be complex or nonroutine and require a high quality of subordinate acceptance or involvement. It therefore seems fair to say that participative leader behavior, much like supportive behavior, can often have positive effects on job satisfaction and performance, but is based on contingency factors—the task and personality of subordinates.

INSTRUMENTAL STYLE

Instrumental leader behavior is characterized by managers who plan, organize, control, and coordinate the activities of subordinates in order to foster group accomplishment. Some typical behaviors of instrumental leaders that have been identified by researchers at Ohio State include:

Assigning of members to particular tasks.
Establishing of standards of job performance.

Informing subordinates of the job requirements.

Scheduling work to be done.

Encouraging the use of uniform procedures to be followed.[18]

Like the results found in the previous sections on supportive and participative leader behavior, the evidence is mixed. Reviews of the literature on instrumental leader behavior have concluded that this style has its most positive effects when any of the following conditions are present:

1. There is a high degree of pressures for output due to demands imposed by sources other than the leaders;
2. The task is satisfying to subordinates;
3. The subordinates' attitudes, expectations, or personalities predispose them toward being told what to do and how to do it;
4. Subordinates' tasks are nonroutine;
5. The number of people working together for the same leader is high (span of control greater than 12).[19]

These reviews obviously suggest that there are several critical contingencies that a leader must consider before using this style of leadership. The real strength of the instrumental leader lies in his or her ability to control available resources and to use them in the most effective way for the group's task accomplishment.

Contingency Approaches

So far we have shown that analyses of the situational demands are important to understanding the process of leadership. Attempts to determine the kinds of leader traits or leader behavior that are characteristic of effective leaders have continually encountered problems. The leadership problem is apparently more complex. We now begin to look at a number of characteristics that are essential to a contingency approach of leadership. These characteristics are based on some of the things in previous approaches that we have reviewed and from more general knowledge about both the functioning of groups and individual behavior.

Figure 12.2 shows a general "road map" to the leadership process. The three important elements are followers, leader, and the situation. The needs, behavior patterns, and goals of followers combine with characteristics of the situation to provide a framework of variables within which the leader must operate. In addition, the leader's own perceptions of these characteristics and his or her own needs, behavior, and goals determine the type of influence used to affect the behavior of subordinates. These three elements form the basis for the contingency models we will discuss.

FIEDLER'S CONTINGENCY MODEL

The first contingency model of leadership effectiveness was developed by Fiedler and his associates.[20] This model, a departure from the trait and behavioral models of leadership, specifies that a group's performance is contingent on the motivational system of the leader and the degree to which the leader has control and influence in a particular situation. The effectiveness of

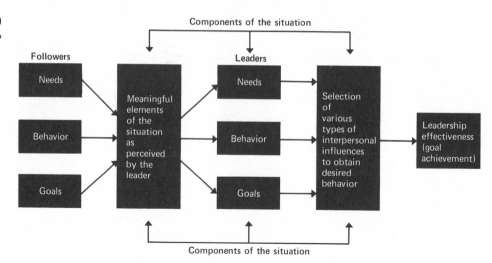

Components of the situation

Followers

Leaders

Fig. 12.2. Components of the leadership process. (Adapted from R. Tannenbaum, I. R. Weschler, and F. Massarick, *Leadership and Organization: A Behavioral Science Approach,* New York: McGraw-Hill, 1961, p. 32. Used with permission.)

a leadership style depends on the interaction of the leader's behavior with three situational variables: task structure, leader-member relations, and leader's position power.

Assessing Leadership Style. A person's leadership style is determined by his or her esteem for the "least preferred coworker" (LPC). LPC is measured by asking the manager to think of all coworkers he or she has ever had and to describe the person with whom he or she could work least well. Fiedler asserts that the LPC score is an index of a motivational system, or behavioral preferences. The high-LPC person, one who describes his or her least preferred coworker in a more favorable light, has the basic goal of desiring to be related with others. This leader seeks to have strong emotional ties with coworkers. The leader who reaches this goal will want to reach the secondary goals of status and esteem and have subordinates show admiration and recognition.

The low-LPC person has a different motivational system. This person's basic goal is task accomplishment. Self-esteem is gained through achievement of task-related goals. However, as long as accomplishing the task presents no problems, this person also tends to be friendly and have pleasant relations with subordinates. It is only when task accomplishment is threatened that good interpersonal relations assume secondary importance to accomplishing the task.

Variables

1. *Task structure.* This variable focuses on the extent to which the task is simple (or routine), can be done only one (or numerous) ways, and is highly specific (or vague). A routine task is likely to have clearly defined goals, only

a few steps or work procedures, be verifiable, and have a correct solution. An axle asembler in an auto plant who secures front and rear assemblies to chassis springs is performing a highly structured task; the goals are clearly spelled out, the method to accomplish the task is detailed and specific, and correct task performance is verifiable. Under these conditions, the leader's ability to influence the group is restricted, because the task's structure reduces the leader's potential influence.

At the other extreme is the complex or nonroutine task. In this condition, the leader may possess no more knowledge than the subordinates. The goals are unclear, the means to achieve the goals are multiple, and the task cannot be done by the "numbers." Tasks performed by social workers, detectives, policy makers, executives, marketing researchers, and other managers are examples of complex tasks.

2. *Leader-member relations.* This refers to leaders' feelings of being accepted by the group. The leader's authority depends partly on his or her acceptance by the group, which may depend on referent power, for example—the leader's personality, trustworthiness, and other personal characteristics.

3. *Leader's position power.* Position power is the extent to which the leader possesses reward, coercion, and legitimate sources of influence. Does the leader have the right to promote or demote a subordinate? Can the leader instruct the subordinates concerning task goals? In most business organizations, foremen, supervisors, and managers have high position power. In most voluntary organizations, committees, and other social organizations, leaders tend to have low position power.

Determinants of Favorable Situation. The three aspects of the situation that appear to be the most important in determining the leader's influence and control are: (1) the work group's acceptance or rejection of the leader (group atmosphere); (2) whether the task is relatively routine or nonroutine (task structure); and (3) whether the leader has high or low position power (power position). A particular group may be classified first by its leader-member relations, then by its task structure, and finally by its leader's position power. The higher each of these is (i.e., the more pleasant the leader-member relations, the more structured the task, and the greater the leader's position power), the more favorable the situation for the leader.

Figure 12.3 shows Fiedler's contingency model of leadership. The three basic contingency variables are shown on the horizontal axis. The eight numbered blocks represent combinations of the three variables and are arranged in order of leader favorableness, from most favorable to least favorable. The model assumes that a leader will have the most control and influence in groups that fall into block 1; the leader is accepted and has high position power, and subordinates perform relatively structured tasks. A leader will have somewhat less control and influence in block 2; the leader is accepted, has little position power, and the task is structured. In block 8, the leader's control and influence are very limited; the leader is not accepted by the group, has little position power, and the group performs an unstructured task.

Telephone offices, craft shops, meat departments, and grocery departments are typical of blocks 1 and 5; team games, surveying parties, of blocks 2 and

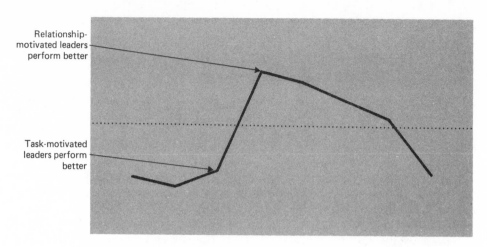

Leader-member relations	Good	Good	Good	Good	Poor	Poor	Poor	Poor
Task structure	Structured		Unstructured		Structured		Unstructured	
Leader position power	Strong	Weak	Strong	Weak	Strong	Weak	Strong	Weak
	(1)	(2)	(3)	(4)	(5)	(6)	(7)	(8)

Fig. 12.3. Basic contingency model. (Fred E. Fiedler, "Engineer the Job to Fit the Manager," *Harvard Business Review* **45** (September-October 1965): 118. Reproduced with permission. Copyright © 1965 by the President and Fellows of Harvard College. All rights reserved.)

6; general foremen, ROTC groups, research chemists, military planning groups, of blocks 3 and 7; racially divided groups, disaster groups, church groups, and mental health groups, of blocks 4 and 8. The critical question is: What kind of leadership style is most effective in each of the different group situations?

Effectiveness of Different Leadership Styles. The average results of the various studies conducted by Fiedler and his associates are plotted in Fig. 12.3. The horizontal axis indicates the favorableness of the situation, ranging from most favorable, on the far left, to least favorable, on the far right. The vertical axis indicates the leader's LPC score. The solid line on the graph above the midline indicates a positive relationship between LPC and group performance. That is, high-LPC leaders performed better than low-LPC leaders. The solid line below the midline indicates that low-LPC leaders performed better than high-LPC leaders. The solid line represents the best predictions between a leader's LPC score and work-group effectiveness.

Low-LPC leaders are task-motivated and perform most effectively in the very favorable situations (blocks 1, 2, and 3) and in the least favorable situation (block 8). In favorable situations, there is good group atmosphere, the leader's power position is high, and the task is structured. The leaders, by being motivated to accomplish the task, will strive to develop pleasant work relations and will seem friendly and considerate toward coworkers. In unfavorable situations, in which the task is unstructured, the leader lacks group support, has low position power, and will strive to achieve the primary goal of the group.

Figure 12.3 also indicates situations in which a high-LPC leader is most likely to perform better. High-LPC leaders obtain best group efficiency under conditions of moderate or intermediate favorableness (blocks 4, 5, 6, and 7). Blocks 4 and 5 describe situations in which (1) the task is structured but the leader is disliked and must demonstrate care for the emotions of subordinates, or (2) the leader is liked but the group has an unstructured task and the leader must depend on the willingness and creativity of the group's members to accomplish the goals.

Implications. There are several important implications of this model. First, both relationship-motivated and task-motivated leaders perform well under certain contingencies but not others. An outstanding manager at one level who gets promoted to another level may fail at higher levels because his or her motivational base does not match the demands of the situation. For example, an outstanding foreman may prove to be a poor production manager. The contingency model suggests that the foreman's failure in the new position reflects a change in leadership situation; the structure of the task has probably lessened considerably, and the person's leadership style no longer "fits" the situation. The new situation may call for a relation-centered style rather than a task-centered style.

Second, it is not totally accurate to speak of a "good" or "poor" leader. Rather, one must think of a leader who performs well in one situation but not in another. Third, the performance of a leader depends on both his or her motivational system and the situation. The organization can change leadership effectiveness by attempting to change the motivational system of the leader or by modifying the favorableness of the leader's situation. The real challenge for management is to recognize that effective leadership is contingent on the three variables described by Fiedler—leader-member relations, task structure, and leader's position power.

Evaluation of the Model. A number of fairly detailed reviews to validate the model have been published.[21] Studies to determine the validity of this model have been conducted in a wide variety of groups, teams, and organizations (e.g., research teams, department stores, military units, basketball teams, hospital wards), and several important issues have been raised.

First, what does "LPC" mean? Early in his research, Fiedler assumed that it was a measure of the leader's personality, but his most recent interpretation is that it reflects an individual's motivation system with respect to need gratification from groups. Despite the fact that the interpretation of a leader's LPC score is cloudy, it does seem to reflect a leader's underlying motivational system and not cognitive ability or a basic personality. Although the debate over the meaning of LPC continues, it has been highly related to group productivity.

Second, how stable is a leader's LPC score over time? It seems hardly worthwhile to change a work situation on the basis of a leader's LPC score if the leader's LPC score is likely to change soon and can vary according to group performance. High performance of a group can increase a leader's LPC score; low performance can cause a decrease. Although changes in the LPC score do occur as a result of changes in an individual's life and the leader's success or failure, we cannot engineer the job to fit the manager if the manager's motivational systems are continually changing.

Third, the model does not take into account that the leader can influence the task structure because of his or her knowledge of the situation. A leader can take a nonroutine task and provide some structure to it before assigning it to subordinates. They, in turn, perceive the task to be more structured than unstructured. The leader can also affect the group's atmosphere through a particular style of behavior. A leader whose style is supportive or participative may facilitate the development of group harmony and high group cohesiveness. On the other hand, a leader who is aloof, unapproachable, and unfriendly may create hostility and resentment in the work group.

Fourth, LPC is unidimensional; the concept suggests that an individual highly motivated toward task accomplishment must be completely unconcerned with relations among group members or oriented away from social concerns, and vice versa. As discussed earlier, however, it is possible for an individual to be both task- and relations-motivated. Thus a leader's orientation on one dimension should not completely determine the orientation on the other. The leader may well be one who is motivated to both task and relational concerns.

In summary, Fiedler's contingency model stresses that both relations-oriented and task-oriented leaders can perform well, but under different conditions. The task-motivated leaders perform best in situations in which their power and influence are either very high or very low, as well as in situations in which their task is highly structured and there are good leader-member relations. Relations-motivated leaders perform best under conditions of moderate favorableness, in which the power and influence they have are mixed, leader-member relations are low, and the structure is either high or low.

HOUSE'S PATH-GOAL MODEL

Puzzled by the contradictory findings in the leadership area, House developed a model of leadership based on Vroom's expectancy theory of motivation (see Chapter 11). House's model of leadership effectiveness does not indicate the "one best way" to lead, but suggests that a leader must select a style most appropriate to the particular situation and the needs of his or her subordinates.[22] His model uses two styles of leadership: supportive and instrumental.

Supportive leadership is demonstrated by a friendly and approachable leader who shows concern for the status, well-being, and needs of subordinates. A supportive leader does little things to make the work more pleasant, treats members as equals, and is friendly and approachable. *Instrumental* leadership is demonstrated by letting subordinates know what is expected of them, giving specific guidance as to what should be done and how it should be done, making the leader's part in the group understood, scheduling work to be done, maintaining definite standards of performance, and asking that group members follow standard rules and regulations.

In other words, one of the functions of a leader is to enhance the personal satisfactions of subordinates that result from the motivation to perform a task or in satisfaction with the job. The leader's function consists of increasing the personal satisfactions to subordinates for work-goal attainment and making the means to achieve these satisfactions easier to obtain. The leader accomplishes these ends by clarifying the nature of the task, reducing the roadblocks from successful task completion, and increasing the opportunities for the subordinates to obtain personal satisfactions. The model states that to the extent that the leader accomplishes these functions, subordinates' motivation will increase. Subordinates are satisfied with their jobs to the extent that performance will lead to things that they value highly. The function of the leader, therefore, is to help subordinates reach these highly valued job-related goals. The specific style of leader behavior is determined by two contingency variables—characteristics of the subordinates and the task structure.

Characteristics of Subordinates. The model states that leader behavior will be viewed acceptable to subordinates to the extent that they see such behavior as either an immediate source of satisfaction or as needed for future satisfaction. For example, if subordinates have a high need for self-esteem and affiliation, supportive leader behavior may serve as an immediate source for satisfying these needs. On the other hand, subordinates with high need for autonomy, responsibility, and self-actualization are more likely to be motivated by leaders whose style is instrumental rather than supportive.

Task Structure. The second major contingency variable in House's model is the task's structure. Where means-ends relationships are apparent because of the routine nature of the task, attempts by the leader to further clarify these relationships will be perceived by subordinates as unnecessarily close control. Although such close control may increase performance by preventing "goofing off," it will also result in decreased job satisfaction. The axle assembler in an auto plant who secures front and rear assemblies to chassis springs is performing a highly structured and repetitive task. Indeed, many workers cannot obtain any intrinsic satisfaction (i.e., esteem, self-actualization) from the performance of a highly structured task. If a leader uses an instrumental style of behavior, it is likely to be perceived by the workers as redundant, excessive, and directed at keeping them working on unsatisfying tasks. Within this task structure, a leader who is supportive is likely to have more satisfied employees. A supportive leadership style is likely to increase the worker's intrinsic satisfaction (e.g., satisfaction with the supervision of the company, company policies) on a job that provides little intrinsic satisfaction.

On the other hand, when the tasks are highly unstructured, i.e., more complex and varied, a more instrumental leadership style is appropriate to the extent that it helps subordinates cope with task uncertainty and clarifies the paths leading to highly valued goals. A manager of an industrial relations team who gives subordinates guidance and direction on how to process a grievance for arbitration is attempting to clarify the direction of subordinates for the attain-

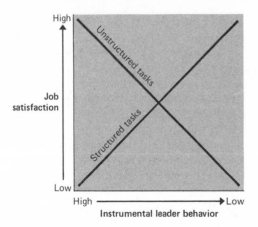

Fig. 12.4. A path-goal leadership model.

ment of an organizational goal. This style of leadership is not perceived as excessive and/or redundant, since it helps the subordinates reach their goals, a source of intrinsic job satisfaction.

Figure 12.4 illustrates the effect of task structure on leader behavior and subordinates' job satisfaction. Task structure moderates the relationship between leader behavior and subordinate job satisfaction. When the task is highly structured, the leader who does not give direction and excessive coaching is likely to have highly satisfied subordinates. On the other hand, when the task is unstructured, an instrumental leadership style is likely to increase subordinates' job satisfaction. (There are several other variables, e.g., performance, supervisor satisfaction, promotion satisfaction, that could replace job satisfaction without changing the relationships in the figure.)

Implications. The kind of leadership style needed varies according to the situation. Thus, for example, although shop-floor personnel may prefer a supportive leader in order to gain some extrinsic satisfactions from performing routine and often boring tasks, middle and professional employees work better when their leader uses an instrumental style of leadership. At these levels, job descriptions are usually written without much specification, and a directive leader can clarify the task(s) and the goal(s) for the subordinates. It does not seem unreasonable that different leadership styles will be required for different occupational groupings and levels of the organization's hierarchy.

Evaluation of the Model. It is too early to make anything but a preliminary assessment of House's path-goal theory of leadership, because so little research data are available. However, the early research findings have been encouraging. Workers performing highly structured tasks have reported high job satisfaction when their immediate supervisor uses a supportive (as opposed to instrumental) leadership style. On the other hand, managers performing in unstructured task environments are more productive when their immediate supervisor uses a more instrumental leadership style. However, this instrumental style does not always lead to high job satisfaction.[23]

There are many questions still to be answered about the leadership process. Perhaps the foremost question concerns the contingency variables that make a particular style of leader behavior less effective or, in some instances, unnecessary. A wide variety of individual, task, and organizational characteristics have been mentioned throughout this chapter as important contingency variables affecting the leadership process. Some of these contingency variables, such as job pressures or routineness of the task, act primarily to influence which leadership style will be most effective. The effect of other contingency variables, however, is to act as "substitutes for leadership." Generally, a substitute for leadership can be any characteristic that makes leader behavior irrelevant or does not seem to affect an employee's motivation to perform. Thus a substitute for leadership tends to nullify or decrease the leader's ability to exert influence over subordinates in a meaningful way.

Table 12.1 gives a partial list of substitutes for leadership that have been identified by Kerr.[24] The substitutes are in the personal characteristics of the subordinates, the requirements of the task, and the formal structure of the organization. The two styles of leader behavior are *participative* and *instrumental*. An X indicates that a particular leadership style can be substituted when that contingency variable exists. For example, instrumental leader behavior can be substituted for when subordinates have a great deal of ability, work experience, training, and knowledge and are indifferent toward organizational rewards. The greater the subordinate's ability to perform the task, for example, the less she or he relies on the supervisor for directions to perform the task.

Subordinate Characteristics

As indicated in Table 12.1, when a leader has subordinates who have the ability, experience, training, and knowledge to actually complete the task, instrumental leader behavior will not have much affect on their motivation and/or performance. The individual working behind the counter at McDonald's, Hardee's, or Burger King as a short-order cook usually can master the basic requirements of the task within a short period of time. During this learning period, instrumental leader behavior will have an impact on the trainee's job performance. After the person has learned the job, this style of leader behavior will not increase the employee's motivation to perform. The employee has already acquired the needed abilities, experience, and talents, to perform the task, and these now substitute for instrumental leader behaviors. On the other hand, the participative leadership style will probably have a greater impact on employees' behavior because they cannot derive any intrinsic satisfaction from the task itself. To obtain job satisfactions, the employees turn toward their supervisor.

Task Characteristics

As indicated in Table 12.1, four task characteristics may act as substitutes for leader behavior. Three of these act as substitutes for instrumental leader be-

Table 12.1. Substitutes for leadership

| | Will tend to neutralize | |
Contingency variables	Participative	Instrumental
Subordinates		
1. Ability		X
2. Work experience		X
3. Training		X
4. Knowledge		X
5. Indifferent toward organizational rewards	X	X
Task		
6. Unambiguous and routine		X
7. Simple, machine-paced, highly standardized methods		X
8. Provides its own feedback concerning accomplishment		X
9. Intrinsically interesting	X	
Organization		
10. Formalization (explicit plans, goals, and areas of responsibility)		X
11. Rigid (unbending rules and regulations)		X
12. Closely knit work groups	X	X
13. Organizational rewards not within the leader's control	X	X
14. Spatial distance between leader and superior	X	X

Adapted from S. Kerr, "Substitutes for Leadership: Their Meaning and Measurement." Paper presented at Eighth Annual Conference, American Institute for Decision Sciences, San Francisco, November 1976.

havior; one acts as a substitute for participative leader behavior. Continuing with our example of the short-order cook, the task of making hamburgers (Big Mac's, Whopper's, etc.) is routine. (In fact, one of the goals of McDonald's is to ensure that each hamburger is made exactly the same throughout the country.) In order to see that this goal is achieved, the method used to make the hamburger is simple and routine. In this instance, the short-order cook also gets immediate feedback from the task itself as to whether or not the task has been accomplished.

The routineness of the task, its simplicity, and the fact that the task provides feedback to the individual—all act as substitutes for instrumental leader behaviors. In this case, participative leader behavior will motivate employees to perform at higher levels. If the task is intrinsically satisfying, participative leader behavior would be redundant. Employees enjoy performing the task and need some directions on how to increase their effectiveness.

Organizational Characteristics

Finally, Table 12.1 shows there are five organizational contingencies (numbers 10–14) that might act as substitutes for a particular style of leader behavior. To the extent that the organization has explicit goals, plans, rules, and regulations, it makes instrumental leader behavior less necessary. The goals, plans, etc., act as guidelines for subordinates, thus reducing the importance of instrumental leader behaviors. In essence, the "mechanistic" organization (see Chapter 5 for a review of this organizational structure) makes instrumental leader behavior less appropriate, because the structure of the organization greatly influences the subordinate's behavior.

If the leader cannot control the rewards for the subordinates, his or her influence bases will be eroded.[25] One of the basic premises of the leadership process is that it is an exchange between a leader and subordinate. The leader brings desired rewards to the group or individual, and in turn the group or individual permits the leader to exert influence. Unless the leader can control the rewards that the group considers valuable, why follow the leader's orders?

Although this explanation may be an oversimplification of what happened in the Vietnam war, let's assume that the primary goal of the American army was to win a war. Let's also assume that the primary goal of the individuals on the front lines was to get home alive. What happened? How did the soldiers in Vietnam reach their goal? When was their tour of duty over? The soldiers returned home whether the war was won or not. Furthermore, the chances of getting home alive by obeying orders compared to the chance of getting home alive by not obeying orders was not great. Mutineers in Vietnam were frequently assigned rest and rehabilitation rather than facing courts-martial, firing squads, etc. Officers in the field often did not have control over the rewards that American soldiers wanted, thus rendering any particular leadership style ineffective.

Summary

This chapter suggests that there is no "one best way to lead." Five major points about the nature of managerial leadership can be made. First, leadership is a process that is necessary when two or more people seek to accomplish a common goal. In this respect, leadership is built on a mutually dependent relationship. Subordinates depend on leaders for rewards, and the leader depends on subordinates for rewards. Successful leadership depends on the motivation of subordinates to accomplish the goal(s) of the organization. To this extent, leaders must link the individual's objectives to those of the organization.

Second, there are no physical characteristics or personality traits that are universally evident in all leadership situations. A specific leader emerges because of a mixture of personal characteristics, the elements of the situation, and the characteristics of the followers. Thus leadership is not a mechanical process in which specific characteristics are successful in all situations.

Third, there are at least three styles of leader behavior—supportive, participative, and instrumental. The supportive leader seeks to gain acceptance of organizational goals by treating subordinates with respect, helping them with their personal problems, and seeing that they are rewarded for jobs well done. The participative leader shares information with subordinates and allows them equal participation in the decision-making process. The instrumental leader is one who plans, organizes, and controls the activities of subordinates. Each of these styles is effective in only certain situations.

Fourth, two contingency approaches to the study of leadership were presented. Fiedler's model emphasizes the importance of the task, group, and power position of the leader to give or retain rewards from subordinates. House's model, by contrast, emphasizes the role of the task and the characteristics of the subordinates. Both of these approaches seem to be heading in the right direction.

Finally, there are various substitutes for the leadership process that reduce the impact of a particular style of leader behavior. Three major classes of contingency variables—subordinates, task, and organizational—act as substitutes for the leadership process.

Discussion Questions

1. Define leadership. What are the important elements in your definition?

2. "All managers are leaders." Is this statement true or false? Support your position.

3. What are the sources of influence in the leadership process?

4. What is the traitist approach to studying leadership? Are there any traits that you feel are universal among all leaders?

5. What is meant by the "behavioral" approach to the study of leadership?

6. How do the supportive, participative, and instrumental styles of leader behavior differ?

7. Is there one best style to follow in order to become an effective leader?

8. What are the basic elements in Fiedler's model?

9. Identify some of the problems in Fiedler's model.

10. Compare House's approach to that of Fiedler's. Where are these two simi-
    lar/dissimilar?

11. Discuss the notion that substitutes to leadership are important.

Management Incidents

HOT AND ROCK JUNK YARD

The Hot and Rock Junk Yard, a medium size junk yard in Washington, had been taking steps to improve the effectiveness of its management. It contracted with a private consulting firm for some leadership training. Some of the sessions involved familiarization with the various approaches to leadership. The managers were asked to rate themselves, and their subordinates were given an opportunity to comment on the leadership ability of their supervisors. Larry Hottenstein, one of the managers, was rated as high in supportive leader behavior by his subordinates. John Carzo, another participant, was rated as high on instrumental leader behavior.

When this phase of the leadership program was over, the trainers took these basic styles and tried to explain why each particular style was effective. Larry, foreman in the yard, and John, the manager of the yard, couldn't understand why one style wasn't better than another. Each had excellent proficiency ratings, and both had been told that they would be promoted within the next year.

1. What answer would you give to John and Larry? Why?
2. What are some of the contingencies probably facing these men in their daily work?

THE PRIZE

Marie Straka has been president of the company for seven years, and initially things had gone very well. Sales increased on an average of 14 percent per year, and return on investment during this period had never been lower than 10 percent. Slowly other firms began to realize the kinds of profits that could be attained in the weight-control industry and began moving in. As they did, competition increased and the big profit margin began to shrink. Prices dropped as each company tried to capture and retain a large number of clients who wanted to lose weight. Many of these newcomers used gimmicks ("One week free"; "Guaranteed to lose up to ten pounds in two weeks"; "Free beauty advice") to attract their clientele. Marie's firm was barely able to keep its head above water. It was during its June 1976 meeting that the Board of Directors decided to let Marie go.

This was not an easy decision for the directors to make. Everyone liked Marie, who was pleasant, easy-going, and friendly to clients and employees. Nevertheless, the board felt that she was unable to turn the company around and that someone who could was needed.

The board's choice was Ildiko Booney, the president of a competitor. Ildiko told the board that she would take the job only if she were able to do things her way. In turn, she promised results.

Within the first six months of her appointment, Ildiko had fired over 40 percent of the old management that Marie had recruited. She did not replace them. If someone quit or was fired, the work load was redistributed among the remaining employees. Ildiko's reasoning was quite simple. She came to this company when it was almost bankrupt. There were too many chiefs and not enough Indians. She changed all this and tightened up the management ranks.

When the board met in June 1977, it was difficult to argue with her, because her leadership style seemed to be getting results. The company had begun to attract new customers, and its return on investment was returning to previous highs.

Some of the members of the board felt that Ildiko's style was too rough. They believed that the company was heading for trouble if this style of leadership continued. One of the directors asked, "Doesn't this style run the risk of driving off the best workers?" The chairman of the board answered, "We decided to select Ildiko in order to protect the investment of our stockholders. Besides, we have to evaluate a person's leadership style by how effective it is. And she has sure been effective."

1. Why was Marie ineffective in turning the company around?
2. How do you account for Ildiko's results?
3. Do you think that Ildiko should be retained or fired?

THE BOSTON ELECTRONICS COMPANY

The James Donaldson plant of the Boston Electronics Company has been experiencing low productivity and high costs compared to the company's other plants. Richard Fenton, manager of the James Donaldson plant, believes that if costs are to be reduced and productivity increased, employees must be willing to put more effort into their work for the same amount of pay each day.

During a discussion with Fenton about his approach for improving productivity, union leaders at the plant realized that the manager considered his viewpoint to be very logical and rational. The union leaders pointed out to the manager that there had been a large number of employee grievances within the past four months. In addition, most had concerned contractual agreements on overtime work and job descriptions that specify who was qualified to perform certain jobs in the plant. The union leaders noted that since management had done nothing about these grievances, employee morale had worsened. Now there is a high degree of mistrust between the workers and managers, and the union and management.

The plant manager has analyzed the situation and feels that the problem of low productivity is caused by poor leadership and communications between the first-line foremen and the workers. If the first-line foremen could explain management's position to the workers for trying to reduce costs and increase productivity, Fenton feels that the plant's effectiveness would increase. Thus as Fenton sees it, the solution is to train first-line managers to be more supportive and participative in their leadership style. Further, communication between workers could be improved if their spouses were informed of the necessity for higher productivity.

Fenton also feels that his staff must show the rest of the plant that they are concerned about increasing costs. In fact, he is planning to cut top-management salaries by 10 percent and slow down merit and annual pay increases throughout management ranks.

1. Is Fenton's analysis correct? What do you see as the plant's basic problem?
2. Do you feel that Fenton's solution to the problem is reasonable? Would you suggest another approach? If so, what?

REFERENCES

1. R. Stogdill, *Handbook of Leadership: A Survey of Theory and Research* (New York: Free Press/Macmillan, 1974), p. 9.

2. G. Homans, *Social Behavior: Its Elementary Forms* (New York: Harcourt, Brace and World, 1961), p. 286.

3. J. French and B. Raven, "The Bases of Social Power," in *Studies in Social Power,* ed. D. Cartwright (Ann Arbor, Michigan: Institute for Social Research, 1959), pp. 150–167.

4. D. Mechanic, "Sources of Power for Lower Participants in Complex Organizations," *Administrative Science Quarterly* **7** (1962): 352–358.

5. A. Sloan, Jr., *My Years with General Motors* (New York: Macfadden, 1965).

6. For excellent reviews of these various approaches to the study of leadership, *see* R. Stogdill, *Handbook of Leadership: A Survey of Theory and Research* (New York: Free Press/Macmillan, 1974); C. Schriesheim, S. Kerr, "Theories and Measures of Leadership: A Critical Appraisal of Current and Future Directions," in *Leadership: The Cutting Edge,* ed. J. Hunt and L. Larson (Kent, Ohio: Kent State University Press, 1978); and V. Vroom, "Leadership," in *Handbook of Industrial and Organizational Psychology,* ed. M. Dunnette (Chicago: Rand McNally, 1976), pp. 1527–1552.

7. R. Stogdill, "Personal Factors Associated with Leadership," *Journal of Psychology* **25** (1948): 35–71.

8. G. Saunders and J. Stanton, "Personality as an Influencing Factor in Decision Making," *Organizational Behavior and Human Performance* **15** (1976): 241–257; and L. Sank, "Effective and Ineffective Managerial Traits Obtained as Naturalistic Descriptions from Executive Members of a Super-Corporation," *Personnel Psychology* **27** (1974): 423–434.

9. R. White and R. Lippett, "Leader Behavior and Member Reaction in Three 'social climates,'" in *Group Dynamics: Research and Theory,* 3rd ed., ed. D. Cartwright and A. Zander (New York: Harper & Row, 1967), pp. 318–336.

10. This section draws on the literature reviewed by A. Filley, R. House, and S. Kerr, *Managerial Process and Organizational Behavior* (Glenview, Ill.: Scott, Foresman, 1976), pp. 211–239.

11. *Ibid.,* p. 215.

12. A. Korman, "Consideration, Initiating Structure and Organizational Criteria: A Review," *Personnel Psychology* **19** (1966): 349–362; and S. Kerr and C. Schriesheim, " 'Consideration, Initiating Structure and Organizational Criteria: An Update of Korman's 1966 Review," *Personnel Psychology* **27** (1974): 555–568.

13. R. House and T. Mitchell, "Path-Goal Theory of Leadership," *Journal of Contemporary Business* **3** (1974): 81–97.

14. Filley, House, and Kerr, *op. cit.*, p. 215.

15. N. Maier, *Problem Solving and Creativity in Individuals and Groups* (Belmont, Calif.: Brooks/Cole, 1970); and T. Mitchell, "Motivation and Participation: An Integration," *Academy of Management Journal* **16** (1973): 160–179.

16. R. House, "Leader Initiating Structure and Subordinate Performance, Satisfaction and Motivation: A Review and a Theoretical Interpretation," unpublished working paper, 1974.

17. S. Kerr, C. Schriesheim, C. Murphy, and R. Stogdill, "Toward a Contingency Theory of Leadership Based upon the Consideration and Initiating Structure Literature," *Organizational Behavior and Human Performance* **12** (1974): 62–82; T. Ruble, "Effects of One's Locus of Control and the Opportunity to Participate in Planning," *Organizational Behavior and Human Performance* **16** (1976): 63–73; and A. Abdel-Halim and K. Rowland, "Some Personality Determinants of the Effects of Participation: A Further Investigation," *Personnel Psychology* **29** (1976): 41–55.

18. C. Schriesheim, R. House, and S. Kerr, "Leader Initiating Structure: A Reconciliation of Discrepant Research Results and Some Empirical Evidence," *Organizational Behavior and Human Performance* **15** (1976): 310–311.

19. Kerr, Schriesheim, Murphy, and Stogdill, *op. cit.*; and House, *op. cit.*

20. F. Fiedler and M. Chemers, *Leadership and Effective Management* (Glenview, Ill.: Scott, Foresman, 1974).

21. A. Ashour, "The Contingency Model of Leader Effectiveness: An Evaluation," *Organizational Behavior and Human Performance* **9** (1972): 339–355; and J. Stinson, and L. Tracy, "Some Disturbing Characteristics of the LPC Score," *Personnel Psychology* **27** (1974): 477–486.

22. R. House, "A Path-Goal Theory of Leader Effectiveness," *Administrative Science Quarterly* **16** (1971): 321–338.

23. K. Downey, J. Sheridan, and J. Slocum, "The Path-Goal Theory of Leadership: A Longitudinal Analysis," *Organizational Behavior and Human Performance* **16** (1976): 156–176; and C. Schriesheim and M. VonGlinow, "The Path-Goal Theory of Leadership: A Theoretical and Empirical Analysis," *Academy of Management Journal* **20** (September 1977).

24. S. Kerr, "Substitutes for Leadership: Their Meaning and Measurement." Paper presented at the Eighth Annual Conference, American Institute for Decision Sciences, San Francisco, November 1976.

25. S. Kerr, "On the Folly of Rewarding A, While Hoping for B," *Academy of Management Journal* **18** (1975): 770–771.

13

13

Group Process

Managerial styles
Philosophies
Contingencies
Perceptions
Individual problems
Interpersonal communi-
cations

Chapter 10

Motivation
Needs
Satisfiers and dis-
satisfiers
Expectancies and con-
tingencies
Management by objectives
Job enrichment

Chapter 11

Leadership
Power and influence
Traits
Contingency models
Substitutes for leadership

Chapter 12

Groups
Roles
Models
Contingencies
Procedures for group
problem solving

Chapter 13

Conflict
Contingency model
Role conflict
Interpersonal conflict
Intergroup conflict

Chapter 14

The objectives of this chapter are to:

discuss the nature of formal and informal groups and the positive and negative viewpoints often expressed toward them;

present two basic group models that can help you understand how groups operate;

show you how to improve problem-solving processes within groups;

demonstrate the effects of group size, cohesiveness, and norms on group performance;

emphasize that any one group's behavior needs to be analyzed and understood in terms of certain contingencies, e.g., group size, norms, and type of technology.

"Since I became a supervisor, I've had to attend management meetings. It took me a while to get the hang of things. I noticed that everyone has to say at least one joke—usually an ethnic joke—and then when all the jokes are over, we can all sit down and get on with the business. So I went along with it, and now I mark down an ethnic joke or two before a meeting, and when the meeting comes, I'll tell my joke—kind of a ticket of admission—so that I can sit down and get to work.

"There's a lot of back-slapping and forced phony friendship at these meetings. It's meaningless, and I wish they'd skip all that and get down to business, but I go along with it and shake hands and 'buddy' everyone to prove that I'm a regular guy."

These comments suggest the focus of this chapter—groups and their effects on individuals and organizations. The overall objective of this chapter is to develop your conceptual skills in understanding groups within organizations and to help you in being an effective group member and leader of a group.

As you read this chapter, keep in mind that business firms represent only one type of organization in which groups operate. Many of our comments are also relevant for managers operating in small groups within governmental, educational, religious, and voluntary organizations.

NATURE OF GROUPS

There are several ways of thinking about the nature of groups. Let's start by considering the major ways by which groups differ from organizations. First, a group is usually within a physical space that permits the members to hear and see one another. Second, each member can usually verbally communicate with every other member. Third, a group does not have many hierarchical levels found in an organization.[1]

These characteristics are necessary, but not sufficient, conditions for the existence of a group, however. For example, if five strangers start playing basketball together, they probably still do not constitute a group. A group exists if the members are mutually aware of one another and perceive themselves to be members of a group.[2] Thus we can define a *group as two or more individuals who come into personal, meaningful, and purposeful contact on a relatively continuing basis.* If five individuals play basketball together on a continuing basis, share a common goal of winning games, communicate freely among themselves, and the like, they are a group.

It has been estimated that the average individual belongs to six groups.[3] At work, the individual might be a member of two or three groups. The first might be made up of one's immediate superior and fellow workers; the second, of the people with whom one interacts on a social basis. For example, such an informal social group might be the five or six workers who sit together every day during breaks to eat and play cards and who are members of the same bowling or golf league.

But so far we have not said anything about whether the group is effective or ineffective. An effective group is likely to have the following characteristics:

1. It knows why it exists.
2. It has an environment in which its work can be accomplished.

3. It has guidelines or procedures for making decisions.
4. It has established conditions under which the members can make their contributions.
5. It has achieved communication among its members.
6. The members have learned to receive and give help to one another.
7. The members have learned to deal with conflict within the group.
8. Members have learned to diagnose their processes and improve their own functioning.[4]

The degree to which a group is weak in one or more of these characteristics provides a rough measure of the relative immaturity and possible ineffectiveness of the group.

Formal and Informal Groups

There are several ways of classifying groups, but here we will simply distinguish between formal and informal groups. *Formal groups* have goals specifically related to achieving the goals of the organization. Formal groups are usually part of the formal structure of the organization and are created to accomplish specific goals of the organization.

Informal groups, on the other hand, develop out of the activities, interactions, and sentiments of individuals. Membership in informal groups is normally voluntary. The purposes of informal groups are not necessarily related to the formal organizational goals. Nonetheless, the formal organization often has considerable influence on the development of informal groups. Some of the contingency factors from the formal organization include the physical layout of work, the leadership practices of superiors, and the type of technology used. For example, the move of a department from one building to another is likely to have an impact on the membership of informal groups that existed before the move occurred. Or, a new manager taking over a department might tell the members to "shape up or face being shipped out." With this type of threat, the informal groups may band together in a united front to try and protect themselves from this new manager.

Views of Groups

Some managers see groups as providing a number of benefits to the organization. Thus groups might increase employee creativity and problem solving, stimulate work motivation when the group members accept the goals of the organization, and decrease turnover and absenteeism because of the satisfactions the individuals experience from their group membership.[5] However, some managers believe that close-knit groups have undesirable effects on the organization. These managers often view groups as a potential source of antiestablishment power, as a means for holding back information when the group does not identify with organizational goals, and as a means of pressuring individuals to hold down the amount of work produced.

Groups may also be considered from the perspective of their members. Thus groups can provide several desirable outcomes, e.g., security and protection for members. Some groups enforce production quotas on each member, fearing that higher management might use the outstanding worker as a standard for output and that increased production might lead to some workers being laid off. A group can also help an individual define and test reality through the corrective or reinforcing feedback provided by other members. The all too common belief in the United States that higher productivity will work against the interests of workers is kept alive and enforced by some informal groups within organizations. Third, a group may provide an individual with higher-level need satisfactions and serve as a means for helping the individual to acquire needed skills, knowledge, and attitudes.

It is also common to hear of the undesirable effects that groups can have on individual members. These undesirable effects usually fall into two categories. First, a group may be able to manipulate rewards and punishments and thus pressure members to conform to its standards of behavior. For example, in 1976 a Detroit policeman quit his job rather than accept bribes when stopping people for traffic violations. After a bribe had been offered and refused three times, he would arrest the party for attempting to bribe an officer. He told the press that the harassment and pressure for doing this from his fellow policemen was so intense that he had to quit the force. Second, a group may restrict an individual's freedom by filtering and evaluating the ways by which these needs can be satisfied. To obtain esteem from other members, some gangs require each individual to engage in various types of antisocial and possibly violent acts. Work groups have been known to ridicule individuals for not conforming to their standards of "acceptable" output. Such treatment may threaten the individual's physiological, security, and social needs.

The specific viewpoints of groups mentioned for managers and members may hold true in some group situations but not others. It is inappropriate to stereotype groups in organizations as always desirable or undesirable. From a managerial point of view, it is probably best to consider ways of minimizing the undesirable effect of informal groups rather than engaging in the futile task of trying to eliminate them.

INDIVIDUALS IN GROUPS

Entering Groups

In Chapter 10 (see Table 10.1), we discussed the major classes of problems experienced by individuals entering a new organization or group, the types of feelings these problems may generate, and the major types of reactions that may be stimulated by these feelings. These major classes of problems pertain to identity, control and influence, needs and goals, and acceptance and intimacy. Naturally, not every individual who joins a group experiences these types of problems or feelings. The intensity of the problems and feelings, as well as the types of responses, will depend on contingency factors, such as the individual's personality and the relative importance of the group to the individual. An understanding of the problems encountered in entering groups should help you to: (1) diagnose and take corrective action with respect to your own behavior when entering new groups; (2) understand the emotional problems and behavioral patterns that are likely to exist and need to be worked through in new groups before you and other members can effectively engage

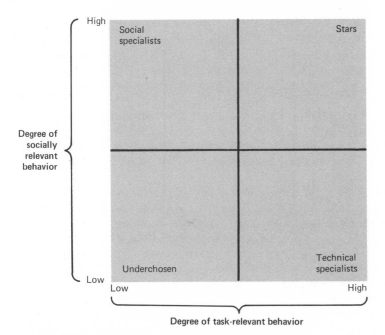

Fig. 13.1. Roles of individuals in groups. (Adapted from
D. Moment and A. Zalenznik, *Role Development and Interpersonal Competence: An Experimental Study of Role Performance in Problem-Solving Groups,* Boston: Division of Research, Graduate School of Business Administration, Harvard
University, 1963, pp. 10–18.)

in task issues; and (3) understand the need for special support and encouragement new members require when they enter well-formed groups.

The problems of a newly formed group or of adding a new member to a
group have special implications for the leaders of those groups. A manager
(formal leader) of a work group can help reduce these emotional problems.
First, she or he can give the group an opportunity to work out its emotional
problems rather than immediately imposing or legislating the supposed solution.[6] Second, the manager might make special efforts to provide entering
members of a work group, such as new or transferred employees, with a sense
of belonging by introducing them to the other members, inviting them out to
lunch with others, and extending a specific invitation to chat at the end of the
week. Third, the manager should realize that the group's productivity might
temporarily decline until the emotional problems associated with integrating
the new members of a group are worked through. Fourth, when appropriate,
the manager can enlarge the members' area of free activity (see Fig. 10.2)
through the constructive use of disclosure and feedback.

Role Orientations

Once individuals have become full-fledged members of a group, they generally act out different roles. Figure 13.1 presents a framework for describing

and analyzing these different types of role behavior in groups. This framework was developed from a study of middle- and upper-level managers in problem-solving groups.[7] One variable is the degree to which the individuals are engaged in task-relevant behavior; another is their socially relevant behavior. Cross-classifying these two variables results in four role types, as shown in Fig. 13.1.

Stars, who rate high on both social and task behaviors, are active group members and exhibit a variety of behaviors. Stars let others know where they stand and show open and honest involvement without appearing too anxious. They address other members personally and neither avoid nor are excessive in task or social behaviors.

Technical specialists avoid confronting social and emotional problems and display little interpersonal expression, being neither hostile toward nor supportive of other group members. For the most part, they are relatively withdrawn and quiet. When they do speak, they tend to elaborate at length on the task. Their small amount of social contact is attempted through joking that seems to meet their personal rather than group needs.

Social specialists concentrate on social behaviors by showing a great deal of feeling and support for others. They avoid disagreeing, criticizing, and expressing aggression toward other group members and are interested in keeping the group operating as one "happy family."

Underchosen participants are uncommitted to the group and tend to show interest only in their personal needs. They are relatively serious and are the most aggressive and hostile of the four types, but not the quietest of the four types. They participate more than the technical and social specialists, but less than the stars. Their perceived lack of importance to the other group members is due more to the ineffectiveness of their actions than to an "invisibility" factor. Stars are relatively satisfied with the decisions reached by the groups; the reverse is true for the other types. However, there is little difference among the four role types as to their satisfaction with the procedures and ways in which the groups operate.

These findings have several implications for managers. First, it is highly unlikely that all individuals can or will play the same role in groups. Some individuals prefer to be technical specialists; others, to be social specialists. What role group members play is a function of their personality, communication style, level of need satisfaction, and leadership style. Second, this framework provides a useful diagnostic tool for the manager when a group is operating poorly. Is the group overwhelmed by underachievers, task specialists, or social specialists? Domination by any of these three roles may lead to ineffectiveness in problem solving. The probability of a group's effectiveness should increase as more members are capable of performing the star role. Third, the manager may use this framework to gain insight about his or her own behavior in work groups.

If the manager wonders why no one ever questions his or her decisions and discussions are short-lived, it could be that the manager is playing the underchosen role. In this role, the need to be aggressive, dominant, and assertive may hinder group communication.

BASIC GROUP MODELS

Among the many models for describing and analyzing groups, two widely used for considering groups within organizations are Homans's systems model and Bales's Interaction Process Analysis (IPA) model. Both models: (1) provide at least partial explanations of why people act as they do within groups; (2) suggest that groups are different from and more than the sum of their members; (3) provide managers with a framework for diagnosing group processes within their organizations; (4) consider contingency factors likely to affect the processes and outputs of groups; and (5) suggest how groups are likely to change over time.

Homans's Systems Model

This model was first presented in full form in 1950 and was modified and developed further in a book Homans published in 1961.[8] His concepts are few in number and as close as possible to common observations of group life. The model consists of two major parts—the internal system and the external system. Of course, these distinctions are relative, and the systems are interdependent. This model has most often been used to analyze and predict the behavior of informal groups. However, it is also relevant to formal groups that meet our definition of a group.

INTERNAL SYSTEM

The internal system develops from the external system, which represents the "givens" that existed before the group came into being. For example, the New York Jets football team might draft and keep a total of ten new football players each year. Most of them are likely to form one or more new informal groups. Several may also become members of established informal groups. In this situation, the informal groups would probably not have developed if there was no formal organization (i.e., New York Jets).

More important, the formal organization of the New York Jets is likely to influence the issues of concern to these informal groups and their very survival. Management may decide to cut four of the six members of a particular informal group because of their playing ability, effectively "killing" that group. However, once the internal system is established, it is likely to act on the external system as well. For example, if the new football players on the New York Jets feel that they are being unfairly treated by one of the coaches, they might join together and present *their* complaint to the head coach. A favorable response would be an example of the internal system (a group of unhappy players) affecting the external system (Jet management).

The basic variables in the internal system are activities, interactions, sentiments, and norms. These variables are interrelated (i.e., a change in one will result in a change in the others). Groups need to be considered as systems and not simply as a sum of member behaviors. It is the interrelationships of the members that substantially influence their effectiveness as a group. The relative power of the internal system (compared to that of the external system) on individual member behavior can vary widely.

Activities are what individuals do to or with other individuals or with inanimate objects (machines). Within business organizations, task activities required by one's position are likely to be dominant in terms of the expenditure of time. The civil engineer is likely to be most concerned with the typography, soil conditions, and site preparation for the construction team. Socially relevant activities, such as playing cards or pitching pennies, may be important to the group as well.

Interaction, the starting actions and the following reactions between two or more individuals, is essentially concerned with the pattern of communication between group members. This variable can be considered through such questions as:

1. With whom do the individuals have relationships?
2. How often do the members interact, e.g., talk to one another?
3. How long do they interact?
4. Who starts the interaction?

Sentiments, a broad category, can include current feelings (such as anger, happiness, sadness) as well as deep-seated values (such as the meaning of equality, freedom, courage).

Norms usually develop out of the group's functioning. A norm is a standard that is widely shared by members of the group. It sets specific expectations or limits for the members on what they "ought to do" under certain circumstances. Norms are quite comparable to the decision rules of an organization. Work groups often have norms defining how much and how little output of work is acceptable for their members.

As suggested in Fig. 13.2, activities, sentiments, interactions, and norms can interrelate in a variety of ways. Some of these basic interrelationships can be summed up as follows:

> The more frequently persons interact with another, the stronger their sentiments of friendship for one another are apt to be. . . . Persons who feel sentiments of liking for one another will express those sentiments in activities over and above the activities of the external system. . . . Persons who interact with one another frequently are more like one another in their activities than they are like other persons with whom they interact less frequently.[9]

The pattern of sentiments, activities, and interactions is likely to differ for each group member. These differences form the group's *social structure,* which is determined by such factors as the relative contribution of each member to the group's goals, the degree to which each member accepts the norms of the

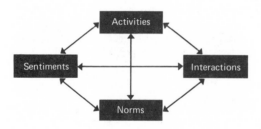

Fig. 13.2. Internal system of Homans's model.

group, and the personal characteristics of the members. An analysis of a group's social structure requires an evaluation of the differential ranking (or statuses) assigned to members, group leadership, and communication patterns. Some of the relationships among sentiments, activities, and interactions in relation to the internal social structure are suggested in the following statements:

> The higher the rank of a person within a group, the more nearly his/her activities conform to the norms of the group. . . . The higher a person's social rank, the wider will be the range of his/her interactions. A chef in a restaurant usually communicates to more employees than does a waiter/waitress. . . . A person of higher social rank than another originates interaction for the latter more often than the latter originates interaction for him/her. . . . The sentiments of the leaders of a group carry greater weight than those of the followers in establishing a social ranking.[10]

EXTERNAL SYSTEM

The second part of Homans's model is the external system, the "givens" that existed before the group was formed. These "givens" would likely continue to exist if the group should cease to function. For work groups, these "givens" might include such contingency factors as the values of the members, the interactions and activities required by the technology, the physical setting, and the structure and control system of the formal organization. The external system of work groups, compared to that of gangs or friendship groups, is likely to be relatively explicit.

Technology as a Contingency. The relative degree of freedom of groups in organizations can vary greatly. The type of technology (i.e., unit or small batch, mass production, or continuous process) is likely to be an important contingency factor influencing the relative freedom of the group. In unit-production technology, the firm is engaged in the custom manufacturing of individual items, with each item built to the customer's specifications. Since the firm manufactures different items, standardization of procedures and work flows is difficult to establish. In mass-production technology, firms are engaged in producing a large volume of goods that are either identical or so similar that it is practical for management to build the technology and work flow around these particular items (e.g., automobile assembly). Continuous-process technology demands that activities be performed constantly. Thus a chemical plant cannot shut down without incurring heavy start-up costs. The continuous-process technology is also distinct in that the worker does not handle the material itself, except for occasional testing, but instead monitors the work flow and diagnoses how the process is progressing from automatic meters and charts. The workers need to cooperate in preventing breakdowns, but once one does occur, they need to move quickly as a team in getting the process started again. As suggested in Fig. 13.3, groups functioning within a unit- or small-batch technology have a greater potential for the formation of highly autonomous groups than do those in mass-production technology, because the workers have a high degree of control over the pace of their work, how their tasks are performed, and often need to interact with others to get the job done.

With the mass-production technology, groups are likely to have little autonomy and therefore scant opportunity for developing much of an internal

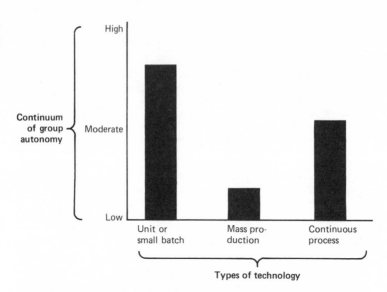

Fig. 13.3. Technology as a contingency affecting group autonomy.

system.[11] This is because workers must stay at their work stations and perform their own individual operations on the materials that are continually passing by them on the line at a fairly constant speed. The opportunities to interact with fellow workers on the line may also be made difficult by the high noise levels and distance between workers. Finally, the degrees of autonomy of groups in a continuous-process technology (e.g., an oil refinery) can be somewhat greater. With this technology, work-group members are highly interdependent and must communicate with one another on a continuing basis. Continuous-process technologies might permit giving the work group considerable control over the allocation of certain tasks, including self-selection of members (after initial requirements established by management have been met) and election of a leader by the group members. To management, who performs what tasks is not as important as encouraging workers to act as a team in keeping the process going, preventing breakdowns, and restoring production as soon as possible when a breakdown does occur. Here, the group leader's role might be limited to coordinating the tasks assigned to the group, leading discussions requiring group decisions, and serving as the group's spokesperson with management.[12]

The actions of a group can be understood and predicted only by analyzing both the internal and external systems. Homans's model is a useful framework for pulling together a number of observations and findings about groups. For the practicing manager, its main contribution may be in providing a mental map for understanding and predicting the behavior of groups with which he or she is involved. The statements illustrating the relationships among sentiments, interactions, activities, and social structure should be useful in suggesting the patterns of behavior to be expected in groups. For example, a manager who issues an order that is inconsistent with a group norm (such as changing the dress code of employees) may well face a united group to have the order changed. Or, if a manager tries to change or eliminate established interaction or communication patterns, the consequences may range from complaints to increased absenteeism or turnover.

On a more positive note, the manager may serve more in a group leadership role by encouraging the establishment of group norms that reinforce the formal goals of the department. Where there is high task interdependency and a great need for cooperation among group members, the manager may increase the use of group rewards rather than emphasize individual rewards. These rewards could be in the form of praise and recognition to the group as a whole or even a compensation system based on group outputs.

APPLICATION

The Homans systems model can be applied to a case study of an industrial work group, based on a participant observation study of a small work group on the night shift in a food-processing plant.[13] This case focuses on the changes in the internal system over 15 months, especially on the impact of the external system (i.e., management-initiated changes) on the internal system. This study is somewhat unique because it started very soon after the plant was open and before informal groups had been formed.

External System. The factory, which employed about 600 people, was the newest and most modern of a large national food corporation. The plant was non-union, but the pay and fringe benefits were better than comparable union plants in the same area. The group normally consisted of 12 individuals who worked in the Sanitation Department. This department had a total of about 50–65 individuals and was divided into three work groups. The primary task of the department was to clean all of the equipment, floors, windows, and walls in the plant. The jobs were divided into two basic categories. The higher job category involved disassembling equipment for cleaning, washing it, and reassembling it. The lower job category involved more washing tasks, including washing floors and windows. Eligibility and assignment to the higher job category was based on seniority. The main difference between the two job categories was the amount of technical knowledge and skill required to disassemble and reassemble the product pipelines and other equipment. The lower job category could be learned in one day; the higher job category, about two weeks.

Emergence of Internal System. The new hires of the group were relatively similar—white native-born American males under 30 years of age. But as they began to interact, the members became differentiated on an informal basis. Initially, these differences showed up in personality characteristics, background experiences, and nonwork social positions. Some of the members had military experiences, others had traveled, one became known for his heavy drinking on weekends and another for his self-proclaimed sexual exploits. Over time, the relative skill and speed in job performance became the primary factor for placing individuals in the developing social structure of the group. Gradually, a dominant shared norm of the group became the speed in which one could perform his job. There was a continuing effort to improve their speed, and members would even race each other to get finished. Most members could eventually finish their work 30 minutes to an hour before quitting time. In brief, speed in task performance became a major group norm and the most important factor in the informal ranking of members in the social structure.

Fast workers were given high group status; slow workers, low status. Quality of work also emerged as an important basis of informal ranking. A reward for the speedy (and quality) workers was the "free" time at the end of the shift, when workers would relax and engage in social activities. The foreman did not object to this so long as all of the work was done properly and the members didn't make it *too* obvious. At the end of the work shift, rewards were provided for conforming to the group's norms or punishments for failure to conform. Those who finished early often teased or joked (in a friendly way) about those not yet finished. During this first period, the internal system encouraged a fairly high commitment to the job management wanted done and also provided for the social needs of the members. This period lasted about six months and was characterized by a rather lenient and permissive supervisory style.

Changes by the External System. After this first period, several major changes in the external system disrupted the internal system and eventually led to a new internal system. The first change, supervisory style, resulted from the findings of a time-and-motion study conducted on all jobs in the plant. During this study, the workers continued enthusiastically to try to complete their work as fast as possible. As a result, top management pressured the immediate supervisor to become less permissive and more authoritarian. For example, at the end of the shift, the foreman would assign miscellaneous special projects (e.g., wiping grease off electric motors, scrubbing water hoses, cleaning light fixtures, etc.) to those workers who finished their regular jobs early. This change dramatically disrupted the informal social life of the group. The extra work projects were perceived as menial busywork and extremely distasteful. The workers soon realized that speedy work was costly rather than rewarding. Workers in the higher job category also complained bitterly that their rank was no longer associated with the privileges of autonomy and freedom from busywork.

Following this change in leadership style, two technical changes were imposed by the external system. One change, developed by the Quality Control Department, permitted considerable work simplification in performing certain tasks. The second change involved the installation of new equipment, which was to be cleaned by one person. Previously at least two individuals were required to work together to clean equipment. However, there were no time-and-motion studies conducted for determining how long it should take to clean this equipment. The supervisor simply determined the time requirements by observing and questioning the workers. In responding to the supervisor, the workers had previously banded together and agreed to define the time requirements in the maximum terms they thought the supervisor would accept. The workers' consensus was that the cleaning of each piece of this new equipment would take between one and two hours, depending on the condition of the machines. In practice, each machine could usually be cleaned within 30 minutes. Through this collective effort, the group was able to regain some of the autonomy (freedom) it had previously possessed.

New Internal System. From these informal adaptations to the external system, there emerged a new primary norm and ranking system within the group. This new norm emphasized the need to pace the work so that it would be completed just before quitting time. This new norm was associated with the excessively fast and excessively slow workers being given low informal status. Either of these patterns of working was expected to attract unfavorable attention from the supervisor. Most of the fast workers in the first period successfully adapted by slowing down their pace and retaining their high status.

The new informal patterns of the group could not provide nearly so well for the purely social-emotional and recreational needs of the group. Horseplay in the group was practically eliminated, and the lively and boisterous conversations involving the entire group took place less often. The decline in morale and satisfaction was apparent.

Summary. This study clearly illustrates several of the generalities made by Homans as part of the discussion of his model.

1. If individuals continue over time to be together in a common situation, they develop their activities, interactions, and sentiments beyond that which is required by the environment for sheer survival. This gives rise to an internal system, or informal culture and social structure.
2. Freedom for the development of the internal system in a task group is positively related to fulfillment of members' social-emotional needs, group morale and individual satisfaction, and commitment to the task.
3. Changes in the external system of a group generate changes in its internal system. The external system refers to the activities, interactions, and sentiments imposed by the environment and required for the group's survival.
4. There is a close relationship between a group's internal system and external contingency factors, such as organizational structure, formal leadership practices, and technology.

One obvious implication of this case study for management practice is that individuals in industrial work groups may exert a greater effort to fulfill management's goals if they are allowed some degree of autonomy (consistent with formal job requirements). Conversely, if group autonomy is severely reduced, members may well reduce their commitment to management's goals. However, the groups may continue to perform satisfactorily, but with minimal commitment.

Bales's Interaction Process Analysis

The second major model for discussion is Bales's Interaction Process Analysis (IPA). The major goal of IPA is to provide a framework for observing and analyzing the process of problem solving within groups. By "process," we mean the methods, steps, or operations and their interrelations.[14] Since formal and informal groups carry out significant amounts of important problem-solving activities, IPA is a useful model for any student of management. Furthermore, group problem solving within an organization is especially likely when the problems are novel, unique, or nonroutine.

IPA considers six basic problem areas confronting all small groups: *communication* (giving or receiving orientation), *evaluation* (giving or asking for opinions), *control* (giving or asking for suggestions), *decision* (agreeing or disagreeing), *tension reduction* (showing tension release or tension), and *reintegration* (showing solidarity or antagonism). These problem areas are dealt with by classifying each act of communication and interaction within the group into one of twelve observational categories, or acts. An *act* is any behavior of an individual, verbal or nonverbal (e.g., wringing one's hands, tapping a foot, smiling), that is communicated to at least one other individual in the group. For example, showing agreement may be illustrated by nodding of the head or simply by the statement "I agree with you."

FRAMEWORK

The overall framework of IPA is shown in Fig. 13.4. The *task area* is concerned with both questions and answers, whereas the *social-emotional area* is concerned with positive and negative reactions. As a formal tool for observing group process, IPA requires the individual to record (typically on a moving tape) who communicates with whom in terms of the 12 types of interaction. The observer does not focus on the content or subject matter being communicated. This suggests two possible limitations of IPA. First, it deliberately ignores the content and quality of the interactions, which may be critical for an evaluation of the group's effectiveness. Second, each act is recorded in a single category, though it may actually be serving several purposes. At a meeting, the billing department manager might say, "Sales were not up by 10 percent in December, but by only 5 percent, according to our records." This comment supplies information as well as refutes what another individual has said.

BENEFITS

Despite these limitations, a number of findings obtained through the use of IPA are of potential value to the manager.

Channels of Communication. The quantity of communication intake and output tends to be unequal between group members, even when they are of equal formal status. Despite the tendency toward centralization of communication in small groups (three to seven members), the difference becomes especially pronounced as group size increases. With increased size, a large proportion of the communication tends to be directed to a single member, such as an informal or formal leader. In addition, the comments by the leader increasingly become directed to the group as a whole rather than to specific members within the group.[15] This is probably the result of the leader's not wanting to show favoritism or be accused of picking on specific individuals.

Centralization of communication may become even greater when the group consists of members with unequal formal status, e.g., a manager and sub-

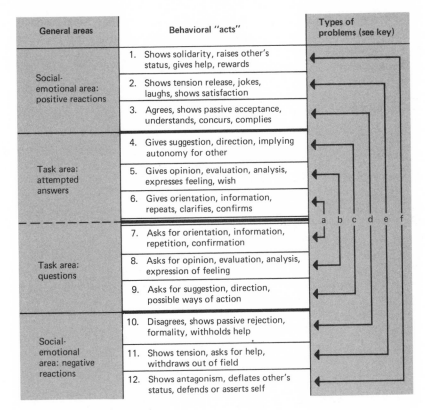

Fig. 13.4. Bales's IPA system. (R. Bales, *Interaction Process Analysis*, Cambridge, Mass.: Addison-Wesley, 1950, p. 9. Reprinted by permission of the author.)

ordinates. A manager can probably "open up" the communication by providing positive social-emotional reactions and minimizing negative ones, e.g., antagonism, tension, or disagreement. In terms of the task area, the manager can probably reduce the tendency for communications to centralize around him or her by focusing on questions (i.e., asking for suggestions, opinions, or orientations), with relatively less emphasis on providing answers (i.e., giving suggestions, opinions, or orientations). These suggestions assume that the manager sincerely desires participation by the subordinates and that the purpose of the group session is to engage in some problem-solving activity rather than just to exchange information.

A manager should not bring a large number of individuals—20 or more—together if he or she wants each of them to actively participate in a problem-solving activity through a group process. The manager who does so should not become disappointed if the interactions are dominated by a half dozen or so individuals. A possible alternative is to break the large group into subgroups of seven or so individuals. Each subgroup might consider the same basic problem. After a certain time, the subgroups could come back together, with a representative from each reporting its findings. The ideas and findings from the subgroups might then become the basis for further interaction in the larger group. This technique increases the probability of inputs and interactions by all members.

Group Phases. Bales found that as a group engages in problem-solving activity, it goes through several distinct phases: Groups tend to move in their interaction from relative emphasis upon problems of orientation to problems of evaluation and subsequently to problems of control; and that concurrent with these transitions, the relative frequencies of both negative reactions and positive reactions tend to increase.[16] These findings are shown in Fig. 13.5.

In an effective group, there are usually two positive reactions to one negative reaction.[17] This provides the basis for showing the relative emphasis on positive reactions in Fig. 13.5. The group starts with a task emphasis on prob-

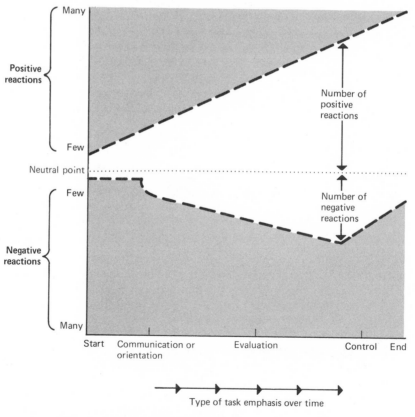

Fig. 13.5. Phases in group problem solving.

lems of communication and orientation, moves to a focus on problems of evaluation, and concludes with a concern for problems of control. After a group reaches a decision, there is likely to be a further surge in positive reactions and a corresponding dropoff in negative reactions, which results in re-integration.

These phases in problem-solving groups are most valid if the members have similar goals and do not have fixed, preconceived ideas about how the problem(s) should be solved. In contrast, when members of management and the union come together, there may be a much greater initial emphasis on negative reactions and less positive reactions than indicated in Fig. 13.5; the two groups are often perceived as being in conflict. For example, the strike by the maids, waiters and waitresses, and doormen during the holiday season in Miami Beach in 1976 was over improved economic conditions. The initial reaction by the management of the hotels was that they could not meet the union's demands and still maintain their place in the market. Thus there was a high level of negative reactions between the parties from the very start of the group problem-solving process to end the strike.

If the goal preferences of the group are basically compatible, these findings have several managerial implications. First, the manager needs to allow time for the expression of feelings and questions. The group may feel that a decision was "dictated" to them if the percentage of "answers" rises too high or comes too soon. On the other hand, the avoidance of attempted answers may lead the members to believe that the session was a waste of time. Second, a manager should be permissive, up to a point, toward negative and positive reactions. The manager can overcorrect on either side by stating: "Let's keep feelings out of this"; "There is no need to be upset"; or "Let's not have any more goofing off here." A manager needs to avoid the extremes; a mutual admiration situation (in which there is an unwillingness to express any disagreement) may be as unproductive as one which becomes a name-calling session. Task and social-emotional acts are interdependent, and both are necessary for effective group functioning. The average ratio for many problem-solving groups is about two task-oriented acts for each social-emotional act.

Different Roles. Bales's approach has provided insight into the different roles individuals might take on within problem-solving groups. As a group develops, *two* leadership roles often develop. The *task-oriented leader,* in Bales's framework, concentrates mainly on the problems of orientation, evaluation, and control, as in the *instrumental* leadership style discussed in Chapter 12. The *social-emotional leader* concentrates primarily on problems of decision, tension reduction, and reintegration, as in the *participative* style discussed in Chapter 12. In satisfied groups, the task and social-emotional leaders complement and support each other. Because of the potentially competing requirements of the task and social-emotional functions, it may be difficult for one individual to act as the leader in both roles. In Bales's view, there could be an effective group without any members being classified as "stars" (see Fig. 13.1).

The implications of the two leadership roles are twofold. A manager filling the task-oriented role might be supportive of a subordinate who begins to perform the social-emotional leadership role rather than become anxious and defensive over the prospect of "shared" leadership. Second, the manager should not assume that by virtue of formal position, he or she must always dominate as the task leader. If another individual has more expertise about the problem being considered by the group, the manager might serve more as the facilitator and coordinator within the group session. This view implies that leadership in a group can be dynamic and shifting.

GROUP PROBLEM SOLVING

So far in this chapter, we have suggested that the existence of groups in organizations is inevitable. We also implied that one of the major purposes of groups within organizations is to deal with problems. The manager usually has some discretion over whether to use a group rather than an individual approach to problem solving. We now turn to a discussion of the contingencies under which each approach is appropriate and the effectiveness of groups for problem solving. The forces operating in groups for effective problem solving can be assets, liabilities, or contingent, depending on the effectiveness of the members and the leader(s).[18]

Assets

GREATER KNOWLEDGE

A group's information and knowledge should be greater than that of any one member's. If the group's members have varying sources of expertise related to their problem, each person might be able to fill in the knowledge gaps of other individuals. Thus, for example, the needed decisions on the design of a product are likely to require group meetings among individuals from such fields as marketing (customer acceptance), engineering (design), production (production feasibility), accounting (cost considerations), personnel (labor requirements), legal (safety and patent consideration), etc.

MORE APPROACHES

Individuals tend to become "tunnel-visioned" in their thinking and approach to a problem; that is, they regard only their own part of the problem as important. Although all individuals in a group may have the same problem, their interaction and communication can stimulate the search for more alternatives. By challenging one another's thinking, members of a problem-solving group may arrive at a decision that takes into account all viewpoints, i.e., a workable compromise.

INCREASED ACCEPTANCE

Group problem solving, by its very nature, may lead to increased acceptance of the decision by the members and thus more effective implementation of the solution. A person who has had a chance to influence the group's decision may have a greater commitment to that decision and assume responsibility for making it work. Thus a high-quality solution "handed down from on high" may not be as effective as a low-quality solution arrived at more democratically. This conclusion is somewhat dependent, however, on the relative power of the group to resist and/or implement the solution. Thus the individual who solves the problem has the additional task of persuading others to accept it.

The relative effectiveness of participation is far from clear. It is clear that a simple claim that increased participation in decision making is always needed or desirable is so sweeping that it can't be proved or disproved without considering various contingency factors.[19]

BETTER UNDERSTANDING

An individual who problem solves alone usually needs to communicate the decision reached to others. Often, organizational problems are caused by the inadequate communication of decisions from managers to their subordinates. But if the individuals who must implement the decision have participated in making it, the probability of failures in communication may be reduced. Since the individuals saw or participated in the development of the solution, they are more likely to have a firm understanding of it and the surrounding factors. Of course, this asset may hold only so long as the individuals have some expertise to offer or power to influence the implementation of the chosen alternative.

Liabilities

OVERCONFORMITY

Because of social pressures for consensus and friendship and avoidance of disagreement, groups can become instruments for maintaining conformity. Conformity is especially a problem when the solution should be based primarily on facts rather than on feelings or wishes. Thus agreement on and acceptance of a decision by group members are not necessarily related to the quality of the decision reached. If a group is advisory or is used as part of the management system, the manager might serve as a check on the group's decisions or might encourage the group members to engage in a diagnosis and analysis of their group processes. (Some ways of doing this are discussed in Chapter 15.)

DOMINATION BY AN INDIVIDUAL

The effectiveness of groups can be reduced by allowing one individual to dominate the interactions through a high volume of communication, persuasive ability, or persistence (tiring the opposition). These factors are not necessarily related to problem-solving ability. The best problem solver may be unable to upgrade and influence the group's decisions, having been cut off from the group. This problem may be increased when a group has an appointed leader who believes that it is his or her duty to control the group and provide the major input to its decision. Managers need to be aware of their possible domination of the group.

GOAL DISPLACEMENT

One major goal of a problem-solving group is to create an effective solution. To accomplish this, the members need to consider alternatives. But some members may become zealous proponents of an alternative, attempting to win support rather than find an optimal solution. This type of goal displacement can lower the quality of the decision, and it would probably be desirable to start over again by generating alternatives and avoid, for the time being, evaluating them. If the evaluation is clouded by the lack of facts or controversy over them, the group session can be disbanded until the needed clarifications can be made. (Other suggestions are provided in the next chapter.)

Contingencies in Group Problem Solving

ROLE OF LEADER

Group problem solving can be made more effective if the leader differentiates the leadership role from membership role. Being the focal point does not require the leader to dominate the group.

For a leader, such functions as rejecting or promoting ideas according to his personal needs are out of bounds. He must be receptive to information contributed, accept contributions without evaluating them (posting contributions on a chalkboard to keep them alive), summarize information to facilitate integration, stimulate exploratory behavior, create awareness of problems of one member by others, and detect when the group is ready to resolve differences and agree to a unified solution.[20]

This type of role may be strange to many managers. It is certainly not consistent with the popular image of what it means to be "a manager." This role for the manager is possible when:

1. the manager sincerely wants the subordinates to participate as a group to resolve or provide suggestions on a problem;
2. the problem is related to the tasks performed by the subordinates;
3. the subordinates can provide meaningful inputs to the problem's solution;
4. the subordinates can influence success in implementing the proposed solution;
5. the goals of the group members are basically compatible with respect to the problem.

DISAGREEMENTS

A skillful group leader will create an atmosphere for disagreement that will stimulate innovative solutions. At the same time, the leader must minimize the risks of some members leaving the group with bitter feelings, especially if these members will participate in implementing the decision.

Disagreements can be "managed" if the leader permits differences within the group, delays the reaching of a decision, and separates idea generation from idea evaluation. This last technique reduces the tendency for an alternative solution to be perceived as "belonging" to one individual rather than to the group.

TIME REQUIREMENTS

The leader must strike a proper balance between permissiveness and control. Rushing through a group session can prevent full discussion of the problems and lead to negative feelings. On the other hand, unless the leader keeps the discussion moving, members are likely to become bored and arrive at poor solutions. Unfortunately, leaders tend to push for an early solution because of time constraints. This ends the discussion, however, before the full potential of the group has been achieved.

When there are disagreements in a group, some members will have to change their minds in order for the group to reach a consensus. This change process can be either an asset or a liability. If members offering the best alternatives are persuaded to change, the outcome suffers. The leader of the group can play an important part in protecting individuals with a minority view by discouraging the expression of hostilities toward them. The leader can also increase the opportunity of the persons with a minority view to influence the majority position. This can be done by keeping the minority view before the group, encouraging communication about that view, and reducing misunderstandings.

Procedural Approaches

A group's decision-making procedures have a direct impact on its interaction and communication patterns. If problems cannot be solved through standardized procedures or through appeal to facts, procedures encouraging increased interaction often lead to better decisions than do those involving less interaction.[21] This is partially due to the error-correcting potential of group interaction that is less common with individual problem solving. There are four major categories of procedures.

DECISION BY PERSON WITH POWER

Here the manager obtains the views and feelings of others and then announces the solution. This approach is characteristic of a mechanistic rather than an organic management system. The topic of many cartoons, this type of manager may even go so far as to begin the group session by announcing the proposed solution and then invite alternative solutions or comments.

Although the manager eliminates the possibility of a solution that he or she doesn't like, there is also an increased probability of lower commitment to the implementation of the decision. This may occur even if the manager believes that the best decision has been made. The meaning of "best" can vary among individuals and will depend in part on what they think will happen to them as a result of the proposed solution.

This technique may work efficiently when:

1. the group has simple goals and the decision is relatively routine;
2. the group has a clear-cut division of labor;
3. there are strong external pressures toward conformity (e.g., pending bankruptcy);
4. group members see speedy action as necessary (crisis situation);
5. group members expect the manager to make the decision;
6. the decision will be unpopular (e.g., layoff of group members).[22]

DECISION BY MINORITY

This approach occurs when a small part of the group forms a coalition, either before or during the group session, to continuously push and force its solution. A *group coalition* consists of two or more individuals who band together to maintain or increase their outcomes (such as money, time to goof off, etc.) relative to another person or group. In popular terms, the minority group's effort to push its position is often called "railroading" and may entail ridiculing, name calling, and charging others with foot-dragging. The minority group is likely to prevent voting by fostering boredom, fatigue, or resignation in the rest of the group.

This approach may have several harmful effects. Over the short run, the decision-by-minority approach may lead to the lack of any personal commitment by the majority to the decision. Over the long run, the other group members may be motivated to form their own coalitions, which is likely to lead to a hostile atmosphere within the larger group.

Under certain contingencies, the decision-by-minority approach has some advantages, however. These are likely to occur when:

1. everyone cannot meet to deal with the problem;
2. the group is under such time pressure that it must delegate responsibility to a committee;
3. only a few group members have the needed knowledge and resources;
4. broad member commitment is not needed to implement the decision;
5. the problem is relatively routine and simple.

DECISION BY MAJORITY

In very large groups, face-to-face interaction may be difficult or impossible, and here the decision-by-majority approach is often necessary and desirable. The approach is so popular that it is often used in small-group problem-solving situations as well. Majority voting usually involves making a motion, debating it, and voting.

Often, however, discussion is soon closed on issues that are highly complex and important for the group. There are several limitations in this process. First, the group spends relatively little time on the development of ideas and alternatives and therefore moves too quickly to the evaluation stage. Second, the group members are motivated to divide too rapidly into separate coalitions of those for, against, or neutral with respect to the motion. The interaction tends to be dominated by the "for" and "against" coalitions, leaving the neutrals with little influence in the discussion. Third, this approach reduces the middle ground for the introduction of new alternatives or compromises. Finally, the problem of commitment continues. A small group whose members are evenly divided still has a problem about gaining acceptance of the decision. Those with the minority view might be hostile or become indifferent toward implementing the decision. If the minority continues to have intense negative feelings, it is probably best to reconsider the problem.

If the limitations of this approach can be minimized, it may be a useful approach when:

1. group members have somewhat conflicting goals;
2. the problem must be dealt with on the basis of judgment;
3. several solutions are likely to be effective;
4. the members believe in the appropriateness of a "democratic" approach;
5. there is not enough time to reach a consensus;
6. the problem is not important enough to justify the additional expenditure of time that would be necessary to reach a consensus.

Consensus emerges from alternatives being raised, discussed, and modified until agreement on one solution is reached. Members respect one another's views, even when there are serious disagreements. Members recognize that all of the alternatives are tentative until the group is ready to make the final choice, to which the members are likely to be highly committed. This does not mean that everyone totally agrees with the final decision. Rather, the opposed members are more likely to implement it because they feel they have been fairly treated and listened to. This approach uses the resources of all members and helps ensure the future decision-making ability of the group.

One problem for the manager is that of weighing the costs in additional time required for the consensus approach versus the benefits obtained from higher commitment and understanding of the decision. On some problems this approach may be impractical because of the number of decisions that must be made, time pressures, and situations requiring quick responses. Since the consensus approach requires trust and the full exchange of information among members within as well as outside of their group sessions, it is more likely to be used in an organic than in a mechanistic management system.

Decision by consensus is most likely to be effective when:

1. innovative, creative, and high-quality decisions are needed;
2. the members agree on basic goals but not on the best means for reaching those goals;
3. the problem is important, complex, and all of the member resources must be tapped to solve it;
4. member commitment is crucial for the successful implementation of the solution;
5. it is desirable to increase the capacity for problem solving throughout the group so that there is less dependency on the survival or presence of one or two members.

Although the consensus approach may be the ideal for problem-solving groups, particular contingencies may require the use of the other approaches. This is especially true for the decision by the person with power and/or expertise approach and the decision-by-majority approach.

CONTINGENCIES AFFECTING GROUP PERFORMANCE

Turning now from problem-solving groups, we will further consider the contingency variables that can influence the performance of *all* types of groups.[23] For any group performance is its output, which might vary from member satisfaction to the production of decisions that permit the attainment of organizational goals. There is no requirement that group performance be consistent with or necessarily related to the organization's goals. However, our focus will be on the task performance of groups in organizations. Several of the major contingency variables affecting group performance are group size, group cohesiveness, and group norms.

Size

As suggested earlier, a number of changes occur in groups and in their performance as they increase from two to twenty members. The critical change point seems to be about seven members. In larger groups it becomes increasingly difficult for the members to interact with all of the other members at once. In general, *as group size increases:*

1. the greater the demands on the leader and the more the leader is differentiated from the membership at large;
2. the greater the group's tolerance of direction by the leader and the more centralized the proceedings;
3. the more the ordinary members inhibit their participation and hence the less exploratory and adventurous the group's discussion;
4. the less friendly the group atmosphere, the more impersonal the actions, and generally the less satisfied the members as a whole;
5. the longer it takes to get to the nonroutine and judgmental decisions;
6. the more subgroups (coalitions) form within the membership and the more formalized the rules and procedures of the group.[24]

These findings suggest that managers can influence group performance by controlling group size. For groups engaged in intensive problem solving, the ideal size is seven to twelve members.[25] If the group has 20 or more members, the manager might break it up into smaller groups to help the process of analyzing task-related information by all members. The larger group might then be used to confirm one or more subgroups' decisions.

A large-group manager needs to recognize the existence of several subgroups each with its own informal leader. Thus although there are more potential resources available in large groups, they often have negative effects on overall group performance.[26] In addition, it is probably necessary to use some type of formal procedure, e.g., Robert's Rules of Order, to keep the agenda moving in large problem-solving groups. Voting to obtain an overall assessment of members' positions is also useful. Unfortunately, merely voting may not reveal the intensity of members' feelings, either positive or negative.

Large groups may be efficient when the primary purpose of the group is to begin to communicate or reinforce new policies, procedures, plans, and the like. With an adequate opportunity for questions from the members, the objective "to inform" may be well satisfied.

In sum, the manager's behavior will need to be substantially different in small-group and large-group sessions. With large groups, a more guiding and structured approach is usually desired and necessary.

Cohesiveness

Group pride, solidarity, loyalty, team spirit, teamwork, and mutual attraction between members can all be defined as cohesiveness.[27] Cohesion is a matter of degree and can arise from many sources in groups. Individuals may simply enjoy interacting with one another, may receive mutual support on some task or emotional issues, or obtain their goals most effectively through group action.[28]

Table 13.1. Factors affecting group cohesiveness

Factors increasing cohesiveness	Factors decreasing cohesiveness
1. Group provides status and recognition for members	1. Disagreement over the ways to solve group problems
2. Attack from the outside	2. Unpleasant experiences resulting from group membership
3. Favorable evaluation of the group by outsiders	3. Failure of the group to move toward its objectives
4. Personal attractiveness of members to one another	4. Dominating or self-oriented behavior on the part of group members
5. Intergroup competition	5. Intragroup competition
6. Opportunity for interaction	

Whatever the source, cohesion increases the satisfaction of individuals' needs or goals through a group. In general, the more the individuals perceive the group as a means to their need satisfaction, the greater the cohesiveness of the group. Table 13.1 summarizes the factors that tend to increase and decrease cohesiveness.

EFFECTS ON PERFORMANCE

The effects of low or high cohesiveness on performance can be pronounced. Cohesiveness frequently increases after the group has performed some task successfully, thereby increasing members' motivation to achieve success in the future. Championship athletic teams usually have a high degree of cohesiveness. Task or goal failure may tend to lower cohesiveness, which in turn becomes a possible reason for failing to reach certain goals in the future. Failures may be due to changes in the external environment that the group doesn't have the power or ability to influence. For example, a group of grinder operators in a large steel plant had been recognized in many ways within the plant, e.g., union positions, an attractive incentive plan, and excellent working conditions.[29] But the significance of the group's operation declined substantially when management made some technological changes in the production process. This led to serious political disputes within the group, especially over seniority, which shattered the group's cohesiveness for many years and virtually eliminated its influence in plant affairs.

In other instances, however, task or goal failure may result in an *increase* of cohesiveness, especially if the failure was caused by an external threat or grievance. For example, if good workers feel that promotions are being given out on the basis of favoritism rather than merit, they may band together and present a case to management that seniority should be the basis for promotion.

A key variable seems to be the group members' belief that a united front will be effective in dealing with the threat or grievance. If the group perceives that it has little power, the members are more likely to become fatalistic about the threats or grievances and experience a decrease in cohesiveness.

Managerial actions can have a significant impact on group cohesiveness. A reward system based on group output tends to increase group cohesiveness. A five-person work crew paid on the basis of the group's output makes all members somewhat dependent on other coworkers for their total compensation. By contrast, a reward system based on individual output may reduce cohesiveness, because the emphasis is on the individual rather than on the group.

CASE APPLICATION[30]

A study of group cohesiveness was undertaken at the plant of a large manufacturer of heavy machinery. Of the firm's 10,000 employees, about 90 percent were directly involved in production operations. The study focused on the individuals filling factory jobs classified "skilled" and "semiskilled."

The firm was generally regarded as having progressive personnel policies. The factory employees' hourly rates were average for the area. Sixty-three percent of the employees belonged to an active local of a major international union known for its vigorous contract negotiations and grievance handling. The employees regarded both the company and the union quite favorably.

A factorywide survey of employee attitudes toward their group was conducted. The questionnaires were given to the employees on company time, and extensive safeguards were taken to ensure that all responses would be confidential and not made available to the company.

The results showed that there was less individual variability in productivity within groups characterized by high group cohesiveness than in those of low cohesiveness. This suggests that the degree of cohesiveness affects the power of the group to enforce conformity to a norm of individual productivity. The relationship between group cohesiveness and the variance in productivity also differed between groups. High-cohesive groups differed more in output rates than low-cohesive groups did. A partial explanation for this is that high cohesiveness was found to be associated with high or low productivity, depending on the degree to which the members *felt secure* in their relation to the company. High-cohesive groups that felt confident in the company performed better than high-cohesive groups that viewed management as being nonsupportive of the group.

Norms

Norms are ideas or standards that exist in the minds of the members. They are decision rules indicating what members *should do* under specific circumstances.[31] Some norms may be "logical" consequences of the values shared by members of a group. For example, a group that values democracy may also hold the norm that individuals ought to vote.

Group norms exist when three criteria have been met.[32] First, *standards exist* about appropriate behavior for individuals as group members. For example, a work group may share norms as to the amount of output that is appropriate. However, these norms would not apply to a member's part-time job in another company. Second, there must be a relatively high degree of *agreement among the members* as to the norms. This does not mean that *all* members of a group need to share the norms. But if most of the members have significantly different sentiments (feelings) about the amount of output that is appropriate, the group does not have an output norm. Third, the members need to be *aware* that the group supports a particular norm through a reward and punishment system. Norms are reinforced by punishments following violations and rewards following compliance.

The ability of a group to enforce its system of norms is partially dependent on the *intensity* of rewards and punishments and the *probability* that they will be used.[33] The intensity and probability factors have to be considered from the point of view of the members. Individuals who value the group might still violate its norms if they believe they can do so without being caught, especially if they perceive rewards associated with violating the norms. For example, a salesperson whose work group punishes for bringing in orders above a certain norm might still do so, because of the low perceived probability of being caught and the opportunity for earning additional income.

Intensity reflects the significance of the group to the individual. An individual who does not value the rewards or punishments provided by the group may have little motivation to follow its norms. This is particularly true if the rewards and punishments are inconsistent with the individual's own standards. For example, a college graduate who strongly identifies with management might be placed in a work group as part of the company's training program. If this work group is antagonistic toward management and has a number of norms to keep production down, the college graduate may reject these norms, not caring about the work group. This individual's output could remain far above the norms, even though the group continues to try to punish the violator through harassment or fear techniques.

In some instances, individuals who deviate from group norms may be brought back into line by a controlled flow of needed materials or information. For example, one of the authors once had a summer job at a huge distribution center for the Goodyear Tire and Rubber Company. His job was to unload automobile tires from railroad boxcars during the afternoon shift, which had three towmotor drivers and six unloaders working the rail dock. The towmotor drivers brought and removed the pallets on which the tires were stacked. During his first week, he was unloading three to four boxcars a day. Then word got out! Several workers told him to lower his output to two to two and a half boxcars a day—the group's norm. He didn't cut his output. By the middle of the second week, the towmotor drivers had reduced the flow of pallets to him and let loaded pallets stack up outside of the boxcar. The other workers were able to enforce their own norms without ever creating intense interpersonal conflicts or engaging in threats.

Within work groups, norms can focus directly on the quality or quantity of desired output or, by focusing on interpersonal relations, may have an indirect effect on output. In the latter instance, a work group with norms that encourage social interaction may indirectly reduce task performance.

In sum, norms are ideas about what people think behavior ought to be under specific circumstances. Norms are not descriptions of behavior itself! Within cohesive work groups, there are often norms specifying the range of acceptable performance. Depending on the group's sentiments toward the organization and management, these norms may specify restrictions on the quality or quantity of output or may be neutral, if not supportive, about high output.

Summary

This chapter has emphasized small groups. Managers must relate to and understand both individual members and groups within organizations. Managers are also continuously working as members of groups.

Groups are inevitable in organizations, and their impact on organizations and management can be wide-ranging. Groups can be a source of resistance and antagonism from the manager's point of view, or they can supplement the formal motivational and control system by reinforcing quality and quantity performance standards. Various contingency factors influence these different outcomes.

A number of guidelines exist for helping managers work with and use groups more effectively. These guidelines can be used to identify the major contingencies that need to be evaluated by the manager when interacting with groups and the likely consequences of using different approaches to group problem solving. Some of these contingencies are technology, formal leadership, group size, group cohesiveness, and group norms. Four approaches to group problem solving are decision by the person with power, decision by a minority, decision by the majority, and decision by consensus. The effectiveness of these approaches depends on the contingencies involved.

Discussion Questions

1. Identify one formal and one informal group to which you belong and use the eight characteristics of effective groups identified at the beginning of the chapter to evaluate the two groups. You might want to start by ranking your informal and formal groups as high, medium, or low on each of these characteristics. Then identify at least one example for each characteristic that illustrates your ranking.

2. Based on your personal experience, do you feel that the work groups you have belonged to had desirable or undesirable effects on you and the organization? Explain.

3. How well did your last superior help you meet the emotional problems often experienced when entering a new group? What did he or she do or fail to do in terms of the types of steps that can be taken to reduce emotional problems?

4. Why is it necessary for both task-relevant and socially relevant behaviors to take place in a group?

5. What are the similarities and differences between Homans's systems model and Bales's IPA model?

6. Under what conditions can a highly cohesive group help the manager achieve the formal goals of the department?

7. Joe described his work group as "friendly, just great. All the guys get along together, and we bowl and play softball after work." However, production records show that Joe's group is one of the poorest in the plant. Why might this be?

8. Under what circumstances do you believe that the decision-by-majority approach would be effective and ineffective?

9. How might group size, degree of cohesiveness, and norms be interrelated in affecting the behavior of group members?

10. What is meant by goal displacement in group decision making? Give an example of this from your personal experience.

Management Incidents

THE NEW MANAGER

Since Sara Platou got her bachelors degree in business with a major in management five years ago, she has had positions in the purchasing, quality control, and work standards departments of a national firm that manufactures auto parts. Because of her outstanding performance, she has been offered and has accepted a position as a departmental manager of 40 employees. After a three-week orientation to her department and the plant as a whole, she assumed full responsibilities as the departmental manager.

Sara found that the department was fairly efficient, except for one small group of younger male employees. This group was made up of six employees and has an indirect influence over a fringe group of about six more. The main cause of the inefficiency seems to be the amount of time the employees in this group spend off the job in non-work-related activities.

Correcting this problem will be difficult; the union-management labor contract specifies that employees will not be held responsible for a specified number of units per day, but are expected to remain on the job except for reasonable personal delays. No specific times for breaks are spelled out. It is up to each employee to set his or her own break times.

Sara decided to attack the problem by picking out the worst offender in the group and noting his time off the job for a 12-hour period—almost four hours. Armed with this data and the fact that the employee had been verbally warned twice before, Sara issued a written reprimand to him, whereupon he requested and received aid from the union steward. As a result, a written grievance was filed, charging her with discrimination against the employee. The next day, at the start of the shift, this employee's peer group and the fringe group requested aid from the union steward.

For three more days, these ten employees and the union steward subjected Sara to mental pressure and harassment in an effort to have her remove the reprimand from the employee's work record. The reprimand was not removed. Oddly, however, though the production output of the 11 disgruntled employees directly involved fell drastically, the other employees in the department continued at about the average rate of output; they even gave her verbal support and encouragement.

1. What should Sara Platou do now?
2. What concepts and approaches in this chapter can you draw on that would provide guidance in selecting a course of action?
3. Would you have initially dealt with this problem in the same way as Sara? What concepts and approaches in the chapter serve to "back up" your position?

HOW TO CONDUCT A GROUP MEETING

You have just completed a week-long supervisory training program put on by the personnel department of your organization. As part of this program, you received the following information as a handout instructing you on how you should conduct a group meeting:

Restating the problem: You should be a good clarifier and identifier of subproblems during the meeting. Ask each member to write a statement of the problem. Record for all to see.

Metaphoric vacation: After working for a time on the problem, ask everyone to "put it out of their minds." Draw on one of the written subproblems for a lead and create an artificial, instant vacation from the problem. "Can anyone think of a striking image in the world of weather?"

Toward the solution: Bring the vacation to a close by asking the group to return to the subproblem which suggested the "metaphoric vacation." Continue toward solutions to the problem.

Rules for the supervisor:
1. Never compete with group members.
2. Listen to the group members.
3. Don't permit anyone to be put on the defensive.
4. Keep the energy level high.
5. Keep the members informed about where they are and what is expected of them.
6. Keep your eye on the expert; when he or she shows interest in an idea, give him or her some time.
7. Do not manipulate the group.

List of steps:
1. State the problem.
2. Discuss it with possible solutions.
3. Restate the problem as each participant understands it.
4. Select one of the restatements.
5. Take the group on a vacation.
   a) Select one key element (a striking image, say).
   b) Pick out an area in which to concentrate (e.g., weather).
   c) Then ask for examples of the key element (e.g., striking images in weather).

6. Select an example (e.g., "thunderhead") and ask for further examination.
7. End the vacation and ask for possible solutions to the original problem.
8. Make a decision.

1. Which of the guidelines, rules, and steps are consistent with the materials in this chapter?
2. Which of these guidelines, rules, and steps are inconsistent with the material in this chapter?
3. What contingencies exist, and how might they influence your decision whether to follow all of these guidelines, rules, and steps?

THE COHESIVE GROUP

You are the manager of a group of 20 production employees for a major steel fabricator. These employees have the same ethnic origin and form a fairly close-knit group, both in and out of the plant. In the past several months you have experienced several problems with this particular group: (1) an increase in production schedules required the hiring of several part-time workers, who were subjected to much verbal abuse and quit after several days; (2) refusal by the crew to work overtime, because of their daily gathering at a neighborhood bar; (3) sabotage of a new machine (which was rumored to be capable of replacing two workers), which you suspect your crew of. Nonetheless, your supervisor has just sent you a memo commending you for your fine yearly production record.

1. What group forces seem to be operating in this situation?
2. Which forces appear to be beneficial and which act to the detriment of the company?
3. What actions would you take?

REFERENCES

1. G. Miller, "Living Systems: The Group," *Behavioral Science* **16** (1971): 302–398.

2. E. Schein, *Organization Psychology*, 2d ed. (Englewood Cliffs, N.J.: Prentice-Hall, 1970).

3. M. Mills, *The Sociology of Small Groups* (Englewood Cliffs, N.J.: Prentice-Hall, 1967), p. 2.

4. L. Bradford and D. Mial, "When Is a Group?" *Educational Leadership* **21** (1963): 147–151.

5. P. Bernstein, "Workplace Democratization: Its Internal Dynamics," *Organization and Administration Sciences* **7** (1976): 1–127.

6. W. Schutz, "Interpersonal Underworld," *Harvard Business Review* **36** (1958): 123–135.

7. D. Moment and A. Zalenznik, *Role Development and Interpersonal Competence: An Experimental Study of Role Performance in Problem-Solving Groups* (Boston: Division of Research, Graduate School of Business Administration, Harvard University, 1963), pp. 10–18.

8. G. Homans, *The Human Group* (New York: Harcourt, Brace, 1950); *Social Behavior: Its Elementary Forms* (New York: Harcourt, Brace, 1961).

9. Homans, *The Human Group, op. cit.*, pp. 133, 134, 135.

10. *Ibid.*, pp. 141, 145, 181.

11. L. Sayles, *Behavior of Industrial Work Groups: Prediction and Control* (New York: Wiley, 1958); J. Goldthorpe, D. Lockwood, F. Bechhofer, and J. Platt, *The Affluent Worker: Industrial Attitudes and Behavior* (London: Cambridge University Press, 1968), pp. 43–53.

12. G. Susman, *Autonomy at Work: A Sociotechnical Analysis of Participative Management* (New York: Praeger, 1976).

13. D. Johnson, "Social Organization of an Industrial Work Group: Emergence and Adaptation to Environmental Change," *Sociological Quarterly* **15** (1974): 109–126.

14. R. Bales, *Interaction Process Analysis* (Cambridge, Mass.: Addison-Wesley, 1950); J. Heinen, and E. Jacobson, "A Model of Task Group Development In Complex Organizations and a Strategy of Implementation," *Academy of Management Review* **1** (1976): 98–111.

15. R. Bales, "Some Uniformities of Behavior in Small Social Systems," in *Readings in Social Psychology,* rev. ed., ed. G. Swanson, T. Newcomb, and E. Hartley (New York: Holt, 1952), p. 155.

16. R. Bales, and F. Strodtbeck, "Phases in Group Problem Solving," *Journal of Abnormal and Social Psychology* **46** (1951): 485.

17. H. Philp, and D. Dunphy, "Developmental Trends in Small Groups," *Sociometry* **22** (1954): 162–174.

18. N. Maier, "Assets and Liabilities in Group Problem-Solving: The Need for an Integrative Function," *Psychology Review* **74** (1967): 244; M. Sashkin, "Changing Toward Participative Management Approaches: A Model and Methods," *Academy of Management Review* **1** (1976): 75–86, 239–249. *See also* H. Kelley and J. Thibaut, "Group Problem Solving," in *Handbook of Social Psychology,* 2d ed., ed. G. Lindzey and E. Aronson (Reading, Mass.: Addison-Wesley, 1960), pp. 1–101.

19. A. Lowin, "Participative Decision-Making: A Model, Literature Critique, and Prescriptions for Research," *Organizational Behavior and Human Performance* **3** (1968): 69–99; H. Van De Ven, "Group Decision Making and Effectiveness: An Experimental Study," *Organization and Administrative Sciences* **5** (1974): 1–110.

20. Maier, *op. cit.*, p. 246.

21. C. Holloman and H. Hendrick, "Adequacy of Group Decisions as a Function of Decision-Making Process," *Academy of Management Journal* **15** (1972): 175–184.

22. H. Wilensky, "Human Relations in the Work Place," in *Research in Human Industrial Relations,* Vol. XII, ed. C. Arensburg (New York: Harper & Row, 1957), p. 35.

23. Adapted from L. Sayles, "Research in Industrial Human Relations," *Industrial Relations Research Association* (New York: Harper & Row, 1957), pp. 131–145.

24. B. Berelson and G. Steiner, *Human Behavior: An Inventory of Scientific Findings* (New York: Harcourt, Brace and World, 1964), p. 358.

25. G. Manners, "Another Look at Group Size, Group Problem Solving and Member Consensus," *Academy of Management Journal* **18** (1975): 715–724.

26. J. Davis, *Group Performance* (Reading, Mass.: Addison-Wesley, 1969), p. 73.

27. S. Seashore, *Group Cohesiveness in the Industrial Work Group* (Ann Arbor, Mich.: Survey Research Center, Institute for Social Research, 1954), p. 11.

28. D. Cartwright and A. Zander, *Group Dynamics: Research and Theory* (New York: Harper & Row, 1968).

29. Sayles, *op. cit.,* p. 101.

30. This section is adapted from Seashore, *op. cit*

31. Homans, *The Human Group, op. cit.,* p. 123.

32. A. Athos and R. Coffey, *Behavior in Organizations: A Multidimensional View* (Englewood Cliffs, N.J.: Prentice-Hall, 1975).

33. Davis, *op. cit.*

14

Conflict Process

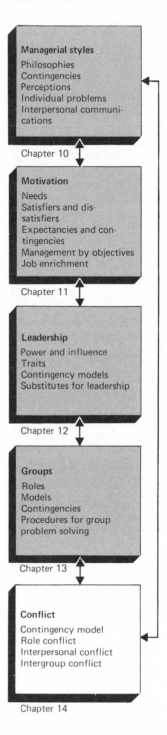

Managerial styles

Philosophies
Contingencies
Perceptions
Individual problems
Interpersonal communi-
cations

Chapter 10

Motivation

Needs
Satisfiers and dis-
satisfiers
Expectancies and con-
tingencies
Management by objectives
Job enrichment

Chapter 11

Leadership

Power and influence
Traits
Contingency models
Substitutes for leadership

Chapter 12

Groups

Roles
Models
Contingencies
Procedures for group
problem solving

Chapter 13

Conflict

Contingency model
Role conflict
Interpersonal conflict
Intergroup conflict

Chapter 14

The objectives of this chapter are to:

present and evaluate the different points of view often taken toward conflict;

develop your conceptual skills in diagnosing basic conflict situations through the presentation of a contingency conflict model;

explain the nature of three different levels of conflict—role conflict, interpersonal conflict, and intergroup conflict;

discuss some of the causes, effects, and ways of managing each of the three levels of conflict;

provide a contingency approach to the successful management of conflict.

What do you think of when you read or hear the word "conflict"? To many people, the word suggests negative situations—war, destruction, aggression, violence, and competition. For other individuals, the word may have the positive connotations of excitement, intrigue, adventure, and challenge. A third set of responses to "conflict" might stimulate mixed feelings, and this is probably the most realistic and useful point of view for a manager.

The classical writers on organization (see Chapter 3) typically viewed conflict as undesirable, to be minimized or eliminated through careful selection of people, training, detailed job description, elaborate rules to specify the relationships among employees, and incentive systems. These prescriptions are often still useful for reducing and possibly preventing some undesirable conflicts. In our view, however, conflict management is *relative* rather than absolute. To us, conflict is a certainty in organizations and may sometimes be highly desirable for all parties. Although it may be possible to prevent many conflicts, others will need to be managed so that conflicts between coworkers, superiors and subordinates, two or more departments, the organization and external groups (such as major customers, unions, and government agencies) can be resolved.

The overall objective of this chapter is to develop your skill in recognizing the major causes and types of conflicts and the need for different approaches to prevent and resolve conflicts. Since much of Chapter 2 focused on conflicts between organizations, that topic is not discussed here. We do, however, note how conflicts between organizations can be a cause of conflict *within* an organization.

There is no single definition of conflict that reflects the spirit or complexity with which we would like to use the word. But as a starting point, we can say that conflict *refers to the awareness of all kinds of disagreements, opposition, or antagonistic interaction within one individual or between two or more individuals.*[1] In later sections of this chapter, we will introduce more restricted definitions of various levels (role, interpersonal, intergroup) and types of conflict.

VIEWPOINTS TOWARD CONFLICT[2]

Negative View

An employee who experiences frequent and high levels of conflict may show psychological withdrawal (apathy, indifference, and alienation) and physical withdrawal (turnover, tardiness, and absenteeism). In other cases, aggressive and hostile behavior may result, being expressed by concealing information needed by others, stealing and damaging property, and striking.

From a decision-making standpoint, conflicts can lead to gross distortions of reality, resulting in biased perceptions of information and possibly the decision to take actions that increase rather than reduce or resolve the conflict. From a control standpoint, managers might dislike conflict because they believe that it interferes with productivity and efficiency. In sum, many managers believe that conflict disrupts organizational goal achievement and is therefore undesirable.

Positive View

Conflict may stimulate the parties to search for ways to reduce or resolve their disagreements, a process that often leads to innovation and change. Conflict may provide individuals with the opportunity to attain various monetary and personally meaningful rewards. For example, status and esteem needs might be met by managers successfully competing on performance objectives, achieving a promotion over other candidates, and meeting or exceeding objectives they have set for themselves.

From a decision-making standpoint, conflict may result in better choices because of the need to offer evidence and arguments when there is a diversity of viewpoints. From a control standpoint, conflict can indicate the need for adjustments in managerial processes (such as organizations' structures, decision systems, planning processes, and goals) or behavioral processes (such as motivation, communication, or leadership patterns). In addition, the expression of conflict provides managers with information about the operations for which they are accountable and where corrective actions might be needed. In sum, the positive viewpoint toward conflict is that it is a necessary condition for the attainment of individual and organizational goals.

Balanced View

More realistically, conflict has both positive *and* negative aspects and must therefore be managed. The proper management of conflict can often minimize its negative effects and enhance its positive effects. This balanced view is at the heart of the contingency model of conflict.

CONTINGENCY MODEL OF CONFLICT

Managers must be able to diagnose the basic conflict situations they are likely to face. The distributive and integrative contingency variables can be used to distinguish four basic conflict situations.[3] The *distributive variable* refers to the degree to which one or more goals of each of the parties are *perceived* as incompatible. In other words, one person's gain is another's loss; most games, for example, are played until one person or team wins and the other loses. The *integrative variable* refers to the degree to which one or more of the goals of each of the parties are *perceived* as compatible. Each of these contingency variables varies along a high-low continuum.

By cross-classifying these two variables, we can construct a four-cell basic contingency model of conflict, as shown in Fig. 14.1. Before discussing each of the types of conflict situations, a word about the entire model might be helpful.

First, the total relationship between any two individuals or groups need not be restricted to only one cell. Although the pattern in one of the cells is likely to dominate, the parties may be placed in different cells for different issues. In a collective bargaining relationship, for example, management and the union may feel that the wage issue is a win-lose situation (cell 1). Gain by

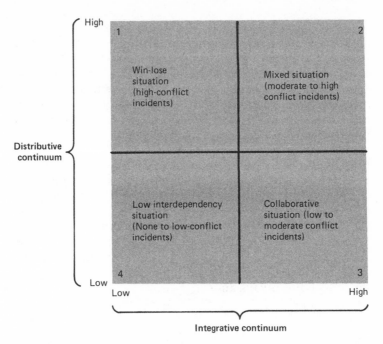

Fig. 14.1. Contingency model of conflict.

the union is loss to management, and vice versa. On other issues, such as adjusting to technological changes, the two parties may perceive a mixed situation (cell 2). The union and management may need to cooperate in introducing technological changes so that the firm can remain competitive and survive, provide workers with jobs, and keep on earning profits. But intense conflicts may still exist over who will gain the most benefits from the new technology. Thus this conflict situation consists of both high-distributive and high-integrative relationships.

Second, the particular management approach used is contingent on the particular conflict situation. At one extreme, the manager can take a negative approach, regarding all problems or conflicts as win-lose situations; at the other extreme, regarding all conflict as basically collaborative situations. A more realistic approach is to carefully evaluate the nature of the conflict situation and *then* decide on the most appropriate approach.

Conflict Situations

The four major conflict situations presented in Fig. 14.1 represent extreme positions on the grid. Real-life conflict situations may occur at any point on the grid, including "borderline" positions.

WIN-LOSE SITUATION

Cell 1 is characterized by high-distributive and low-integrative relationships. One party's gain is another party's loss. Typically, a win-lose situation occurs when there is a direct conflict in goals. Organizations often try to avoid creating win-lose situations internally because of their negative effects on employee performance and attitudes. Nonetheless, win-lose situations may occur when: (1) an immediate cutback of the work force is ordered; (2) only one of two contending executive vice-presidents can become president; or (3) having another firm perform services provided by one of the organization's departments will result in all departmental employees being retained or all being fired.

A major factor influencing the perception of a win-lose situation is the reward system. The potential effects of the reward system on soldiers' perception of a win-lose versus mixed situation in World War II and the Vietnam war has been described as follows:

> What did the GI in World War II want? To go home. And when did he get to go home? When the war was won! If he disobeyed the orders to clean out the trenches and take the hills, the war would not be won and he would not go home. Furthermore, what were his chances of attaining his goal (getting home alive) if he obeyed the orders compared to his chances if he did not? What is being suggested is that the rational soldier in World War II, whether patriotic or not, probably found it expedient to obey.

> Consider the reward system in use in Vietnam. What did the man at the bottom want? To go home. And when did he get to go home? When his tour of duty was over! This was the case *whether or not* the war was won. Furthermore, concerning the relative chance of getting home alive by obeying orders compared to the chance if they were disobeyed, it is worth noting that a mutineer in Vietnam was far more likely to be assigned rest and rehabilitation (on the assumption that fatigue was the cause) than he was to suffer any negative consequence. In light of the reward system used in Vietnam, would it not have been personally irrational for some orders to have been obeyed? Was not the military implementing a system which *rewarded* disobedience, while *hoping* that soldiers (despite the reward system) would obey orders?[4]

This example suggests that the reward system used by management can have a strong influence on whether the employees (or soldiers) perceive their goals as being consistent or inconsistent with those of the organization (or military unit).

MIXED SITUATION

The mixed situation (cell 2) occurs when there is both a high-distributive and high-integrative relationship, e.g., union-management relationships. The distributive issue often concerns the allocation of rewards (rather than punishments) created out of two groups' joint efforts. The integrative part of the relationship includes the parties': (1) jointly deciding on the terms for relating to each other; (2) obtaining rewards from their mutual association and recognizing that losses would occur from a termination or deterioration in it; and (3) realizing that they might be able to increase the rewards for each other through association.[5] The parties may tend to move toward a win-lose situation (cell 1) or (less likely) toward a collaborative situation (cell 3). The direction of this movement is heavily influenced by the attitudes, communication patterns, and decision processes established between the parties.

COLLABORATIVE SITUATION

In the collaborative situation (cell 3), there is a high-integrative relationship and a low-distributive relationship. The actions of one party have desirable effects on the other party, and vice versa. Since the goals of the parties are compatible and often mutually reinforcing, goal attainment by one party helps goal attainment by the other, and vice versa.

Conflicts will probably not be as intense or long-lasting as in the win-lose or mixed situations. However, conflicts are still likely to occur because of interpersonal difficulties, task interdependencies, and debates over the most effective means to reach the common goals. The collaborative situation is frequently found in organizations and probably typifies behavior within organizations.

LOW-INTERDEPENDENCY SITUATION

The low-interdependency situation occurs when there are both low-integrative and low-distributive relationships. Conflict is at a minimum or non-existent, because there is little reason for the parties to get together.

Case Application[6]

This case study is concerned with the relations between the sales and production departments within two districts of the same organization. The two districts are similar with respect to technology, economic and market conditions, structure of the departments, and basic tasks. Integration between the two departments was primarily an *ad hoc* arrangement in each of the districts, which were concerned with the production of a wide variety of metal windows, doors, and sashes for sale to industrial customers and to the building industry. The primary areas of task interdependence between production and sales were acceptance of new orders, scheduling, and quality control. These task interdependencies were especially important because items were usually produced only on request from customers. The orders could include standard industry items or products made to the specification of customers. The size of the orders could vary from several dozen to several thousand items. These factors created a potential for both collaboration and conflict between the production and sales departments.

Table 14.1 summarizes the contrasting relationships between the sales and production departments in the two districts. The Elgin district can be characterized as a win-lose situation; the Bowie district, a collaborative situation. Each of the four dimensions listed in the table describes a relationship that was self-reinforcing, mutual, and lasting. The relationships were self-reinforcing because suspicious and unfriendly attitudes reinforced the tendency to avoid and distort information or to focus on competing goals. Mutuality occurred because when one department distorted information, considered only its own narrow goals, or tried to limit the activities of the other department, the other did likewise. Finally, the relations at each operation were lasting; the experience, attitudes, and "appropriate" behavior of older workers were communicated to new members. Informal rewards and punishments in both districts also supported the established relationships.

Several factors helped collaboration at Bowie and increased win-lose conflicts at Elgin. First, with its better relations and task assistance from the home office, Bowie was able to produce more items for inventory. This reduced the

Table 14.1. Contrasting examples of intergroup relations

Dimensions	Elgin: win-lose situation	Bowie: collaborative situation
1. Goals and orientation to decision making	1. Each department emphasized the requirements of its own particular task	1. Each department stressed common goals whenever possible and in other cases tried to balance goals.
2. Information handling	2. Each department (a) minimized the others' problems or tended to ignore them when recognized and (b) minimized or distorted the information communicated.	2. Each department tried to (a) understand the other's problems and give consideration to them and (b) provide the other with full, timely, and accurate information relevant to joint decisions.
3. Freedom of movement	3. Each department tried to gain maximum freedom for itself and to limit the freedom for the other through such tactics as: (a) circumventing formal procedures; (b) emphasizing jurisdictional rules; (c) trying to fix the future performance obligations of the other department; (d) restricting interaction patterns; (e) using pressure tactics, such as hierarchical appeals; (f) blaming the other for past failures in performance.	3. Each department tried to increase its freedom to attain goals through the following actions: (a) accepting informal procedures which facilitated task achievement; (b) blurring of the differences between production and sales; (c) avoiding trying to fix the department's future performance; (d) encouraging relatively open interaction patterns; (e) searching for solutions rather than employing pressure tactics; (f) focusing on the diagnosis and correction of defects in rules rather than placing blame.
4. Attitudes	4. Each department developed negative feelings toward the other. Desires to threaten, vent hostilities, and retaliate were common.	4. Each department adopted trusting and positive attitudes toward the other.

peak-load pressures on the production department that often stimulated conflicts between sales and production. Second, Bowie's equipment and physical plant were better. Third, there was a greater status gap between sales and production managers at Elgin, in terms of age, education, and experience, than at Bowie. Finally, managerial styles at Elgin differed more than did those at Bowie. For example, Elgin's sales manager had an aggressive personal style, and the production manager lacked human and conceptual skills. These differences may be important factors for explaining how their relationships developed as basically collaborative or competitive.

One of the most important implications of this case is that the parties, through their actions and attitudes, can *move* toward a different situation. In this case, we started with the assumption that the relationship between sales and production was basically a mixed situation. Through their actions and attitudes, the parties at Elgin moved it to a win-lose situation and at Bowie to a collaborative situation.

Summary

The contingency model of conflict can be a useful framework for *diagnosing* the nature of the conflict between two or more parties. The model suggests that different conflict-management approaches are appropriate for different types of conflict situations. For example, a win-lose conflict situation may be partially dealt with by some form of third-party intervention, such as the conflicting parties' superior or an agreed on arbitrator. On the other hand, the conflict in a mixed conflict situation might be dealt with through improved problem-solving and confrontation approaches to reduce the development of negative attitudes and stereotypes.

ROLE CONFLICT[7]

A *role* is a particular set of related activities carried out by an individual. These roles may occur within organizations (superior, subordinate, peer) or outside of organizations (husband or wife, father or mother, female or male). Roles do not exist or function independently of the people in them.

Role Set

The collection of roles directly related to the role(s) of any one individual in an organization is called the person's *role set*. For example, the role set of a press foreman in a plant producing trim parts for automobiles consists of 19 other roles: general foreman, superintendent, sheet-metal foreman, inspector, shipping-room foreman, and 14 press operators.[8]

The members of a person's role set are typically affected by the individual's performance and actions. Thus they may experience rewards or punishments because of this individual's actions and may require certain actions from this person in order to perform their own tasks. For a quarterback to complete a pass, for example, the line must block and the receivers must be able to hold onto the ball. Since the members of a role set are influenced by this person's performance and actions, they develop attitudes about what should and should

not be done as part of the role. These "do's" and "don'ts," called *role expecta-*
tions, vary from expectations about how the person should dress to how much
or how little should be produced. A professor telling students to read each
chapter in the text at least three times is an example of a role expectation.
Expectations are communicated by the members of the role set (*role senders*)
to the individual whose role is under consideration (*focal person*).

Of course, in addition to providing information, role senders also exert
pressure on the focal person to carry out their expectations; these acts are
called *role pressures.* A professor telling the students that they must have a
90 or higher average for an A grade is an example of a role sender creating role
pressure. Pressures are exerted through the use of one or more types of power,
i.e., reward power, coercive power, legitimate power, referent power, and
expert power (see Chapters 9 and 12). The nature and intensity of role conflicts are likely to be influenced by the type of power used by the parties and
their relative power in the conflict.[9] For example, if two parties can provide
rewards to each other in meaningful quantities, we might expect them to be
strongly motivated to resolve their conflicts by seeking a win-win solution.

So far we have suggested that the role sender and the focal person are two
different individuals. But in actuality, one person can fill both roles. One's
"inner voice" provides the do's and don'ts associated with each role a person
fills. Thus an individual might have (1) an idea of his or her own "ideal" role
as a student and (2) perceptions of his or her "actual" role as a student. A role
conflict may arise if there is a large gap between the two and the student can't
figure out how to reduce it.

SIMPLIFIED MODEL

Figure 14.2 provides a simplified model of a *role episode,* which is a continuous process of a role sender's attempts to influence the behavior of a focal
person. In turn, the actual behavioral responses by the focal person influence
the succeeding expectations by the role sender.[10] The *expectations* of the role
sender are translated into *pressures* that are sent to the focal person. The
focal person has both emotional and cognitive responses to these pressures.
The *emotional response* is the individual's feeling about the perceived pressures—good, angry, frustrated, happy. The *cognitive response* is the person's
perception of what the role sender wants done. The focal person will respond
to the role sender on the basis of these perceptions. The nature of the response
by the focal person becomes a new input to the role sender's future expecta-

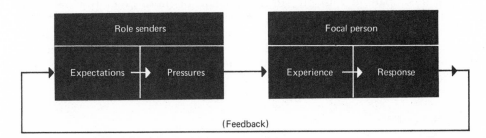

Fig. 14.2. Model of role episode.

tions and pressures. For example, a sales manager who responds to pressures with hostile counterattacks toward the production manager is likely to be thought of and responded to differently by the production manager than one who responds with submissive acceptance. If the sales manager shows signs of tension and anxiety from the pressures, the production manager is likely to "lay off."[11]

Given the numerous role episodes most people participate in, the experience of role conflict becomes almost inevitable. *Role conflict* occurs when a (role sender's) role expectations are incompatible with those of the focal person. These pressures may lead to conflict within the focal person and possibly with one or more of the role senders as well. Such role conflict may be of various types and stems from various causes.

Causes and Types of Role Conflicts

Role conflicts occur because two or more sets of pressures are placed on the individual at the same time. By responding to one set of pressures, the person finds it difficult, if not impossible, to respond to one or more other sets of pressures. The intensity of the role conflict depends on the absolute and relative strength of the role pressures (i.e., power of the role senders) and the focal person's desire to respond to the various types of pressures. Pressure from two fellow workers may be relatively easy to deal with, but pressure from two supervisors may result in severe role conflict.

INTRASENDER CONFLICT

This type of role conflict occurs when the do's and don'ts from a single role sender are incompatible. A manager might tell a subordinate that a particular task is to be completed today and a short time later assign another task to be completed today. This may make it difficult, if not impossible, to complete the first assignment. Of course, there is no problem if the manager changes the initial time deadline. Another example is when one spouse pressures the other to cut down on expenditures for food and then complains about the poor meals. A final example occurs when your professor assigns a paper or case to be handed in the same week as he or she is giving an examination. If you haven't planned your time well, you may experience intrasender conflict from not having enough time to adequately prepare for both assignments.

INTERSENDER ROLE CONFLICT

This type of conflict occurs when pressures from one role sender are perceived as being incompatible with pressures from one or more other role senders. The following incidents are representative of intersender role conflicts. A design engineer reported inconsistent orders from the engineers and shop people. A general supervisor in an automobile assembly reported feeling "right in the middle" when management demands certain work standards and the union objects to them. A salesperson was in a dilemma when a customer wanted a better price but management wouldn't allow it.[12]

INTERROLE CONFLICT

Here, role pressures associated with membership in one group or organization are in conflict with those stemming from membership in other groups or organizations. Pressures requiring overtime or take-home work may conflict with pressure from one's spouse or children to give more attention to family matters during the evening or on weekends. When this type of conflict becomes intense, the focal person may simply "withdraw" from one of the roles. For example, a spouse might change jobs or get a divorce.

PERSON-ROLE CONFLICT

Incompatibilities may arise between the demands of the role(s) and the focal person's own needs, attitudes, values, and abilities. The college student who, because of parental pressures, enrolls in a management program rather than in a course for mechanics may experience person-role conflict.

Person-role conflict may also arise when professional persons are required to do certain types of work. The conflict arises because the expectations of the mechanistic (bureaucratic) organization (which follows rules and regulations, hierarchy of power, etc.) are at odds with the individuals' expectations as professionals (e.g., freedom and participation in decision making). The following contrasts are characteristic of the conflicts between expectations in a mechanistic system and those by professionals:

1. emphasizing the similarity rather than the uniqueness of clients' problems;
2. focusing on procedures and keeping records rather than on change and the development of knowledge;
3. appealing to the need for increasing the efficiency of techniques and established processes rather than for *achieving goals* based on a client orientation;
4. demanding loyalty to the organization and superiors rather than to professional associations and standards;
5. deriving authority on the basis of occupying position (office) rather than on personal expertise.[13]

When managers attempt to apply mechanistic-system expectations to professionals, they are likely to encounter conflict with them. Most of these conflicts can be reduced by adopting more of an organic system, which is characterized by a high degree of participation by subordinates in decision making and goal setting, open channels of communication throughout the organization, and authority based on the knowledge of the individual rather than on one's position in the hierarchy. With this management system, there may be considerable compatibility perceived between professional expectations and organizational goals.[14]

Some conflicts are likely to exist and may well be desirable up to a point.[15] For example, conflict may continue over the best ways to handle tough problems. If handled properly, this form of conflict could stimulate creative decision making.

Effects of Role Conflict

Frequently, role conflicts are minor, and the resulting frustrations are probably essential for the development of competent and mature individuals. But *excessive* role conflicts can have adverse effects for the individual and possibly for the organization as well.

An in-depth study of 53 managers from four industries compared data on the emotional reactions for managers in high- and low-role-conflict situations.[16] The high-role-conflict group experienced greater job-related tensions, *less satisfaction* with the job, and *less confidence* in superiors and in their organization than did the low-conflict group. The primary source of role conflicts came from higher levels in the organization, and the managers' emotional reactions led to lower levels of trust, respect, and liking for the role senders.

However, it has also been found that external groups (e.g., customers, suppliers, government agencies) can also be a major source of role conflict for managers and other employees, such as salespeople.[17] For example, two major customers might pressure a salesperson for early delivery of their orders, with the implied threat that they will go elsewhere in the future if their order isn't delivered.

Managing Role Conflicts

There is no single pattern used by individuals or organizations to manage intense role conflicts. The personality of the person and the characteristics of interpersonal relationships with the role senders are important contingency variables influencing the approaches used to manage role conflicts.

PERSONAL TACTICS

Unlike an extrovert, an introvert is more likely to withdraw or to avoid the people creating the role conflicts. The act of withdrawal may worsen the conflict by making it more difficult to find satisfactory solutions. Communication has been stopped, and distrust, apathy, and disrespect may follow. But if the interpersonal relationships between the focal person and role sender are characterized by trust, respect, and friendship, resolution of role conflicts is more likely to be successful. Under these conditions, communications will continue to flow between the people in an attempt to find a mutually agreeable solution.

The reduction in contacts and communication between the focal person and the role sender may be a relatively passive and subconscious process or active, persistent, and aggressive. An employee who is absent excessively, requests a transfer, or quits the organization may illustrate the passive approach to managing role conflict.

A person under high role conflict is also likely to resort to defense mechanisms, such as projection and rationalization, to manage (by avoiding) role conflicts. *Projection* refers to the protection of one's self from feelings of guilt by blaming other individuals for one's own faults. Thus the immediate superior may be blamed for the employee's not getting a promotion. The employee might also gripe that the boss is always out to get him or her or that the boss never really liked him or her. *Rationalization,* by contrast, refers to creating a socially desirable reason for one's behavior that the individual believes is less ego-deflating than the true reason. An employee whose output is significantly lower than that of coworkers might believe that the cause is poor machinery or obsolete equipment rather than his or her own deficiency.

From a managerial point of view, these personal approaches to managing intense role conflicts may have negative effects on job performance, absentee-

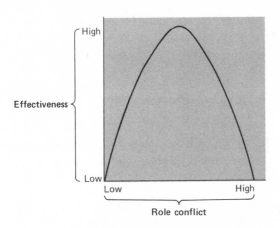

ism, and turnover. Avoidance behavior may be especially bad on the performance of the focal person. As a result, the role senders are likely to increase pressure on the focal person to produce or try to eliminate their dependency on the focal person. Individuals who use avoidance mechanisms for managing their role conflicts may be defeating themselves over the long run.

The relative effect of role conflict on overall organizational effectiveness has not been established to date.[18] This is not especially surprising, since organizational effectiveness is also influenced by many other factors, such as planning, decision making, controlling, leadership, and reward systems. As suggested in Fig. 14.3, there is a curvilinear relationship between level of role conflict and organizational effectiveness. If there is no or very low role conflict throughout the organization, the members have probably accepted the status quo and are not challenging one another in a positive way. At the other extreme, role conflict can become so intense that the members are continually either fighting one another through win-lose power struggles or avoiding one another, and there is little cooperation, sharing of information, or trust. A moderate to high amount of each of these factors is usually necessary for organizational effectiveness.

ORGANIZATIONAL TACTICS

Management can use a variety of tactics to keep role conflicts at tolerable levels. For example, structural changes in the organization can be made to reduce the interdependencies between jobs and departments. Manufacturing organizations often use expediters to coordinate the marketing department's desires with those of the production department. At Standard Steel Corporation, expediters are assigned to large sales orders to ensure that they are manufactured to specification and shipped on time to the customers. Another tactic might be the development of new selection and placement criteria. Personality tests for jobs with high levels of objective role conflict can be used to screen out applicants with a low tolerance for pressure. Or, the organization can try to increase the tolerance and coping abilities of individuals toward role conflict through interpersonal skill training. There might also be efforts to improve the interpersonal relationships among organizational members through more considerate leadership practices and opportunities for social get-togethers. Several of the organizational tactics for managing role conflict are developed further in the following sections on interpersonal conflict and intergroup conflict.

INTERPERSONAL CONFLICT

This section on interpersonal conflict is an extension to, rather than a departure from, the previous section on role conflict. Here, the focus is on some patterns of communication between the focal person and role senders and their attitudes and behaviors toward each other.

Interpersonal conflicts can be broadly defined to include: (1) disagreements over policies, practices, or plans; and (2) emotional issues involving negative feelings, such as anger, distrust, fear, rejection, and resentment.[19] The two types of conflict are often interrelated. However, each type may require different strategies of resolution. Resolving planning, goal, and policy conflicts should emphasize problem solving and compromise (bargaining); emotional conflict, modification of the parties' perceptions and increasing positive feelings for each other. Both types of conflict might benefit from interventions by third parties. In union-management relations, the third party could be a mediator, arbitrator, or even a court judge; in family matters, a counselor or lawyer.

Effects of Win-Lose versus Collaborative Interpersonal Relations

The basic nature and effects of win-lose versus collaborative interpersonal relations are outlined in Table 14.2. Keep in mind, however, that these are pure types and thus may not reflect real-life interpersonal relations. Also note that this presentation is an extension of our contingency model of conflict (see Fig. 14.1 and Table 14.1).

The two types of interpersonal relations have several implications for managers. First, when the parties believe that their relationship is purely win-lose, or competitive, the manager might try to get them to redefine and perceive the situation as a "mixed" one. Unless this occurs, the relations are likely to remain fragile and explosive. Both parties may desire to dominate each other through the use of threats, if necessary. If emotional issues come to dominate the relationship, the parties may refuse to even consider compromising on the various goals, plans, and policies.

Second, many situations are mixed, containing both distributive and integrative elements. Therefore, the manager can influence the persons involved by helping them to perceive the conflict as being relatively more collaborative than win-lose. Thus the manager might emphasize the parties' mutual interests, show a friendly attitude and trust in both parties, communicate in a relatively open and honest manner, and respond positively to the needs expressed by both parties.[20]

The point of view and attitudes of the parties can create a self-fulfilling prophecy. If they approach their relationship as a win-lose conflict-filled situation, it is likely to become so. Third, a basically collaborative relationship

Table 14.2. Effects of win-lose and collaborative interpersonal relations

Dimensions	Interpersonal relationships	
	Win-lose	**Collaborative**
Task orientation	Emphasis on antagonistic interests; the minimization of the other's power becomes an objective.	Highlighting of mutual interests, coordinated effort with division of labor and specialization of function; substitutability of effort rather than duplication; the enhancement of mutual power becomes an objective.
Attitudes	Suspicious, hostile attitudes with a readiness to exploit the other's needs and weakness and a negative responsiveness to the other's requests.	Trusting, friendly attitudes with a positive interest in the other's welfare and a readiness to respond helpfully to the other's needs and requests.
Perception	Increased sensitivity to opposed interests, to threats, and to minimizing the awareness of similarities.	Increased sensitivity to common interests while minimizing the opposed interests, a sense of convergence of beliefs and values.
Communication	Little communication or misleading communication; espionage or other techniques to obtain information the other is unwilling to give; each seeks to obtain accurate information about the other but to mislead, discourage, or intimidate the other; coercive tactics are used.	Open, honest communication of relevant information; each is interested in accurately informing as well as being informed; communication is persuasive rather than coercive in intent.

Adapted from M. Deutsch, "Socially Relevant Science: Some Reflections on Some Studies of Interpersonal Conflict," *American Psychologist* **24** (1969): 1078.

in terms of substantive issues may be *interpreted* as being win-lose because of emotional issues that create negative attitudes and perceptions between the parties.

In the collaborative relationship, one person's chances for goal attainment increase or decrease along with the other person's chances. In contrast, the interdependencies in the win-lose relationship are such that as one person's chances for goal attainment increase, the other person's chances decrease. In the extreme win-lose situation, the parties are likely to have difficulties in solving problems and may engage in tactics resulting in ineffective performance for the entire organization. When the Pennsylvania Railroad and the New York Central Railroad "merged" to create the Penn-Central, for example, the two groups are reported to have continually fought each other. Cooperation was at such a low level that the two groups could not integrate their computer-based information systems, which resulted in thousands of goods-filled railroad cars being lost, late deliveries, and billing errors. As you might expect, many customers sought other means for shipping their goods, which ultimately contributed to the bankruptcy of the Penn-Central. On the other hand, we need to reemphasize that it is naive and futile to assume that a relationship is basically collaborative when there are real differences between the parties in terms of goals, policies, plans, and procedures.

In the mixed situation, the parties are faced with dilemmas concerning secrecy versus openness, deceit versus honesty, and distrust versus trust. There is some evidence that individuals often deal with these dilemmas, in part, by adopting middle-of-the-road behaviors. They are neither entirely open nor secretive, trusting nor distrustful, honest nor deceitful.[21] It has not been determined whether this is the most desirable approach for the parties when they are in a mixed situation.

Interpersonal Styles for Managing Conflict[22]

The interpersonal styles to manage conflicts may be used when managers are parties to the conflict or when they are coming into a conflict situation, such as between two subordinates. We will discuss five major interpersonal styles for managing conflict: avoidance, compromise, smoothing, forcing, and confrontation.

AVOIDANCE

Most simply, the manager may withdraw from the conflict, being unavailable for conference, deferring answering a disturbing memo, or refusing to take sides in the conflict. The avoidance-prone manager may act merely as a communication link by transmitting messages between superiors and subordinates. When asked to take a position on controversial issues, he or she is likely to say: "There has not been time to study the problem fully"; or "I would need more facts before making a judgment"; or "Perhaps the best way is to proceed as you think best."[23]

When unresolved conflicts can affect the tasks for which the manager is responsible, the avoidance style is likely to have a negative impact on organizational effectiveness. However, conflict avoidance may be desirable when:

1. the issue is so minor or of passing importance that it's not worth the time or energy to confront the conflict;

2. the power is so low relative to the other party that the manager perceives little opportunity to affect a change (such as major, top-level organizational policies);

3. others can more effectively resolve the conflict than the manager, e.g., the subordinates themselves.

COMPROMISE

Compromise is "splitting the difference." There may be several problems with the *early* use of this conflict-resolution style, however. First, the manager may be encouraging compromises on the *expressed* issues rather than on the underlying conflicts. The early use of compromise results in less diagnosing and exploring the nature of the real conflict. Oftentimes, the first issues raised are not the real ones, but are used merely as openers. For example, a student's telling the prof that his or her course is really tough and challenging may be a way of trying to negotiate a better grade in the course. Second, there is a tendency to accept the initial positions presented, rather than exploring and searching for additional alternatives acceptable to all. Third, compromise may be inappropriate to all or part of the conflict situation. There may be better means of resolving the conflict than suggested by either of the parties. Much more problem solving may be needed in the search for additional alternatives. Thus the conflict issue might require both the confrontation and compromise styles. Finally, the early use of compromise may leave the parties feeling uneasy and somewhat dissatisfied.

Our concern is primarily with the use of this style too early in the conflict situation and when another style may be more appropriate. But if the parties to a conflict have relatively equal power and are in a win-lose or mixed situation, such as a typical union-management relationship, it is likely that compromise through the bargaining process will be useful. Thus compromise might be desirable when:

1. both parties perceive the possibility of reaching an agreement in which each party would be better off or no worse off than if no agreement is reached;

2. both parties perceive that there is more than one such agreement that could be reached; and

3. both parties perceive that their goals are conflicting or their interests opposed with regard to the different agreements that might be reached (distributive part of the relationship).[24]

SMOOTHING

In the smoothing style, the manager acts as though the conflict will pass with time and appeals simply to the need for cooperation. This manager tries to reduce tensions by reassuring and providing support to the parties. Although some concern is expressed with the emotional aspects of the conflict, there is little recognition and interest in working on the goals, plans, and policies that are part of the conflict. The smoothing style simply encourages the parties to cover up and avoid expression of their feelings and therefore is not typically effective as an overall style. The smoothing style is based on an attitude of "our friendship shouldn't be disrupted by this problem, so let's not worry too much about it, because things will work out."[25] However, the smoothing style may be effective when:

1. the parties are in a potentially explosive conflict situation, and smoothing is used to defuse it;
2. keeping harmony and avoiding disruption are especially important; and
3. the conflicts are based primarily on personality characteristics of the parties and can't be dealt with in the prevailing organizational climate.

FORCING

Forcing is based on coercive power, and the solution reached is satisfactory to only one of the parties. The manager assumes that the conflict involves a win-lose situation and when dealing with conflicts between subordinates or between departments may threaten or actually apply punishments, e.g., demotion, dismissal, or the threat of a poor performance evaluation. Forcing is suggested in such phrases as: "If you don't like the way things are run, get out"; "If you two can't learn to cooperate, I am sure others can be hired who will." When conflicts are between peers, the individuals might try to get their own way by appealing to a common superior. In this manner, a superior is used to force the decision on the opposing party.

Overreliance on forcing may lessen the motivation of the party whose interests have not been considered. Furthermore, relevant information and other possible alternatives may be ignored (also see the effects of win-lose relationships in Table 14.2). However, there are some contingencies under which the forcing style may be necessary, e.g., when:

1. there are extreme emergencies and quick action is necessary;
2. unpopular courses of action must be taken for long-term organizational effectiveness and survival (such as cost cutting and dismissal of employees for unsatisfactory performance); and
3. others are trying to take advantage of someone, and the person needs to take quick action for self-protection.[26]

CONFRONTATION

In the confrontation, or problem-solving, style of conflict management, the conflict is recognized openly so that it can be evaluated by all of the parties. Sharing, examining, and assessing the reasons for the perceived conflict may lead to a more thorough development of alternatives that can be discussed by those involved. This process increases the probability of discovering an alternative that effectively resolves the conflict and is acceptable to all of the conflicting parties. One manager describes the use of confrontation for resolving inter-departmental conflicts this way: "In recent meetings we had a thrashing around about manpower needs. At first we didn't have much agreement, but we kept thrashing around and finally agreed on what was the best we could do."[27]

If confrontation is so effective, one might ask, why isn't it used more frequently? Some of the barriers to using the confrontation style are:

1. task requirements (e.g., time limits inhibit direct confrontation of feelings and issues involved in a conflict);

2. group norms (e.g., shared feelings that managers should not express negative feelings toward others);

3. personal role concepts (e.g., a boss who feels the ability to engage in conflict with a subordinate is nonetheless limited by her or his supervisory role).[28]

The use of confrontation is likely to be influenced by the type of management system (mechanistic versus organic) and the leadership style of one's superior. The supportive and participative manager is more likely to encourage and utilize the confrontation style than is an autocratic manager. The confrontation style is likely to be used more frequently and may possibly be more necessary in the organic than in the mechanistic managerial system. If external factors, such as type of management system or leadership style, do not prevent the use of confrontation, is it simply a matter of "opening up" and "going at it"? The answer is yes, but only when the conflicts are limited to goals, plans, policies, and procedures. When emotional issues enter in (which is usually the case), confrontation can backfire and increase interpersonal conflicts.

Several confrontation guidelines that may be useful in managing interpersonal conflicts are the following:

1. Don't just complain; ask for a reasonable change.
2. Ask for and give feedback on the major point.
3. Be tolerant.
4. Consider compromise after the analysis of the "real" problems and the generation of alternatives. Remember, the other's view of reality may be just as real as yours, even though you may differ.
5. Never assume that you know what the other person is thinking until you have checked out the assumption in plain language.
6. Never put labels (e.g., "coward," "neurotic," or "child") on the other person.
7. Forget the past and stay with the here-and-now. What either of you did last year or last month or yesterday morning is not as important as what you are doing and feeling now.[29]

These guidelines are easy to state, but often quite difficult to practice in a spontaneous and natural manner. Effective confrontations require more than opening up to others; they demand opening up to oneself and gaining self-insight as well. The confrontation style of conflict management is likely to be very effective when:

1. the parties have common goals (i.e., a basically integrative relationship) but are experiencing conflict over the *means* to achieve these goals;
2. a consensus is likely to lead to the best overall solution to the conflict; and
3. there is a need to make decisions on the basis of the best expertise and information available.

In sum, the confrontation style often has great potential for effectively managing conflicts, but the parties should be ready and willing to abide by the types of guidelines presented. Otherwise, the adoption of a confrontation style may lead to a deterioration in relationships and increase conflict. Although confrontation is often regarded as the "best" style, each style may be useful under different contingencies.[30] Finally, the parties may need assistance of third parties—external consultants or internal specialists in organizational behavior—to assist them in developing the skills and self-insights necessary for effective use of the confrontation style.

INTERGROUP CONFLICT

The third level of conflict focuses on differences and clashes between groups, departments, or divisions within an organization. But before exploring some of the causes, effects, and mechanisms for managing intergroup conflicts, let's briefly consider the interrelationships between the three levels of conflict emphasized in this chapter.

Interrelationships in Levels of Conflict

From a systems viewpoint, there is no simple cause-and-effect or beginning-and-ending relationship between role conflict, interpersonal conflict, and intergroup conflict (see Fig. 14.4). We have gone from the simple to the complex in considering the levels of conflict. Intrasender role conflict (i.e., incompatible expectations of the role sender toward the focal person) on plans, policies, and goals could lead to broader interpersonal conflicts involving emotional issues of distrust, secrecy, and the lack of communication. Interpersonal conflicts, e.g., between two managers, could be enlarged to influence the relations between all of the two managers' subordinates. The managers might limit the exchange of needed information between the two groups of subordinates or, by expressing bitter and hostile attitudes toward the other department, influence the development of similar feelings within their subordinates.

Finally, intergroup conflicts could trigger role conflicts. For example, the sales department might have large orders from two customers who are both pressuring for an early delivery of their order and threatening to take their future business elsewhere if their demands are not met. As a result, members of the sales department pressure the production department to meet *both* delivery dates, but production finds it difficult, if not impossible, to meet both time schedules within the normal workweek. This leads to intrasender role conflict for members of the production department. The sales department responds that there is really no problem, since production can work overtime. However, intersender role conflict could become a problem if the production manager finds it difficult to meet the department's efficiency standards because of the relatively higher labor costs with overtime. Thus production is under pressure

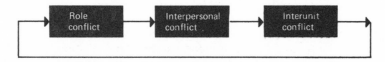

Fig. 14.4. Interrelationships between three levels of conflict.

from the sales department for overtime and from the formal department goals

to keep per-unit labor costs within certain limits. One of the more obvious ways for managing this situation is to push the conflict up the line for resolution by the two departments' common superior.

The discussion of the interrelationships between the three levels of conflict is illustrative rather than exhaustive. Our aim is to caution that a fuller understanding of conflict situations can be gained by diagnosing them in terms of all three levels of conflict. The initial cause of a conflict can stimulate other levels of conflict. This, in turn, can increase the intensity of the initial cause of the conflict and compound the problems in resolving the total conflict situation.

Causes of Intergroup Conflict[31]

Our discussion has already suggested that role conflicts and interpersonal conflicts can "cause" intergroup conflict. Some of the other "causes" of intergroup conflicts are: task interdependencies, task dependencies, inconsistent performance criteria and rewards, and intergroup differences and problems in sharing scarce common resources. Naturally, conflict between groups can stem from more than one of these causes.

TASK INTERDEPENDENCY

A major cause of work-related conflicts—between groups, peers, or superiors and subordinates or intraunit *task interdependency* refers to the extent to which two groups rely on and need each other for service, information, and goods to accomplish their own tasks and goals. Although task interdependency should suggest a collaborative situation, the groups can encounter severe conflicts. An increase in demand may increase pressure on one or both groups to provide the necessary added services and/or to provide them more quickly. This overloading may increase tension and frustrations and lead to intergroup conflicts. It is not unusual to find this taking place between the computer-processing and other departments during certain peak periods. The production, marketing, personnel, and finance departments may all be demanding and needing programming assistance and computer runs at the same time.

Interdependent groups may also engage in conflicts because of the ambiguities or uncertainties as to the tasks each is to perform. The following is an example of ambiguity over the jurisdictions of the commercial department and plant department in a telephone company.

> The commercial department receives recognition for sales orders that it handles. The plant department receives credit for additional or replacement orders made by its installation men. If the customer takes a replacement (say, a princess phone rather than a slim-line phone), then the commercial department loses recognition for its sales; therefore, it is important to the commercial department that the plant department installation men carry the proper equipment on their trucks and follow installation orders. Even then, there is ambiguity about who can initiate substitute service ideas for the customer's consideration.[32]

In this study, the lack of clarity about which department had responsibility for particular tasks was the most consistent source of conflict. The department responded to the ambiguity by trying to avoid responsibility for tasks requiring time and personnel. Where it was advantageous to control the tasks, there was conflict because of mutual attempts to claim jurisdiction over common areas.

TASK DEPENDENCY

Task dependency occurs when one group must rely on another group for services, information, and goods. Since the independent group has less incentive to cooperate with the dependent group, the latter may generate pressure to gain the needed assistance. This could lead to either cooperation or a negative response by the independent group. For example, the assembly departments at Mack Truck are dependent on the flow of parts (doors, engines, tires, etc.) from other departments. If the parts do not arrive as needed or if they vary from specification, the assembly department has difficulty in performing its tasks. The assembly department might then pressure other departments and possibly create conflicts. Maintenance of an inventory of parts at each work station could serve to minimize this type of conflict. But because of the costs involved, inventories are likely to be kept at a minimum. Thus a major breakdown in a supplying department will influence the assembly department in short order. It may then respond by putting heavy pressure on the supplying departments to get into business again.

In a study of line and staff conflicts, one researcher found that staff departments could justify their existence only by providing services to the line departments.[33] But since the staff departments could not require the use of their services, they had to promote their ideas and follow a policy of understanding the problems of the line departments. Because none of these relations required reciprocity by the line, the staff departments felt frustrated and were often in conflict with the line.

INCONSISTENT PERFORMANCE CRITERIA AND REWARDS

Interdependent groups may be evaluated and rewarded on the basis of criteria that motivate them to concentrate on their self- (or competing) interests rather than on common interests. The greater the interdependency of two groups and the more higher management emphasizes the separate rather than combined performance of the groups, the more conflict is likely.

Line-staff conflicts are often made worse by the reward system. Staff departments push for change in order to prove their worth to top management. To line departments, change may imply that their previous activity was below standard.

Another example of the way performance criteria can stimulate conflict between units is provided by the previously mentioned telephone company study.

The plant department maintains all equipment; failure in some pieces of equipment subtracts directly from its efficiency indices; failure in others reduces indices of the traffic department, which must often request the plant department to give priority to maintenance or repair work on equipment that is especially vital to the performance of the traffic department. If other maintenance work is also required, which is important to the efficiency and evaluation indices of the plant department, then there is strong conflict of interest in this situation.[34]

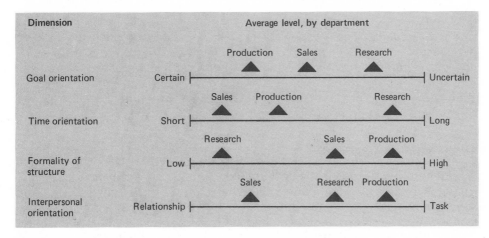

Fig. 14.5. Interdepartment differences in the plastics industry.

INTERGROUP DIFFERENCES

Groups may differ significantly because they perform different tasks and deal with different parts of the organization's task environment. (See Chapter 5 for a detailed discussion of differentiation.) These differences are a potential cause of intergroup conflict. Differences between the research, sales, and production departments, for example, have been classified into four categories: goal orientation, time orientation, department structures, and interpersonal orientation.[35] *Goal orientation* could differ in terms of scientific knowledge (research department) versus customer problems and market opportunities (marketing department) versus costs of producing units (production department). *Time orientation* refers to how long it would take the department to know the results of its decisions. The research department is likely to have a long time horizon, the sales department a short to moderate time horizon, and the production department a moderate to short time horizon. The formality of *structure* of departments refers to their relative tightness of rules, span of control, and frequency and specificity of supervisory control. The research department is likely to have the least formal structure (organic system), the production department the most formal structure (mechanistic system), and the sales department somewhere in between. *Interpersonal orientation* refers to the relative openness, sociability, and permissiveness in relationships within the department. The sales department is likely to be the most open and sociable interpersonally, the production department the least, and research in between. Figure 14.5 summarizes the relative differences in these categories for the production, sales, and basic research departments of six organizations in the plastics industry.[36] The figure suggests that the greater the differentiation between departments, the greater the potential difficulty of integrating tasks between them. In turn, these differences may be causes of intergroup conflicts.

SHARING COMMON RESOURCES

Conflicts often arise because scarce resources must be shared. Thus departments might compete for physical space, equipment, operating or capital funds, and centralized services (typing, printing, or computer time).

Intergroup conflict has a variety of causes: task interdependencies, task dependencies, inconsistent performance criteria and rewards, intergroup differences, and the need to share common resources. It is probably not possible to eliminate all these sources of intergroup conflict. But appropriate managerial actions and decisions can do much to reduce them when they occur and keep them at levels that do not cause poor performance.

Effects of Intergroup Conflict

A summary of the possible effects of conflicting intergroup relationships is shown in Table 14.3. In addition, other characteristics may influence a conflict situation. For example, competition between two groups may stimulate aggression or withdrawal by one of them, depending on the personalities of the members involved in each group. To some managers, conflict is a major threat; for others, it stimulates energy and involvement. If the conflicting groups are highly interdependent and either has the ability to conceal and distort information needed by the other, a major negative result may be less timely and poorer quality decisions.

If the groups cannot resolve even minor issues and continuously appeal to a common superior, this individual may soon be overloaded with their tasks. This can have serious negative effects. The superior has to keep working on day-to-day instead of on long-range problems. On the other hand, the common superior may want to become involved in important conflicts between the groups because it increases awareness about the operations and subordinates.

In sum, the characteristics of conflicting intergroup relationships may have positive or negative effects, or in some cases, both types of effects.[37] To evaluate the likelihood of these effects, it is necessary to consider other situational variables, such as the degree of task interdependency between the groups, personal attributes of the members, differences in goals, and the relative power of the groups.

Managing Intergroup Conflict

Mechanisms used to manage role and interpersonal conflicts may also be useful in managing intergroup conflicts. In particular, the most effective interpersonal styles for managing intergroup conflicts are confrontation and compromise.[38]

Although our focus throughout the chapter has been on mechanisms that do not basically alter the assigned goal structures or task interdependencies, conflict can also be reduced by structural changes, e.g., an altered reward system, better selection, and more effective training programs. A reward system that places greater emphasis on acts of collaboration is likely to encourage that type of behavior. Multiple group incentives, e.g., bonuses, based on plantwide productivity are likely to encourage departmental collaboration. Separate and different departmental incentives, especially when the departments are interdependent, can lead to undesirable competition between the groups. Task interdependencies, one of the principal sources of all conflict, can be reduced by such means as: (1) reducing dependence on common resources; (2) loosening

Table 14.3. Effects of intergroup conflict

Characteristics of intergroup conflict	Positive effects	Negative effects
Competition	Increases motivation Contributes to a system of checks and balances Increases number of new ideas to compete with established ones Decreases collusion among groups	Decreases motivation May deprive higher-level management of information
Concealment and distortion of information		Lowers quality of decisions
Appeals to superiors for decisions	Superior becomes more informed about operations and subordinates, may lead to confrontation with superior as a third-party facilitator	Superior may become overloaded by referrals; may lead to forcing with superior handing down edicts without full knowledge
Rigidity and formality in decision procedures	May increase stability in the system	May lower adaptability to change
Decreased rate of intergroup interaction	May decrease problem *if* a group or person is used to provide the necessary liaison	Hinders coordination and implementation of tasks
Low trust, suspicion, hostility	Increased cohesion within group contributing to cooperation within group	Psychological strain and turnover of personnel

Adapted from R. Walton and J. Dutton, "The Management of Interdepartmental Conflict: A Model and Review," *Administrative Science Quarterly* **14** (1969): 73–83.

up schedules, establishing inventories, or using contingency funds; and (3) simply reducing pressures for consensus.[39] Each of these techniques has its own set of costs. Managers must evaluate whether the benefits gained from decreased conflicts are greater than the costs of the techniques used to reduce them.

There are, of course, a variety of other mechanisms for managing intergroup conflicts, e.g., interventions by superiors and/or use of superordinate goals, separate integrating groups, and standardized practices. As might be expected, the greater the differences between groups and the more they need coordination, the greater the emphasis on and use of a variety of conflict-management tactics.

INTERVENTIONS BY SUPERIORS

In one high-performing container (beer cans and cardboard boxes) organization, the knowledge needed to resolve intergroup conflicts was found to exist primarily at the top levels of the organization.[40] The task environment of the container organization was characterized by relatively few uncertainties about technology, customers, legal regulations, and the like. The main competitive issues—delivery times and quality—required tight coordination between the sales and production departments, and only the top executives had the necessary knowledge to balance all the factors involved. With their broad understanding and responsibility for resolving conflicts and making the needed decisions, these superiors kept the sales and production departments informed of critical problems and kept them from persisting in their problems or reaching poor decisions. They also intervened by modifying departmental goals and task interdependencies.

This case shows that when groups with moderately different structures and orientations have conflicts, they can probably be effectively resolved through intervention by a common superior. In such cases, the use of more involved mechanisms may simply make integration and conflict resolution more difficult.

SUPERORDINATE GOALS

Superordinate goals are the shared goals that can be achieved only through cooperation. For example, in dealing with conflicts between marketing and production, a president might emphasize that the cooperation of *both* groups is necessary if the firm is to earn profits, survive, and grow. These outcomes are examples of superordinate goals for the production and marketing departments.

If groups are engaged in intense conflicts, it may be difficult to get them to perceive any superordinate goals *unless* a "common threat" appears on the scene. A common threat acts as a superordinate goal when the parties realize that they will all lose something unless they cooperate. A common threat for conflicting groups within a firm might be a new competitor that could make substantial inroads on the firm's market. For example, IBM's introduction of its new line of high-quality copiers in the early 1970s was generally regarded as a major long-term threat to Xerox, then dominating the copier market. Similarly, competing national political parties may present a united front if the country goes to war. The two groups set aside some of their differences and conflicts in order to beat the enemy, a superordinate goal.

If accepted, superordinate goals are likely to have a quick impact on the level of emotional conflict between the conflicting groups.[41] Unless other steps are taken, it is not likely that the use of superordinate goals alone will resolve the long-term conflicts between the parties, however. For example, once the war is won, the political parties are likely to bring to the surface their old conflicts.

SEPARATE INTEGRATING GROUPS

A separate integrating group may help to resolve conflicts and achieve coordination between two groups. Use of this third group would be necessary only when the groups are highly interdependent, require tight integration (coordination), and are highly differentiated from each other.

In the study of the six plastics-industry organizations mentioned previously, the two most successful organizations had integrating groups. The successful integrating groups had the following characteristics:

1. In terms of their goal, time, and interpersonal orientations and their degree of structure, the integrating personnel were midway between the members of the linked groups. This intermediate position enabled the integrating groups to communicate with all other groups and gave them a "neutral," objective posture.
2. The integrating personnel had relatively high influence, based on their expertise and formal authority.
3. The integrators felt that higher-level superiors evaluated and rewarded them on overall performance measures, which included the activities of the groups they were responsible for integrating. In contrast, the integrating managers in the poor-performing organizations thought that individual performance or performance of their subordinates was more important.
4. The more effective organizations openly confronted differences between groups rather than smoothed or forced them.[42]

These findings suggest that the creation of integrating groups requires careful judgment by higher-level managers.

STANDARDIZED PRACTICES[43]

There are a number of formal procedures and practices that can aid in managing intergroup conflicts.

1. Permanent teams or committees consisting of representatives from the interdependent groups and the integrating group, if one exists, should meet on a regular basis. This reduces the tendency of parties to "withdraw" from conflicts in the short run and avoids the tendency of conflicts to build up before they are finally confronted.
2. Higher-level managers might encourage direct contact of individuals across groups and between levels. This may aid problem solving and prevent the development of intense conflicts between groups or individuals.
3. Procedures may be established for appealing to a common superior. One of the potential weaknesses of such procedures, however, is the possibility that the parties or groups will perceive the conflict as a win-lose situation.
4. Training sessions in interpersonal and intergroup dynamics and/or the use of third-party interventions by behavioral scientists may be effective. (More will be said about this in the next chapter.)

There is no single mechanism for managing intergroup conflict. A manager can err by creating a too elaborate conflict-resolution network, which could result in too much time being spent on minor conflicts and confusion for the conflicting parties. On the other hand, an elaborate conflict-resolution network may be desirable when there is high differentiation between the groups as well as high needs for coordination.

Summary

In focusing on internal organizational conflict, we also noted the effect of the external environment. Since conflict is neither good nor bad in and of itself, use of the contingency model is a starting point for diagnosing any level of conflict. The model presents three major types of conflict situations—win-lose, mixed, and collaborative—and considers the causes, effects, and tactics for managing role conflicts, interpersonal conflict, and intergroup conflicts. Role conflicts, which occur because of excessive or inconsistent pressure on the individual, are of four types: intrasender, intersender, interrole, and person-role. High levels of role conflict can have negative effects, such as poor performance and job dissatisfaction. Role conflicts are often dealt with through such personal tactics as avoidance, rationalization, and projection, but can also be dealt with more positively through confrontation and various organizational tactics.

Causes of interpersonal conflicts may range from disagreements over policies, practices, or plans to emotionally based issues. Among the interpersonal styles for managing conflicts are avoidance, compromise, smoothing, forcing, and confrontation (problem solving).

At a more complex level, intergroup conflicts may be "caused" by task interdependencies, task dependencies, inconsistent performance criteria and rewards, differences between groups, and problems in sharing common resources. The ultimate effect of high levels of intergroup conflict is probably lower profits, poor service, and reduced long-term effectiveness. Some of the tactics for managing intergroup conflicts are interventions by superiors, superordinate goals, separate integrating groups, and standardized practices.

Since these conflict levels are quite interrelated, a manager should not rush to a conclusion about "the" cause of a particular conflict. Rather, a manager needs to first diagnose the conflict in terms of each of these levels and then develop a more meaningful course of action for dealing with it.

Discussion Questions

1. Why is conflict inevitable in organizations?

2. Give an example of a "mixed-conflict" situation from your past, using the contingency model of conflict. Identify those elements that contributed to the distributive nature of the conflict.

3. Why is it important to diagnose a conflict situation prior to entry into it, if possible?

4. Drawing on your own experience, give an example of intergroup conflict. What were its causes?

5. Discuss the likely relationships between the relative power of individuals and intensity of their perceived role conflicts.

6. How does personality act as a contingency between role senders and focal persons in influencing the mechanisms for managing conflicts?

7. When can conflict help individuals, groups, and organizations be more effective?

8. When can conflict hurt the effectiveness of individuals, groups, and organizations?

9. Why is avoidance or withdrawal so commonly used as an interpersonal mechanism for managing conflicts?

Management Incidents

PANTHER INN*

In October 1972 Midland University became a member of the Small Business Institute, an experimental program under the auspices of the Small Business Administration. The objective of the institute was to provide university students to give management assistance to small businesses. The student consultants thus had the opportunity to complement their academic experience through exposure to "real world" problems.

One of the 20 cases assigned to the students at Midland University was the Panther Inn (PI), a family restaurant and lounge located at the intersection of I–88 and State Route 127 near Bloomfield, Illinois. Located in the Panther Valley, PI has a scenic view of rolling farmland. PI is located in Midland County about 40 miles from Midland University.

PI was assigned to a team of three management students: Dave, Helen, and Jim. All three were a little older than the average student, having pursued other careers before continuing their educations, and all three had prior small-business consulting experience. The institute's policy was for each team to work on two cases per quarter. In addition to Panther Inn, the team was consulting with Alpha Electronics, a small electronics repair shop. The team enjoyed an excellent working relationship with Alpha Electronics.

PI was founded by Harvey Adams, who had secured a loan of $300,000 from the SBA. The loan was 90 percent guaranteed by the SBA, with an interest rate of 8 percent on the unpaid balance. Four months later, he secured a loan of $350,000 from the SBA. The first $300,000 of this loan was to cancel the original note; the remaining $50,000 was for additional financing. An additional $10,000 was borrowed from relatives in order to provide working capital. The

---

*This case was prepared by Professor Thomas F. Urban (Texas A&M University) and Harvey J. Brightman (Georgia State University). Copyright © 1973 by Thomas F. Urban and Harvey J. Brightman. Used with permission.

restaurant and surrounding property had a current net worth of $700,000, but was expected to reach $1,000,000 at completion.

Since Mr. Adams was involved in other business activities, he handed PI over to his son, Chuck, who became owner and manager. Chuck was 22 years old, married, a high school graduate, and had no prior business education or experience.

In their initial meeting, both Mr. Adams and Chuck enthusiastically welcomed the proposed counseling by the team. Chuck admitted that he knew nothing about a restaurant business. He had originally just wanted to be the bartender for the lounge. Since the restaurant was entering the operational phase, Dave, Helen, and Jim outlined their approach to the problems of PI. Their initial conclusion was that special attention should be directed toward market research, inventory control, financial and accounting operations, and overall management of the restaurant and the lounge.

In touring the facility, the team noted that there were two distinct operations located at PI: restaurant on the main floor and the lounge on the lower level. Seating capacity for the restaurant included two counters with 15 seats each and a table capacity of 175 customers. The party rooms were not operating at full capacity (approximately 200 persons). The lounge area was currently operating at its 100-person capacity, but when fully completed, two bars will be operating with a capacity of 200 customers.

Chuck stated that there were 24 full-time and part-time employees. Because of the continual turnover and anticipated increases in personnel needs, Chuck had been spending a lot of time interviewing and filling positions.

After touring the restaurant facilities, the team began to discuss the specific needs of PI. Chuck stated that although he didn't know much about business, he thought he should be making a profit because so many customers came in, but there didn't seem to be any money left over. He was too busy hiring people and tending bar "to look into money matters." Chuck wasn't sure where the customers were coming from, but many seemed to be tourists. He also wanted to know how to order the supplies needed for the restaurant. Sometimes they ran out of food; at other times the employees had to eat it in order to keep it from going to waste. Chuck concluded by stating, "I want to be a good manager, but how? I never have any time left over to take care of anything. Just tell me what to do and I'll do it."

The team told Chuck that they needed to develop a cost analysis of the restaurant and lounge, as well as a labor analysis of the current wage structure. Since Chuck had no idea as to whether the restaurant and/or lounge was making a profit, he relied on his accountant to provide these figures. The team indicated that they would need more data and figures to analyze the situation. Chuck said that they could get this from the accountant if he had it, adding that the accountant was an old family friend of his father and was a "nice guy." In addition, the team recommended a market research program in order to determine the extent of PI's potential market share. Finally, Chuck wanted an analysis of his parking lot layout and facilities in order to efficiently park the customers. The first meeting closed on a friendly note as Chuck had to return to the lounge and tend bar. He promised to get all the records from the accountant and said, "You can do anything you want. I just don't know that much about business and you're the experts. I'm glad the SBA put you in to do the work for me."

Several weeks later, Dr. Urman, the team's faculty adviser, was grading papers when he was interrupted by Dave, Helen, and Jim. "We're quitting PI," said Jim. "He's not going to get any more cheap labor from us. He never does anything, and now he's taken off for Florida—a two-week vacation because he 'had to get away.' " "Yeah!" said Helen, "we drove all the way up there and he's in Florida. That's it! He never does anthing we want him to."

"Hold on a second," said Dr. Urman, "we just can't drop a case because its too tough. We have a contract with the SBA and that's one of our cases. Let's start at the beginning."

"Okay," said Jim. "The first time we went out, we told him what we were going to do and what we needed. He never did anything. He wants us to do everything. When we went back a few days later, he hadn't gotten the records from the accountant. In fact, the accountant hadn't even filed a tax return for PI. We told him to place a register at the door to have people sign it. We could get our market information from this as to where the customers come from— tourists, families. We drew up a plan for his parking lot. He wanted us to go out and paint the lines for parking spaces for him. Us—management students!"

"Yeah!" said Helen. "Look at our progress reports. We tell him to do something, and it's never done. The only way we get him to do anything is to do it ourselves. Look at that accounting mess! We finally drove out to his accountant's and got the books. That dumb bookkeeper! He even wears green eye shades! He still uses a single-entry system. We analyzed the books, and he didn't have any of the data we needed. We finally worked up a cost analysis by collecting the data ourselves. Then we found he made a $2300 error. He didn't post figures in the ledger and when he did post, he put the figures in the wrong places. We finally broke the figures down into separate listings for the lounge and restaurant. When we told Chuck to get rid of him, he said that he can't because the accountant is a friend of his father."

"I took care of his personnel problems," said Dave. "We prepared a wage analysis. Then I wrote the ads for the papers and went to the employment agencies myself. I made up an organization chart and job descriptions for each position. All Chuck wants to do is tend bar. He keeps saying, 'Do what you want to do. The SBA sent you in. You're the experts.' He just thinks that everything will work out. He doesn't have any experience and wants us to take care of everything. He doesn't want to be a manager!"

"I had to take care of his marketing," said Jim. "I wrote the ads and put them in the paper. He can't rely on tourists all year. We designed the billboard for him and he never put it up. We have to do everything for him. We advertise low prices and he raises everything on his menu by $1.00 to $2.50. He didn't need to do that without asking us. Then we advertise a family restaurant, and he still won't put in a kid's menu. We wanted him to give out balloons or panthers or something, and he still hasn't even looked into it. Chuck apologizes to us for not carrying through and he admits that he's lazy. All he wants to do is tend bar."

"If we can't quit this case, Dr. Urman, how can we get him to do the things we want him to? We've done more work on this than any of our other courses, and we don't have anything to show for it. He just wants us to do the busy-work—and now he goes to Florida."

1. What types of conflicts are there in this case?
2. What are the causes of these conflicts?
3. What mechanisms for managing these conflicts might be used?

THE NEW ENGINEER*

The following is an actual letter written by a student to his professor of management about six months after graduation. Although the names of the companies have been altered, the text of the letter has not been changed, shortened, or edited in any way.

Dear Professor:

I hope this note finds you in good health.

I am presently working for ABCD Corporation, a subsidiary of WXYZ Corporation, a large conglomerate in the bio-chemical field.

ABCD is just coming out of the dark ages.

They do not have a time clock, but they do have two older gentlemen who watch what happens. They both come early and leave late. One, Mr. B, had been Chief Engineer but was replaced (he is a good engineer—very poor at human relationships). He still tries to exert his opinions and watches the office. The second is Mr. C. He is a competent engineer and influences the Chief Engineer by riding to and from work with him and talking.

The Chief Engineer is an old line type who had it hard most of his life. He does not believe in creature comforts such as air conditioning, luxury cars, neat rest rooms, carpets, etc. He does not mix with anyone much. His secretary is an older, long-time employee, not too tactful—she issues the order (not too reliably sometimes). Most of the people in the engineering office were job shoppers until I came. Between 1 May 1975 and 1 May 1976 they have hired about six engineers and draftsmen, also two female office workers; neither is outstanding.

This has presented an interesting sociometric situation. Mrs. E, who is the long-time ABCD employee and secretary to Mr. K, the Chief Engineer, is very authoritarian and not overwhelmingly liked. Mrs. J, the newer girl, is younger and has been insidiously undermining Mrs. E. It came to a head when Mrs. J thought she had won enough support and she threatened to quit. Mr. K did not fire Mrs. E. (I believe Mr. K allows Mrs. E to bear the dislike that would otherwise go to him.) Mrs. J has developed the habit of speaking to Mr. K about people who come in late, are absent, talk on the phone, etc. I am sure that she is still trying to oust Mrs. E, but she has lost her influence with the draftsmen and engineers because they feel she is using them.

Once Mr. K does become disenchanted with someone, he fires them without notice. This is typical throughout the plant.

They also play a little power game with things like issuing drafting lead, tape, paper, erasers, etc. Each thing is under lock and key. The Xerox can only be used by Mrs. E and Mrs. J, as the draftsmen and engineers are incompetent.

I believe this must cost the parent company a great deal of money, but it would be as reasonable for a Jew to have offered help to the Nazis as it would for me to make a suggestion here.

Motivation is another area that could stand some improvement. I received a raise (the maximum) without any review. I have no idea what they think of my work. I presume that it is alright.

I wonder if this could be worked into something concrete? There are a number of interesting subjects to be covered.

Some of the things I see now would have escaped my notice before I had your course.

Sincerely,
The New Engineer

1. What types of role conflicts is the new engineer apparently experiencing?
2. What interpersonal styles of conflict management seem to dominate in this situation?
3. How would you characterize the power system, based on this letter?
4. What do you think the new engineer should do?

LOIS BURGER

Lois Burger was raised in Texas and attended Texas A&M University, where she majored in petroleum engineering. Lois graduated in the top ten percent of her class and was immediately hired by one of the largest oil companies in America. Initially, Lois planned to work for the company for four or five years and then return to her home state and join her father's small oil-exploration firm.

After ten years, Lois has received several promotions and raises and is well on her way to becoming a member of top management. To return to her father's business would almost certainly mean taking a large pay cut, which she could probably never make up. Six months ago, her father suffered a heart attack, and the survival of the small company has been in danger ever since. Lois's desire to return to Texas is as strong as ever, and she has said that she wishes she were not doing so well, so that her decision would be easier. Since her father's illness, Lois has become increasingly depressed and has considered consulting an analyst in order to reach a decision.

1. What are the probable causes of Lois's conflict?
2. What type of conflict is she probably experiencing?
3. What course of action should she take?

REFERENCES

1. S. Robbins, *Managing Organizational Conflict: A Nontraditional Approach* (Englewood Cliffs, N.J.: Prentice-Hall, 1974), p. 23.

2. This discussion is modified and adapted from K. Boulding, *Conflict Management and Organizations* (Ann Arbor, Mich.: Foundation for Research on Human Behavior, 1961); M. Deutsch, *The Resolution of Conflict: Constructive and Destructive Processes* (New Haven: Yale University Press, 1973); and R. Walton, *Interpersonal Peacemaking: Confrontations and Third-Party Consultation* (Reading, Mass.: Addison-Wesley, 1969).

3. Adapted from R. Walton and R. McKersie, *A Behavioral Theory of Labor Negotiations: An Analysis of a Social Interaction System* (New York: McGraw-Hill,

1965). *Also see* S. Schmidt and T. Kochan, "Conflict: Toward Conceptual Clarity," *Administrative Science Quarterly* **17** (1972): 359–370.

4. S. Kerr, "On the Folly of Rewarding A, While Hoping for B," *Academy of Management Journal* **18** (1975): 777.

5. Modified from R. Walton and R. McKersie, "Behavioral Dilemmas in Mixed-Motive Decision-Making," *Behavioral Science* **11** (1966): 370–384.

6. Adapted from J. Dutton and R. Walton, "Interdepartmental Conflict and Cooperation: Two Contrasting Studies," in *Managing Group and Intergroup Relations*, ed. J. Lorsch and P. Lawrence, Homewood, Ill.: Richard D. Irwin and the Dorsey Press, 1972, pp. 285–304.

7. Adapted from R. Kahn, D. Wolfe, R. Quinn, and J. Snoek, *Organizational Stress: Studies in Role Conflict and Ambiguity* (New York: Wiley, 1964).

8. R. Merton, *Social Theory and Social Structure*, 2d ed. (Glencoe, Ill.: Free Press, 1957).

9. J. Nagel, *The Descriptive Analysis of Power* (New Haven: Yale University Press, 1975); V. Murray, "Some Unanswered Questions on Organizational Conflict," *Organization and Administrative Sciences* **5** (1974/1975): 35–53.

10. Kahn *et al.*, *op. cit.*, p. 26.

11. *Ibid.*, p. 29.

12. *Ibid.*, pp. 57–58.

13. R. Corwin, "Militant Professionalism, Initiative, and Compliance in Public Education," *Sociology of Education* **28** (1965): 310–331.

14. R. Likert and J. Likert, *New Ways of Managing Conflict* (New York: McGraw-Hill, 1976); E. Harrison and J. Rosenzweig, "Professional Norms and Organizational Goals: An Illusory Dichotomy," *California Management Review* **14** (1972): 38–48.

15. E. Gross, "When Occupations Meet: Professions in Trouble," *Hospital Administration* **12** (1967): 40–59.

16. Kahn *et al.*, *op. cit.*, p. 66.

17. D. Rogers and J. Molnar, "Organizational Antecedents of Role Conflict and Ambiguity in Top Level Administrators," *Administrative Science Quarterly* **21** (1976): 598–610.

18. R. Miles, "A Comparison of the Relative Impacts of Role Perceptions of Ambiguity and Conflict By Role," *Academy of Management Journal* **19** (1976): 25–35.

19. A. Filley, *Interpersonal Conflict Resolution* (Glenview, Ill.: Scott, Foresman, 1975).

20. M. Deutsch, "Socially Relevant Science: Reflections on Some Studies of Interpersonal Conflict," *American Psychologist* **24** (1969): 1076–1092.

21. H. Kelley, "Interpersonal Accommodation," *American Psychologist* **23** (1968): 384–410.

22. Adapted from R. Blake and J. Mouton, *The Managerial Grid* (Houston: Gulf, 1964).

23. *Ibid.*, p. 95.

24. Deutsch, *The Resolution of Conflict*, *op. cit.*, p. 216.

25. P. Lawrence and J. Lorsch, *Organization and Environment* (Homewood, Ill.: Richard D. Irwin, 1967), p. 75.

26. K. Thomas, "Conflict and Conflict Management," in *Handbook of Industrial and Organizational Psychology*, ed. M. Dunnette (Chicago: Rand McNally, 1976), pp. 889–935.

27. Lawrence and Lorsch, *Organization and Environment, op. cit.*, p. 74.

28. R. Walton, *Interpersonal Peacemaking: Confrontation and Third-Party Consultation* (Reading, Mass.: Addison-Wesley, 1969), p. 76.

29. *Ibid.*, pp. 94–115.

30. H. Bernardin and K. Alvares, "The Managerial Grid As a Predictor of Conflict Resolution Method and Managerial Effectiveness," *Administrative Science Quarterly* **21** (1976): 84–92.

31. This section is heavily based on the literature review in Walton and Dutton, *op. cit.*, pp. 73–83.

32. R. Walton, J. Dutton, and T. Cafferty, "Organizational Context and Interdepartmental Conflict," *Administrative Science Quarterly* **14** (1969): 527.

33. M. Dalton, *Men Who Manage* (New York: Wiley, 1959).

34. Walton, Dutton, and Cafferty, *op. cit.*, p. 527.

35. Lawrence and Lorsch, *Organization and Environment, op. cit.*, pp. 36, 91.

36. *Ibid.*

37. S. Lourenco and J. Glidewell, "A Dialectical Analysis of Organizational Conflict," *Administrative Science Quarterly* **20** (1975): 489–508.

38. J. Rubin and B. Brown, *The Social Psychology of Bargaining and Negotiation* (New York: Academic Press, 1975); J. Lorsch and S. Allen, III, *Managing Diversity and Interdependence: An Organizational Study of Multidivisional Firms* (Boston: Graduate School of Business Administration, Harvard University, 1973).

39. L. Pondy, "Organizational Conflict: Concepts and Models," *Administrative Science Quarterly* **12** (1967): 264–319.

40. Lawrence and Lorsch, *Organization and Environment, op. cit.*, pp. 110–124.

41. J. Hunger and L. Stern, "An Assessment of the Functionality of the Superordinate Goal in Reducing Conflict," *Academy of Management Journal* **19** (1976): 591–605.

42. Lawrence and Lorsch, *Organization and Environment, op. cit.*, pp. 54–83.

43. R. Walton, "Third-Party Roles in Interdepartmental Conflict," *Industrial Relations* **7** (1967): 24–43.

IV

IV

The Process of Change

CHANGE PROCESSES

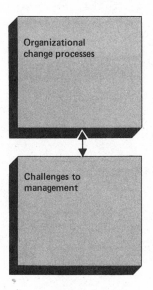

The growth and change of an organization have been compared to a painter working on a landscape. Managers cannot build an organization, nor does it grow, by starting with particular activities that are arranged in an orderly sequence of events. Instead, managers build an entire organization by simultaneously molding, structuring, and fitting personnel, capital, and talent together. Similarly, the artist paints a landscape by fitting the pieces in the total landscape together while keeping in mind the total scene that he or she is trying to capture.

In Chapter 15, we will consider the meaning of planned organizational change. The reasons why organizational change is necessary, as well as the resistances to change, are examined. A model of change is presented and discussed. Finally, four strategies to achieving organizational change are examined. Implications and case studies are presented as a further means to give you an insight into the change processes used by organizations.

During the past decade, managements have faced many challenges of their values, practices, and policies. Among other things, we have seen a rise in shear size of organizations, the growth of the multinational organizations, changes in the make-up of the labor force, and society's demands on managements to be more socially responsible. Chapter 16 discusses these changes and their likely impact on the behavior of managers in the future. Organizations are placing different demands on their managers, requiring them to perform more and varied tasks with less time to plan, than they have in the past. Career planning is discussed as one means of trying to assist managers to cope with these new problems.

15

Organizational Change Processes

The objectives of this chapter are to:

discuss the objectives for understanding planned organizational change;

present a model for understanding the process of organizational change;

explore reasons why individuals and organizations may resist change;

discuss various change strategies available to managers, including technology, structure, task, and people;

indicate various ways managers may achieve change.

Organizations are never really static, since they are continually in contact with other groups that are making demands on them that change over time. Some of these groups are competitors, suppliers, outside pressure groups, governments, employees, and customers. Shifts in attitudes of customers, technical breakthroughs, and demands from diverse groups in society are a sampling of the forces that underlie organizational change. The pace of change will vary from organization to organization, but the fact of change will not. Many changes, of course, will be beyond the control of the organization; others can be created and guided by the organization. One author has stated that:

> change has always been a part of the human condition. What is different now is the pace of change, and the prospect that it will come faster and faster, affecting every part of life, including personal values, morality, and religion, which seem almost remote from technology. . . . So swift is the acceleration, that trying to "make sense" of change will become our basic industry.[1]

Some of the areas of change are noted in Fig. 15.1.

In his penetrating book *Future Shock,* Alvin Toffler argues that humanity is now a part of an environment so unfamiliar and complex that it is threatening millions with "future shock."[2] Future shock occurs when the types of changes and their speed of introduction overpower the individual's ability to adapt. The problem comes not from a particular change that one cannot handle, but from the fact that since so many things are changing, new ways of dealing with the "temporary society" are needed. This temporary society is characterized by temporary housing, jobs, friendships, neighborhoods, etc. Things move so quickly that there is no time for long-term stability, and values become a part of a "throw-away" society.

No one can escape change. Change is so rapid that there is no time to adjust before more change takes place. The decade of the 1960s has been

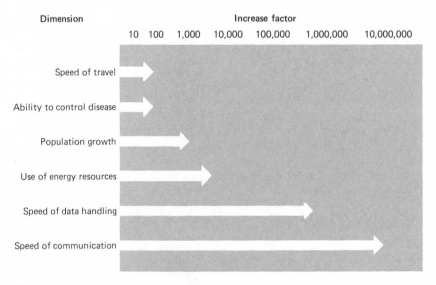

Fig. 15.1. Dimensions of change during the past 100 years.

called the decade of the explosion—in knowledge, technology, communications, and economics. In addition, the dramatic change among youth and minority groups, in morals and politics contribute to the challenge of the 1970s. For the modern organization, the lesson is clear. Given the facts of rapid change, the static organization cannot survive. Yesterday's successes mean very little in a world of rapidly changing markets, products, values, and life-styles. In order to survive, organizations must devise means of continuous self-renewal. They must be able to recognize when it is necessary to change, and above all they must possess the competency to bring about change when it is required. Some companies have created specialized units whose primary purpose is organizational planning. These units spend a great deal of time developing and implementing new structural, technological, and motivational programs for the organization to improve its level of adaptation to its environment, as well as to make changes in the behavioral patterns of employees. To achieve successful change, both of these goals must be satisfied.

Planned organizational change is a deliberate attempt to modify the functioning of the total organization or one of its major parts in order to bring about increased effectiveness. Change of this type can be initiated by organizational members or external change agents. Excluded from consideration in this chapter are changes created by forces such as fire, bombings, sabotage, strikes, lockouts, or government decrees. For example, the Food and Drug Administration learned that a line of children's sweaters was highly flammable. The clothing manufacturer in New York City responsible for merchandising this line was forced to discontinue production, creating drastic organizational changes, such as decreasing the number of employees and adversely affecting the image of the company. This kind of change lies beyond the scope of this chapter.

OBJECTIVES OF ORGANIZATIONAL CHANGE

If asked why an organization was changing, a manager might respond: "to achieve higher performance, get a new product accepted in the marketplace, increase the productivity of employees, reduce turnover, increase the motivation of employees to work for the company's goals, and to be socially responsible." Organizational changes are frequently aimed at one or more of these general goals.

Underlying these more obvious goals are two objectives: (1) changes in the organization's level of adaptation to its environment; and (2) changes in the behavioral patterns of employees.

Adapting to Environmental Changes

Since the environment is composed of groups and organizations outside the immediate influence of the organization, the organization must try to adapt itself to the demands of these groups by introducing internal organizational changes that will allow the organization to be more effective. The environment of the organization may change as a result of innovation, changes in consumer preferences, changes in legal requirements, and pressure from outside groups.[3]

In some industries, such as electronics and pharmaceutical, innovation is a way of life. The competitive nature of the market changes how organizations will adapt to new products and ideas. The development of microcircuitry made it possible to reduce the cost and size of computers and pocket calculators. The development of optical scanners to read cost, item type, and size data from food packages by National Cash Register makes it possible to use data processing and computers at supermarket checkout counters. The main reason that store owners have decided to switch to automated checkout is the elimination of human error. The average tired checker can make errors on 1.5 percent on his or her checkouts.

The implications of such a move in the supermarket industry may be tremendous. The nature of the checker's job will change from performing the actual checkout for a customer to monitoring the groceries, meat, and produce as they pass through the electronic eye. The shelf check by a stock clerk to determine the amount of items sold, at what price, and on what day will now be performed by an inventory manager who will be able to have inventory levels determined almost instantaneously. Ordering of products can be more responsive to the sudden shifts in customers' preference. The computer readout will tell the manager percentage of sales in each department, when to reorder, how consumers responded to store coupons, and how many food stamps, manufacturers coupons, and bottle refunds were cashed.

Such an innovation will have implications for the manufacturers of both cash registers and scanning equipment. These companies will have to devise new marketing strategies to deal with the problem of integrating these new systems into the existing structure of the supermarket and the data-processing capabilities of the computer firm. All of these advantages have costs associated with them. James Edleman, National Cash Register account manager, says that equipment for each checkout costs about $9500 and the computer is about $30,000. NCR claims that savings alone from clerk error should pay for the system within a short time for high-volume stores.[4]

CHANGING CONSUMER PREFERENCES

The nature of the market may change with shifts in consumer tastes. The women's fashion industry has long been noted for frequent and radical changes in consumer tastes. In the early 1970s, when the "mini" skirt was popular, clothing manufacturers were producing short skirts by the thousands. The trend was short-lived, however, and within two years, the mini was no longer considered fashionable. Cothing styles for men are also more varied than they were in the past. The introduction of the leisure suit and the double knit, for example, have been major style changes in this segment of the industry. If consumer preferences keep changing, it is difficult for manufacturers to predict sales levels as accurately as they were able to in the past. Production methods and purchasing of materials have to be responsive to shifts in taste. Few manufacturers want to be left with large inventories of clothing that are soon out of style.

CHANGES IN LEGAL REQUIREMENTS

There have been instances where certain products were made illegal by new laws. Perhaps the classic example was banning of the sale of alcoholic beverages by the United States during the late 1920s and early 1930s. During Prohibition, the rise of illegal "speak-easies," home-made stills, the underworld's interest, and the people's open defiance of the law made the government reverse its decision in 1933. In 1977 the government banned the use of saccharine as a food additive. This act, which would devastate the diet soft drink industry, led to a frantic search for a replacement. To avoid air pollution, California has passed stringent laws designed to curb emissions of certain chemical compounds by automobiles. This has forced automobile manufacturers to alter the emission systems for cars sold in California.

OUTSIDE PRESSURE GROUPS

In some cases, the organization has been forced to adapt its internal operations because of the pressures exerted by outside groups. In 1969 the National Environmental Act was passed. This Act states that public policy should be aimed at achieving a balance between population and resource use that will permit high standards of living. The National Audubon Society used this legislation to force Florida to drop its proposed planned jet aviation port in the Florida Everglades. Similarly, a group of environmentalists and conservationists concerned about San Francisco Bay were successful in gaining passage of a state law creating a regional Conservation and Development Commission, which has the power to plan for the maximum usefulness of San Francisco Bay while preserving its recreational and scenic values. Oregon has passed legislation prohibiting the sale of nonreturnable bottles in that state. Firms selling products in Oregon had to undertake modifications in their manufacturing processes. Because of their desire to sell soft drinks in Oregon, Coca-Cola Bottling Company and Reynolds Metals undertook deliberate efforts to make it economically feasible to recycle bottles and cans.

Modifying Employee Behavior

The second goal of organizational change is to alter employee's behavioral patterns. The need for this goal becomes evident if one recognizes that an organization's level of adaptation to its environment cannot be improved unless many of its employees change their behavior. Organizations do not operate through computers or elaborate electronic circuits, but through employees making decisions. Every organization has its unique pattern of decision-making behaviors. These patterns are influenced by the values of top management, the leadership practices of managers, the reward system used to motivate employees, and informal group rules. Any change in an organization, whether it is introduced through a new structural design or a training program, is basically trying to get employees to change their behavior and ground rules for relating to one another. For the change to be successful, these new behavioral patterns must emerge throughout the entire organization. In the final analysis, all organizational change efforts must take account of the fact that people are being called on to do things differently. In this sense, behavioral change is involved in all organizational change efforts.

We see the problems of organizational change as twofold. First, organizations must learn to adjust effectively to meet the changing demands of the environment. Managers who see themselves as change agents and who know how to function effectively in this role are clearly among the most valuable members of the organization. Second, when we consider the problems inherent in changing the behavior of organizational members, we also need to study the processes that should be considered by a manager when attempting to create change.

A MODEL FOR ORGANIZATIONAL CHANGE

Figure 15.2 presents an eight-stage overview of the total change process as it relates to organizations. Each stage is dependent on the prior one. Since successful change is likely to be greater when the manager considers each of these stages in logical order, we will explore each stage separately.

Changes in External Environment

An organization's external environment is in a state of flux, and one of the primary functions of a manager is to reduce the uncertainty in the organization's environment. In Chapter 5, we noted that two of the basic sources of uncertainty in the external environment are market and technological changes.

The market structure of an organization may be homogeneous (with respect to price, materials and supplies, suppliers, customers, governmental regulations, and so forth) or heterogeneous. Homogeneous markets can be found in the brewing, insurance, and commercial baking industries; in each of these industries, the products, customers, suppliers, methods of distribution, and the price are similar. Extensive advertising campaigns are carried on by firms in these industries in an attempt to differentiate products and create a demand for their products. Miller Brewing Company makes a "Lite" beer, and the Joseph P. Schlitz Company sells "Light" beer. These two firms are competing for the same

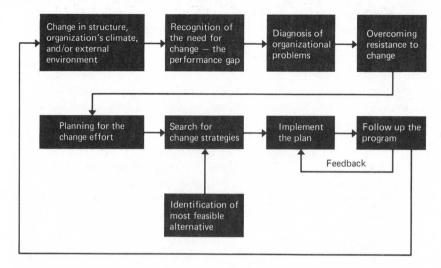

Fig. 15.2. A model for the management of change.

type of beer drinker, charge similar prices, negotiate with the same international union, and face similar distribution problems. Insurance premiums of the large companies, such as State Farm, Allstate, Prudential, Travelers, Hartford, are very similar. The difference among these firms is in the service that each insurance agent promises to give to the client.

Conglomerates are examples of firms facing relatively heterogeneous markets. Gulf & Western Industries, Inc., Textron, Northwest Industries, AMF, United Technologies, and IT&T are examples of firms operating in highly different markets. Gulf & Western owns Collyer Wire, Bliss Hydraulic Press, Titanium Corporation, Kayser-Roth, Schrafft's Candy, Muriel Cigars, Paramount Pictures, among others, and each of these markets presents a unique challenge for Gulf & Western in terms of customers, prices, channels of market distribution, suppliers, and government regulations. Kayser-Roth, which manufactures "No Nonsense" and "Supp-hose" hosiery, "Catalina" swimwear, and "Paris" belts, faces a different environment than does Paramount Pictures, producers of *The Great Gatsby, Chinatown,* and the television series "Mannix," "Happy Days," and the "Odd Couple." The task of Gulf & Western's top management team is to provide integration of these diverse companies where necessary.

The second major source of uncertainty for the firm is technology. The rapid rate of technological change is suggested by the fact that 93 percent of all scientists who ever lived are alive today. Most industries have undergone tremendous technological advances since World War II. In some industries, the technology of 20 years ago is now outdated. Consider the rapid rise of computers and related management information systems in the insurance industry during the past 20 years. Before the development of computers, most of the work was done by hand or processed on elementary accounting posting machines. Since the computer entered the picture, most insurance firms have undergone several structural as well as job-design changes. High rates of obsolescence have encouraged many organizations to adopt a short-term payback period, so that they will not be caught with outmoded equipment. Slowness in adapting to a new technology, which could have effects on reduction in costs and improvement in quality, might well lead to decreased profitability.

Changes in Organization's Climate and Structure

An organization is made up of individuals, each of whom has his or her own belief system. Through interaction with other members in the organization, the organization's climate is formed. The leadership style of top management; the norms, values, practices, and attitudes of the organization's employees; and the structure of the organization all contribute to the development of an organization's climate. Organization effectiveness can be increased by creating a climate that satisfies employees' needs and at the same time directs their behavior toward the achievement of the organization's goals. At its simplest, organizational climate refers to the typical day-to-day characteristics of a particular organization.[5] Some terms commonly used to describe an organization's climate are "warm," "conservative," "impersonal," "go-getter," and "employee-centered." These depict the quality and style of interpersonal relations among an organization's members. Let's briefly look at three different types of organizational climate—power, affiliation, and achievement.

In a *power-motivated* organizational climate, communication lines are clearly defined, all decisions are centralized and made at the top, lines of authority are clearly established and used frequently, and there is little room for individual discretion. An organization set up along democratic lines, emphasizing warm working relations more than task accomplishment through the formal organization, may be classified as *affiliation-oriented*. In this type of climate, employees are encouraged to talk over interpersonal issues on a daily basis. Managers encourage employees to bring their problems to them. A company in which top management formulates objectives in collaboration with other managers, permits groups to set their own procedures and establish rewards for task performance, and continually communicates a high-performance expectation to employees would be an *achievement organization*. Top management is interested in providing employees with career-growth ladders and continually feeds back data to employees on their task performance.

Performance levels and satisfaction have been found to vary among these climates. Job satisfaction is high in the achieving and affiliation climates and low in the power climate. In terms of effectiveness measured through profits, the employees operating in an achieving climate are more productive than those in either of the other types of organization. In terms of achieving change, different tactics may be used depending on the organization's climate. Human-relations training, which emphasizes participative decision making, open communication channels, and participative leadership styles, has been found successful if the employees perceive that their organization's climate is achievement-oriented. This type of training has not been successful if the organization's climate is perceived as power-oriented. Thus one goal of the manager is to continually diagnose the organization's climate and make sure that changes in it are in the direction wanted by the organization.[6]

The impact of changes in work design on employee behavior were discussed in detail in Chapter 11. It was stressed that changes in a task can significantly alter employees' behavior and attitudes. Experience from a number of organizations has shown that efforts aimed at redesigning jobs usually lead to a surfacing of other organizational problems that may have been hidden from management. The process of task change through job redesign may uncover preexisting problems of supervision, pay, intergroup relationships, organizational structure, and even authority relations.

Since an organization is continuously relating to its environment, one might also expect that the internal structure of the organization will change. The dimensions of an organization's structure were discussed in detail in Chapters 4 and 5. In Chapter 5, it was indicated that a popular structural device for top management's achieving change is to use "task forces," "project teams," and "matrix" organization structures. The movement toward a matrix organization can begin as a result of the organization's inability to coordinate across different functional areas in product development and marketing. With these new organizational forms, a number of new problems *must* be solved: (1) authority and decision-making responsibility, (2) work and production flows, (3) standards and control, and (4) employee appraisal and rewards.

In summary, the first step in the change process is for the manager to correctly evaluate the changes that are occurring in the task environment and the organization's climate. If a manager incorrectly diagnoses the problem, the next steps will be directed toward solving the wrong problem. Too often managers speed through this diagnosis and solve the wrong problem well.

Performance Gap

The second step in the change process is to determine the performance gap—the difference between what the organization could do by virtue of its opportunity in its market and what it actually does in taking advantage of that opportunity. The gap may be characterized by new marketing opportunities brought about by changes among consumers or by loss of market because of new competition. It may also occur when new technical specifications are required by governmental regulatory agencies.

The performance gap may persist for some time before it is recognized. In fact, it may never be recognized. The gap also must be perceived as having significant consequences for the firm if the gap is not narrowed or bridged. In Chapter 3, we discussed the rise and fall of W. T. Grant's, as well as the phenomenal rise of K-Mart in the retailing market. It was obvious that Grant's top management did not recognize the performance gap until it was too late for the organization to take corrective action. On the other hand, K-Mart was able to close the gap quickly and take advantage of a new market.

The awareness and need, in effect, unfreeze functions within the organization that are most closely associated with the change. When this occurs, conditions are present for altering the structure and function of the organization. Thus, for example, Playboy Enterprises, Inc., has changed the internal structure of its hotel and food business without making any changes in its *Playboy* magazine policy.[7] Profits from Playboy Clubs had decreased steadily since 1971, and the hotel business had also proved to be a money-loser. In the 1960s, the decision for Playboy Clubs International to move into clubs and hotels was based on a feeling that the successful magazine's proclaimed life-style should be expressed in real house-party atmospheres. The first Playboy Club in Chicago was an instant success, and it was followed by clubs in other cities. At the same time, Playboy Clubs International purchased hotels in Lake Geneva, Wisconsin, Miami Beach, and Great Gorge, New Jersey. Miami Beach was intensely competitive for a while with local hotels, but attendance in all the hotels began to slip off as the public lost interest in live entertainment. Playboy was then saddled with hotels and a dwindling market. In 1976 Playboy sold its Miami hotel and started advertising its Lake Geneva and Great Gorge hotels under a "time-sharing plan" whereby customers are guaranteeing for themselves certain weeks of their own vacation at the resort annually in exchange for installment payments. The entire family, including children under 18, who want a vacation in a rural, restful area is being appealed to. If the sales success during the initial months at Lake Geneva in late 1976 is duplicated in New Jersey, Playboy will have successfully narrowed the performance gap.

Diagnosis of Organizational Problems

As suggested in the first two steps, it is essential that management make the proper diagnosis of the organization's problem areas. In the Playboy Club illustration, the problem was not with the magazine, but with the hotels and clubs. Therefore, no changes have been proposed to change the magazine. Diagnosis of problems will continue to take place after the change program has been initiated, especially if unanticipated problems arise and/or new data become available for the manager's decision-making framework. The change process often gets under way early in the diagnostic step, depending on who does the diagnosis and the methods chosen for analyzing the problem areas.

The objective of the diagnostic step is for management to essentially agree on the nature and extent of the problem area(s) before taking any action. Diagnosis should precede action. This may sound obvious, but it is nonetheless important. Often harassed and results-oriented, managers let impatience push them toward attempting solutions before the problem is clear. By now, you should have recognized that problems often have multiple causes. In organizations, as in life, there is seldom one, simple, obvious cause for organizational problems. To aid in the identification of problems, several general questions may be asked:

1. What are the specific problems to be corrected?
2. What are the determinants of these problems?
3. What must be changed to resolve the problem?
4. What are the forces likely to work for and against change?
5. What goals or objectives are expected from the change, and how will these be measured?

The approach that management uses to diagnose the problem plays a crucial part in determining the problem(s) to be analyzed. A variety of data-gathering techniques have been successfully used—such as attitude surveys, conferences, informal interviews, and team meetings. The central concern of these approaches is to gather data that are not biased by a few dominant persons in the organization or consultants. Conference meetings between the manager and his or her subordinates may quickly highlight technical problems. However, interpersonal problems usually involve extensive attitude surveys and/or the use of outside consultants.

Attitude surveys can usually tap the feelings of the employees most effectively. This method may enable management to evaluate the organization's climate and employees' attitudes toward pay, work, and related working conditions. Use of this technique requires that the surveys be answered anonymously so that the employees can express their genuine attitudes without the fear of management reprisal. Because this technique can prove insightful for many potential problem areas, management should spend time in formulating the proper questions on a wide variety of work-related factors.

Overcoming Resistance to Change

Managers often feel that subordinates tend to resist all change because of the difficulties in implementing new methods and procedures or the belief that change will hurt them. Change is resisted primarily when the results of the change are perceived as negative or uncertain. The feeling of uncertainty may create feelings of insecurity and therefore opposition. Even though the public may have benefited from the technological advances in the electronics field, employee resistance to change may occur. In 1972 the United States Coast Guard decided that it would automate its 200 lighthouses, thereby eliminating the job of lightkeeper. Employees resisted this change, but by 1977 only 15 lighthouses had not been fully automated.

If automation in the past has resulted in layoffs and less reliance on the worker, probably no amount of propaganda will convince the individual otherwise. Resistance to change is difficult to overcome. Insecurity brings on emotional reactions where logic and reason should prevail.

Sometimes management is also reluctant to change because of the strong commitment to current activities and product lines. The sunk costs in current operations are often tremendous. Roles, norms, expectations, and structural factors are all sources of pressure for conformance to existing values and behavioral patterns. Change often results in a redistribution of power. Accordingly, individuals will resist such a reorganization if they expect to lose out.

Organizational change can be brought about successfully only if the manager understands the resistances by the individual and the organization. The purpose of this section is to focus on some of those resistances to change.

Figure 15.3 represents the forces that operates within an individual to resist change: habit, selective perception, dependence, and insecurity and regression. Figure 15.4 represents the forces that operate within an organization to resist change: the stability of the system, resource limitations, sunk costs, and interorganizational agreements. Of course, there are also many other reasons why people and organizations resist change, why change fails to be undertaken by individuals and organizations, and why they may not perform adequately once changes are adopted.

INDIVIDUAL RESISTANCES[8]
Once a *habit* is established, it may become a source of satisfaction for the individual, who will continue to react to his or her work until there is some

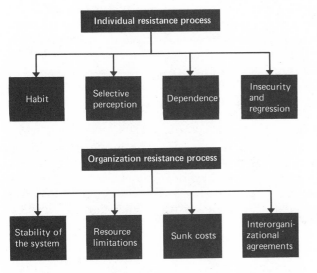

Fig. 15.3. Individual resistance forces.

Fig. 15.4. Organizational resistance forces.

reason to change. If an organization were to suddenly announce that every employee was to receive an immediate 20 percent pay raise, few would object. However, if the company were suddenly to announce that every employee was to immediately receive a 20 percent pay reduction, many would object. In the latter case, many habits—taking vacations, buying new cars, enjoying leisure activities, buying convenience foods—would have to be changed because of the individual's inability to finance these purchases adequately.

Once an attitude has been established, a person responds to others' suggestions within the framework that has been established—*selective perception*. Situations may be perceived as reinforcing the original attitude when they actually do not. Individuals successfully resist the possible impact of change on their lives by reading or listening to what agrees with their present views. People resist change by conveniently forgetting any learning that could lead to opposite viewpoints and by misunderstanding communications that if correctly perceived, would not be consistent with preestablished attitudes. Many managers who enroll in training programs and are exposed to different managerial philosophies may do very well at discussing and answering questions about these philosophies. But they may carefully segregate in their minds the new approaches which "of course would not work in my job" and those which they are already practicing.

A change will usually be opposed by an employee unless he or she has specifically requested the change. Since the employee's status, prestige, or job may be at stake with the coming change, the employee must be convinced of the need for it. The employee must see some personal benefit to be gained before he or she is willing to participate in the change process.

All human beings begin life *dependent* on adults. Parents sustain life of the helpless infant and provide major satisfactions. For this reason, children tend to accept the values, attitudes, and beliefs of their parents. The dependency of an individual on others can be a resistance to change if the individual has not developed a sense of self-esteem. The adult who is highly dependent on others and lacks self-esteem is likely to resist change until significant others endorse the changes and make them a part of their managerial behavior. The worker who is highly dependent on his or her boss for feedback on performance will probably not incorporate any new techniques or methods unless the boss personally okays the decision and indicates to the employee how these changes will improve his or her performance.

The last obstacle to change is the tendency of some individuals to seek *security* in the past. When life becomes frustrating, individuals think with nostalgia about the happy days of the past. The irony is that this frustration-regression sequence occurs just when old ways no longer produce the desired outcome, and experimentation with new approaches is most needed. Even under these conditions, individuals with a high degree of insecurity are likely to cling even more desperately to the old, unproductive behavior patterns. The male manager who does not recognize the effects of equal-opportunity legislation on his policy of hiring only white males or of the changing composition of the labor force seeks somehow to find a road back to the old days when he ran the shop according to his personal likes.

Most organizations have been designed to be innovation-resisting. That is, like fully automated factories, organizations have customarily been designed to do a narrowly prescribed assortment of things and to do them consistently. As you will recall, these are some of the characteristics of mechanistic management systems. To ensure consistency, the organization may create strong defenses against change.

The first resistance to change by organizations are their desires for *stability*. The typical bureaucratic organization narrowly defines jobs, delimits lines of authority and responsibility, and emphasizes the hierarchical flow of information and orders from the top to the bottom. It stresses discipline through the use of rewards and punishments. Novel ideas and/or the use of resources in a new way may be perceived as threats to the internal distribution of power and status. For example, the conservative financial policy of Montgomery Ward immediately after World War II ensured great organizational stability. But since the retail environment was changing, this drive for economic stability was instrumental in Ward's decline in the merchandising field. On the other hand, Sears assumed that risk taking, in terms of opening new stores in suburban areas and adding new lines of merchandise, was needed to gain prominence in the market. As a result of these different strategies, Sears' sales in 1976 were about 5½ times Ward's. In Chapter 3, we indicated that A&P had a strategy to concentrate in cities and not in the expanding suburbs. To maintain this strategy, A&P promoted executives from within the firm. This policy had worked for many years and provided A&P with management stability. But as the environment changed, A&P had to make major organizational changes in order to survive in this highly competitive market.

Although some organizations desire to emphasize stability, others would change their structure and behavior if they had available the *resources* necessary to implement a change. Bethlehem Steel Corporation made a decision to close its Johnstown, Pa., operation rather than expend huge sums of money to comply with the environmental standards proposed by state and federal governmental agencies. Only after the agencies modified their environmental regulations was Bethlehem able to continue its Johnstown operations. Of course, another interpretation of Bethlehem's behavior is that its position was simply a power play to get the government to make concessions. Another example is the decline in central business districts. Many firms watch their customers desert them for the greater convenience of suburban shopping centers. Yet the companies find themselves unable to raise the funds needed to provide the public parking facilities and rapid transit systems required to counter this trend.

Resource limitations obviously are not confined to organizations lacking assets. Rich organizations may find themselves as hard put because they have invested much of their capital in fixed assets (e.g., equipment, building, land, etc.). They may be locked into the present by their assets, for those represent *sunk costs*. Again, the plight of many central business districts illustrates this resistance. Most American large cities grew haphazardly in the era before automobiles, and they can hardly begin to handle today's automobile traffic. Therefore, these cities have had an increasingly difficult time meeting the competition of suburban shopping centers.

Sunk costs are not always limited to physical things. They can also be expressed in terms of people. What happens to an employee who is no longer making a significant contribution to the organization but has enough seniority to maintain his or her job? Unless the employee can be motivated to higher task performance, he or she will likely stay with the company until retirement. Fringe benefits, salary, and the like are payments to the individual for past services and represent sunk costs for the company.

Interorganizational agreements usually create obligations on managements that can act as restraints on their behavior in the future. Labor contracts are the most common examples, because some things that were once considered major rights of management (right to hire and fire, assignment of personnel to jobs, promotions, etc.) now have become subjects of negotiation. Labor contracts are not the only kinds of contracts that create obligations for management. Advocates of change may find their plan delayed by arrangements with competitors, commitments to suppliers, pledges to public officials in return for licenses or permits, promises to contractors, and unions. Although agreements can be ignored or violated, potential legal costs may be expensive, lost customers might be hesitant to buy the product again, and credit-rating declines can be disastrous.

Does it follow, therefore, that managers must be forever saddled with the task of trying to achieve change in organizations or individuals that resist change? Our answer is no. Resistances to change will probably never cease completely, but managers can learn to succeed and to minimize the resistance by planning the change.

Planning the Change Effort

The fifth step is to develop procedures to measure the change. The change experience must be transferred to the job situation if it is to be effective. The problem of assessing the effects of a change program are twofold: criterion development and research design.

If a change effort is to be effective, objectives or goals must be clearly stated before the change program is under way. Where possible, the objectives should be stated in quantifiable terms so that they can be measured. The objectives should be (1) based on realistic organizational and employee needs, (2) clearly stated, and (3) consistent with the organization's policies. If an objective of a change program is to help foremen reduce machine downtime to an acceptable level, one of the organization's tasks is to train its foremen and then delegate maintenance procedures to them. If the change program cannot do this, why undertake the change program? Many change efforts have failed because the objectives were not clearly stated or understood by all involved members of the organization.

Managers have generally used two classes of objectives—internal and external—to assess the effectiveness of an organization change program. *Internal objectives* refer to changes in attitudes, improved decision-making ability, increased motivation, and increased job satisfactions. These are changes that occur within the individual. *External objectives*—turnover, grievances, absenteeism, profits, new customers, rate of production—measure the change in employee performance in the job. The external objectives attempt to measure directly the effects of the change program on employee job behavior. Changes in attitudes, for example, must be shown to be related to improved performance. If it is desired to change managers' attitudes to making them more considerate to the needs of subordinates, the change should be related to productivity, grievances, or any other external objectives. If the objectives of the change effort are spelled out in this fashion, the sequence of learning activities and the most appropriate change strategy can be adopted by the organization.

To measure the change, the manager should establish both experimental and control groups. The *experimental group* receives the training, has its job enriched, market tests a new product, is given a new task, or participates in a university executive education program. The *control group* receives no "treatment." Its members usually do not know that they are involved in a study. The purpose of the control group is to assess more accurately the overall effectiveness of the changes in the experimental group. By matching the groups on important corporate variables, such as salaries, number of promotions, level in the hierarchy, and performance-appraisal records, it is possible to measure the results of the change program more effectively.

To illustrate this point, suppose that one group of employees receives MBO training (experimental group) and another group does not (control group). After the training is completed and some time has elapsed, a measure is taken that indicates that the employees who received MBO training are more effective planners now than before the training program was started. Without a control group, it would be impossible to tell whether this observed change would have occurred naturally or whether something happened within the organization to influence the results of the training program. The need to establish experimental and control groups and the need for before-and-after measures is of major importance for effective evaluation of the change program.[9]

Search for Change Strategies

The sixth step is to look for available change strategies that management might use. An organization's direction and status are determined by existing internal and external forces. Change in an organization can be accomplished only by modifying these forces. The forces and strategies are shown in Table 15.1. An organization is composed of four interrelated forces—task, structure, people, and techonology as indicated in Fig. 15.5. A change in any one force usually results in a change in one or more of the others. A structural change, for example, toward decentralization of decision making should result in assignment of different people to certain organizational tasks. But decentralization of decision making will also probably change the technology for performing certain tasks, as well as the attitudes and behaviors of the employees performing the task.

Table 15.1. Forces and strategies affecting change

Forces	Change strategies
Tasks	Modify nature of tasks Job redesign Team development
Technology	Modify production methods Modify machinery Automation
People	On-the-job training Management development courses Organizational development programs
Structure	Change position descriptions Modify organization's authority and responsibility structures Modify organization's structure

Adapted from H. Carlisle, *Management: Concepts and Situations* (Chicago: Science Research Associates, 1976), p. 450.

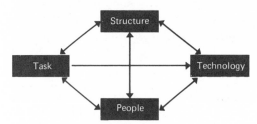

Fig. 15.5. Forces in organizational change. (H. Leavitt, "Applied Organizational Change in Industry: Structural, Technological and Humanistic Approaches," in *Handbook of Organizations,* ed. J. March, Chicago: Rand McNally, 1965, p. 1145. Used with permission.)

TASK AND CHANGE

Modifying tasks has come to the forefront as one of the most common change methods, for two reasons. First, it is often easier for a manager to change tasks than people or the norms of the entire organization. Second, programs such as job enrichment (see Chapter 11) have demonstrated that improved performance and job satisfaction can result from combining tasks to make jobs more challenging.

The effects of new methods, new materials, and improved work-flows and information systems can be felt throughout the organization. Volvo's redesign of the assembly line for the manufacturing of cars would be one example of a technological change. In some industries, such as electronics, pharmaceutical, and toys, technical change proceeds at a quicker pace than social change. One problem for management is to keep these two forces of change matched up.

PEOPLE AND CHANGE

The people strategy attempts to change organizations by modifying the attitudes, values, behavior, and interpersonal processes of employees. If work-related knowledge is essential for the change, on-the-job training and job rotation have been used by organizations. In recent years, university management development and organization development programs have been introduced to more completely help the manager understand the process of changing attitudes and perceptions of employees.

STRUCTURE AND CHANGE

Managers have traditionally looked to altering the formal organization structure when a change is required. Many reorganizations are aimed at capturing the unique advantages of another form of organizational design. Typical is the situation of a large, centralized organization that decentralizes decision making in order to capitalize on the advantages of teamwork and self-control. However, even though changing the formal structure will change people's tasks and job descriptions, often it does not go deep enough to change individual attitudes and group norms.

Implementing and Following the Process

The final step in the change process is to implement and follow the change over a period of time. Designing the change process so that the best method can be used requires that the revision be sustained over a period of time. The results of a change depend to a considerable extent on the degree to which the manager assists his or her team members to learn and practice their newly acquired skills. The degree to which the organization has the opportunity to reinforce this learned behavior during and after the development effort will affect the desired results.

In discussing the planning phase, we indicated that managers often use both internal and external criteria to measure the impact of the change process on the organization. The major source of feedback is the firm's information system. It is quite possible that productivity can increase while morale is declining. A manager should not blindly assume that an increase in productivity and morale are directly related; rather, the change effort should consider both productivity and morale as criteria to be evaluated.

The problem of deciding when the change process has been a success depends on the trend in improvement over a period of time. This trend has three dimensions: (1) the level of satisfaction, productivity, new product development and market share before the change process is undertaken; (2) the magnitude of the improvement or decline; and (3) the duration of the improvement or decline. It is critical that the organization establish benchmarks before the program is started that adequately measure the firm's objectives. This should be accomplished in the diagnostic phase of the change process. A well-designed change process should also specify the magnitude of the change expected and some time period (after the formal change process has been completed) when the objectives will be measured.

The manager, ideally, should closely monitor the change process. However, this may be too costly and time-consuming. Therefore, managers usually measure the change process at predetermined time intervals after the program has been started. One measurement is usually taken immediately after the change. If a "people" change strategy is used, changes in attitudes, knowledge, skills, and the emotional makeup of the employees can be tapped at this time and compared against the predetermined objectives of the change program. To avoid the danger of overreliance on only temporary changes in attitudes, another measurement of attitudes should be taken later, after the immediate effect of participating in the process has worn off. Often, the second measure will indicate attitudinal changes that the first measure did not reveal. This is because the organization did not have the opportunity to reinforce (or try to eliminate) newly acquired employee attitudes. Participants in a human-relations training program might show an initial increase in their sensitivity to others. Unless the organization reinforces this behavior over a period of time, through salary increases and promotions, it is doubtful that the attitudes acquired in the traning program will be permanent.

In the eighth, or follow-up step, the internal objectives are related to the external ones; otherwise, dangerous errors could be made. Change-program effectiveness should not be determined only by measures of behavior or measures of performance improvement. Rather, a composite index, made up of both behavioral and performance objectives, should be used. Following up on the change process over a period of time involves measuring both objectives.

Now that we have reviewed the major processes in achieving organizational change, let's turn our attention to the strategies for achieving change and examine the various methods used to achieve change in each strategy. It might be helpful if you tried to work through our model when analyzing the methods used by managers.

STRATEGIES FOR ORGANIZATIONAL CHANGE

The strategies to change organizations and employees considered in the next few pages are representative of the strategies indicated in Table 15.1. Some of the strategies have been woven into previous chapters, such as job enrichment in Chapter 11, MBO in Chapters 8 and 11, structural changes in Chapter 5, and thus will not be discussed at length here.

There is no ready-made or agreed-on formula for determining the strategy to utilize in changing an organization's adaptation to its environment or changing the behavior of its employees.[10] One key contingency should be the nature of the problem the organization is attempting to solve. With this in mind, we will discuss change strategies that have been utilized by managements.

Changing the Technology

Changing the technology of an organization can have far-reaching effects throughout the entire organization. Marketing, personnel, and other areas outside of the basic processing or manufacturing of goods are often affected. Almost any partially or totally automated manufacturing plant, mill, or office would serve as a valuable case history about the impact of technology on organizational change. Here we will highlight two examples of technological change.

A two-year study of a 1200-employee baking plant undergoing a transition from an old-type mill to a new, highly automated facility offers a large-scale example of a technological change.[11] Several actual changes could be related to the change in technology.

CHANGE IN SUPERVISORY RESPONSIBILITY

Under the new technology, it became apparent to management that one mistake could easily affect the entire organization. Although the span of control had been reduced for the first-line foremen, the consequence of employee errors was magnified because of the speed of the line and the tremendous cost of breakdowns. Prior to automation, foremen had more time to correct errors. The increased speed of the line and the reduced mobility of the machine operators reduced opportunities by the foremen to avoid substantial scrap. The new machinery made it impossible to detect errors early in the production process. The foremen's increased responsibility made them more dependent on one another to accomplish their tasks. Each foreman became more aware of his role in the system.

Another change was the ratio of supervisors to workers. The most vivid example of the increased number of supervisors to workers took place in the baking and mixing department (the area experiencing the greatest technological change). Before automation, approximately 70 employees were supervised by a foreman and an assistant foreman. After automation, three foremen were responsible for only 25 men.

CHANGE IN WORK-GROUP STRUCTURE

Automation had a dramatic effect on the total number of workers and communications among them. The size of the work teams in the baking department was reduced. Much of the work was now accomplished by machines. Helpers were reduced in number or entirely eliminated. Teamwork was required only when machines broke down. Many workers were now doing individual work. This greatly restricted their mobility because they were tied more closely to their machines. Any failure to observe correctly the dials and various gauges could have resulted in serious product loss and/or costly machine damage. This led to a feeling of isolation among the workers.

After the automation, machine tenders were assigned to monitor one or more machines within a limited area. Because of this physical restriction, new friendship arrangements had to be formed. Workers were spread out among three floors. It became physically difficult to chat. Employees were relieved for rest breaks at varying times, depending on their particular work station. The rather minimal amount of talk time provided by the brief 30-minute lunch period also reduced opportunities for widespread close interpersonal relationships. In some departments, informal free-time periods had been stopped, thus reducing the amount of interaction time by almost 20 minutes a day. The changes in the work groups created morale problems.

The effects of computer technology on organization behavior has also been the subject of several large-scale studies. *The Impact of Computers on Organizations* by Thomas Whisler discusses the widespread outgrowths of computers on a variety of companies in the life insurance industry.[12] The findings provide another illustration of how changes in technology bring about changes in an organization's structure, the content of jobs, and employee motivation.

ORGANIZATION STRUCTURE

If computers were eliminated from the insurance industry and the industry desired to maintain the same quality of service to customers, 60 percent more clerical personnel, 9 percent more supervisory personnel, and 2 percent more managerial personnel would be required. When the computer was introduced, many of the functions of the companies were centralized. Although the span of control declined at lower levels in the organization, it remained about the same for higher managerial levels. An implication of this was a tightening of control over an individual's behavior, especially in clerical jobs.

DECISION MAKING

As might be expected, decision making moved to higher levels in organizations and was significantly quantified and rationalized. This had the primary impact on middle management, which lost many of its decision-making rights. Top-management decision making showed little change except that substantial new problems of inflexibility in decision making resulted from computer use. Although the use of the computer stimulated ideas for change, the cost of implementing such changes greatly increased.

JOB CONTENT

Job content was influenced by the use of computers, but its impact was a function of job level. Clerical jobs tended to become more routinized, whereas the job of the first-line supervisor tended toward increased autonomy, feedback, and significance. In general, skill levels were upgraded, but approximately one-third of clerical jobs showed a downgrading. Skill levels were relatively uninfluenced at the top-management levels. At the time these studies were conducted (mid-1960s), the focus of computer systems was still at the level of clerical jobs.

Changing Organizational Structure

Changing the organization's structure is another method of attempting to improve the functioning of the organization. The reasons behind such a reorganization typically include:

1. The pressure of competition on margins and profits has put a premium on efficient organizational structure. Overlapping departments have been combined, product divisions consolidated, and marginal functions eliminated.
2. The booming international trade market has required more and more companies to change export departments to international divisions, to establish regional management groups, and to restructure the corporate staff.
3. Mergers and acquisitions have generated strong pressures for reorganization in parent companies as well as in newly acquired subsidiaries.
4. New developments in technology often require new organizational arrangements to realize their ultimate potential for improving corporate performance.[13]

General Dynamics offers a large-scale example of a structural change.[14] The company is the fifth largest major airframe maker in the world and has passed through several management crises (see Chapter 4). Traditionally, the aerospace business is like a game of musical chairs: It has more players than chairs, and when the music stops, some of the players are forced out of the game. On the military side of the aerospace business, which accounts for more than 80 percent of the industry's volume, there are not enough prime contracts to go around. A similar situation is found in the commercial sector of the market. Some companies, such as North American Aviation, Douglas Aircraft, and Republic Aviation, have vanished as independent companies and have been forced to merge with larger manufacturers. Martin Marietta Corporation, on the other hand, was forced to withdraw from the production of aircraft. Lockheed Aircraft Corporation, Grumman Corporation, Fairchild Industries, Inc., and LTV Corporation's Vought division are companies facing financial crises. Thus the environment facing most airframe manufacturers is highly unpredictable.

In 1970 General Dynamics was a prime candidate for extinction. Its major defense contracts were saddled with massive cost overruns, an ill-advised acquisition of the Quincy, Mass., shipyard had drained more than $230 million from earnings in three years, and the company's nondefense business—mostly concrete and other building materials—was slipping because of poor management. General Dynamics reported a $6.9 million deficit on $2.2 billion sales in 1970. Moreover, the company's backlog was down to dangerously low levels, and its general financial condition was shaky.

Prior to 1970, when David Lewis became chairman and chief executive officer, General Dynamics was a sprawling collection of autonomous operating divisions. A corporate philosophy of decentralization was practiced (see Chapter 4 for a detailed summary of this). Top management did not know what was going on in significant product areas. This was evidenced by the fact that 75 percent of defense sales contributed almost no profit to the company. Inadequate financial controls, preoccupation with sales to the government, and production-line problems were the pitfalls of this loosely organized decentralized management.

When Lewis took charge, he quickly reshaped General Dynamics into a highly centralized corporation. Lewis replaced all but one of the corporate vice-presidents and all but one of the 12 operating division heads. He also introduced a new layer of management—three executive vice-presidents to closely monitor the operating divisions. To further centralize the organization, he increased the size of the corporate staff by about 15 percent, to 340 persons. The key staff jobs have been changed from counselors and advisers to individuals with direct line responsibilities to their technical areas.

These responsibilities are carried out by an exhaustive series of managerial reviews that Lewis has initiated. Each month a team of staff financial specialists visits the operating divisions to check performance. Quarterly meetings with key executives are held in the home office in St. Louis.

Lewis has also cut products that are no longer profitable and diversified the commercial product line so that General Dynamics could sustain the periodic downturns in military business. For example, Stromberg-Carlson, which is the leading producer of equipment for independent domestic telephone companies, has expanded its product line into foreign markets with advanced telecommunications equipment. Datagraphic, Inc., which manufactures machines to store and retrieve computer data on microfilm, has dropped several unprofitable lines and updated and expanded its computer lines.

Changing Tasks

Whenever a job is changed—whether because of a new technology, an internal reorganization, or managerial whim—task redesign has taken place. Task redesign is used to refer to any activities that involve the change of specific jobs with the intent of increasing both the quality of the employees' work experience and their on-the-job productivity. The basic strategy has been described in Chapter 11, but we shall briefly review the major points and cite two examples.

There are four unique aspects to the redesign of tasks.[15] First, task redesign changes the basic relationship between a person and what he or she does on the job. Job enrichment enables workers to break out of the "givens" in a job. Job enrichment is based on the assumption that work itself may be a very powerful influence on employee motivation, satisfaction, and productivity. It provides a strategy for moving away from satisfying only the lower-order needs (or hygiene factors) toward higher-order needs (or motivators) that cause the individual to do the work because she or he finds it interesting, challenging, and intrinsically rewarding. Second, task redesign directly changes behavior. The basic feature of job enrichment is to change the behavior of the worker in a way that gradually leads to a more positive set of attitudes about the work, the organization, and the person's own image. Because enriched jobs usually bring about increased feelings of autonomy and personal freedom, the individual is likely to develop attitudes that are supportive of his or her new on-the-job behaviors.

Third, task redesign offers numerous opportunities for initiating other organizational changes. Technical problems are likely to develop when jobs are changed. This offers management an opportunity to refine the work. Interpersonal issues almost inevitably arise between supervisors and subordinates and sometimes between coworkers who have to relate to each other in different ways. These issues offer opportunities for developing new supervisory skills and teamwork. Finally, work redesign can humanize the organization. Job enrichment can help individuals regain the chance to experience the kick that comes from doing a job well and to care about developing competence in their work. Individuals are encouraged to grow and stretch themselves.

BELL TELEPHONE COMPANY

This is a case of clerks who assembled information for telephone directories at Indiana Bell Telephone Company.[16] Prior to the change, a production-line model was used to assemble directory information. Information was passed from clerk to clerk as it was processed. Each clerk did only a small part of the entire phone directory. There was a total of 21 different steps in assembling a telephone directory. Jobs were changed so that each qualified clerk was given the responsibility for all clerical operations needed to assemble an entire directory—including receiving, processing, and verifying all information. The new work arrangement improved not only the clerks' job satisfactions, but the efficiency of the operation as well.

PET FOODS

When plans were being developed for a new plant in the late 1960s, top management at Pet Foods decided to use behavioral science knowledge to design and manage the plant.[17] The physical design and layout of the plant, the type of management style desired, the information and feedback systems, and the compensation systems designed were all developed on this basis.

A key part of the plan was the development of teams. Each team (consisting of seven to fourteen workers) was given nearly total responsibility for a significant task. A processing team and a packaging team operated during each shift. The processing team unloaded and stored materials, got materials from storage to mix them into products, and then actually produced the products. The packaging team's responsibilities included the finishing stages of the manufacturing—packaging operations, warehousing, and shipping. In addition to actually carrying out the work required to perform these tasks, team members performed many activities that had been traditionally reserved for management, e.g., solving production problems, assigning team members to jobs, screening and selecting new team members, and counseling those team members who did not meet team standards.

The basic jobs performed were designed to be as challenging as possible, and employees were encouraged to broaden their skills further in order to be able to handle even more challenging tasks. For example, each team member maintains the equipment he or she runs and housekeeps the area in which he or she works. Each team member has the responsibility for performing quality control tests and ensuring that the product meets standards. Pay increases are geared to an employee mastering an increasing proportion of jobs, first in the team and then in the total plant. Because there were no limits on the number of employees who can qualify for higher pay brackets, employees were encouraged to help each other out. Although not without some problems, the Topeka plant of Pet Foods appears to be profitable, and many employees are experiencing pleasant work experiences for the first times in their lives.

Changing People

The people-oriented approach to change chiefly takes the form of various educational and developmental programs intended to improve one or more of the three basic skills that underlie managerial effectiveness—technical, human, and conceptual. As we indicated in Chapter 1, mastery of technical skills is central to understanding production methods, equipment, work processes, and techniques. Indeed, a worker may well be promoted to first-line supervision because he or she is the most technically qualified worker. To bridge the gap to middle management will primarily require the development of human-relations skills. The employee must be able to show effective interpersonal skills, to work as a team member, and to build cooperation in a group. At the top-management level, the conceptual skill is very important. The members of the top management team must be able to see the organization as a whole and understand how the various functions fit together in relation to the firm's environment.

As we indicated in Chapter 1, these three classes of skills are not mutually exclusive. An effective chief executive officer should possess certain technical and human relations skills as well as conceptual ones, but successful upward movement and performance require a shift in emphasis. Various programs exist for developing these three skills.

ORGANIZATION DEVELOPMENT

Organization development (OD) refers to a variety of behavioral science approaches used to move organizations toward more open and honest communication among individuals and groups. Essential to organization development is the acquisition of self-critical attitudes toward present policies, procedures, and behavioral patterns. Members of the developed organization are, ideally, more open, explicit, and direct in their dealing with one another.

Organization development can be achieved by a variety of methods and techniques. Approaches to redesigning work described early in this chapter and also in Chapter 11 can rightfully be called OD techniques, because they enable an organization to resolve behavioral problems that are negatively affecting its overall effectiveness. The two widely practiced approaches to organization development we will discuss are the Managerial Grid and behavioral modification.

We wish to caution you, however, that not all activities given the label OD refer to the types of activities described in the following pages. Many industrial organizations (such as TRW Systems, Exxon, Corning Glass Works, Mack Trucks, and Shell Oil Corporation) have OD units within their personnel departments that may or may not conduct OD sessions that we shall describe. Some of these personnel departments are essentially involved in labor planning, career planning, pensions, and other employee-related benefits.

The Managerial Grid. Since the early 1960s, the Managerial Grid has been used by nine of the ten largest corporations in the world and has widespread application throughout the world.[18] The Grid technique assumes that it is possible for managers and the organizations of which they are members to maximize both production and concern for human values. That is, organizational and individual goals are compatible rather than at odds.

The Grid is a graphic representation of five styles of managerial behavior. These styles are based on two key variables—concern for production or output and concern for people. These two variables and some of their possible combinations are shown in Fig. 15.6. The number one (1) represents minimum concern on the scale; the nine (9), maximum concern.

The lower left corner (1,1) indicates a person with minimum concern for both people and production. This managerial style is characterized by withdrawal from the organization; the manager is simply a communication link

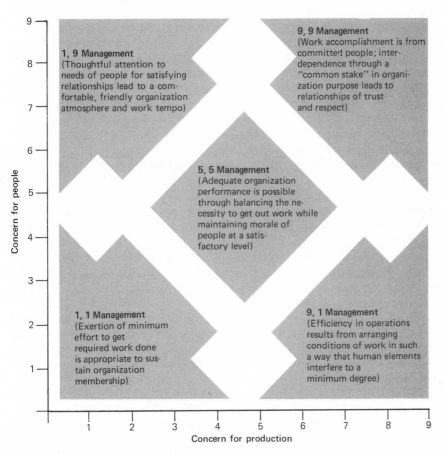

Fig. 15.6. The Managerial Grid. (Robert R. Blake, Jane S. Mouton, and Larry E. Greiner, "Breakthrough in Organization Development," *Harvard Business Review* **42** (November-December 1964): 136. Used with permission from the Harvard Business School. Copyright 1964 by the President and Fellows of Harvard College. All rights reserved.)

between the subordinates and higher management. Production will be limited, because it is assumed that people don't want to work and there is little reward in work accomplishment with others.

The upper left (1,9) represents minimum concern for production and maximum concern for people. Here the manager assumes that production requirements are not compatible with the needs of people and therefore are secondary to people considerations. Human relationships are an end in themselves. It is assumed that if people are made comfortable and secure in a warm way, production will take care of itself. Conflict is avoided or smoothed over by not pressuring people.

The lower right corner (9,1) represents maximum concern for production and minimum concern for people. People are viewed as instruments of the task, and human interactions are minimized. This management style also assumes that people basically resist production. Unlike the 1,9 manager, however, the 9,1 manager exerts heavy pressures and controls on people to get high production.

At the center point (5,5), the management style balances the concerns for production and people. Decisions are made by compromise and are guided by precedents. This management style also assumes that there is conflict between the needs of people and production. The manager resolves this conflict through splitting the difference, compromise, and similar measures.

The upper right corner (9,9) represents a high concern for both production and people. According to the Managerial Grid, it represents the ideal managerial style. This manager assumes that people are basically mature and responsible and, if given rewarding work to which they are committed, will produce at maximum level. This manager basically believes that the needs of the organization and its members are compatible.

There are six phases of Grid development. The educational content of Phase 1 includes self-evaluation forms, placing oneself on the "Grid," and organizational problem-solving exercises. The problems typically attempt to simulate organizational conditions in which interpersonal behavior affects task performance. To simulate organizational life, teams of five to nine members, representing all levels of the organization, are formed. They are responsible for developing solutions and improving their own problem-solving effectiveness. Effectiveness is measured against objective standards. After the teams have been informed of their performance, the members return to their separate rooms and critique their operational effectiveness. Weaknesses and strengths are identified and analyzed. Plans for increasing effectiveness are introduced. This process is repeated throughout the first phase, emphasizing learning through critique. Thus Phase 1 serves as a trigger to create the readiness to really work with the human problems of production, and it is not intended to produce immediate organizational improvement.

Phases 2 and 3 concentrate on the application of behavioral science knowledge to teamwork and intergroup development. The most common barriers to increasing team effectiveness are failure to fully communicate, improper planning, unwillingness to listen to others' opinions, and interpersonal friction. Improvement in behavioral skills is necessary to overcome these problems. In these phases, each member analyzes the climate and problems of the team and proposes solutions. A self-evaluation by each member of his or her job performance and that of others on the team is made. The team then discusses these problems and evaluations and develops its own solutions. Each member of the team attends at least two team meetings, in one playing a subordinate's role and in the other a superior's. The focus is on improving relationships between groups, among people at the same level, and between superiors and subordinates. For example, although competitiveness may increase organizational effectiveness, it may also result in departmental goals being placed ahead of more important organizational goals. A goal of these phases is to avoid the "win-lose" pattern of problem solving and to introduce joint problem-solving activity, in which both teams benefit from the relationship.

The fourth phase stresses organizational goals that require commitment at all levels of the organization. Goals discussed in this phase pertain to union-management relations, basic policy development, safety, promotions, and determining the proper structure of the organization. The specific goals to be introduced are identified by the teams. Departmental groups may also help to define goals and problems.

The final success of Phase 5, implementation of the corporate model for effectiveness, is based on the quality and character of the achievements resulting from all of the preceding phases. At this point, behavioral theories must have been understood, communication roadblocks removed, and a full understanding and commitment to corporate excellence obtained. The manager's primary goal is to help achieve the goals established during Phase 4 and also recognize previously undefined problems.

The final phase of the developmental process is stabilization. During this phase, the organization must be supportive of the changes brought about in the earlier phases. These changes are assessed and reinforced so as to prevent slipping back or regressing.

The effectiveness of the Grid Organization Development program is open to question. Although many corporations, such as British-America Tobacco Company, Texas Instruments, Pillsbury, Chas. Pfizer and Company, Union Carbide and Company, and Honeywell, among others, have participated in the Grid program, its effectiveness has not been rigorously tested. In many of the reported studies using the Grid approach, the exact causes of the changes were not reported, nor was the effect of any particular phase of the change program evaluated for its contribution to the total change. Measurements of attitudes and knowledge of behavioral concepts do not always lead to behavioral change.[19]

Grid Organization Development has produced many positive results, however. Productivity, profits, and attitudes have been shown to improve in those companies where the executives participated in the program. In many of the companies, more time was being spent on team problem solving where managers became aware of increased alternatives available for solving managerial problems. Similarly, subordinates have reported that their managers became more understanding of their problems.

Behavior Modification. Behavior modification is based on the premise that organizational behavior is largely a function of the contingent consequences.[20] Coming or not coming to work are behaviors and, therefore, a function of environmental consequences. If employees are sick, the consequence of staying home is that they will get better; the consequence of going to work is that they will become sicker.

There are three general categories of consequences that affect employee behavior: positive, negative, and nothing. A positive consequence will strengthen the behavior and increase its frequency of occurrence. This is called *positive reinforcement*. A positive reinforcer that is applied as a consequence of coming to work (such as satisfaction of one's higher-order needs, the "kick" out of doing a job) will increase the employees' attendance and job performance. A positive reinforcer for staying home or at the corner bar will increase the frequency of the employee absenteeism. In essence, the more frequently employees are positively reinforced for coming to work, the more they will do so.

Negative reinforcement, which also leads to increases in behavioral frequency, should not be confused with punishment. A simple example of negative reinforcement is a student who works hard to avoid parental nagging. If by working harder, the student's parents do stop nagging for higher grades, the working-hard response is said to be negatively reinforced; removal of the nagging resulted in an increase in grades. The parents' nagging is called a negative-reinforcement strategy.

Employees soon learn which consequences available to managers have real "clout" and which are almost meaningless. For example, when B. F. Goodrich started a program that rewarded attendance, it became a cue to employees that attendance was important. Likewise, the employee can associate the attendance program with consequences that are available for attendance and absence behaviors.

A *negative or punishing* consequence results in weakening the behavior and decreasing the frequency of its occurrence. An employee who experiences a negative consequence for coming to work will decrease attendance behavior. By the same token, if the employee is punished for not coming to work (loss of pay, seniority, vacation time, etc.), absenteeism will decrease. A bright young woman who stops telling her manager about a new technique she developed because every time she has done so in the past the manager has warned her for wasting time has been punished. The actions of the manager are called punishers because of the effect they have on the employee's behavior. A punishment strategy is designed to decrease the frequency of behavior.

The third possible consequence (*nothing*) will also decrease the behavior. If the door-to-door encyclopedia salesperson stops calling on a house after four different tries because no one is at home, the response of calling on that particular house has been stopped. The response has stopped because it has not been reinforced (the reinforcer in this case is someone answering the door).

Figure 15.7 shows a five-step behavioral modification model that has been proposed as a technique for organizational change.[21] The initial step is defining the problem. This involves naming behaviors that can be identified, measured, and reinforced, punished, or ignored. Absenteeism, shoddy workmanship, grievances, and amount of machine downtime should be behavioral measures. Contributing problems for absenteeism may be illness, hang-overs, lack of transportation, family problems, religious beliefs, alcoholism, and no day-care facilities for workers' children. In any change model, unless the manager is sure

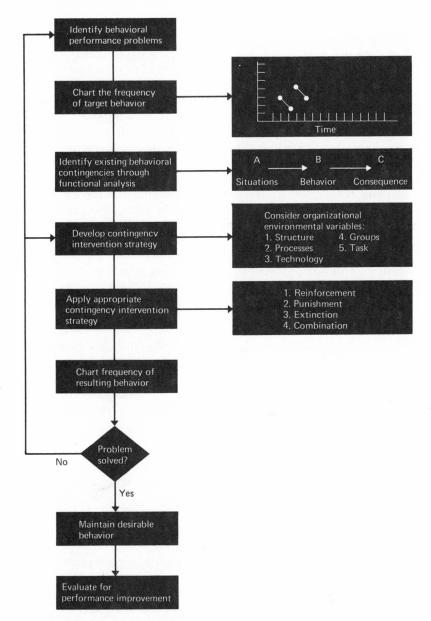

Fig. 15.7. Behavioral modification model. (Adapted from F. F. Luthans and R. Kreitner, "The Management of Behavioral Contingencies," *Personnel* **4** (1974): 13. Used with permission of the authors.)

that the behavior(s) that are targeted for change impact on attendance, grievances, or shoddy workmanship, the subsequent steps of the model are meaningless.

The keeping of accurate records is needed to establish baseline measures against which to determine how often the behaviors are occurring under existing conditions. The records are usually converted to frequency charts in step 2. From this, it might be possible to find out that absenteeism is high the day after payday, right before a three-day weekend, first day of hunting or fishing, or when weather is hot.

The next step is an analysis of the situations and consequences influencing past and present employee behavior. Inspection of the charts obtained in step 2 will tell if behavior improves or worsens. The situations control behavior. Managers can control behavior because behavior is associated with certain consequences that are available to the manager. Note that in Table 15.2, the situations, behavioral events, and consequences are identified. Thus a verbal reprimand for absenteeism is a punisher only if it decreases absenteeism. If absenteeism increases subsequent to the verbal reprimand, the reprimand is actually a reinforcer, despite the fact that it is normally considered to be an undesirable consequence. The employee may actually see this as one means of getting the manager to pay attention to him or her.

The fourth step is to develop contingency strategies to solve the problem. This would involve considering properties of the task, organization's structure, group processes, technology, and the people themselves. If the problem is one of poor work design, job enrichment might be a good strategy. If employees are having trouble with their supervisors' management style, Grid training may be appropriate.

The fifth step is to implement the appropriate strategy through the use of various consequences: positive, negative, punishment, extinction, or some combination of all four. If top management initiates a Grid program, managers who train themselves to be more effective supervisors (9,9) should be promoted and get larger raises than managers who do not change their supervisory (1,1)

Table 15.2. Functional analysis of absenteeism behaviors

Situation(s)	Behavior(s)	Consequence(s)
A ⟶	B ⟶	C
Illness/accident	Getting up late	Discipline programs: verbal reprimands, written reprimands, pay docks, layoffs, dismissals
Hang-over	Sleeping in	
Lack of transportation	Staying home	
No day-care facilities	Fishing/hunting	Escape from working
Family problems	Visiting	Nothing
Religious beliefs	Caring for sick child	

Adapted from F. Luthans and M. Martinko, "An Organizational Behavior Modification Analysis of Absenteeism," *Human Resource Management* **15** (1976): 15.

style. Data should be compiled and presented in an understandable manner so that each person can see how managerial style and work-group performance directly affects him or her. In other words, in step 5, the appropriate contingency strategy must be reinforced and the precise consequences of this spelled out.

Behavior modification was used in Valleyfair Park, a large family entertainment center near Minneapolis, Minnesota.[22] Before the park opened its door to the first customer, the Valleyfair management set about to develop a work-place climate dedicated to good human relations between guests and employees and between employees themselves. Part of this effort was to foster Theory Y management of the park. First names were used, few titles were used, and management helped out whenever needed. Each person was trained in all park operations—from sweeping the lavatories to running all the rides. One of the major strategies to maintain an achievement-motivated climate was to develop a performance feedback/positive reinforcement system.

Guests entering the park receive small gold-colored cards saying "Nice Going Award" and are asked to give the cards to Valleyfair employees who make the guests' day more pleasant. Supervisors carry and award blue "Fuzzy Tickets" for good performance. These tickets are also awardable on an employee-to-employee, employee-to-supervisor, supervisor-to-supervisor, and employee-to-manager basis to recognize good performance. Fuzzy Tickets can be awarded just for niceness, but supervisors are encouraged to award them for very specific behaviors, all of which are indicators of the four factors that management believes contribute most to the effectiveness of the park—friendliness, service, park cleanliness, and show.

Employees who receive Fuzzy Tickets and Nice Going Awards jot the date and reason for the award on the back of the awards and later redeem them with the general manager for Fuzzies—small brightly colored fluff balls which employees fasten to the nametags on their costumes. The tickets also give the employees points toward prizes, ranging from pizza discount coupons to $50 gift certificates in a clothing store.

How did the system work? According to the management, great. Management asked a random sample of guests 36 very specific questions about park/employee performance. The guests gave them high marks on all four performance measures—friendliness, service, show, and cleanliness.

Summary

This chapter has focused on several global change-related issues. One is that there are two objectives of organization change—adapting to the environment and changing the behavior of employees in the organization. Various environmental factors generate the necessity for change. An eight-step model for organizational change can be used to indicate the need for systematic analysis by a manager of both the firm's external environment and its internal structure and organizational climate. The manager is often aware of the need for change because of the performance gap, or the difference between what the organization could do by virtue of its opportunity in its market and what it actually does in taking advantage of that opportunity. Not all organization change is warmly received by employees, and change efforts may be resisted by employees and the entire organization. Once these reasons have been explored, management must actually plan the change strategy and examine the alternative strategies it has available.

We identified four change strategies. A *technology* strategy focuses on change in workflows, methods, materials, and information systems, as might occur in most companies. The *organizational structure* strategy emphasizes the internal changes in the operation of the firm that are brought about by the realignment of jobs within the organization. General Dynamics' recent reorganization illustrates this change strategy. *Task* strategies focus on specific job activities that have been changed to increase both the quality of the employees' work experience and their on-the-job productivity. Bell Telephone and Pet Foods used job enrichment to increase employees' job satisfactions and productivity. *People* strategies usually are directed toward improving communications and relations among individuals and groups to achieve increased organizational effectiveness. The Managerial Grid and behavior modification are people-oriented strategies.

We have emphasized that the manner in which the manager diagnoses the problems and how accurately he or she recognizes the need for change will affect the change process. Important to the success of the change program are the current levels of dissatisfaction with the firm, support by top management for the change effort, and the correct diagnosis of the sources of resistance to the change effort. Successful programs generally involve the individuals directly affected by the change in the process from the start. If change is successful, individual goals, social ties, and economic rewards may be altered. Altering the steps in the change process can introduce serious doubt that the overall objectives of the change program can be accomplished without involvement of all employees who will be affected by the change.

Discussion Questions

1. Why do organizations change?

2. What are some of the external pressures faced by top managements?

3. What are attributes of an organization's climate? How do these relate to change?

4. Why do organizations resist change?

5. Why do people resist change?

6. What factors influence whether or not a manager sees a performance gap?

7. Review your understanding of the change model by using it to evaluate a change that you implemented recently in your approach to getting a college degree.

8. Discuss the forces and strategy involved in determining and implementing large-scale organization changes.

9. Which step in the change process is the most difficult and most likely to be ignored by management because of its difficulty? Why?

10. What are the assumptions of organization development?

11. What are the differences between the "people" and "structural" change strategies?

12. What are the differences between job enrichment and behavioral modification change strategies?

Management Incidents

PHELPS PLANT

The manufacturing operations at the Phelps plant of the Macungie Corporation consist of fabricating and assembling trucks—over-the-road, fire engines, and panel trucks. Traditionally, the manufacturing systems have been designed and built around an assembly-line operation.

As general production manager of the Phelps plant, Mr. Schaadt, who has developed through the management ranks largely by following the basic principles of management, must give final approval to all system changes that will affect the operations of this plant. A new design for an engine of the over-the-road truck has been completed by product engineering. In turn, it has been released to manufacturing engineering for implementation into the assembly-line system.

The manufacturing engineering group recently studied the available research relative to the advantages of job enrichment and how it compares to the traditional method of an assembly line, in terms of providing the workers with more challenging tasks, relief from boredom, and greater responsibility for the product. Management realized that job satisfaction and motivation continued to be an apparent problem on assembly-line work, and a system that included job enrichment was developed to assemble the new components of the engine along with the traditional conveyor-paced system. After the systems had been in operation for six months, the results of each system were presented to Mr. Schaadt for his approval. The manufacturing engineering group recommended that he adopt the job enrichment system because it relieved workers from performing dull, meaningless, and repetitive tasks. Mr. Schaadt, being aware of the perceived monotony and boredom of the assembly line, decided to accept the recommendation from the manufacturing engineering group.

As the production date arrived, the facilities were completed, and a number of operators moved from the assembly line process to a new job. They, in turn, were told to completely assemble the engine and stamp their work with a personalized identification stamp that Macungie had provided.

Output and quality during the first week were 10 percent below that expected, and during the next few weeks very little improvement was shown. In fact, the output was significantly below that of similar engine work at an adjacent conveyor-paced system.

Mr. Schaadt's boss was upset, since efficiency was low and excessive overtime was necessary to meet the heavy demands for trucks. Mr. Schaadt, realizing that he is responsible for the production at the Phelps plant, is trying to determine what happened and what course of action to take.

1. What should Mr. Schaadt do?
2. What factors should Mr. Schaadt consider changing?

THE ANDY CAPP MANUFACTURING COMPANY

Andy Capp Manufacturing Company is a medium-sized conglomerate that has followed a policy of growth by acquiring smaller firms. Five years ago, it took over Hagerty Plastics as a subsidiary. Previously Hagerty Plastics had been the second largest plastics manufacturer in the United States, but at the time of takeover by Andy Capp, its sales and profit were rapidly deteriorated. Andy Capp's management team felt that Hagerty Plastics was a good buy for the money in this depressed condition, and they were confident that they could turn Hagerty around to again be a real competitor in the plastics field.

The first new general manager Andy Capp assigned to Hagerty Plastics tried for four years to change the profit picture, but met with little success. Hagerty operates three plants in rural areas in the Northwest, Midwest, and Southwest. Each plant employs about 500 people. At all plants, the employees and management are very set in their ways and not receptive to new, innovative ways. In fact, last year at one plant the work force initiated a "wild-cat" strike that lasted about 30 hours. This was in opposition to the general manager Andy Capp assigned to the plant.

1. What are some of the resistances to change in this company?
2. If you were appointed as the new general manager of this company, what would you do?
3. How can new ideas become accepted at the Hagerty plants?

THE ACE RACKETBALL COMPANY

Absenteeism and lateness at Ace had been staggering for the last year. For 1977 the average employee was 20 minutes late for work twice a week and absent one and a half days per month. Given the intense market competition from foreign imported racketballs, gloves, and other athletic equipment, Barbara Harrison decided that something had to be done.

The problem was turned over to Marcy Ruth of the personnel department. After thinking about the situation for a few weeks, Marcy suggested to Barbara and the other members of the management team that an incentive program might solve the problem. She proposed that every worker who was on time during the month would be eligible for a cash award of $75. A worker maintaining perfect attendance throughout the year would be eligible for a cash award of $400. Marcy thought that the cash awards might be enough of an incentive to keep the 400 workers coming to work on time. Within one week after the announcement of the cash awards, absenteeism declined to a lower level than it had ever been for the past seven years. Furthermore, throughout the next eight months, the firm continued to maintain its award policy, and the lateness problem almost disappeared. Absenteeism was also low. Early in 1978, after the firm had issued its first annual perfect attendance award and 13 monthly cash awards, the firm dropped both awards. In March 1978, absenteeism and lateness soared to an all-time high, but returned to its former low level in April, when the award system was reinstated.

1. Has management actually modified the workers' behavior?
2. Why did absenteeism and lateness increase when management dropped its award plan?
3. Is money the only motivator that management could have used?

REFERENCES

1. M. Ways, "The Era of Radical Change," *Fortune* **79** (1964): 113.

2. A. Toffler, *Future Shock* (New York: Random House, 1970).

3. These have been adapted from H. Tosi and S. Carroll, *Management: Contingencies, Structure, and Process* (Chicago: St. Clair Press, 1976), pp. 493–500.

4. C. Varkonyi, "Computer Checkout Debuts in Coopersburg," *Centre Daily Times,* December 27, 1976.

5. B. Schneider, "Organizational Climates: An Essay," *Personnel Psychology* **28** (1975): 447–480.

6. H. Hand, M. Richards, and J. Slocum, "Organizational Climate and the Effectiveness of a Human Relations Training Program," *Academy of Management Journal* **16** (1973): 185–195.

7. W. Jones, "Playboy Courting a Family Image," *Washington Post,* September 19, 1976.

8. G. Zaltman, R. Duncan, and J. Holbek, *Innovations and Organizations* (New York: Wiley/Interscience, 1973), pp. 94–103.

9. J. Campbell, M. Dunnette, E. Lawler, and K. Weick, *Managerial Behavior, Performance, and Effectiveness* (New York: McGraw-Hill, 1970), pp. 271–326.

10. C. Alderfer, "Change Processes in Organizations," in *Handbook of Industrial and Organizational Psychology,* ed. M. Dunnette (Chicago: Rand McNally, 1976), pp. 1591–1938; for an excellent discussion of numerous change strategies, *see* E. Huse, *Organization Development Change* (St. Paul, Minn.: West, 1975).

11. O. Lipstreu and K. Reed, "A New Look at Organizational Implications of Automation," *Academy of Management Journal* **8** (1965): 24–31.

12. T. Whisler, *The Impact of Computers on Organizations* (New York: Praeger, 1970).

13. D. Daniel, "Reorganizing for Results," *Harvard Business Review* **44** (1966): 96.

14. "General Dynamics: Winning in the Aerospace Game," *Business Week,* May 3, 1976, p. 86 ff.

15. J. R. Hackman and L. Suttle, *Improving Life At Work: Behavioral Science Approaches to Organizational Change* (Santa Monica, Calif.: Goodyear, 1977), pp. 100–106.

16. R. Ford, "Job Enrichment Lessons from AT&T," *Harvard Business Review* **51** (1973): 96–106.

17. R. Walton, "How to Counter Alienation in the Plant," *Harvard Business Review* **50** (1972): 70–81.

18. R. Blake and J. Mouton, *The Managerial Grid* (Houston, Texas: Gulf, 1965).

19. A. Filley, R. House, and S. Kerr, *Managerial Process and Organizational Behavior* (Glenview, Ill.: Scott, Foresman, 1976), pp. 505–506.

20. F. Luthans and R. Kreitner, *Organizational Behavior Modification* (Glenview, Ill.: Scott, Foresman, 1975); *also see* "Behavior Modeling Symposium," *Personnel Psychology* **29** (1976): 325–370.

21. F. Luthans and M. Martinko, "An Organizational Behavior Modification Analysis of Absenteeism," *Human Resource Management* **15** (1976): 11–18.

22. R. Zemke, "A Warm, Fuzzy Feedback System Helps Meet Clearcut Organizational Goals," *Training* **13** (1976): 22–23.

16

16

Challenges to Management

CHANGE PROCESSES

**Organizational
change processes**

Need for changes
Resistance to change
Change model
Approaches

Chapter 15

**Challenges to
management**

Changing world
Changing managerial
processes
Changing behavioral
processes

Chapter 16

The objectives of this chapter are to:

discuss the changing world in which we live and the implications this has for managements;

indicate how managerial functions might change to meet these changing conditions;

suggest some changes in how to create conditions for employee motivation in the future;

review some topics discussed in previous chapters, in terms of the future.

It is impossible to forecast with certainty and in detail the future development of organizations and their managers. There are simply too many forces in both the external environment and within the internal structure of the organization to do so. However, there are certain factors that might have an impact on the future of management and organizations. Projection of these factors is not haphazard, but is derived from a study of trends and changes that have been taking place in the twentieth century. Managements have been both the initiators and responders to these changes.

Throughout this book, we have stressed that the nature of the external environment will help define the structure of the organization and the behavior of employees. The external environment of an organization includes all classes of people—the owners, stockholders, the members of the organization, and its various publics. As these classes of people change their values, the requirements they place on the organization also change. Demands for social responsibilities, pollution control, participation in decision making, among others, will have real impact on the behavior of tomorrow's company. Organizational structure evolves with economic development, expanding size, new technology, and increased management education.

MANAGING IN THE CHANGING WORLD

The world is continually changing—politically, socially, and technologically—and these changes seem to have accelerated in recent years. Alfred P. Sloan, past president of General Motors, has said, "To deliberately stop growing is to suffocate."[1] What Sloan is telling us is that if managements are to survive in an ever-changing world, they must be aware of the changing pressures in firms' environments. Although the exact meaning of "change" is nebulous, certainly increases in the sheer size of an organization may be taken as one indicator that change has taken place. The hospital that has added beds, nursing personnel, or patients treated per year is growing. Kodak Company's introduction of a self-developing camera similar to Polaroid's, coupled with extensive advertising campaigns and active research and development programs, may indicate that Kodak is changing and growing. Other companies with extraordinary growth are franchise operations, such as McDonald's, Kentucky Fried Chicken, Holiday Inn, and conglomerates.

Expansion of Organizations

Perhaps the first factor that will be relevant to future managerial practices is the sheer size of organizations.[2] Organizations in the future will be larger than they are today. An example of two companies in the brewing industry may help you understand how companies can grow. Heileman Brewing, Inc., and Lone Star Brewing are moderately large regional brewers. Both firms, initially single-region brewers with one major brand, suffered in the 1950s from declining per capita consumption, competitive pressures from the major national brands, and cost-price pressures. Although showing a small increase in sales from 1953 to 1961, Heileman's earnings per share slipped from $2.87 to $1.27. By 1971 earnings per share had risen to over $15.00, return on assets almost doubled, and sales increased about five times over 1961 levels. Starting in the early 1960s Heileman responded to the changes in the market with a major expansion program based on acquisition. As small brewers found that they could not meet the competition, Heileman purchased their facilities at prices much lower than the cost of starting a new brewery. In addition to capacity, Heileman also acquired brand names with regional significance. By the late 1960s Heileman was marketing more than 30 brands in the North, Northeast, Midwest, and South in all three price segments (local, national, and premium beers). In the late 1960s, Heileman also diversified into unrelated areas, primarily baking and machine toolings. Throughout this period, a strong commitment to growth dominated Heileman's corporate actions.

Lone Star's 1970 earnings per share of $1.14 represented only a small increase from the 1956 level of $1.08; return on assets had fallen about 40 percent during the same period. Lone Star attempted to grow primarily by expanding existing facilities in the same geographical area. The company attempted to increase penetration in Texas, Oklahoma, and Arkansas by continuing with its single premium-price beer, with heavy promotion and with a strong commitment to quality. Lone Star's paternalistic and socially oriented management engages in several large-scale civic and historically oriented projects. The difference between these two firms appears to be largely a function of their differing growth strategies: growth through acquisition and diversification into new geographical areas versus internal expansion.

A comparison of the W. R. Grace and duPont chemical companies reveals a different growth pattern. After an initial period of declining income during the early 1950s, Grace's income increased at a yearly rate of 27 percent from 1955 to 1965, and its sales increased more than 30 percent a year. DuPont's income increased at a rate of only 2 percent a year, sales about 5 percent per year, and return on gross plant investment dropped from the 25 to 30 percent range to 7 to 8 percent during the same period. During this time the environment was characterized by such factors as increased number of competitors, excess capacity, and severe price cutting.

In light of unfavorable antitrust rulings, e.g., forced divestiture of duPont's General Motors holdings and an unfavorable ruling on a duPont–Imperial Chemical agreement, expansion through acquisition was not undertaken by duPont. Rather, its strategy was to rely on its strong R&D capacity to provide growth by internal development of products. As competitors developed strong R&D programs themselves and duPont's patents began to expire, a strong ownership of patent rights became more difficult to maintain, and rapid growth ceased. For example, Corfam, duPont's synthetic leather product, was on the market only six months when B. F. Goodrich countered with Aztran, a modification of the duPont product. The Corfam project eventually lost about $8 million. The company's size meant that major projects, which usually involve increased risk, were necessary to have a significant effect on sales and profits.

Grace expanded in the chemical industry primarily by acquiring well-managed, established firms with proven products and growth potential. Once a company was acquired, large capital expenditures were made to expand and to modernize facilities. Expansion was financed largely by the sale of traditional, but less profitable, lines of business. Grace also emphasized expansion in rapidly growing foreign countries and a higher degree of diversification than duPont did.

The performance of these firms suggests the relative effectiveness of two growth strategies, but even more the extreme importance of management's responding to uncontrollable factors—primarily external environmental constraints. A victim of its tremendous size, duPont was forced to expand internally at a time when its competitive advantages were weakening and when competition was never more fierce. Grace, not burdened by antitrust and other environmental constraints, was able to grow successfully through a sound acquisition program.

The development of large-scale companies and conglomerates with activities in a wide diversity of industrial fields is another example of increased size and expansion. Conglomerates, such as Gulf & Western Industries, ITT, AMF, United Technologies, encompass within their organizational structures a number of unrelated businesses operating in different market segments. By expanding into diverse market segments, these organizations have been able to increase their stability, improve their profit picture by purchasing equipment and services from other firms within the conglomerate, increase their sales effort by distributing the selling capabilities more equitably among salespeople, and thereby gain increased sales productivity. Unneeded products, personnel, and facilities have been reduced through the use of extensive planning systems.[3] Because of poor management, other conglomerates, such as Avco, LTV, and Whittaker, have become financial nightmares.

Change in Goals

Changes in organizational goals have caused firms to increase their scope. The goals of hospitals, for example, have undergone a steady transformation. In early times, a hospital's goal was to take care of the poor and sick who could not afford private medical assistance. During the last century, hospitals transformed this goal to give greater emphasis on preventive treatment. Today, the objectives of hospitals usually emphasize quality care, the coordination of various activities of the physician and the hospital staff, and the recruitment of physicians oriented to hospital practice. Hospitals have also expanded their range of influence by taking on the objective of maintaining optimum health-care service for *all* people in a community rather than simply the care of individual patients. Similarly, the modern prison has expanded its scope to include not only activities related to prisoner confinement, but the training and rehabilitation of prisoners as well.

The Multinational Organization

The development of the multinational corporation has significantly changed the operation of many companies. A multinational organization is one that is headquartered in one nation, but has its business operations spread over many countries.[4] These types of corporations came into existence during the 1960s, when it became profitable for American firms, such as IBM, Singer Company, Colgate-Palmolive, Heinz, Hoover, to cross national boundaries. Approximately 6000 American corporations currently operate in foreign countries, and virtually every large corporation has overseas operations. Corning Glass Works, for example, has plants in Mexico, France, Japan, India, Brazil, and Italy. In the past few years, several Japanese firms and most recently Volkswagen have opened plants in the United States.

Since multinational organizations are basically holding companies, they must conform to the requirements of the particular countries in which they operate. In turn, ownership portions are directly related to the control that the parent company can usually maintain. For example, the Singer Company, manufacturer of sewing machines, computer systems, laundry products, knitting machines, computerized cash registers, and Friden calculators, sells its products in 180 political jurisdictions, with its foreign operations accounting for nearly 40 percent of its $2.1 billion in sales during 1975. The chairman and chief executive officer of the company states that his market is the world. It is his philosophy that Singer must satisfy the needs of each country in which it operates. In South Africa, for example, the government decreed that imports would be 20 percent of those allotted in 1969. Singer changed its corporate strategy accordingly and has eliminated all but five of its retail stores, tightened its credit policy, and limited its assets in South Africa.[5]

Among the many reasons why multinational corporations have expanded are the following:

1. an expanding world population that desires a higher standard of living;
2. high transportation costs prohibiting the long-distance shipping of many products;
3. the easier establishment of new markets when domestic markets are saturated with a product;
4. international laws facilitating world trade;
5. increased world demand and personal income.[6]

Foreign operations create more uncertainty for the firm than do domestic operations. For example, the rise of nationalism in South America has led to greater regulation of the multinational firms (especially the oil companies) operating in that part of the world. Pressures from business persons and labor unions are forcing governments to discourage the inflow of foreign capital by adopting selective controls and stricter regulations on such investments. Consequently, multinational firms are faced with the problem of reconciling their activities with the interests and desires of the nations in which they are investing. Success and survival in international markets depend on the sensitivity and adaptation to local circumstances, as indicated in the Singer sewing machine case.

Changes in Values

One of the major forces at work in organizations is the desire of personnel to participate in decisions affecting them. The growing student demands for participation in university affairs and the collective-bargaining activities of school teachers, local, state, and federal employees, nurses, and engineers are examples of this desire for organizational participation. There appear to be several reasons for this desire to participate.

There seems to be a gradual erosion of Western society's basic belief about the need for work and its primary importance for workers. The "Protestant ethic" holds that men and women were created to work and that to satisfy their basic needs, they have to work hard. This belief is now seriously questioned by many groups in society. Some people see technology as being capable of providing their material needs without any real effort on their part.

This change implies that the use of individuals by an organization to satisfy its economic goals is no longer a universally accepted societal goal. Many people will not let themselves be used by the organization. They want other things out of the work place in addition to material rewards, e.g., pay, fringe benefits, workmen's compensation, and unemployment benefits. Material rewards do not provide a cleaner atmosphere, a better urban transportation system, better educational facilities, and improved health services. In a large sample of blue-collar workers, it was found that workers value (1) interesting work (most important); (2) opportunity to develop their own special abilities; and (3) chance for promotion over (1) job security; (2) whether their jobs let them forget their personal problems; and (3) being asked to do excessive work.[7] (Chapter 2 discussed values held by successful American managers and how various values from countries affect management practices.)

The effects of these changing values are already evident in society. In recent years, for example, college students have become increasingly concerned with social issues, and for some students this concern has taken the form of sit-ins, marches, demonstrations, and active participation in political processes. One study found that students want to do things for people, share and be generous, be compassionate toward the unfortunate, and oppose militarism and conformity; business executives also show a strong desire for the emphasis on individual rights and responsibilities.[8] Because of their expectations about their work, some college students turn down jobs that would put them on the corporate payrolls and instead take jobs with the Peace Corps or nonprofit organizations. If people do not find things as they want, they often leave their present positions. At Union Carbide Corporation, the turnover rate for one job was 150 percent during the first two years, because people wanted a job that was relevant and significant.

This same emerging value system has also been observed in blue-collar workers. At the Lordstown, Ohio, plant of Chevrolet, workers struck for several days in 1972 because they were rebelling against the "system," performing unchallenging tasks, and resisting "speed-up" attempts by management. At one Ford plant, the quit rate hit 125 percent per year; some workers did not even return to get their back pay. Feelings are also vented through absenteeism, shoddy work, sabotage, and grievances. In some plants, absenteeism on the assembly line had become so bad that lines had to be closed temporarily because there were not enough workers to keep them going. Though somewhat of an exaggeration, the philosophy of these workers has perhaps been best stated by Walter Reuther, late president of the United Auto Workers: "Young workers . . . get three or four days' pay and figure, 'Well, I can live on that. I'm not really interested in those material things anyhow. I'm interested in the sense of fulfillment as a human being.' "[9]

The same feelings have also been observed among the unemployed, who seem to be as selective about accepting employment as the employed are about changing jobs. One reason for this is that society has provided a means for the jobless to subsist—welfare—which may provide more money than the jobs available.

Another change has been the general souring of attitudes toward business by society in general. Sampling more than 4000 persons, the Public Opinion Research Corporation found that Americans are generally cynical toward organizations making profits; 60 percent disapprove of many of the actions taken by businesses, 34 percent have little confidence in corporate leadership, 32 percent feel that the government should limit corporate profits, and 60 percent agree that the government should control prices.[10]

Changes in Work-Force Composition

WOMEN IN MANAGEMENT

Opportunities for women in management have been developing gradually, but progress has been slow. To date, only a small segment of the female work force has penetrated managerial ranks. However, women are increasingly demanding and obtaining equal opportunity. This is being brought about by a combination of circumstances, including (1) enforcement of legal sanctions against discrimination; (2) increased educational attainment by women; (3) greater sexual and social freedom, with a marked reduction of different expectations, standards, and norms for men and women; and (4) more favorable attitudes toward women as colleagues and supervisors of men at work.[11]

Why haven't these forces altered the picture more rapidly? The most obvious answer seems to be that traditional male attitudes toward women at the professional and managerial level continue to block change. The traditional attitude is that women should be adaptable to new environments, good hostesses, and active participants in civic and social activities of the community. Such attitudes reflect a combination of feelings about what women's place should be in our society and other attitudes that result from men's experience with women who have achieved managerial status. Many women, especially older women, are ambivalent about how they should relate to men in the typical business organization. However, this will not be true of the younger women desiring careers, who are not the least bit bound by traditional imagery and who want change.

Another block to equal status has been the lack of clear-cut career patterns for women who seek jobs leading to work at the managerial level. From 1950 to 1960, for example, the number of female executives increased from 8875 to 24,475, but the proportion of female to male executives remained the same.

Working women today are found primarily in white-collar occupations, but only a very small percentage of them are in prestigious white-collar jobs. There are very few women in most professional fields, with the exception of nursing and teaching. In the field of architecture, 1981 out of 56,000 are women. Of the 1.2 million engineers, fewer than 20,000 are women. Women make up only

13 percent of the life and physical scientists, 19 percent of the social scientists, and only 33 percent of the writers, artists, and entertainers.[12]

Some firms are trying to improve the situation. But in most cases, the pressure for change is coming from the federal government. When the Equal Pay Act was passed in 1963, the government said that if jobs were substantially equal, the pay between sexes should also be equal. Several large corporations, most notably Wheaton Glass, Pacific Telephone and Telegraph, RCA, and American Can, were found to have violated the Equal Pay Act and have had to pay women "back pay." In addition to seeking action through the courts, women are also employing union power; women constitute majorities in the International Ladies' Garment Workers, Communications Workers, and the Clothing Workers.

HIRING THE HARD-CORE UNEMPLOYED

Many business firms have voluntarily responded to the challenge of the National Alliance of Businessmen (NAB) to reduce their barriers for employment.[13] The NAB was formed in 1968, and one of its goals was to find employment for 100,000 hard-core unemployed. Using a "community chest" type of drive, it established quotas for cities around the country and then canvassed each city, calling on businesses to pledge a specific number of jobs. In particular, it asked each business to review and modify its hiring policies so that it would take on hard-core applicants. As a result, the NAB was able to announce in its 1973 annual report that the program had found work for more than 1.3 million people since 1968.

How successful has this voluntary business venture been? Despite some problems, such as determining who is going to pay to train these hard-core unemployed and who will give them the special support they sometimes need, the program has been successful. In New York City, approximately 50 percent of Consolidated Edison's new employees are Puerto Rican or black. The Bank of America in California increased its minority-group personnel from 11 percent in 1965 to 22 percent by mid-1970. The federal government, through the Department of Labor, has tried to help firms that hire the hard-core unemployed by awarding subsidy contracts to them.

THE TEMPORARY EMPLOYEE

Until World War II, there were very few temporary employees. By contrast, approximately two to three million people worked as temporaries during 1977.[14] Eight out of ten American firms now occasionally use temporaries, with a typical firm purchasing nearly 250 days of temporary office help per year. Temporary help has become a $1.5 billion-a-year industry. Most of the jobs that temporary employees fill are clerical, and most of these employees are women. For example, International Transportation hires clerical employees who are bilingual and places them in organizations where the use of two languages is essential. Salespower, a division of Manpower, furnishes salespersons on a temporary basis. Kelly Services and Typing Service guarantees its temporaries a full week of work so that its customers are assured of service at any time.

Who is drawn to this type of work? Some individuals want this type of work situation and would find a permanent job bothersome or impossible. Others

report that they like this type of employment because it provides them with
freedom of movement, a continually changing environment, flexibility in work
hours, and the ability to meet more people and make more friends. According
to several large surveys, temporary workers report that they have very little
interest in becoming full-time employees.

Why do firms hire temporary employees? One major advantage associated
with the use of temporary employees is that the hiring firm is not responsible
for fringe benefits (such as life and health insurance, vacation time, stock bonuses, and discounts at company shops). Another attraction is that the firm can
hire an individual as a regular employee if he or she performs well. Conversely,
there is no problem of terminating an employee who is performing at an unsatisfactory level. Temporary employees are frequently used to fill in for full-
time employees who are ill or on leave, to aid the firm during peak periods
(such as the postal service hiring of college students during the Christmas rush),
or to handle special jobs. The one major disadvantage associated with hiring
the temporary employee is the training and orientation of the worker. If the job
is complex, it is often wasteful to provide the needed training to a short-time
worker.

CHANGES IN THE WHITE-COLLAR WORK FORCE

Presently the number of professional and technical workers is increasing the
fastest, with an estimated increase of 50 percent between 1968 and 1980. The
number of service workers and sales persons is also increasing more rapidly
than is the number of craftsmen and foremen, factory workers, and farm
workers. There has also been a corresponding change in workers' educational
levels. It has been estimated that most adults will have completed high school
and attend some sort of college before the mid-1980s. There is likely to be a
rapid growth of junior colleges, whose goal is to provide continuing education
for many individuals.

Increased Foreign Competition

United States firms are facing increased foreign competition, especially in the
automobile industry. Other products, such as cameras, sewing machines, shoes,
radios, and televisions are among the latest group of products to face stiff foreign competition. The rapidly improving quality of some of these goods, as well
as lower prices, have made competition difficult for some domestic producers
to cope with. Since World War II, foreign competitors have been able to build
modern plants and use the latest management techniques and practices to keep
prices low. Their labor forces are often equally or more highly motivated and
may work for wages substantially lower than most United States workers. In
1975 the average hourly compensation for an employee in the motor vehicle
industry was $9.29 in the United States, $4.99 in Italy, and $3.61 in Japan.[15]

Increased foreign competition requires more attention by domestic producers to costs and technological improvements. Foreign competition also involves the federal and state governments because of the potential impact that
foreign firms have on the national economy. When Volkswagen decided to
locate its first American plant in New Stanton, Pennsylvania, the state posted a

bond that enabled Volkswagen to buy an old plant from the Chrysler Corporation and pay a very low interest rate. The monies for the new plant were drawn from the state's Teacher's Retirement Fund. Volkswagen decided to locate in the United States because fluctuations in the foreign exchange rate priced the VW at the upper end of the small-car price range in the United States.

Changes in Government-Business Relations

In the future, there will be a greater emphasis on problems involving government and business. John Kenneth Galbraith foresees a closer interrelationship between business and government and the continued development of an industrial system based on cooperation:

> Given the deep dependence of the industrial system on the state and the nature of its motivational relationship to the state . . . the industrial system will no longer be regarded as something apart from government. Rather, it will be increasingly seen as part of a much larger complex which embraces both the industrial system and the state.[16]

Although you may not agree with his statement about the extent of industrial-governmental cooperation, there have been numerous instances of such cooperation. Consider the case of the supersonic transport (SST) or the government's 1972 decision to lend Lockheed $250 million to hold its competitive position in the airplane market and maintain its work force in an industry that had been hard hit by unemployment.

The case of the SST illustrates government-business cooperation and determination of national priorities. In 1962 President Kennedy announced his decision to commit the United States to the development of a supersonic plane. This announcement was clearly a response to the joint effort by the British and French to build the Concorde, another supersonic plane. The United States Congress appropriated $750 million for development purposes. Three airframe manufacturers and three engine companies submitted initial design proposals in January 1964. In May, President Johnson directed the FAA (Federal Aviation Administration) to award airframe contracts to Boeing and Lockheed and told General Electric and Pratt & Whitney to revise their bids on engines. These companies submitted their revised bids in November 1964. After six more months of review, President Johnson announced an 18-month design program and requested from Congress an additional $140 million appropriation for the program. On December 31, 1966, the FAA announced that Boeing and General Electric had been selected to construct the SST; after a government commitment of $311 million and expenditure of $244 million, in addition to the $70 million spent by the plane manufacturers, the SST program was ready to go. Contracts were signed in May 1967, and Congress was asked to appropriate an additional $198 million to help finance the prototype construction phase of the program. In the fall of 1968, after nearly $500 million had been spent, Boeing announced that its design would have to be scrapped.

Although it would be beyond the scope of this book to examine all of the ramifications of these negotiations, let's briefly examine four areas: balance of payments and international affairs, economics, environmental and sociological impact, and technological advancement.

The government projected that sales of the SST to foreign governments would improve the United States's balance of payments by about $70 billion (depending on the competition) from its introduction in 1978 to 1990. Because of the noise pollution created by the Concorde, the government felt that it could bar the Concorde from the major United States airports and thus create a further market for the SST. In 1976 the Concorde made its maiden flight to the United States. Congress quickly enacted legislation that prohibited the Concorde from landing at all American airports except Dulles, outside of Washington, D.C., and Kennedy, in New York. (The New York Port Authority, however, has barred use of Kennedy by the Concorde.) Congress will ultimately decide whether the plane can land on a regular flight schedule in the United States. The Concorde is also facing a financial dilemma. By 1973 Air Canada, Pan Am, TWA, and United had all cancelled their options to buy the $60 million plane. In 1976 Air France lost $32 million operating the plane. Most travelers are not going to be willing to pay $801 to get, for example, from New York to Paris in 3½ hours instead of 6 hours.

The economic benefits which would have accrued to the airline industry were also projected to be substantial. Between 1962 and 1967, the rate of return on investment for the airline industry had been about 7.7 percent and was declining steadily. It was estimated that airlines buying SST's could earn 25 percent before taxes, which would substantially improve their profit outlook. It was also projected that an additional one hundred thousand workers would be employed in the aerospace industry to manufacture these planes. This employment figure would be concentrated in highly skilled and managerial positions.

The effects of technological fallout from the SST program were identified as flight-control systems and structures, materials, aerodynamics, aircraft engines, etc. This would improve the aircraft industry in general, would benefit other industries, and would have military applications.

Social Responsibilities of Organizations

During the last decade or so, society has been placing demands on large business firms for greater social responsibility. What is meant by a socially responsible management of a business organization? The managers of such an organization have agreed to three actions.[17] First, they must have an awareness of the firm's obligations to solve some of the problems facing society. This awareness of social problems has to exist in the firm's relationships with its customers, owners, employees, creditors, community, government, and society in general. Second, the firm must be willing to help solve some of these social problems. Obviously, not all problems can be solved by business organizations, but the firm must be willing to tackle some of society's problems. Third, and more specifically, the firm must attempt to make decisions and actually commit resources of various kinds in some of the following problem areas: pollution (air, water, solid waste, land, and noise), poverty and racial discrimination (minority groups, black capitalism, and urban problems), and consumerism (product safety, misleading advertising, consumer complaints).

As problems such as these continue to mount, managers of the future will be faced with being more socially responsible. In addition to the belief that power implies responsibilities, there are other reasons why the corporation will be looked toward for help in solving society's problems. By the 1960s, America was the most affluent nation the world had ever known. With this affluence came a social awakening. People started asking questions about conditions in America and started demanding that corrective action be taken in such areas as equal opportunity, ecology, and consumerism. Feeling that the business community had the resources and the know-how to handle these problems, the public insisted, through local, state and federal laws, that business become involved in social issues. Some of the largest corporations, e.g., IBM, Chase Manhattan Bank, Xerox, Eli Lilly and Coca-Cola, have become very active in major social-action programs. However, companies may also engage in social programs to avoid harassment by social groups. The Wonder Bread Bakery plant in Boston, for example, became more sensitive to minority employment problems as a result of a threatened boycott of its products in minority areas.

LIMITATIONS TO SOCIAL RESPONSIBILITY

Despite the strong arguments for social responsibility by organizations, there are also some powerful arguments against it. Some people question whether public problems *should* be placed on the shoulders of corporate managers. These critics argue that businesspeople are not held responsible to the voters for their decisions and could, in determining what is best for society, turn into paternalistic rulers. Many people believe that business may suffer serious profit consequences by accepting a heavy burden of social responsibility. Capital and managerial talent may be drained by those activities that may be against the profit motive of the firm and to the firm's stockholders. Milton Friedman, the Nobel Prize winning economist from the University of Chicago, believes that a corporate manager is an agent of the stockholders and that any diversion of resources from the task of maximizing stockholder wealth amounts to spending the stockholders' money without their consent.[18] Moreover, he argues, government rather than business is the institution best suited for solving social problems. Friedman's point is that managers' actions are constrained by the economic need of their companies. Profit and positive cash flow are still the baselines for all firms. Friedman stresses that no executive can afford to jeopardize the firm's financial position in the name of social involvement. Boise Cascade Corporation, for example, promoted a minority enterprise in the heavy-construction industry. The venture resulted in a pretax loss of approximately $40 million to Boise Cascade. As a result, the corporation's stock fell 60 points, and the stockholders were demanding the resignation of the corporation's officers.

Managers may find themselves on the horns of a dilemma. When they attempt to become involved in society's problems, they may face an angry group of stockholders who maintain that companies have no right to use their earnings for such uses. Since they, the stockholders, are the legal owners of the company, only they can make such decisions. On the other hand, when managers attempt to maximize profit for stockholders, they may face the wrath of many groups which claim that managers have no respect for the needs of society as a whole and are failing to safeguard the environmental conditions that provide for the survival and growth of the entire business community.

It is probably necessary to find a middle position. Thus the firm will have to broaden its perspective to encompass different cultural, social, economic, and political problems. Society is posing problems and assigning priorities to the allocation of scarce resources which may require firms to cooperate and compete with other organizations, such as universities, foundations, governmental agencies, and institutes. Thus business firms may have to develop ways of measuring their performance in activities that affect society rather than be concerned solely with profits.

One of the most recent approaches to measuring performance is the corporate social audit. Some companies, including BankAmerica Corporation and American Telephone and Telegraph, are preparing statements of their social commitments, environmental resources consumed, pollution control, etc., which reflect their total commitment to society. They are also trying to measure these commitments in terms of performance, costs, profits, human assets available, and the like. The American Institute for Certified Public Accountants has appointed an eight-member committee to develop standards and techniques for measuring and auditing a firm's social responsibilities. These companies are adopting the model of the "well-tempered corporation"; the claims of stockholders and creditors will be more likely to be met if the company develops a socially responsible attitude.[19] This can be done only if management integrates the factors of production with respect to the primary interests of the owners and the prevailing norms and values of society.

Technology Changes

Technology has advanced extremely rapidly in recent years, and this trend can be expected to continue. These technological changes have shortened the life of many products and services. Every customer has had the experience of trying to buy certain items in the supermarket only to find that the product is impossible to locate or that the brand does not even exist any more. Approximately 55 percent of the products sold today did not even exist ten years ago, and of the products sold then, about 40 percent have been taken off the shelf. In the high-technological-change industries, such as the pharmaceutical and electronics fields, a product is often obsolete within six months. For example, in 1976–77 the swine flu vaccination program undertaken by the federal government required the major pharmaceutical firms to make a product that was virtually unknown to most people prior to early 1976. In the pocket calculator market, it seems that almost every month a new, less expensive, more complex instrument is being introduced into the market, rendering older ones obsolete to some extent. When product life cycles are shortened, organizations must be able to shorten their "lead times" to get into production. Thus when the government undertook the vast inoculation program against swine flu in 1976–77, the pharmaceutical firms wanted a long enough lead time to perfect the product. Liability insurance was provided by the federal government because the "lead time" was not sufficient for testing the vaccine. The firms that participated in the program set up production facilities that could produce the desired amounts of vaccine on a short time basis.

CHANGES IN MANAGERIAL PROCESSES

In the first part of this chapter, we briefly outlined some of the major conditions that will impact on the organization and its managers in the future. The effects of these conditions are likely to vary from organization to organization. No two organizations are identical; therefore, no two organizations will respond to these conditions in the same ways. Since most organizational environments are subject to dynamic changes, structures will not only differ, but should be designed through a contingency approach. The contingency approach depends on the prevailing culture of the organization, its state of readiness for the change, its technology, its expectations about the future, and its value system. In this part of the chapter, we shall discuss how these conditions may affect the managerial processes.

Structural Changes in the Future

Most organization charts reflect the pyramid-shaped structure in which there are fewer people at higher levels than at lower levels. However, this pyramid is not recognizable in all organizations. If an organization is in a rapidly changing environment, the pyramid is likely to be effective only if it can adapt to the changes in its environment. As indicated in Chapter 5, the ability to organize resources around problems in temporary structures is the focus of "project management." Once the project is completed, the workers, equipment, resources, etc., will be reassigned to other departments in the organization. This type of structure minimizes the role of the organization's hierarchy and is formed on the basis of technical direction and expertise. Each department within the organization will farm out specialized activities to task forces for assistance. The manager becomes a linking pin between the various task forces within the organization. The manager will often be a person who can speak the language of the people in various task forces, relay information, and mediate disputes between task forces. This type of structure is presently being used in the aerospace industry, construction industries, and in many professional and consulting firms.

One set of predictions about the future design of large organizations suggests a structural form similar to a diamond balanced on top of a pyramid. As shown in Fig. 16.1, the lower part of the diamond reflects how middle-management positions in the organization will be affected by the advancement of the computer and information technology. The main changes that have been forecast by the advancement of the computer and information technology are:

1. Information should be pushed upward in the organization structure to close the gap between the planning and implementation functions. A significant amount of the planning activities is currently being done by middle management. In the future, planning specialists will be located at the top of the hierarchy.

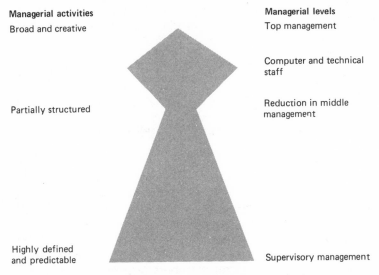

Managerial activities
Broad and creative

Partially structured

Highly defined
and predictable

Managerial levels
Top management

Computer and technical
staff

Reduction in middle
management

Supervisory management

Fig. 16.1. Structural changes in organizations of the future.
(Adapted by permission from R. Trewatha and M. Newport,
Management: Functions and Behavior, Dallas: Business Publi-
cations, 1976, p. 507.)

2. The availability of high-speed computers along with new mathematical and statistical techniques will enable organizations to recentralize many of their activities, such as purchasing, planning, budgeting, and transportation. This recentralization trend will allow the top-level managers to take on activities that call for more creativeness, innovation and risk taking.

3. The line separating top and middle management will be drawn more clearly. The managers who are the innovators and coordinators will be found at the top echelons of the organization's hierarchy.[20]

One word of caution is needed on this forecast. In some organizations where managers are performing relatively routine and repetitive tasks, the impact of information technology on their jobs will have a greater effect than on managers who are performing unstructured and innovative jobs. As indicated in Chapter 5, some industries, such as insurance, baking, and banking, have been affected more than others because their tasks are more suitable for computer programming. However, even in these industries, computerized information systems have had their primary impact at lower levels rather than at upper managerial levels. Information-decision systems at these higher levels will not be completely amenable to computational decision-making strategies, as pointed out in Chapter 3. Rather, they will provide the managers at these levels with the necessary information for decisions involving motivation, leadership, and conflict.

It is also likely that organizations will use more than one hierarchy more frequently in the future than in the immediate past. Instead of having only one hierarchical structure within the organization, two or three hierarchies may be used to maintain the firm's adaptiveness and flexibility. One hierarchy might be used for professional personnel, another for production personnel, and still another for those personnel concerned with auditing the corporation's social responsibilities. In many hospitals, one hierarchy is composed of the medical staff (physicians and specialists), another of the nursing staff (licensed practical nurses, practical nurses, registered nurses, nurse's aides, etc.), and another of professional management representing such traditional managerial functional areas as finance, personnel, and accounting. Within each structure, personnel could be advanced consistent with their abilities and skills within their sphere of expertise.

The major implication of this concept is that the traditional notion of the single chief executive is changing. Because of the sheer volume of work and the demand for different talents and skills by the varying interest groups within the organization, the concept of the "executive office" is appearing more frequently. The executive office typically handles the job of coordinating (integrating) the various decision-making centers. At the Caterpillar Tractor Company, for example, four members in the executive office have the authority to speak for the entire corporation.[21] The four members operate within broadly established policies and are in continual communication with one another. The major advantage of this system is that it eliminates delays in decision making. One vice-president toured South America for a budget review trip while another vice-president was touring Europe for the same purpose. Decisions were made on the spot, thus making decentralization effective.

Changes in Planning

An organization operating in a stable environment can plan its activities with a high degree of certainty. As indicated in Chapter 8, planners project the past into the future and perceive, consolidate, and design the appropriate structure of operations of the firm for the future.

With a changing environment, however, many more uncertainties are introduced into the organization. To cope with these uncertainties, a different—entrepreneurial—type of planning activity may be needed. The activity of entrepreneurial planning is different from that of traditional planning. The major functions of this type of planning activity are indicated in Fig. 16.2. Searching for new opportunities and establishing new and challenging goals are the major ingredients of this type of planning activity. Entrepreneurial planners search for new business opportunities which will enhance the growth potential for the firm. These types of planners are more concerned with the future than with the past and with opportunities outside the firm rather than problems within. Entrepreneurial planning involves risk taking, creating new possibilities for the firm, and enlarging its sphere of influence. At duPont, for example, the entrepreneurial planning activity has taken on more importance. DuPont, which had built its reputation on the long time span of its proprietary inventions, has found that its latest inventions are quickly taken over by competition. As the product life cycle shortens, duPont is confronted with technical obsolescence of its products and is looking at new markets for growth.

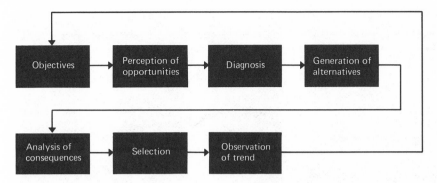

Fig. 16.2. Entrepreneurial cycle. (H. Ansoff and R. Brandenburg, "The General Manager of the Future," *California Management Review* **11** (1969): 64. Reprinted by permission of R. Brandenburg and *California Management Review*.)

Changes in Decision Making and Control

One of the consequences of the changing environment may be the alteration of the process by which decisions are made in organizations. If many of the manager's routine decisions can be programmed, more time will be available to the manager to think about environmental problems which have ill-defined solutions. An increasing number of novel decisions will be made requiring imaginative analysis and judgment rather than formulas based only on applications of past experience. New techniques will have to be developed to provide management with accurate information, requiring the blending of knowledge from computer sciences with the knowledge of the behavioral sciences.

Let's consider some of the changes that will likely occur in the structure of decision making in terms of three areas: content, processes, and information. Table 16.1 contrasts where we are today and where we may be tomorrow, in terms of these areas.

When all parts of the decision-making process are viewed in the perspective of accelerated change, management today is seemingly confronted with two major decision-process problems: (1) to design a system that will enable it to process an increased and growing volume of decisions; and (2) to rely increasingly on experts without losing control over the decisions. In the past, corporate staff grew in size to assist other managers in decision-making activities. As a result of management's dependence on staff personnel for improvement in decision-making techniques, the manager had to relinquish control of certain parts of the decision-making process and instead depend on staff experts. The trend to the corporate or executive form of office structure has significance beyond merely alleviating managerial overload or regaining control over the decision-making process. In the future, decisions may be made which will enable the firm to remain fully responsible, innovative, and competitive in tomorrow's environment. The decision maker of the future will adopt a systems framework that will require this individual to be an entrepreneur, statesman, planner, and organizational designer.

Table 16.1. The changing characteristics of decision making

Firm of today	Firm of the future
Content of decisions	
Operating issues, corporate policies	Strategy formulation, design of systems for strategy implementation
Exploitation of firm's current position	Innovation in patterns of firm's products, markets, and technology
Economic, technological, national, intraindustry perspective	Economic, sociopolitical, technological, multinational, multiindustry perspective
Decision process	
Emphasis on historical experience, judgment, past programs for solving similar problems	Emphasis on anticipation, rational analysis, pervasive use of specialist experts, techniques for coping with novel decision situations
Personnel-intensive process	Technology-intensive process
Information for decisions	
Formal information systems for internal performance history	Formal systems for anticipatory, external-environment information
One-way, top down, flow of information	Interactive, two-way communication channels linking managers and other professionals with knowledge workers
Computer systems emphasizing volume and fast response information for general management	Computer systems emphasizing richness, flexibility, and accessibility of information for general management
Emphasis on periodic operations plans, capital, and operating expenditure budgets	Emphasis on continuous planning, covering operations, projects, systems resource development. Control based on cost-benefits forecasts

Adapted from H. Ansoff and R. Brandenburg, "The General Manager of the Future," *California Management Review* **11** (1969): 69. Reprinted by permission of R. Brandenburg and *California Management Review*.

Nature of Managerial Work[22]

Traditional descriptions of work focused on the formal aspects of the organization's structure while minimizing the effect of the employee. In the future, it will not be possible to simply insist on viewing the manager simply as a decision maker.

Managerial work has several distinctive components. Each has a significant bearing on the manager's ability to manage the organization in the future.

QUANTITY OF WORK

Despite the semblance of normal working hours, the manager performs a great many activities at an unrelenting pace. One study of five managers found that they processed an average of thirty-six pieces of mail each day, participated in eight meetings, engaged in five telephone calls, and took one plant tour. Free time appears to be rare. During their "off" time, managers spent a considerable amount of time on work-related reading.

VARIETY, FRAGMENTATION, AND BREVITY OF ACTIVITY

There seems to be no pattern to managerial activity. Rather, variety, brevity, and fragmentation appear to be characteristics of a manager's work. In effect, the manager must be prepared to shift gears quickly and frequently. In a typical day, a manager will receive a call from someone asking for a favor, hear from a subordinate the current events in the plant, be asked to speak to a visiting group of dignitaries, and handle complaints from an important customer about the quality of the company's products. Throughout the day, there is a continual variety of activity.

Furthermore, these managerial activities are brief; half of them last less than nine minutes, and only ten percent exceeded one hour's duration. Thus frequent interruption is normal, and the manager becomes accustomed to the flow of "instant communication" that cannot be delayed. Managers are often plagued by what they might do and what they must do.

CURRENT, SPECIFIC ISSUES ARE PREFERRED

The managerial environment is one of stimulus and response. It breeds not reflective planners, but adaptable, action-oriented information manipulators who prefer live, concrete situations. Ad hoc reports receive considerable attention. Current gossip, speculation, or hearsay are considered by managers in making decisions. These types of communications receive first consideration by many managers because of the need to make decisions based on incomplete information.

VERBAL MEDIA

The typical manager has five media to use—mail, telephone, unscheduled meetings, scheduled meetings, and tours. Most managers have expressed a strong desire for oral forms of communications and dislike of the documented form of communication (mail) because it is slow and tedious. Most of the mail generated by managers is sent in reaction to mail received—a reply, a request, an acknowledgment—or information forwarded to all members of the organization. The less formal means of communication—the telephone and the unscheduled meeting—are used frequently to transmit information to outsiders and subordinates. However, these are usually brief in duration; the average telephone call lasts six minutes and the unscheduled meeting lasts only twelve minutes. Scheduled meetings are used primarily when the participants are unfamiliar to the manager (e.g., presentation of a speech at a national convention), when a large quantity of information has to be transmitted (e.g., presentation of the company's annual report to stockholders), when a ceremony has to take place (e.g., the retirement of a long-time employee), or when a complex strategy meeting has to be undertaken (e.g., the Ford Motor Company negotiating with the United Auto Workers). An important source of information for managers is the comments made by the audience prior to and after the formal meeting. In general, each medium is used for particular purposes. Managers prefer verbal media, which provide greater flexibility, require less effort, and bring faster responses.

As we have outlined, managerial work assumes a number of distinctive characteristics. The quantity of work is great; the pace is fast and unrelenting; the manager's work activities are varied and brief; the manager relies on issues that are current, specific, ad hoc, and to do so, finds that the verbal forms of communication are preferred. Managers in large, complex bureaucratic organizations face the real danger that the structure of the organization will become the major obstacle in the flow of decisions and information.

CHANGES IN BEHAVIORAL PROCESSES

Over the past decade, business organizations have proved that they are very effective in accomplishing goals. Consider the tremendous productive capacity of the industrial system, the rise of the gross national product, and the number of men and women employed in organizations of all sizes and financial resources. In the future, another goal may assume equal importance. Can organizations make effective use of their human resources while satisfying their profit-making goals? According to Henry Schacht, president of Cummins Engine Company, organizations will have to think of people as their key assets and realize that an organization's future depends not solely on its particular technical skills, location or product line, but on its employees as well.[23] Increasingly, managements will have to emphasize their human resources. An unprecedented opportunity exists for behavioral scientists to apply their skills to seeking solutions to the problems in industry. In this part of the chapter, we shall explore some of the behavioral problems facing managers in the future and some of the approaches that managements are using to deal with these problems.

Approaches to Job Design

The nature of work in America is in the public eye.[24] A great deal of attention has been focused on such things as job design, the quality of working life, job satisfaction, and productivity. Numerous aspects of job design have been advocated and implemented. As indicated in Chapter 11, proponents of job enrichment see it as a way of reducing the high degree of specialization brought about by scientific management. It is felt that reducing the amount of specialization will make the work more meaningful and satisfying and may result in desirable changes in productivity, quality, and other work patterns.

The results of job enrichment are generally positive. Increases in positive attitudes toward the company are usually found, and in some instances increases in the quality and quantity of work and reductions in turnover and absenteeism have been reported. As we pointed out in Chapter 11, technology is an important factor determining job design, as well as influencing opportunities for the individual to satisfy his or her high-order needs on the job. If job enrichment emphasizes changes that would require the replacement of expensive capital equipment, the program is not likely to be implemented. If the employees are not concerned about satisfying their higher-order needs on the job, it is likely that job enrichment will not have a positive effect on their behavior.

Modified Workweeks

Modifications of the standard five-day workweek have been started by a number of firms. The modified workweek appeals to management because it may lead to the reduction in the costs of doing business, through increased production, decreased turnover, decreases in start-up time, increased motivation, and decreased absenteeism. The modified workweek appeals to employees because it redistributes their free time into more meaningful patterns. Although an employee may work the same number of hours, as in a traditional schedule, the time pattern is changed.

Perhaps one of the most promising systems is the flexitime system, a way of arranging work time that gives the employees some freedom in choosing the hours they will work each day.[25] A typical example is the system used in Westinghouse's Nuclear Energy Systems division for 1500 hourly, clerical, and administrative personnel. They can report to work in the morning between the hours of 7:00 and 9:00, but they must be there between 9:30 and 11:30. Lunch can be taken between 11:30 and 1:00, as long as at least 30 minutes are used. All employees are required to be at work during the afternoon hours of 1:30 to 3:30 P.M., and they may leave work any time between 3:30 and 6:00. Total hours must balance monthly against the worktime requirement.

An employee may work as little as 5½ hours or as much as 10½ (excluding ½ hour for lunch) in any one day and as little as 27½ or as much as 52½ hours in any one week. The only requirement is that the employee be present every day during the core time of 9:30 and 11:30 and 1:30 to 3:30. If the usual monthly work requirement is 168 hours and the employee works more than 178 hours, she or he can carry over only ten hours as a credit balance. In general, time credit has been applied only to working days and has not been added to vacation time, but this is another option.

The idea of flexible time started in Europe and Canada and is spreading rapidly in the United States, where Hewlett-Packard, Scott Paper, Westinghouse, Occidental Insurance, Sun Oil, Nestle, Lufthansa Airlines, and Samsonite have adopted the system. There is considerable variation in the implementation of systems. The results of the flexible time system have been encouraging. Where the system has been adopted, the firm reports that absenteeism has been reduced, customer service and satisfaction have actually increased, and communication problems have decreased.

The key to success appears to be that employees have an opportunity to take some responsibility for their own performance and to coordinate their personal time with their work time. People have a stake in making the system work and can clearly see the benefits of the system. To succeed, the flexible working-hours systems requires that members of an organization have mutual trust and confidence in the management. Unlike other benefits that are given to employees and are passively accepted (such as life and health insurance, vacations, and company discounts plans), flexible hours require the employees to live up to their performance expectations. Companies report that there are fewer meetings and that those that do take place take less time. The companies do report, however, that there are instances when the people who are needed are not available.

Changes in Compensation Systems

Increasingly, American society is becoming more permissive about the freedom of the individual to meet his or her needs in the manner most personally appropriate and satisfying. "Doing your own thing" is now even being innovatively applied to executive compensation plans. Although an organization cannot afford to operate in a manner designed to be all things to all people, it can be more flexible and responsible to the needs of its members.

The need for a variety of executive compensation plans and flexibility in modifying and implementing those plans has long been recognized. The assumption has been that the needs of the manager should be a factor in determining the nature of the compensation package. The investment made by the organization in the individual's compensation package would be realized through an increase in effective performance.

The approach that promises the greatest amount of responsiveness to employee needs (as determined by the employee) is what may be called the *cafeteria* approach. Under this plan, employees select from a number of compensation systems those most appropriate for themselves. Certainly, the nature of probable alternatives offered would have to be based on an analysis of the costs and benefits and the current IRS tax laws.[26] A typical cafeteria approach to employee need satisfaction that has been used by General Electric is as follows:

Options with a Cost of about $600 to Company

1. $600 salary increase, no vacation increase, no increase in company contribution to employee savings plan;
2. no salary increase, 12 additional days of vacation, no increase in company contribution to employee savings plan;
3. no salary or vacation increase, increase in company contribution to employee savings plan from 3 to 9 percent;
4. $300 salary increase, six days of vacation, no increase in company contribution to employee savings plan;

5. $300 salary increase, no vacation increase, increase in company contribution to savings plan from 3 to 6 percent;
6. no salary increase, six additional vacation days, increase in company contribution to employee savings from 3 to 6 percent.[27]

Each manager at General Electric was told to assume that he or she would get a raise in the form of one of these six options and was asked to choose among them. What is being advocated at GE, TRW Systems, and other companies that have tried this type of motivational system is to let the individual employee participate in his or her own compensation system. Although there are some IRS limitations to this plan, it may be possible for companies to provide an individual with more benefits that he or she prefers at no extra cost to the company.

Emphasis on Career Development

One of the manager's prime responsibilities is to manage subordinates effectively. To do this, a manager should know about subordinates' career goals. A career is what the individual perceives to be the consequences associated with his or her work-related activities over the span of the person's life. A person tends to see job and organizational situations in relation to the ways they will affect him or her personally, not just in relation to what is best for the company. Therefore, a manager who understands the career goals of subordinates can be more effective in managing people than the manager who doesn't.

IMPORTANCE OF CAREER DEVELOPMENT

There are several reasons why an understanding of subordinates' careers is important.[28] First, a career represents a person's entire life in the work setting. For most people, the quality of their personal lives is determined by their work. Work provides the setting for the satisfaction or dissatisfaction of the entire range of human needs—physiological, safety, belongingness, self-esteem, and self-actualization, and the need for achievement. A second reason is the fundamental belief in society about social equality and personal liberation. Civil rights groups are seeking equality in job hiring and promotion practices. Organizations may be forced to pay more attention to the nature of career experiences that they provide for their employees. Third, there is a marked increase in the mobility of people. Taking advantage of better opportunities and looking for a better match between the individual's personal interests and the organization's job characteristics can cause frequent job changes. Related to this tendency is the growing reluctance to sacrifice personal and family pleasures for the sake of one's career. This is reflected in the refusal of job transfers, promotions, and an increase in the importance of location and physical characteristics of the individual's environment. Finally, by being sensitive to the career needs of employees, the manager will be able to bring about change more effectively.

CAREER STAGES FOR MANAGERS

Individuals progress through three career stages: early, middle, and late. During early career development, the individual needs to develop managerial skills so that he or she can apply the concepts and learnings obtained in schools. These are the years for creativity and innovation. From age 22 to the mid-40s, the person is usually encouraged to develop in depth one area of specialty. However, the specialty could be a trap for a person who becomes indispensable in the area and the organization cannot reward the person for his or her performance. Therefore, in some cases, rotation to a new specialty after a few years is advisable for the person to avoid becoming too narrow or even obsolete in a particular job.

Once a person becomes established in his or her career, the next stage is the midcareer stage (age 40s to retirement). In contrast to the fierce competition and achievements of the early career period, the midcareer period is characterized by holding one's own or maintaining a level of performance that has already been achieved. This is not a tranquil period. This is the stage at which many people embark on a new career rather than maintain the old one. Elliot Jacques has noted that age 37 seems to be critical in the lives of most creative artists.[29] He found a sudden surge in the death rate between 35 and 39 and a sudden drop between the ages of 40 and 44. This would indicate that the peak performance crisis would come from these artists between 35 and 39. Why was this so? By this age, a person has a pretty good idea of how far she or he will advance in the field. A person who has not attained his or her goals needs to adjust level of aspiration or find a new field of work or, perhaps, commit suicide.

There are changes in the awareness of death. Many people report that they feel that life is half over and now that they are "middle-aged," time is a more precious resource. The person's body is also undergoing changes. Aches and pains become more frequent, and physical performance and stamina drop off. While the individual's body is changing, so too are conditions in the manager's personal life. Children are now teenagers, and the manager's spouse is not quite the attractive person he or she was ten years ago. The manager is no longer looked at as the "bright young individual" on the way up the organization's ladder. Young subordinates are now the new wave of the future. Not only does this make a person feel older, but it can also lead one to question one's own competence.

The third critical stage for most workers is the late-career stage, which marks the transition to retirement. Because work is so much a part of the person's life, especially so for professional and managerial people, the loss of one's work role can be traumatic. The difficult transition into retirement may be eased by part-time work, hobbies, and a new career devoted to the creative use of leisure time.

As a way of tying together what we have said about these career stages, let's consider these stages in terms of the individual's needs. Table 16.2 summarizes much of what has been written in this area. The two basic need categories—task and emotional—are related to the three development stages in one's career. As a person progresses through these career stages, the importance of task and emotional needs varies. In the early career stages, task needs are important. Competence in work and the application of educational training to the first demands of corporate life are important. Younger managers want support from their superiors, but also want to make decisions (autonomy)

Table 16.2. Developmental needs in early, middle, and late career

Stage	Task needs	Emotional needs
Early career	Develop action skills Develop a specialty Develop creativity, innovation Rotate into new area after 3–5 years	Support Autonomy Deal with feelings of rivalry, competition
Middle career	Develop skills in training and coaching others (younger employees) Training for updating and integrating skills Develop broader view of work and organization Job rotation into new job requiring new skills	Opportunity to express feelings about midlife (anguish, defeat, limited time, restlessness) Reorganize thinking about self (morality, values, family, work) Reduce self-indulgence and competitiveness Support and mutual problem solving for coping with midcareer stress
Late career	Shift from power role to one of consultation, guidance, wisdom Begin to establish self in activities outside the organization (start on part-time basis)	Support and counseling to help see integrated life experiences as a platform for others Acceptance of one's one and only life cycle Gradual detachment from organization

D. Hall, *Careers in Organizations* (Pacific Palisades, Calif.: Goodyear, 1976), p. 90. Copyright © by Goodyear Publishing Company. Reprinted by permission.

because of their strong desire to achieve. During the manager's midcareer, the development of leadership skills is important, because now the executive is a manager of managers. There is a need to develop a broader perspective of the organization than one's own specialty and to upgrade oneself and develop new skills. On the emotional side, the person needs opportunities to cope with the midcareer crisis. In the late-career stage, the task of the individual is to provide wisdom and guidance for younger managers. On the emotional side, the individual must prepare oneself for leaving the organization.

Summary

In this chapter, we discussed the challenges that managers will be facing in the future. Some of these challenges will require organizations to structure themselves differently, to change their internal operating procedures, and to modify their values and assumptions about their employees.

Various external pressures face the organization—the trend for organizations to grow in size, the rise of the conglomerate and the multinational corporation, increased foreign competition, and changes in the composition of the work force. These environmental changes will likely affect the various managerial processes, such as planning, decision making, controlling, and the nature of the manager's work. However, knowledge of the future in and of itself is no guarantee of success. The challenges management is facing are too great to be solved simply by rules and regulations. The awareness of various contingencies that can affect the managerial process can improve the overall effectiveness of the organization. The issues of job design, modification of the workweek, and career development are important behavioral processes challenging the manager of the future.

Discussion Questions

1. Why are organizations growing in size and how are they doing this?

2. Why are changing values important to managers?

3. In what way has the Equal Pay Act been of value in promoting equal opportunity?

4. What role has the National Alliance of Businessmen played in the business world?

5. What is the role of the temporary employee?

6. What is meant by the term "social responsibility"? How would you go about assessing a firm's social responsibility?

7. Do you agree with the experts on the role that technology will have on the organization's structure? Support your answer.

8. What is the difference between entrepreneurial and traditional planning?

9. What are some characteristics of managerial work that resemble your own work patterns?

10. What are some limitations of flexitime systems?

11. What are some of the arguments that can be raised against job enrichment programs?

12. What is the purpose of career development programs?

13. What organizational actions (policies, rules, regulations) would improve the career development of individuals at various stages of their careers?

14. What is the cafeteria compensation plan?

Management Incidents

THE KELLEY CORPORATION

Your organization has traditionally been very attractive to young Ph.D.'s as a place to work. The turnover among new employees has been about average for your industry. However, a recent study of your personnel conducted by your vice-president for personnel has revealed that your turnover is now occurring among your highest-performing employees. The people you'd like to lose are staying, and those you want to keep are leaving.

Exit interviews indicate that these employees are frustrated by the low challenge, low advancement opportunities, and numerous meetings and committee reports. You have a lot of people in their late forties and early fifties who are blocking promotions now and who feel threatened by these sharp new Ph.D.'s. But you won't have any good middle managers in the next ten years if all your good people leave. Business has been rather slow, and no new positions through growth seem likely.

1. What should you do to retain more promising productive employees?
2. If you were a new Ph.D., would you be attracted to this company?

YEARGOOD TIRE COMPANY

Dear _____:

We are glad to inform you that you are a finalist for the Vice-President of Planning at Yeargood Tire Company. As I indicated in our telephone conversation, all of the members of the Office of the President were quite impressed with you during the first interview and more than satisfied with your education and experience. Thus we would like to invite you to meet with the members of the Office of the President and several members of the Board of Directors for a final interview.

Some of the things we would like to explore with you are:

1. What role do you envision for this formal planning role, and how might this relate to the planning responsibilities of other members of Yeargood Tire Co.?
2. What issues, problems, and developments do you see in society and in our immediate environment which should be of concern to Yeargood Tire Company during the next ten years?
3. In what ways might these issues and problems affect our growth, survival, and profitability?
4. What priorities would you assign to these issues and problems?

We fully recognize that these questions are unanswerable in any finalized or definitive sense. However, we do feel that these types of questions need to be made operational by the individual who becomes our first Vice-President for Planning. You might also anticipate that some members of the board, since they didn't meet you during your first visit, will possibly repeat some of the territory we covered previously.

We are looking forward to visiting with you on _____ at _____ in the Board Room of Yeargood Tire Company. Please feel free to call me regarding any questions concerning the interview.

Sincerely,

President
Yeargood Tire Company

1. Outline the points you would be prepared to set forth in explaining your views on each of the four questions posed by Yeargood's president.

THE SHADOW COMPANY*

Rodney Hardy, president of the large insurance company, was quite distressed. He had thrown a party at his home over the weekend for some associates, and during the party he was cornered by one of his wife's friends, who spent the better part of the evening discussing "women's lib." Most of what she said was common sense and was of little direct interest to Rod. However, she did ask him how many women managers the firm employed. Rod had to admit that he did not know. She said that because he didn't know, there probably weren't any on the executive staff.

Rod was bothered by her comments and thought about the statement during the Sunday afternoon football game on TV. The first thing Monday morning, he called the Personnel Department for the answer. The Personnel Department ran through its list of managers and reported that indeed women were in the executive ranks. When pressed further by Rod, the Personnel Department admitted that less than 1 percent of all women employed by the firm were in executive positions and that all the rest were clerks, typists, receptionists, and secretaries.

The reply started Rod thinking about the role of women in management. He asked his secretary to gather some information about industry standards, and he read these materials. When he was finished doing his homework on the subject, he concluded that the only way to ensure equal advancement opportunities for women was to give the matter some personal attention. Before doing so, he decided to find out how much the top managers of his office really knew about women in business. Therefore, he gave the following questionnaire to all employees.

---

* Adapted from R. Hodgetts, *Management: Theory, Process and Practice* (Philadelphia: Saunders, 1976), p. 524.

The Women As Managers Scale (WAMS)

Instructions	Rating scale

The following items are an attempt to assess the attitudes people have about women in business. The best answer to each statement is your *personal opinion*. The statements cover many different and opposing points of view; you may find yourself agreeing strongly with some of the statements, disagreeing just as strongly with others, and perhaps uncertain about others. Whether you agree or disagree with any statement, you can be sure that many people feel the same way you do.

1 = Strongly disagree
2 = Disagree
3 = Slightly disagree
4 = Neither disagree nor
   agree
5 = Slightly agree
6 = Agree
7 = Strongly agree

Using the numbers from 1 to 7 on the rating scale to the right, mark your personal opinion about each statement in the blank that immediately precedes it. Remember, give your *personal opinion* according to how much you agree or disagree with each item. Please respond to all 21 items. Thank you.

_____ 1. It is desirable for women rather than men to have a job that requires responsibility.

_____ 2. Women have the objectivity required to evaluate business situations properly.

_____ 3. Challenging work is equally as important to men as it is to women.

_____ 4. Men and women should be given equal opportunity for participation in management training programs.

_____ 5. Women have the capability to acquire the necessary skills to be successful managers.

_____ 6. On the average, women managers are as capable of contributing to an organization's overall goals as are men.

_____ 7. It is acceptable for women to assume leadership roles as often as men.

_____ 8. The business community should, some day, accept women in key managerial positions.

_____ 9. Society should regard work by female managers as valuable as work by male managers.

_____ 10. It is acceptable for women to compete with men for top executive positions.

_____ 11. The possibility of pregnancy does not make women less desirable employees than men.

_____ 12. Women would no more allow their emotions to influence their managerial behavior than would men.

_____ 13. Problems associated with menstruation should not make women less desirable than men as employees.

_____ 14. To be a successful executive, a woman does not have to sacrifice some of her femininity.

(cont.)

The Women As Managers Scale (WAMS) (cont.)

_____ 15. On the average, a woman who stays at home all the time with her children is as good a mother as a woman who works outside the home at least half-time.

_____ 16. Women are as capable of learning mathematical and mechanical skills as are men.

_____ 17. Women are ambitious enough to be successful in the business world.

_____ 18. Women can be assertive in business situations that demand it.

_____ 19. Women possess the self-confidence required of a good leader.

_____ 20. Women are competitive enough to be successful in the business world.

_____ 21. Women can be aggressive in business situations that demand it.

Adapted from J. Terborg, L. Peters, D. Ilgen, and F. Smith, "Organizational and Personal Correlates of Attitudes Toward Women as Managers," _Academy of Management Journal_ **20** (1977): p. 93. The higher your score, the more favorable your attitude toward women as managers.

The average score on the questionnaire was a 54, indicating that most of Rod's top managers had negative attitudes about women as managers.

1. What do the results of this tell Rod?
2. What initial steps do you recommend he take to correct these attitudes?

REFERENCES

1. A. Sloan, _My Years With General Motors_ (Garden City, N.Y.: Doubleday, 1963).

2. D. Schendel and C. Patton, "Corporate Stagnation and Turnaround," _Journal of Business and Economics_ **28** (1976): 236–241.

3. R. Pitts, "Diversification Strategies and Organizational Policies of Large Diversified Firms," _Journal of Economics and Business_ **28** (1976): 181–188; and J. Pfeffer, "Beyond Management and the Worker: The Institutional Function of Management," _Academy of Management Review_ **1** (1976): 36–41.

4. J. Daniels, E. Orgram, and L. Radebaugh, _International Business: Environments and Operations_ (Reading, Mass.: Addison-Wesley, 1976).

5. "Global Companies: Too Big to Handle," _Newsweek_ **80** (November 20, 1972): 96–104.

6. R. Pehlman, J. Ang, and S. Ali. "Policies of Multinational Firms," _Business Horizons_ **16** (1976): 14–18.

7. S. Zagoria, "Searching for the Meaning of Work: Rebellion and Reform," _Washington Post_, February 1972.

8. R. Taylor and M. Thompson, "Work Value Systems of Young Workers," *Academy of Management Journal* **19** (1976): 522–536; and M. McCall and E. Lawler, "High School Students' Perceptions of Work," *Academy of Management Journal* **19** (1976): 17–24.

9. P. Doeringer, "Ghetto Labor Markets and Manpower Problems," *Monthly Labor Review* **22** (1969): 55–56.

10. "America's growing Antibusiness Mood," *Business Week,* June 17, 1972, pp. 89–91, 103, 116; J. Bowman, "Managerial Ethics in Business and Government," *Business Horizons* **19** (1976): 48–54.

11. B. McCord, "Identifying and Developing Women for Management Positions," *Training and Development Journal* **24** (1971): 2; L. Putnam and J. Heinen, "Women in Management: The Fallacy of the Trait Approach," *MSU Business Topics* **24** (1976): 47–54; and R. Loring and T. Wells, *Breakthrough: Women Into Management* (New York: Van Nostrand Reinhold, 1972).

12. J. Veiga and J. Yanouzas, "What Women in Management Want: The Ideal vs. the Real," *Academy of Management Journal* **19** (1976): 137–143. The entire issue of the *Monthly Labor Review* **97** (1974), was devoted to women in the workplace. The *AFL-CIO American Federationist,* July 1974, pp. 9–16, had an excellent article on women workers. This section draws heavily on those works.

13. R. Hodgetts, *Management: Theory, Process and Practice* (Philadelphia: Saunders, 1976), p. 503.

14. Y. Halberstam, "Temporary Jobs—A Way of Life," *The Washington Post (Parade Magazine),* November 21, 1976.

15. "Special World Trade Outlook," *Commerce Today* **20** (1975): 4–48.

16. J. K. Galbraith, *The New Industrial State* (Boston: Houghton Mifflin, 1967), p. 392.

17. R. Hay, E. Gray, and J. Gates, *Business and Society* (Cincinnati, Ohio: South-Western, 1976), pp. 15–16. *Also see* V. Buehler and Y. Shetty, "Managerial Response to Social Responsibility Challenge," *Academy of Management Journal* **19** (1976): 66–78.

18. M. Friedman, "The Social Responsibility of Business Is to Increase Profits," *New York Times Magazine,* September 13, 1970, pp. 122–126.

19. H. Fogler and F. Nutt, "A Note on Social Responsibility and Stock Valuation," *Academy of Management Journal* **18** (1975): 155–160; and R. Johnson, J. Monsen, H. Knowles, and B. Saxberg, *Management, Systems, and Society: An Introduction* (Pacific Palisades, Calif.: Goodyear, 1976).

20. H. Leavitt and T. Whisler, "Management in the 1980s," *Harvard Business Review* **36** (1958): 41–48.

21. R. Hulme and J. Maydew, "A View from the Top: A Study of Collective Management Organization," *Business Horizons* **15** (1972): 19–31.

22. For a more detailed description of the nature of these managerial activities, *see* H. Mintzberg, *The Nature of Managerial Work* (New York: Harper & Row, 1973).

23. H. Schacht, "The Impact of Change in the Seventies," *Business Horizons* **13** (1970): 31.

24. G. Susman, "Why Millions Hate Their Jobs—and What's Afoot to Help," *U.S. News and World Report* **81** (September 27, 1976), 87ff.

25. A. Elbing, H. Gadon, and J. Gordon, "Flexible Working Hours: It's About Time, *Harvard Business Review* **52** (1974): 18ff; M. Evans, "Notes on the Impact of

Flexitime in a Large Insurance Company," *Occupational Psychology* **47** (1973): 237–240; R. Donahue, "Flexible Time Systems: Flextime Systems in New York," *Public Personnel Management* **41** (1975): 212–215; and E. Tellinger, "Flexi-time at Westinghouse." Unpublished paper, Penn State University, 1977.

26. For an excellent review of these types of plans, *see* P. Greenlaw and B. Biggs, *Modern Personnel Management* (Philadelphia: Saunders, in press; and W. Werther, "Flexible Compensation Evaluated," *California Management Review* **19** (1976): 14–20.

27. Adapted from S. Adams and R. Solaski, *The Psychological Value of Compensation Increases Options Among Exempt Salaried Employees* (New York: General Electric Behavioral Research Service, 1964).

28. This section draws heavily from an excellent book by D. Hall, *Careers in Organizations* (Pacific Palisades, Calif.: Goodyear, 1976). *Also see* J. VanMaanen and R. Katz, "Individuals and Their Careers: Some Temporal Considerations for Work Satisfactions," *Personnel Psychology* **29** (1976): 601–616.

29. E. Jacques, "Death and the Mid-Life Crises," *International Journal of Psychoanalysis* **46** (1965): 502–514.

Glossary

Acceptance theory of authority. A theory of authority Barnard proposed, according to which the ultimate source of authority is the decision of the subordinate to accept the superior's orders.

Accountability. Responsibility for results.

Adaptation decision model. A way of explaining how individuals modify their goals as a consequence of their experience. It suggests that adjustments can occur in both goals and alternatives as a result of experience.

Administrative management. A closed-system view of organizations that focused on similarities in structure and processes among organizations in an attempt to find tasks common to all successful managers. This was proposed by Henri Fayol.

Analogies. The heuristic approach used for creatively dealing with unstructured problems. Personal, symbolic, or direct analogies are often used in creative decision making by individuals.

Anarchic control structure. An organization in which the amount of control for all hierarchical levels is relatively low.

Authority. The tool by which a manager can exercise considerable discretion by providing for the direction and control of decisions within the organization. Authority is always limited by the organization's policies and procedures and the rules of the larger society.

Automation. The process for converting inputs to outputs that are primarily self-regulating. It usually involves joining machines with other machines, especially some type of computer.

Autonomy. The ability to operate independently of others. A manager may have a great deal of autonomy in his or her job, or one can speak of a subsidiary of a conglomerate having limited autonomy.

Avoidance style. A conflict-management style whereby the individual simply withdraws from the conflict.

Bales's Interaction Process Analysis. A framework for observing and analyzing the process of problem solving within groups. It identifies 12 behavioral acts that are broken down into task and social/emotional categories. The task area is concerned with questions and answers; the social/emotional area, with positive and negative reactions.

Behavioral change. Planned change in employees' attitudes, motives, and knowledge.

Behavioral modification. A process by which a manager increases the desired patterns of employee behavior by using rewards and punishments.

Beliefs in causation. This contingency variable refers to the amount of agreement or disagreement between two or more individuals as to the cause-and-effect relationships of past, present, or future actions. It is a key variable in the contingency organizational decision model.

541

Bounded rationality. The tendency of decision makers to satisfice, engage in a limited search of alternatives, and to make decisions with inadequate information and control of the factors that are likely to influence the outcome of their efforts.

Break-even model. It shows the basic relationships between units produced, dollars of sales revenue, and the resulting level of costs and profits for an entire firm or one of its product lines. It may be useful for decisions concerned with projecting profits, controlling expenses, and determining prices.

Break-even point. The point at which total costs equal total sales. It may be expressed in terms of total dollar revenues or total units produced.

Budget. A control technique used to establish financial targets desired by the organization in the future. These target characteristics are usually expressed in terms of dollars.

Bureaucracy. A form of organization characterized by highly specialized jobs, adherence to rules and regulations, career orientations, and rigid lines of authority.

Cafeteria compensation approach. Under this plan, an employee selects from a number of compensation options to determine his or her salary increase.

Centralization. The extent to which responsibility and authority in an organization reside with top management.

Certainty. Condition of decision making whereby the decision maker has complete knowledge of the results or consequences of each alternative that might be used in solving a problem.

Classical management. The first identifiable school of management thought. It includes bureaucracy, administrative management, and scientific management.

Closed decision model. This describes a situation in which there is a known set of alternatives and the decision maker selects a decision by a rational process.

Closed-system approaches. Management concepts and practices that represent the earliest attempts to define and describe management principles. Closed-system approaches to management look for the "one best way" and largely ignore environmental variables. Bureaucracy, administrative management, scientific management, and human-relations approaches are examples of closed-system approaches.

Coercive power. This form of power is based on a leader's ability to create fear in a subordinate who does not follow his or her orders. The subordinate is afraid to deviate from the order because of the leader's ability to reward and sanction subordinates who do not follow orders.

Cohesiveness. A relative quality of a group. The degree to which a group is characterized by such things as pride, solidarity, loyalty, team spirit, and mutual attraction between members.

Collaborative situation. This is a situation characterized by a high integrative relationship and a low distributive relationship. The actions of one party have desirable effects on the other party, and vice-versa.

Communication channel. The particular flow of information, messages, and decisions within a group or organization.

Compromise strategy. A decision approach used when the parties may perceive and interpret the "facts" in a similar manner. But they are at odds over the desirability of the goals and values that will be served by the available alternatives.

Compromise style. A conflict-management style that attempts to resolve conflicts through "splitting the difference" between the parties.

Computational strategy. Well-established procedures and decision routines that can be systematically followed to arrive at a decision. This is often used for decisions that are repetitive and routine.

Conditional value. This refers to what would happen if each strategy and each state of nature did occur. It is used in the payoff-matrix model.

Conflict. All kinds of disagreements, opposition, or antagonistic interaction within one individual or between two or more individuals.

Confrontation style. A conflict-management style in which there is an attempt to reach a mutually satisfactory solution. There is an attempt to approach the conflict from a problem-solving standpoint.

Conglomerate. An organization comprising two or more companies that produce unrelated products.

Consensus. A decision-making approach within groups that involves alternatives being raised, discussed, and modified until everyone feels that the group is ready to make a choice.

Contingency model of conflict. A framework to aid managers in diagnosing basic conflict situations they are likely to face. It consists of two key contingency variables —the distributive variable and the integrative variable—and distinguishes four basic conflict situations—win-lose, mix, low interdependency, and collaboration.

Contingency organizational decision model. An integrating decision model based on the interaction of two basic contingency variables—beliefs in causation and goal preferences. The four basic decision strategies identified in this model are computation, compromise, judgment, and inspiration.

Contingency theories of leadership. Models of leadership that focus on the role of the leader and the situation in which he or she is facing. Fiedler's and House's models are contingency models.

Contingency theory of design. An approach that assumes that the type of organizational structure depends on the nature of the organization's task environment, technology, and the needs of the members of the organization. Contingency design focuses on what is best for the particular organization.

Contingency view of strategic planning. An overall framework that suggests that the nature of the strategic planning process will vary in different situations. Its two variables are the degree of stability continuum and the degree of homogeneity continuum.

Continuous-process technology. A technology involving the continuous flow of activities for transforming inputs into outputs, with virtually all physical activities being performed by machines.

Control. The process by which a person, group, or organization consciously determines or influences what another person, group, or organization will do.

Control graph. A technique for charting the relative amount of control held by each hierarchical level in the organization.

Coordination. The development of cooperative relationships between individuals and groups whose work overlaps.

Corrective control. The mechanisms designed to return the individual, department, or organization to some predetermined condition.

Corrective model of control. The process of detecting and correcting deviations from preestablished goals or standards. It consists of six interconnected elements: defining the subsystems, identifying characteristics, setting standards, collecting information, making comparisons, and diagnosing and implementing corrections.

Critical path. An element in the Program Evaluation and Review Technique, it is the path with the longest elapse time for completing a project.

Decentralization. The degree to which responsibility and authority are delegated to lower-level managers in the organization. Each organization practices a certain amount of decentralization.

Decision-making process. From a prescriptive standpoint, it refers to the series of steps that should be undertaken in reaching a decision. These steps are: establishing goals, searching for alternatives, comparing and evaluating alternatives, choosing among alternatives, implementing decisions, taking corrective action if necessary, and following up and controlling.

Decision-tree model. A decision-making tool that highlights the interactions between future decision strategies, possible states of nature, and present decision strategies. It is particularly useful when a decision problem can be broken down into a sequence of smaller problems, which follow each other in some logical order.

Deductive decision process. The development of a model to show an outcome that was not apparent from an analysis of the real world. It starts with the development of premises or assumptions.

Defense mechanisms. An individual who is blocked in attempts to satisfy needs, may use one or more defense mechanisms, e.g., rationalization, withdrawal, aggression, repression, and projection.

Delegation. The process a manager uses to assign a task or part of a task to one of his or her subordinates.

Delphi technique. An approach to systematically refine experts' opinions to arrive at a general consensus concerning the future. An important forecasting method.

Democratic control structure. An organizational situation in which the amount of control rises with lower levels in the hierarchy. The superiors function primarily with the consent of the "governed."

Department. A basic subunit of an organization frequently used in formal title of some subunits, e.g., marketing, production, finance.

Departmentation. The process of grouping or joining together jobs on some common basis; typically, function, product, clientele, or geographical factors.

Descriptive decision model. This decision model attempts to explain reality. The census of the population is a descriptive decision model.

Deterministic model. A model is deterministic when all of the variables and their interrelationships are known. All of the variables taken into account in the model are assumed to be exact, or determinate, quantities.

Differentiation. The tendency of open systems to divide themselves into various parts (departments). Each department tends to develop a structure in relation to the requirements posed by its relevant external environment.

Division of labor. The method of dividing a task into specialized subtasks, with different people doing different subtasks so that they may become very efficient at performing their task and thereby contribute to accomplishing the overall job at least cost.

Effectiveness. The extent to which the desired result is realized.

Efficiency. Output divided by input, or the extent to which the result produced was produced at least cost.

Entropy. A movement to disorder, complete lack of resource information, and death. To offset this process, organizations acquire inputs from their environments.

Environment. The external setting in which a business operates. Of special importance are the factors that may have a large impact on the business's success—the task environment.

Equifinality. A characteristic of open systems; profits, sales, growth, etc., may be reached from different initial conditions and in different ways.

Expectancy theory. A motivation theory that assumes that an individual's motivation is a function of two expectancies—that effort will lead to successful performance and that successful performance will lead to desired work-related outcomes.

Expected value. Provides a weighted average outcome for each strategy; the sum of all outcomes (conditional values) after they have been multiplied by their probability of occurring.

Experiment. A research design having two major elements, namely, an independent and dependent variable. The variable being manipulated is the independent variable, and the results are evidenced by changes in the dependent variable.

Experimental group. The group scheduled to receive a treatment. Especially useful in planned change programs.

Expert power. A person's or group's perception that another person or group has greater knowledge or expertise and is thus worthy of following with respect to the specific area of ability.

Extrapolation. The attempt to project some tendency from the past into the future.

Feedback. The property of an organization that permits managers to determine whether progress is being made toward goal attainment.

Fixed costs. Costs that remain relatively constant, regardless of the number of units produced.

Flexitime. A way of scheduling work under which an employee must be present during certain "core" hours of the day, but can begin work and end work any time before and after these core hours.

Focal person. Individual for whom role senders create expectations and pressures.

Forcing style. A conflict-management style in which one party attempts to coerce the other party into accepting his or her preferred solution. A solution satisfactory to only one of the parties is reached.

Forecasting. The process of predicting, projecting, or estimating future events or conditions in the organization's environment that are outside of the direct control of management. A major component to any planning process.

Formal group. Those groups whose objectives are specifically related to achieving the goals of the organization. They are usually identified as part of the formal structure of the organization.

Formal organization. The structure that indicates to whom each person in the hierarchy reports; frequently diagrammed in an "organization chart."

Frustration. This occurs when individuals are unable to satisfy their needs. The result of frustration may be to use defense mechanisms.

Functional authority. Authority based on a business function whose exercise may require compliance by persons who are not subordinates of the person exercising authority. For example, a person in the accounting department may require persons in another department to follow its procedures for submitting travel expenses.

Functional foremanship. The application of the division of labor at the foreman level suggested by Frederick Taylor. It involves splitting the task of the foreman into eight areas and having each worker report to several foremen.

Functional organization. A way of organizing a business that makes the manufacturing, selling, engineering, accounting, and other business departments defined by business function the basic subunits of the organization.

Functions of management. According to Fayol, these are the specific activities (e.g., planning, controlling) that a successful manager must perform.

Future shock. What happens when the types of changes and their speed of introduction overpower the individual's ability to adapt. The problem is that so many things are changing.

Goal. A desired future end(s) or objective(s).

Graicunas' law. A mathematical formulation of the relationship between the number of subordinates (N) and the number of potential superior-subordinate contacts (C):

$$C = n(2^n/2 + n - 1).$$

"Great man" theory. An approach to the study of leadership asserting that leaders possess certain traits and that these traits are possessed by "great men."

Group. Two or more individuals who come into personal, meaningful, and purposeful contact on a relatively continuing basis.

Group coalition. Two or more individuals or groups that band together to maintain or increase their goals relative to another person or group.

Halo effect. The tendency in forming an impression of a person to be influenced by a general impression of that person.

Hawthorne studies. These studies, which began the human-relations movement, were conducted by a group of researchers from Harvard University at the Chicago Hawthorne plant of Western Electric. The conclusion pointed to the need for managers to study the human relationships that are formed on the job in order to understand worker motivation and performance.

Heuristic decision model. Helps to explain some of the ways by which individuals can and do deal with unstructured decision problems. It focuses on sophisticated trial-and-error approaches that rely heavily on the knowledge and judgment of the individual decision maker.

Hierarchy. The levels in an organization that make some individuals subordinate to others.

Hierarchy of goals. This framework, often referred to as a means-end chain, provides a way to systematically link the goals of lower-level departments with higher-level departments in the organization.

Holism. A characteristic of an open system that suggests the need for recognizing a system as something different from and more than the sum of its parts. It is an integration of these parts that is important.

Homans's systems model. A framework for understanding group processes and behavior. It consists of two major parts: the internal system and the external system. The external system represents the "givens" that existed before the group formed. The internal system is formed and developed out of the external system. The basic variables in the internal system are activities, interactions, sentiments, and norms.

Human relations. A school of management whose basic proposition was that the attitudes formed by individuals in informal groups are critical to understanding workers' productivity. The school, founded after the Hawthorne experiments, took the opposite view from bureaucracy, scientific management, and administrative management in that it focused on the individual and small group instead of on rules and regulations and other administrative characteristics as important determinants of productivity.

Hygiene factors. In Herzberg's two-factor theory, extrinsic sources of motivation (e.g., air conditioning, salary, supervision, etc.) do not directly affect productivity and motivation. These are necessary but not sufficient to create job satisfaction.

Imperfect competition. A market structure having some of the characteristics of perfect competition and oligopolies.

Inductive decision process. This involves creating a model from which an existing outcome can be predicted. It is consistent with the scientific method. The elements of the inductive process are observation, hypothesis, experiment, results, and theory.

Inequity decision model. Provides a partial explanation for individual decisions and actions as a consequence of perceiving conditions of justice or injustice. Problems in inequity can arise in any situation involving a direct relationship and comparison between two or more individuals.

Informal group. It develops out of the activities, interactions, and sentiments of individuals. Membership is normally voluntary.

Inspiration strategy. A decision approach that may be necessary and effective in decision situations characterized by confusion. The individuals cannot agree on cause-and-effect relationships or goal preferences.

Institutional-level managers. Dealing directly with the firm's external environment, managers (presidents, board members) at this level link the organization to various groups outside the firm—unions, customers, suppliers, governments, etc.

Instrumental leadership. This style is characterized by managers who plan, organize, control, and coordinate the activities of subordinates in order to achieve the group's purpose.

Intergroup conflict. Differences or clashes between groups, departments, or divisions within an organization.

Interpersonal conflict. Conflict between two or more individuals over policies, practices, or plans and including emotional issues involving negative feelings, such as anger, distrust, fear, rejection, and resentment.

Interrole conflict. The conflict experienced when pressures associated with membership in one group or organization are in conflict with pressure stemming from membership in other groups or organizations.

Intersender role conflict. The conflict experienced when pressures from one role sender are perceived as being incompatible with pressures from one or more other role senders.

Intrasender conflict. Conflict experienced because the do's and don'ts from a single role sender are incompatible.

Irrationality. Defying the laws of reason and logic or going against something considered "rational" by other groups or individuals.

Job description. An outline of the duties and responsibilities inherent in a particular job.

Job enrichment. Suggested by Herzberg as a means for building greater personal achievement, recognition, and responsibility for workers. The increase in tasks makes the job more interesting and challenging, and therefore the work becomes psychologically more meaningful.

Johari window. An information-processing model that can be used to diagnose variable interpersonal communication styles used by managers. The model has feedback and exposure as its two major parts.

Judgment strategy. An approach to decision problems when the relative effectiveness of available alternatives cannot be proved. The decision makers have the same goal preferences but are in disagreement or are uncertain about cause-and-effect relationships.

Leader-member relations. Proposed by Fiedler, this dimension of leadership refers to the degree of confidence that followers have in their leaders.

Leadership. The ability of one person to influence the behavior of another.

Least preferred coworker (LPC). An integral part of Fiedler's leadership model, it refers to the motivational system or behavioral preferences of the leader. High-LPC leaders are relations-oriented; low-LPC leaders are task-oriented.

Legitimate power. The belief by one person or group that it is rightful or desirable for another person or group to influence their actions within specific areas.

Line function. Managers and employees directly involved in the production of the final or service the organization produces. In a university, the faculty members are line managers.

Loss. The excess of total dollar costs over total dollar sales associated with certain level of production.

Low interdependency situation. A situation in which there is both a low integrative and low distributive relationship. Conflict is likely to be at a minimum or nonexistent.

Management. The process of coordinating individual and group activity toward organizational goals.

Management By Objectives. A philosophy of management, as well as a process, emphasizing the central role of objectives for each department, manager, or employee by placing a high value on employee participation in work-related matters. Basic elements include objective setting, action planning, self-control and correction, and periodic reviews.

Management philosophy. A system of thought that is logically applied to a problem, decision, or activity. Theories X and Y are examples of different management philosophies.

Managerial Grid. An organizational change approach that assumes that leaders should be both people- and production-centered.

Mass-production technology. The manufacture of large volumes of identical or similar goods through an assembly-line process.

Matrix organization. An organization design that combines departmentation by product and function. Functional managers exercise technical control and authority over projects; the product managers have responsibility for budgets and final completion of projects. The functional managers lend project managers employees as needed to complete the project.

Means. The specific tactics or approaches used to achieve the organization's goals or objectives. Roles, procedures, and standard operating plans are examples of means intended to help achieve goals.

Mechanistic structure. An organization having a high degree of functional specialization of jobs, a centralized decision-making structure, formal and standardized procedures, economic incentives for motivation, and formal and impersonal relations between groups and individuals. Successful if used in a stable task environment.

Mix situation. A conflict situation in which there is both a high distributive and a high integrative relationship, as in union-management relationships.

Model. A simplified representation of a complex or abstract process that can be changed to explore the range and quality of solutions to a problem.

Monopoly. A market structure in which virtually all of a service or good is provided by a single organization.

Motion study. The process of analyzing work in order to determine the preferred motions to be used in the completion of tasks. Motion study is a major contribution of scientific management.

Motivation. The inner state that activates or moves the individual toward goals.

Motivational factors. In Herzberg's two-factor theory of motivation, those job-related factors which, if present, operate to build high achievement motivation and performance, e.g., achievement, challenge, recognition, advancement, and interesting work.

Multinational firm. A firm with branches, divisions, and subsidiaries in foreign countries.

Need hierarchy. Abraham Maslow's theory of motivation, which holds that human needs are arranged in a hierarchy. Individuals seek to satisfy basic needs before attempting to satisfy higher-order needs.

Negative feedback. This exists when a department collects information about its behavior and compares it with predetermined standards. The purpose of negative feedback is to bring the department back into line with standards.

Network. An element in the Program Evaluation and Review Technique. It is a diagram of the sequential steps that must be performed to accomplish a project or task.

Nominal-group technique. An approach especially used for dealing with planning tasks that require idea generation, creativity, and the exercise of judgment by a group. It helps improve the judgments of individuals with different backgrounds and skills.

Norm. A standard that is widely shared by members of a group. It sets specific expectations or limits for the members of what they ought to do or should not do under certain circumstances.

Normative decision model. A model that prescribes what "should be" and how decisions should be made. It sets forth a broad framework of standards against which acts or decisions should be judged.

Objective probabilities. A decision-making condition under risk which assumes that the decision maker is confronted with a situation in which he or she can assign the probability or likelihood that each of the possible states of nature will occur.

Oligopolies. A market structure in which a few firms provide most of the output of the particular product or service.

Open decision model. This model views the decision process and outcomes as relatively uncertain. It assumes that goals are not necessarily predetermined, but may represent an important part of the decision problem.

Open system. A set of processes whose operation is influenced by sources outside of management's immediate control. The open-system study to management suggests that an organization can be seen as a number of interdependent parts (departments) and that each part contributes something to the whole. The open-system perspective views the organization as securing inputs, transforming them into goods or services, and then exporting them to the customers.

Organic structure. An organization design having enriched jobs, a decentralized decision-making structure, economic and noneconomic sources of motivation, flexible jobs and procedures, informal and personal relations between individuals and groups, and both vertical and lateral communication. This design is most appropriate in an unstable or changing task environment.

Organization chart. The pictorial representation of the formal organization.

Organization design. The structure of an organization that provides the framework for tasks and lines of authority, responsibility, and accountability.

Organization development (OD). The name given to a variety of behavioral science techniques directed toward moving organizations toward more open and honest communication among individuals and groups. Both the structure of the organization and the behavioral processes used within the organization are examined.

Organizational change. The process of diagnosing and implementing changes in the organization's structure, task, technology, and/or people.

Organizational climate. Perceptions people have about the day-to-day events that are characteristic of a particular organization.

Organizational-level managers. A group of managers in the managerial system that controls and services the technical-level managers. Managers (department heads) at this level are concerned with integrating the internal activities of the firm to ensure that the technical system performs its funcion.

Organizational structure. The formally defined system of task and authority relationships. Through the hierarchy, there are varying degrees of authority at different organizational levels.

Organizing. The process of creating a formal organization structure or of breaking a task to be performed into subtasks.

Output goals. The specific types of consumer goods, educational services, and the like that the organization actually produces.

Participation. The process of involving employees in decision making and objective setting, particularly as related to their own work and organizational unit.

Participative leadership. The sharing of information, power, and influence between supervisors and subordinates.

Participative management. The behavioral science notion that employees at all hierarchical levels should be allowed to participate in decisions affecting their jobs.

Payoff-matrix model. A tool for helping evaluate the alternatives in a particular decision situation. It assumes that the decision maker is able to identify his or her desires and goals as well as to specify the alternatives (strategies) for dealing with the decision problem. It involves the development of a two-dimensional array of figures or symbols arranged in rows and columns.

Perceptual defense. The process by which individuals put on blinders to defend themselves from seeing those events that might disturb them.

Perceptual process. How individuals form impressions of others through selectivity.

Perfect competition. A market structure in which there are many buyers and sellers, and price is a key variable in consumers' purchase decisions.

Performance. The accomplishments of an individual, group, or organization.

Personality. The general sum of characteristics of an individual. It is an important determinant of motivation, leadership, and communication.

Person-role conflict. A conflict arising from incompatibilities between the demands of the role(s) and the individual's own needs, attitudes, values, and abilities.

Planning. The formalized decision-making process of establishing goals and strategies at various levels in the organizations. The major concerns of planning are to anticipate and avoid problems in the future, to identify opportunities in the future, and to develop courses of action that will help the organization or unit reach its desired goals.

Planning activities. Conscious decision processes characterized by establishing goals, identifying opportunities and anticipated problems, accumulating information, relating bits of information and beliefs, establishing assumptions, forecasting future conditions, developing and choosing among alternative courses of action, and ranking or selecting total plans that will achieve the best balance between ultimate and secondary objectives.

Policy. A general guide for carrying out action. It is generally qualitative, conditional, and relational. An example of a policy is "promotions will be based on merit."

Polyarchic control structure. An organization in which the amount of control would be relatively high and relatively flat for all organizational levels. All groups are considered to have considerable control.

Power. The source of a superior's ability to persuade subordinates to follow a particular order. The five types of power are: coercive, expert, legitimate, referent, and reward.

Preferences about possible goals. A contingency variable referring to the priority of goals held by the parties to a decision situation. It is a key variable in the contingency organizational decision model.

Preventive control. The mechanisms designed to minimize the need for taking corrective action, e.g., rules, regulations, and training programs.

Principles of management. In closed-system theory, principles of management refer either to rules of conduct that should guide manager's behavior or to the underlying laws that determine the structure of organizations.

Product goals. The characteristics of goods and/or services being produced, e.g., quality, quantity, availability, uniqueness, and innovativeness.

Profits. The excess of total dollar sales over total dollar costs associated with certain levels of production.

Program Evaluation and Review Technique. A planning and control tool often used in production activities. It consists of five major elements: the network, resource allocation, time and costs considerations, network paths, and the critical path.

Project management. An organization design in which each employee is used only for the life of the project. When the project is completed, the employee either goes to another project or returns to his or her functional area.

Projection. A defense mechanism designed to protect one's self from feelings of guilt by casting them toward other individuals and blaming them for the faults that one has about oneself.

Protestant work ethic. A belief that the human being was created to work; to satisfy one's basic needs, the individual has to work hard.

Rationality. The making of decisions or the use of a decision process that serves to maximize goal achievement.

Rationalization. A defense mechanism involving the creation of a socially desirable reason for one's behavior that the individual believes is less ego-deflating than the true reason.

Referent power. Leadership power based on attractiveness or charismatic qualities. That is, the leader's orders are followed because of some personal qualities which the followers closely identify with.

Responsibility. Performance areas in which a person or department is expected by the organization to produce results.

Reward power. A person's or group's perceptions that another person or group has the ability to provide varying amounts and types of rewards (promotions, status symbols, salary increases). A reward can be anything that is desired by the individual or group.

Reward-punishment system. The form of control strategy employed to help direct individuals to fulfill the requirements of the organization.

Risk. The decision-making situation that assumes that enough information exists to predict the likelihood of different states of nature (future conditions).

Role. A particular set of related activities that are carried out by an individual.

Role conflict. A conflict arising when two or more sets of pressures are placed on the individual at the same time. By responding to one set of pressures, a person finds it difficult if not impossible to respond to one or more other sets of pressures.

Role expectations. The do's and don'ts prescribed for an individual in his or her role by other role senders.

Role pressures. The tactics used by role senders to get the focal person to perform as desired. Pressures may be exerted through the use of one or more types of power.

Role set. The collection of roles directly related to the role of any one individual in an organization.

Rule. A specifically required course of action or conduct that must be followed. It is much more specific than a policy and is set forth by the organization.

Satisficing. Using a solution to a problem by examining only a limited number of alternatives and selecting the first one that appears to be minimumly acceptable. There is no attempt to find the best possible solution.

Scalar chain. The chain of direct authority relationships from managers to subordinates throughout the organization. Every employee should know his or her area of responsibility in the organization.

Scanning. The exposure to and perception of information through undirected viewing, condition viewing, informal search, and formal search.

Scientific management. The closed-system perspective whose supporters argued that there is an ideal way of performing any job, which, if followed, will yield the "one best" way. Time-and-motion study was the means to achieve the one best way. Work should be organized into its simplest elements, and systematic improvement of the worker's performance of each of these elements would result in higher levels of output per worker.

Selection. The process of hiring, promoting, or transferring employees in the organization.

Simulation model. An approach for obtaining the essential qualities of reality without actually experiencing the particular reality. It enables management to explore a number of "if-then" relationships. A useful aid in planning.

Smoothing style. A conflict-management style in which the individual acts as though the conflict will pass with time and simply appeals to the need for cooperation between the parties.

Social/emotional leader. An individual who concentrates primarily on problems of decision, tension reductions, and reintegration within Bales's Interaction Process Analysis framework.

Socialization. The process by which employees learn their "ropes" in an organization.

Social responsibility. Business involvement in solving both social and ecological problems (pollution, poverty, discrimination, and consumerism). Socially responsible managers should be: (1) aware of firm's obligations facing society, (2) willing to help solve some of these, and (3) committing resources to these areas.

Span of control. A structural variable that refers to the number of people reporting to a single superior.

Staff. Employees who advise and assist line managers and employees. The staff employees are not directly engaged in the production of the final good or service.

States of nature. The future set of conditions that could prevail in the environment that are relevant to the decision problem, e.g., different levels of expected market demand.

Stereotypes. Preconceived notions about people, often based on superficial characteristics (e.g., height, weight, sex, race, ethnic background) that can distort communication between individuals.

Strategic planning. The process of deciding on the objectives of the organization, on changes in these objectives, on the resources used to attain these objectives, and on the policies that are to govern the acquisition, use, and disposition of these resources. It usually receives primary emphasis at the top level of the organization.

Strategy. The means an organization uses to achieve its overall goals and objectives.

Structural change. Planned changes in the formally prescribed task and authority relationships.

Structure. The arrangement and interrelationships of processes and functions within the company. The methods used vary, including the functional approach, decentralization, and matrix forms.

Structured decision problems. A decision situation in which goals and alternatives are objective and tend to be ready-made.

Subjective probabilities. A decision-making situation under conditions of risk. The decision maker assigns probabilities to the alternative states of nature on the basis of his or her belief that each will occur.

Suboptimization. The tendency to seek maximum goal attainment in one area, with the consequence of reducing overall goal attainment for the system as a whole.

Substitute for leadership. A substitute for leadership tends to decrease the leader's ability to exert influence over subordinates in a meaningful way. Major substitutes include: (1) personal characteristics of subordinates, (2) requirements of the task, and (3) formal structure of the organization.

Superordinate goals. Shared goals that cannot be achieved by groups without their mutual cooperation. A mechanism sometimes used to reduce conflict between two or more individuals or groups.

Supportive leadership. Managers who give consideration to the needs of their subordinates and are concerned with their well-being, status, and comfort. These leaders seek to create a friendly and pleasant working climate for employees.

Systems theory. An approach to management that assumes that an organization: (1) is a system of departments that interact with one another and depend on one another for survival, and (2) is an open system interacting with its external environment and dependent on it.

Tactical planning. The process concerned with current activities and those in the near future (one year or less), the control and integration of current activities, and the current allocation of resources (especially through the budget process). It is usually undertaken by managers and specialists in the organizational and technical subsystems.

Task dependency. A situation that occurs when one individual or group must rely on another individual or group for services, information, and goods.

Task environment. Those specific environmental forces that are relevant to the decision-making processes of the organization; they are beyond the immediate control of the organization, but can affect the organization's survival.

Task interdependency. The extent to which two or more individuals or groups rely on and need one another for service, information, or goods to accomplish their own tasks and goals.

Task-oriented leader. An individual who concentrates primarily on the problems of orientation, evaluation, and control within Bales's Interaction Process Analysis framework.

Task structure. The extent to which the task is simple (routine) or complex (nonroutine). An important contingency in both Fiedler's and House's models of leadership.

Technical-level managers. Those who are involved with the actual production of the firm's goods and/or services, e.g., foremen and general foremen.

Technological change. The use of new methods, equipment, information systems, and work flows to achieve planned changes.

Technology. The techniques, methods, and processes used for transforming inputs into outputs. A typical classification of technology is unit, mass production, and continuous process.

Theory X. The managerial assumption that employees are lazy, avoid responsibility, need direction, and must be coerced to work.

Theory Y. The managerial assumption that employees seek responsibility, do not dislike work, do not want to be controlled and threatened, and want to satisfy their esteem and self-actualization needs on the job.

Training. The attempt by the organization to change the skills, knowledge, attitudes, values, or motivations of individuals to help achieve the organization's goals.

Trait theory. A view of leadership that assumes that leaders differ from other people in specific physical, social, personality, and personal traits. The approach relies on research that relates these classes of traits to leader-success criteria.

Two-factor theory. Frederick Herzberg's theory of motivation based on two separate components—satisfiers (motivators) and dissatisfiers (hygienes).

Uncertainty. A decision-making situation in which the individual has no information or insight to use as a basis for assigning probabilities to each state of nature.

Unit-production technology. A type of technology emphasizing the custom manufacturing of individual items.

Unity of command. A management principle that states that each subordinate should report to only one superior.

Unstructured decision problems. A decision situation in which goals and alternatives tend to be subjective and constructed by the individual decision maker.

Valences. Anticipated satisfactions that the individual wishes to either avoid or obtain after performing at some level of behavior.

Variable cost. The costs that tend to change with changes in the number of units produced.

Vroom's model. A basic expectancy model of motivation. It views motivation as a process governing choices and explains how the goals of individuals influence their efforts.

Win-lose situation. A conflict situation in which there is a high distributive relationship and a low integrative relationship. One party's gain is another party's loss.

Appendix:
Case Studies

Tulsa Motor Inn

Mr. Jim Baggett had heard about Oklahoma's penal reform plans. One phase of the plan involved the establishment of prisoner prerelease centers in both Tulsa and Oklahoma City. This idea seemed to make sense in some ways; the cost of rehabilitating a man might be lowered, and the percentage of parolees who made the transition from tax-using regimented prisoner to useful tax-paying citizen might be increased. The basic idea was to provide a "half-way" house, a boarding house for parolees who had no family anxiously awaiting their release, which would give them an opportunity to readjust to a new job and make new friends; in short, fit into the society which had labeled them previously as misfits.

But as Jim scanned the newspaper that morning, his acquiescence toward one particular prisoner prerelease center (PRC) began to change. The headline catching his eye read: TULSA MOTEL TO BECOME PRISONER PRERELEASE CENTER. The article went on to explain that the State had entered into a long-term lease with the owners of an existing mismanaged and floundering motel to use that facility as the Tulsa PRC. Another PRC was to be located in Oklahoma City. The most important information in the article to Jim, however, was the location of the PRC motel. It was *next door,* not 50 yards away from his own motel, the Tulsa Motor Inn.

The Baggetts had acquired the Tulsa Motor Inn 18 months prior to the PRC announcement. After successfully managing a motel in the Oklahoma City area, they had purchased this one in Tulsa, which at the time was also mismanaged and losing money. Jim carefully planned and financed its remodeling and renaming under a nationally franchised motel chain. After investing $1,250,000 and a year and a half of hard work, the operation was beginning to show promise of success. "And now the State wants to locate 20 to 30 parolees within 50 yards of my guests, dozens of new cars, vacation-enlarged billfolds, and dressed-for-the-pool swimmers!" The thought brought with it a vision of empty rooms, forced room-rate reductions, and higher overhead stemming from new security precautions.

During the last 12 months the Tulsa Motor Inn had grossed $197,000, permitting a net profit before taxes of $41,000. Although he considered this to be

This case was prepared by James C. Johnson and Howard A. Thompson of the University of Tulsa as the basis for class discussion and not to illustrate either effective or ineffective handling of an administrative situation. Expenses involved in developing this case were funded by the Office of Reseach, The University of Tulsa. Presented at the Case Workshop of the Southern Case Writers Association and Intercollegiate Case Clearing House, Washington, D.C., 1972. Distributed by the Intercollegiate Case Clearing House, Soldiers Field, Boston, Mass. 02163. All rights reserved to the contributors. Printed in the U.S.A. Used with permission.

less than half of its potential profitability, assuming occupancy percentages continued to improve, Mr. Baggett believed the Motor Inn to be "on target" according to his forecast nearly two years earlier. The PRC, however, was definitely not part of the "game plan." He had little doubt but that the excellent repeat business with commercial travelers (sales representatives), now believed to constitute about one-half of total revenue, would shift to a "safer" location once the prisoners were known to be 50 yards away. An earlier advantage of being located near an expressway within 15 minutes of downtown Tulsa while still out of the congested part of the city now seemed almost a disadvantage.

Mr. Baggett's business associates counseled him to seek an injunction to prevent the State from locating an "undesirable" facility next door. He, with his son, a management major at the University of Tulsa, had been wrestling with questions of social responsibility, environmental pollution, and the like only a few weeks ago. He was very much in favor of business committing itself to the pursuit of these goals and ideals. But if he failed to act quickly against the State's announced plan for the new PRC, Mr. Baggett was certain this could mean a severe financial reversal for the Motor Inn.

What counsel would you give Mr. Baggett?

Supplementary Information

Two broad types of travelers are customers of the Tulsa Motor Inn, transient or through travelers and business travelers making frequent trips to Tulsa. In terms of room-occupancy percentages, the business traveler is slightly more important. This is true except during the summer months of June, July, and August, when through travelers are most numerous. Through travelers, however, are most important in terms of annual gross rental income. During the only full calendar year of operational experience under the present management, 56.8% of gross rental income was from through travelers and 43.2% from business travelers. Multiple occupancy among through-traveler customers creates a total gross rental income greater than that received from the more numerous business traveler rentals.

Average monthly room occupancy increased from about 30% at the time of purchase to 60.2% last year.

At present the Tulsa Motor Inn enjoys a fine reputation with its repeat customers, the business travelers. Comments such as "clean," "well managed," "best beds in town," and "best motel for your money in the area" are frequently filled in on rating cards left in their rooms by business travelers.

Among business travelers "previous experience" was a strong factor influencing the choice of the Tulsa Motor Inn. Approximately 72% indicated that this was the reason which drew them back to Tulsa Motor Inn whenever they were in the Tulsa area. Other business travelers volunteered the information that they had only recently started staying at the Tulsa Motor Inn as a result of advice from other salesmen. Such indicators as these suggest that the present business volume at the Tulsa Motor Inn is healthy and growing especially among this customer group.

Atlas Aircraft

I. OBSERVATIONS

"It's sure too bad about Willis, Ball, and Conrad," Bob Harris said to George Mathews, who was stirring his coffee when Bob joined him on a Friday afternoon break. George shook his head in apparent disbelief at the news. The three managers mentioned had just been fired as a result of a disastrous bid on a proposal which they had worked on. Mathews then asked, "What do you suppose really went wrong on that bid?" It was now Harris's turn to shake his head. "We'll probably never know the whole story," he said. "Oh sure, somebody has to be responsible for goofs, but it really shakes you up to think of those guys, all of them with over 20 years here, and all at once out on their butts!" Nodding his head in agreement, George said, "Boy, we really gotta watch what the hell we're doing, from now on!"

II. BACKGROUND

Atlas had been a successful airframe manufacturer—one of the five largest—for 40 years. The firm took pride in the fact that 85% of its managers were engineers. This feeling seemed to stem from the idea that such a manager could better cope with the technical aspects of airplane manufacture than could a nonengineer manager.

III. TROUBLE

A. The Swing-Wing

About one year prior to the above conversation, Atlas had submitted a bid on a giant cargo plane for the Air Force. At the time of the bid, the engineering was not yet complete on the internal materials-handling equipment which would be used to load a wide variety of cargoes. Cargoes would range from heavy tanks or trucks to the bulk-loading of small, irregularly shaped packages. To ensure submission of the bid on time, the Atlas executive committee insisted on getting a "safe but competitive" price from engineering, on the loading system.

Atlas was awarded the contract on the cargo plane, but the estimated costs on the loading system were nowhere near the actual costs. The additional R & D needed to make the loading system operational and efficient ran to about $160,000, compared to the $20,000 estimate. Also, the production costs of the system were over $135,000 per plane, in contrast to the $27,000 per unit estimate. These increased costs amounted to nearly $1.5 million for the

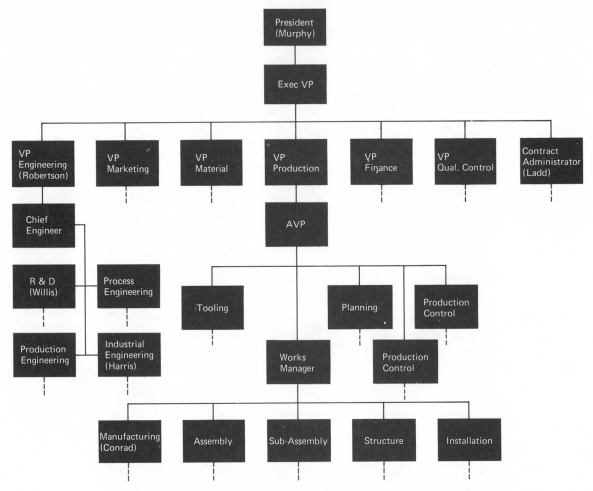

Fig. 1. Abstract from organization chart for Atlas Aircraft, at beginning of case time period.

12-plane contract, and the air force admitted only $600,000 for additional billing on this system. This meant that Atlas' potential profit on the contract was reduced by nearly $1 million.

Henry Murphy, the president, was furious at this result, which he blamed on poor engineering and on irresponsibility on the part of those who put the loading-system estimate together. In order to shake up the entire management, and to force the managers and staff to accept responsibility, Murphy insisted on seeing "some heads roll." Consequently, the Chief of R & D was fired, along with the Chief of Production Engineering and the manager of Manufacturing.

Murphy was correct in expecting management to be shaken, but the event did not seem to be followed by any noticeable improvement in decision making.

It has been the practice among U.S. planemakers for a prime contractor* to subcontract 40% to 60% of the contract value to other manufacturers. In keeping with this practice, Atlas prepared plans and requested proposals for various subcontracts on a new fighter plane—the NFX-3. The total amount of electronic gear on this sophisticated plane was considerably greater than had appeared on any previous Atlas plane. The electronics manufacturers who commonly subcontracted for Atlas were not able to handle the physical volume required by the NFX-3 schedule. Consequently, Atlas was forced to seek new electronics manufacturers for this purpose. The usual "Requests for Bids" were sent out, and several companies responded with proposals. After correspondence regarding specifications and costs, Atlas dispatched some electronics engineers and production coordinators to physically evaluate the potentialities of the interested electronics firms. Out of the five firms evaluated, the team determined that two of the five were fully qualified as subcontractors and wrote their report to that effect. They had found that both firms were currently in production of sophisticated army and navy electronics, and that their production lines were not "contaminated" with civilian consumer items. The investigation suggested a highly satisfactory on-time delivery record.

After the scheduling was completed and all subcontracts had been let for the NFX-3, the manufacturing and the assembly operations were commenced. These, and the subcontracting and purchasing deliveries, were closely observed and checked with the PERT charts. The first deliveries of the electronic equipment from the two new subcontractors were due in the 38th week of the NFX-3 schedule. Delivery from Firm A came in, a few days early, while Firm B's delivery missed the deadline. Following the PERT schedule, Production Control had checked with Firm B two weeks before the scheduled delivery. Production Control was told that some purchased component parts had been unacceptable and had been returned to the maker, who had promised immediate replacement. Since the PERT dates for these items included some slack, the delay seemed to be relatively minor, and quickly correctible, with rush work on the part of Firm B.

Unfortunately, Week 42 went by with still no delivery from Firm B. Now, things began looking a little hairy; by Week 44, additional equipment would have to be installed, which could go in only after the gear from Firm B had been installed. This meant that a real possibility existed that a line-stoppage would occur unless the delayed electronics arrived almost immediately.

An electronics engineer and a production planner were dispatched to Firm B to get an actual look at the situation and to try to devise means to accelerate deliveries.

The subsequent report was grim; according to the troubleshooters, Firm B's production line was very primitive, and an educated guess would put earliest delivery at around Week 58!

Murphy really blew his top. As after the loading-system fiasco, he thought that drastic action was necessary. Therefore, the Senior Electronics Engineer

---

* Holder of the airplane contract from the customer.

and the Production Control Chief were fired. Again, the reason was to inspire the remaining managers and staff to approach the decision making more seriously and to accept responsibility more completely.

A couple of days later, George Whyte, Board Chairman of Atlas, called Murphy. "I hear that heads have rolled again," he said. "I'm afraid so," replied Murphy, as the weight in his stomach seemed to get heavier. "You may have good reason to be afraid," said Whyte, "if this action doesn't start bringing in some answers. I hope that you have not lost control."

C. The Swing-Wing

In the following year, nearly all production seemed to slow, although almost imperceptibly. Schedules became more difficult to maintain; new development, bids, and proposals seemed excruciatingly slow. Several times, requests for extensions in bidding deadlines were forwarded by Atlas, because of behind-schedule conditions. Investigations into the reasons for such delays seemed to always suggest a nearly unanimous feeling among managers that the increasingly complex technology in nearly every aspect of airframe design and manufacture seemed to require greater precision and certainty in decision making. This, of course, would require more research, more data, and more time to come up with optimum decisions and their implementing plans.

Since *time* was one thing which Atlas surely could not spare, the only solution occurring to top management was an increase in the number of managers and staff experts to get the work out.

The resulting organization structure turned out to have nearly one manager or staff person for each three hourly workers at Atlas. This is in contrast to the two-year earlier proportion of one manager/staff member to each 3.46 hourly workers (at the start of this case history). This can be seen as an increase of almost 1/7th in administrative salaries.

In the meantime, the air force was soliciting bids for a swing-wing fighter. Atlas was very eager to get such a contract. In fact, overhead expenses were so high that new contracts seemed imperative to maintain an acceptable cash-flow.

As the swing-wing bid deadline approached, no proposal from Atlas had been finalized. The president called in his top-level people and asked, "Why the delay?" All reasons suggested were centered on new technology and the need for more data. Murphy emphasized the need for a timely bid and suggested an all-out effort.

Five days before the deadline, the bid was still not finished, and the need for more data was again insisted on. Through political contacts, Murphy was able to get a two-week extension on the deadline, but at the cost of some strained friendships. Upon receiving the extension, Murphy put out the word that the proposal *must* be ready, this time.

Three days before the extended deadline, President Murphy received a copy of a report sent to Contracts Administration by the group responsible for the proposal figures. The third paragraph caught his eye: it read:

3. The production technology for the swing-wing hinge is in flux, at this time. It is necessary to combine great strength with optimum weight. There are two or three

firms which might be able to make the hinges with a forging-press. The tooling for this may run to $180,000, but we have no firm commitment as to the cost of tooling, the unit cost, or delivery schedule.

There are several firms interested in the carbon-filament technique, but time has not permitted the necessary stress-analyses to determine optimum size and weight. Here, the cost of tooling is estimated at from $40,000 to $115,000.

If neither of these processes is available and appropriate, we can hog the hinges from 8" titanium stock. The tooling here would probably be below $20,000, but there is a great waste in scrap, from which there is little salvage.

If we are able to get a forging for the hinges, we can produce the hinges for about $17,000 (direct cost) per plane. If we could seek a manufacturer to produce them from carbon-filament, we can expect about $29,000 per plane. If neither of these techniques is available, we shall have to machine them from titanium plate, at about $48,000 per set.

After a very deep sigh, Murphy murmured to himself, "What the hell kind of a proposal is this?"

A few minutes later, Murphy rang his secretary and told her, "Cancel all of my appointments. Get hold of Ladd* and Robertson†—tell them to cancel *their* appointments and to plan to spend the next 48 hours with me, to get this proposal finalized."

Shortly thereafter, Chairman Whyte called Murphy. "How's the proposal?" Murphy explained the situation as briefly as possible. Whyte responded with, "You'd better meet that deadline!"

Hanging up, Murphy heaved another sigh, as his ulcers burned, then sat motionless for five minutes. "Where did I go wrong?" he thought. "What have I solved?" He then phoned a nationally known management consulting firm and talked with one of the partners. "We seem to have lost our capability for making decisions," Murphy said. "Can you help me?"

---

* Contract Administrator
† VP, Engineering

Financial Data Systems (B)

INTRODUCTION

In the fall of 1972 a team of students in management information systems at a local university received approval from Executive Vice-President Tom Dickinson of Financial Data Systems (FDS) to study current operating requirements and future trends in his company, which provides data-processing services to banks and other users. The team included graduate students in computer science, business data processing, personnel, and management.

This case was prepared by Professor August W. Smith of Texas A&M University and Rae Albertini, a graduate student at Texas A&M University, College Station, Texas, as a basis for class discussion rather than to illustrate either effective or ineffective handling of an administrative situation. Presented at the 1975 Case Workshop of the Southern Case Research Association and Intercollegiate Case Clearing House, New Orleans, Louisiana, Nov. 11–13, 1975. Distributed by the Intercollegiate Case Clearing House, Soldiers Field, Boston, Mass. 02163. All rights reserved to the contributors. Printed in the U.S.A. Used with permission.

At that point in time the board members of FDS were considering and evaluating a few prospects for further growth and development of the company. Since 1967, when FDS was founded to provide data-processing services to several owner banks in a central Texas community of 50,000 population, it has steadily grown and expanded its services and operations in the area. The company has developed a Demand Deposit Accounting (DDA) system, which is currently in use in a number of banks in surrounding communities. The company has expanded operations to meet some individual requirements of users whenever users have requested additional services, such as processing of interest accruals to savings accounts, dividend statements, and some special reports.

In addition to financial institutions, several small businesses, including retail stores, private doctors, and pharmacies, use the basic processing services which FDS provides, primarily in the areas of accounting and billing. In contrast with high-volume financial institutions, which receive preferential customer status, other customers usually represent lower volume, more specialized operations representing higher overhead and higher costs per unit transaction, which they pay for these services.

The four financial institutions which share equal ownership of FDS provide a spokesman president for the company on a revolving basis. As a result, the Executive Vice-President, Tom Dickinson, serves as the chief operating officer on a continuing basis. He had five years' data-processing experience with a commercial bank before joining FDS. Other job experiences included electrical engineering and computer process control at Union Carbide.

Over a period of five years the organization has grown from 7 to 15 full-time employees in three marketing, programming, and operation divisions, which all report to Tom Dickinson. All major planning decisions are made by the board through Dickinson.

In the beginning the board did not list specific job duties or goals for Dickinson or for the other division heads. It was felt that as the organization evolved these duties and goals would become more evident and would eventually be formalized. All equipment, facilities, and some personnel hiring decisions require prior approval by the board.

The company has been quite profitable every year since it was founded. In 1971 the net operating profit after federal income taxes amounted to $49,556.13 after major payments for equipment and all administrative expenses, including a consultant's feasibility study of about $1500.00. Retained earnings have varied considerably each year, depending on board policies regarding dividends. The owners had received dividends surpassing their original investments of $32,500 by 1971, and remaining profits had been set aside for future growth.

By September 1972 the Burroughs B-500 system installed in 1971 was operating at near full capacity during the peak night-shift hours and was being used more and more on special projects by the programmers during the day-shift hours as well.

In conducting the study, various students investigated the prospects for continued growth and development of the company. Dickinson and the board members cooperated fully and provided information in interviews.

STUDY APPROACH

It was felt that any comprehensive planning effort should include information from several sources representing different points of view. For this reason, open-ended interviews were held with a large-user institution, an owner on the board of directors, and the key operating officer, Dickinson. From these viewpoints certain planning alternatives emerged and were reviewed relative to technical and other supporting considerations. Finally, additional information about the banking industry, noting trends in the sources banks use for their data processing and in the functions banks are automating now, was obtained using a questionnaire to Federal Reserve Districts. All of this information went into the final report to the top management of FDS to help them in their current planning efforts.

A USER'S VIEWS

In order to gain a complete view of Financial Data Systems, it seems necessary to briefly investigate the perspectives of some user institutions. It was felt that interviews provided a way to examine and evaluate different views held by both users of FDS services and also those who have primary stock holdings in FDS. Several interviews were held. The first interview was with Earl Lewis, officer with a user bank.

Earl Lewis works directly with FDS and was able to point out numerous strong and weak aspects of his bank's relations with FDS as a service company. He mentioned several points on which he is particularly pleased:

1. FDS is the most economical means available for his bank to obtain current data-processing capabilities.
2. The local service is quite convenient and nearby should problems arise.
3. FDS personnel understand banks—their combined banking background is valuable in helping to resolve any bank-related problems. They even anticipate some problems in advance.
4. Errors and other problems have decreased since the functions were first automated.
5. Minor changes, exceptions, and corrections are made at the expense of FDS.
6. Security is adequate for protecting bank records.

At the same time, Lewis recognized some areas where improvements could be made:

1. Reports are somewhat difficult for typical bankers to pick up and use—the user must learn where to find the significant data on his own.
2. When FDS installs any service, it should provide more training of the user's personnel.
3. If accounts do not balance, there is some question and disagreement about which party is further responsible—sometimes this is hard to determine.
4. Any major changes in the basic bank services requires agreement by all users—which is getting harder to obtain as the users grow and diversify.

5. Minor changes and corrections in accounts are sometimes quite slow and costly in customer goodwill.
6. Several minor shortcomings exist in FDS's programs. For example:
    a) If an erroneous entry is deleted in the Demand Deposit Accounting (DDA) system, the correction appears in the next day's report three times. Lewis does not understand why this is so, even though there may be a valid reason.
    b) Occasionally when a bank customer's address is updated, only three of four address lines are altered, leaving a fourth line of garbage.
    c) Reports are not streamlined enough to permit quick identification of exceptions—yet is this a fault of the users or FDS? Users often lack an understanding of ways to streamline their own internal systems which FDS supports.

Relations between FDS and this bank had been somewhat strained, but have recently improved. Lewis feels that their overall service has been satisfactory, and he is confident that it will continue to be adequate for his needs.

A DIRECTOR'S VIEWS

Another interview was held with Scott Smith of Valley Bank and Trust, a major stockholder in FDS who uses their data-processing services. He provided some insight into the attitudes and activities of the four members of the board of directors—representing the four owner institutions who established FDS to handle their own data-processing needs and to earn a reasonable return on their investments in specialized equipment and personnel. Since then, they have placed equal weight on these two goals and are reasonably pleased with the results of FDS operations in meeting these goals.

Yet the board is presently reconsidering short-range plans to meet the firm's current work load and projected needs for the next several years. One possibility is to install a second computer system, but some directors are reluctant to take such a step only a year after installing the Burroughs B-500 system in 1971. Some thought is being projected by the board about bringing in a follow-up consultant at this point. They had a consultant do a study earlier, which encouraged them to buy the B-500 system originally. Various directors view FDS's need to expand differently, and they are beginning to develop alternative plans on their own.

AN OPERATING OFFICER'S VIEWS

Persons who have direct working contact with FDS all seem to have continuing respect for the financial and other success that the company's management has achieved to date. They share some of the enthusiasm Dickinson has about the future of the FDS organization.

An interview with Dickinson, the operating executive of FDS, provided still other views. Dickinson's observations are not entirely positive. He notes that "we can only be paid out of the money we make. The more income we generate, the more we can be paid, and we're all human enough to want to expand as much as possible." At the same time, he recognizes a basic contradiction in the policies espoused by the board of directors when he observes, "The main obstacle to our growth now is the fact that the board of directors give their first loyalty to their separate bank employers. They see FDS primarily as a tool for promoting their individual banks and not as a joint profit-making firm and business."

PLANNING ALTERNATIVES

Several alternatives became quite evident as the study progressed. One alternative was to maintain the status quo. FDS has been very successful in providing typical services in a limited area and probably could remain profitable for some time without making any changes at this time. Profit is not the only goal for FDS, and a decrease in profits could be sustained without jeopardizing the firm and its continued operation.

A second alternative is to increase services offered to the present users and then expand services to nonbanking customers. There should be some future demand for additional services as the banks increase their volume of business in certain functions. One key user of FDS services, Earl Lewis, mentioned several services which his bank will be interested in receiving in the near future. These services include handling of certificates of deposit, which FDS presently offers on a limited loan, and commercial loans, on which FDS has already done some preliminary development work. A third one relates to a type of credit-card system which would permit the bank to offer new banking services to military personnel stationed around the world from this area. This function is growing rapidly in his bank and may soon justify automation. The bank would like for FDS to provide this service and feels confident that it can meet this new request.

One primary user of FDS services, Valley Bank & Trust, indicated that it will soon need additional services and support in the automation of some aspects of their general ledger accounts. He also notes the need for more intensive and extensive analyses of accounts. Finally, he foresees FDS eventually offering more nonfinancial services in payroll, accounts receivable, and accounts payable, especially to customers other than owner banks.

Banking has increasingly become more of a service industry—one in which the range of services offered to customers encompasses a much broader area of activity than the traditional banking function. Still the 1950s processing services to banks have increased in volume and types of services. This will likely continue through the 1970s.

The key decision facing FDS is not whether to expand services or to remain with the existing ones, but rather to determine just how far to go in extending and in increasing its services. This question is paramount to all short-term and long-term planning. It is also a major factor influencing capital budgeting and planning for equipment. In the past, decisions have been short-sighted to resolve existing problems and concerns. FDS now hopes to avoid defensive actions through offensive long-range planning.

A third alternative for the company might be to expand geographically, without any major diversification in services. FDS could investigate the possibil-

ity of establishing new centers in other Texas cities and perhaps later in surrounding states. As an aid in viewing this possibility, a study concerning the
industry outlook is presented later.

The most ambitious alternative for FDS would be to attempt expanding
into a major, regional general data-processing service organization. This alternative could lead FDS into several competing directions: toward the use of
time-sharing or facilities management, or outside consultants, and so forth.
Considerations of this sort would require major changes in both hardware and
personnel requirements, and operations, and new hardware would likely be
required.

TECHNICAL AND SUPPORTING CONSIDERATIONS

The technical aspects of planning for hardware and software and support needs
for the next few years was of particular concern to operating officers. Any
short-range plans must include hardware considerations and must relate to
overall long-range plans as well as additional considerations.

Several questions must be resolved at FDS concerning its hardware needs.
Tom Dickinson and the board of directors must decide the overall question
of data-processing needs within the next five to ten years. Then, they should
relate this to hardware requirements and the present Burroughs B-500 system
that was installed in 1971. For example, when will they need to expand or replace this system based on projected growth?

The key question is to determine growth requirements and their role as
a banking service organization. What direction will FDS take in the future?
This will also have to be decided from two standpoints—as an organization
serving banks and a diversity of the regional users of their services both now
and in the future.

The relative volumes and multiplicity of accounts will determine the overall hardware and monitoring software required. A major increase in either
volume or types of transactions would undoubtedly require a system capable
of multiprogramming and peripherals of a direct-access nature. At present only
the sort/merge operations are the critical operations performed on the B-500
system.

Also, no simple guidelines exist by which to determine exact needs for a
peripheral system and the economic tradeoffs with and without such a system.
A peripheral system would prove necessary if the firm expands rapidly and
requires a back-up system to buffer workloads and meet time requirements
imposed by the users of FDS services.

Personnel and support requirements can vary considerably, depending on
which type of equipment is used. Also, training varies according to technical
equipment and operating priorities. Specialists in programming and other supportive skills depend on technical operating requirements. The trend in the
data-processing industry is toward more sophisticated equipment, but less
programming skill requirements and operating complexity and with accessibil-
ity and personal flexibility by the user.

In order to effectively develop future plans for FDS, external factors must be carefully considered and evaluated. A brief look at the banking industry, which FDS primarily serves, is important. Any bank which contemplates the acquisition of data-processing or computer capabilities has four general options:

1. On-premises computer—in this case the bank provides its own hardware, software, and staff.
2. Another bank—a single bank shares its own data-processing facilities with other institutions. The prime user takes full responsibility and provides all hardware, software, and personnel. System costs are usually prorated over the entire user group on a time, item, or volume basis. This method is often used by city correspondent banks for the banks which they serve.
3. Cooperative—a group of banks exercises joint ownership and operation and prorates the cost of the facility.
4. Service bureau—generally, a bank takes its work to the bureau's installation to be processed.

FDS functions as both a cooperative and a service bureau. This rather unusual marriage has proved quite successful in building its business in the past. But it seems inevitable that in the future, one of these functions must ultimately be given priority over the other.

Numerous factors determine which of these four computer sources a bank will choose. Generally, on-premise computers are restricted to relatively large banks; smaller banks tend to utilize the other sources. Another bank is an attractive choice, if it is available. Correspondent banks (banks accepting deposits from other banks and in return offering services to those banks) are a good possibility—in Federal Reserve District 10, 90% of the correspondent banks offer data-processing services. However, only 46% of the small banks use these services, probably because of the distance between banks. [1]

In order to obtain a feel for how these four DP sources are distributed among automated banks, a questionnaire was sent by several graduate students studying alternatives for FDS to seven Federal Reserve Districts. These districts were expected to roughly match Federal Reserve District 10, in which FDS banks operate in terms of the mix of banks served. The results of this research are summarized in Table 1. In an effort to obtain meaningful averages, two approaches were taken. First, the data for District 9 was excluded because it was based on a biased sample. A second average was obtained by excluding any widely divergent percentages, on the assumption that they resulted from highly irregular situations or different interpretations of that particular category. The results derived should provide some indication of the state of the art of bank data processing in the Southwest.

One question included in the questionnaire asked federal reserve officials to note any prevailing trends. Such trends could then be related to areas which FDS services or might service in the future. Although the research is not comprehensive enough to draw final conclusions, it is quite significant that all three respondents to this question chose alternative B—"Another bank." This

Table 1. Banking DP questionnaire summary

	DP source						Automated functions										
	% banks using DP	On-premise	Another bank	Co-operative	Service bureau	Other	Demand deposits	Regular savings	Installment loans	Certificates of deposits	Club accounts	Investments	Mortgage loans	Credit card loans	Safe deposits	Trust department	Number of samples
11—Dallas[1]	89	27	40	10	15	8	93	91	88	67	13	21	28	15	33	10	15
10—Kansas City	40	25	60	5	10	0	100	60	100	25	20	70	85	100	85	0	90
9—Minneapolis[2]	75	4	63	7	26	0	93	NA	61	100	NA	NA	12	0	2	NA	3
8—St. Louis[3]	72	16	72	6	20	0	90	75	25	80	10	10	10	100	15	NA	10
6—Atlanta[4]	91	38	46	4	12	0	90	88	85	NA	NA	NA	14	NA	12	NA	24
Average (excluding District 9)	73	26	54	6	14		93	78	74	57	14	34	34	72	36	5	35
Average (excluding divergent values)	73	26	56	6	17		93	78	83	82	14	15	16	100	20	5	13

[1] Data based on 1971 Functional Cost Analysis Program.
[2] Data based on 1970 FCA Program, for banks with deposits less than $50 million only.
[3] Data based on State member banks.
[4] Data based on 1970 FCA Program.

is reflected in the data-processing source breakdowns in Table 1. Among the reasons given for a bank preferring B were:

1. Prepackaged services are available.
2. Only a short lead time is required before utilization is possible.
3. The location is often convenient.
4. The other bank performs the same services for its own operations and understands bank-management needs.
5. Costs are very competitive (particularly when compared to purchase or lease) mainly because many larger banks have excess computer capacity and can offer very attractive rates.

Questionnaire results further indicated that some banks actually utilize the services of more than any one source—note that distribution for District 8 adds up to more than 100%.

The banking situation within Texas should be particularly relevant to FDS's future. According to a study performed by the American Banking Association [4], the state had a total of 1142 banks in 1966. During the period from 1956 to 1965, Texas' percentage of the total banks in the United States increased from 6.9% to 8.27%. The average total assets for a Texas bank in 1965 was $17.5 million, compared to an average of $27.3 million for the entire United States. Using a stratified sample of 212 banks, this study obtained the following results:

1. 20% had one or more computers installed and operating, including 19% of those banks with deposits of $10–49 million.
2. 12% had no computer, but used an off-premise computer. This included 15% of those with deposits less than $10 million and 11% with deposits from $10–49 million. Only a negligible number of larger banks fell in this category.
3. 11% had no computer processing, but had computers on order or had contracted for off-premise services. All these had deposits less than $100 million, and most were in the $10–49 million range.
4. 59% had no computer processing and no plans for using computers.

In considering these figures, it must be noted that some of the respondents which had no computer processing, and no plans for such, have undoubtedly decided in favor of such processing since the survey. This is also true of banks not involved in the study. Comparison of these results with those from the questionnaire should give some indication of the recent growth in banking automation.

One fact that places firms selling computer services to banks in a favorable light is the financial loss associated with most on-premise facilities. As mentioned earlier, full-service banking can require a bank to engage in activities that are not fund-raising in a banking sense—activities that are not using funds as loans or investments. With very few exceptions, these activities have shown losses in recent years, for banks of all sizes. [9] Data processing is a case in point. For the average bank participating in the 1970 Functional Cost Analysis program, the rate of net earnings from on-premise computer services are as follows [6]:

Deposits up to $50 million: 17.05%
Deposits of $50–200 million: 14.21%
Deposits over $200 million: 7.52%

The justification for retaining these unprofitable activities is that they contribute to the growth and profitabiliy of other functions. Even though the development of computer service can be expensive (especially in its early stages), in the longer run increased efficiencies do evolve, which lower overall processing costs. Banks not willing to endure this initial unprofitability usually continue to rely on a data-processing service bureau to meet their needs.

FINAL INQUIRY

The final study report presented to FDS management included all of the industry facts as being relevant to future growth and development of the company's short-range and long-range plans. In accepting the report, several operating officers, including Dickinson, indicated that this new information would be shared with the board of directors, who were presently analyzing alternative courses of overall action for the company in the immediate years ahead. Clearly the company is at a crucial turning point. Its future growth is uncertain and unknown. What should the company do in the short run? In the long run? Specifically, what objectives and plans should it follow if one considers its prevailing external environment and present technical, operational, and industry trends?

BIBLIOGRAPHY

1. Robert S. Aldom, *et al., Automation in Banking* (New Brunswick, N.J.: Rutgers University Press, 1963).

2. *Automating Bank Operations* (Park Ridge, Ill.: NABAC Research, 1962).

3. *The Check Collection System* (Park Ridge, Ill.: Bank Administration Institute).

4. Lawrence L. Crum, *Transition in the Texas Commercial Banking Industry, 1956–65* (Austin: Bureau of Business Research—University of Texas, 1970).

5. *Demand Deposit Accounting EDP Manual* (Prepared by FDS staff).

6. *Function Cost Analysis—1970 Average Banks* (Federal Reserve System).

7. Robert E. Knight, "Correspondent Banking," *Monthly Review* (November 1970): 3–14.

8. W. B. Rossnagel, *Checklist for Management, Engineering, Manufacturing, and Product Assurance* (New York: Spartan Books, 1971).

9. Carla M. Warberg, "Functional Profitability Varies with Size of Bank," *Business Review* (November 1971): 5–11.

Where Do We Get Workers for a Third Shift?

Petro Manufacturing, located in the Houston area, was an independent machine shop specializing in production metal working. It operated 13 automatic screw machines, 5 numerical control machining centers, numerous conventional machine tools, and an extensive grinding shop. The typical shift employed 25–40 workers depending on the work available. Most of these workers were skilled machinists. The proposed expansion of Petro Manufacturing sales had been effective during the summer and fall of 1974, to the point that the typical shop work week had stretched to two ten-hour shifts a day, six days a week. Sunday work was not unusual. At this point, management was giving serious thought to the possibility of starting a third shift.

Several advantages of a third shift were evident to management:

1. work at regular rates rather than overtime rates;
2. workers to work fewer hours, with less fatigue and perhaps higher overall efficiency;
3. maximum utilization of existing machine tools and equipment. Even with a third shift, some desire for overtime could still be satisfied, at least partly, by working Saturday and possibly part of Sunday. If the ten-hour shift that workers were accustomed to ceased, some workers would look for additional moonlighting jobs in other competitive plants. In this particular industry, during busy times it was not unusual for workers to work eight hours at one plant and an additional four hours at another plant.

At the same time, any move to a third eight-hour shift would likely incur several difficulties and disadvantages:

1. Some of the better workers, accustomed to a high level of overtime, would become dissatisfied as the amount of overtime would be reduced;
2. Current slack in work schedules, that could be made use of by working more than ten hours a shift on a machine, would no longer be available, because the machines would be scheduled to run continuously 24 hours a day. The only time available for catch-up or extra work would be during Saturday or Sunday.

It was decided that the biggest stumbling block would be in obtaining sufficient manpower. The Houston area had lower unemployment rates compared to other cities in the nation (as noted in Table 1). In fact, the types of workers Petro Manufacturing needed to hire had a local unemployment rate of almost zero percent.

Petro's personnel people described their workers this way:

Machine shop workers are a nomadic group, tending to move from one shop to another and back again as the work load in the individual shops vary. Many of these

This case was prepared by Howard Chamberlain and A. W. Smith of Texas A&M University. It is designed to be used as a basis for class discussion rather than to illustrate either effective or ineffective handling of an administrative situation. Presented at a Case Workshop and distributed by the Intercollegiate Case Clearing House, Soldiers Field, Boston, Mass. 02163. All rights reserved to the contributors. Printed in the U.S.A. Used with permission.

Table 1. Unemployment rates for selected cities

	Los Angeles	Detroit	Cleveland	Houston
July 1974	7.7	9.3	5.6	4.2
Aug. 1974	7.4	9.5	5.0	4.0
Sept. 1974	6.9	7.6	4.7	4.2
Oct. 1974	6.6	8.1	4.8	3.7
Nov. 1974	7.6	9.3	6.1	4.5
Dec. 1974	7.9	12.2	6.4	4.0
Jan. 1975	9.1	14.9	7.4	4.6

Note 1: These unemployment rates are representative of the greater city and are not seasonally adjusted.

Note 2: The Los Angeles, Detroit, and Cleveland Standard Metropolitan Statistical Areas (SMSA's) had substantial unemployment, where: (1) Unemployment in the area equaled 6 percent or more of its labor force, discounting seasonal or temporary factors; and (2) It is anticipated that the rate of unemployment during the next two months will remain at 6 percent or more, discounting temporary or seasonal factors.

Note 3: The Houston SMSA was categorized as having moderate unemployment, or an unemployment rate between 3.0 and 5.9 percent.

Source: *Area Trends in Employment and Unemployment,* published by the U.S. Department of Labor, Manpower Administration Division.

workers actively seek situations where a high level of overtime is required. If they are working for a shop that can support them only eight hours a day, five days a week, they will keep their ear open to the grapevine to find out who is busy and attempt to hire on in a shop that is working five ten-hour shifts or possibly even six ten-hour shifts per week. If that is not available, they may well take moonlighting work in shops with a higher work demand. A fair percentage of these employees have less loyalty to their company than to their trade. A significant proportion of Petro Manufacturing production workers were in their second or third and a few cases in their fourth employment with Petro in the last few years.

While the Houston area was experiencing a very "tight" labor market situation, other areas in the United States were in a general recession. Larger cities—Los Angeles, Detroit, and Cleveland—were identified as areas where Petro could obtain unemployed workers for use in its operation. The aerospace industry had experienced severe cutback, causing widespread unemployment in the Los Angeles area. The automotive industry had also experienced cutback, causing unemployment in the Detroit area. This was also evident in other manufacturing communities, such as Cleveland. It was felt that each of these industries would employ machinists with the skills necessary to help Petro meet its demand.

The personnel department's problem was to plan for these visits to the three cities in order to make the most effective use of Petro people's time and to try to produce the greatest number of potential employees. How should they go about recruiting employees in a distant area? How could they convince prospective employees to move up to 2000 miles to go to work for an unknown employer?

The Unity Group, Inc.

In the spring of 1971, Bill Dixon was reviewing the history of The Unity Group, Inc., searching for answers to the very severe problems that currently faced the organization. After five years, The Unity Group was confronted with the most serious crisis of its existence. Bill Dixon knew that some significant action on his part would be necessary soon if The Unity Group survived.

THE UNITY SINGERS

The Unity Group was born as The Unity Singers, a singing group composed of high school and college students in west Texas. Bill conceived the idea of a "folk choir" from his experience with choral groups while studying speech and fine arts at a local college. In 1964 approximately 50 youngsters were selected for the singing group. Aside from singing ability, other requirements were that they had the time, the discipline, and the desire to help build the choir "from the ground up."

Success was quickly achieved in terms of popularity in the extended local area. In 1965 the Singers chartered a bus for a month and went to Hollywood, hoping to extend their success to a much wider audience. This goal was only partially achieved. Back in Texas, the Singers were trimmed to 18 members. These 18 were selected for their ability as well as their attitude. Dedication, ambition, and loyalty were considered particularly important personal attributes for group members.

In 1966 the 18 Singers returned to Hollywood, this time to live. Thus began the five-year history that Bill was thinking about.

HOLLYWOOD

With only $1800 to begin with, it was necessary to be frugal with their money. Because of this and also because some of the members were underage and Bill had promised their parents they would be strictly supervised, they rented a ten-room house and lived together. Bill, at this time 22 years old, was one of the older members and was married. There were also nine single boys, five single girls, and one other married couple—Bill Dixon's brother and his wife.

This case was prepared by Assistant Professor John Todd of the University of Arkansas as a basis for class discussion rather than to illustrate either effective or ineffective handling of an administrative situation. Presented at the Houston Case Workshop of the Southern Case Research Association and the Intercollegiate Case Clearing House, November 6–8, 1973. Distributed by the Intercollegiate Case Clearing House, Soldiers Field, Boston, Mass. 02163. All rights reserved to the contributors. Printed in the U.S.A. Used with permission.

Strict rules were imposed by Bill Dixon, prohibiting alcohol, drugs, and sexual relations among the unmarried members. The girls' dating was subject to Bill's approval. "The Strip" was out of bounds except when somebody had to go for groceries. Bill explained the necessity of the rules as follows: "These strict rules were imposed for two reasons: (1) my own sense of rather strict moral codes, and (2) the group members' parents held me fully accountable for their conduct. I was expected (by the parents) to act as surrogate father figure and monitor the conduct of their children. They were, after all, 15 to 18 years old for the most part." A newspaper story described Bill as a "patriarch, running the household as a Puritanical dictatorship—a condition which came about when 18 small-town youngsters got their first glimpse of 'sinful city.'" Daily routines were established, and household chores were divided among the members.

Professionally, the Singers achieved a certain amount of success. They were recognized in a show-business newspaper as "young, fresh, and qualifying for the kids-next-door genre—enthusiastic, but obviously well disciplined." They appeared on network TV shows and played rodeos, fairs, and resort hotels across the country. Between the "feasts," however, were some "famines." Bookings were often difficult, and money was correspondingly short. Several members supplemented the treasury with outside jobs, contributing their earnings to the common fund.

After two years of Hollywood, interest of the members in show business waned. The intense competition and tiresome routine of show business resulted in a general lack of fulfillment. Only two of the original 18 members had left the group in the first two years. (Replacements had been made.) Now, without the common bond of show business, the future of the group had to be questioned. Since the group had originally come together for a specific purpose, was there any reason to continue?

Bill Dixon described the answer to this question from his perspective, as follows: "The focus of attention on the internal make-up of the group had been as important to me as the achievement of show business success and it took fully as much of my energy. As I mentioned, the group members' parents imposed some heavy responsibilities on me, which I full well intended to discharge; this, then, necessitated a great deal of thought and careful planning as to how we would function in the close living situation.

"In the process of all this, my personal emphasis gradually drifted away more and more from show-business success, as such, and more toward the awareness that we had accidentally stumbled onto a formula for living productively that was extraordinary. In this lifestyle I had observed that people could be taught through the environment to be more sensitive, have greater reliability, and more significant sense of responsibility for the common good, that they could more easily set aside petty personal conflicts. In other words, we had accidentally created a formula that just might hold answers for a number of people and might have the potential, at its most megalomaniacal extreme, of making a significant contribution to society if we could figure out how to use it.

"We could have stayed in show business indefinitely. As a matter of fact, when we did leave California, I had to cancel three two-week rodeo dates we had been booked for. We simply chose to get out and focus all of our energy on the group structure that we had witnessed coming into being and to figuring out how we could make the broadest possible use of it. Hence the decision to leave show business and use our talents in a less cut-throat type of show business and still grow in the direction of the more idealistic fulfillment."

Most others in the group shared Bill Dixon's ideas and ideals. Faced with the choice of continuing in show business on their own, returning to Texas, or staying with the group, practically all opted for the last of the three alternatives. They defined their style of living "for each other" as the ultimate form of Christianity. The "sharing" and "caring" that resulted were believed by them to be unique with their group. The Unity Singers thereby became The Unity Group, often abbreviated to simply "Unity."

Attracted by a newspaper advertisement, the group considered a move to southern Missouri. Bill Dixon and another member made a trip to Missouri to investigate and brought back pictures and a recommendation to lease a guest ranch there. It appeared to them that "the ranch would be a good place to make a living in a creative and peaceful atmosphere." The recommendation was approved by the other members, and the move was made in the winter of 1968.

SHADY RIVER GUEST RANCH

Seventeen adult Unity Group members and two children made the move to Missouri. Of the 17, there were five married couples. The average age was 21 years.

They found a restaurant-lodge, five cabins, rental boats, and camping facilities. The rental was $400 per month. The nearest city of over 10,000 population was approximately 100 miles away. Accessibility was a major problem, particularly in wet weather. The highway was five miles away and could only be reached over a rocky, packed-clay road. Largely due to this barrier, profitable operation of the ranch could not be achieved in the first year. Members took whatever jobs they could find—primarily farm labor and factory work with occasional singing engagements. Approximately half of the group had to spend several months in Chicago in order to meet the group's financial obligations.

The reaction of the community to the group ranged from curiosity to hostility. One group of nightriders paid the ranch a visit shortly after their arrival, breaking windows and causing other property damage.

The size of the group was gradually increasing during this year, particularly drawing individuals who were disillusioned and looking for a more emotionally satisfying lifestyle. Bill Dixon explains the appeal of The Unity Group at that time as follows: "Many joined us because they became disillusioned with the swinging life of sensual pleasure in a spiritual vacuum. Others came looking for an alternative lifestyle, people who cared or others who found that drugs didn't offer inner peace. They stayed because we were sincere, not fashionable." Among the new members were several with more education and job experience than the original members. Mark Peters, a successful ad executive from New York, and his wife, a highly paid fashion model, were attracted by the potential for personal growth and freedom they saw in the group. Richard

Palmer, a college graduate working for General Electric, stated his motivation to join the group as follows: "I saw people talking about what they might have done and what they could do, but they weren't doing them; I felt sad, and I didn't want this. Many people find themselves caught in a rut. At the commune, they can withdraw and look at themselves, find love of others and gain strength." Thus, after the move to Missouri, The Unity Group was increasing in both size and diversity, with new members ranging from ex-drug addicts to "dropout" executives.

BLUE MOUNTAIN LODGE

Early in 1970, Unity Group was offered the opportunity to manage all the facilities at a mountain resort approximately one hour from Shady River. This appeared to provide an answer to the economic problems of the group. It provided employment for 40 people as well as an entrepreneurial opportunity to make a profit above salaries. In addition, the type of work was interesting, in contrast to the menial work often necessary in the past, and all the members could be together again.

Unity Group accepted the one-year resort concession enthusiastically. Buildings were renovated and redecorated. Grounds were cleaned up. Comedy and singing acts were developed to entertain guests. Unity members worked long hours in the summer of 1970 at Blue Mountain Lodge. The financial results reflected a success for the 1970 season. With this experience, a new ten-year management contract was negotiated with the owner of Blue Mountain Lodge. Four hundred acres of undeveloped timber land on one side of Blue Mountain was purchased by Unity, and architects were engaged to draw up plans for communal living facilities there. With a financial income secured and prospects for future expansion of facilities and employment opportunities, Bill Dixon instructed the architects to draw up plans for a 200-person community. This community was to serve as a base for Unity Group in its economic endeavors and personal-development activities. It was hoped that other bases could be established in other parts of the United States as finances permitted.

THE TRAGEDIES

When the summer resort season ended, Unity members moved back to Shady River Guest Ranch, which they still leased. They planned to spend the winter there and then move back to the more isolated Blue Mountain area in the spring.

Then, the first of two tragedies hit Unity. On February 3, 1971, Blue Mountain Lodge was completely destroyed by a fire. (The fire was set by an escaped convict who had used the Lodge as a hideout.) The Unity Group incurred a heavy financial loss from equipment and personal belongings that were stored there. More seriously, the owner of Blue Mountain decided not to rebuild the lodge, at least in 1971. Thus plans for Unity's financial security and growth were victims of the fire. As Bill Dixon said at that time: "This just about wipes us out." A newspaper article at that time said: "The lodge fire February 3 was more than a routine property loss. It may have ended an experiment in communal living by 60 young persons in the remote pine-covered mountains."

Two days later, the second tragedy struck. Eight Unity members were returning from jobs they held in a town approximately 75 miles away. A drunken driver struck their vehicle head-on, and five Unity members were killed. The financial loss of the wreck created a further drain on Unity's limited resources. The personal and emotional loss to Unity members was even more devastating. Four widows and three children suffered the most direct effects of the deaths. All members of Unity were shocked and saddened, however, at the loss of these members with whom they had shared their lives. February was a month of depression and bewilderment about the future. A shortage of food made the time even more difficult.

During this time, the Unity members reaffirmed their belief in the philosophy of the group as well as their desire to continue as participants. The tragedies seemed to pull Unity members even closer together as they helped each other through the difficult times. About this, Richard Palmer said: "Members had to reexamine the strength of their feelings, because things were very difficult for all of us at that point."

MARCH–APRIL 1971

Because of financial necessity, 20 of the 60 adult members of Unity moved to St. Louis. This move was at the invitation of a Catholic priest to live in Church facilities and help him develop a ghetto ministry. While a few members assisted the priest, in exchange for lodging of the whole group, the remainder sought other jobs that provided badly needed income. Richard Palmer was the appointed leader of the St. Louis wing of Unity. Trying to develop some group self-sufficiency, various small-business opportunities were being investigated in St. Louis. The most promising possibilities seemed to be a boutique, a health food store, and a restaurant. No decision had yet been made on these businesses.

The remainder of the Unity members stayed at Shady River, working when possible. Bill Dixon was actively seeking a new business that would provide some financial stability for the organization. He was currently investigating the leasing of a restaurant on Beaver Lake, a relatively new lake in northwest Arkansas. The restaurant had not been successful in its two years of operation, and the owner believed that new management with new ideas was needed. He was willing to lease the 200-chair restaurant for 10% of its gross income. The area impressed Bill as one which had considerable potential as the lake grew in popularity. Already, two large resort communities were being developed within one-half hour of the restaurant. He believed the restaurant could be converted into a dinner theater to attract customers as well as to utilize the talents of the group members.

LIFE IN UNITY

Except for the rules against drugs and promiscuous sex, there are no rules. (One member was expelled for violation of the latter rule.) In lieu of a list of rules, one policy is followed: "The common good always comes first." Although each member is encouraged to express himself or herself, it must not be at the expense of others.

All possessions are considered to be owned by the group, except for personal items and other items not needed by the overall group. Assets and debts of the new members are likewise assumed by The Unity Group. There are 12 married couples and 14 children in the group in 1971. Most new members have been friends or relatives of other Unity members.

Bill Dixon is concerned about not only the future of Unity but also his role in the group. From the autocratic state of the California days, he has attempted to move toward more self-government on the part of the members. The Unity Group was legally incorporated in 1970—with Bill Dixon as president. This action gave Unity members a greater legal voice in the affairs of the organization. Bill believes that his decreased leadership has been dysfunctional for the group, in terms of cooperation and effectiveness, because of conflicts over power. Therefore, he is wondering whether he should step back into his previous role or try another leadership structure.

In reply to a question about the major problems faced by the group in the past (besides economic), Bill noted the following:

1. power trips by would-be leaders;
2. rip-offs by persons who take advantage without contributing;
3. lack of skills;
4. trouble with suspicious authorities and neighbors.

The Jack Daily Case

Jack Daily is driving home from a two-day seminar on managerial leadership. While he drives, Jack thinks about what went on at the seminar and how he can use the material that was presented to be a better manager.

Most of the time at the seminar was devoted to discussion and lecture about certain "leader behaviors." Jack thinks that one of the most important concepts that he learned was the idea that a leader can have a *variety* of leader behaviors that are independent of one another. That is, leadership can be described as more than a *single* leader behavior, and a good leader may be "high" or "low" in a number of distinct leader behaviors. Jack finds this concept useful, because his previous concept about leadership had been vaguely defined as being "participative" versus "dictatorial," somewhat similar to the old "Theory Y/Theory X" concept.

Although many different types of leader behaviors were discussed, the seminar usually focused on two dimensions that Jack thinks of as "directiveness" and "supportiveness." Several names were brought out that related somewhat to these two dimensions: for example, "consideration" and "concern for people" were similar to "supportiveness." Also, "initiating structure" and "concern for production" seemed to relate to "directiveness." In particular, the concept of the "Managerial Grid" was useful to Jack, because it taught him that a manager could be "high" on both "concern for production" *and* "concern for people."

Prepared by Henry P. Sims, Jr., Penn State University as a basis for class discussion. Used with permission.

In general, Jack liked the seminar and found it useful because it stimulated him to think about his own managerial (leadership) style and because he was now able to articulate some concepts that until now had been only vague notions. Despite this generally positive feeling, Jack has some doubts about how he will take what he's learned and put it into practice. For the most part, Jack thinks that the new knowledge he has acquired is "nice to know," but he's having some problems in determining precisely how he can use this knowledge to improve the motivation of his subordinates.

Jack has a very real and a very specific problem in mind. Jack is an engineering manager and supervises several engineers, architects, and draftsmen. In his mind, Jack is contrasting the performance and attitudes of two of his subordinates—Jim Perkins and Fred Jones. Both Jim and Fred are about the same age, have similar engineering educational backgrounds, and have both been working for Jack for about two years. The basic ability of both men is about the same, but the contrast in performance, especially recently, has been substantial. Jim's performance has been on a rising curve; his projects are completed on time, he spends time in developing new skills when needed, and his time at work is efficiently task-oriented. Fred, on the other hand, has had a decline in performance. Fred's time at work involves too much "fooling around" with unimportant tasks, and he has had trouble completing his projects on time. Fred also spends a lot of time "B.S'ing" with fellow employees. Several times, Jack has warned Fred about excessive "socializing" while on the job. These warnings, which have been none too gentle, have had an effect for a few days, but then Fred backslides into his typical "I don't give a damn" attitude.

As he drives, Jack is thinking about the contrast between Jim and Fred and how he can use the leadership concepts to bring Fred's performance up to where it should be. In the seminar, there seemed to be an "unwritten prescription" that "concern for people" might be the best motivational strategy. Jack considers the question of whether he has had sufficient "concern for people" when it comes to Fred. He deliberates whether he should use more "consideration" in dealing with Fred. Jack decides to give it a try; tomorrow morning he will make a special point to be friendly with Fred. He promises himself that he will take a greater interest in Fred's personal life and will make a sincere attempt to be sympathetic to Fred's problems. Having made the decision, Jack turns into his driveway with a sense of optimism and relief. He believes the leadership seminar was time well spent, and he is confident that his intention to be more "considerate" to Fred will improve Fred's performance.

The Pepper Bush

Sherman Kent was an engineer with an idea. Not an idea to push back the frontiers of knowledge in electrical engineering, but an idea for a specialized food-

This case was prepared by William V. Rice, Jr., Assistant Professor of Economics and Management, and Robert McGlashan, Associate Professor of Management, University of Houston at Clear Lake City, as a basis for class discussion rather than to illustrate either effective or ineffective handling of an administrative situation. Presented at a Case Workshop and distributed by the Intercollegiate Case Clearing House, Soldiers Field, Boston, Mass. 02163. All rights reserved to the contributors. Printed in the U.S.A. Used with permission.

service operation. Though he was an electrical engineer and a graduate of one of the foremost universities in the Southwest, he had determined that his future lay in operating a restaurant.

This idea did not come from a lifelong ambition to be in food-service operation or from family background. It evolved by accident over a period of time when Sherman did the cooking for hunting and fishing trips with friends. In his cooking, he used jalapeno pepper liberally to flavor the foods being prepared. The jalapeno was used in bread and combined with cheese to form a spread to enhance the flavor of meat.

His hunting and fishing companions suggested, perhaps jokingly at first, that he should market his product. As the discussions became more serious, they agreed to back him financially if he would establish and manage a restaurant specializing in hamburgers with the special recipe, jalapeno cheese sauce. Thus the Pepper Bush was born.

EARLY OPERATIONS

Sherman opened the small restaurant, the Pepper Bush, in the spring of 1973. He was the operating partner with two other partners who helped finance the business and were instrumental in securing a small loan from a local bank. The Pepper Bush is located in a suburban community of approximately 15,000 near a large metropolitan area. He secured a building with a seating capacity of 50 and equipped it to serve the usual line of short-order food services. Though he specialized in the hamburger with the special jalapeno and cheese sauce, he also served the usual line of hamburgers, french fries, beverages, etc. His principal competition was the franchise-food operations, such as McDonald's and Burger King, which were also located on the local "franchise row." His customers were a cross-section of the local community. For the noon meal, the customers were primarily white-collar employees from the local business community and a nearby federal installation. These were people who could afford the $1.75, plus beverage and tip, for the jalapeno special. Customers for the evening meal were primarily family groups and young people. These young people came either with a date or just in groups of four to ten.

Sherman felt that he had catered to the right groups. He was especially catering to the young group in his long-range plans. As he stated, "Most of these young people have been trained to eat in fast-food places, and they won't change after they establish their own families. By cultivating them now, I'll get their business later."

By the summer of 1975, business was increasing to an expected gross of $125,000, and Sherman was thinking of expanding. The present location is too small for the volume of business that is being generated. Customers are standing in line for tables during the noon meal Monday through Friday and for the evening meal every day. He serves only the noon meal and evening meal, operating from 11:00 a.m. until 10:00 p.m. every day. Financing could be secured from the bank, and a newer and larger site could be found in the vicinity of the present restaurant.

The personnel policies of the Pepper Bush could be described as highly unstructured. When Sherman opened the restaurant, he hired a cook, three waitresses, and a dishwasher by running ads in the local papers. He did much of the cooking himself and performed all of the management functions. An accounting firm keeps the books on a contract basis. His employees presently consist of two cooks, five full-time waitresses, two part-time waitresses, and three part-time dishwashers. One of the cooks is Alvin Marsh, who also serves as Assistant Manager.

Alvin was one of the first employees hired and has been with Sherman throughout the 2½-year existence of the Pepper Bush. He serves as manager in Sherman's absence and for the past six months has been actively involved with Sherman in hiring new employees. Alvin has had no previous management experience, but has worked in two other restaurants. Sherman feels that by having Alvin participate with him in some of the management decision making, Alvin can become an effective manager. When a vacancy occurs, one of the present employees brings a friend to Sherman to be interviewed or Sherman runs an ad in the local paper.

He also has placed a "help wanted" sign in front of his restaurant. He stated that this had been a most effective way to secure part-time help. Many young people live in a large apartment complex near the restaurant and are able to walk to and from the restaurant. For those who do not have transportation, the Pepper Bush offers a place to earn money even by working odd shifts. This method has been especially effective in securing part-time waitresses and dishwashers.

The job interview, whether conducted by Sherman or Alvin, is relatively brief. No formal written application is required. Sherman explains the operation of the Pepper Bush, the duties expected of the applicant, and secures from the applicant some general background data, such as experience in fast-food service and previous employment. The principal criteria for employment, however, is Sherman's subjective opinion of how well the applicant will fit into the Pepper Bush team. He feels that he can train anyone to do the work, but it is of primary importance that the applicant can work well with his other employees and work effectively in a relatively unstructured environment. The applicant is either hired or refused employment at this interview. Sherman's technique of instinctive interviewing has been successful at the present level of operations, since turnover of full-time employees has been remarkably low for a fast-food operation. In addition to Alvin, two of the full-time waitresses have been with the Pepper Bush since it opened. Sherman believes that the low turnover rate is due to the fact that he takes a personal interest in each of his employees and tries to take into account individual differences. For example, in contrast to many of the franchise operations, he does not require his employees to dress uniformly. The waitresses wear jeans and a blouse, and the male employees may wear their hair any length they desire. He also allows a very flexible schedule of work. The various classes of employees work out their own shift substitutions, as long as each category is covered during the appropriate hours. Sherman is proud of the fact that though two of his original waitresses quit to take "better" jobs, they returned to the Pepper Bush because of the more informal working conditions.

Sherman has no formal job descriptions, and his training consists of on-the-job training. For example, all waitresses are expected to be able to work the cash register, wait tables, clean the tables, and if on the last shift, clean up for the night. But if the waitresses are busy, the cook may also work the cash register or clean the tables. All employees are expected to do whatever needs doing.

Sherman estimates that the waitresses average $3.00 per hour, including tips. This hourly wage compares favorably with wages paid by other fast-food establishments on "franchise row." He also pays competitive wages to the cooks and dishwashers. Sherman and Alvin are discussing the proposed expansion; Sherman attempts to summarize the things he considers both positive and negative.

"I have located a newer building which will almost double our seating capacity and also has a better kitchen arrangement. Financing has been arranged with the local bank. Our product will meet the competition, at least it has for the past two and a half years. I know some of our competitors have had labor problems, since a majority of their employees are part-time high school and college students. I feel that we have had a significantly lower turnover rate because we emphasize the individuality of each employee. What worries me is that if we expand to 25 or 30 employees, can we still continue with this philosophy? Is it practical with an expanded organization, even granting that I believe it is desirable?"

The Rose Company*

Mr. James Pierce had recently received word of his appointment as general manager of the Jackson Plant, one of the older established units of The Rose Company. As such, Mr. Pierce was to be responsible for the management and administration at the Jackson Plant of all functions and personnel except sales.

Both top management and Mr. Pierce realized that there were several unique features about his new assignment. Mr. Pierce decided to assess his new situation and relationships before undertaking his assignment. He was personally acquainted with the home-office executives, but had met few of the Jackson personnel. This case contains some of his reflections regarding the new assignment.

The Rose Company conducted marketing activities throughout the United States and in certain foreign countries. These activities were directed from the home office by a vice president in charge of sales.

Manufacturing operations and certain other departments were under the supervision and control of a senior vice president. These are shown in Fig. 1.

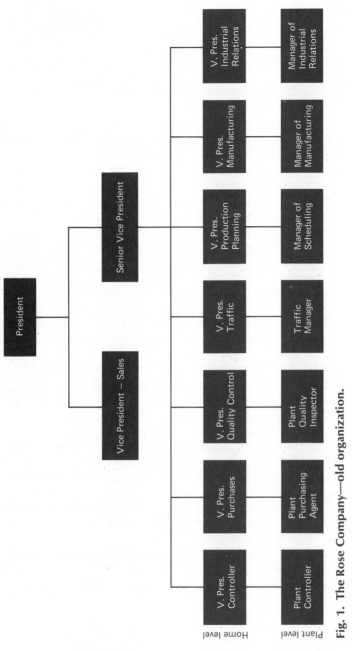

Fig. 1. The Rose Company—old organization.

For many years the company had operated a highly centralized-functional type of manufacturing organization. There was no general manager at any plant; each of the departments in a plant reported on a line basis to its functional counterpart at the home office. For instance, the industrial relations manager of a particular plant reported to the vice president in charge of industrial relations at the home office, and the plant controller to the vice president-controller, and so on.

Mr. Pierce stated that in the opinion of the top management, the record of the Jackson Plant had not been satisfactory for several years. The Rose board had recently approved the erection of a new plant in a different part of the city and the use of new methods of production. Lower costs of processing and a reduced manpower requirement at the new plant were expected. Reduction of costs and improved quality of products were needed to maintain competitive leadership and gain some slight product advantage. The proposed combination of methods of manufacturing and mixing materials had not been tried elsewhere in the company. Some features would be entirely new to employees.

According to Mr. Pierce, the top management of The Rose Company was beginning to question the advisability of the central control of manufacturing operations. The officers decided to test the value of a decentralized operation in connection with the Jackson Plant. They apparently believed that a general management representative at Jackson was needed if the new experiment in manufacturing methods and the required rebuilding of the organization were to succeed.

Prior to the new assignment, Mr. Pierce had been an accounting executive in the controller's department of the company. From independent sources the case writer learned that Mr. Pierce had demonstrated analytical ability and general administrative capacity. He was generally liked by people. From top management's point of view, he had an essential toughness described as an ability to see anything important through. By some he was regarded as the company's efficiency expert. Others thought he was a perfectionist and aggressive in reaching the goals that had been set. Mr. Pierce was aware of these opinions about his personal behavior.

Mr. Pierce summarized his problem in part as follows: "I am going into a situation involving a large number of changes. I will have a new plant; new methods and processes, but most of all I will be dealing with a set of changed relationships. Heretofore all the heads of departments in the plant reported to their functional counterparts in the home office. Now they will report to me; I am a complete stranger, and in addition this is my first assignment in a major 'line' job. The men will know this.

"When I was called into the senior vice president's office to be informed of my new assignment, he asked me to talk with each of the functional members of his staff. The vice presidents in charge of production planning, manufacturing, and industrial relations said they were going to issue all headquarters instructions to me as plant manager and they were going to cut off their connections with their counterparts in my plant. The other home-office executives admitted their functional counterparts would report to me in line capacity. They should obey my orders and I would be responsible for their pay and promotion. But these executives proposed to follow the common practice of many companies of maintaining a dotted-line, or functional, relationship with these men.

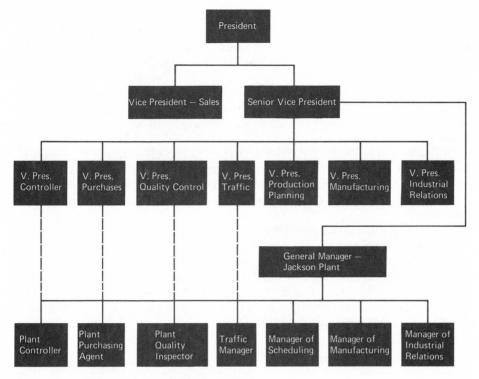

Fig. 2. The Rose Company—new organization.

I realize that these two different patterns of home-office plant relationships will create real administrative problems for me."

Figure 2 shows the organization relationships as defined in these conferences.

Bankers Trust Company (A)

BACKGROUND

Founded in 1903 by a group of American financial leaders, Bankers Trust Company was originally established to handle trust business which many existing banks could not accept due to charter limitations. Since its founding the bank had grown steadily in terms of the amount of deposits, as well as in terms of

This case was prepared as a basis for class discussion rather than to illustrate either effective or ineffective handling of an administrative situation. It was made possible through the cooperation of the Bankers Trust Company, and with help from the following sources: William W. Dettelback and Philip Kraft, "Organization Change Through Job Enrichment," *Training and Development Journal* **25** (August 1971): 2–6; and W. Philip Kraft, Jr., "Job Enrichment for Production Typists—A Case Study," *New Perspectives in Job Enrichment*, ed. John R. Maher, New York: Van Nostrand Reinhold, 1971, pp. 115–128. Copyright © 1972 by the President and Fellows of Harvard College. Distributed by the Intercollegiate Case Clearing House, Soldiers Field, Boston, Mass. 02163. All rights reserved to the contributors. Printed in the U.S.A. Reproduced by permission.

the scope of its activities. In 1905 deposits were $18.5 million; in 1930 they totaled $537.8 million; and by 1970, following two mergers and its incorporation in 1967, the bank had deposits of $7,219.0 million and it ranked among the top ten U.S. banks in amount of deposits and in terms of permanent capital funds.

In 1970 the Bankers Trust New York Corporation was the second largest bank holding company in the country (based on amount of deposits). Under its organization, Bankers Trust Company was affiliated with six banks in New York State. These banks together had 60 offices located in 42 different communities in 15 counties in the state. Total deposits in 1970 were $493.0 million. The bank also had several international branches as well as numerous affiliated institutions throughout the world. In addition to the bank and its affiliates, the corporation included a mortgage investment firm and a trust advisory and administrative service.

The bank's headquarters were located in the New York City financial district, with staff and operating units situated in five separate locations in lower Manhattan, as well as over 100 banking offices throughout the city. Plans were under way to centralize the staff and operating units in one facility, while still maintaining the present headquarters. A site had already been acquired for a 40-story building, which would include a spacious plaza and a footbridge to the World Trade Center Building.

COMMUNITY INVOLVEMENT

Bankers Trust Company had taken an active role in various areas of the New York community. Included among its activities were a mortgage lending plan for disadvantaged areas of the city and a special lending service to help businessmen meet antipollution requirements. The bank was also involved in the loan programs of the Small Business Administration. The 11,643 employees at Bankers Trust were encouraged to work with organizations confronting social and environmental problems, and the bank had organized its own volunteer program to facilitate employee involvement and participation. Other employees had benefited from the bank's new programs to improve recruitment and promotion procedures. In 1970 job posting was initiated, and in order to keep a competitive benefits position, a restructured profit-sharing plan was established for employees, as well as a savings incentive plan whereby the bank would match a certain percentage of the employees' savings.

Bankers Trust was the first New York City bank to join Plans for Progress, an "organization designed to assist in making equal opportunity a reality for every American." The bank also worked closely with the U.S. Veterans Administration, and, with the added help of other sources, it had found jobs for over 1000 veterans, 70% of them from minority groups and many of them disabled. As a result of this work, Bankers Trust was the only bank cited by the Veterans Administration for its contribution.

CORPORATE AGENCY DIVISION

The bank offered a wide variety of services to its customers. Along with regular banking features, Bankers Trust performed a stock-transfer service for a large number of corporations. This service was carried out by the Corporate Agency Division (CAD) of the bank. Within CAD there were approximately 1000 employees, 150 supervisors, and 33 bank officers. Twenty percent of the division was administrative; the remaining staff were involved in operations. (See Figs. 1 and 2 for organization charts.)

The Corporate Agency Division had 300 clients, and the service provided for these clients consisted primarily of the various clerical and bookkeeping tasks involved with the transfer of ownership of securities. There were eight account officers who dealt directly with the clients, coordinating the present accounts and acquiring new ones. The major job, however, performed by CAD was the issuance of stock certificates to new holders and the corresponding cancellation of the old certificates of the previous owners. Two related jobs were the maintenance of stockholders' records and the distribution of dividends, stock splits, annual reports, etc., for the division's clients.

ISSUING DEPARTMENT

The bulk of the transfer of stock was done in the issuing department. Several steps were involved and these were performed by different groups of personnel. First the old stock certificates and the appropriate transfer information were paired with the new certificates. Clerks "pulled" and "issued" the new certificates, which were located in a large cage in the center of the department. The new certificates were filled out by one set of typists and passed on to another set, the production typists. These employees typed the transfer data

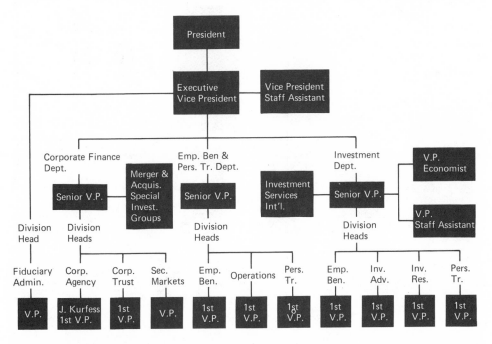

Fig. 1. Bankers Trust Company (A) fiduciary departments.

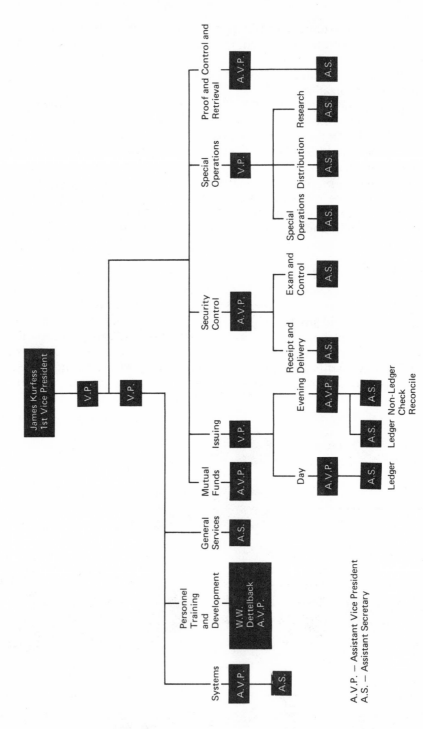

Fig. 2. Bankers Trust Company (A) Corporate Agency Division—Operations.

onto large sheets. This data was then recorded onto magnetic tapes, which would eventually be fed into the computer for the official recording of the stock transfer.

Prior to this official transfer, however, the completed stock certificates were punched and date-stamped by the preparation clerks, or "preppers." The certificates, along with the transfer sheets, had to be reviewed by a checker. There was approximately one checker for each typist. If errors were discovered, the incorrect form or certificate was marked and sent on to a special group of typists who worked only on such corrections. Following a second check after the corrections had been made, the certificates would then be signed by one of the six stock signers who worked among the typists and checkers. Occasionally a few typists were permitted to work as "preppers," when illness or vacations caused a temporary shortage. Any unusually complicated transfers, or "specials" as they were called, were assigned to certain selected typists.

The personnel in the issuing department were divided into two shifts. The typists worked in groups of 14, led by a group leader. The checkers were organized in the same manner. A group of typists and a group of checkers formed a section, with a section head in charge. There were two head supervisors for the ten sections, one for each shift. An assistant supervisor was assigned to the day shift. The cage employees, primarily clerks, numbered 18 (14 day, 4 night) with two supervisors. Finally there was approximately one "prepper" for each section. All personnel were situated in one large room, with the cage located in the center. Every member of the department, and of the entire division, had to wear a bank identification card, and there were security guards at all entrances and exits. The reason behind this was the millions of dollars of blank stock certificates and negotiable securities in the offices and especially in the issuing department.

The group leaders devoted their time to organizing the work of the typists or checkers under their supervision. They were in charge of assigning work to their subordinates, and this was usually done on a random basis. They were also responsible for changing the computer input tapes; the typists raised their hands when the tapes needed to be changed. In addition, the group leaders decided when the group took its coffee and lunch breaks, and the employees had to get their permission to use the rest rooms. Another aspect of the group leaders' job was talking to their subordinates about any problems or errors. When these were discovered, the group leader would usually get the entire group together. One leader commented that this was done even if only one or two of the employees were involved. Leaders also held meetings with their groups to give out information on changes in procedure or policy, etc.

Despite the high number of checkers in the issuing department and the frequency of reviews, division management felt that production was low and the quality of the work poor. Any errors left unnoticed created several problems, including incorrect stock registrations and/or cancellations, misplaced certificates, lost dividend checks, and annoyed customers. Employee attitudes were poor. There was considerable tension among certain employees, and this had led to a few fist fights in the lounges. Absenteeism and turnover were high. The latter ran as much as 63% a year, and management estimated that this was costing the bank about $1.0 million. Turnover was not noticeably greater among the minority-group employees, who totaled 51% of the work force. While the majority of personnel in the issuing department were women, there were 30 men working in the department, 25 as checkers and five as supervisors. All employees were high school graduates, and the average age was 25.

JOB ENRICHMENT

In October 1969, James Kurfess, First Vice President in charge of the Corporate Agency Division; William Dettelback, Assistant Vice President of Personnel and Training; and other division officers had come to the decision that certain measures should be taken to improve the productivity of the issuing department. They were aware of the work that had been done in the area of job enrichment. In an effort to discover if this type of approach would be appropriate, they called in a consulting firm whose work in job enrichment and job design was well known to some of the division officers.

In their investigation of the department and what might be done to increase its productivity, the consulting-firm team examined the flow of work, the quality of the work, and how to measure it. They were interested in how a transfer was processed and how the issuing department handled over 20,000 items a day. Due to how the work was completed, it was difficult to assess quality, and no method had previously been developed to provide this information for management.

The consulting team wanted to find out how the employees felt about their work. In the course of the interviews, one of the typists expressed her surprise at being asked her opinion. However, others were willing to volunteer their views on their work.

Employee A: Sometimes I get tired. It's boring. I think it would be better if we could have different kinds of jobs. Sometimes I don't feel like working at all because it is the same thing over and over. I get a headache—the people aggravate me and I don't feel like doing nothing.

Employee B: I don't see anything good in the job . . . not anything . . . The same thing. What could you learn from typing stock; typing names and addresses? It is very simple, you don't learn anything from that. I don't see nothing good.

Employee C: How can I explain? What's there to do? There is nothing to do, right? Because that's your job. Typing the stock. You can make no decision because it is there. You have to do it.

Employee D: Same sheeting every day. Don't know when you make errors. Some you are told about, some you are not. Maybe a correction girl will say, "What are you doing over there? You are making 12 errors a day." The work is just routine. I find that this is the main reason for transfers or girls leaving the jobs. You have no say in the programming of the work. Just told to sheet it like this and that's that. You have four or five errors on a sheet that you know yourself can be corrected before the sheets are sent out. Girls just send out—they know they won't get the corrections back so they just let them go that way.

Employee E: Nothing much good except the breaks that we get, which totals three. Outside of that nothing good. I have five bosses to account to; it is ridiculous. I like to be treated like an adult. Not a child in kindergarten. That is exactly the way I feel when I come in in the morning—like I'm going to school.

One typist had put in for a transfer prior to being interviewed by the consulting team. She said that many people had requested transfers, but that the supervisors would often "lose" the requests. She added that not very many of these were transferred and if they were, it was after a long wait. While talking about her job she said that most of the typists sat around and griped to each other. They considered their work "a drag," and if a group leader other than their own asked them to help out, they would rarely volunteer. She noted that leaders frequently had trouble getting help from outside their group. At the end of the interview she remarked: "I don't see why I should have to leave my brain on the desk in the morning when I punch in and pick it up on the way out at night."

The consulting team also invited the supervisors in the issuing department to express their views. While many were enthusiastic about the idea of job enrichment when it was presented to them, they did express some reservations about its possible practice in the issuing department. One group leader said: "I don't think it's possible. The employees are still going to need careful supervision and constant checking." She commented that undetected errors could result in a "big mess." Pat had just been promoted from a typist job which she had held for 11 years. In discussing her experiences as a typist, she said: "Supervisors didn't have the time to listen. They were very production-oriented and all they thought about was getting the work out." She also remarked that there was little communication between typists or checkers and leaders, or between leaders and section heads. She added that people were secretive and that some of the employees feared their supervisors. According to one of the typists, most supervisors were easy to spot in the department. They were either "little old ladies," she revealed, 30-year veterans of the office who had spent most of their time as typists or the supervisors were "aspiring young men."

FUTURE ACTION

As the consulting team reviewed its findings, the members considered the various ways in which jobs in the issuing department could be enriched. They were also concerned with how such enrichment could be assessed after its implementation. At management's request, the team was focusing its attention on the production typist job; however, the members realized that all personnel in the issuing department would be affected to some degree by any changes which were instituted. Other personnel from CAD would be involved as well, specifically the bank officers to whom the head supervisors in the issuing department reported. While division management had given the team its full support, it was unclear what contribution, if any, they would make to a job enrichment program in the issuing department. Concerning this, Mr. Kurfess commented: "Job enrichment is allowing people to contribute as much as they can. We have to be as flexible as we can."

The consulting team was especially interested in the role of the supervisor. In projects for other organizations, first- and second-level supervisors had made an important contribution in helping determine what could be done and in participating in its implementation. The team had asked various supervisors what they thought might be done to change the production typist job. Most of those questioned mentioned only a few items which they thought might improve the typing job. The consulting team, however, was confident that with encouragement these same supervisors would be able to contribute extensively in planning and implementing an enrichment project. In fact, the team was considering holding a series of meetings with all of the supervisors in order to talk at great length about possible changes in the issuing department.

The team would be discussing the position of the supervisors, as well as several other issues, with division management within a week. While it was not mandatory to present a thorough and detailed proposal at this time, the team nevertheless wanted to clarify its thinking on what changes should be made in the issuing department, and how these changes could best be implemented and assessed.

Author Index

Subject Index

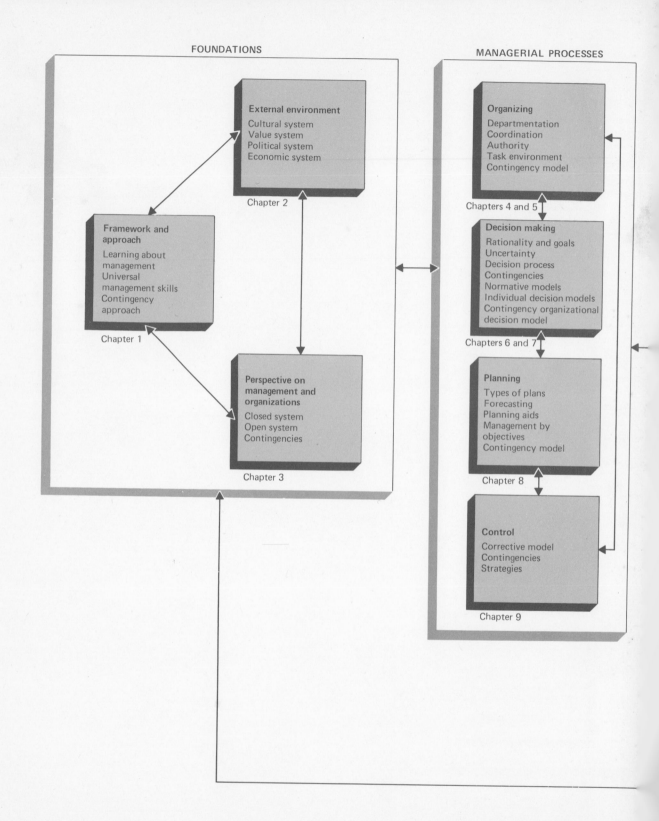

External environment

Cultural system
Value system
Political system
Economic system

Chapter 2

Organizing

Departmentation
Coordination
Authority
Task environment
Contingency model

Chapters 4 and 5

Framework and approach

Learning about
management
Universal
management skills
Contingency
approach

Chapter 1

Decision making

Rationality and goals
Uncertainty
Decision process
Contingencies
Normative models
Individual decision models
Contingency organizational
decision model

Chapters 6 and 7

Perspective on
management and
organizations

Closed system
Open system
Contingencies

Chapter 3

Planning

Types of plans
Forecasting
Planning aids
Management by
objectives
Contingency model

Chapter 8

Control

Corrective model
Contingencies
Strategies

Chapter 9